W9-AVE-742

ANNUAL REVIEW OF

INFORMATION SCIENCE AND TECHNOLOGY

VOLUME 34 1999

ISBN: 1-57387-093-5
ISSN: 0066-4200
CODEN:ARISBC
LC No. 66-25096

ANNUAL REVIEW OF
INFORMATION SCIENCE AND TECHNOLOGY

Volume 34, 1999

Edited by

Martha E. Williams
University of Illinois
Urbana, Illinois, USA

Published on behalf of the
American Society for Information Science and Technology
by Information Today, Inc.

Information Today, Inc.
Medford, New Jersey

ISBN: 1-57387-093-5
ISSN: 0066-4200
CODEN: ARISBC
LC No. 66-25096

Published and distributed by:
Information Today, Inc.
143 Old Marlton Pike
Medford, NJ 08055-8750
for the
American Society for Information Science and Technology
8720 Georgia Avenue, Suite 501
Silver Spring, MD 20910-3602, U.S.A.

*LSL
REF
Z
699
.A1
A65
V.34
1999/2000*

ARIST Production staff, for ASIST:
Charles & Linda Holder, Graphic Compositors
Cover design by Sandy Skalkowski
Printed in Canada

Contents

I
Planning Information Systems and Services

II
Basic Techniques and Technologies   101

Preface

PUBLISHING HISTORY

This is the 34th volume of the *Annual Review of Information Science and Technology (ARIST)*. It was produced for the American Society for Information Science (ASIS) and published by Information Today, Inc.

ASIS initiated the annual review series in 1966 with the publication of Volume 1 under the editorship of Carlos A. Cuadra, who continued as Editor through Volume 10. Martha E. Williams assumed responsibilities of Editor starting with Volume 11 in 1976. ASIS is the owner of *ARIST*, maintains the editorial control, and has the sole rights to the series in all forms.

Through the years several organizations have been responsible for publishing and marketing *ARIST*. Volumes 1 and 2 were published by Interscience Publishers, a division of John Wiley & Sons. Volumes 3 through 6 were published by Encyclopaedia Britannica. Volumes 7 through 11 were published by ASIS itself. Volumes 12 through 21 were published by Knowledge Industry Publications, Inc. Volumes 22 through 25 were published by Elsevier Science Publishers B.V., Amsterdam, The Netherlands. With Volume 26 Learned Information, Inc. assumed the role of publisher of *ARIST* for ASIS. In 1995 Learned changed its name to Information Today, Inc.

Each volume of the *Annual Review of Information Science and Technology* has a unique volume number and is intended for completion and publication in a specific year. The volume number and the year associated with it appear on the title page and half title page, in each chapter within the book, and on the book cover and spine. In all but a few cases the copyright year coincides with the intended publication year. As happens occasionally with other serial publications, such as journals and conference proceedings, a delay in publication may cause the copyright date to be later than the year associated with the volume. Volume 34 was delayed because of an unusual number of very late chapter cancellations requiring very late invitations of additional authors to prepare chapters. In addition *ARIST* staff and some immediate family members experienced an unusual number of illnesses. Consequently, Volume 34 will have a combined cover date of 1999-2000, and Volume 35 will be the 2001 volume. When an author of a chapter cites another chapter in the same or earlier volume of *ARIST*, the volume number and the year associated with the volume appear in the citation (not the copyright year).

As Editor of *ARIST* I apologize for the delay and assure the readers that the quality of the books is in every way commensurate with the standards we have maintained from volume 11 to date.

POLICY

ARIST is an annual publication that reviews numerous topics within the broad field of information science and technology. The contents vary from year to year; no single topic is treated on an annual basis. Inasmuch as the field is dynamic, the contents (chapters) of the various *ARIST* volumes must change to reflect this dynamism. *ARIST* chapters are scholarly reviews of specific topics as substantiated by the published literature. Some material may be included, even though not backed up by literature, if it is needed to provide a balanced and complete picture of the state of the art for the subject of the chapter. The time period covered varies from chapter to chapter, depending on whether the topic has been treated previously by *ARIST* and, if so, on the length of the interval from the last treatment to the current one. Thus, reviews may cover a one-year or a multiyear period. The reviews aim to be critical in that they provide the author's expert opinion regarding developments and activities within the chapter's subject area. The review guides the reader to or from specific publications. Chapters aim to be scholarly, thorough within the scope defined by the chapter author, up to date, well written, and readable by an audience that goes beyond the author's immediate peer group to researchers and practitioners in information science and technology, in general, and ASIS members, in particular.

PURPOSE

The purpose of *ARIST* is to describe and to appraise activities and trends in the field of information science and technology. Material presented should be substantiated by references to the literature. *ARIST* provides an annual review of topics in the field. One volume is provided each year. A master plan for the series encompasses the entire field in all its aspects, and topics for each volume are selected from the plan on the basis of timeliness and an assessment of reader interest.

REFERENCES CITED IN TEXT AND BIBLIOGRAPHY

The format for referring to bibliographic citations within the text involves use of the cited author's name instead of reference numbers. The cited author's surname is printed in upper case letters. The reader, wishing to find the bibliographic references, can readily locate the appropriate reference in the bibliography (alphabetically arranged by first author's last name). A single author appears as SMITH; co-authors as SMITH & JONES; and multiple authors as SMITH ET AL. If multiple papers by the same author are cited, the distinction is made by indicating the year of publication after the last name (e.g., SMITH, 1986), and if a further distinction is required for multiple papers within the same year, a lower case alpha character follows the year (e.g., SMITH, 1986a). Except for the fact that all authors in multi-authored papers are included in bibliographic references, the same basic conventions are used in the chapter bibliographies. Thus, the reader can easily locate in the bibliography any references discussed in the text.

Because of the emphasis placed on the requirement for chapter authors to discuss the key papers and significant developments reported in the literature, and because *ARIST* readers have expressed their liking for comprehensive bibliographies associated with the chapters, more references may be listed in the bibliographies than are discussed and/or cited in the text.

The format used for references in the bibliographies is based on the *American National Standard for Bibliographic References*, ANS Z39.29. We have followed the ANSI guidelines with respect to the sequence of bibliographic data elements and the punctuation used to separate the elements. Adoption of this convention should facilitate conversion of the references to machine-readable form as need arises. Journal article references follow the ANSI guide as closely as possible. Conference papers and microform publications follow an *ARIST* adaptation of the format.

As the information world becomes more networked and as publishing becomes increasingly electronic, more publications are appearing on the Internet with no complementary hard copy version. In such cases the only option for citing the publication is a cite to the uniform resource locator (URL). Unfortunately, most of these publications are not permanently archived, and many of the sites (e.g., World Wide Web (WWW) sites) are not maintained or updated, and they do not retain permanent addresses. Some move to other servers, and others die as sponsorship or funding wanes. The *ARIST* staff verifies all cited URLs during the course of editing chapters, but by the time this volume is published some URLs will undoubtedly no longer be valid. While *ARIST* has always required page numbers for quotations, electronic documents do not consistently have explicit pagination noted; thus some quotes from URLs are cited without page numbers.

STRUCTURE OF THE VOLUME

In accordance with the *ARIST* master plan, this volume's eight chapters fit within a basic framework: I. Planning Information Systems and

Services; II. Basic Techniques and Technologies; and III. Applications. Chapter titles are provided in the Table of Contents, and an Introduction to each section highlights the events, trends, and evaluations given by the chapter authors. An Index to the entire volume is provided to help the user locate material relevant to the subject content, authors, and organizations cited in the book. An explanation of the guidelines employed in the Index is provided in the Introduction to the Index. A Cumulative Keyword and Author Index of *ARIST* Titles to this and all prior volumes follows the Index.

DATABASES AND ABSTRACTING AND INDEXING SERVICES COVERING *ARIST*

ARIST as a whole and/or individual chapters are included in a number of abstracting and indexing (A&I) journals both within the United States and internationally. Databases that both cover *ARIST* and are available through major online services in the United States are:

BIOSIS (Biological Abstracts)
Current Contents
ERIC (Educational Resources Information Center)
Information Science Abstracts
INSPEC (Computer and Control Abstracts)
Library Literature
LISA (Library and Information Science Abstracts)
Social SciSearch (Social Sciences Citation Index)

Publishers of other A&I journals and databases who would like to include *ARIST* in their coverage are encouraged to contact the publisher for a review copy and notify the editor who will add the database name(s) to this list when appropriate.

Martha E. Williams
Editor, *Annual Review of Information Science and Technology*

Acknowledgments

The American Society for Information Science and the Editor wish to acknowledge the contributions of the three principals on the editorial staff and the technical support staff.

Linda Schamber, Copy Editor

Debora Shaw, Index Editor

Linda C. Smith, Bibliographic Editor

Technical Support Staff

Mary W. Rakow, Technical Advisor

Sheila Carnder, Assistant

Linda Holder, Compositor

Appreciation

Appreciation is expressed not only to the editorial and technical support staff but also to many individuals and organizations for their roles in creating this volume. First and foremost are the authors of the individual chapters who have generously contributed their time and efforts in searching, reviewing, and evaluating the large body of literature on which their chapters are based. The *ARIST* Advisory Committee Members and *ARIST* Reviewers provided valuable feedback and constructive criticism of the content. The Dialog Corporation plc generously provided the authors with online access to databases.

Advisory Committee for *ARIST*

Marcia Bates

Blaise Cronin

John Hearty

Mark T. Kinnucan

Edie Rasmussen

Ronald E. Rice

Linda C. Smith

Karen J. Sy

Judith E. Weedman

Contributors

Sally Jo Cunningham
University of Waikato
Department of Computer Science
Private Bag 3105
Hamilton, New Zealand

Peter Ingwersen
Royal School of Library and
    Information Science
Department of Information
    Studies & Center for
    Informetric Studies
Birketinget 6
DK-2300
Copenhagen S. Denmark

Donald W. King
4915 Gull Lane Dr.
Ann Arbor, MI 48103

James Littin
University of Waikato
Department of Computer Science
Private Bag 3105
Hamilton, New Zealand

Robert E. Molyneux
University of South Carolina
College of Library and Informa-
    tion Science
113 Davis College
Columbia, SC 29208

Albert N. Tabah
Université de Montréal
École de bibliothéconomie et des
    sciences de l'information
C.P. 6128 Suce Centre-Ville
Montréal, Quebec
Canada H3C 3J7

Carol Tenopir
University of Tennessee
School of Information Sciences
804 Volunteer Blvd.
Knoxville, TN 37996-4330

Walter J. Trybula
International SEMATECH
4621A Pinehurst Drive So.
Austin, TX 78747

Peiling Wang
University of Tennessee
School of Information Sciences
804 Volunteer Blvd.
Knoxville, TN 37996-4330

Robert V. Williams
University of South Carolina
College of Library and Informa-
    tion Science
113 Davis College
Columbia, SC 29208

Concepción S. Wilson
The University of New South
    Wales
School of Information Systems,
    Technology and Management
UNSW Sydney NSW 2052
Australia

Ian H. Witten
University of Waikato
Department of Computer Science
Private Bag 3105
Hamilton, New Zealand

Chapter Reviewers

Bryce L. Allen

Nicholas J. Belkin

Michael K. Buckland

Blaise Cronin

Pauline A. Cochrane

Raya Fidel

John Hearty

Peter Hernon

Carol A. Hert

Donald W. King

Michael E. D. Koenig

Gary Marchionini

Katherine W. McCain

Jessica L. Milstead

Ronald E. Rice

Judith E. Weedman

ASIS and Its Members

For over 50 years the leading professional society for information professionals, the American Society for Information Science is an association whose diverse membership continues to reflect the frontiers and horizons of the dynamic field of information science and technology. ASIS owes its stature to the cumulative contributions of its members, past and present.

ASIS counts among its membership some 4,000 information specialists from such fields as computer science, management, engineering, librarianship, chemistry, linguistics, and education. As was true when the Society was founded, ASIS membership continues to lead the information profession in the search for new and better theories, techniques, and technologies to improve access to information through storage and retrieval advances. And now, as then, ASIS and its members are called upon to help determine new directions and standards for the development of information polices and practices.

I

Planning Information Systems and Services

Section I includes two chapters: "Cognitive Information Retrieval" by Peter Ingwersen of the Royal School of Library and Information Science and the Department of Information Studies & Center for Informetric Studies in Denmark, and "Methodologies and Methods for User Behavioral Research" by Peiling Wang of the University of Tennessee, Knoxville.

Ingwersen's chapter reviews, largely, the developments of the cognitive approach to information retrieval (IR) research and theory with emphasis on analytic and empirical research on the nature of the formation and situation of information need and their association with relevance. He covers, for the most part, the time period 1992-2000. Ingwersen's chapter has five major sections: The Individual Cognitive View, The Holistic Cognitive View, Information Structures, Dimensions of the Holistic View, and Integration of Models.

Ingwersen divides the developments of the cognitive approach to IR into two distinct periods, 1977-1991 built on Marc de Mey's original thesis that processing of information is mediated by a system of categories that is a model of the world of the processing device, and 1992-2000 when de Mey's basic evolutionary view gained importance. Peter Ingwersen notes that a central assumption of the cognitive view is that the cognitive state of an individual is affected by one's past and one's social context. This affects the way an individual classifies objects. He further cites A. R. Luria's demonstration of how one's education and work influence the way that one classifies objects and separates their relationships into "*situational* and *categorical* (generic and part-whole) categories" as seen, for example, in the way that knowledge is organized in libraries. According to Ingwersen IR should "bring into accord the cognitive structures of authors, systems designers, and indexers with those of the intermediary (human or computer) and the user, in order to cope with the [user's] information need." In the first time period most researchers concentrated on the *individual* nature of cognitive structures in empirical studies of behavior and cognitive structures, and the studies were on small-scale tests that did not involve real users.

1

In the section on The Individual Cognitive View Ingwersen covers Major Research Results and Critical Issues. He describes the essential aspects of some 20 research efforts and says that they led to two lines of research in the IR community—intelligent retrieval and supportive IR systems. He notes that automated knowledge acquisition in complex queries is so far unsolvable. According to Karen Sparck Jones the supportive systems are easier to design and to implement than expert systems and the traditional retrieval systems produce better results than do question-answering expert systems. Ingwersen sees the research results of the first period as lacking in realism, theory integration, and holistic perspective. In the balance of the chapter Ingwersen covers some of the problems addressed in the second time period.

The second chapter in Section I of this volume is Peiling Wang's "Methodologies and Methods for User Behavioral Research." She introduces the chapter first by explaining the difference between the terms methodology and method. Methodology is a theory of methods for "guiding the description, explanation, and justification of methods" used in empirical studies whereas "methods refers to the actual design and specific scientific techniques" employed in a study. Wang notes some current concerns regarding methodologies and research designs for library and information science (LIS) studies. Included are: the limited influence that methodological research has had on LIS research; the dearth of methodology papers in core LIS journals; an increasing awareness of the importance of methodology; and an increase in efforts to promote LIS research and to explore new methods. Wang reviews the literatures of methodology in social and behavioral research and of empirical studies of user behaviors.

The majority of the chapter is devoted to the sections on Research Paradigms and Methods Used in User Behavioral Studies. She notes that there are two paradigms—one quantitative and the other qualitative. The first is said to be empirical, objective, scientific, and quantitative. The second or new paradigm is said to be naturalistic, sensemaking, illuminative, and qualitative. In order to help the reader better understand these two paradigms, Wang provides a table outlining some 15 points of comparison found in the papers of several authors. Wang's treatment of methods used in user behavioral research is done in terms of survey methods, interview methods, observation of users through experiments, observation of users in natural settings, and multiple-phase studies and emerging methods. In conclusion Peiling Wang observes that current methodologies and methods need to be strengthened and deepened to study the complexities of information and user behavior and consequently to advance the field as such advancement depends on methodological development.

1 Cognitive Information Retrieval

PETER INGWERSEN
Royal School of Library and Information Science

INTRODUCTION

This chapter reviews and discusses critically the development during the last decade of the cognitive approach to information retrieval (IR) research and theory. The focus is analytic and empirical research on the complex nature of information need formation and situation, their inherent association with the concept of relevance, and the development of cognitive and related IR theory and evaluation methods. The time span is largely 1992-2000 (references to earlier works are provided as needed). Thus, the review complements and extends the previous *ARIST* chapters on cognitive research (ALLEN, 1991) and the user-oriented perspectives of IR research and analysis methods (SUGAR).

Since its start in 1977, the cognitive approach to information science has developed in two periods. The first covers 1977-1991 and can briefly be characterized as user- and intermediary-oriented. The second period is 1992-2000 (the major concentration of this chapter), when the approach turns into a holistic view of all the interactive communication processes that occur during information transfer.

Following the introduction, the review falls into five major sections. The first section highlights the scientific developments, characteristics, and substantial results of the cognitive approach in the first period. This section also includes drawbacks and criticisms of the approach, that is, the lack of realism, theory integration, and holistic perspective. This is followed by a section covering the development in the second period about the focus shift into a holistic cognitive view, with a subsection on views of information processing. The third section covers information structures, with a subsection on information need. The fourth section looks into the dimensions of cognitive IR theory in a holistic perspec-

Annual Review of Information Science and Technology (ARIST), Volume 34, 1999
Martha E. Williams, Editor
Published for the American Society for Information Science (ASIS)
By Information Today, Inc., Medford, NJ

tive. Subsections concern polyrepresentation of information objects, the cognitive space and IR interactions, and relevance and evaluation issues. This section includes work task conceptions and issues concerned with feedback and query modification. The fifth section approaches the integration of cognitive models of information seeking, IR, and scientific communication, including a discussion of critical issues. A concluding section ends the review.

THE INDIVIDUAL COGNITIVE VIEW

The cognitive approach in information science and IR research started at the end of the 1970s. It was influenced by discussions of cognitive science in the early 1970s, the establishment of the journal *Cognitive Science*, and De Mey's epistemological contributions on the cognitive viewpoint in general (DE MEY, 1977, 1982) and its relation to information science (DE MEY, 1980). While initially the cognitive viewpoint influenced theory building in information science as such (see, for instance, BROOKES's equation), it soon became useful to the growing user-centered IR research community. The viewpoint was here clearly seen as an alternative to the mainstream system- and document-driven IR research tradition. Reviews and discussions of the cognitive approach to IR during the 1980s can be found in BELKIN's (1990) overview, ELLIS's (1989; 1992) critical essays, and INGWERSEN's (1992) book. Belkin outlines the major contributions of an analytic and empirical nature that have been rather explicitly based on the cognitive approach. Ellis (1992) contrasts the system-driven mainstream tradition in IR, which he calls physicalistic, with the user-oriented and the cognitive school, both merged under the label of a cognitive paradigm. One may argue that the concept of paradigm in a Kuhnian sense is an exaggeration with respect to the cognitive approach. However, in relation to the system-driven tradition in IR, there is no doubt that it possesses paradigmatic properties. Ingwersen (1992) discusses in detail the cognitive viewpoint and its implications for the concept of information in information science, the understanding of information need development leading to user modeling—the Mediator Model—and, in particular, its theoretical potential for IR research.

One may divide the development of the cognitive approach to IR into two distinct periods. During the first period, 1977-1991, cognitive IR research built on DE MEY's (1977; 1980) original theses, mainly his central point: "that any processing of information, whether perceptual or symbolic, is mediated by a system of categories or concepts which, for the information processing device, are a model of his (its) world" (1977, p. xvi-xvii). To this Ingwersen adds that the world model consists of cognitive structures that are determined by the "individual and social/collective experiences, education, training etc." (INGWERSEN, 1982, p. 168).

During the second period, 1992-2000, De Mey's core evolutionary view, consisting of four stages through which thinking on information processing has developed (DE MEY, 1980, p. 49), gained importance, for example, in relation to the conceptualization of information and the understanding of the limitations of information processing by computers (INGWERSEN, 1992, 1995, 1996).

Clearly, the current cognitive state of the individual is affected by the past and the social context. This understanding of the central assumption of the cognitive view was influenced by the Russian cognitive psychologist LURIA and his empirical work in the 1920s on humans' classification of objects. Luria demonstrates how educational background as well as work routines and situations trigger the way humans classify objects and separate their relationships into situational and into categorical (generic and part-whole) categories. Naturally, such classificatory behavior impacts the perception by individuals (users) of, for instance, knowledge organization in libraries.

The cognitive view assumes a variety of individual differences in cognitive structures. According to INGWERSEN (1982), the task of IR is to bring into accord the cognitive structures of authors, systems designers, and indexers with those of the intermediary (human or computer) and the user, in order to cope with the actual information need. Ingwersen emphasizes that collective cognitive structures, the result of social interaction and subject domains, as well as scientific and social paradigms, also influence the structure of indexing systems and the relations of topics and concepts treated in the body of literature and in information needs. This notion of bringing into accord cognitively different structures immediately ought to have ensured the establishment of a dominant and workable holistic approach to IR. With the exception of BROOKES, this was unfortunately not the case during the first period. Instead, the main bulk of researchers focused on the individual nature of the cognitive structures in a range of empirical studies of the behavior and cognitive structures of users, human intermediaries, their interactions (including interactions with operational Boolean IR systems), and individual information need formation. The goal was to obtain an improved understanding of such interactive phenomena and factors affecting the actors in order to improve IR performance from a stand different from that of the prevailing system-driven research. One must bear in mind that researchers taking the system view did not involve real users in their experiments, which at that time were carried out on small-scale test collections as a means to find and tune the best retrieval algorithm.

Major Research Results

The results of several studies highlight applications of the individual cognitive view. BELKIN ET AL. (1982a) originated the Anomalous States of Knowledge (ASK) hypothesis, which concerns the development of individual information needs founded in the notion of a problem situation. As a quite novel approach in user-centered research, BELKIN ET AL. (1982b) applied a best-match (non-Boolean) system in their empirical investigation matching structures of users' need descriptions with document abstract structures. The idea was that the user narrative should provide context to the ASK in the form of a problem description. Although the results of these comprehensive experiments were unsatisfactory, they led the IR community to new knowledge concerning the role of the intermediary mechanism and systems design. In similar studies, FENICHEL investigated on a pragmatic psychological basis the influence of different types of experience on end-user online searching and BATES (1981) produced her well-known search tactics for online retrieval. Quite comprehensive empirical investigations of user or of intermediary communications with online systems (BORGMAN; FIDEL, 1991a, 1991c; SARACEVIC ET AL., 1990, 1991) led to a detailed understanding of interactive processes and use of feedback by end users. INGWERSEN (1984) demonstrated how frequency analyses of indexing terms and other representative structures may aid users in their understanding of the information contents of IR systems. Cognitive subject representation and feedback mechanisms are further explored by INGWERSEN & WORMELL and by MCALPINE & INGWERSEN in relation to supportive interface designs. To a great extent WORMELL (1981; 1984) builds her implementation of the inherent natural-language features of monographic material on the cognitive approach in combination with semiotics in the Subject Access Project and database system. The application of controlled vocabulary versus natural language during online searching was further investigated empirically by FIDEL (1991b). At the same time, T. D. WILSON (1980) started his empirical studies of nonscientific information seeking processes with the INISS project, which pursued quite a different track in investigating the task-driven information seeking behavior of social workers in community environments. T. D. Wilson's (1981) analyses were to a great extent inspired by the cognitive approach. One may find that, in particular, the ASK work as well as the INISS project point to the present state of research in which the integration of broader information seeking processes and IR interaction based on domain work tasks and problem situations is an emerging research issue (VAKKARI, 1999, 2000).

Based on empirical evidence and international cooperation during the mid-1980s, BELKIN ET AL. (1983) and BROOKS (1986) investigated the possibility of creating a user-oriented and cognitively based framework for intelligent interface design based on discourse analyses of user-intermediary-system interactions: the Monstrat Model. Similar protocol analyses led Ingwersen to the discovery of the Label-Effect and the influence of context concerned with information requests (INGWERSEN, 1982) and to a typology of information needs (INGWERSEN, 1986). The Label-Effect means that users, even those with well-defined knowledge of their information gap, tend to label their initial requests for information verbally by means of very few terms or single concepts. This implies two obstacles to successful IR. First, intermediary mechanisms have difficulty in reaching out into the proper directions in information space where data are located relevant to a particular user. Due to the lack of context in the request, a multitude of directions are indeed possible. This was observed in the scientific online age 10 to 20 years ago, and the same phenomenon is dominant today in web searching. Second, intermediary mechanisms may not be capable of distinguishing between users with detailed, some, or no knowledge about their information requirements, that is, whether the user's ASK is intrinsically well- or ill-defined. Independently of Belkin et al. (1982a; 1982b), Ingwersen's observations (1982) of the situational influence of context on information need descriptions and perceptions, for instance in the form of reasons for having a knowledge gap, confirmed the problem situation conception in the ASK hypothesis by Belkin et al. (1982a). Also, the investigations point to contextual perceptions of users leading to problem situations, e.g., perceived goals or interests, and a certain randomness and nonrationalism in the cognitive behavior of searchers. The information need typology consists of three categories, depending on the nature and strength of the conceptual cognitive structures of the user: verificative, conscious topical, and intrinsically muddled or ill-defined. The importance of distinguishing between levels of retrieval knowledge (from novices to experts) and status of conceptual or subject-domain knowledge was originally analyzed in BATES's doctoral dissertation (1972) on catalog search success. The effect of the two distinctive types of knowledge was confirmed— also as a result of BORGMAN's and MARCHIONINI's detailed studies of user-system interaction. Borgman investigates online searchers with different knowledge levels while Marchionini focuses on novice users of full-text encyclopedias (1989), later generalized in 1995. Mainly due to the ASK hypothesis, the development of the Monstrat Model, and the user-need typology, a great deal of interest was invested in the area of cognitive user modeling. DANIELS, as part of the Belkin team, produced an extensive overview of research on cognitive models, including her own, and OFORI-DWUMFUO stressed the importance of dialogue modeling, an issue already investigated by ODDY (1977a; 1977b).

These research efforts led to two novel lines of research within the IR community. First was the intelligent retrieval attempts, as reviewed by BROOKS (1987). These were carried out by researchers such as CROFT & THOMPSON and FOX in projects where artificial intelligence (AI) tools were used to create knowledge-based IR systems and experiments. Although belonging to the cognitivistic Strong-AI tradition, not the information science cognitive view, these designs demonstrated an interesting similarity to the otherwise user-driven and empirical Monstrat Model. The second line of research was the supportive IR systems approach, in which interface and systems design aid the user by means of a detailed empirical analysis of user, domain, and retrieval characteristics. This approach was shown, for instance, by PEJTERSEN (1980; 1989) in her Bookhouse project on fiction. Pejtersen's and similar lines of research into systems design (e.g., BATES, 1989) completely contrast with the approach taken by RICH (1979) in the Grundy project, which was also on fiction retrieval, but founded in the cognitivistic AI tradition of user stereotype applications. While the supportive systems approach has developed into a comprehensive model for general systems design based on ideas from cognitive engineering in the area of human-computer interaction in the 1990s (FOX ET AL.; RASMUSSEN ET AL.), the former intelligent IR perspective ran out of steam in the 1980s along with other complex expert system-based design attempts. The main reasons are that automatic knowledge acquisition in complex IR scenarios thus far is unsolvable and presumes the same user and domain analyses carried out as for supportive systems. The supportive systems are easier to design and implement than expert systems and, according to SPARCK JONES (1987; 1990), traditional retrieval systems yield better IR results than the knowledge gained by the expert system from question-answering. In a cognitive sense, this outcome is not surprising given that the user is the only truly intelligent and dynamically knowledge-based actor in interactive IR.

Critical Issues

From the results of this first period of cognitive research, it is apparent that the individual cognitive approach falls short in three ways: realism, theory integration, and holistic perspective.

Lack of realism. Too much emphasis was put on the analysis of user and human intermediary behavior during interaction without also including the cognitive structures embedded into the system side and the contextual environment. Further, the systems under investigation were mainly Boolean, large-scale online systems, not experimental best-match retrieval engines. The most interesting and promising exception was the THOMAS retrieval system, or rather program as ODDY put it

(1977a; 1977b). THOMAS represented an approach quite different from traditional online or experimental IR to the nature of interaction between user and database. IR was meant to be facilitated not by issuing orders to the system, but rather by forms of dialogue that should resemble personal communication. Thus, comprehensive IR theory-building was not really attempted, and the predictive power of the cognitive viewpoint in collaboration with best-match techniques leading to novel workable research questions and investigations was in general not put to use. For instance, during this first period it would have been appropriate to ask which (combination of) retrieval engines and relevance feedback methods best suit different types of information needs, and *why*. Only the BELKIN & KWASNIK work comes to mind as an explicit example of addressing such issues. Although CROFT & THOMPSON's famous I³R system actually made use of both clustering and probabilistic models, this was done to improve precision and recall but not founded in any particular cognitive theory of, say, user relevance. Also, the prevailing methods of IR systems evaluation and testing (the Cranfield methodology) suffered from lack of user involvement—that is, lack of realism—which was not improved by cognitive researchers. One critical reason was perhaps that only a few of the researchers, even the pragmatic user-centered investigators, knew enough about best-match retrieval principles, probabilistic and vector space models, or logic. This changed substantially during the second period in connection with the upscaled TREC experiments, initiated in 1991-1992. Generally, too much ignorance prevailed in most sectors of the IR research community, particularly about results obtained in other sectors. An exception from this gloomy picture was the result of a workshop held at Rutgers University (BELKIN ET AL., 1987). A number of leading IR researchers from various approaches came together to exchange views on the current state of affairs in IR research and to attempt to bring together the variety of views, from intelligent IR over traditional experimental research to cognitive and user-oriented pragmatic views.

Lack of theory integration. During the first period other scientifically based approaches to information transfer were proposed. In 1986 DERVIN & NILAN presented their sense-making theory in a substantial *ARIST* chapter based on communication theory and regarded as an alternative to pragmatic and cognitive approaches. Also in 1986 WINOGRAD & FLORES published their more general socio-hermeneutic approach to systems design. Where Dervin & Nilan's work became highly influential in information need and seeking studies (although hardly in IR research), Winograd & Flores' ideas did not penetrate heavily, except into certain metatheoretical approaches to information science (BRIER) and into the reopening of the relevance discussion by SCHAMBER ET AL. in 1990. Perhaps due to its broader scope, Dervin & Nilan's sense-making theory was not sufficiently compared to nor integrated into the cognitive approach, although both theories deal profoundly with information need formation by individuals and its underlying rationale. Now it is possible to observe mutual agreements between the sense-making and the cognitive approaches, because both fundamentally concern communication phenomena and acts of interpretation in a social context (DERVIN).

Lack of holistic perspective. With researchers conducting empirical studies on the individual cognitive properties of end users, intermediaries, and their interactions, the cognitive approach became open to various kinds of criticism. Because IR consists of a human side *and* a system side it is evident that any (new) theory for IR *must* circumscribe both sides. Retrieval systems require search engines and research into such engines, including their underlying assumptions as well as strengths and weaknesses.

ELLIS (1989) raises some critical questions associated with the individual cognitive approach as a theory for IR. He questions the ability of the viewpoint on its own to support cognitive empirical investigations that are different from the traditional pragmatic user-system studies carried out in operational IR environments. Ellis (1992; 1996) merges cognitive and pragmatic user-oriented research into one line of cognitive research and development in IR, but essentially his arguments are the same.

It is important to understand that from a methodological point of view, the user-centered studies and the cognitive studies have data collection methods in common, including direct observations, recordings of thinking/talking aloud, post-search interviews, and transaction logs. Due to Belkin and colleagues (BELKIN, 1984; BELKIN ET AL., 1982a, 1982b, 1983; BROOKS, 1986), INGWERSEN (1982), and T. D. WILSON (1981), among others, the methodological issues concerned with the widespread use of these inherently obtrusive methods, mainly in combination, became evident to the user-centered research community. The major problem lies in the treatment of the collected data during data analysis. Micro as well as macro protocol analyses and discourse analyses were used both at qualitative and quantitative levels by cognitive researchers to produce both descriptive results and causal cognitive explanations of, for instance, user-librarian interactions (BELKIN & VICKERY; PEJTERSEN, 1989). It is essential to uncover the kind of cognitive factors or structures that trigger users' information needs and problem statements, for instance, the reasons for users' (mis)conceptions of classification structures or icons in systems. The cognitive nature of representative structures of information objects or knowledge sources are thus of direct interest. Common semantics, that is, social or collective cognitive structures influencing the IR outcome, can then easily be detected. Causality analyses require models in order to function. However, several so-called pragmatic studies are actually based on phenomenological approaches or general social science investigative models. Hence, their outcomes may be quite similar to, but often more descriptive than, those of more "pure" cognitive studies. Evidently, the results of pragmatic investigations are of high value when their hypotheses and assumptions are clearly stated. INGWERSEN & PEJTERSEN discuss the utility of a variety of qualitative and quantitative methods, and INGWERSEN (1993) provides a list of cognitively inspired empirical research in response to ELLIS's (1992) questions. SANDSTROM & SANDSTROM present a detailed discussion and exemplification of anthropological methods, including their misuse and proper use in information science. YUAN & MEADOW investigate the use of the variety of variables pertaining to IR user studies, and PORS argues for the introduction of more rigorous social science-based experimental models in interactive IR research, including the application of the classical setting of control groups, also known from medical drug testing.

THE HOLISTIC COGNITIVE VIEW

The reasons for initiating the second period of cognitive research at the beginning of the 1990s are several. (1) The SCHAMBER ET AL. article on situational relevance in 1990 inspires an increasing amount of hitherto unanswered or ignored questions about relevance phenomena in fora outside the algorithmic IR domain. For instance, HARTER proposes in 1992 the conception of psychological relevance and its relationship to information need formation. With respect to the concept of information need, he challenges the ASK hypothesis proposed a decade earlier by BELKIN ET AL. (1982a). However, he misinterprets the central point of the hypothesis, that is, that the system design in the paper by Belkin et al. is based on the idea of a constantly changing ASK, exactly by virtue of the interaction process over IR session time. Essentially, Harter (p. 610) restates the Belkin et al. view and adds nothing new to the information need and ASK discussion. What is important is the quite comprehensive understanding of the relevance issue seen as a dynamic and complex phenomenon. (2) This discussion of relevance complexity is in direct contrast to the view on relevance and interaction taken in the large-scale mainstream TREC experiments that start in 1991-1992 (HARMAN). In TREC, continuing the empirical Cranfield tradition, relevance is regarded as a binary, topical, and stable, manifestation. TREC forces IR research to reconsider the nature of IR and IR theory. IR theory is not simply algorithmic solutions to technical problems in settings without realism, nor just socio-psychological theories of user behavior in more realistic settings. Both mainstream, cognitive and user-centered theorists recognize the fragmented often black-box like state of affairs at this point in time, and some serious attempts are made during the ensuing years to clarify and understand the situation. (3) ROBERTSON & HANCOCK-BEAULIEU point to three recent revolutions in IR that, in their opinion, are crucial to understand in order to proceed toward a more holistic theory of IR: the cognitive, the relevance, and the interactive revolutions. The cognitive and relevance revolutions in empirical IR require realism with reference to the processes of information need development and human relevance assessments. This means that an information need ought to be treated as a potentially dynamic concept, and that the multidimensional and similarly dynamic nature of relevance should be taken into account. Relevance ought to be judged against the information need situation, not the query or request, by the person who owns the information need or problem situation. The interactive revolution points to the fact that (even experimental) IR systems have become increasingly interactive, due to actual applications of dynamic relevance-feedback and query-modification techniques by users over IR session time. Thus, experimental or evaluative IR settings, as well as theory, have to incorporate this realism that would incorporate the context or situation surrounding the IR activity, i.e., seeking processes. At the same time, experiments must maintain a degree of control. The question is, what do IR researchers wish to observe, analyze, measure, or make theories about? The revolutions can thus be seen as the real challenge to the IR community. (4) DE MEY's (1980; 1982) original view of cognition in contextual social interaction as well as his stages of information processing, their effect on the concepts of information and information need formation, and their association with IR research are not fully explored. An attempt is thus made by INGWERSEN in 1992 and 1996 to discuss in detail the state of IR theory and research from an interactive perspective, hereby following up on the work by BELKIN & VICKERY.

By contrasting the usual relevance notion of topicality with the concept of situational relevance, SCHAMBER ET AL. also stress the importance of context in IR. Situational relevance derives from P. WILSON's original concept in 1973. Context may come from the information objects or knowledge sources in systems, but may also be influenced by the actual information seeking situation adhering to a domain. Situational also implies a series of dynamic cognitive states in the mind of the user during an IR session. Essentially, this means that if relevance evaluation is dynamic, the corresponding information need is dynamic as well. During an IR session, an information object may thus be topically relevant in the sense of the TREC experiments (HARMAN), but may not be useful to the situation the end user is facing at that time. Obviously, only the user can assess this type of relevance.

There is some similarity between situational relevance and LURIA's situational classification of objects. For example, one can easily detect situational assessments in the empirical studies of user-intermediary-system interactions. The user's current perception of the situation, rather than the user per se, becomes the focal point for IR interaction. The intentionality of the user (in the sense presented by SEARLE, i.e., the user's goal or purpose) and background knowledge at a given time can be seen as the crucial components in IR interaction. IR implies a continuous process of interpretation and cognition. In a holistic sense such processes take place both on the user side and on the system side during human-machine interactions. However, DE MEY's (1980; 1982) stages of understanding information processing in a broad sense define the limitations and characteristics involved on both sides in a cognitively asymmetrical way. The shift into a holistic cognitive view implies that the belief that the variety of cognitive structures in IR (e.g., indexing structures, information object structures by authors, or users' cognitive interpretations) can be commonly understood shifts to the acceptance that such structures are inherently different. The goal is to explore and employ the cognitive differences of structures in such a way that IR can be facilitated and improved. At its current level of cognition, i.e., recognition and algorithmic processing following implemented rules, the machine cannot become aware of and understand what the user is looking for, in particular when the user's ASK initially is ill-defined. The machine may, however, be designed to support the user during the interactive process of IR in order to make the user interpret and learn so he/she feeds data back to the machine, which eases its way of further supporting the user. Ultimately, information retrieval in its real sense takes place only in the mind of the information seeker, that is, information is seen as process or as knowledge and cognition, as discussed by BUCKLAND (1991a; 1991b). The road is constantly uphill from the machine point of view.

Information Processing

Generally, the shift into a situational context assumes consideration of intentionality and processes of interpretation. We are thus seeking an understanding of phenomena that pertain to both machine functions and human cognition. To this end, INGWERSEN (1992, p. 33) proposes a model of the cognitive communication system for information retrieval originally put forward by BELKIN (1977), and, later made more detailed in INGWERSEN (1996, p. 6). The latter model is depicted in Figure 1. It shifts the focus of the cognitive viewpoint into the four

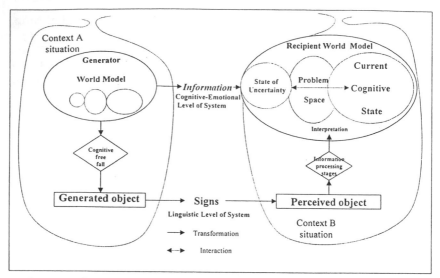

Figure 1. The cognitive communication system for information retrieval
at a given point in time (extension of INGWERSEN, 1996, p. 6)

generalized evolutionary stages proposed by DE MEY (1980): monadic,
structural, contextual, and cognitive. These are seen as stages of information processing consistent with the similar common evolutionary
levels of language understanding (SMEATON): morpho-lexical, syntactic, semantic, and pragmatic.

In human information processing, the world model constitutes the
cognitive space, consisting of highly dynamic autopoietic and changeable cognitive structures, that controls the perception and further processing of external input, for instance during communication and IR
interaction. Originating from BOULDING, the individual cognitive space
and, in particular, the individual's current cognitive/emotional structures and states, are determined by the experiences gained over time in
a social and cultural context through social interaction. In computerized information processing, the computer's world model is not self-
contained. It consists of the human cognitive structures embedded in
the system prior to processing. Its cognitive structures (e.g., algorithms
or textual symbolic strings) may interact with one another and with
structures generated by humans external to the system, according to the
capabilities of the system's algorithms. However, the processing constantly takes place at a linguistic sign level of communication, never at a
cognitive level (see Figure 1). The linguistic sign levels consist of the
morpho-lexical, the syntactic, and the semantic levels of language understanding. For human recipients of communicated signs, perception
may also take place at a cognitive-emotional level. In this case, the signs

provide information that may transform the current cognitive states into new states of knowledge. During any act of human or computerized communication, all communicated messages are regarded as signs transferred at a morpho-lexical linguistic level. Only perception and interpretation by humans in their current cognitive states can transform signs into information at a cognitive level. This implies that any intentionality and meaning underlying the communicated messages are immediately lost (SMEATON) in what is known as a cognitive free fall (Figure 1). The message must be rebuilt, or interpreted, by individuals (or the computer) based on the presuppositions, in context, that they bring to the communication act. Cognitive free fall means that essentially all cognitive manifestations in messages are lost when uttered or transmitted, whether from machine or any other entity. The messages consist of signals, data, or signs at a monadic stage. This is the reason we may not, or only partly, perceive and understand people's, nature's, or machines' messages, which inherently are ambiguous. However, we may give meaning to or interpret (also erroneously) perceived messages or objects according to our current presuppositions in a situational context. Naturally, machines constantly suffer from similar problems of correct recognition and interpretation at the linguistic sign-processing levels. Figure 1 shows one instance of communication between a sender or generator and a recipient. In true interaction the recipient role becomes the sender role at the following instance (summarized from INGWERSEN, 1992, 1996).

Computers (or books for that matter) hold fixed human presuppositions, while those of humans are unpredictable, formed by episodic, semantic, and tacit knowledge, or emotional experiences in context. The semantic level is identified as the stage of language understanding in which a domain or culture shapes the common interpretation of a sign at a given point in time by means of social interaction in a common context (context A overlapping context B).

Four fundamental characteristics are of crucial importance to IR:

- All interactive communication activities during IR can be regarded as processes of cognition, which may occur in all the information processing components involved, but at different levels of cognition.
- The presuppositions and intentionality underlying messages are vital for the perception and understanding of such messages, but are lost by any transmitting system between sender and recipient, whether human or machine.
- Uncertainties and unpredictabilities are inherent in IR interaction and associated with all acts of interpretation

> carried out by senders and recipients, whether human or machine.
> - Direct and real information retrieval, as opposed to text retrieval performed at a linguistic level, Figure 1, is possible only by the individual user in context.

Because of these characteristics, IR systems may be most successful only when they support IR by humans. Further, because of the dynamic nature of cognition, time becomes an important issue in interactive IR.

DE MEY's (1980) four information processing stages stated above limit the level of cognition for machines to a linguistic sign level, up to and including the contextual (or semantic) stage. Communicative discrepancies may occur between humans and between humans and machines because machines cannot reach the same level of understanding as humans unless the meaning of a sign is common to both. To be understood by human or machine, a text or image must be interpreted at a certain linguistic stage. The lower the stage, the larger the semantic openness of the object or sign. This means that an object or sign does not necessarily yield the same information to the recipient as intended by the sender or, for that matter, does not yield the same information to different recipients at the same time.

INFORMATION STRUCTURES

In the comprehensive cognitive view, the concept of information, building on WERSIG, BROOKES, BELKIN (1978), and SEARLE, must satisfy two conditions simultaneously (INGWERSEN, 1992, p. 33): "on the one hand information being the result of a transformation of a generator's knowledge structures (by intentionality, model of recipients' states of knowledge, and in the form of signs); and on the other hand being something which, when perceived, affects and transforms the recipient's state of knowledge." The satisfaction of these two conditions means that information goes beyond meaning. A sentence or an image may have several meanings or semantic values, and each meaning may provide many different interpretations and transformations of the state of knowledge. In machine translation, the attempt is to establish the one correct linguistic meaning (semantics) by means of textual context. In IR, the goal is to give recipients access to plausible meanings or values for interpretation at a pragmatic level in their specific situational context. The information is associated with the situation in context, not just with its general semantic value.

The implication for the interactive communication process taking place between human and machine is that messages sent by machines or humans to a human recipient can become information in the real sense; however, signs communicated by machines or humans to a machine can *never* become information, although they are perceived and affect the embedded cognitive structures. Such signs stay signs, or remain as potential information (BELKIN, 1978; INGWERSEN, 1984, 1992) at a linguistic surface level. Figure 1 demonstrates the two conditions that must be met. The first condition is found at the sign level and corresponds to the information concept applied by SALTON and others who conduct system-driven research. Texts and text features *are* information; hence the possibility of retrieving information in text retrieval by means of term weighting and similarity measures in the algorithmic approach. The second condition corresponds to information concepts centered on reduction of uncertainty and similar transformations of cognitive structures. In a very generic sense LOSEE ends his information understanding discussion by viewing information "as the result of a process." The process may be any process, such as chemical, biological, mental, etc. In our cognitive framework each condition is a process involving intentionality—and both conditions must be met. Hence, our information concept, like BROOKES's and BUCKLAND's (see below), is a limited case in terms of Losee's almost universal concept. Further discussions of the cognitive information understanding are provided by Ingwersen (1992; 1996) and, in connection to Popper and Shannon, by COLE in a recent analysis.

BROOKES's and BUCKLAND's (1991a; 1991b) information concepts have properties in common. Brookes regards information as an increment of knowledge where information interacts with the existing cognitive structures of an individual. The result is a modified set of structures: $K(S) + \delta I = K(S + \delta S)$. This, BROOKES's equation, is in pseudo-mathematical form and acts like a model. It states in a very general way that the knowledge structures $K(S)$ are changed into a new modified state of knowledge $K(S + \delta S)$ by the information δI, the δS indicating the effect of the modification. In other versions the equation symbol is replaced by an arrow pointing to the right, whereby its irreversible aspects are stressed. The equation can be illustrated by the dynamic interaction at the cognitive levels of information between generator and recipient (Figure 1). By introducing Popper's Three World Ontology into information science, Brookes suggests a dual model of knowledge: Objective knowledge (World 3), that is, man-made data structures, such as books or computer files; and Subjective knowledge (World 2), that is, the cognitive spaces of individuals. The interaction between the two constitutes the information processes and the focus for information science. Brookes places the focus on World 3. (World 1, i.e., artifacts, is not discussed.) The problem with his model is the omission of the forces driving the information processes, for example, intentionality and interpretation, the reasons for information transfer.

A similar flaw occurs in BUCKLAND's (1991a; 1991b) tripartite notion of information. Without reference to Brookes' 1980 contribution, Buckland divides the world into similar concepts. (1) Information-as-Thing, that is, the words, texts, images, man-made data structures, exhibitions of natural artifacts, etc. equals Objective knowledge. (2) Information-as-Knowledge is analogous to Brookes's Subjective knowledge. (3) Information-as-Process is like Brookes's interactions, or the informing acts during which data structures transform into cognition and knowledge. Also, Buckland introduces an additional notion of information processing, which signifies the tangible manipulation of data at a linguistic sign level (Figure 1) and may take place in computers. In contrast to Brookes, Buckland discusses whether a natural artifact such as an animal or a DNA molecule is Information-as-Thing. In my opinion, this question is about how sensory data can become information, that is, can inform and become cognition and knowledge. With the two-conditional concepts in mind, one would suggest that this is possible if an intentional hypothesis exists concerning an object. For example, a person observing an object, such as a star, with a hypothesis in mind, acts both as sender of a message (a test) and as recipient of data (the test result). Depending on the person's perceptions and presuppositions (a theory), influenced by a domain, this process affects and transforms the state of knowledge. The test data becomes information on the object.

According to his holistic cognitive model (INGWERSEN, 1992, p. 16), later enhanced (1996, p. 9) to attempt a cognitive IR theory, IR interaction consists of interactive communication processes involving five major cognitive actors: (1) information objects or knowledge sources, including their representations, originating from author and indexer knowledge structures; (2) system structures, such as retrieval algorithms, generated by designers, system owners, etc.; (3) interface functionalities, made by system designers or consisting of human intermediary cognitive structures; (4) the user's cognitive space, consisting of work task and situational perceptions, current state of knowledge, problem and uncertainty states, etc.; and (5) the socio-organizational environment, including the situational context, domain structures, work tasks, strategies, and preferences. The model emphasizes that the last two components interact and influence human behavior and the generation of new information objects over time.

This cognitive model illustrates BUCKLAND's (1991a; 1991b) tripartite notions. Foremost, the information objects as well as the system setting encompass his concept of Information-as-Thing. His Information-as-Knowledge equals the cognitive space, and the interactions occurring during information transfer between the components illustrate Information-as-Process. Information processing, his other notion, coincides with the interaction of information objects and the setting. Only the socio-organizational environment is not dealt with explicitly by Buckland.

Information Need

According to the cognitive approach, an individual information need is a function of the current knowledge state of the individual (BELKIN ET AL., 1982a; BELKIN & VICKERY; WERSIG; WILSON, 1981).

Information needs may be stable and well-defined, as is often the case in patent searching and selective dissemination of information (SDI) or information filtering. However, frequently information needs are variable, especially in initial exploratory search sessions where they may be vaguely stated or ill-defined (BORLUND & INGWERSEN; SCHAMBER ET AL.; SU).

According to INGWERSEN (1996, p. 15) four types of information need initiation cases may occur, each of which affects subsequent inter-action and information need development. If the cognitive structures behind the information need are strong, the probability that the need can be well-defined is high; the information need may then be either (1) stable or (2) variable. If it is variable, the user is not sure whether the initial information need is adequate but is willing to learn. However, if the structures are weak, that is, the user scarcely knows how to define the lack of information, two cases occur: (3) the need is intrinsically ill-defined or muddled and the user feels the need as stable, or (4) the user is motivated for change, that is, willing to learn. Ill-defined stable information needs (case 3) can be observed in cases of librarians carry-ing out retrieval on behalf of users, as shown by INGWERSEN (1982). All four cases represent different problems to the computer interface/human intermediary and the retrieval system.

Under the individual cognitive view, the suggestion would have been to provide feedback to the user about the information space, such as characteristics of the knowledge resources stored in or retrieved by the system; see for example, proposals by INGWERSEN (1984) and evaluations by EFTHIMIADIS (1995). Under the holistic view, this might work for the two cases in which the user's information need is well-defined. In the two cases in which the user's cognitive structures are weak, the information need may be too ill-defined to be useful for interactive system activities such as providing relevance feedback or assisting in query modification, expansion, or enhancement. In such cases of cognitive confusion, additional means for information transfer and cognition are required. According to the cognitive view, one way is to provide exploratory means for learning and cognition in IR systems, e.g., by browsing and navigation, as proposed by BATES (1989), and supported by plausible inference networking (TURTLE & CROFT). It is important to be aware of the distinctions between (1) the real work tasks, problem situations, or simply interests that lead people to engage in information seeking behavior; (2) the intrinsic perception or understanding of such situations or tasks presumably of more stable nature than a need for information triggered by such perceptions; and (3) the statements concerned with the perception of the information need. WILSON (1981) makes similar distinctions between the intrinsic information need and the perceived reasons underlying it in his cognitively based analyses of information need characteristics.

Current interactive TREC experiments involve feedback from systems; relevance feedback to systems; and query modification, expansion, or enhancement. Because noninteractive TREC experiments typically evaluate IR systems based on stable and well-defined topics, one may argue that the results basically pertain only to stable and well-defined information need statements. The most recent interactive experiments, however, allow for variations in information need and its perception over IR session time. Generally, the interactive TREC experiments as well as the OKAPI evaluation studies (ROBERTSON) provide useful results that demonstrate (1) the actual limitations of TREC, in particular concerning its noninteractive tracks; and (2) how searcher inconsistency, feedback, and query modification can support a holistic cognitive IR theory.

Preliminary interactive TREC experiments on the retrieval performance of combined query versions generated by several searchers, but deriving from the same well- and pre-defined information need statement (i.e., a TREC topic), demonstrate a performance result similar to that of the best-performing single query. This single-query result is, of course, always unknown beforehand and hence unpredictable (BELKIN ET AL., 1993). IIVONEN also looks into searcher and search-term inconsistencies in applying interactive TREC topics. This interesting research on intersearcher consistency, similar to the interindexer consistency and hypertext interlinker consistency experiments made outside TREC (ELLIS ET AL.), strongly indicates that the individual cognitive nature of the request formulation is rooted in intrinsic situational causality. Following the cognitive view, the intrinsic causality concerns the perception and interpretation in context of the incoming messages, say a TREC topic and the ensuing interactive feedback from the system. With scarce or no situational context provided around the test topic— the why of the search—the user must provide for it him/herself. This may be the reason for the variations and inconsistency observed in the experiments. More realistically, the most recent interactive TREC experiments ask the test persons to retrieve aspects of topics over session time (HARMAN). This makes room for more dynamics in the IR processes. In a cognitive sense the next step toward more realism during experimentation would be to introduce problem situations or work tasks to be solved by the test persons. In this way the test persons would have cause for their retrieval behavior, and one might make use of the persons' work-task perceptions in the form of statements or search activities, in addition to often vague descriptions of the information gaps. From empirical research outside TREC we obtain strong indications that feedback from systems is used differently during IR sessions (SPINK & LOSEE; SPINK & SARACEVIC, 1998). During the session users increasingly tend to focus on the perceived underlying situation, problem, or task leading to information seeking in the first place, or other aspects of the interaction (ROBINS)—and less on the topic. This conception of utilizing the "problematic situation"—but less explicitly the perceived work task—essentially refers to WERSIG's (1979) original ideas, the ASK hypothesis (BELKIN ET AL., 1982a), and the Monstrat Model (BELKIN ET AL., 1983).

DIMENSIONS OF THE HOLISTIC VIEW

During this second period the understanding of information as a situational phenomenon is quite clear. A direct consequence of the situational approach and the enhanced cognitive model is a shift away from the idea of simply bringing cognitive structures into accord. Instead, the new cognitive IR theory focuses on the explicit application of the cognitive structures of different origin involved in IR interaction. The objective is to point to the potential value of matching the multidimensional variety of representations inherent in or extracted/interpreted from information objects and from the cognitive space of a user in a social and situational context. The work task and its perception by a user is regarded as just as valuable as the information need in the form of requests (INGWERSEN, 1996).

Polyrepresentation of Information Objects

Cognitive IR theory favors all kinds of variations in information structures, and particularly favors retrieval overlaps between such variations. The assumption is that the more disparate the structures in cognitive origin, logic, functionality, and time, the smaller the overlap and the better and probably more relevant the retrieval outcome (INGWERSEN, 1996). The concepts of cognitive retrieval overlaps, data fusion (BELKIN ET AL., 1995b), and request fusion are essential elements of a theory framed by the cognitive perspective. For example,

SARACEVIC & KANTOR point to retrieval overlaps and their potential for improved retrieval outcome in a combined information seeking and retrieval user study.

The overlaps are based on a principle of multiple evidence or polyrepresentation. The principle originates from the arguments proposed by TURTLE & CROFT in 1990 with regard to their generic inference network proposal. The network implies different ways of referring to the same concept and of linking different concepts in the form of a conceptual net thrown over the underlying information objects. Following INGWERSEN (1992, p. 201), the principle implies analog representations in a variety of different forms of one information object, or of an information requirement. Fundamentally the representations are forms of the different cognitive structures noted above.

Representations of different cognitive origin and type are generated via a variety of well-known retrieval and (automatic) indexing methods applied to IR systems. Different indexing methods, for example, natural language versus controlled vocabulary, applied to the same text collection retrieve different sets of text or passages for the same query. A passage can equal a paragraph, a section, or a figure in a full-text object. In online bibliographic databases, human indexing with a small number of controlled terms per document results in a representation based on human interpretation and domain expertise of the entire full-text object. As such, this leads to a heavy reduction in access possibilities, although new facets of potential informative value may have been added by the indexer. The automatic natural-language processing (NLP) approach provides many more access points, but generated by the author. The author's terms in section headings or titles are assumed to have greater weight than similar words in the text body. Hence, the writing style in scientific communication influences the NLP result differently due to its domain dependence. The NLP result can be automatically filtered through a domain-specific thesaurus of controlled terms. Thesauri are actually interpretations of a domain by experts different from the indexers (INGWERSEN, 1996).

Several empirical investigations carried out in the operational Boolean environment demonstrate clearly that the combination or the overlap of controlled index terms and natural-language representations yields better retrieval results than the two separately (KATZER ET AL.; LANCASTER; TENOPIR). The more variety in cognitive origin of representation, the more different the results and narrower the overlaps. Because of individual variance in interpretation, human indexing results in retrieved sets rather different from those based on automatic indexing. INGWERSEN (1996) exemplifies how the mixing of author-generated title and abstract terms with indexer-generated terms can be applied following a Boolean quorum logic combined with the cognitive principle of polyrepresentation or multiple evidence in traditional online bibliographic databases. AHLGREN (1998; 1999) proposes how to improve and logically simplify this cognitive online approach.

One of very few investigations of the overlap in retrieval of journal articles using term indexing and citation indexing was carried out by MCCAIN. As expected, for the same queries in Medline and the citation databases, the two very different cognitive structures of indexers and citing authors yielded an overlap of only 11% on average. PAO's (1993; 1994) similar investigations of the overlap between indexing and citation analysis went further by clearly demonstrating that up to 90% of retrieved documents in the narrow overlap set were judged relevant by experts. HARTER ET AL. investigated two confirmatory representative structures associated with scientific communication—those of citing and cited authors—and observed their semantic relationships or overlaps. SWANSON's 1986 methodology for examination of scientific communication patterns to discover hitherto unknown connections between two medically remote research communities belongs to the same kind of multiple evidence approach. There is a small but increasing interest in these approaches to retrieval based on different types of citation indexing. When invented three decades ago, citation indexing was seen as an alternative to text retrieval (GARFIELD). Now in light of current cognitive theory and information technology, they appear to offer far more in combination than anticipated.

With respect to overlaps between sets of texts retrieved via different best-match (and Boolean) techniques or search engines for the same user statement, the picture is identical. From a cognitive perspective, this evidence of variety is obvious. This is the idea behind data fusion as discussed by KANTOR and first put into practice in the I³R system developed by CROFT & THOMPSON.

An interesting line of research is proposed by VAN RIJSBERGEN & LALMAS and LALMAS & RUTHVEN. Van Rijsbergen & Lalmas suggest the application of uncertainty logics, including abduction, because uncertainty and unpredictability are fundamental obstacles to effective access to information in IR. They go on to propose the application of the Dempster-Schafer theory of evidence as a logical tool in IR. The proposal is carried on by Lalmas & Ruthven. In many ways their approach seems associated with or complementary to cognitive theory, primarily with regard to the use of uncertainty and multiple evidence or polyrepresentation of information objects. A comprehensive cognitive IR theory should not only attempt to bridge or associate with prevailing theories in mainstream research, but it ought also to be able to explain some fundamental problems that occur in such theories. One example is the well-known but unrealistic assumptions of term and relevance-assessment independence concerning probabilistic and vector-space techniques (ELLIS, 1996). The term-independence assumption implies that each term or feature in an information object is independent of other features. Terms are the entities on which probabilistic or vector calculations are made, and they seem to yield a better performance result on average than the use of concepts or composite terms or phrases. Similarly, each relevance assessment of a ranked list of objects is assumed to be independent, or not to influence other assessments. The first assumption is in fact realistic in a cognitive sense if we assume that authors actually write meaningful texts and the query is rich. In such cases (INGWERSEN, 1996), when a text passage is retrieved containing a vast number of independent query terms, the probability that we reach a meaningful text entity is high and correct topicality is assured. Clearly, we have not necessarily retrieved information in a cognitive sense, but conceivably a meaning quite identical to the query. DRETSKE's semantic information theory comes to mind, in which information (seen as the text itself, as opposed to the cognitive information conception) leads to meaning, that is, to making sense. In addition, although phrases are more concise and precise features, they are more semantically closed than single terms. In a cognitive sense, the bigger the context, the more disambiguation at the semantic linguistic level (Figure 1), and the fewer the paths into information space of possibly useful nature to the user. Hence, phrases limit recall. The relevance-independence assumption should be seen in the light of the Cranfield-like experiments in which titles or short abstracts were presented to users. In that case the assumption does not necessarily hold because each assessment will be as fast and possible to remember as the ensuing one. This depends, of course, on the presentation mode of objects. However, if full-text objects are assessed, the independence assumption may very well hold due to cognitive overload during assessments.

Cognitive Space and IR Interactions

Two particularly important structures in the cognitive space of the user are the perceptions of the work task and the information need that drive the user's seeking behavior. Various researchers are finding ways to observe and understand the relationship of work task to information need with the goal of designing more responsive IR systems that employ mechanisms such as feedback and query expansion.

Work task. As part of the situational context surrounding the world model of the user (Figure 1) are the work tasks imposed by the social-organizational environment and perceived by the user by means of his or her current cognitive state as an interest, problem, or task to be pursued (INGWERSEN, 1996). This act of perception can be seen as a dominant component of the problematic situation conceived in the ASK hypothesis (BELKIN ET AL., 1982a), or the component regarded as the cause for information need development. In a cognitive sense the user's perception of a work task is likely to be more stable over IR session time than the corresponding dynamic information need. The perception of work task is thus appropriate to utilize, as it may provide the context necessary for the system to retrieve relevant information, i.e., information useful to that user in carrying out the work task. This conception of context and information use is associated with WILSON (1981). In this respect we may see how decade-old conceptions, proposals and observations often are resurfacing and tuned into new shapes due to the ongoing process of research in the field.

Several extensive studies of the influence of work task on IR have been made. BYSTRÖM & JÄRVELIN, in a study based partly on the cognitive view and partly on sense-making theory, investigated the complexity of work tasks and how it affects not only IR but also information seeking and use in decision making. Their results show that, in the case of complex and ad hoc work tasks, both the information need and corresponding problem perception are extremely weak or nonexistent. The user can describe only the perceived work task itself. Evidently, any IR design and/or evaluation ought to take that factor into consideration. Researchers should investigate the socio-organizational environment and domains with respect to characteristics of work tasks and preferences as well as their associated problem and need manifestations. This type of domain analysis can be carried out by means of common social science data collection and analysis methods, such as process analysis. A detailed model for work-task analyses is provided by RASMUSSEN ET AL. (p. 206) in their empirically based cognitive ecological framework, which covers both design and evaluation issues of information systems and is both analytical and empirical.

In evaluation of IR systems, BORLUND & INGWERSEN (1997) created simulated work-task situations, or cover stories, that were employed by test users to generate their own information needs. Although the study was small in scale, the results indicate that IR systems can be tested applying simulated task frames. Currently, the technique of applying real information needs generated by test users in response to simulated work tasks is being studied in large-scale IR system evaluation experiments involving full-text and best-match algorithms including query modification (BORLUND; BORLUND & INGWERSEN, 1999). ALLEN (1996a, 1996b) and HERSH ET AL. use the work-task approach in a more pragmatic and user-centered study, while JOSE ET AL. rely on the Borlund technique of simulated tasks and information situations in an evaluation study of image retrieval. REID supports Borlund's technique in promoting a task-oriented approach to IR evaluation in general. It should be noted that a task can be understood in two ways in

IR: (1) as a work task that originates external to the user from an information and domain situation and (2) as one or several different retrieval or search tasks of specific conceptual or retrieval nature to be performed in connection with searching for information. Hersh et al. study the task phenomenon in its latter capacity as does MARCHIONINI, who regards information seeking as a process in which the search task consists of a series of actions in pursuit of an aim. The aim is identical to the work task or interest. Search tasks are also (re)investigated in relation to online searching, i.e., searching virtual environments, such as digital libraries or the World Wide Web. Various approaches to investigating cognitive style are recently discussed. FORD introduces the use of neural networks to handle fuzzy navigational behavior, while PALMQUIST & KIM observe search performance in terms of time spent and number of nodes traversed, and S. PARK looks into the role of integrated interaction and user control of the distributed environment including database selection.

The work task and its effect on the user's perception constitutes a valuable dimension of the cognitive space of the user, in line with problem and information need perceptions. Conceivably, this multidimensionality can be further exploited in building request models to extract descriptions of various user perceptions.

Feedback and query expansion. SPINK ET AL. (1998a) conducted a large-scale empirical investigation of elicitations of information from users by search intermediaries in standard online IR situations. By means of 40 mediated IR interactions and more than 1500 elicitations, the authors establish a categorization of purpose and strategies for mediated questions from users with real needs and monitor the transition sequences from one type of question to another. Their conclusions are compared to previous interaction studies and models (BELKIN ET AL., 1987; INGWERSEN, 1982, 1996; SARACEVIC, 1996a; SARACEVIC ET AL., 1990) and stress in a very detailed manner the importance of extracting information from the user on search terms, domain knowledge level, previous information seeking experience, and search knowledge. SPINK & SARACEVIC (1997) found that search terms evaluated from systems feedback and later applied to query expansion were found to be highly productive, as was the interactive IR session in teams of users.

Feedback from IR systems is thus a fundamental element both in standard online retrieval and in relation to best-match IR, for instance, in TREC. Based on the cognitive approach and cybernetics theory, SPINK analyzes three different feedback frameworks applied in information science research. She suggests enhancing the feedback concept within the cognitive understanding of information, thus illuminating the information seeking and retrieval context. In an *ARIST* chapter,

SPINK & LOSEE present a comprehensive overview of feedback issues in IR. SPINK & SARACEVIC (1998) provide a smaller but highly structured review related to human-computer interaction in IR.

Manual query modification during experimentation, for example, in the OKAPI experiments (HANCOCK-BEAULIEU ET AL.), combined with relevance feedback, demonstrates highly interesting results from a cognitive view. It provides the basis for improved cognition and expression by the user of the underlying problem or work task and, possibly, of the actual need for information, by forcing the user to interpret the search outcome (SPINK ET AL., 1998a). This outcome does not have to be monolithic, that is, one simple ranked list, but may also contain pointers to several conceivable routes into information space, for example, hypertext links, class names, condensed or structured lists of concepts, and analogous means of conceptual feedback. The structures of monolithic term lists have been empirically evaluated by EFTHIMIADIS (1995) from a cognitive and user-centered view. Simple frequency-ranked term lists seem less valuable than lists ranked with the "best" search terms first.

The results of some investigations disagree on the effect of query modification on retrieval outcome. BELKIN ET AL. (1996a) maintain that interactive query modification adds to the performance of the total IR system, measured as recall and precision in interactive TREC experiments. In contrast, HANCOCK-BEAULIEU ET AL. claim that manual query expansion in various forms does not increase overall performance but rather decreases it. The latter result has been confirmed by MAGENNIS & VAN RIJSBERGEN. However, the investigations on this matter are very few and, due to the experimental settings, difficult to compare. We have indications that successful use of ranked retrieval systems depends heavily on the users' mental models of how such systems operate, including functionality like relevance feedback and query modification (BELKIN ET AL., 1996b).

It should be noted that equal treatment, accumulation, or fusion of request versions (or relevance feedback) over IR session time, as done in noninteractive best-match algorithms, is incompatible with a cognitive theory for information transfer. Because cognitive theory assumes that dynamic interpretations, learning and cognition take place during information interaction, the latest versions of requests should be given higher priority or weighting than previous versions in interactive best-match algorithms. This does not make objects redundant that previously have been judged relevant and still are seen as useful by the user. The systems design should obviously allow for a return path or save functions, consistent with the observations of relevance behavior by FLORANCE & MARCHIONINI. CAMPBELL and CAMPBELL & VAN RIJSBERGEN propose an application of a probabilistic model, called the Ostensive Model, that reduces the weights given to previous relevance feedback results, thus conforming to the realistic concept of information need and situational variation during IR. The implemented system is intended to work without query reformulations by the user, a conception similar to that of the THOMAS system (ODDY, 1977b); instead it displays image representations of the information objects in the form of clusters of candidate objects generated by the highest-ranked objects based on the previous relevance feedback actions with falling probabilistic weights. In the effort to reduce clutter, the candidates are only shown around the current object chosen by the user. The path of previously assessed clusters is the sequence of objects from the starting point to the current object. The user is thus free to select any object at any time as the new current object (CAMPBELL).

Relevance and Evaluation

The TREC and other interactive investigations and experiments demonstrate the problematic issues concerned with the concept of relevance and the evaluation methods generally applied in IR. Until recently a basic drawback of the cognitive approach has been a lack of discussion directed toward these issues. Yet, the number of journal articles on relevance alone has increased tremendously since the SCHAMBER ET AL. article in 1990: in that year 9 articles were published and in 1996-1997 the trend peaked with more than 50 articles per year. Schamber reviews the issue of relevance in *ARIST* (SCHAMBER, 1994) and has herself contributed to the empirical study of relevance assessment criteria from a cognitive approach (SCHAMBER, 1991), along with others, including BARRY, BARRY & SCHAMBER, BRUCE, and T. K. PARK. A thorough discussion of evaluation of IR systems can be found in the *ARIST* 32 chapter by HARTER & HERT.

The relevance experiments and investigations, including those associated with TREC, led SARACEVIC (1996b) to produce the most comprehensive model of relevance types and IR interaction. The model is seen as an alternative to but strongly associated with the cognitive models proposed by INGWERSEN (1992; 1996) and BELKIN ET AL. (1995a). Saracevic's model is at least two-dimensional. One dimension is occupied by three communication levels. The (1) processing level corresponds roughly to SMEATON's morpho-lexical and syntactic linguistic levels, and the (2) interactive and (3) cognitive levels to Smeaton's semantic and pragmatic levels. The other dimension consists of five increasingly subjective types of relevance: from (1) algorithmic, which is similar to ranked machine output, e.g., in TREC; through (2) topicality; (3) pertinence to information needs; and (4) situational relevance. Situational relevance corresponds to the work-task situation. Saracevic also introduces (5) an emotional/intentional type of relevance that can be seen as a socio-cognitive assessment category referring to the domain and its collective preferences (COSIJN & INGWERSEN). Later SPINK ET AL. (1998b) add two new dimensions to the model: time and relevance scaling. BORLUND & INGWERSEN (1998) propose the application of scaling during IR experimentation and two new performance measures built on the Saracevic model: relative relevance, which compares different types of relevance assigned by users to the same ranked output; and ranked half-life measures, which measure the capacity of the system to rank the most relevant object as high on the list as possible. From a more logical and structured stand, MIZZARO (1996; 1997) analyzes the variety of conceptualizations of relevance, including cognitive contributions in IR.

INTEGRATION OF MODELS

The holistic cognitive approach to IR attempts to cover both the information object and system facets of the retrieval processes as well as the user and socio-organizational environment. Information is seen as situational and contextual. Only recently we begin to observe a trend of integrating information retrieval with its natural context: information seeking processes and behavior. The question of integration has always been there, for instance already modeled implicitly by WILSON (1981). Another integrative approach can be seen in connection to the field of scientific communication and informetrics, for which IR has been an essential means to data collection. However, prior to looking into those integrative efforts we will deal with the critical issues of the cognitive view, mainly arising from a meta-theoretical stand.

Critical Issues

VICKERY outlines the individual cognitive approach, mainly belonging to the first period, 1970s to 1990s, and compares it to other epistemological views on information science. His main criticism of the approach is that it is said to lack predictability and practical investigations along its theoretical lines. Since the cognitive view does not adhere to a natural science research tradition, no formal ways exist to model IR and IR interaction from that standpoint. Nevertheless, at a theoretical conceptual level—as a middle-range theory—the holistic cognitive view predicts that deliberate simultaneous use of several different formal IR techniques or algorithms will produce retrieval overlaps that are more relevant (useful) to a user, the more cognitively different the techniques. The condition is that the user's cognitive space is also represented in IR by different but causal cognitive structures in terms of polyrepresentation or multi-evidence. We have seen some empirical indications that this prediction may be correct (MCCAIN; PAO) when applying citation and term representations simultaneously. Another prediction is that simulated work-task situations or cover stories may function just as well as real needs, and more realistically than simple queries, during controlled investigations of interactive IR activities (BORLUND & INGWERSEN, 1997), mainly due to their situational and contextual nature. So far this assumption seems not to have been falsified (BORLUND). The building and use of cognitive user and request models that successfully guide researchers through large-scale studies of interaction with IR systems seem successful in the sense that we know of their functional limitations (BELKIN ET AL., 1983; BROOKS, 1987; INGWERSEN, 1992). Hence, more elaborated models, based on empirically investigated successes, errors, or limitations of the former models have been proposed, discussed, and empirically tested (BELKIN ET AL., 1995a; BORLUND & INGWERSEN, 1997; HARTER & HERT; INGWERSEN, 1996; MIZZARO, 1996, 1997; RASMUSSEN ET AL.; SARACEVIC, 1996a; SPINK ET AL., 1998b; WILSON, 1999). This is perhaps the major contrast to the prevailing black-box system-driven research tradition in IR. The crude Cranfield model (CLEVERDON ET AL.) has hardly changed for decades, although the same tradition increasingly produces evidence that suggests including variables of more interactive nature than simplistic relevance feedback. The complexity on the user side, framed by social interaction in dynamic situational contexts, forces the cognitive researcher to finely grain the investigative models in order to observe and analyze the dependent variables between system elements, properties of information objects, and actors in context. One should note that the context surrounding the actor actually includes both the socio-environmental (domain) influence and the information objects embedded in system settings produced by that environment. Some research concepts are common to both types of context, but with quite different connotations. For instance, uncertainty is a dominant concept in formal probabilistic retrieval models. However, uncertainty is regarded as a state of mind during social interaction, information seeking, and IR activity. This uncertainty during interpretation of knowledge sources was predicted earlier (BELKIN ET AL., 1982a; INGWERSEN, 1992; WERSIG) and is found empirically to increase during the initial stages of interaction, dependent on the knowledge state of the user (KUHLTHAU, 1991, 1999). Comprehensive cognitive models should operate with both kinds of uncertainty.

One may agree with VICKERY and ELLIS (1992) that both cognitive (and user-oriented) research as well as system-driven R&D (named physicalistic by Ellis (1992)) suffered from a kind of theory weakness or, at least, theory fragmentation. With respect to the individual cognitive approach Ellis's objections concern mainly two aspects of the theory. First, he disapproves of the attempt to view cognitive structures in systems and information objects, seen as artifacts, and human cognition under the same model (1992, p. 59). In a cognitive theory for IR this unified conception is, however, regarded as a strength, exactly in order to understand the differences between and limitations of such structures that prohibit the interaction. In contrast to traditional IR research, the cognitive view does not per se regard user behavior as highly rational, well-defined, and purposeful. Rather, random action and vagueness are seen as typical elements of retrieval behavior, due to uncertainties and ambiguities as, for instance, demonstrated by the label effect. Second, Ellis indicates that the cognitive view lacks empirical research results (1992, p. 53). This observation is surprising exactly because cognitive modeling is empirically based, for instance by studying the activities and language use during interaction as manifestations of cognitive processes. The modern holistic cognitive view continues to build a unified theory that circumscribes interactive IR processes in which one of the cornerstones is the understanding of the complexity of relevance, relevance assessments, and information use over time. With the recognition of the three revolutions by ROBERTSON & HANCOCK-BEAULIEU, i.e., the cognitive, the interactive, and the relevance revolutions, and the proposed research perspectives by VAKKARI (1998; 1999), VAKKARI & HAKALA, and WILSON (1999) on information behavior, the possibility of creating a unified theory of ISR (information seeking and retrieval)—or at least a comprehensive research framework or program—has increased. The strength of the cognitive approach is its encouragement to engage in empirical investigations at both general and quite detailed levels of study due to its models, assumptions, hypotheses, and hitherto obtained results. Typical to cognitively inspired research is the diversity of data-collection methods, including case-based, observation, and interviewing, and qualitative and quantitative analyses at various levels, including talking-aloud protocol, log, contents, and discourse analyses. However, as in other complementary information research perspectives or approaches, such as the sense-making framework (DERVIN & NILAN), one must be aware of the pitfalls of investigation. For instance, when studying variables in interactive IR or information behavior and seeking processes it is important not only to focus on the correlation of some selected variables, but also to ask whether such variables in fact happen to be marginal, or possibly related to other known variables recognized in earlier work. Similarly, it is important not to invent new names for old concepts, and to relate really novel conceptions to already existing ones.

VICKERY and ELLIS (1992) are critical of the cognitive view in IR because they do not observe a drastic improvement in the theoretical basis of the field. They both wish to see theory proceeding into a better understanding of phenomena, applications, and information practice. A quite different critical view of the individual cognitive view derives from metatheoretical and philosophical approaches to information science. Observations start with FROHMANN (1990), who argues that the individual cognitive view shows heavy signs of mentalism, signifying that reality and the social context are a mental construct. Frohmann (1992) takes his critique further by implying that the view as applied in IR (and in the sense-making framework of DERVIN & NILAN) signifies the "erasure of the social" (FROHMANN, 1992, p. 376), mechanistic instrumentality and, indeed, cognitivism (p. 380), also known as Strong AI. Frohmann's critical views are based on discourse analysis of a variety of articles produced in the 1980s, foremost by Belkin and his teams. HJØRLAND (1992) sees the approach as subjective idealism— close to the mentalistic position—as opposed to his own (1997) method-ological collectivist point of view. In our view, such metatheoretical criticism is unavoidable in a research field which, in reality, is heavily technology-dependent but progressing from a natural science-like IT-focused framework into the domains of social science with all its variety of philosophical attributes and schools.

The essential research problem in information science, IR and infor-mation seeking, and like fields is to understand the reality and func-tionality of complex formal technologies, such as best-match retrieval systems, in interaction with a multitude of interlinked and unstruc-tured knowledge resources, some even constantly changing like the World Wide Web, and individuals in a situated social context. In such information fields and sciences, the system/knowledge source/actor/ domain/social context of interactivity is most often seen as a phenom-enon in which the totality of activities becomes fragmented into sepa-rate elements. This is unfortunate because it reduces the potential for understanding the complexity of information phenomena.

HJØRLAND & ALBRECHTSEN propose domain analysis as a "new horizon in information science" as opposed to the individual cognitive view. Domain analysis in their sense assumes that the domain and social-cultural structures are the determining factors for information transfer and communication. From a cognitive stand, however, such structures only influence the symbolic and perceptual cognitive struc-tures of individuals in their current situations. The actors in context, i.e., all the derived human knowledge structures involved in IR interaction and seeking of information, are the determining factors that change the domain. For instance, the World Wide Web changes over time due to individual contributions in social interaction. Human social domains can only be dynamic and changeable if individual cognitive structures change, and when they involve and change other structures collectively. The critique is recently summarized by JACOB & SHAW in connection to document representation in an *ARIST* review, in particular with respect to the linguistic issues of representation.

The major differences between the (holistic) cognitive approach in information science and the critical approaches of social realism, including critical hermeneutics, semiotics, and social constructivism (TALJA), are that the latter theoretical constructs thus far have not generated workable empirical research methodologies.

Converging Models

During the 1990s several models of an integrative nature have emerged. The production of convergent models takes place in two dimensions: vertically, by placing interactive IR as an integrative part of information seeking processes, framed by information behavior (VAKKARI 1998, 1999; WILSON, 1999); and horizontally, by modeling interactive IR as seeking strategies or episodes (BELKIN ET AL., 1995a), or by viewing interactive IR in a stratified way (SARACEVIC, 1996a), including the modeling of relevance (1996b).

WILSON (1999) outlines earlier models of information seeking and other aspects of information behavior, initiated by his model (1981). He demonstrates the relationship between communication and information behavior in general with information seeking and retrieval in IR systems in the form of a nested model, arguing that the earlier models address issues at various levels of information behavior. By investigating and discussing the sense-making framework (DERVIN & NILAN), ELLIS's (1989) feature model, KUHLTHAU's (1991) phenomenological stage process model, BELKIN ET AL.'s (1995a) episodic model, INGWERSEN's (1996) cognitive communication model for interactive IR, SARACEVIC's (1996a) stratified IR processing model, and SPINK's feedback framework, Wilson succeeds in bringing together and generalizing the variety of central aspects involved in information behavior in context (1999, pp. 257, 264). In this comprehensive study Wilson further views uncertainty stages in the transition process of (pragmatic) problem solving as an alternative way of approaching information behavior and thus IR. On this issue Wilson relies on the comparison or merge of Ellis's feature and Kuhlthau's stage process models. In relation to uncertainty and problematic situations and solutions Wilson might, for example, have pointed to the ASK hypothesis (BELKIN ET AL., 1982a). Wilson suggests that the discussed models are complementary rather than conflicting, and that his problem-solving model (p. 266) provides a basis for relating the models in appropriate research strategies. In a pioneering effort, VAKKARI (1998) provides a detailed analysis of theory growth in information seeking, in particular the growth of a theoretical research program on the relation between work-task complexity and information seeking. Vakkari follows up on this effort by explicitly addressing and emphasizing the processes and theoretical aspects that link information retrieval theory to information seeking research frameworks (1999).

BELKIN ET AL.'s (1995a) episodic model of information seeking strategies (ISS) or behavior considers the types of search a system must support. It might br considered a model of IR interaction behavior rather than an information seeking model, depending on the level of generalization at which one regards it. The idea behind the model is that people commonly engage in multiple searching behaviors both during IR sessions and across sessions. The goal of the model is to support retrieval (or seeking) by making design and implementation of IR systems adapt to the changing requirements of the systems. Implementation was done in the so-called MERIT system. The model consists of 16 types of behaviors or episodes within a four-dimensional classification of IR modes. Each mode contains a binary number of values and each type of behavior is defined by the four-dimensional values. The four modes are method of searching (scanning or browsing); mode of retrieval (recognition or specification of relevant objects); the goal of retrieval (learning about the system and information space or finding relevant information); and the resource considered (information objects or meta-information). The model has been applied to Web searching and navigation studies, for instance by PHARO. Pharo's test seems to show that the model is not exhaustive and that there is a potential for interdependency between the method of searching and mode of retrieval (p. 211).

SARACEVIC's model of stratified interaction displays a three-level structure consisting of surface, cognitive, and situational strata (1996a). The surface stratum deals primarily with the computational data processing based on a query. The cognitive stratum embraces the process of perceiving information during human-machine interaction in relation to the perceived need for information, and the situational stratum refers to the information use with respect to a perceived work task in context of the environment. The model is clearly associated with that of INGWERSEN (1996, p. 9) and is seen as an alternative model for interactive IR. It is made more comprehensive by incorporating a typology of relevance (1996b), consisting of five different types of relevance: algorithmic, in relation to the system output; topical, in relation to aboutness of information objects and query; pertinence or cognitive relevance, associated with the perceived information need of the user; situational, seen as the usefulness of the objects to the current interest of the user; affective/motivational, associated with the goal of the user.

This model has recently inspired several empirical studies and further modeling of relevance phenomena. For instance, BORLUND & INGWERSEN (1997) explored the possibility of applying situational relevance and topicality assessments in interactive IR experiments using nonbinary relevance assessments and by modeling SARACEVIC's typology (1996b) in relation to real as well as simulated work tasks. That model was later (1998) modified to emphasize the relation between a perceived work task, the dynamic information need developing over time, and relevance categories for test persons as well as assessors in IR experiments. The Borlund & Ingwersen approach also suggests performance measures that incorporate types of relevance (1998). SPINK ET AL. (1998b) empirically investigate what they call regions of relevance, including the application of nonbinary assessments in large-scale interactive studies. Very recently, COSIJN & INGWERSEN re-analyze Saracevic's typology and propose to replace the affective/motivational relevance type with a socio-cognitive category, directly associated with the contextual environment and domain, and originating from ØROM.

With the re-incorporation of situational relevance and situated context into IR and information seeking models, the issue of information use becomes paramount as a research topic. This issue extends the time line commonly observed during IR investigations and makes it increasingly necessary to view information seeking and retrieval as a whole (VAKKARI, 1998). Longitudinal studies of information behavior and search processes should hence play a more central role as an empirical foundation for information seeking and retrieval (ISR) models. KUHLTHAU's (1999) investigations of problem solutions and information behavior over time come to mind, as do the more retrieval-oriented longitudinal studies by WANG and WANG & WHITE. Kuhlthau's study included observations of uncertainty developments in relation to the knowledge state of the user. Wang investigates the alterations of the perceived information needs over research project time, represented by the distribution of articulated unique and novel versus overlapping search terms. Also in an empirical research environment, VAKKARI (2000) and VAKKARI & HAKALA follow the development of relevance, relevance criteria, and contributing information types of searched documents in task performance over an academic term period. Similarly, Wang & White investigate and provide a cognitive model of the actual application of documents at the reading stage, in particular in relation to decisions of citing the works used.

As a special case, one may regard author co-citation maps as adequate indicators of actual interpretations of information and its use. NOYONS ET AL. demonstrate the technique in a bibliometric sense but also with reference to citation mapping that can be applied as a visual IR gateway to the underlying information. WHITE & MCCAIN and

DING ET AL. visualize the clustering of the most co-cited authors in information science and IR respectively. The maps visualize the cognitive authority over a given time period in a scientific community and inform about how the community makes use of scholarly works as well as how it perceives closeness of relationships among works through co-citations on reference lists. In principle, maps of words or other representative means, like journals, produced by identical multidimensional scaling methods and factor analysis from document data, have similar meanings, i.e., how terms or journals are used in connection with one another in information objects that all are results of interpretation and information use.

CONCLUSIONS

The cognitive research approach, based on the epistemological cognitive view, has made significant contributions to a more comprehensive understanding of retrieval processes. As stated by JACOB & SHAW (p. 131), this approach has been instrumental in shifting the focus from the system per se to the interaction between user and the system. However, we cannot claim that the view has completely penetrated the frameworks applied to mainstream research on IR. This fact can easily be observed in the co-citation maps published recently (WHITE & MCCAIN; DING ET AL.) that show the amount and concentration of purely system-driven researchers. Only recently can we detect a more comprehensive view of information retrieval in the context of information seeking, that is, in the context of the social and cultural environment (BYSTRÖM & JÄRVELIN; VAKKARI, 1998, 1999; WILSON, 1999).

Generally speaking, the cognitive approach has from its start in the 1970s been associated with the user and intermediary mechanism configuration in the universe of IR research. Later, in the 1990s, the cognitive view broadens its scope by also seeking to encompass and understand the formal and experimental dimensions of IR by concentrating on all the processes of interaction that take place between the complex variety of actors in interactive IR. Thus, there appear elements of a holistic theory for IR that attempts to view such interactions between representative structures of information objects, symbolic structures in systems, and the user's cognitive space in context of the work or interest domain in a situated manner.

In a more detailed manner we may regard the years 1977-1982 as a time when the cognitive view is established as a theoretical perspective that moves into a research program with initial research models and empirical investigations carried out in accordance with those models. During the period 1982-1986 we find the next wave of empirical research and theoretical analyses, which achieve the ASK hypothesis

(BELKIN ET AL., 1982a), the Monstrat Model for knowledge-based intermediary and systems design (BELKIN ET AL., 1983), and the observation of the Label-Effect and information need typologies (INGWERSEN, 1982, 1984, 1986). The central issue is the user-system interaction via an intermediary mechanism (BELKIN & VICKERY). From 1987 to 1991 we observe the drawbacks of the so-called intelligent (knowledge-based) IR approach (BROOKS, 1987) and attempts to integrate the variety of investigative models in IR (BELKIN ET AL., 1987). We can observe a shift in user-driven research toward exploratory information behavior (BATES, 1989) and situated context (SCHAMBER ET AL.). The period 1992-2000 can be characterized by the increasing interest in phenomena of relevance and uncertainty (SARACEVIC, 1996a, 1996b; SCHAMBER, 1994; WILSON, 1999), the TREC experiments that reinforce the discussion of measures of relevance, realism, and control in experimental settings (HANCOCK-BEAULIEU ET AL.; INGWERSEN, 1996; ROBERTSON & HANCOCK-BEAULIEU), and in particular the focus on a comprehensive perspective on IR interaction in work-task and domain context (BORLUND; BYSTRÖM & JÄRVELIN; VAKKARI, 1999). During this period we further observe remodeling of interactive IR as well as information seeking, based on solid empirical studies of a broad nature in both fields. The critique of the individual cognitive view also appears during this period (HJØRLAND & ALBRECHTSEN; TALJA).

The history of the cognitive view in IR and information studies thus covers nearly 25 years of impressive activity of both theoretical, analytic and, foremost, empirical nature. Although still weak on aspects of information seeking and behavior, the viewpoint increasingly demonstrates the potential of contributing interesting and valid research questions, directions, and solutions to the integrated study of information seeking and retrieval (ISR) in situated context. "We shall not cease from exploration and the end of all our exploring will be to arrive where we started and know the place for the first time."

T. S. Eliot "Little Gidding V" in *Four Quartets*

BIBLIOGRAPHY

AHLGREN, PER. 1998. A Note on Search Formulation Redundancy. Journal of Documentation. 1998 June; 54(3): 352-354. ISSN: 0022-0418; CODEN: JDOCAS.

AHLGREN, PER. 1999. On Cognitive Search Strategy. In: Aparac, Tatjana; Saracevic, Tefko; Ingwersen, Peter; Vakkari, Pertti, eds. CoLIS 3: Proceedings from the 3rd International Conference on Conceptions of Library and Information Science: Digital Libraries: Interdisciplinary Concepts, Challenges and Opportunities; 1999 May 23-26; Dubrovnik, Croatia. Lokve, Croatia: Naklada Benja; 1999. 245-254. ISBN: 953-6003-37-6.

ALLEN, BRYCE L. 1991. Cognitive Research in Information Science: Implications for Design. In: Williams, Martha E., ed. Annual Review of Information Science and Technology: Volume 26. Medford, NJ: Learned Information, Inc. for the American Society for Information Science; 1991. 3-37. ISSN: 0066-4200; ISBN: 0-938734-55-5; CODEN: ARISBC.

ALLEN, BRYCE L. 1996a. From Research to Design: A User-Centered Approach. In: Ingwersen, Peter; Pors, Niels Ole, eds. CoLIS 2: Proceedings of the 2nd International Conference on Conceptions of Library and Information Science; 1996 October 13-16; Copenhagen, Denmark. Copenhagen, Denmark: Royal School of Librarianship; 1996. 45-59. ISBN: 87-7415-260-2.

ALLEN, BRYCE L. 1996b. Information Tasks: Toward a User-Centered Approach to Information Systems. San Diego, CA: Academic Press; 1996. 308p. ISBN: 0-12-051040-5.

BARRY, CAROL L. 1994. User-Defined Relevance Criteria: An Exploratory Study. Journal of the American Society for Information Science. 1994; 45(3): 149-159. ISSN: 0002-8231; CODEN: AISJB6.

BARRY, CAROL L.; SCHAMBER, LINDA. 1998. Users' Criteria for Relevance Evaluation: A Cross-Situational Comparison. Information Processing & Management. 1998; 31(2/3): 219-236. ISSN: 0306-4573; CODEN: IPMADK.

BATES, MARCIA J. 1972. Factors Affecting Subject Catalog Search Success. Berkeley, CA: University of California, 1972. 287p; (Ph.D. dissertation). Available from: UMI, Ann Arbor, MI (UMI order no. 74-15639).

BATES, MARCIA J. 1981. Search Tactics. In: Williams, Martha E., ed. Annual Review of Information Science and Technology: Volume 16. White Plains, NY: Knowledge Industry Publications, Inc. for the American Society for Information Science; 1981. 139-169. ISSN: 0066-4200; ISBN: 0-914236-90-3; CODEN: ARISBC.

BATES, MARCIA J. 1989. The Design of Browsing and Berrypicking Techniques for the Online Search Interface. Online Review. 1989; 13(5): 407-424. ISSN: 0309-314X.

BELKIN, NICHOLAS J. 1977. Internal knowledge and external information. In: de Mey, Marc; Pinxten, Rik; Poriau, M.; Vandamme, Fernand, eds. CC77: International Workshop on the Cognitive Viewpoint; 1977 March 24-26; Ghent, Belgium, University of Ghent. Ghent, Belgium: University of Ghent; 1977. 187-194. OCLC: 6906871.

BELKIN, NICHOLAS J. 1984. Cognitive Models and Information Transfer. Social Science Information Studies. 1984 April/July; 4(2/3): 111-129. ISSN: 0143-6236; CODEN: SOSSD3.

BELKIN, NICHOLAS J. 1990. The Cognitive Viewpoint in Information Science. Journal of Information Science. 1990; 16(1): 11-15. ISSN: 0165-5515.

BELKIN, NICHOLAS J.; BORGMAN, CHRISTINE L.; BROOKS, HELEN M.; BYLANDER, TOM; CROFT, W. BRUCE; DANIELS, PENNY J.; DEERWESTER, SCOTT; FOX, EDWARD A.; INGWERSEN, PETER; RADA, ROY; SPARCK JONES, KAREN; THOMPSON, ROGER; WALKER, DONALD. 1987. Distributed Expert-Based Information Systems: An Interdisciplinary Approach. Information Processing & Management. 1987; 23(5): 395-409. ISSN: 0306-5817; CODEN: IPMADK.

BELKIN, NICHOLAS J.; BROOKS, HELEN M.; DANIELS, PENNY J. 1987. Knowledge Elicitation Using Discourse Analysis. International Journal of Man-Machine Studies. 1987; 27: 127-144. ISSN: 0020-7373.

BELKIN, NICHOLAS J.; COOL, COLLEEN; CROFT, W. BRUCE; CALLAN, JAMES P. 1993. The Effect of Multiple Query Representations on Information Retrieval Performance. In: Korfhage, Robert; Rasmussen, Edie; Willett, Peter, eds. SIGIR '93: Proceedings of the Association for Computing Machinery Special Interest Group on Information Retrieval (ACM/SIGIR) 16th Annual International Conference on Research and Development in Information Retrieval; 1993 June 27-July 1; Pittsburgh, PA. New York, NY: ACM Press; 1993. 339-346. ISBN: 0-89791-605-0.

BELKIN, NICHOLAS J.; COOL, COLLEEN; KOENEMANN, JÜRGEN; NG, KWONG BOR; PARK, SOYEON. 1996a. Using Relevance Feedback and Ranking in Interactive Searching. In: Harman, Donna K., ed. Proceedings of the 4th Text REtrieval Conference (TREC-4); 1995 November 1-3; Gaithersburg, MD. Gaithersburg, MD: National Institute of Standards and Technology; 1996. 181-188. (NIST Special Publication 500-236). OCLC: 36640879.

BELKIN, NICHOLAS J.; COOL, COLLEEN; KOENEMANN, JÜRGEN; PARK, SOYEON; NG, KWONG BOR. 1996b. Information Seeking Behavior in New Searching Environment. In: Ingwersen, Peter; Pors, Niels O. eds., CoLIS 2: Proceedings of the 2nd International Conference on Conceptions of Library and Information Science: Integration in Perspective; 1996 October 13-16; Copenhagen, Denmark, Royal School of Library and Information Science. Copenhagen, Denmark: Royal School of Library and Information Science; 1996. 403-416. ISBN: 87-7415-260-2.

BELKIN, NICHOLAS J.; COOL, COLLEEN; STEIN, ADELHEIT; THIEL, ULRICH. 1995a. Cases, Scripts, and Information Seeking Strategies: On the Design of Interactive Information Retrieval Systems. Expert Systems with Applications. 1995; 9(3): 379-395. ISSN: 0957-4174.

BELKIN, NICHOLAS J.; KANTOR, PAUL; FOX, EDWARD A.; SHAW, J. A. 1995b. Combining the Evidence of Multiple Query Representations for Information Retrieval. Information Processing & Management. 1995; 31: 431-448. ISSN: 0306-4573; CODEN: IPMADK.

BELKIN, NICHOLAS J.; KWASNIK, BARBARA. 1986. Using Structural Representations of Anomalous States of Knowledge for Choosing Document Retrieval Strategies. In: Rabitti, F. ed. Proceedings of the Association for Computing Machinery Special Interest Group on Information Retrieval (ACM-SIGIR) 9th Annual Conference on Research and Development in Information Retrieval; 1986 September 8-10; Pisa, Italy. New York, NY: ACM Press; 1986. 11-22. ISBN: 0-89791-187-3.

BELKIN, NICHOLAS J.; ODDY, ROBERT N.; BROOKS, HELEN M. 1982a. ASK for Information Retrieval: Part I. Background and Theory. Journal of Documentation. 1982 June; 38(2): 61-71. ISSN: 0022-0418; CODEN: JDOCAS.

BELKIN, NICHOLAS J.; ODDY, ROBERT N.; BROOKS, HELEN M. 1982b. ASK for Information Retrieval: Part II. Results of a Design Study. Journal of Documentation. 1982 September; 38(3): 145-164. ISSN: 0022-0418; CODEN: JDOCAS.

BELKIN, NICHOLAS J.; SEEGER, THOMAS; WERSIG, GERNOT. 1983. Distributed Expert Problem Treatment as a Model for Information Systems Analysis and Design. Journal of Information Science. 1983; 5: 153-167. ISSN: 0165-5515.

BELKIN, NICHOLAS J.; VICKERY, ALINA. 1985. Interaction in Information Systems. London, UK: British Library; 1985. 250p. ISBN: 0-7123-3050-X.

BORGMAN, CHRISTINE L. 1989. All Users of Information Retrieval Systems Are Not Created Equal: An Exploration into Individual Differences. Information Processing & Management. 1989; 25(3): 237-252. ISSN: 0306-4573; CODEN: IPMADK.

BORLUND, PIA. 2000. Experimental Components for the Evaluation of Interactive Information Retrieval Systems. Journal of Documentation. 2000 January; 56(1): 71-90. ISSN: 0022-0418; CODEN: JDOCAS.

BORLUND, PIA; INGWERSEN, PETER. 1997. The Development of a Method for the Evaluation of Interactive Information Retrieval Systems. Journal of Documentation. 1997 June; 53(3): 225-250. ISSN: 0022-0418; CODEN: JDOCAS.

BORLUND, PIA; INGWERSEN, PETER. 1998. Measures of Relative Relevance and Ranked Half-Life: Performance Indicators for Interactive IR. In: Croft, W. Bruce; Moffat, Alistair; Van Rijsbergen, C.J.; Wilkinson, Ross; Zobel, Justin, eds. SIGIR '98: Proceedings of the Association for Computing Machinery Special Interest Group on Information Retrieval (ACM/SIGIR) 21st Annual International Conference on Research and Development in Information Retrieval; 1998 August 24-28; Melbourne, Australia. New York, NY: ACM Press; 1998. 324-331. ISBN: 1-58113-015-5.

BORLUND, PIA; INGWERSEN, PETER. 1999. The Application of Work Tasks in Connection with the Evaluation of Interactive Information Retrieval Systems: Empirical Results. In: Dunlop, Mark, ed. Mira '99: Final Mira Conference on Information Retrieval Evaluation; 1999 April 14-16; Glasgow, UK. Glasgow, UK: Department of Computing Sciences; 1999. 29-46. Avail. WWW: http://www.dcs.gla.ac.uk/mira/workshops/conference.

BOULDING, KENNETH E. 1956. The Image. Ann Arbor, MI: University of Michigan Press; 1956. 175p. OCLC: 376662.

BRIER, SØREN. 1996. Cybersemiotics: A New Interdisciplinary Development Applied to the Problems of Knowledge Organization and Document Retrieval in Information Science. Journal of Documentation. 1996; 52(3): 296-344. ISSN: 0022-0418; CODEN: JDOCAS.

BROOKES, B. C. 1980. The Foundation of Information Science: Part 1: Philosophical Aspects. Journal of Information Science. 1980; 2: 125-133. ISSN: 0165-5515.

BROOKS, HELEN M. 1986. Developing and Representing Problem Descriptions. In: Intelligent Information Systems for the Information Society. Amsterdam, The Netherlands: North-Holland; 1986. 141-161. ISBN: 0-444-70050-1.

BROOKS, HELEN M. 1987. Expert Systems and Intelligent Information Retrieval. Information Processing & Management. 1987; 23(4): 367-382. ISSN: 0306-4573; CODEN: IPMADK.

BRUCE, HARRY W. 1994. A Cognitive View of the Situational Dynamism of User-Centered Relevance Estimation. Journal of the American Society for Information Science. 1994; 45: 142-148. ISSN: 0002-8231; CODEN: AISJB6.

BUCKLAND, MICHAEL K. 1991a. Information as Thing. Journal of the American Society for Information Science. 1991; 42(5): 351-360. ISSN: 0002-8231; CODEN: AISJB6.

BUCKLAND, MICHAEL K. 1991b. Information and Information Systems. New York, NY: Praeger; 1991. 225p. ISBN: 0-275-93851-4.

BYSTRÖM, KATRIINA; JÄRVELIN, KALERVO. 1995. Task Complexity Affects Information Seeking and Use. Information Processing & Management. 1995; 31(2): 191-214. ISSN: 0306-4573; CODEN: IPMADK.

CAMPBELL, IAIN. 2000. Interactive Evaluation of the Ostensive Model Using a New Test Collection of Images with Multiple Relevance Assessments. Information Retrieval. 2000; 2(1): 87-114. ISSN: 1386-4564.

CAMPBELL, IAIN; VAN RIJSBERGEN, C. J. 1996. The Ostensive Model of Developing Information Needs. In: Ingwersen, Peter; Pors, Niels Ole, eds. CoLIS 2: Proceedings of the 2nd International Conference on Conceptions of Library and Information Science: Integration in Perspective; 1996 October 13-16; Copenhagen, Denmark. Copenhagen, Denmark: Royal School of Librarianship; 1996. 251-268. ISBN: 87-7415-260-2.

CLEVERDON, CYRIL W. 1967. The Cranfield Test on Index Language Devices. Aslib Proceedings. 1967 June; 19(6): 173-194. ISSN: 0001-253X.

COLE, CHARLES. 1999. Activity of Understanding a Problem during Interaction with an "Enabling" Information Retrieval System: Modeling Information Flow. Journal of the American Society for Information Science. 1999; 50(6): 544-552. ISSN: 0002-8231; CODEN: AISJB6.

COSIJN, ERICA; INGWERSEN, PETER. 2000. Dimensions of Relevance. Information Processing & Management. 2000; 36: 533-550. ISSN: 0306-4573; CODEN: IPMADK.

CROFT, W. BRUCE; THOMPSON, ROGER H. 1987. I³R: A New Approach to the Design of Document Retrieval Systems. Journal of the American Society for Information Science. 1987; 38(6): 389-404. ISSN: 0002-8231; CODEN: AISJB6.

DANIELS, PENNY J. 1986. Cognitive Models in Information Retrieval. An Evaluative Review. London, UK: City University; 1986. 67p. OCLC: 17620605.

DE MEY, MARC. 1977. The Cognitive Viewpoint: Its Development and Its Scope. In: de Mey, Marc; Pinxten, Rik; Poriau, M.; Vandamme, Fernand, eds. CC77: International Workshop on the Cognitive Viewpoint; 1977 March 24-26; Ghent, Belgium, University of Ghent. Ghent, Belgium: University of Ghent; 1977. xvi-xxxi. OCLC: 6906871.

DE MEY, MARC. 1980. The Relevance of the Cognitive Paradigm for Information Science. In: Harbo, Ole; Kajberg, Leif, eds. Theory and Application of Information Research: Proceedings of the 2nd International Research Forum on Information Science; 1977 August 3-6; Copenhagen, Denmark, Royal School of Librarianship. London, UK: Mansell; 1980. 48-61. ISBN: 0-7201-1513-2.

DE MEY, MARC. 1982. The Cognitive Paradigm: An Integrated Understanding of Scientific Development. Dordrecht, The Netherlands: D. Reidel Publishing Co.; 1982. 314p. ISBN: 90-277-1382-0.

DERVIN, BRENDA. 1997. Given a Context by Any Other Name: Methodological Tools for Taming the Unruly Beast. In: Vakkari, Pertti; Savolainen, Reijo; Dervin, Brenda, eds. Information Seeking in Context: Proceedings of an International Conference on Research in Information Needs, Seeking and Use in Different Contexts; 1996 August 14-16; Tampere, Finland, Department of Information Studies. London, UK: Taylor Graham; 1997. 13-38. ISBN: 0-947568-71-9.

DERVIN, BRENDA; NILAN, MICHAEL. 1986. Information Needs and Uses. In: Williams, Martha E., ed. Annual Review of Information Science and Technology: Volume 21. White Plains, NY: Knowledge Industry Publications, Inc. for the American Society for Information Science; 1986. 3-33. ISSN: 0066-4200; ISBN: 0-86729-209-1; CODEN: ARISBC.

DING, YING; CHOWDHURY, GOBINDA; FOO, CHUBERT. 1999. Mapping the Intellectual Structure of Information Retrieval Studies: An Author Co-citation Analysis, 1987-1997. Journal of Information Science. 1999; 25(1): 67-78. ISSN: 0165-5515.

DRETSKE, FRED I. 1981. Knowledge and the Flow of Information. Oxford, UK: Basil Blackwell; 1981.

EFTHIMIADIS, EFTHIMIS N. 1995. User Choices: A New Yardstick for the Evaluation of Ranking Algorithms for Interactive Query Expansion. Information Processing & Management. 1995; 31(4): 605-620. ISSN: 0306-5817; CODEN: IPMADK.

EFTHIMIADIS, EFTHIMIS N. 1996. Query Expansion. In: Williams, Martha E., ed. Annual Review of Information Science and Technology: Volume 31. Medford, NJ: Information Today, Inc. for the American Society for Information Science; 1996. 121-187. ISSN: 0066-4200; ISBN: 1-57387-033-1; CODEN: ARISBC.

ELLIS, DAVID. 1989. A Behavioural Approach to Information Retrieval System Design. Journal of Documentation. 1989; 45(3): 171-212. ISSN: 0022-0418; CODEN: JDOCAS.

ELLIS, DAVID. 1992. The Physical and Cognitive Paradigms in Information Retrieval Research. Journal of Documentation. 1992 March; 48(1): 45-64. ISSN: 0022-0418; CODEN: JDOCAS.

ELLIS, DAVID. 1996. Progress and Problems in Information Retrieval. London, UK: Library Association Publishing; 1996. 220p. ISBN: 1-85604-123-9.

ELLIS, DAVID; FURNER-HINES, JONATHAN; WILLETT, PETER. 1994. On the Creation of Hypertext Links in Full-Text Documents: Measurement of Inter-Linker Consistency. Journal of Documentation. 1994 June; 50(2): 67-98. ISSN: 0022-0418; CODEN: JDOCAS.

FENICHEL, CAROL HANSEN. 1981. Online Searching: Measures That Discriminate among Users with Different Types of Experience. Journal of the American Society for Information Science. 1981; 32(1): 23-32. ISSN: 0002-8231; CODEN: AISJB6.

FIDEL, RAYA. 1991a. Searchers' Selection of Search Keys: I. The Selection Routine. Journal of the American Society for Information Science. 1991; 42(7): 490-500. ISSN: 0002-8231; CODEN: AISJB6.

FIDEL, RAYA. 1991b. Searchers' Selection of Search Keys: II. Controlled Vocabulary or Free-Text Searching. Journal of the American Society for Information Science. 1991; 42(7): 501-514. ISSN: 0002-8231; CODEN: AISJB6.

FIDEL, RAYA. 1991c. Searchers' Selection of Search Keys: III. Searching Styles. Journal of the American Society for Information Science. 1991; 42(7): 515-527. ISSN: 0002-8231; CODEN: AISJB6.

FLORANCE, VALERIE; MARCHIONINI, GARY. 1995. Information Processing in the Context of Medical Care. In: Fox, Edward A.; Ingwersen, Peter; Fidel, Raya eds., SIGIR '95: Proceedings of the Association for Computing Machinery Special Interest Group on Information Retrieval (ACM-SIGIR) 18th Annual Conference on Research and Development of Information Retrieval; 1995 July 9-13; Seattle, WA. New York, NY: ACM Press; 1995. 158-163. ISBN: 0-89791-714-6.

FORD, NIGEL. 2000. Cognitive Styles and Virtual Environments. Journal of the American Society for Information Science. 2000; 51(6): 543-557. ISSN: 0002-8231; CODEN: AISJB6.

FOX, EDWARD A. 1987. The Development of the CODER System: A Testbed for Artificial Intelligence Methods in Information Retrieval. Information Processing & Management. 1987; 23(4): 341-366. ISSN: 0306-4573; CODEN: IPMADK.

FOX, EDWARD A.; HIX, DEBORAH; NOWELL, LUCY T.; BRUENI, DENNIS J.; WAKE, WILLIAM C.; HEATH, LENWOOD S.; RAO, DURGESH. 1993. Users, User Interfaces, and Objects: Envision, A Digital Library. Journal of the American Society for Information Science. 1993; 44: 480-491. ISSN: 0002-8231; CODEN: AISJB6.

FROHMANN. BERND. 1990. Rules of Indexing: A Critique of Mentalism in Information Retrieval Theory. Journal of Documentation. 1990 June; 46(2): 81-101. ISSN: 0022-0418; CODEN: JDOCAS.

FROHMANN, BERND. 1992. The Power of Images: A Discourse Analysis of the Cognitive Viewpoint. Journal of Documentation. 1992 December; 48(4): 365-386. ISSN: 0022-0418; CODEN: JDOCAS.

GARFIELD, EUGENE. 1998. From Citation Indexes to Informetrics: Is the Tail Wagging the Dog?. Libri. 1998; 48: 67-80. ISSN: 0024-2667.

HANCOCK-BEAULIEU, MICHELINE; FIELDHOUSE, MARGARET; DO, THIEN. 1995. An Evaluation of Interactive Query Expansion in an Online Library Catalogue with a Graphical User Interface. Journal of Documentation. 1995 September; 51(3): 225-243. ISSN: 0022-0418; CODEN: JDOCAS.

HARMAN, DONNA K., ed. 1999. TREC Publications. Gaithersburg, MD: National Institute of Standards and Technology; 1999. Available WWW: http://trec.nist.gov/pubs.html.

HARTER, STEPHEN P. 1992. Psychological Relevance and Information Science. Journal of the American Society for Information Science. 1992; 43: 602-615. ISSN: 0002-8231; CODEN: AISJB6.

HARTER, STEPHEN P.; HERT, CAROL A. 1997. Evaluation of Information Retrieval Systems: Approaches, Issues and Methods. In: Williams, Martha E., ed. Annual Review of Information Science and Technology: Volume 32. Medford, NJ: Information Today, Inc. for the American Society for Information Science; 1997. 3-94. ISSN: 0066-4200; ISBN: 1-57387-047-1; CODEN: ARISBC; LC: 66-25096.

HARTER, STEPHEN P.; NISONGER, THOMAS E.; WENG, AIWEI. 1993. Semantic Relationships between Cited and Citing Articles in Library and Information Science Journals. Journal of the American Society for Information Science. 1993; 44(9): 543-552. ISSN: 0002-8231; CODEN: AISJB6.

HERSH, WILLIAM; PENTECOST, JEFFREY; HICKAM, DAVID. 1996. A Task-Oriented Approach to Information Retrieval Evaluation. Journal of the American Society for Information Science. 1996; 47(1): 50-56. ISSN: 0002-8231; CODEN: AISJB6.

HJØRLAND, BIRGER. 1992. The Concept of "Subject" in Information Science. Journal of Documentation. 1992 June; 48(2): 172-200. ISSN: 0022-0418; CODEN: JDOCAS.

HJØRLAND, BIRGER. 1997. Information Seeking and Subject Representation: An Activity-Theoretical Approach to Information Science. Westport, CT: Greenwood Press; 1997. 213p. ISBN: 0-313-29893-9.

HJØRLAND, BIRGER; ALBRECHTSEN, HANNE. 1995. Toward a New Horizon in Information Science: Domain Analysis. Journal of the American Society for Information Science. 1995; 46(6): 400-425. ISSN: 0002-8231; CODEN: AISJB6.

IIVONEN, MIRJA. 1995. Consistency in the Selection of Search Concepts and Search Terms. Information Processing & Management. 1995; 31(2): 173-190. ISSN: 0306-4573; CODEN: IPMADK.

INGWERSEN, PETER. 1982. Search Procedures in the Library Analysed from the Cognitive Point of View. Journal of Documentation. 1982 September; 38(3): 165-191. ISSN: 0022-0418; CODEN: JDOCAS.

INGWERSEN, PETER. 1984. A Cognitive View of Three Selected Online Search Facilities. Online Review. 1984; 8(5): 465-492. ISSN: 0309-314X.

INGWERSEN, PETER. 1986. Cognitive Analysis and the Role of the Intermediary in Information Retrieval. In: Davies, R., ed. Intelligent Information Systems. Chichester, West Sussex, UK: Ellis Horwood; 1986. 206-237. ISBN: 0-85312-896-0.

INGWERSEN, PETER. 1992. Information Retrieval Interaction. London, UK: Taylor Graham; 1992. 246p. ISBN: 0-947568-54-9.

INGWERSEN, PETER. 1993. The Cognitive Viewpoint in IR. Journal of Documentation. 1993 March; 49(1): 60-64. ISSN: 0022-0418; CODEN: JDOCAS.

INGWERSEN, PETER. 1995. Information and Information Science. In: Kent, Allen, ed. Encyclopedia of Library and Information Science: Volume 56, Supplement 19. New York, NY: Marcel Dekker; 1995. 137-174. ISBN: 0-8247-2056-3.

INGWERSEN, PETER. 1996. Cognitive Perspectives of Information Retrieval Interaction: Elements of a Cognitive IR Theory. Journal of Documentation. 1996 March; 52(1): 3-50. ISSN: 0022-0418; CODEN: JDOCAS.

INGWERSEN, PETER; PEJTERSEN, ANNELISE MARK. 1986. User Requirements: Empirical Research and Information Systems Design. In: Ingwersen, Peter; Kajberg, Leif; Pejtersen, Annelise Mark, eds. Information Technology and Information Use. London, UK: Taylor Graham; 1986. 111-124. ISBN: 0-947568-06-9.

INGWERSEN, PETER; WORMELL, IRENE. 1988. Means to Improved Subject Access and Representation in Modern Information Retrieval. Libri. 1988; 38(2): 94-119. ISSN: 0024-2667.

JACOB, ELIN K.; SHAW, DEBORA. 1998. Sociocognitive Perspectives on Representation. In: Williams, Martha E., ed. Annual Review of Information Science and Technology: Volume 33. Medford, NJ: Learned Information, Inc. for the American Society for Information Science; 1999. 131-186. ISSN: 0066-4200; ISBN: 1-57387-065-X; CODEN: ARISBC.

JOSE, JOEMON M.; FURNER, JONATHAN; HARPER, DAVID J. 1998. Spatial Querying for Image Retrieval: A User-Oriented Evaluation. In: Croft, W. Bruce; Moffat, Alistair; van Rijsbergen, C. J.; Wilkinson, Ross; Zobel, Justin, eds. SIGIR '98: Proceedings of the Association for Computing Machinery Special Interest Group on Information Retrieval (ACM/SIGIR) 21st Annual International Conference on Research and Development in Information Retrieval; 1998 August 24-28; Melbourne, Australia. New York, NY: ACM Press; 1998. 232-240. ISBN: 1-58113-015-5.

KANTOR, PAUL B. 1994. Information Retrieval Techniques. In: Williams, Martha E., ed. Annual Review of Information Science and Technology: Volume 29. Medford, NJ: Learned Information, Inc. for the American Society for Information Science; 1994. 53-90. ISSN: 0066-4200; ISBN: 0-938734-91-1; CODEN: ARISBC.

KATZER, JEFFREY; MCGILL, MICHAEL J.; TESSIER, JUDITH A.; FRAKES, WILLIAM; DASGUPTA, PADMINI. 1982. A Study of the Overlap among Document Representations. Information Technology: Research and Development. 1982; 1: 261-274. ISSN: 0144-817X.

KUHLTHAU, CAROL COLLIER. 1991. Inside the Search Process: Information Seeking from the User's Perspective. Journal of the American Society for Information Science. 1991; 42: 361-371. ISSN: 0002-8231; CODEN: AISJB6.

KUHLTHAU, CAROL COLLIER. 1999. The Role of Experience in the Information Search Process of an Early Career Information Worker: Perceptions of Uncertainty, Complexity, Construction, and Sources. Journal of the American Society for Information Science. 1999; 50(5): 399-412. ISSN: 0002-8231; CODEN: AISJB6.

LALMAS, MOUNIA; RUTHVEN, IAN. 1998. Representing and Retrieving Structured Documents Using the Dempster-Shafer Theory of Evidence: Modelling and Evaluation. Journal of Documentation. 1998 December; 55(5): 529-565. ISSN: 0022-0418; CODEN: JDOCAS.

LANCASTER, F. W. 1991. Indexing and Abstracting in Theory and Practice. London, UK: Library Association Publishing; 1991. 328p. ISBN: 1-85604-004-6.

LOSEE, ROBERT M. 1997. A Discipline Independent Definition of Information. Journal of the American Society for Information Science. 1997; 48: 254-269. ISSN: 0002-8231; CODEN: AISJB6.

LURIA, A. R. 1976. Cognitive Development: Its Cultural and Social Foundations. Cambridge, MA: Harvard University Press; 1976. 175p. ISBN: 0-674-13731-0.

MAGENNIS, MARK; VAN RIJSBERGEN, C. J. 1997. The Potential and Actual Effectiveness of Interactive Query Expansion. In: Belkin, Nicholas J.; Narasimhalu, A. Desai; Willett, Peter, eds. SIGIR '97: Proceedings of the

Association for Computing Machinery Special Interest Group on Information Retrieval (ACM/SIGIR) 20th Annual International Conference on Research and Development in Information Retrieval; 1997 July 27-31; Philadelphia, PA. New York, NY: ACM Press; 1997. 324-332. ISBN: 0-89791-836-3.

MARCHIONINI, GARY. 1989. Information-Seeking Strategies of Novices Using a Full-Text Electronic Encyclopedia. Journal of the American Society for Information Science. 1989; 40(1): 54-66. ISSN: 0002-8231; CODEN: AISJB6.

MARCHIONINI, GARY. 1995. Information Seeking in Electronic Environments. Cambridge, MA: Cambridge University Press; 1995. 224p. ISBN: 0-521-44372-5.

MCALPINE, GORDON; INGWERSEN, PETER. 1989. Integrated Information Retrieval in a Knowledge Worker Support System. In: Belkin, N. J.; van Rijsbergen, C. J., eds. SIGIR '89: Proceedings of the Association for Computing Machinery Special Interest Group on Information Retrieval (ACM/SIGIR) 12th Annual International Conference on Research and Development in Information Retrieval; 1989 June 25-28; Cambridge, MA. New York, NY: ACM Press; 1989. 48-57. ISBN: 0-89791-321-3.

MCCAIN, KATHERINE W. 1989. Descriptor and Citation Retrieval in the Medical Behavioral Sciences Literature: Retrieval Overlaps and Novelty Distribution. Journal of the American Society for Information Science. 1989; 40: 110-114. ISSN: 0002-8231; CODEN: AISJB6.

MIZZARO, STEFANO. 1996. A Cognitive Analysis of Information Retrieval. In: Ingwersen, Peter; Pors, Niels Ole, ed. CoLIS2: Proceedings of the 2nd International Conference on Conceptions of Library and Information Science: Integration in Perspective; 1996 October 13-16; Copenhagen, Denmark. Copenhagen, Denmark: Royal School of Librarianship; 1996. 233-250. ISBN: 87-7415-260-2.

MIZZARO, STEFANO. 1997. Relevance: The Whole History. Journal of the American Society for Information Science. 1997; 48(9): 810-832. ISSN: 0002-8231; CODEN: AISJB6.

NOYONS, E. C. M.; MOED, HENK F. LEWEL, M. 1999. Combining Mapping and Citation Analysis for Evaluative Bibliometric Purposes: A Bibliometric Study. Journal of the American Society for Information Science. 1999 February; 50(2): 115-131. ISSN: 0002-8231; CODEN: AISJB6.

ODDY, ROBERT N. 1977a. Information Retrieval through Man-Machine Dialogue. Journal of Documentation. 1977; 33: 1-14. ISSN: 0022-0418; CODEN: JDOCAS.

ODDY, ROBERT N. 1977b. Retrieving References by Dialogue Rather Than by Query Formulation. Journal of Information Science. 1977; 1: 37-53. ISSN: 0165-5515.

OFORI-DWUMFUO, G. 1984. Using a Cognitive Model of Dialogue for Reference Retrieval. Journal of Information Science. 1984; 9: 19-28. ISSN: 0165-5515.

ØROM, ANDERS. 2000. Information Science, Historical Changes and Social Aspects: A Nordic Look. Journal of Documentation. 2000; 56(1): 12-26. ISSN: 0022-0418; CODEN: JDOCAS.

PALMQUIST, RUTH A.; KIM, KYUNG-SUN. 2000. Cognitive Style and On-line Database Search Experience as Predictors of Web Search Performance. Journal of the American Society for Information Science. 2000; 51(6): 558-566. ISSN: 0002-8231; CODEN: AISJB6.

PAO, MIRANDA L. 1993. Term and Citation Searching: A Field Study. Information Processing & Management. 1993; 29(1): 95-112. ISSN: 0306-4573; CODEN: IPMADK.

PAO, MIRANDA L. 1994. Relevance Odds of Retrieval Overlaps from Seven Search Fields. Information Processing & Management. 1994; 30(3): 305-314. ISSN: 0306-4573; CODEN; IPMADK.

PARK, SOYEON. 2000. Usability, User Preferences, Effectiveness, and User Behaviors When Searching Individual and Integrated Full-Text Databases: Implications for Digital Libraries. Journal of the American Society for Information Science. 2000; 51(5): 456-468. ISSN: 0002-8231; CODEN: AISJB6.

PARK, TAEMIN KIM. 1993. The Nature of Relevance in Information Retrieval: An Empirical Study. Library Quarterly. 1993; 63(3): 318-351. ISSN: 0024-2519.

PEJTERSEN, ANNELISE MARK. 1980. Design of a Classification Scheme for Fiction. In: Harbo, Ole; Kajberg, Leif, eds. Theory and Application of Information Research: Proceedings of the 2nd International Research Forum on Information Science; 1977 August 3-6; Copenhagen, Denmark, Royal School of Librarianship. London, UK: Mansell; 1980. 146-159. ISBN: 0-7201-1513-2.

PEJTERSEN, ANNELISE MARK. 1989. A Library System for Information Retrieval Based on a Cognitive Task Analysis and Supported by an Icon-Based Interface. In: Belkin, N. J.; van Rijsbergen, C. J., eds. SIGIR '89: Proceedings of the Association for Computing Machinery Special Interest Group on Information Retrieval (ACM/SIGIR) 12th Annual International Conference on Research and Development in Information Retrieval; 1989 June 25-28; Cambridge, MA. New York, NY: ACM Press; 1989. 40-47. ISBN: 0-89791-321-3.

PHARO, NILS. 1999. Web Information Search Strategies: A Model for Classifying Web Interaction. In: Aparac, Tatjana; Saracevic, Tefko; Ingwersen, Peter; Vakkari, Pertti eds. CoLIS 3: Proceedings of the 3rd International Conference on Conceptions of Library and Information Science: Digital Libraries: Interdisciplinary Concepts, Challenges and Opportunities; 1999 May 23-26; Dubrovnik, Croatia. Lokve, Croatia: Naklada Benja; 1999. 207-218. ISBN: 953-6003-37-6.

PORS, NIELS O. 2000. Information Retrieval, Experimental Models and Statistical Analysis. Journal of Documentation. 2000; 56(1): 55-70. ISSN: 0022-0418; CODEN: JDOCAS.

RASMUSSEN, JENS; PEJTERSEN, ANNELISE MARK; GOODSTEIN, L. P. 1994. Cognitive Systems Engineering. New York, NY: Wiley; 1994. 378p. ISBN: 0-471-01198-3.

REID, JANE. 1999. A New, Task-Oriented Paradigm for Information Retrieval: Implications for Evaluation of Information Retrieval Systems. In: Aparac, Tatjana; Saracevic, Tefko; Ingwersen, Peter; Vakkari, Pertti, eds. CoLIS 3:

Proceedings of the 3rd International Conference on Conceptions of Library and Information Science: Digital Libraries: Interdisciplinary Concepts, Challenges and Opportunities; 1999 May 23-26; Dubrovnik, Croatia. Lokve, Croatia: Naklada Benja; 1999. 97-108. ISBN: 953-6003-37-6.

RICH, ELAINE A. 1979. User Modelling via Stereotypes. Cognitive Science. 1979; 3: 329-354. ISSN: 0364-0213.

RICH, ELAINE A. 1983. Users Are Individuals: Individualizing User Models. International Journal of Man-Machine Studies. 1983; 18: 199-214. ISSN: 0020-7373.

ROBERTSON, STEPHEN E., ed. 1997. Overview of the Okapi Projects. Journal of Documentation. 1997 January; 53(1): 3-8. ISSN: 0022-0418; CODEN: JDOCAS.

ROBERTSON, STEPHEN E.; HANCOCK-BEAULIEU, MICHELINE. 1992. On the Evaluation of IR Systems. Information Processing & Management. 1992; 28(4): 219-236. ISSN: 0306-5817; CODEN: IPMADK

ROBINS, DAVID. 2000. Shifts of Focus on Various Aspects of User Information Problems during Interactive Information Retrieval. Journal of the American Society for Information Science. 2000; 51(10): 913-928. ISSN: 0002-8231; CODEN: AISJB6.

SALTON, GERARD. 1989. Automatic Text Processing: The Transformation, Analysis and Retrieval of Information by Computer. Reading, MA: Addison-Wesley; 1989. 530p. ISBN: 0-201-12227-8.

SANDSTROM, ALAN R.; SANDSTROM, PAMELA EFFREIN. 1995. The Use and Misuse of Anthropological Methods in Library and Information Science Research. Library Quarterly. 1995; 65(2): 161-199. ISSN: 0024-2519.

SARACEVIC, TEFKO. 1996a. Modeling Interaction in Information Retrieval (IR): A Review and Proposal. In: Hardin, Steve, ed. ASIS '96: Proceedings of the American Society for Information Science (ASIS) 59th Annual Meeting: Volume 33; 1996 October 21-24; Baltimore, MD. Medford, NJ: Information Today, Inc. for ASIS; 1996. 3-9. ISSN: 0044-7870; ISBN: 1-57387-037-4; CODEN: PAISDQ.

SARACEVIC, TEFKO. 1996b. Relevance Reconsidered '96. In: Ingwersen, Peter; Pors, Niels Ole, eds. CoLIS 2: Proceedings of the 2nd International Conference on Conceptions of Library and Information Science: Integration in Perspective; 1996 October 13-16; Copenhagen, Denmark. Copenhagen, Denmark: Royal School of Librarianship; 1996. 201-218. ISBN: 87-7415-260-2.

SARACEVIC, TEFKO; KANTOR, PAUL. 1988. A Study of Information Seeking and Retrieving, III: Searchers, Searches, and Overlaps. Journal of the American Society for Information Science. 1988; 39(3): 197-216. ISSN: 0002-8231; CODEN: AISJB6.

SARACEVIC, TEFKO; MOKROS, HARTMUT; SU, LOUISE. 1990. Nature of Interaction between Users and Intermediaries in Online Searching: A Qualitative Analysis. In: Henderson, D., ed. ASIS '90: Proceedings of the American Society for Information Science (ASIS) 53rd Annual Meeting: Volume 27; 1990 November 4-8; Toronto, Ontario, Canada. Medford, NJ: Learned Information, Inc. for ASIS; 1990. 47-54. ISSN: 0044-7870; ISBN: 0-938734-48-2; CODEN: PAISDQ; LC: 64-8303.

SARACEVIC, TEFKO; MOKROS, HARTMUT; SU, LOUISE; SPINK, AMANDA. 1991. Nature of Interaction between Users and Intermediaries in Online Searching. In: Williams, Martha E., ed. Proceedings of the 12th National Online Meeting; 1991 May 7-9; New York, NY. Medford, NJ: Learned Information, Inc.; 1991. 329-341. ISBN: 0-938734-51-2.

SCHAMBER, LINDA. 1991. Users' Criteria for Evaluation in a Multimedia Environment. In: Griffiths, José-Marie, ed. ASIS '91: Proceedings of the American Society for Information Science (ASIS) 54th Annual Meeting: Volume 28; 1991 October 27-31; Washington, DC. Medford, NJ: Learned Information, Inc. for ASIS; 1991. 126-133. ISSN: 0044-7870; ISBN: 0-938734-56-3.

SCHAMBER, LINDA. 1994. Relevance and Information Behavior. In: Williams, Martha E., ed. Annual Review of Information Science and Technology: Volume 29. Medford, NJ: Learned Information, Inc. for the American Society for Information Science; 1994. 3-48. ISSN: 0066-4200; ISBN: 0-938734-91-1; CODEN: ARISBC.

SCHAMBER, LINDA; EISENBERG, MICHAEL B.; NILAN, MICHAEL. 1990. A Re-Examination of Relevance: Toward a Dynamic, Situational Definition. Information Processing & Management. 1990; 26(6): 755-776. ISSN: 0306-5817; CODEN: IPMADK.

SEARLE, JOHN R. 1984. Intentionality and Its Place in Nature. Synthese. 1984; 61: 3-16. ISSN: 0039-7857.

SMEATON, ALAN. 1992. Progress in the Application of Natural Language Processing to Information Retrieval Tasks. Computer Journal. 1992; 35: 268-278. ISSN: 0010-4620.

SMEATON, ALAN; HARMAN, DONNA. 1997. The TREC Experiments and Their Impact on Europe. Journal of Information Science. 1997; 23(2): 169-174. ISSN: 0165-5515.

SPARCK JONES, KAREN. 1987. Architecture Problems in the Construction of Expert Systems for Document Retrieval. In: Wormell, Irene, ed. Knowledge Engineering: Expert Systems and Information Retrieval. London, UK: Taylor Graham; 1987. 34-52. ISBN: 0-947568-30-1.

SPARCK JONES, KAREN. 1990. Retrieving Information or Answering Questions: The 8th British Library Annual Research Lecture. London, UK: The British Library; 1990. 12p. ISBN: 0-7123-3215-4.

SPINK, AMANDA. 1997. Information Science: A Third Feedback Framework. Journal of the American Society for Information Science. 1997; 48(8): 728-740. ISSN: 0002-8231; CODEN: AISJB6.

SPINK, AMANDA; GOODRUM, ABBY; ROBINS, DAVID. 1998a. Elicitation Behavior during Mediated Information Retrieval. Information Processing & Management. 1998; 34(2/3): 257-273. ISSN: 0306-4573; CODEN: IPMADK.

SPINK, AMANDA; GREISDORF, HOWARD; BATEMAN, JUDY. 1998b. From Highly Relevant to Not Relevant: Examining Different Regions of Relevance. Information Processing & Management. 1998; 34(5): 599-621. ISSN: 0306-4573; CODEN: IPMADK.

SPINK, AMANDA; LOSEE, ROBERT M. 1996. Feedback in Information Retrieval. In: Williams, Martha E., ed. Annual Review of Information Science and Technology: Volume 31. Medford, NJ: Information Today, Inc. for the American Society for Information Science; 1996. 33-78. ISSN: 0066-4200; ISBN: 1-57387-033-1; CODEN: ARISBC.

SPINK, AMANDA; SARACEVIC, TEFKO. 1997. Interaction in Information Retrieval: Selection and Effectiveness of Search Terms. Journal of the American Society for Information Science. 1997; 48(8): 741-761. ISSN: 0002-8231; CODEN: AISJB6.

SPINK, AMANDA; SARACEVIC, TEFKO. 1998. Human-Computer Interaction in Information Retrieval: Nature and Manifestations of Feedback. Interacting with Computers. 1998; 10: 249-267. ISSN: 0953-5438.

SU, LOUISE. 1994. The Relevance of Recall and Precision in User Evaluation. Journal of the American Society for Information Science. 1994; 45: 207-217. ISSN: 0002-8231; CODEN; AISJB6.

SUGAR, WILLIAM. 1995. User-Centered Perspective of Information Retrieval Research and Analysis Methods. In: Williams, Martha E., ed. Annual Review of Information Science and Technology: Volume 30. Medford, NJ: Information Today, Inc. for the American Society for Information Science; 1995. 77-109. ISSN: 0066-4200; ISBN: 1-57387-019-6; CODEN: ARISBC.

SWANSON, DONALD R. 1986. Undiscovered Public Knowledge. Library Quarterly. 1986; 56(2): 103-118. ISSN: 0024-2519.

TALJA, SANNA. 1997. Constituting "Information" and "User" as Research Objects. In: Vakkari, Pertti; Savolainen, Reijo; Dervin, Brenda, eds. Information seeking in Context. Proceedings of an International Conference on Research in Information Needs, Seeking and Use in Different Contexts; 1996 August 14-16; Tampere, Finland. London, UK: Taylor Graham; 1997. 67-80. ISBN: 0-947568-71-9.

TENOPIR, CAROL. 1989. Issues in Online Database Searching. Englewood, CO: Libraries Unlimited; 1989. 188p. ISBN: 0-87287-709-4.

TURTLE, HOWARD; CROFT, W. BRUCE. 1990. Inference Methods for Document Retrieval. ACM-SIGIR Forum. 1990 June; 1-24. ISSN: 0163-5840.

VAKKARI, PERTTI. 1994. Library and Information Science: Its Contents and Scope. Advances in Librarianship. 1994; 18: 1-55. ISSN: 0065-2830; ISBN: 0-12-024618-X.

VAKKARI, PERTTI. 1998. Growth of Theories on Information Seeking: An Analysis of Growth of a Theoretical Research Program on the Relation between Task Complexity and Information Seeking. Information Processing & Management. 1998; 34(3): 361-382. ISSN: 0306-5817; CODEN: IPMADK.

VAKKARI, PERTTI. 1999. Task Complexity, Problem Structure and Information Actions: Integrating Studies on Information Seeking and Retrieval. Information Processing & Management. 1999; 35(6): 819-837. ISSN: 0306-5817; CODEN: IPMADK.

VAKKARI, PERTTI. 2000. Relevance and Contributing Information Types of Searched Documents in Task Performance. In: Belkin, Nicholas J.; Ingwersen, Peter; Leong, Mun-Kew, eds., SIGIR '2000: Proceedings of the Association for Computing Machinery Special Interest Group on Information Retrieval (ACM-SIGIR) 23rd Annual Conference on Research and

Development in Information Retrieval; 2000 July 24-28; Athens, Greece. New York, NY: ACM Press; 2000. 2-9. ISBN: 1-58113-226-3.

VAKKARI, PERTTI; HAKALA, NANNA. 2000. Changes in Relevance Criteria and Problem Stages in Task Performance. Journal of Documentation. 2000 September; 56(5): 540-562. ISSN: 0022-0418; CODEN: JDOCAS.

VAN RIJSBERGEN, C. J.; LALMAS, MOUNIA. 1996. Information Calculus for Information Retrieval. Journal of the American Society for Information Science. 1996; 47(5): 385-398. ISSN: 0002-8231; CODEN: AISJB6.

VICKERY, BRIAN C. 1997. Metatheory and Information Science. Journal of Documentation. 1997 December; 53(5): 457-476. ISSN: 0022-0418; CODEN: JDOCAS.

WANG, PEILING. 1997. Users' Information Needs at Different Stages of a Research Project: A Cognitive View. In: Vakkari, Pertti; Savolainen, Reijo; Dervin, Brenda, eds. Information Seeking in Context: Proceedings of an International Conference on Research in Information Needs, Seeking and Use in Different Contexts. 1996 August 14-16. Tampere, Finland. London, UK: Taylor Graham; 1997. 307-318. ISBN: 0-947568-71-9.

WANG, PEILING; WHITE, MARILYN DOMAS. 1999. A Cognitive Model of Document Use during a Research Project. Study II. Decisions at the Reading and Citing Stages. Journal of the American Society for Information Science. 1999; 50(2): 98-114. ISSN: 0002-8231; CODEN: AISJB6.

WERSIG, GERNOT. 1973. Informationssoziologie. Pullach bei München: Verlag Dokumentation; 1973.

WHITE, HOWARD D.; MCCAIN, KATHERINE W. 1998. Visualizing a Discipline: An Author Co-Citation Analysis of Information Science, 1972-1995. Journal of the American Society for Information Science. 1998; 49(4): 327-355. ISSN: 0002-8231; CODEN: AISJB6.

WILSON, PATRICK. 1973. Situational Relevance. Information Storage & Retrieval. 1973; 9(8): 457-471. ISSN: 0020-0271.

WILSON, THOMAS D. 1980. Information Systems Design Implications of Research into the Information Behaviour of Social Workers and Social Administrators. In: Harbo, Ole; Kajberg, Leif, eds. Theory and Application of Information Research: Proceedings of the 2nd International Research Forum on Information Science; 1977 August 3-6; Copenhagen, Denmark, Royal School of Librarianship. London, UK: Mansell; 1980. 198-213. ISBN: 0-7201-1513-2.

WILSON, THOMAS D. 1981. On User Studies and Information Needs. Journal of Documentation. 1981; 37(1): 3-15. ISSN: 0022-0418; CODEN: JDOCAS.

WILSON, THOMAS D. 1999. Models in Information Behaviour Research. Journal of Documentation. 1999 June; 55(3): 249-270. ISSN: 0022-0418; CODEN: JDOCAS.

WINOGRAD, TERRY; FLORES, FERNANDO. 1986. Understanding Computers and Cognition: A New Foundation for Design. Norwood, NJ: Ablex; 1986. 207p. ISBN: 0-89391-050-3.

WORMELL, IRENE. 1981. SAP—A New Way to Produce Subject Descriptions of Books. Journal of Information Science. 1981; 3: 39-43. ISSN: 0165-5515.

WORMELL, IRENE. 1984. Cognitive Aspects in Natural Language and Free-Text Searching. Social Science Information Studies. 1984 April/July; 4(2/3): 131-141. ISSN: 0143-6236; CODEN: SOSSD3.

YUAN, WEIJING; MEADOW, CHARLES T. 1999. A Study of the Use of Variables in Information Retrieval User Studies. Journal of the American Society for Information Science. 1999; 50(2): 140-150. ISSN: 0002-8231; CODEN: AISJB6.

2

Methodologies and Methods for User Behavioral Research*

PEILING WANG
University of Tennessee, Knoxville

INTRODUCTION

A substantial body of literature exists on empirical studies of human behavior in various disciplines: social sciences, psychology, cognitive science, and information science. In behavioral research, there has been a strong orientation toward quantitative methodology as a scientific approach, especially in the nineteenth century and early twentieth century. Since the 1960s, however, many researchers have been searching for alternative methodologies to overcome limitations and respond to criticisms of this traditional approach to research. Regardless of the topics and objectives of the research, all inquiries must deal with methodological issues. The purpose of this chapter is to examine the methodologies and methods applied in empirical research on user behavior.

It is necessary to distinguish between methodology and method. Methodology is a theory of methods that guides the description, explanation, and justification of methods in empirical studies, while method refers to the actual design and specific scientific techniques used in an empirical study. The aim of methodology is to describe methods and analyze them in terms of limitations, presuppositions, consequences, and potentialities (KAPLAN). It seeks to answer the question, "what kinds of investigative methods and strategies should be used to answer the research question(s) for a given purpose?" or briefly, "how should the data be obtained and interpreted?" A methodology also addresses the strategies and measures used to strengthen the research design.

*I dedicate this chapter to my advisor, Professor Dagobert Soergel of the University of Maryland, College Park, and my mentor, Professor Carol Tenopir of the University of Tennessee, Knoxville. Sincere gratitude goes to Professor Martha E. Williams for her strong support in the process of writing. Special thanks are due to the reviewers for their thoughtful comments. Thanks also go to Margaret Goodbody for editorial help.

Annual Review of Information Science and Technology (ARIST), Volume 34, 1999
Martha E. Williams, Editor
Published for the American Society for Information Science (ASIS)
By Information Today, Inc., Medford, NJ

Methodology is also referred to as a set of methods or the general approach to methods. DERVIN (1997) cautions researchers: "In recent years the term methodology has been used as a substitute for methods when it is more usefully referred to as the theoretical analysis of methods. In essence, methodology is theory for research step-taking, including theory of the methods of theorizing as well as theory of observing and analyzing" (p. 28).

Current Concerns

HERNON & SCHWARTZ, editors of *Library & Information Science Research*, call for more studies on methodologies and research designs in library and information science (LIS). They point out the limited influence of methodological research on LIS research practice and a tendency of published research to focus on the findings and their implications rather than on the methods used and issues of reliability and validity. JÄRVELIN & VAKKARI found that little had been published in core LIS journals on methodology and there was even a decline from the mid 1960s to the mid 1980s (8% for 1965, 3% for 1975, and 1% for 1985, respectively). Research methods are underdebated and underappreciated in LIS.

The last decade witnessed the increasing awareness of the importance of methods, especially qualitative methods. After the volume on qualitative research and methods in LIS edited by GLAZIER & POWELL, the *Library Quarterly* published a symposium issue on qualitative research in 1993 and printed additional copies for distribution (BRADLEY & SUTTON). In 1999, the *Journal of the American Society for Information Science* scheduled a special topic issue titled, "Qualitative Methodologies for Information Science Research," but canceled it due to insufficient submissions. The Library Research Seminar I, a conference to promote LIS research and to explore new methods, was held at the Florida State University in 1996 and the second seminar is scheduled for 2001 at the University of Maryland.

Scope

In this first *ARIST* chapter on the topic, two bodies of literature are reviewed: literature on methodology applicable to social and behavioral research, and literature reporting empirical studies of user behaviors. This chapter discusses methodological issues in empirical studies of information-related behavior in six specific research areas: information needs and uses, information seeking, relevance judgment, online searching (including online public access catalog (OPAC), online database, and the Web), human-system interactions, and reference transactions. Reference transactions involve intermediaries, who are not usually considered as users; this line of research is included because intermediary behavior cannot be isolated from user behavior, and methods used in the studies of reference transactions are important to user studies.

Comprehensive searches of DIALOG databases (ERIC, PsycINFO, Sociological Abstracts, Information Science Abstracts, Library Literature, and Library and Information Science Abstracts) were conducted as a starting point and also to verify completeness. Reading lists of courses on research methods and information seeking at several doctoral programs were also consulted. Selected recent dissertations on user behavioral studies are included.

Selection Criteria

The review covers publications from the following two categories: (1) works discussing methodological issues and (2) original empirical studies on user information-related behavior considered as basic research. For the latter, four additional criteria are applied: (2.1) publications with detailed descriptions of research design; (2.2) key papers that reported projects financed by large grants, received awards, were frequently cited, and were selected as readings in doctoral courses; (2.3) studies that provide good illustrations of specific methods or techniques; or (2.4) studies that are related to selected studies. Research on information systems, using human subjects as measuring instruments, such as usability testing, is not included.

In presenting how researchers conducted their research in selected empirical studies, this review emphasizes data collection more than data analysis. This does not imply that data analysis is not important; rather, it reflects several facts. Within the positivist research paradigm, a detailed description of data collection is necessary for replicating the study. Researchers using a quantitative approach need not articulate why a specific test was used, because it is assumed that readers know, for example, what a nonparametric test (e.g., Chi-square) is and where it should be used. In qualitative research, however, standards and procedures are not as uniformly applied as those that guide quantitative research. In documenting research design, researchers are often less extensive or explicit in their description of analytic procedures than in data collection. Some qualitative studies mention little about how content analysis was done (e.g., what was the analysis unit or coding scheme?). FIELDING & FIELDING criticize most textbooks on qualitative methods for focusing on data collection or mechanical procedures rather than on procedures for linking operational and theoretical definitions.

Organization of the Chapter

The remainder of this chapter is organized into three major sections. The first section provides a brief review of research paradigms and their corresponding methodologies. The second section presents selected empirical studies classified into four major research designs based on observational methods: surveying users, interviewing users, observing users through experiments, and observing users in natural settings. Research designs using multiple methods and some emerging new methods are covered in a fifth subsection. For each type of research design, the discussion is organized based on the six research areas listed in the Scope. Special techniques are covered as separate sub-sections in the type of research design or where the selected studies used these techniques. For example, critical-incident technique is in Surveying Users; time-line interview and qualitative data analysis are covered in Interviewing Users. A summary of each research design is given at the end of that part. The final section summarizes the methodological trends of user behavioral research and identifies the needs to advance research methodologies and methods.

RESEARCH PARADIGMS

Paradigms are worldviews or general frameworks that guide researchers in scientific inquiry. Paradigms also refer to universally accepted models of inquiry and specific tools, instruments, and procedures for doing research in scientific disciplines. Research paradigms have philosophical roots—a researcher consciously or unconsciously follows a paradigm that structures his/her thinking toward one general approach. That is, a research problem can take different directions as decided by the researcher. Within a paradigm there are objections to and acceptances of certain methods. Currently, two basic paradigms shape research in social and behavioral sciences: the traditional positivist paradigm, and the emerging alternative paradigm.

The Two Paradigms

The positivist paradigm—also called empiricism, objectivism, quantitative, or scientific paradigm—can be traced back to the early nineteenth century. It dominates research in the natural sciences and penetrates almost all disciplines in social and behavioral sciences. Recent developments in social and behavioral sciences have resulted in criticisms of positivism: theories must be presupposed prior to observation; theories are reduced to only observable elements; entities are isolated from their contexts; the complexities of human behaviors in real life are ignored; only cause-and-effect relationships are studied; there is no such thing as a neutral observer who is capable of objective measurement of the observed; and statistics can be manipulated to support any position. These criticisms have resulted in the adoption of an alternative or a new paradigm, called variously, the naturalistic paradigm (LINCOLN & GUBA; WILLEMS & RAUSH), the sense-making approach (DERVIN, 1983), qualitative methodology (BRADLEY & SUTTON; FIDEL, 1993; GLAZIER & POWELL), and the illuminative paradigm (FORD). Other frequently encountered names, such as ethnography, hermeneutics, phenomenology, constructivism, contextualism, postmodernism, postpositivism, and so on, reflect the perspective of a specific discipline or origin. For example, ethnography originated in anthropology and has since penetrated nearly all the behavioral sciences. Hermeneutics, originally the theory and method of interpreting the Bible, was later extended to the interpretation of human history and life and is now a method used to interpret human behavior. Phenomenology originated in philosophy and is now an important research approach in psychology and sociology; it focuses on human experiences perceived by the informants who live them and provides techniques to identify structural invariants of a particular type of experience across individuals.

Some social scientists such as LINCOLN & GUBA and WILLEMS & RAUSH use the term naturalism to mean that human behaviors should be observed in natural settings and interpreted within that context; positivist methods based on natural science methodology are not appropriate for naturalistic inquiry. On the contrary, most philosophers of social sciences use the term naturalism as more or less identical to or associated with the term positivism. Specifically, epistemological naturalism believes that the social life of humans is knowable in the same way as the natural world is; methodological naturalism applies natural science methodology in the social sciences (BENTON).

It seems fruitless, if not impossible, to draw a clear-cut line between the two paradigms. The debate on the appropriateness of each paradigm suggests that both paradigms developed and advanced valuable methods and techniques for conducting research and that neither approach alone can provide a complete understanding of user behavior. Many researchers advocate methodological pluralism or dual paradigms to take advantage of the strengths of each approach and let them complement one another in user studies (BATES; DERVIN, 1997; LIEBSCHER; MCGUIRE; SCHWARTZ & OGILVY; SUTTON; WILDEMUTH). Dervin's sustained work on sense-making as a methodology aims to bridge the gap between metatheory and methods in studying human information seeking and use. According to DERVIN, in using sense-making approach, it "is not necessary to privilege either realism-based or interpretative-based methodologies" (1999, p. 732).

Comparison of Quantitative and Qualitative Methodologies

The two research paradigms adopt different methodologies in scientific inquiry. It is possible that a researcher may use a predominant approach to his/her research problems but also adopt methods or techniques from another approach. Textbooks or references on quantitative methodology, such as BABBIE and MILLER, provide explicit prescriptions for standard methods and techniques. Qualitative methodology, however, is not a unified doctrine. Instead of providing a definition, FIDEL (1993) describes qualitative methods as nonmanipulative and noncontrolling, holistic and case-oriented, focused on processes, open and flexible without an a priori conceptual framework, using multiple methods for triangulation, coding data into categories derived from content analysis, humanistic in that the observer and the observed have a good rapport, and inductive in data analysis. She asserts that qualitative methodology is scientific although not by traditional standards. Several writers compare the differences between the two methodologies (CRESWELL; FORD; MERRIAM). Table 1 brings together the major points of comparison.

Citing 152 publications on methodologies and empirical studies, SANDSTROM & SANDSTROM (1995) voice concerns that qualitative methods have been translated to library and information science with "unfortunate" misconceptions and a fashionably narrow focus. Their main criticisms are that the majority of LIS researchers missed important methodological works on qualitative methods and followed radical relativists in rejecting positivist science and the idea that an objective understanding of human behavior is possible or desirable. They suggest that the current characterization of the distinctions between quantitative and qualitative approaches is artificial and false and that it should be abandoned. THOMAS & NYCE, in response to this article, argue that the Sandstroms's notion of ethnography is positivist, which would not help LIS research, but weaken it. SANDSTROM & SANDSTROM (1998) defend their views and expand the discussion. This kind of debate seldom reaches an agreement but can advance the thinking and understanding of the methodological concerns in research. More such debates are needed.

METHODS USED IN USER BEHAVIORAL STUDIES

Unlike paradigms or methodologies, it is difficult to categorize methods in a satisfactory way. A cursory glance at the contents of major textbooks and references of research methods for the social and behavioral sciences confirms this fact (BABBIE; BUSHA & HARTER; CRESWELL; DENZIN & LINCOLN; GLAZIER & POWELL; KERLINGER & LEE; MELLON; PATTON; POWELL; SCHUTT;

Table 1

Two Methodologies Compared

Point of comparison	Quantitative	Qualitative
Ontology	Reality is objective and singular	Reality is subjective and multiple
Epistemology	Researcher is independent from what is researched	Researcher interacts with what is researched
Axiology	Inquiry is free of value judgment and biases	Inquiry is value-bound
Rhetoric	Formal and impersonal voice	Informal and personal voice
Purpose	Generalization and prediction Universal laws	Rich description and theory development Context-bound understanding
Outset	We know that we don't know	We don't know that we don't know
Phenomenon	Atomistic (focusing on parts) Low complexity	Holistic (focusing on whole) High complexity
Logic	Hypothetico deduction	Analytic induction
Theory	Free of time and context Cause-and-effect relationship	Time- and context-bound Mutual simultaneous factors
Measurement	Reliability Internal validity External validity Objectivity	Dependability Credibility Transferability Confirmability
Sampling	Random sampling	Selective purposive sampling
Setting	Experiment (control, treatment)	Natural settings (field)
Data	Quantitative data (numerical)	Qualitative data (various formats)
Data collection	Questionnaires, tests Inanimate instruments (scales, computers, recorders)	Interviews Field observation Discourse
Data analysis	Objective statistical analysis for hypothesis testing	Content analysis Description Interpretation to provide insights and understanding

SOMMER & SOMMER). Different classifications have been used in analyzing research articles published in LIS core journals (FEEHAN ET AL.; JÄRVELIN & VAKKARI; JULIEN). POWELL's recent paper reviews traditional and new methods used in LIS research and the methodological trends. He uses two broad categories: quantitative research methods (survey, experiment, bibliometrics, content analysis, etc.) and qualitative research methods (case study, historical method, ethnography, grounded theory, phenomenology and hermeneutics, discourse analysis, etc.).

Accepting the lack of a unified classification of research methods, this section discusses research designs based on how behaviors are observed and data are obtained and analyzed: surveying users, interviewing users, observing users through experiments, observing users in natural settings, and research designs using multiple phases and emerging methods. The six specific user-study areas include information needs and uses, information seeking, relevance judgments, online searching (OPAC, database, and the Web), human-system interactions, and reference transactions. The selected studies are illustrative examples because they provide detailed descriptions of research designs, are key papers, apply specific methods or techniques, or are related to the selected studies.

Surveying Users

The survey method is a standard quantitative design used in the social and behavioral sciences. It uses structured questionnaires as instruments to measure variables to test a hypothesis or simply measure a population parameter of interest. A survey measures users' self-perceived and reported behavior. Originally developed in the social sciences, it is now one of the main methods used in LIS studies. Based on a sample of user studies published between 1990 and 1994, JULIEN found that the survey method accounted for 56% of research designs, compared to studies using the field-study method (9%) and experimental method (6%). An earlier investigation of research articles published in core LIS journals in 1980 by NOUR also reported the survey as the most frequently used method (over 40%).

Information needs and uses. Early classic studies of information needs and uses were conducted within the communication framework at a macro level starting in the 1960s; the survey method was frequently used with large samples. This line of research was based on a communication model that depicted information being transferred from sources to users, and grouped users by disciplines, professions, or communities. The variables in these studies were time allocation (how scientists spent their work time on information), information channels (personal contact, formal publications, etc.) and frequency of use, information sources, information habits, etc. GARVEY and colleagues conducted a series of surveys of several thousand scientists from nine disciplines over a four-and-one-half-year period. The questionnaires were designed to guide respondents to systematically describe an information exchange associated with a critical event (e.g., a scientist gave a conference presentation, then published it as a journal article and the article was requested by others, etc.). KING ET AL. conducted sustained research on the use of scientific and technical information in six related surveys. SHUCHMAN and colleagues conducted a national study of engineers' information needs in which they distributed a self-administered questionnaire to 3,371 engineers (1,315, or 39%, returned the survey) after having interviewed thirty-nine engineers. Surveys continue to be the major method to study information needs of various user populations, such as the general public (C.-C. CHEN & HERNON; DERVIN ET AL.), health professionals (MARSHALL; SALASIN & CEDAR), and health information users (ISAACS).

Information uses in critical incidents. ALLEN and colleagues studied engineers in R&D laboratories using questionnaires along with a self-administered solution-development record to log information use in relation to tasks. The solution-development record is an instrument based on the critical-incident technique developed in psychology (FLANAGAN). Engineers who completed the solution-development records in a fifteen-week period were further interviewed. Using the critical-incident technique in a survey, WHITE studied academic economists' information-gathering behavior during a research project. In this study, survey questions on information needs and uses focused on a recently completed research project, asking the economists how they sought and used information in the three stages of their research: problem definition, methodology and data collection, and presentation of results.

Information seeking. Using the survey method to study information seeking often results in descriptive statistical data, such as type of sources used and rating of the sources. JOHNSON ET AL. used questionnaires to collect data to test a proposed model, the Comprehensive Model of Information Seeking (CMIS), and applied LISREL (a statistical technique for estimating linear relationships) to analyze data. The model had three components: antecedents, information-carrier factors, and information-seeking actions. The questionnaire included nine factors (thirty-two questions) and used a 10-point scale. Three hundred eighty respondents (74% return rate) completed the survey; they were from a large state governmental agency responsible for providing engineering and technical services.

Surveys and Delphi technique. Most survey studies collect data once from a sample. The Delphi technique provides a mechanism for communication among experts to reach consensus on issues with a multiround survey or a focus group (see Interviewing Users for information about the focus-group method). NEUMAN examined high-school students' use of databases, assuming that, in a school environment, teachers and school librarians are the experts on student information needs and uses. Between May 1992 and October 1993, she conducted a fourround Delphi study, including a panel of twenty-five media specialists from twenty-two selected schools across the United States. Based on previous studies, her survey instrument included eighteen categories and 226 statements using a five-point Likert scale. The first two rounds used similar instruments to obtain consensus. The results were used to substantially revise third- and fourth-round instruments to include sixty-one statements.

Surveys using the Internet to collect data. In the past, questionnaires have been distributed through mail, at conferences, or via telephone calls. Recently, researchers found Web surveys a less expensive method that can include more geographically diverse respondents (PITKOW & RECKER). ZHANG developed a Web-based survey to automate data collection and processing to increase completeness by immediately prompting the respondent to reenter an answer for an unanswered question. Multiple submissions and loss of data due to system failure were problems unlikely in mail or phone surveys. She suggests assigning a unique ID to each invited respondent to identify multiple submissions and sending follow-up requests to the respondents whose responses were lost.

Surveys combined with other methods. To study how chief executive officers (CEOs) use information sources in actual decision situations, AUSTER & CHOO (1993, 1994) first conducted a survey sent to 207 CEOs in firms with sales of more than five million (Canadian) dollars in Canadian publishing and telecommunication industries. In the following stage, they selectively interviewed thirteen CEOs (see Interviewing Users). Similarly, WILKINS & LECKIE studied the information needs and seeking behavior of academic professional and managerial staff, also using both a survey and follow-up interviews.

More often questionnaires are based on interview results. CHU (1999b) studied literary critics' information-seeking behavior in two phases. In the first phase, she developed a six-stage process model of production and use of literary criticism, based on interviews with a random sample of thirty-one literary critics. The second phase of the study tested the model using a questionnaire structured with both closed and open-ended questions. The survey was mailed to a systematic random sample of 800 academic literary critics, with 171 usable questionnaires (21%) returned.

The Council on Library Resources sponsored a cooperative (five organizations), multiyear, in-depth investigation into library users and OPAC use. This project applied multiple methods: transaction log analysis, focus-group interviews, and national surveys (LARSON; MARKEY; MATTHEWS ET AL.; TOLLE).

Diaries or journals kept by the respondents over a period of time have also been used to collect data along with questionnaires. As an example, the solution-development record was a structured diary maintained by the engineers in ALLEN's study. BYSTRÖM & JÄRVELIN used diaries in combination with questionnaires to study information seeking and uses. The participants were given semistructured guidelines to facilitate the recording of relevant data. Because the diaries were self-administered, only 27% of the collected diaries were usable in Byström & Järvelin's study, and 58% of Allen's participants completed the fifteen-week period.

Sampling. An important methodological issue is to insure representative samples so that the results can be generalized. Low return rates have been a problem for many reported survey studies (SEYMOUR). DERVIN ET AL. reported extra efforts to include the hard-to-reach respondents in a telephone survey: the average contacts for one subgroup was 5.0 as compared to 2.7 for the population. In three national surveys of the information use of scientists, phone calls to reach nonrespondents were able to increase response rate to over 50 percent (TENOPIR & KING).

In summary, the survey method is a typical quantitative design to ask users about their information needs and uses, and information-seeking activities from large samples. In user studies, most surveys provide descriptive results at a macro level based on users' perceptions. A few researchers tested models using survey data. LIS researchers also use the survey method along with other methods in a single study. To deal with context in information seeking and use, several researchers have adopted the critical-incident technique in developing questionnaires. The survey method will continue to play an important role in user studies along with other methods and should be improved to deal with methodological issues, such as low return rate.

Interviewing Users

Like the survey method, the interview method is based on users' perceptions, but it adds the interaction between the interviewer and the interviewee. Interviews used in a survey as a data-collection technique are considered as an alternative to self-administered questionnaires to improve data quality. This section focuses on semistructured in-depth interviews that use predefined guidelines and include open-ended questions allowing interviewees to address issues not considered before.

Time-line interviews are also semistructured, focusing on an important event and its temporal sequences. Interviews are frequently conducted in a one-on-one setting.

Focus-group interviews bring together a group of six to twelve selected individuals who are led by an experienced moderator in an open in-depth discussion. Well-conducted focus-group interviews can provide researchers with spontaneous thoughts of group members. Because the sample is small, the purpose of the research is not to generalize the findings, but to use the findings to design follow-up studies of larger samples, such as through surveys.

Information needs and uses. CASE interviewed twenty historians to understand their information uses. He conducted interviews mostly in respondents' offices where he also observed their information organization. LECKIE interviewed forty-two female farmers selected on the basis of stratification by enterprise type to investigate their information needs, information channels, and information uses. In a study of information needs and uses of low-income communities, BISHOP ET AL. conducted twenty-six household interviews involving thirty-four participants and many focus groups involving 116 adults and forty-eight teens. Focus groups were held during a two-day computer-training program; participants of the program received a free computer sponsored by the Community Networking Initiative. WILLIAMSON ET AL.'s study of the information needs of blind people began with two focus groups (ten and six participants respectively) drawn from people who worked with the blind. These results identified issues for subsequent interviews with fifteen visually impaired individuals.

Understanding children's information needs can be challenging because children are frequently unaware of their information needs or unable to articulate them. Based on the assumptions that children have information needs and that their needs are ministered to by their significant adults, WALTER conducted in-depth interviews with twenty-five adults who worked with children in a variety of capacities (e.g., caretaker, teacher, librarian, police officer, social worker, nurse, etc.). Children of immigrant families form a different user group. They play an important role in satisfying the information needs of their families and their parents who do not speak or read English. CHU (1999a) conducted a series of studies of this group. She and her colleagues interviewed seventy-seven immigrant children in their preferred languages (English, Spanish, or Korean); she also interviewed thirty-three librarians working as facilitators of immigrant children. Her sample of children ranged from age three (the youngest) to twenty-nine (the oldest was considered a child by the ethnic group by dint of being unmarried and still living with the family).

Information uses in critical incidents. AUSTER & CHOO (1993, 1994) applied the critical-incident technique to interview thirteen CEOs from the 113 survey respondents based on willingness, geographical proximity, and availability (see the previous section). The interviewees were asked to recall a recent incident in which information played a critical role. The discussion focused on factors surrounding the incident. WANG & WHITE interviewed researchers for document uses in relation to a recently completed research project. They conducted interviews in respondents' offices so that interviewees had access to their personal collections or other information cues. Both researchers participated in the interview: one assumed the interviewer's role and the other took notes and asked follow-up questions when needed (WANG & WHITE; WHITE & WANG).

Information seeking. Focusing on incidental information acquisition of everyday life, WILLIAMSON recruited 202 older adult participants (ages sixty and over) to record incoming and outgoing telephone calls for a two-week period. The phone diaries included the purpose and the topic of the phone call. All participants were also interviewed in depth on their information needs and sources over the past five years. The phone diaries revealed participants' personal networks and the structured interviews provided data on their information needs and sources. To understand how information is sought and used in everyday life situations, SAVOLAINEN also interviewed two contrast groups: eleven teachers representing middle-class citizens with university degrees and eleven industrial workers representing working-class citizens with only limited vocational education. In-depth interviews lasting about ninety minutes covered information situations and information seeking in everyday life. The respondents were also asked to recall a recent problem and how information was used in solving the problem.

Information seeking and relevance judgment using time-line interviews. Time-line interviews in combination with the critical-incident technique focus on a specific past incident in order to reconstruct an information-need situation and the step-by-step activities related to information gaps and gap bridging. Over the last three decades, DERVIN (1992) and colleagues have conducted and articulated this line of research, called the sense-making methodology and a quantitative-qualitative approach to information seeking in real-life situations. The sense-making methodology assumes that information is a user construct and information seeking is a user's action/movement through space and time. The methodology focuses on situations in which information seeking is used for problem solving. In a time-line interview, an information-seeking event is reconstructed by the user: when and how it occurred, what gaps were perceived, what kind of help was needed, what was the result. The time-line interview was developed from the critical-incident technique, but goes beyond it by establishing a micro-moment time-line. The analysis of data focuses on individual events rather than individual users. Adapting DERVIN's (1992) sense-making time-line interview technique, SCHAMBER (1991) conducted in-depth interviews with thirty professionals of various occupations who were regular users of weather information. Her focus was on their use of relevance criteria in evaluating multimedia weather information in potentially life-and-death situations. Her recent methodological discussion (SCHAMBER, 2000) details the combination of time-line interviews and content analysis technique applied to relevance research.

Computer-assisted focus-group interviews. Similar to Web-based surveys, computer technology makes focus-group studies easier to manage. ABELS ET AL. carried out a focus-group study using an advanced teaching laboratory equipped with the VisionQuest software for the session. Two researchers moderated the session with semistructured questions. The brainstorming data were aggregated immediately for a subsequent rating.

Qualitative data analysis. In-depth interviews produce unstructured verbal data, which are open to interpretation by the researcher. Few researchers agree on a precise procedure to analyze qualitative data. Most reported studies omit details on data analysis in order to focus on findings. Frequently, researchers name the research design to indicate the use of the inherent modes for data analysis. For example, a grounded-theory study may identify and compare categories based on coding incidents (STRAUSS & CORBIN). In case-study research, data analysis focuses on the search for patterns, explanations of causal relationships, and analysis of changes over time (YIN). Ethnographic researchers use domain analysis to find semantic relationships, to develop taxonomies, and to identify differences across the respondents (SPRADLEY). In the phenomenological approach, the data-analysis procedure may take typical steps, such as the classification of a random sample of protocols, reduction and linguistic transformation, elimination of irrelevant elements, identification of an experience, and application of the description to randomly selected cases (POLKINGHORNE). To help researchers to grasp the phenomenological bracketing technique, DUKES explains that a researcher should focus on the experience rather than the cause of the experience, based on the idea that the cause is irrelevant for phenomenological research purposes. WATSON suggests a three-step reading technique of phenomenological interview texts: a quick reading, a close reading, and insights. The second reading, also called a hermeneutic reading, interprets for meaning. The final reading aims at a higher level of interpretation with new perspectives. KRIPPENDORFF emphasizes that content analysis of text is a research technique for making replicable and valid inferences from data to their context. It requires sound decisions on units of analysis, coding scheme, and analytical procedures, as well as appropriate measures to ensure reliability and validity.

In summary, interviews are an important research design to study behaviors that are context-dependent, such as information seeking and uses, and the user groups that are unlikely or unable to answer a survey, such as semiliterate families and children. An important methodological development is to combine the critical-incident technique with the time-line interview technique to examine micro-level information-seeking behavior and processes. The interview method allows in-depth discussions with the users and provides informative and rich data that often reveal thoughts and reasons underlying behavior. It is labor-intensive in both data collection and analysis. Therefore, studies using in-depth interviews often include a small number of respondents who were often self-selected. It is difficult to draw conclusions about the behavior of the population. A major challenge to researchers is the lack of standards for data analysis. Many published studies provide little explanation of procedures and techniques used in data analysis. Because the nature of qualitative data analysis is inductive, it is important to document the steps, instruments, techniques, and measurements used to reach findings.

Observing Users through Experiments

In experiments, a standard quantitative design in psychology, subjects are observed in laboratories. Experiments are designed to test hypotheses or establish causal relations. Two issues are important in experimental design: treatment and randomization. Behaviors are observed under a controlled condition (called treatment) and subjects are assigned randomly to conditions (called randomization). Both the treatment and randomization are critical factors to ensure reliable results, so that findings are replicable under the same condition. True experiments are not always feasible or desirable, however. An alternative is the quasi-experimental design or field experiment carried out in the real world; both control and randomization are compromised to some extent. It is often difficult to classify a study into observing users through experiments or observing users in natural settings. In general, a study is considered as an experiment if the participants were recruited to perform a search and did not approach the IR system due to a task-related need even if they searched for their own topics. A study is considered as observing users in natural settings if the participants had real information needs related to tasks at hand rather than hypothetical questions based on topical interests.

Data-collection techniques. In the positivist tradition, observation is concerned only with overt behaviors. In information retrieval and human-system interaction research, researchers believe that it is important to know the underlying thoughts and cognitive processes related to behavior (INGWERSEN, 1982, 1992). A verbalization technique for studying thoughts and cognitive processes while performing tasks, called think-aloud protocol, was developed to provide valid and reliable thought data (ERICSSON & SIMON). To collect think-aloud protocols, subjects are instructed to verbalize whatever comes into their minds while performing a cognitive task. Despite being criticized as "soft" data, verbalization is the only method to obtain subjects' thoughts while they perform specific tasks. It has been used successfully in advancing cognitive research beyond the traditional simple measures such as latency and correctness of responses in experiments. Concurrent verbalization adds to the subject's cognitive load and may interfere with his/her performance and behavior, especially with complex tasks such as database searching. An alternative is the stimulated recall technique: the subject is interviewed while viewing a replay of the recorded session. The replay must be done immediately after the session or the subject may not recall the elements of his/her thinking process. Even with immediate replay, subjects cannot remember what actually happened at some points (MARCHIONINI ET AL., 1990).

Today, two standard data recording techniques are used in experiments: audio/video recording and online monitoring. Audio/video recording of information-seeking transactions can capture the process to be replayed during data analysis. To minimize effects of the presence of recording equipment or observers, many human-system interaction research laboratories hide cameras or observers, such as behind a one-way mirror. The online monitoring technique provides an automatic transaction log of searches including all the commands and system responses. This technique is often used for unobtrusive observation of online searching (OLDROYD & CITROEN; PENNIMAN & DOMINICK; RICE & BORGMAN).

Measurement techniques. Category rating scales (i.e., dichotomous or Likert scales) have been widely used to solicit subjects' responses to stimuli. EISENBERG investigated magnitude estimation for relevance judgments in order to overcome the limits and biases associated with predefined categories. The magnitude measurement technique uses an open-ended scaling method in which subjects can assign any number that corresponds to their estimated intensity to a stimulus. It produces ordinal and interval data. As EISENBERG noted, magnitude measures can be obtained by placing a mark on a line (BATEMAN; JANES). BRUCE implemented this technique using a handgrip pressure dynamometer to measure the magnitude of satisfaction of information seeking on the Internet.

Information needs and uses. In experiments, circulation records are often used to measure information uses. To test whether users tend to select displayed books over those in stacks, several experiments were conducted in public libraries. A sample of books, carefully selected using criteria such as publication date, length, circulation history, and physical condition, was placed in various display, such as primary with easy access and nonprimary with difficult access, for a period of time. Parallel experiments were also administered at two similar public libraries in the same area (BAKER; GOLDHOR 1972, 1981).

Information seeking. An early investigation of information seeking from the cognitive viewpoint was carried out in the late 1970s to tackle many complex factors: information needs, search process, user-librarian negotiation, and information organization (INGWERSEN, 1982). This field experiment captured search processes of thirteen librarians and five users in public libraries. The participant librarians searched for information on two written test questions. Five users with limited library experience were recruited for the experiment. They were instructed to search for their own information needs first and to interact with librarians after they failed to find needed information. Subjects wore a tape recorder to record think-aloud protocols during the processes. Experimenters observed and recorded the processes with detailed step-by-step notes.

A large-scale multiphase experiment of information seeking and retrieval by Saracevic and colleagues examined five classes of variables (user, question, searcher, search, and retrieved items) to understand the nature of information seeking in real-life situations. Forty end users participated in this study. Each submitted a request and was interviewed about the problem and intended use of retrieved information. Thirty-six recruited paid searchers plus three staff searchers performed searches for the forty requests. Each question had five searches done by outside searchers and four searches by staff searchers. These nine searches were captured in log files to produce a union set of search results by removing duplicates. All searchers also took cognitive traits tests. Users evaluated both relevance and utility of the results based on full records. This project examined forty variables quantitatively and qualitatively (SARACEVIC & KANTOR, 1988a, 1988b; SARACEVIC ET AL.). The raw data collected in this research were further analyzed by other researchers. For example, WU analyzed the data corpus on reference interviews and focused on users' question-elicitation behavior during interviews. SPINK ET AL. adopted and expanded Wu's coding scheme and focused on the nature of intermediaries' elicitation behavior.

To test a proposed user measure of success of information retrieval (IR) and to compare it with traditional measures of recall and precision, SU designed a field experiment with forty self-selected academic participants. Her participants were primarily doctoral students conducting dissertation research who paid for the online searches that were conducted by intermediaries. Subjects were asked to evaluate the searches using a quantitative measure with twenty indicators of search success, such as worth of search results in dollars, searcher's contribution, and completeness. Postsearch interviews solicited the evaluation and the reasons for the assigned ratings; the interviews were audiotaped.

To investigate how personal knowledge and database uses affect problem solving, WILDEMUTH ET AL. conducted a longitudinal experiment to observe students in three cohort bacteriology classes. Students were given six problems (each involving several specific questions) to answer prior to the course. At the end of the course, they were given the same six problems again with the incorrect or incomplete answers from the first assignment. At that time, the subjects were asked to solve the problems using the INQUIRER database. The effects of knowledge on problem solving and on database searching were examined.

Relevance judgment. Two large-scale projects on relevance judgments were carried out in the 1960s (CUADRA & KATTER; REES & SCHULTZ). Each project consisted of a series of experiments involving several hundred participants with different educational backgrounds. Subjects were given retrieved documents and asked to make relevance judgments based on given hypothetical queries. At the outset, more than forty variables that might affect relevance judgments were suggested from the following categories: judges, requests, documents, use orientations, and judgment conditions; each of the two studies examined a subset of the variables. The interest in relevance judgment research was renewed in the 1990s with a shift from the system-oriented view to a user-centered approach. Researchers found users' relevance judgments can only be studied in natural settings rather than experiments (see Observing Users in Natural Settings).

Online searching. OPACs were among the first online systems in libraries designed for end users. BORGMAN conducted a 2 x 2 experiment to examine effects of training methods and gender on novice users' search of a sample bibliographic database with records extracted from the OCLC database. Two different training methods were used: the introduction of an analogical model of the card catalog, and the introduction of mechanical procedures typically provided in an IR system manual. Two tasks were given: a simple search that required the use of one index and no more than one Boolean operator, and a complex search that required two or more indexes and one or more Boolean operators. Forty-three undergraduates participated in the experiment; only thirty-two completed it. In another experiment designed to examine users' misconceptions of OPACs, H. CHEN & DHAR recruited thirty business-school students to perform a search for documents within a subject area of their interest. The process was captured with log transactions and simultaneous think-aloud protocols. Content analysis of data derived a taxonomy of misconceptions. Another experiment (BORGMAN ET AL.; HIRSH) investigated children's online searching behavior in relation to topics, complexity, prior knowledge, and search methods. Children were selected from two different environments: a school with a library but without a computer lab, and a school without a library but with a computer lab. The sample of sixty-four fifth-grade students balanced gender and level of science knowledge. Each student was given eight different science topics to search. The study collected data through interview, observation, and online monitoring. Prototype systems designed for children were tested and a theoretical model of children's information seeking was refined.

Early online databases were designed for trained intermediaries. FENICHEL designed an experiment examining how overall search experience and knowledge of specific databases affected the search process and outcome. The data were collected via log files of the search processes. A total of seventy-two subjects with different levels of search experience and subject knowledge completed the experiment. To study effects of search experience and subject knowledge on term selection, search monitoring, and query formulation/modification, HSIEH-YEE designed an experiment using a purposive sampling method. Thirty novice searchers and thirty-two experienced searchers completed the experiment. Focusing on both cognitive and affective factors during online searching, NAHL & TENOPIR provided a two-hour training session for their subjects, who subsequently conducted a series of searches (three to four sessions per subject). Think-aloud protocols during the searches were collected in addition to transaction logs. IIVONEN, in a longitudinal experiment, investigated inter- and intra-searcher consistencies of search-term selection. Two months after their first searches, searchers were given the same questions to search again. The two searches of the same questions were then compared to calculate consistencies. HUANG examined how novice searchers searched online databases and what caused them to pause or stop. Forty-four self-selected university faculty and students performed searches for their own information needs. Before beginning their searches, subjects watched a standard training videotape on how to use DIALOG. The search session was logged in a file with time stamps identifying pauses during the search process. Immediately after the search, Huang interviewed the subjects about the reasons for any discernable pauses. A pause was defined as any three-second or longer idling in interaction.

Human-system interactions. MARCHIONINI designed a series of experiments to examine how various user groups interacted with computerized information systems in finding information: experts versus novices, domain experts versus search experts, and children from fourth through eleventh grades. Fifty-two students (twenty-eight third and fourth graders, and twenty-four sixth graders) were given two introductory sessions and demonstrations of an electronic encyclopedia they had not used before. They were then given two factual search questions of different facets/levels to answer using the encyclopedia. Their search keystrokes were logged into a file and an onsite experimenter timed the session (forty-five minutes were allotted for each search question). Search outcomes were measured by success, search time, and number of moves. Nonparametric statistics were used to test effects of age groups and task level on search outcomes (MARCHIONINI). In a series of studies of searching databases by subject experts and experienced searchers, MARCHIONINI ET AL. (1990) captured subjects' interactions with databases and verbalization of their thoughts while searching. Thoughts were solicited either by an immediate replay of the session to stimulate the searcher's recall of his/her thinking at particular points (MARCHIONINI ET AL., 1990), or by thinking aloud while searching (MARCHIONINI ET AL., 1993).

A series of projects under the name of TIPSTER III led by BELKIN in the 1990s investigated various aspects of users' interactions with experimental IR systems. All experiments were carried out with a general design of data collection: subjects (1) filled out a questionnaire on demographic data and IR experience; (2) were interviewed about experiences and told about the goals of the study; (3) were given a tutorial of the system (twenty-five to forty-five minutes); (4) were given search tasks described in detail on paper (search tasks were based on Text REtrieval Conference (TREC) topics); (5) performed searches with concurrent thinking aloud; (6) filled out postsearch questionnaires on the searches; (7) were given an exit interview about the searches. Search transactions were logged, verbalizations and screen views of computer monitors were recorded on videotape, and interviews were audiotaped. Progress reports of these projects, the data-collection instruments, and data analysis are available on the project's Webpage (BELKIN & PÉREZ-CARBALLO). S. PARK reports one of these studies. COOL & XIE adapted this design in a field observation[1] of the information seeking of fourteen managers, engineers, and technical staff at the Boeing Corporation. Because the subjects were not asked to use an experimental IR system, their design modified steps 4 and 5: subjects were given standard forms (called Activity Notes) and verbal instructions; and they self-administered the recording of information activities and information sources used in relation to the actual tasks performed. The subjects' self-administered activities were not audio or video recorded; the interviews were audio recorded.

---

[1]This study belongs in the next section, Observing Users In Natural Settings. It is mentioned here because it adapted Belkin's research design.

An increasing interest in the World Wide Web as an information channel evoked many studies on how users find information on the Web. WANG ET AL. designed an experiment to capture user-Web interaction processes in finding factual information. Twenty-four information science graduate students participated in the study. Each searched for two imposed factual questions (simulating a reference setting). The entire interactions (transactions, URLs, screen actions, and concurrent verbalization) were videotaped synchronously using a videocassette recorder connected to a computer via a UMAX VGA/TV Converter. The subjects were given a cognitive style test (Embedded-Figure Test) and anxiety-level tests before and after each search. They filled out questionnaires on prior computer and IR experience and self-evaluations of the search results and processes. Analysis of both quantitative and qualitative data focused on the searchers' cognitive and affective behavior in relation to the interfaces and the Web. In a similar way, SAITO & OHMURA connected a second monitor to the computer used by the subjects for searching and placed it behind a partition where it was hidden from the subjects. A video camera faced the second monitor to tape the search processes and verbalizations. This experiment investigated the effect of forming an image of target information on searching behavior. Subjects searched in pairs and made decisions as a team. SU & H.-L. CHEN recruited thirty-six university students to perform searches using four Web engines (with a 4 x 4 Latin square design to balance order effect). The subjects were paid to search on a self-selected topic. They made relevance judgments on retrieved information using a three-point scale: relevant, partially relevant, and not relevant. They were then interviewed on their satisfaction with and the value of the searches. RIEH & BELKIN (2000) observed sixteen scholars searching on the Web for four given generic tasks: research project in progress, conference information, information and treatment on a disease, and information on buying a computer. The processes were recorded using ScreenCam. Subjects were subsequently interviewed about the process as it was replayed. This study followed their previous study in which they interviewed fourteen scholars about the criteria for evaluating Web information sources (RIEH & BELKIN, 1998).

Children are also active Internet users. KAFAI & BATES, in an experiment, observed students' interactions with the Web in six elementary classrooms (grades one to six) where students were taught information literacy skills and learned to search the Web and build a Webpage on a specific topic for other children. BILAL studied children's cognitive, affective, and physical behaviors while using the Yahooligans! search engine. Twenty-two students, selected by their teachers, completed the procedure. They attended a training session and conducted a factual search on Yahooligans! (limited to thirty minutes). Three instruments were used to collect data about the participants: (1) a quiz of

Internet/Web knowledge; (2) students' characteristics (defined by teachers); (3) an exit interview with the searcher. The search sessions were captured using ScreenCam. Both the descriptive statistical analysis of actions and moves, and the qualitative observation of the sessions provided insight into children's searching behavior on the Web.

Reference transactions. Reference transactions have been observed in field experiments. The first study of reference transactions in public libraries was conducted in New Jersey in 1968 by CROWLEY, who developed a single-blind field experiment using a set of carefully developed test reference questions. The experimenters, posing as users, visited the selected public libraries to have their questions answered by the reference staff. CHILDERS and other researchers replicated this study on a larger scale and in different settings, including academic libraries. These studies resulted in similar findings (i.e., only about fifty-five percent of the answers were correct). Further, WEECH & GOLDHOR conducted a study assessing whether obtrusiveness had any effect on librarians' behavior. Significant behavioral differences were observed between the two groups: voluntary participants who knew they were observed, and subjects who did not know they were observed. This line of studies raised ethical issues: Should unobtrusive experiments be conducted? Should consent be obtained for such observation? Is there negative impact on the populations studied when the published results of the high rate of incorrect answers reveal the crisis in reference services?

Focusing on the reference process, LYNCH carried out a field observation[2] in which participating librarians wore wireless microphones and their patrons were notified about the study and given the option to turn off the recording. The researcher was not on the scene but could hear and see the transactions from an unobtrusive distance. A total of 309 reference interview transactions was gathered. Content analysis of these data resulted in a better understanding of the reference process in real library settings. DEWDNEY further explored the results of training methods on reference interview behaviors using a 2 x 3 field-experiment design with twenty-four librarian participants. Two kinds of training were given: neutral questioning[3] and microcounseling.[4] A control group did not receive any training. Subjects were observed before and after training.

---

[2]It may be argued that this study belongs in Observing Users in Natural Settings, because no treatment was applied. It is included here so that it precedes the field experiment that followed this study.

[3]Neutral questioning, developed by DERVIN & DEWDNEY, is a strategy for conducting effective reference interviews by asking open yet structured questions to obtain information on specific elements—situations, gaps, and uses.

[4]Microcounseling, by Allen E. Ivey (cited in DEWDNEY), teaches basic listening and questioning skills focusing on open, nondirective questions in order to allow articulation of problems without premature diagnosis.

HARRIS & MICHELL investigated factors that affect users' evaluation of reference services. In this experiment, gender, role, and interaction styles were independent variables: gender of the librarian, gender of the patron, gender of the judge, warmth of the librarian, and inclusion of sources by the librarian when providing an answer. Professional actors played librarians and patrons. Each reference service transaction had four different scripts based on two interaction variables; in each script, the librarian and the patron were performed by both genders. This design resulted in a total of sixteen videotapes. Three hundred twenty adult public library users were recruited as judges. Judges were randomly assigned to one of the sixteen tapes to rate the librarians' behavior in terms of competence, friendliness, and knowledge using a seven-point scale.

Meta-experiments. Most experimental designs focus on a small number of variables and control other variables. GOLOVCHINSKY ET AL. proposed an experimental design, the meta-experimental approach. It compromises experimental control to a certain extent to augment ethnographic elements in research design. Three cases using this design to study human-system interactions are presented in their paper. The researchers collected data involving many variables and used (1) factor analysis to reduce a large number of measured variables into a more manageable set of factors; (2) cluster analysis to group subjects into clusters (this is different from assigning subjects to conditions before an experiment); and (3) discriminant analysis to determine differences between the clusters.

In summary, as a typical quantitative method for behavioral research, experiments are widely used in user studies, especially in human-system interactions. LIS researchers design experiments to test hypotheses guided by theories to identify factors that affect information-related behavior. Most experiments include a small number of self-selected subjects. There are two main criticisms of experiments: (1) behavior observed in experimental conditions may not map to real-life behavior and (2) when a large number of inseparable variables are observed together, it is often difficult to pinpoint specific factors. LIS researchers have gone beyond traditional experimental design by collecting additional data through postexperimental interviews and conducting meta-experiments to study phenomena involving a large number of variables.

Observing Users in Natural Settings

Field studies and case studies are typical qualitative research designs in the social sciences. In contrast to experimental design, user behavior is observed as it occurs naturally, in real-life situations. Two basic observation modes have been used in user studies: (1) the observer does not participate in the process and is as unobtrusive as possible and (2) the observer is involved in the process as a member. The former is often called field observation and the latter participant observation or ethnography. Participants are often instructed or trained to record data on their own behavior, especially when it is difficult to predict where and when information seeking will happen.

Information needs and uses. Wilson and colleagues conducted a study of information needs and uses funded by the British Library R&D Department called Project INISS (Research Project on Information Needs and Services) using both field observations and interviews. Twenty-two professionals in local authority social services departments were observed for one week at their workplaces. Field observation was followed by interviews with 151 members of the population. Results from the field observation were verified by the interview data. The researchers noted that field observation, although unavoidably obtrusive, can be used successfully to collect reliable data for certain situations with appropriate preparation of the participants and observers (WILSON & STREATFIELD; WILSON ET AL.).

A two-phase study observed document selection and use by a group of academic users during their research projects. Twenty-five users from an academic department participated in the first phase of the project. After a reference interview to obtain information needs, DIA-LOG searches were conducted, and the printout of retrieved documents in full bibliographic formats was presented to the user for selection in the presence of the researcher. Concurrent verbal reports of the selection process were audio recorded (WANG; WANG & SOERGEL). In the second phase of the project (two and one-half years later), fifteen of the twenty-five original participants had finished their projects and were available for follow-up interviews (two participants' papers were near completion). A semistructured interview with each of the fifteen users obtained information on how the retrieved and selected documents were used (i.e., read or cited) and why they were (or were not) used. The interviewees were given the bibliographic records of the selected documents and the citations of the written product produced in the project (WANG & WHITE; WHITE & WANG).

Information seeking. The Getty Information Institute sponsored and carried out a two-year project to study humanities scholars' searching of online information systems and use of information for their research. A total of twenty-seven volunteer participants resulted in twenty-eight cases: thirteen from the first year and fifteen the second year (one scholar participated in both years). All participants did their own searching after a one-day training program; they had twenty-four-hour-a-day access to a workstation near their offices. DIALOG databases were used in this study. A program developed in-house recorded the needs statements (not a part of the DIALOG transaction) and search transactions in DIALOG (queries and printouts). A total of 188 natural-language statements of information needs and 5,035 queries was captured. All participants were interviewed in depth about their needs and what they thought of the online retrieval systems. Several coding schemes were developed for content analysis of these data. Participants who did not search any DIALOG databases were also interviewed about their reasons for not using the online databases (BATES ET AL., 1993, 1995; SIEGFIED ET AL.).

CHATMAN (1992) conducted a two-year study into information needs and seeking of retired women using an ethnographic or participant-observation method. Her in-depth interviews with fifty-five retired women and detailed notes of observation resulted in rich and systematic data on this underresearched community. She combined both inductive and deductive reasoning in data analysis. Earlier, in another study of an underresearched user group using the same method, she followed fifty-two custodial workers for two years to understand their information needs and seeking behavior (CHATMAN, 1987). SOLOMON's (1997) participation in a three-year work-planning task as a facilitator and record keeper gave him a rare opportunity to conduct ethnographic research of information seeking. Being involved in the entire process, he engaged in persistent and extended observation. The collected data included field notes, interview transcripts, meeting transcripts, think-aloud protocols, logs, and other documents. A key step in his data analysis was to develop a classification scheme for coding these data using DERVIN's (1992) sense-making framework. He also used two important techniques to establish credibility: (1) peer debriefing, in which researchers in information seeking examined and critiqued the draft research report and (2) member checking, in which the participants were given the draft report for comment.

To understand students' information-seeking processes in completing research assignments, KUHLTHAU designed a series of studies observing a group of high school students over a four-year period using multiple methods: field observation, interviews, and surveys. The first study collected field data: self-administered student journals about feelings and thoughts during their work; search logs of sources and decisions kept by the students; written topic descriptions at the beginning, middle, and end of the assignment; and in-depth interviews with six volunteer students about their journals, search logs, and topic statements. Decisions during the process were illustrated retrospectively using conceptual maps. The teachers provided assessments of the completed projects. Kuhlthau also used questionnaires to survey a larger sample to test her model. A field experiment was designed by

KRACKER[5] to test Kuhlthau's model in an undergraduate course with a research paper assignment. Sections of the course were assigned randomly to two conditions: an introduction to Kuhlthau's model by a guest speaker or a placebo session by a different speaker who had no knowledge of the model. Kracker's instrument was based on the critical-incident technique to measure the aspects of the model twice: once at the beginning of the course when the students were asked to answer the questions based on an experience of a recent research assignment, and again after the completion of their papers for the course.

Relevance judgment. Early relevance studies conducted in the 1960s represented a system-oriented view using mostly experiments. In the 1990s, a shift to user-centered approaches resulted in empirical studies of real users in real situations (SCHAMBER, 1994). These studies often focused on users' relevance criteria, collected verbal data on relevance judgments through think-aloud protocols or semistructured interviews, applied content analysis to textual data, and reached comparable findings. Six dissertations examined relevance judgments of retrieved documents based on IR system records or full-text documents (C. L. BARRY, 1993; BATEMAN; H. PARK; T.K. PARK; TANG; WANG). Several studies examined changes in relevance judgments during the natural span of an information-seeking activity—a course research assignment (BATEMAN; SMITHSON; TANG; VAKKARI).

Online searching. Several studies used online monitoring and collected search logs unobtrusively from a large body of users of an open system, such as OPACs (DICKSON; HUNTER; PETERS), online databases (TENOPIR & READ), and the Web (JANSEN ET AL.). Although it is easy to collect data unobtrusively in transaction logs of searches, it is hard to identify users' real information needs. The boundaries (starting and ending points) of individual searches are unclear in public terminals and the actual uses of the search results are unknown. Instead of collecting unobtrusive transaction logs, CATLEDGE & PITKOW set up a study to log Web searches on a consent basis. During a three-week data-collection period, 107 users (67%) chose to participate in the study. Screen actions and URLs were captured with time stamps.

LARGE ET AL. observed fifty-three students in two sixth-grade classes with a project titled "The Middle Ages." Students were working in seventeen groups over a four-week period. Their search interactions with multimedia CD-ROM databases and conversations during the search were recorded simultaneously and unobtrusively on videotapes. The students were not instructed to think aloud because the study was

---

[5] This study belongs in Observing Users through Experiments. It is mentioned here because it tests Kuhlthau's model.

designed as an unobtrusive field observation. Students evaluated their information use of the systems. A total of fifty hours of search sessions was recorded. The analysis focused on search strategies, use of information (including other sources listed on the postproject questionnaire), and navigation of hypertext systems in relation to the finished student projects.

SOLOMON (1993) conducted a participant-observation study of students' OPAC searching behavior in a school media center where he was also a volunteer. He observed students enrolled in the first to sixth grades of an elementary school for a school year when various training sessions on OPAC searching were given to students. To ensure that the collected data represented the population, he randomized his observation days so that his samples covered all the grades for a period of time. He observed a total of 902 transactions involving approximately 500 students. Although he originally planned to be an objective observer in the field, he soon assumed the role of participant observer because the children expected him to help them. This, in turn, helped him obtain data otherwise inaccessible to him.

Case-study method. Case studies focus on a group, an organization, and sometimes a single individual. The case-study method is appropriate for studying a phenomenon with a large variety of factors and relationships, and with no theory to determine important factors or relationships (FIDEL, 1984a). FIDEL (1984b, 1991) set out to explore how intermediaries performed searches for end users. She intensively observed five intermediary searchers on the job, capturing search transactions and verbalizations during their search processes. She also conducted in-depth follow-up interviews to triangulate her observations and to gain additional information about what was not observed during the process. FIDEL ET AL. formed a research team (the instructor plus her seven students) and conducted a field observation on the Web-searching behavior of high-school students in completing course assignments. Each researcher observed one student for two to three searches. This project obtained a larger sample than a single researcher could have and also trained students to conduct real research. WIBERLEY & JONES participated in a year-long seminar for eleven scholars in humanities conducting one-person research projects to understand their information-seeking behavior. In her dissertation research, FITZGERALD followed five second-year doctoral students through the process of searching a topic for a literature review paper. She observed and interviewed her participants three times during the six-week process to understand how and why they used information systems in the library, selected retrieved documents, and used information. She analyzed each case in depth and all cases collectively to identify elements

of the cognitive process and information-seeking strategies. TANG &
SOLOMON observed one graduate student's information seeking during completion of a term paper for a course.

In summary, observations in natural settings have gained great favor
in user studies in recent years, because it records what actually happened during a process. The method requires the researcher to gather
data intensively and frequently. Researchers often apply multiple data-
collection methods in a single study across a natural span of cases or
activities. These studies, however, tend to observe a small convenience
sample of users known to the researcher and to produce descriptive
results that cannot be generalized. This method is time-consuming and
labor-intensive, but it is the only method that observes natural behavior
in context. When the presence of an observer is not possible or desirable, the participants are asked to keep self-administered diaries, journals, or activity logs using guidelines. Data analysis faces the same
challenge as interview designs mentioned in the Interviewing Users
section.

Multiple Phases and Emerging Methods

Multiple-phase and longitudinal studies. As noted above, most behavioral studies obtain data by asking for information from users (through
quantitative surveys or qualitative interviews) or observing users
(through quantitative experiments or qualitative field observations). As
evident from the studies reviewed above, user behavioral research
tackles complex issues, often applies more than one data-collection
method, and is conducted over a period of time or in multiple phases.
Multiple methods are used for triangulation, or, in many cases, are
necessary in the context of the phenomenon. A frequently used research design of a multiple-phase study starts with a case study or
focus-group interview to identify potential variables and follows up
with a survey of a large sample representing the population, or with
experiments focusing on fewer variables.

Incorporating multiple methods in a single study is challenging in
data collection and analysis. C. A. BARRY (1997) developed the Research Activity Timeline (RAT) design to collect multiple data in a four-
year longitudinal study of academics' information seeking and uses
related to their work projects. Based on the time-line and critical-incident technique, RAT is implemented in seven stages: (1) diary (a structured form sensitizing participants to implicit and unconscious information activities); (2) activity log (two structured forms recording a six-
month period of research and information activities); (3) research time-
line (a temporal sequence of activities constructed by the researcher
based on the activity log); (4) semistructured interview (based on the

material from the first three stages); (5) bibliography-prompted information access (asking participants about how specific information was
found based on their written products' references); (6) research strand
data analysis (a coding sheet used by the researcher to organize data
surrounding strands (i.e., activities/tasks) across different formats of
collected data) ; (7) research strand map (time-activity map based on
strand sheets and time-lines in the third stage). The seven stages are not
necessarily linear, but are iterative and interwoven. Certain data can
only be collected after the data analysis of previous stages. RAT depends on both participants and researcher in data collection over a
period of time.

Meta-level analysis and synthesis.   In recent years, researchers have
pioneered ways to integrate empirical results from different studies for
a higher level of understanding. Meta-level analysis methods were
developed for this purpose. The term meta-analysis has mainly been
used for quantitative studies (GLASS ET AL.; ROSENTHAL; WOLF).
NOBLIT & HARE use the term meta-ethnography for the method of
synthesizing and integrating qualitative studies to achieve goals similar
to meta-analysis. Meta-analysis is not the same as a standard literature
review aiming at recording progress and identifying gaps for future
work. Nor does it compare the results of two or more studies. As a
research method, meta-analysis reanalyzes data collected by individual
studies on a single or similar phenomenon; it applies appropriate techniques to aggregate findings from different studies (and may include
poorly designed studies).

TRAHAN piloted application of meta-analysis to twenty-five studies to compare effectiveness of searching using computerized systems
versus paper-based systems. SAXTON's meta-analysis included fifty-
nine studies on reference services. To identify invariant underlying
relations of variables from studies with diverse designs and heterogeneous results, C. CHEN & RADA applied meta-analysis techniques to
twenty-three experiments on interactions with hypertext systems. Three
variables were examined: the effects of users' cognitive attributes, the
effects of task complexity, and the effects of hypertext tools. They called
for improvements in empirical studies by developing a user-task taxonomy and by reducing diversity in experimental designs (e.g., using
standard models of hypertext systems).

There is a need to consolidate individual studies on the same phenomenon with similar foci. For example, several empirical studies containing a component of user relevance judgments were conducted with
similar research designs, but used quite different schemes of relevance
criteria in data analysis. While this was unavoidable because these
studies were in progress at about the same time and used different
levels of analyses, meta-level analysis of these results and reanalysis of

original raw data could shed new light on and produce a more coherent understanding of relevance criteria. Although meta-level analysis of research results of individual studies is worth pursuing and should be encouraged, barriers are evident: the field may not accept or appreciate this approach (compared to original research); researchers may be unwilling to share raw data; the participants must be protected; and standards to ensure data integrity must be developed.

Discourse analysis. Discourse analysis is an interpretive research method that collects discourses (published or archived speeches or texts) surrounding a theme and examines these discourses at a macro level. The method focuses on the way in which objects or ideas are spoken about. FROHMANN (1992) identifies several research areas to which discourse analysis can be applied. He argues that discourse analysis can contribute as much to an understanding of user-centric theories of information, users, and information uses as can other methods such as surveys and interviews. Discourse analysis should challenge the traditional way of identifying information user groups (children, women, scientists, CEOs, graduate students, etc.). In another article, FROHMANN (1994) illustrates how the concept of information from the cognitive viewpoint was embedded in LIS literature using discourse analysis. TALJA applied discourse analysis to interview transcripts of library users. In her analysis, the individual user was not the primary analytical unit, nor was the individual question. Rather, her analysis was intended to discover the regularities of user views at a macro sociological level. BUDD & RABER identify two key elements of discourse analysis: form (the structure of language) and function (language as a social phenomenon) of both spoken and written languages. OLSON translates the deconstruction analytical technique used in the humanities into LIS. Deconstruction analyzes the texts that have contributed to contemporary practice of a field to reveal opposite concepts and their relationships. She further illustrates how discourses selected from foundational texts in information storage and retrieval can be analyzed using the deconstruction method and recommends it as a potential method for other LIS research areas, such as relevance research.

Social network analysis. Social network analysis is a research area that uses graph theory to map information use and exchange among entities (individuals or organizations). To support such analysis, data are typically collected through surveys, interviews, citation analysis, and bibliometrics (HAYTHORNTHWAITE; LIEVROUW; SONNENWALD & PIERCE; WEEDMAN).

New methods, mostly qualitative methods, have been applied to user behavioral research in recent years. Many studies were conducted in multiple phases and applied multiple methods, but only a few are truly complementary and interlocking in design so as to provide integrated results.

SUMMARY AND CONCLUSIONS

In this chapter, the four major research methods for behavioral research and their uses in the six research areas of user studies are summarized: (1) studies of information needs and uses use surveys, interviews, experiments, and observations in natural settings; (2) studies of information seeking also use the four methods; (3) relevance judgment studies mainly use interviews, experiments, and field observations; (4) studies of online searching often use experiments and field observations; (5) studies of human-system interactions mostly use experiments; and (6) reference transaction studies also use experiments.

In a short research history, LIS research has made significant progress in applying different methods in user studies. The early adoption of quantitative methods contributed to the understanding of information needs and uses at a macro level, but left many questions unanswered. The adaptation of qualitative methods in the 1970s has brought a new level of understanding of user behaviors in various contexts at a micro level, but also brought difficulties in integrating results of individual studies due to their diverse research designs. Both quantitative and qualitative research approaches are actively applied in the field. There is no strong evidence of an irreconcilable polarity between the two approaches to user behavior. The differences between the two research paradigms remain, but are viewed by most researchers as complementing rather than competing with each other. As POWELL's recent review points out, many new methods, mostly qualitative, have been introduced to LIS research and many are difficult to categorize. Qualitative methods have gained increased popularity in LIS research. Fewer new developments were found in quantitative methods. The current trends in LIS research, such as using qualitative methods and applying multiple methods, are likely to continue. This is also the methodological state of the art in user behavioral research.

In reporting survey and experimental results, the positivist paradigm imposes rigid standards on both elements and formats. In LIS publications, however, the reporting of empirical studies often includes little discussion of the rationale for the methods applied, or descriptions of the research design. Frequently missing elements are time (when was the study conducted? how long was the data-collecting period?), place (where was the study conducted?), sampling (how were the participants or subjects recruited?), setting (what environment was the session carried out in?), stimuli (were the search questions artificial or real?), data-collection procedure (who carried out the interviews, the researcher or other designated staff?), instrument (what did the questionnaire or interview guidelines include?), recording technique (how were data recorded?), process observed (what was the participants' task?) and data analysis technique (what was the analysis unit? what was the analytical scheme? who coded the data and how?). This situation must be improved to facilitate effective communication among researchers and other interested people. BATES stresses that information science is at a historic juncture and is drawing many newcomers who do not have backgrounds in the field. It is important for information scientists to communicate more rapidly and effectively to these newcomers and to people from broader society. Adopting standards for abstracting (using structured abstracts for empirical studies instead of the indicative abstracts seen in most published articles) and for reporting empirical research can contribute to more effective communication. Editors, referees, and researchers can promote consistent use of terminology and standardization in reporting research designs and empirical findings. Empirical studies should be indexed at a deeper level in IR systems so that methods, specific techniques, and tools can be searched.

Information and user behavior related to information are complex phenomena involving large numbers of factors. It is clear that current methodologies and methods need to be strengthened and advanced to study these complex research topics. Compared to other behavioral sciences such as sociology and psychology, user behavioral research in LIS is still young. A deeper treatment of methodological issues for the field is needed, requiring more effort than reviewing publications as in this chapter. More work is needed to examine appropriate or inappropriate uses of research methods. Future work in methodologies is needed to bridge the gaps between theoretical assumptions at the highly abstract level and implementations using specific methods at the practice level (DERVIN, 1999). Comparisons of similarities and differences of different research designs are needed to shed new light on how to improve the use of these research designs. The advancement of a field depends on its methodological development.

BIBLIOGRAPHY

ABELS, EILEEN G.; WHITE, MARILYN DOMAS; HAHN, KARLA. 1997. Identifying User-Based Criteria for Web Pages. Internet Research. 1997 December; 7(4): 256-262. ISSN: 1066-2243 .

ALLEN, THOMAS J. 1977. Managing the Flow of Technology: Technology Transfer and the Dissemination of Technological Information within the R&D Organization. Cambridge, MA: MIT Press; 1977. 320p. ISBN: 0-262-01048-8.

AUSTER, ETHEL; CHOO, CHUN WEI. 1993. Environmental Scanning by CEOs in Two Canadian Industries. Journal of the American Society for Information Science. 1993 May; 44(4): 194-203. ISSN: 0002-8231; CODEN: AISJB6.

AUSTER, ETHEL; CHOO, CHUN WEI. 1994. How Senior Managers Acquire and Use Information in Environmental Scanning. Information Processing & Management. 1994 September-October; 30(5): 607-618. ISSN: 0306-4573; CODEN: IPMADK.

BABBIE, EARL R. 1998. The Practice of Social Research. 8th edition. Westford, MA: Wadsworth Publishing Co.; 1998. 465p. ISBN: 0-534-50486-X.

BAKER, SHARON L. 1986. The Display Phenomenon: An Exploration into Factors Causing the Increased Circulation of Displayed Books. Library Quarterly. 1986 July; 56(3): 237-257. ISSN: 0024-2519.

BARRY, CAROL L. 1993. The Identification of User Criteria of Relevance and Document Characteristics: Beyond the Topical Approach to Information Retrieval. Syracuse, NY: Syracuse University; 1993. 255p. (Ph.D. dissertation). Available from: UMI, Ann Arbor, MI. (UMI order no. 9422230).

BARRY, CHRISTINE A. 1997. The Research Activity Timeline: A Qualitative Tool for Information Research. Library & Information Science Research. 1997; 19(2): 153-179. ISSN: 0740-8188.

BATEMAN, JUDITH ANN. 1998. Modeling Changes in End-User Relevance Criteria: An Information Seeking Study. Denton, TX: University of North Texas; 1998. 206p. (Ph.D. dissertation). Available from: UMI, Ann Arbor, MI. (UMI order no. 9830819).

BATES, MARCIA J. 1999. The Invisible Substrate of Information Science. Journal of the American Society for Information Science. 1999 October; 50(12): 1043-1050. ISSN: 0002-8231; CODEN: AISJB6.

BATES, MARCIA J.; WILDE, DEBORAH N.; SIEGFRIED, SUSAN. 1993. An Analysis of Search Terminology Used by Humanities Scholars: The Getty Online Searching Project Number 1. Library Quarterly. 1993 January; 63(1): 1-39. ISSN: 0024-2519.

BATES, MARCIA J.; WILDE, DEBORAH N.; SIEGFRIED, SUSAN. 1995. Research Practices of Humanities Scholars in an Online Environment: The Getty Online Searching Project Report No. 3. Library & Information Science Research. 1995 Winter; 17(1): 5-40. ISSN: 0740-8188.

BELKIN, NICHOLAS J. 1998. An Overview of Results from Rutgers' Investigation of Interactive Information Retrieval. In: Cochrane, Pauline A.; Johnson, Eric H., eds. Visualizing Subject Access for 21st Century Information Resources: Proceedings of the 34th Annual Clinic on Library Applications of Data Processing; 1997 March 2-4; Champaign, IL. Urbana-Champaign, IL: Graduate School of Library and Information Science, University of Illinois at Urbana-Champaign; 1998. 45-62. Also available WWW: http://mariner.rutgers.edu/tipster3/cladp97.html.

BELKIN, NICHOLAS J.; PÉREZ-CARBALLO, JOSÉ. 1997. Understanding and Supporting Multiple Information Seeking Strategies, a TIPSTER Phase III Research Project: 12 Month Report. New Brunswick, NJ: School of Communication, Information and Library Studies, Rutgers University; 1997. Available WWW: http://mariner.rutgers.edu/tipster3/tip12rep.html.

BENTON, TED. 1998. Naturalism in Social Science. In: Craig, Edward, ed. Routledge Encyclopedia of Philosophy: Volume 6. New York, NY: Routledge; 1998. 717-721. ISBN: 0-415-18711-7.

BILAL, DANIA. 2000. Children's Use of the Yahooligans! Web Search Engine: I. Cognitive, Physical, and Affective Behaviors on Fact-Based Search Tasks. Journal of the American Society for Information Science. 2000; 50: 646-665. ISSN: 0002-8231; CODEN: AISJB6.

BISHOP, ANN P.; TIDLINE, TONYIA J.; SHOEMAKER, SUSAN; SALELA, PAMELA. 1999. Public Libraries and Networked Information Services in Low-Income Communities. Library & Information Science Research. 1999; 21(3): 361-390. ISSN: 0740-8188.

BORGMAN, CHRISTINE L. 1986. The User's Mental Model of an Information Retrieval System: An Experiment on a Prototype Online Catalog. International Journal of Man-Machine Studies. 1986; 24(1): 47-64. ISSN: 0020-7373.

BORGMAN, CHRISTINE L.; HIRSH, SANDRA G.; WALTER, VIRGINIA A.; GALLAGHER, ANDREA L. 1995. Children's Searching Behavior on Browsing and Keyword Online Catalogs: The Science Library Catalog Project. Journal of the American Society for Information Science. 1995 October; 46(9): 663-684. ISSN: 0002-8231; CODEN: AISJB6.

BRADLEY, JANA; SUTTON, BRETT. 1993. Reframing the Paradigm Debate. Library Quarterly. 1993 October; 63(4): 405-410. ISSN: 0024-2519.

BRUCE, HARRY W. 1996. A User Oriented View of Internet as Information Infrastructure. Sydney, Australia: University of New South Wales; 1996. 365p. (Ph.D. dissertation).

BUDD, JOHN M.; RABER, DOUGLAS. 1996. Discourse Analysis: Method and Application in the Study of Information. Information Processing & Management. 1996; 32(2): 217-226. ISSN: 0306-4573; CODEN: IPMADK.

BUSHA, CHARLES H.; HARTER, STEPHEN P. 1980. Research Methods in Librarianship: Techniques and Interpretation. New York, NY: Academic Press; 1980. 417p. ISBN: 0-12-147550-6.

BYSTRÖM, KATRIINA; JÄRVELIN, KALERVO. 1995. Task Complexity Affects Information Seeking and Use. Information Processing & Management. 1995; 31(2): 191-213. ISSN: 0306-4573; CODEN: IPMADK.

CASE, DONALD OWEN. 1991. The Collection and Use of Information by Some American Historians: A Study of Motives and Methods. Library Quarterly. 1991 January; 61: 61-82. ISSN: 0024-2519.

CATLEDGE, LARA D.; PITKOW, JAMES E. 1995. Characterizing Browsing Strategies in the World-Wide Web. Computer Networks and ISDN Systems. 1995; 27(6): 1065-1073. ISSN: 0169-7552.

CHATMAN, ELFREDA A. 1987. The Information World of Low-Skilled Workers. Library & Information Science Research. 1987 October/December; 9: 265-283. ISSN: 0740-8188.

CHATMAN, ELFREDA A. 1992. The Information World of Retired Women. Westport, CT: Greenwood Press; 1992. 150p. ISSN: 0887-3844; ISBN: 0-313-25492-3.

CHEN, CHAOMEI; RADA, ROY. 1996. Interacting with Hypertext: A Meta-Analysis of Experimental Studies. Human-Computer Interaction. 1996; 11: 125-156. ISSN: 0737-0024.

CHEN, CHING-CHIH; HERNON, PETER. 1982. Information Seeking: Assessing and Anticipating User Needs. New York, NY: Neal-Schuman Publishers; 1982. 205p. ISBN: 0-918212-50-2.

CHEN, HSINCHUN; DHAR, VASANT. 1990. User Misconceptions of Information Retrieval Systems. International Journal of Man-Machine Studies. 1990; 32(6): 673-692. ISSN: 0020-7373.

CHILDERS, THOMAS. 1972. Managing the Quality of Reference/Information Service. Library Quarterly. 1972 April; 42(2): 212-217. ISSN: 0024-2519.

CHU, CLARA M. 1999a. Immigrant Children Mediators (ICM): Bridging the Literacy Gap in Immigrant Communities. In: Proceedings of the 65th IFLA Council and General Conference; 1999 August 20-28; Bangkok, Thailand. Available WWW: http://www.ifla.org/IV/ifla65/papers/109-145e.htm.

CHU, CLARA M. 1999b. Literary Critics at Work and Their Information Needs: A Research-Phases Model. Library & Information Science Research. 1999; 21(2): 247-273. ISSN: 0740-8188.

COOL, COLLEEN; XIE, HONG IRIS. 2000. Patterns of Information Use, Avoidance and Evaluation in a Corporate Engineering Environment. In: Kraft, Donald H., ed. ASIS 2000: Proceedings of the American Society for Information Science (ASIS) 63rd Annual Meeting: Volume 37; 2000 November 11-16; Chicago, IL. Medford, NJ: Information Today, Inc. for ASIS; 2000. 462-472. ISSN: 0044-7870; ISBN: 1-57387-108-7.

CRESWELL, JOHN W. 1994. Research Design: Qualitative & Quantitative Approaches. Thousand Oaks, CA: Sage Publications; 1994. 228p. ISBN: 0-8039-5255-4.

CROWLEY, TERENCE. 1985. Half-Right Reference: Is It True? RQ. 1985 Fall; 25: 59-68. ISSN: 0033-7072.

CUADRA, CARLOS A.; KATTER, ROBERT V. 1967. Experimental Studies of Relevance Judgments: Final Reports. Santa Monica, CA: System Development Corporation; 1967. 3 volumes. NTIS: PB 175517, PB 175518, PB 175567.

DENZIN, NORMAN K.; LINCOLN, YVONNA S., eds. 1994. Handbook of Qualitative Research. Thousand Oaks, CA: Sage Publications; 1994. 643p. ISBN: 0-8039-4679-1.

DERVIN, BRENDA. 1983. An Overview of Sense-Making Research: Concepts, Methods and Results to Date. In: International Communication Association Annual Meeting; 1983 May; Dallas, TX. Available WWW: http://communication.sbs.ohio-state.edu/sense-making/art/artdervin83.html.

DERVIN, BRENDA. 1992. From the Mind's Eye of the User: The Sense-Making Qualitative-Quantitative Methodology. In: Glazier, Jack D.; Powell, Ronald R., eds. Qualitative Research in Information Management. Englewood, CO: Libraries Unlimited; 1992. 61-84. ISBN: 0-87287-806-6.

DERVIN, BRENDA. 1997. Given a Context by Any Other Name: Methodological Tools for Taming the Unruly Beast. In: Vakkari, Pertti; Savolainen, Reijo; Dervin, Brenda, eds. Information Seeking in Context: Proceedings of an International Conference on Research in Information Needs, Seeking and Use in Different Contexts; 1996 August 14-16; Tampere, Finland. Los Angeles, CA: Taylor Graham; 1997. 13-38. ISBN: 0-947568-71-9.

DERVIN, BRENDA. 1999. On Studying Information Seeking Methodologically: The Implications of Connecting Metatheory to Method. Information Processing & Management. 1999; 35(6): 727-750. ISSN: 0306-4573; CODEN: IPMADK.

DERVIN, BRENDA; DEWDNEY, PATRICIA. 1986. Neutral Questioning: A New Approach to the Reference Interview. RQ. 1986 Summer; 25(4): 506-513. ISSN: 0033-7072.

DERVIN, BRENDA; ZWEIZIG, DOUGLAS; BANISTER, MICHAEL; GABRIEL, MICHAEL; HALL, EDWARD; KWAN, COLLEEN. 1976. The Development of Strategies for Dealing with the Information Needs of Urban Residents: Phase I—Citizen Study. Final Report. Seattle, WA: School of Communications, University of Washington; 1976. 968p. ERIC: ED 125640.

DEWDNEY, PATRICIA. 1992. Recording the Reference Interview: A Field Experiment. In: Glazier, Jack D.; Powell, Ronald R., eds. Qualitative Research in Information Management. Englewood, CO: Libraries Unlimited; 1992. 122-150. ISBN: 0-87287-806-6.

DICKSON, JEAN. 1984. An Analysis of User Errors in Searching an Online Catalog. Cataloging and Classification Quarterly. 1984 Spring; 4: 26-33. ISSN: 0163-9374.

DUKES, SHEREE. 1984. Phenomenological Methodology in the Human Sciences. Journal of Religion and Health. 1984 Fall; 23(3): 197-203. ISSN: 0022-4197.

EISENBERG, MICHAEL B. 1988. Measuring Relevance Judgments. Information Processing & Management. 1988; 24(4): 373-389. ISSN: 0306-4573; CODEN: IPMADK.

ERICSSON, K. ANDERS; SIMON, HERBERT A. 1992. Protocol Analysis: Verbal Reports As Data. Cambridge, MA: MIT Press; 1992. 443p. ISBN: 0-262-05047-1.

FEEHAN, PATRICIA E.; GRAGG, W. LEE, II; HAVENER, W. MICHAEL; KESTER, DIANE D. 1987. Library and Information Science Research: An Analysis of the 1984 Journal Literature. Library & Information Science Research. 1987; 9: 173-185. ISSN: 0740-8188.

FENICHEL, CAROL HANSEN. 1981. Online Searching: Measures That Discriminate among Users with Different Types of Experiences. Journal of the American Society for Information Science. 1981 January; 32: 23-32. ISSN: 0002-8231; CODEN: AISJB6.

FIDEL, RAYA. 1984a. The Case Study Method: A Case Study. Library & Information Science Research. 1984; 6(3): 273-288. ISSN: 0740-8188.

FIDEL, RAYA. 1984b. Online Searching Styles: A Case-Study-Based Model of Searching Behavior. Journal of the American Society for Information Science. 1984; 35(4): 211-221. ISSN: 0002-8231; CODEN: AISJB6.

FIDEL, RAYA. 1991. Searchers' Selection of Search Keys: I. The Selection Routine; II. Controlled Vocabulary or Free-Text Searching; III. Searching

Styles. Journal of the American Society for Information Science. 1991 August; 42(7): 490-527. ISSN: 0002-8231; CODEN: AISJB6.

FIDEL, RAYA. 1993. Qualitative Methods in Information Retrieval Research. Library & Information Science Research. 1993 Summer; 15(3): 219-247. ISSN: 0740-8188.

FIDEL, RAYA; DAVIES, RACHEL K.; DOUGLASS, MARY H.; HOLDER, JENNY K.; HOPKINS, CARLA J.; KUSHNER, ELISABETH J.; MIYAGISHIMA, BRYAN K.; TONEY, CHRISTINA D. 1999. A Visit to the Information Mall: Web Searching Behavior of High School Students. Journal of the American Society for Information Science. 1999 January; 50(1): 24-37. ISSN: 0002-8231; CODEN: AISJB6.

FIELDING, NIGEL G.; FIELDING, JANE L. 1986. Linking Data. Beverly Hills, CA: Sage Publications; 1986. 96p. ISBN: 0-8039-2518-2.

FITZGERALD, MARY ANN. 1998. The Cognitive Process of Information Evaluation: A Collective Case Study. Athens, GA: University of Georgia; 1998. 265p. (Ph.D. dissertation). Available from: UMI, Ann Arbor, MI. (UMI order no. 9836953).

FLANAGAN, JOHN C. 1954. The Critical Incident Technique. Psychological Bulletin. 1954 July; 51: 327-328. ISSN: 0033-2909.

FORD, NIGEL. 1999. The Growth of Understanding in Information Science: Towards a Developmental Model. Journal of the American Society for Information Science. 1999 October; 50(12): 1141-1152. ISSN: 0002-8231; CODEN: AISJB6.

FROHMANN, BERND. 1992. The Power of Images: A Discourse Analysis of the Cognitive Viewpoint. Journal of Documentation. 1992 December; 48(4): 365-386. ISSN: 0022-0418; CODEN: JDOCAS.

FROHMANN, BERND. 1994. Discourse Analysis as a Research Method in Library and Information Science. Library & Information Science Research. 1994; 16: 119-138. ISSN: 0740-8188.

GARVEY, WILLIAM D. 1979. Communication: The Essence of Science: Facilitating Information Exchange among Librarians, Scientists, Engineers, and Students. New York, NY: Pergamon Press; 1979. 332p. ISBN: 0-08-022254-4.

GLASS, GENE V.; MCGAW, BARRY; SMITH, MARY LEE. 1981. Meta-Analysis in Social Research. Beverly Hills, CA: Sage Publications; 1981. 279p. ISBN: 0-8039-1633-7.

GLAZIER, JACK D.; POWELL, RONALD R., eds. 1992. Qualitative Research in Information Management. Englewood, CO: Libraries Unlimited; 1992. 238p. ISBN: 0-87287-806-6.

GOLDHOR, HERBERT. 1972. The Effect of Display Location on Public Library Circulation of Selected Adult Titles. Library Quarterly. 1972 October; 42(4): 371-389. ISSN: 0024-2519.

GOLDHOR, HERBERT. 1981. Experimental Effects on the Choice of Books Borrowed by Public Library Adult Patrons. Library Quarterly. 1981 July; 51(3): 253-268. ISSN: 0024-2519.

GOLOVCHINSKY, GENE; CHIGNELL, MARK; CHAROENKITKARN, NIPON. 1997. Formal Experiments in Casual Attire: Case Studies in Information

Exploration. The New Review of Hypermedia and Multimedia. 1997; 3: 123-157. ISSN: 1361-4568.

HARRIS, ROMA M.; MICHELL, B. GILLIAN. 1986. The Social Context of Reference Work: Assessing the Effects of Gender and Communication Skill on Observers' Judgments of Competence. Library & Information Science Research. 1986 January-March; 8: 85-101. ISSN: 0740-8188.

HAYTHORNTHWAITE, CAROLINE. 1996. Social Network Analysis: An Approach and Technique for the Study of Information Exchange. Library & Information Science Research. 1996; 18: 323-342. ISSN: 0740-8188.

HERNON, PETER; SCHWARTZ, CANDY. 1994. Editorial: The Need for More Methodological and Research Design Studies in Library and Information Science. Library & Information Science Research. 1994; 16(2): 85-86. ISSN: 0740-8188.

HIRSH, SANDRA G. 1997. How Do Children Find Information on Different Types of Tasks? Children's Use of the Science Library Catalog. Library Trends. 1997 Spring; 45(4): 725-745. ISSN: 0024-2594.

HSIEH-YEE, INGRID. 1993. Effects of Search Experience and Subject Knowledge on the Search Tactics of Novice and Experienced Searchers. Journal of the American Society for Information Science. 1993 April; 44(3): 161-174. ISSN: 0002-8231; CODEN: AISJB6.

HUANG, MU-HSUAN. 1992. Pausing Behavior of End-Users in Online Searching. College Park, MD: University of Maryland; 1992. 270p. (Ph.D. dissertation). Available from: UMI, Ann Arbor, MI. (UMI order no. 9315656).

HUNTER, RHONDA N. 1991. Successes and Failures of Patrons Searching the Online Catalog at a Large Academic Library: A Transaction Log Analysis. RQ. 1991 Spring; 30: 395-402. ISSN: 0033-7072.

IIVONEN, MIRJA. 1995. Consistency in the Selection of Search Concepts and Search Terms. Information Processing & Management. 1995; 31(2): 173-190. ISSN: 0306-4573; CODEN: IPMADK.

INGWERSEN, PETER. 1982. Search Procedures in the Library—Analyzed from the Cognitive Point of View. Journal of Documentation. 1982; 38(3): 165-191. ISSN: 0022-0418; CODEN: JDOCAS.

INGWERSEN, PETER. 1992. Information Retrieval Interaction. London, England: Taylor Graham; 1992. 246p. ISBN: 0-947568-54-9.

ISAACS, STEPHEN L. 1996. Consumers' Information Needs: Results of a National Survey. Health Affairs. 1996 Winter; 15: 31-41. ISSN: 0278-2715.

JANES, JOSEPH W. 1991. Relevance Judgments and the Incremental Presentation of Document Representations. Information Processing & Management. 1991; 27(6): 629-646. ISSN: 0306-4573; CODEN: IPMADK.

JANSEN, BERNARD J.; SPINK, AMANDA; SARACEVIC, TEFKO. 2000. Real Life, Real Users, and Real Needs: A Study and Analysis of User Queries on the Web. Information Processing & Management. 2000 February; 36(2): 207-227. ISSN: 0306-4573; CODEN: IPMADK.

JÄRVELIN, KALERVO; VAKKARI, PERTTI. 1993. The Evolution of Library and Information Science 1965-1985: A Content Analysis of Journal Articles. Information Processing & Management. 1993; 29(1): 129-144. ISSN: 0306-4573; CODEN: IPMADK.

JOHNSON, J. DAVID; DONOHUE, WILLIAM A.; ATKIN, CHARLES K.; JOHNSON, SALLY. 1995. A Comprehensive Model of Information Seeking: Tests Focusing on a Technical Organization. Science Communication. 1995 March; 16: 274-303. ISSN: 1075-5470.

JULIEN, HEIDI. 1996. A Content Analysis of the Recent Information Needs and Uses Literature. Library & Information Science Research. 1996; 18: 53-65. ISSN: 0740-8188.

KAFAI, YASMIN; BATES, MARCIA J. 1997. Internet Web-Searching Instruction in the Elementary Classroom: Building a Foundation for Information Literacy. School Library Media Quarterly. 1997 Winter; 25(2): 103-111. ISSN: 0278-4823.

KAPLAN, ABRAHAM. 1979. The Conduct of Inquiry: Methodology for Behavioral Science. New York, NY: Harper & Row; 1979. 428p. ISBN: 0-352-11700-1.

KERLINGER, FRED N.; LEE, HOWARD B. 2000. Foundations of Behavioral Research. 4th edition. Fort Worth, TX: Harcourt College Publishers; 2000. 890p. ISBN: 0-15-507897-6.

KING, DONALD W.; GRIFFITHS, JOSÉ-MARIE; SWEET, E. A.; WIEDERKEHR, ROBERT R. V.; RODERER, NANCY K. 1984. A Study of the Value of Information and the Effect on Value of Intermediary Organizations, Timeliness of Services and Products, and Comprehensiveness of the EDB. Rockville, MD: King Research; 1984. 131p. NTIS: DE85003670.

KRACKER, JACQUELINE LOU. 2000. Changing Students' Perceptions about Research: Can Thirty-Minutes Make a Difference? Knoxville, TN: The University of Tennessee, Knoxville; 2000. 138p. (Master's thesis). Available from: the author.

KRIPPENDORFF, KLAUS. 1980. Content Analysis: An Introduction to Its Methodology. Beverly Hills, CA: Sage Publications; 1980. 191p. ISBN: 0-8039-1498-9.

KUHLTHAU, CAROL COLLIER. 1993. Seeking Meaning: A Process Approach to Library and Information Services. Norwood, NJ: Ablex; 1993. 199p. ISBN: 0-89391-968-3.

LARGE, ANDREW; BEHESHTI, JAMSHID; BREULEUX, ALAIN. 1998. Information Seeking in a Multimedia Environment by Primary School Students. Library & Information Science Research. 1998; 20(4): 343-376. ISSN: 0740-8188.

LARSON, RAY R. 1981. Evaluating Public Access On-Line Catalogs. Phase I. Development and Testing of Data Collection and Analysis Tools. Final Report. Berkeley, CA: University of California; 1981. 104p. ERIC: ED 234814.

LECKIE, GLORIA J. 1996. Female Farmers and the Social Construction of Access to Agricultural Information. Library & Information Science Research. 1996; 18(4): 297-321. ISSN: 0740-8188.

LECKIE, GLORIA J.; PETTIGREW, KAREN E.; SYLVAIN, CHRISTIAN. 1996. Modeling the Information Seeking of Professionals: A General Model Derived from Research on Engineers, Health Care Professionals, and Lawyers. Library Quarterly. 1996 April; 66: 161-191. ISSN: 0024-2519.

LIEBSCHER, PETER. 1998. Quantity with Quality? Teaching Quantitative and Qualitative Methods in an LIS Master's Program. Library Trends. 1998 Spring; 46(4): 668-680. ISSN: 0024-2594.

LIEVROUW, LEAH A. 1998. Our Own Devices: Heterotopic Communication, Discourse, and Culture in the Information Society. The Information Society. 1998; 14: 83-96. ISSN: 0197-2243.

LINCOLN, YVONNA S.; GUBA, EGON G. 1985. Naturalistic Inquiry. Newbury Park, CA: Sage Publications; 1985. 416p. ISBN: 0-8039-2431-3.

LYNCH, MARY JO. 1978. Reference Interviews in Public Libraries. Library Quarterly. 1978 April; 48(2): 119-142. ISSN: 0024-2519.

MARCHIONINI, GARY. 1989. Information-Seeking Strategies of Novices Using a Full-Text Electronic Encyclopedia. Journal of the American Society for Information Science. 1989; 40(1): 54-66. ISSN: 0002-8231; CODEN: AISJB6.

MARCHIONINI, GARY; DWIGGINS, SANDRA; KATZ, ANDREW; LIN, XIA. 1993. Information Seeking in Full-Text End-User-Oriented Search Systems: The Roles of Domain and Search Expertise. Library & Information Science Research. 1993 Winter; 15(1): 35-69. ISSN: 0740-8188.

MARCHIONINI, GARY; LIN, XIA; DWIGGINS, SANDRA. 1990. Effects of Search and Subject Expertise on Information Seeking in a Hypertext Environment. In: Henderson, Diane, ed. ASIS '90: Proceedings of the American Society for Information Science (ASIS) Annual Meeting: Volume 27; 1990 November 4-8; Toronto, Canada. Medford, NJ: Learned Information, Inc. for ASIS; 1990. 129-142. ISSN: 0044-7870; ISBN: 0-938734-48-2.

MARKEY, KAREN. 1983. Online Catalog Use: Results of Surveys and Focus Group Interviews in Several Libraries. Volume 2. Final Report. Dublin, OH: OCLC Office of Research; 1983. 275p. ERIC: ED 231403.

MARSHALL, JOANNE G. 1992. The Impact of the Hospital Library on Clinical Decision Making: The Rochester Study. Bulletin of the Medical Library Association. 1992; 82(2): 169-178. ISSN: 0025-7338.

MATTHEWS, JOSEPH R.; LAWRENCE, GARY S.; FERGUSON, DOUGLAS K., eds. 1983. Using Online Catalogs: A Nationwide Survey. New York, NY: Neal-Schuman; 1983. 255p. ISBN: 0-918212-76-6.

MCGUIRE, WILLIAM J. 1986. A Perspectivist Looks at Contextualism and the Future of Behavioral Science. In: Rosnow, Ralph L.; Georgoudi, Marianthi, eds. Contextualism and Understanding in Behavioral Science: Implications for Research and Theory. New York, NY: Praeger; 1986. 271-302. ISBN: 0-275-92121-2.

MELLON, CONSTANCE A. 1990. Naturalistic Inquiry for Library Science: Methods and Applications for Research, Evaluation, and Teaching. New York, NY: Greenwood Press; 1990. 201p. ISBN: 0-313-25653-5.

MERRIAM, SHARAN B. 1998. Qualitative Research and Case Study Applications in Education. 2nd edition. San Francisco, CA: Jossey-Bass; 1998. 275p. ISBN: 0-7879-1009-0 .

MILLER, DELBERT C. 1991. Handbook of Research Design and Social Measurement. 5th edition. Newbury Park, CA: Sage Publications; 1991. 704p. ISBN: 0-8039-4219-2.

NAHL, DIANE; TENOPIR, CAROL. 1996. Affective and Cognitive Searching Behavior of Novice End-Users of a Full Text Database. Journal of the American Society for Information Science. 1996 April; 47(4): 276-286. ISSN: 0002-8231; CODEN: AISJB6.

NEUMAN, DELIA. 1995. High School Students' Use of Databases: Results of a National Delphi Study. Journal of the American Society for Information Science. 1995 May; 46(4): 284-298. ISSN: 0002-8231; CODEN: AISJB6.

NOBLIT, GEORGE W.; HARE, R. DWIGHT. 1988. Meta-Ethnography: Synthesizing Qualitative Studies. Newbury Park, CA: Sage Publications; 1988. 88p. ISBN: 0-8039-3022-4.

NOUR, MARTYVONNE M. 1985. A Quantitative Analysis of the Research Articles Published in Core Library Journals of 1980. Library & Information Science Research. 1985; 7: 261-273. ISSN: 0740-8188.

OLDROYD, BETTY K.; CITROEN, CHARLES L. 1977. Study of Strategies Used in On-Line Searching. Online Review. 1977; 1(4): 295-310. ISSN: 0309-314X.

OLSON, HOPE A. 1997. The Feminist and the Emperor's New Clothes: Feminist Deconstruction as a Critical Methodology for Library and Information Studies. Library & Information Science Research. 1997; 19(2): 181-198. ISSN: 0740-8188.

PARK, HONGSEOK. 1995. Inferential Relevance and Its Implications to Inferential Information Retrieval. New Brunswick, NJ: Rutgers University; 1995. 335p. (Ph.D. dissertation). Available from: UMI, Ann Arbor, MI. (UMI order no. 9524200).

PARK, SOYEON. 2000. Usability, User Preferences, Effectiveness, and User Behaviors When Searching Individual and Integrated Full-Text Databases: Implications for Digital Libraries. Journal of the American Society for Information Science. 2000; 51(5): 456-468. ISSN: 0002-8231; CODEN: AISJB6.

PARK, TAEMIN KIM. 1992. The Nature of Relevance in Information Retrieval: An Empirical Study. Bloomington, IN: Indiana University; 1992. 209p. (Ph.D. dissertation). Available from: UMI, Ann Arbor, MI. (UMI order no. 9231644).

PATTON, MICHAEL QUINN. 1990. Qualitative Evaluation and Research Methods. 2nd edition. Newbury Park, CA: Sage Publications; 1990. 532p. ISBN: 0-8039-3779-2.

PENNIMAN, W. DAVID; DOMINICK, WAYNE D. 1980. Monitoring and Evaluation of On-Line Information System Usage. Information Processing & Management. 1980; 16(1): 17-35. ISSN: 0306-4573; CODEN: IPMADK.

PETERS, THOMAS. 1989. When Smart People Fail: An Analysis of the Transaction Log of an Online Public Access Catalog. Journal of Academic Librarianship. 1989 November; 15: 267-273. ISSN: 0099-1333.

PITKOW, JAMES E.; RECKER, MARGARET M. 1995. Using the Web as a Survey Tool: Results from the Second WWW User Survey. Available WWW: http://www.cc.gatech.edu/gvu/user_surveys/papers/survey_2_paper.html.

POLKINGHORNE, DONALD E. 1989. Phenomenological Methodology in the Human Sciences. In: Valle, Ronald S.; Halling, Steen, eds. Existential-

Phenomenological Perspectives in Psychology: Exploring the Breadth of Human Experience. New York, NY: Plenum Press; 1989. 41-60. ISBN: 0-306-43044-4.

POWELL, RONALD R. 1999. Recent Trends in Research: A Methodological Essay. Library & Information Science Research. 1999; 21(1): 91-119. ISSN: 0740-8188.

REES, ALAN M.; SCHULTZ, DOUGLAS G. 1967. A Field Experimental Approach to the Study of Relevance Assessments in Relation to Document Searching: Final Reports. Cleveland, OH: Western Reserve University; 1967. 2 volumes. NTIS: PB 176079; PB 176080.

RICE, RONALD E.; BORGMAN, CHRISTINE L. 1983. The Use of Computer-Monitored Data in Information Science and Communication Research. Journal of the American Society for Information Science. 1983; 34(4): 247-256. ISSN: 0002-8231; CODEN: AISJB6.

RIEH, SOO YOUNG; BELKIN, NICHOLAS J. 1998. Understanding Judgment of Information Quality and Cognitive Authority in the WWW. In: ASIS '98: Proceedings of the American Society for Information Science (ASIS) 61st Annual Meeting: Volume 35; 1998 October 24-29; Pittsburgh, PA. Medford, NJ: Information Today, Inc. for ASIS; 1998. 279-289. ISSN: 0044-7870; ISBN: 1-57387-066-8.

RIEH, SOO YOUNG; BELKIN, NICHOLAS J. 2000. Interaction on the Web: Scholars' Judgment of Information Quality and Cognitive Authority. In: Kraft, Donald H., ed. ASIS 2000: Proceedings of the American Society for Information Science (ASIS) 63rd Annual Meeting: Volume 37; 2000 November 11-16; Chicago, IL. Medford, NJ: Information Today, Inc. for ASIS; 2000. 25-38. ISSN: 0044-7870; ISBN: 1-57387-108-7.

ROSENTHAL, ROBERT. 1991. Meta-Analytic Procedures for Social Research. Revised edition. Newbury Park, CA: Sage Publications; 1991. 155p. ISBN: 0-8039-4246-X.

SAITO, MARI; OHMURA, KAZUNORI. 1998. A Cognitive Model for Searching for Ill-Defined Targets on the Web—The Relationship between Search Strategies and User Satisfaction. In: Croft, W. Bruce; Moffat, Alistair; van Rijsbergen, C. J.; Wilkinson, Ross; Zobel, Justin, eds. SIGIR '98: Proceedings of the Association for Computing Machinery Special Interest Group on Information Retrieval (ACM/SIGIR) 21st Annual International Conference on Research and Development in Information Retrieval; 1994 August 24-28; Melbourne, Australia. New York, NY: ACM Press; 1998. 155-163. ISBN: 1-58113-015-5.

SALASIN, JOHN; CEDAR, TOBY. 1985. Information-Seeking Behavior in an Applied Research/Service Delivery Setting. Journal of the American Society for Information Science. 1985 March; 36(2): 94-102. ISSN: 0002-8231; CODEN: AISJB6.

SANDSTROM, ALAN R.; SANDSTROM, PAMELA EFFREIN. 1995. The Use and Misuse of Anthropological Methods in Library and Information Science Research. Library Quarterly. 1995 April; 65(2): 161-199. ISSN: 0024-2519.

SANDSTROM, ALAN R.; SANDSTROM, PAMELA EFFREIN. 1998. Comment: Science and Non Science in Qualitative Research: A Response to

Thomas and Nyce. Library Quarterly. 1998 April; 68(2): 249-254. ISSN: 0024-2519.

SARACEVIC, TEFKO; KANTOR, PAUL. 1988a. A Study of Information Seeking and Retrieving. II. Users, Questions, and Effectiveness. Journal of the American Society for Information Science. 1988 May; 39(3): 177-196. ISSN: 0002-8231; CODEN: AISJB6.

SARACEVIC, TEFKO; KANTOR, PAUL. 1988b. A Study of Information Seeking and Retrieving. III. Searchers, Searches, and Overlap. Journal of the American Society for Information Science. 1988 May; 39(3): 197-216. ISSN: 0002-8231; CODEN: AISJB6.

SARACEVIC, TEFKO; KANTOR, PAUL; CHAMIS, ALICE Y.; TRIVISON, DONNA. 1988. A Study of Information Seeking and Retrieving. I. Background and Methodology. Journal of the American Society for Information Science. 1988 May; 39(3): 161-176. ISSN: 0002-8231; CODEN: AISJB6.

SAVOLAINEN, REIJO. 1995. Everyday Life Information Seeking: Approaching Information Seeking in the Context of "Way of Life". Library & Information Science Research. 1995 Summer; 17(3): 259-294. ISSN: 0740-8188.

SAXTON, MATTHEW L. 1997. Reference Service Evaluation and Meta-Analysis: Findings and Methodological Issues. Library Quarterly. 1997 July; 67(3): 267-289. ISSN: 0024-2519.

SCHAMBER, LINDA. 1991. Users' Criteria for Evaluation in Multimedia Information Seeking and Use Situations. Syracuse, NY: Syracuse University; 1991. 341p. (Ph.D. dissertation). Available from: UMI, Ann Arbor, MI. (UMI order no. 9214390).

SCHAMBER, LINDA. 1994. Relevance and Information Behavior. In: Williams, Martha E., ed. Annual Review of Information Science and Technology: Volume 29. Medford, NJ: Learned Information, Inc. for the American Society for Information Science; 1994. 3-48. ISBN: 0-938734-91-1.

SCHAMBER, LINDA. 2000. Time-Line Interviews and Inductive Content Analysis: Their Effectiveness for Exploring Cognitive Behaviors. Journal of the American Society for Information Science. 2000; 51(8): 734-744. ISSN: 0002-8231; CODEN: AISJB6.

SCHUTT, RUSSELL K. 1999. Investigating the Social World: The Process and Practice of Research. 2nd edition. Thousand Oaks, CA: Pine Forge Press; 1999. 622p. ISBN: 0-7619-8561-1.

SCHWARTZ, PETER; OGILVY, JAMES. 1979. The Emergent Paradigm: Changing Patterns of Thought and Belief. Menlo Park, CA: SRI International; 1979. 62p. OCLC: 5941888.

SEYMOUR, SHARON. 1991. Online Public Access Catalog User Studies: A Review of Research Methodologies, March 1986-November 1989. Library & Information Science Research. 1991; 13: 89-102. ISSN: 0740-8188.

SHUCHMAN, HEDVAH L. 1982. Information Technology and the Technologist: A Report on a National Study of American Engineers. International Forum on Information and Documentation. 1982; 7: 3-8. ISSN: 0304-9701.

SIEGFRIED, SUSAN; BATES, MARCIA J.; WILDE, DEBORAH N. 1993. A Profile of End-User Searching Behavior by Humanities Scholars: The Getty Online Searching Project Report No 2. Journal of the American Society for

Information Science. 1993 June; 44(5): 273-291. ISSN: 0002-8231; CODEN: AISJB6.

SMITHSON, STEVE. 1994. Information Retrieval Evaluation in Practice: A Case Study Approach. Information Processing & Management. 1994; 30(2): 205-221. ISSN: 0306-4573; CODEN: IPMADK.

SOLOMON, PAUL. 1993. Children's Information Retrieval Behavior: A Case Analysis of an OPAC. Journal of the American Society for Information Science. 1993 June; 44(5): 245-264. ISSN: 0002-8231; CODEN: AISJB6.

SOLOMON, PAUL. 1997. Discovering Information Behavior in Sense Making. I. Time and Timing. II. The Social. III. The Person. Journal of the American Society for Information Science. 1997 December; 48(12): 1097-1138. ISSN: 0002-8231; CODEN: AISJB6.

SOMMER, BARBARA; SOMMER, ROBERT. 1997. A Practical Guide to Behavioral Research: Tools and Techniques. 4th edition. New York, NY: Oxford University Press; 1997. 376p. ISBN: 0-19-510418-8.

SONNENWALD, DIANE H.; PIERCE, LINDA G. 2000. Information Behavior in Dynamic Group Work Contexts: Interwoven Situational Awareness, Dense Social Networks and Contested Collaboration in Command and Control. Information Processing & Management. 2000 May; 36(3): 461-479. ISSN: 0306-4573; CODEN: IPMADK.

SPINK, AMANDA; GOODRUM, ABBY; ROBINS, DAVID. 1998. Elicitation Behavior during Mediated Information Retrieval. Information Processing & Management. 1998; 34(2/3): 257-273. ISSN: 0306-4573; CODEN: IPMADK.

SPRADLEY, JAMES P. 1980. Participant Observation. New York, NY: Holt, Rinehart and Winston; 1980. 195p. ISBN: 0-03-044501-9 .

STRAUSS, ANSELM; CORBIN, JULIET. 1998. Basics of Qualitative Research: Techniques and Procedures for Developing Grounded Theory. 2nd edition. Thousand Oaks, CA: Sage Publications; 1998. 312p. ISBN: 0-8039-5940-0.

SU, LOUISE T. 1991. An Investigation to Find Appropriate Measures for Evaluating Interactive Information Retrieval. New Brunswick, NJ: Rutgers University; 1991. 307p. (Ph.D. dissertation). Available from: UMI, Ann Arbor, MI. (UMI order no. 9125400).

SU, LOUISE T.; CHEN, HSIN-LIANG. 1999. Evaluation of Web Search Engines by Undergraduate Students. In: Woods, Lawrence, ed. ASIS '99: Knowledge: Creation, Organization, and Use: Proceedings of the American Society for Information Science (ASIS) 62nd Annual Meeting: Volume 36; 1999 October 31-November 4; Washington, DC. Medford, NJ: Information Today, Inc. for ASIS; 1999. 98-114. ISSN: 0044-7870; ISBN: 1-57387-091-9.

SUTTON, BRETT. 1993. The Rationale for Qualitative Research: A Review of Principles and Theoretical Foundations. Library Quarterly. 1993 October; 63(4): 411-431. ISSN: 0024-2519.

TALJA, SANNA. 1999. Analyzing Qualitative Interview Data: The Discourse Analytic Method. Library & Information Science Research. 1999; 21(4): 459-477. ISSN: 0740-8188.

TANG, RONG. 1999. Use of Relevance Criteria across Stages of Document Evaluation: A Micro Level and Macro Level Analysis. Chapel Hill, NC:

University of North Carolina at Chapel Hill; 1999. 330p. (Ph.D. dissertation). Available from: UMI, Ann Arbor, MI. (UMI order no. 9954723).

TANG, RONG; SOLOMON, PAUL. 1998. Toward an Understanding of the Dynamics of Relevance Judgment: An Analysis of One Person's Search Behavior. Information Processing & Management. 1998; 34(2/3): 237-256. ISSN: 0306-4573; CODEN: IPMADK.

TENOPIR, CAROL; KING, DONALD W. 2000. Towards Electronic Journals: Realities for Scientists, Librarians, and Publishers. Washington, DC: Special Libraries Association; 2000. 488p. ISBN: 0-87111-507-7.

TENOPIR, CAROL; READ, ELEANOR J. 2000. Patterns of Database Use in Academic Libraries. College & Research Libraries. 2000 May; 61(3): 234-246. ISSN: 0010-0870.

THOMAS, NANCY P.; NYCE, JAMES M. 1998. Qualitative Research in LIS—Redux: A Response to a [Re]Turn to Positivist Ethnography. Library Quarterly. 1998 January; 68(1): 108-113. ISSN: 0024-2519.

TOLLE, JOHN E. 1983. Current Utilization of Online Catalogs: Transaction Log Analysis. Volume 1. Final Report. Dublin, OH: OCLC Office of Research; 1983. 127p. ERIC: ED 231402.

TRAHAN, ERIC. 1993. Applying Meta-Analysis to Library and Information Science Research. Library Quarterly. 1993 January; 63(1): 73-91. ISSN: 0024-2519.

VAKKARI, PERTTI. 2000. Relevance and Contributing Information Types of Searched Documents in Task Performance. In: Belkin, Nicholas J.; Ingwersen, Peter; Leong, Mun-kew, eds. Proceedings of the Association for Computing Machinery Special Interest Group on Information Retrieval (ACM/SIGIR) 23rd Annual International Conference on Research and Development in Information Retrieval; 2000 July 24-28; Athens, Greece. New York, NY: ACM Press; 2000. 2-9. ISBN: 1-58113-226-3.

WALTER, VIRGINIA A. 1994. The Information Needs of Children. Advances in Librarianship. 1994; 18: 111-129. ISSN: 0065-2830.

WANG, PEILING. 1994. A Cognitive Model of Document Selection of Real Users of Information Retrieval Systems. College Park, MD: University of Maryland; 1994. 248p. (Ph.D. dissertation). Available from: UMI, Ann Arbor, MI. (UMI order no. 9514595).

WANG, PEILING; HAWK, WILLIAM B.; TENOPIR, CAROL. 2000. Users' Interaction with World Wide Web Resources: An Exploratory Study Using a Holistic Approach. Information Processing & Management. 2000 February; 36(2): 229-251. ISSN: 0306-4573; CODEN: IPMADK.

WANG, PEILING; SOERGEL, DAGOBERT. 1998. A Cognitive Model of Document Use during a Research Project. Study I. Document Selection. Journal of the American Society for Information Science. 1998 February; 49(2): 115-133. ISSN: 0002-8231; CODEN: AISJB6.

WANG, PEILING; WHITE, MARILYN DOMAS. 1999. A Cognitive Model of Document Use during a Research Project. Study II. Decisions at the Reading and Citing Stages. Journal of the American Society for Information Science. 1999; 50(2): 98-114. ISSN: 0002-8231; CODEN: AISJB6.

WATSON, JINX STAPLETON. 2001. Making Sense of the Stories of Experience: Methodology for Research and Teaching. Journal of Education for Library and Information Science. 2001 Spring; 42(2): 137-148. ISSN: 0748-5786.

WEECH, TERRY L.; GOLDHOR, HERBERT. 1982. Obtrusive Versus Unobtrusive Evaluation of Reference Service in Five Illinois Public Libraries. Library Quarterly. 1982 October; 52(4): 305-324. ISSN: 0024-2519.

WEEDMAN, JUDITH. 1993. On the "Isolation" of Humanists: A Report of an Invisible College. Communication Research. 1993; 20(4): 749-776. ISSN: 0093-6502.

WHITE, MARILYN DOMAS. 1975. The Communications Behavior of Academic Economists in Research Phases. Library Quarterly. 1975 October; 45(4): 337-354. ISSN: 0024-2519.

WHITE, MARILYN DOMAS; WANG, PEILING. 1997. Document Selection and Relevance Assessments during a Research Project. College Park, MD: University of Maryland; 1997. 102p. ERIC: ED 405001.

WIBERLEY, STEPHEN E., JR.; JONES, WILLIAM G. 1989. Patterns of Information Seeking in the Humanities. College & Research Libraries. 1989 November; 50: 638-645. ISSN: 0010-0870.

WILDEMUTH, BARBARA M. 1993. Post-Positivist Research: Two Examples of Methodological Pluralism. Library Quarterly. 1993 October; 63(4): 450-468. ISSN: 0024-2519.

WILDEMUTH, BARBARA M.; FRIEDMAN, CHARLES P.; KEYES, JOHN; DOWNS, STEPHEN M. 2000. A Longitudinal Study of Database-Assisted Problem Solving. Information Processing & Management. 2000; 36(3): 445-459. ISSN: 0306-4573; CODEN: IPMADK.

WILKINS, JANIE L. HASSARD; LECKIE, GLORIA J. 1997. University Professional and Managerial Staff: Information Needs and Seeking. College & Research Libraries. 1997 November; 58: 561-574. ISSN: 0010-0870.

WILLEMS, EDWIN P.; RAUSH, HAROLD L. 1969. Naturalistic Viewpoints in Psychological Research. New York, NY: Holt, Rinehart and Winston; 1969. 294p. OCLC: 2369.

WILLIAMSON, KIRSTY. 1998. Discovered by Chance: The Role of Incidental Information Acquisition in an Ecological Model of Information Use. Library & Information Science Research. 1998; 20(1): 23-40. ISSN: 0740-8188.

WILLIAMSON, KIRSTY; SCHAUDER, DON; BOW, AMANDA. 2000. Information Seeking by Blind and Sight Impaired Citizens: An Ecological Study. Information Research: An International Electronic Journal. 2000 July; 5(4). ISSN: 1368-1613. Available WWW: http://www.shef.ac.uk/~is/publications/infres/paper79.html.

WILSON, THOMAS D.; STREATFIELD, DAVID R. 1977. Information Needs in Local Authority Social Services Departments: An Interim Report on Project INISS. Journal of Documentation. 1977 December; 33(4): 277-293. ISSN: 0022-0418; CODEN: JDOCAS.

WILSON, THOMAS D.; STREATFIELD, DAVID R.; MULLINGS, CHRISTINE. 1979. Information Needs in Local Authority Social Services Departments: A Second Report on Project INISS. Journal of Documentation. 1979 June; 35(2): 120-136. ISSN: 0022-0418; CODEN: JDOCAS.

WOLF, FREDRIC M. 1986. Meta-Analysis: Quantitative Methods for Research Synthesis. Beverly Hills, CA: Sage Publications; 1986. 65p. ISBN: 0-8039-2756-8.

WU, MEI-MEI. 1993. Information Interaction Dialogue, A Study of Patron Elicitation in the Information Retrieval Interaction. New Brunswick, NJ: Rutgers University; 1993. 199p. (Ph.D. dissertation). Available from: UMI, Ann Arbor, MI. (UMI order no. 9320541).

YIN, ROBERT K. 1994. Case Study Research: Design and Methods. Thousand Oaks, CA: Sage Publications; 1994. 192p. ISBN: 0-8039-5662-2.

ZHANG, YIN. 2000. Using the Internet for Survey Research: A Case Study. Journal of the American Society for Information Science. 2000; 51(1): 57-68. ISSN: 0002-8231; CODEN: AISJB6.

II

Basic Techniques and Technologies

The five chapters in Section II are: "Informetrics" by Concepción S. Wilson of The University of New South Wales, Australia; "Literature Dynamics: Studies on Growth, Diffusion, and Epidemics" by Albert N. Tabah of the Université de Montréal, Canada; "Measuring the Internet" by Robert E. Molyneux and Robert V. Williams of the University of South Carolina; "Applications of Machine Learning in Information Retrieval" by Sally Jo Cunningham, Ian H. Witten, and James Littin, all of the University of Waikato, New Zealand; and "Text Mining" by Walter J. Trybula of International SEMATECH.

While in a broad sense informetrics can be viewed as being concerned with all of the quantifiable aspects of information science, it has its roots in bibliometrics and is somewhat related to scientometrics. In order to better answer the question, what is informetrics, Wilson provides an historical survey covering bibliometrics, citation analysis, librametrics, scholarly communication studies, and informetrics. Initially coined by Pritchard, in relation to statistical bibliography, he defined the term as "the application of mathematical and statistical methods to books and other media of communication." Robert Fairthorne widened it to "the quantitative treatment of the properties of recorded discourse and behavior appertaining to it." In a 1989 *ARIST* chapter, H.D. White and Katherine McCain define it as "the quantitative study of literatures as they are reflected in bibliographies. Its task . . . is to provide evolutionary models of science, technology, and scholarship." Concepción Wilson accepts this with the further specifications that it have a subject-independent component and that it chart specific disciplines/subjects by using the framework of indicators and laws.

After the opening sections, Introduction and What is Informetrics, Wilson divides the balance of her chapter into eight major sections: The Content of Informetrics, Citation Analysis (citation performance and usage measures, obsolescence studies, co-citation analysis and literature mapping, co-reference analysis or bibliographic coupling), Word-Related Analyses (including languages, titles, titles and class codes, descriptors, combined analyses (of words in multiple fields, words in full text, and combined co-word and co-citation analyses and content analysis)), Author-Related Analyses, Time and Growth Studies, Informetric Laws (e.g., the inverse power law, stochastic compound distributions), New Trends in Informetrics (e.g., on the World Wide Web), and Conclusion.

In his chapter on literature dynamics Albert N. Tabah covers the topic by looking at: the empirical aspects of literature dynamics (such as the growth of literature, diffusion, epidemics, and fast-growing literatures); methodological issues (such as publication counts, the time factor, and converging indicators); and practical aspects (including paradigm shifts, literature growth, and the growth and development of scientific specialties). Tabah summarizes the main theoretical arguments and empirical results in literature dynamics and concludes that publication counts do measure scientific progress, that quality and quantity of publications are related, and that information science can contribute to a better understanding of scientific progress. Tabah sees the Internet as providing new challenges to understanding the dynamics of the Internet and to the communication patterns of the World Wide Web, and he observes that new tools will be needed to understand the dynamics of growth on the Web.

In a related area Robert E. Molyneux and Robert V. Williams have provided a chapter on "Measuring the Internet." Their chapter surveys the available literature on Internet measurement, and they find that this literature is dispersed, fragmentary, fugitive, and rarely scholarly. Studies of retrospective Internet network traffic make up a scholarly literature, Web characterization activities are approaching the status of scholarly literature and, as might be expected, the two areas are beginning to overlap.

Molyneux and Williams observed that the relevant literature was of four types: factoids; systematic studies; for-profit studies; and scholarly literatures. In general scholarship was seldom encountered while hype and studies with uncertain methodologies were common. As a result, data and conclusions were of varying value. The lack of stable URLs, of an Internet archive, and of scholarly indexing hampered these authors and scholarly studies in this area in general. An attempt was made, based on the available literature, to estimate the size of information on the Internet. Based on data through the end of 1999 the estimate was between 30-44 terabytes.

A substantial part of the literature, particularly that dealing with electronic commerce, was generated by firms whose studies are sold for profit and are not freely distributed. In addition, the methodology of such studies normally is not made available. Information from these studies usually appears in press releases as factoids that are apparently released to stimulate sales of the studies. This information typically disappears quickly. Despite the paucity of scholarly literature Molyneux and Williams have written a chapter that defines the Internet, characterizes the Internet measurement literature, provides a brief history of the Internet, discusses the Internet data environment, discusses the technical characteristics of measuring the Internet, looks at Internet traffic measurement, covers the measurement of information on the Internet, provides demographics on users and use on the net, and characterizes Internet commerce. They observe that, in general, the Internet data environment is not friendly and that in e-commerce, while both the business community and the academic community study the Internet, the academic community is willing to share its data but the business community is not.

Molyneux and Williams look forward to efforts that will: apply scientific sampling to network traffic; provide early release of data to the public so that data will be available to researchers at a reasonable cost; provide funding for measurement studies; make researchers aware of the value of Internet data for social, behavioral, and demographic purposes; develop scholarly indexing of Internet resources; and ensure that data and studies are permanently archived.

"Applications of Machine Learning in Information Retrieval" by Sally Jo Cunningham, Ian H. Witten, and James Littin are largely devoted to the applications in information retrieval (IR), text categorization, query formulation, and information filtering. They introduce the chapter and set the stage by noting that much of information retrieval is automated, such as index generation and expansion of simple queries, while document classification and thesaurus term selection are usually better done by humans. However, there are now algorithms for mining text for index terms, and there are algorithms that model user interests to help them formulate queries. Such algorithms are based in machine learning. Algorithms for machine learning or learning algorithms can replace domain experts for generating rules and explanations, and intelligent agents are providing new roles for the techniques of artificial intelligence (AI).

Machine learning algorithms can discover patterns in large quantities of data and learn from existing examples. Machine learning has a role to play in IR, and the section on IR introduces the basic ideas and underpinnings for the application of machine learning to IR. These are: machine learning paradigms, such as rule induction, instance-based learning, neural networks, and genetic algorithms, with all four used in "intelligent" IR systems; models of text representation, such as term vector models, latent semantic indexing, and sequential models; feature extraction, such as weighted terms, thesauri, phrase identification, and subtopic identification; and collections fusion. All these approaches have been used in limited ways to solve real world problems.

In the section on Models of Text and Text Representation, Cunningham, Witten, and Littin address the use of term vector models wherein a document is represented by a set of terms and each document corresponds to a point in n-dimensional space where n is the number of terms. Terms are usually words. A term vector may be a Boolean vector (representing words in a document) or a numeric vector (based on the number of occurrences of each term in a document). They next look at latent semantic indexing, a technique used to circumvent some of the shortcomings of term vector models by mapping the term vectors into a different space. They then cover sequential models wherein compression algorithms can be used to categorize documents and the degree of compression for each sample can be used to rank the categories.

A major section deals with text categorization, which is the process of classifying documents into one of a set of categories. User queries are similarly classed for matching with the documents. Many algorithms—both standard and specialized— have been used for text categorization. In order to train a classification system a sample of documents must be used because of the impracticality of using the full set of documents. Random sampling is not suitable, particularly when the sample is small. Using a set of training documents based on uncertainty feedback provides much better results. The section on Query Formulation introduces users' articulation of needs, modeling of user concepts, and relevance feedback. Machine learning has been used in information filtering for modeling of user interests, and for information filtering applications, such as news reading, web browsing and searching, and email filtering .

Automation of IR tasks is becoming increasingly dependent on machine learning as a tool of the trade. Machine learning algorithms and techniques are being developed and improved at a rapid pace because the vast amounts of digitized information, available both on the Internet and in digital libraries, are creating a demand for faster ways of finding the right data in response to queries. Software agents can sift through tremendous amounts of textual information to help users with specific needs.

Another response to the tremendous volume of available digital information is text mining. Walter J. Trybula has written the first *ARIST* chapter on "Text Mining." He also wrote the first *ARIST* chapter on "Data Mining and Knowledge Discovery" in 1997. According to Mark Dixon text mining is the process of "finding interesting or useful patterns in a corpus of unstructured textual information, combining many of the techniques of information extraction, information retrieval, natural language processing, and document summarization." The power, speed, and low cost of computers today, combined with the low cost of storage and the volume of available digitized information, provide an excellent climate for data mining. Walter Trybula provides strong rationale supporting the need for text mining.

Trybula's chapter is organized into six major sections. Aside from the anticipated Introduction, Background, and Conclusions, the bulk of the content is contained in the sections called Comparison of Text Mining to Data Mining, Research Areas, and Software Products. An important part of the Introduction covers essential terminology in this field that is still in its infancy. The terms that he defines and explains are database, data mining (DM), knowledge discovery (KD), knowledge discovery of databases (KDD), and undiscovered public knowledge.

Text mining and data mining are compared in order to aid in the understanding of text mining. The major differences are in the information structures being mined and in some of the parts of the mining process. Data mining is of databases, and text mining is of textbases (collections of textual documents). The mining processes are very similar. Text is gathered from textbases in various locations (found), combined, cleaned, and transformed into an organized document repository or target textbase. Similar processes are used to build a database repository in data mining. But when it comes to determining if new knowledge is being found, significantly more understanding is required for text mining than data mining.

Text mining research areas deal with information acquisition, extraction, mining, clustering, and presentation (summaries and visualizations). Acquisition relates to finding and bringing together textual information that will later be processed and mined for information. Extraction is used to develop a textbase that can be mined for insights into the contents of the documents. Mining is the process whereby textbases can be analyzed and methods developed for presenting results to the user. Clustering is used to segment a document collection into subsets on the basis of similar features. The development of knowledge by a user requires that the user be able to distinguish characteristics of the information being presented in order to transform the information into knowledge. Three different approaches for presentation are cross-correlations, summaries, and visualizations.

Software products for text mining are being developed at a rapid rate. Trybula describes about 20 of them and tells what they do. A few with interesting names are iCrossReader, ConSearch, Cambio, CMS TextMap, Intext, Inxight, Perspecta, SemioMap, TextAnalyst, TextSmart, and Xcize. Text mining produces a collection of related documents from the textbase, but assimilating the information and transforming it into knowledge remain a challenge.

3   Informetrics

CONCEPCIÓN S. WILSON
The University of New South Wales

INTRODUCTION

With an uninformed reading, and taking information to be a basic constituent of the universe, informetrics seems a very broad subject. A more informed reading might narrow informetrics to the study of all quantifiable aspects of information science. The reality is (as yet) more modest still. Although it is a part of the discipline of information science (in the sense of modern library science), informetrics is commonly recognized as covering the older field of bibliometrics and perhaps several smaller areas of metric studies, and holds an ill-defined relationship to the field of scientometrics. A first task, then, for this review is to examine the status and scope of informetrics. After this, research in the field is selectively reviewed, drawing mainly from journal articles in English that have been published since the *ARIST* review of bibliometrics by H.D. WHITE & MCCAIN (1989). Greater prominence is given to the informetric laws than to other topics. Finally, some very recent developments that bear on the future of the field are considered. The level of the survey is introductory, always directing the reader to appropriate sources for a deeper treatment.

WHAT IS INFORMETRICS?

Informetrics has been delineated by a listing of its commonly perceived component fields. The reasons for this particular grouping are

I would like to thank William Hood for his work on an earlier version of this chapter and his assistance with parts of this version. I also wish to acknowledge helpful comments from several reviewers.

Annual Review of Information Science and Technology (ARIST), Volume 34, 1999
Martha E. Williams, Editor
Published for the American Society for Information Science (ASIS)
By Information Today, Inc., Medford, NJ

historical, and must be traced from the origins of the oldest component, bibliometrics.

Historical Survey

Bibliometrics. Bibliometrics developed out of the interests of a small number of scientists, during the first half of the twentieth century, in the dynamics of science as reflected in the production of its literature. Their interests ranged from charting changes in the output of a scientific field through time and across countries (COLE & EALES), to the library problem of maintaining control of the output (BRADFORD), to the low publication productivity of most scientists (LOTKA); an extensive account is provided by HERTZEL. Two features characterized this work: (1) the recognition that (scientific) subject bibliographies, the secondary literature sources, contained all the properties of literature necessary for the analyses, clearly a great time-saver; and (2) an orientation to seeking numeric data and analyzing it by statistical or other mathematical methods, as befits scientists. Part of this small but diffuse body of studies, from Cole & Eales to RAISIG, was intended to illuminate the process of science and technology (S&T) by means of counting documents, and was appropriately labeled "statistical bibliography" by HULME. By the late 1960s these varied works had been collated into a common field associated with the documentation strand of librarianship, which was concurrently developing into information science (BOTTLE, discussed below). "Statistical bibliography" seemed ambiguous to PRITCHARD, who proposed an alternative, "bibliometrics," a term with perhaps greater scientific connotation (cf., econometrics, biometrics, etc.). Although OTLET had previously employed "bibliometrie," Pritchard defined the new bibliometrics widely, as "the application of mathematical and statistical methods to books and other media of communication" (p. 348). In the same journal issue, FAIRTHORNE widened the scope even further to the "quantitative treatment of the properties of recorded discourse and behavior appertaining to it" (p. 341). By 1970 bibliometrics had become a heading in both Library Literature and in Library and Information Science Abstracts (PERITZ, 1984), and by 1980 a Library of Congress Subject Heading (BROADUS).

BROADUS observed that PRITCHARD not only originated the new use of the term but also began a long series of definitions for it, frequently wide-ranging and vague with respect to the exact object of study. The definition of bibliometrics by H.D. WHITE & MCCAIN (1989), in the second *ARIST* review on the subject, is unusual in specifying a goal for the field, in the manner of HULME. They define bibliometrics as "the quantitative study of literatures as they are reflected in bibliographies. Its task . . . is to provide evolutionary models of science, technology, and scholarship" (p. 119). This definition is adopted here, but with one qualification: to recognize two components, perhaps two phases, in the meeting of this goal. The first is what might be called a content-free, or at least a subject-independent, component that establishes the structural relationships within literature itself. The second is the charting of specific disciplines or subjects using this framework of indicators and laws. The first component is well described by DE GLAS' definition of all bibliometrics "as the search for systematic patterns in comprehensive bodies of literature" (p. 40). It can be taken as originating with the work of BRADFORD, and contains theoretical (often quite mathematical) and empirical studies (BURRELL, 1990). The second component, with greater affinity to the earlier statistical bibliography stream, consists mainly of empirical studies to date.

Two observations are in order here. First, only with unwarranted emphasis on its second component can bibliometrics be described as a "family of techniques" (LIEVROUW), or be uncertainly located between method and theory (see, e.g., O'CONNOR & VOOS, and strong opposition from EGGHE, 1988). An extension of this view has bibliometrics as an aid for the operation of libraries, leading to the common charge that it is of little use, a solution without a problem (WALLACE). Such charges are overstated, as TAGUE (1988) and MCCAIN (1997) demonstrate. But more generally, this whole perspective is completely misdirected, even if it was encouraged by some earlier bibliometricians. Second, the goal of bibliometrics does not prevent it from contributing to (nor drawing from) other fields, such as its companion field in theoretical information science, information retrieval, with the goal of solving the perennial library problem of how best to retrieve information for users; nor drawing from (nor contributing to) other metric fields, such as econometrics and psychometrics.

The first *ARIST* review fully devoted to bibliometrics is by NARIN & MOLL in 1977, and *ARIST* reviews that treat the subject as a part of information science are by BOYCE & KRAFT and BUCKLAND & LIU. Bibliographies of bibliometrics include HJERPPE (1980; 1982), PRITCHARD & WITTIG, and SELLEN.

Citation analysis. Bibliometrics formed as computers started to impact libraries. Immediate products of their power to manipulate large data files were the citation indexes of the Institute for Scientific Information (ISI), which are in essence the inversion of the reference field of documents from a standard set of journals (GARFIELD, 1979). By allowing for the immediate analysis of citations to documents from this standard set, citation indexes effectively doubled the range of research and the output of bibliometrics. Although the reference lists of actual documents had been studied intermittently from the late 1920s (GROSS & GROSS), such tedious analyses would have little future until citation indexes joined traditional indexes. The role of PRICE (1965) in recognizing the value of citation indexes for the study of science should be noted here. Citation analysis also considerably affected modern information retrieval studies, clearly demonstrating that the respective goals are not disparate. This factor, and the nontraditional nature of citation indexes, contribute to the somewhat ambiguous status of citation analysis. Is it a large sister field of bibliometrics, as would appear, for example, from the reviews of OSAREH (1996a; 1996b) and SHAPIRO (1992), or is it, in the more typical and present view, a very large component of bibliometrics? Other reviews of citation analysis are included in the paragraph on bibliometrics above, and in a later section of this review.

Librametrics. Despite the literal import of its name, bibliometrics does not exhaust quantitative studies associated with the collections of documents, nor of the running of libraries. There may be value in retaining the terms "librametrics" or "librametry" for such studies not specifically analyzing literatures, or at least not specifically directed to the goals of bibliometrics and of information retrieval. These include analyses of book circulation (AJIFERUKE & TAGUE; BURRELL, 1990; RAVICHANDRA RAO, 1988), library collection overlap (MCGRATH, 1988), library acquisitions (BOOKSTEIN ET AL.), fines policy (S. ROUSSEAU & R. ROUSSEAU, 1999), and shelf allocation (EGGHE, 1999), which frequently use optimization techniques from operations research. The term "librametry" was first proposed in 1948 by Ranganathan for the design and development of library buildings and furniture, types and varieties of book sizes and shapes for the housing of books, and library service (GOPINATH); this definition is hardly strained by extending it as suggested. Librametric research is a suitable adjunct or smaller sister field to bibliometrics, which it both contributes to and draws from, within information science; this position is taken, for example, by SENGUPTA in his review of the metric fields of information science. With a wide interpretation of informetrics, librametrics can be subsumed under the informetrics umbrella, as for example in the textbook by EGGHE & R. ROUSSEAU (1990b). This position has not been adopted here, where librametrics is taken to be a specialist branch of management.

Scientometrics. The Russian equivalent, "naukometriya," was coined in 1969 by NALIMOV & MUL'CHENKO. The term gained wide recognition with the founding in 1977 of the journal *SCIENTOMETRICS* by Tibor Braun in Hungary. According to its subtitle, *Scientometrics* includes all quantitative aspects of the science of science, communication in science, and science policy. Scientometrics has typically been defined as "the quantitative study of science and technology," for example, in the recent special topic issue of the *Journal of the American Society for Information Science* (*JASIS*) on S&T indicators, edited by VAN RAAN (1998b, p. 5). (Incidentally, technometrics is recognized as a separate field. The scope of the journal *TECHNOMETRICS*, founded in 1959 in the U.S., is the development and use of statistical methods in the physical, chemical, and engineering sciences.) Clearly, much of scientometrics is indistinguishable from bibliometrics, and much bibliometric research is published in *Scientometrics*. After all, the immediate and tangible output of science and technology into the public domain is literature (papers, patents, etc.). Nevertheless, the focus of bibliometrics, despite many broad definitions, has always been preponderantly on the literature per se of science and scholarship, while there is more to science and technology for scientometrics to measure and analyze than its literature output (e.g., the practices of researchers, socio-organizational structures, research and development (R&D) management, the role of S&T in the national economy, governmental policies toward S&T). A typical example of a nonbibliometric scientometric paper is by GILLETT. Scientometrics correctly belongs to a parallel research tradition, the scientific study of science, even though LEYDESDORFF & WOUTERS (1996, p. 4) express concern that part of the field of scientometrics may have acquired "a more intimate connection with the quantitative library sciences and related specialities in information sciences." A bibliography of current research in scientometrics is the series by SCHUBERT (1996a; 1996b; 1996c; 1996d; 1999), which lists all source items from the Science Citation Index and the Social Sciences Citation Index that cite at least one article from the journal *Scientometrics*. A state-of-the-art paper on scientometrics is provided by VAN RAAN (1997).

Scholarly communication studies. In addition to scientometrics, other components from various traditions in the general study of science and scholarship overlap with bibliometrics through an interest in the quantitative aspects, or their qualitative preliminaries, of published literature. One such field is scholarly communication studies: the "study of how scholars in any field . . . use and disseminate information through formal and informal channels . . . bibliometric methods are applicable only to the study of the formal channels" (BORGMAN, 1990a, p. 14). BORGMAN (1990b) includes a representative series of papers from this domain. A more recent review of the literature with emphasis on the connection to bibliometrics is provided by DING (1998a; 1998b).

Informetrics. The German term "Informetrie" was first proposed in 1979 by NACKE to cover that part of information science dealing with the measurement of information phenomena and the application of mathematical methods to the discipline's problems—in the terms introduced above, to bibliometrics and parts of information retrieval theory— and perhaps more coverage (see also BLACKERT & SIEGEL). In the following year, NACKE ET AL. nominated scientometrics as a sister field of informetrics within information science. In 1984, the All-Union Institute for Scientific and Technical Information (VINITI) established a

Fédération Internationale de Documentation (FID) Committee on Informetrics under Nacke's chairmanship, where "informetrics" was taken as a generic term for both bibliometrics and scientometrics. This usage was adopted in the VINITI monograph by GOR'KOVA with the Russian title *Informetriya [Informetrics]*. At the 1st International Conference on Bibliometrics and Theoretical Aspects of Information Retrieval in 1988, BROOKES suggested that an "informetrics" that subsumes bibliometrics and scientometrics, for both documentary and electronic information, may have a future. *Informetrics 87/88* was adopted as the short title for the published conference proceedings (EGGHE & R. ROUSSEAU, 1988a), with the editors noting that "in promoting a new name, it is a classical technique to use the new name together with the old one." By the second conference (EGGHE & R. ROUSSEAU, 1990a), BROOKES (1990) endorsed "informetrics" as a general term for scientometrics and bibliometrics, with scientometrics taken as leaning toward policy studies and bibliometrics more toward library studies. The status of the term was enhanced in the third conference proceedings in the series, the 3rd International Conference on Informetrics (RAVICHANDRA RAO, 1992), but reduced in the fourth conference title, International Conference on Bibliometrics, Informetrics, and Scientometrics. (The proceedings of the fourth conference were published in four separate volumes, three of which were whole issues of regular journals in English (GLÄNZEL & KRETSCHMER, 1992; 1994a; 1994b)). At this conference, the International Society for Scientometrics and Informetrics (ISSI) was founded, and subsequent conferences (KOENIG & BOOKSTEIN; MACÍAS-CHAPULA; PERITZ & EGGHE) have been held biennially under the society's auspices. As mentioned earlier, a textbook, *Introduction to Informetrics: Quantitative Methods in Library, Documentation and Information Science* (EGGHE & R. ROUSSEAU, 1990b) was published, and a special issue on informetrics appeared in the journal *Information Processing & Management* (TAGUE-SUTCLIFFE, 1992c).

By the mid-1990s, the term "informetrics" clearly enjoyed widespread recognition. The term is slowly gaining acceptance in the literature (Figure 1). From 1995 onward, the use of the term "informetrics" has been rising while the use of "bibliometrics" has been declining; however, "bibliometrics" still clearly occurs more frequently than both "scientometrics" and "informetrics" in the titles and abstracts of publications.

A Terminological Readjustment

A confusion of metrics. It is also apparent that some confusion exists over the exact relationship of informetrics to bibliometrics and

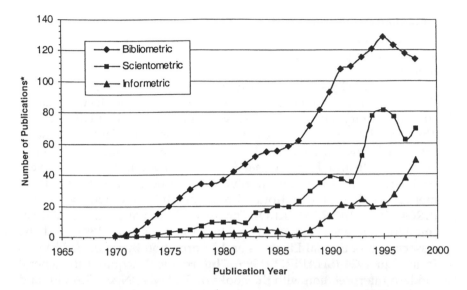

*Based on searching the following truncated terms in the title and abstract fields of the
DIALOG system: (1) bibliometric? (2) scientometric? (3) informetric?. The search was
performed on 11 databases: ERIC, INSPEC, Social SciSearch, LISA, British Education
Index, Information Science Abstracts, Education Abstracts, Library Literature, SciSearch,
PASCAL, and Arts & Humanities Search. The search used DIALOG's duplicate removal
and rank algorithms to produce the frequency distribution of each term by publication
year. The moving three-year average was then calculated to produce the plot points.

**Figure 1. The number of publications using each of the "metric" terms
(bibliometrics, scientometrics, and informetrics) from 1970 to 1998,
employing a moving three-year average.**

scientometrics. One wonders how many other areas of research are
persistently described by an ungainly concatenation of complementary
titles. It is not surprising that the special interest group (SIG) of the
American Society for Information Science (ASIS) recently formed to
cover bibliometrics, scientometrics, informetrics, and metrics related to
the design and operation of digital libraries, should adopt the manageable title SIG/METRICS (GARFIELD, 2000). This terminological confusion is not just a diversion from substantial matters. At least part of the
perception of informetrics as a field in crisis stems from it; see the
discussion paper by GLÄNZEL & SCHOEPFLIN (1994b), where
"bibliometrics" is used synonymously for bibliometrics, informetrics,
scientometrics, and technometrics. Incidentally, the view that the field
is in crisis is not held by the majority in the comments of 29 information
scientists that follow (BRAUN, 1994.) The confusion is not principally
with respect to scientometrics: information scientists with backgrounds
in the hard sciences tend to view scientometrics as distinct from

bibliometrics and informetrics, along the lines of the conceptual separation drawn above. Confusion by other information scientists may lie in a failure to appreciate that there is more to science than its output of literature.

A move to eclipse "bibliometrics" with "informetrics"—as reflected in the titling of ISSI—appears to have its origins in the documentation strand of library science, in or near which bibliometrics actually formed. This strand originated with Paul Otlet and Henri La Fontaine, who in 1903 established the Institut International de Bibliographie (soon to become the Institut International de Documentation), and who actively contrasted its perspective of supplying (scientific) information (in documents) to that of traditional librarianship's "circulating books" (BROOKES, 1990; RAYWARD). The use of "information" in the sense of "modern reference" appeared in libraries as early as 1891, and the Association of Special Libraries and Information Bureaux (Aslib) was formed in 1924 (SHAPIRO, 1995). "Information" acquired its general modern interpretation with the books of SHANNON & WEAVER and of WIENER, both in the late 1940s, and the concurrent rise of modern computer and communication technology. Shapiro traces the origin of "information scientist," essentially a substitute for the scarcely accepted "documentalist," to FARRADANE (1953), and "a science of information" to the same author in 1955. The Institute of Information Scientists was founded in the UK in 1958, and the American Documentation Institute became the American Society for Information Science in 1968. Against this background, it might seem surprising that in 1969 PRITCHARD chose the stem "biblios" rather than a segment of "information" to append to "metrics." FAIRTHORNE's 1969 definition, especially, casts bibliometrics in broad informetric terms.

With the information technology revolution, and the accelerating shift from paper to electronic formats, the notion that bibliometricians were analyzing anything remotely like the traditional book became even more unrealistic and restrictive. A renaming of "bibliometrics" as "informetrics" seems long overdue, even without any immediate change in either its problems or its text-analytical methods, or without any adjustments to its boundary with theoretical information retrieval. So why does the term "bibliometrics" persist? Is informetrics developing a different goal? Or are there reservations about the suitability of the stem of "information" in the title? Do those favoring bibliometrics see information more like propositions (FOX) carried at the clause or sentence level in texts, whereas their object of study is medium-sized packets of information still best described by the document or patent, a generalized book? Do scientometricians wish to maintain a distinction between information in a general sense (e.g., data) from that obtained from publications? Are there connotations, for example, of high-tech commerce, which are repugnant to even numerate students of literature? These questions do not permit immediate answers, but the replacement of "bibliometrics" by "informetrics" can be endorsed. Perhaps if "bibliometrics" is used, it should stand for first-generation work in informetrics. Possible new second-generation subfields of informetrics, such as Webometrics, are introduced in a later section.

Summary. This brief historical excursion justifies the adoption of the initial delineation of informetrics in terms of its (more fully described) subfields. To reiterate, informetrics covers and replaces the field of bibliometrics, including citation analysis, and includes some recent subfields such as Webometrics. It is distinct from theoretical information retrieval with respect to goals, and librametrics with respect to both goals and often its objects of analysis. It overlaps strongly with scientometrics, and less so with scholarly communication studies, with respect to the analysis of scientific literature. More detailed definitions are provided by TAGUE-SUTCLIFFE (1992a) and INGWERSEN & CHRISTENSEN; also see AMUDHAVALLI. Succinct definitions are given by DIODATO (1994) and by KEENAN. Other authors may define informetrics more broadly, including for example, parts of information retrieval and all or parts of librametrics (EGGHE & R. ROUSSEAU, 1990b; KHURSHID & SAHAI, 1991b; Tague-Sutcliffe, 1992a). Also, ISSI conference proceedings usually have included a small number of papers on librametric and even information retrieval topics. Information exchange with these fields is high and goals are often poor bases for drawing distinctions. Informetrics has methodological and certain theoretical similarities to other social science metric studies (EGGHE, 1994b), perhaps tempting the appropriately inclined to see all such studies as manifestations of statistics. But by now the informed reader may well be asking whether the correct conclusion to draw from this discussion is that informetrics and the other fields of concern should be defined by informetric rather than by impressionistic means, perhaps along the lines of the co-citation analysis of information science by H.D. WHITE & MCCAIN (1998). Further comment on this matter is delayed until the conclusion of this review.

THE CONTENT OF INFORMETRICS

The Major Journals

Table 1 shows the top 20 journals, ranked by their numbers of publications on informetrics and/or bibliometrics from 1990 to 1999. The number of publications not in English, and therefore excluded from this review, is apparent. Also, the list itself is incomplete; for example, journals from China have appeared too recently in the searched data-

Table 1. Top 20 Journals With at Least 11 Documents
Related Broadly to "Informetrics" (1990-1999)*

No. of Docs.	Journal Name (JN)	Country of Publication	Primary Language(s)
323	SCIENTOMETRICS	Netherlands	English
67	JOURNAL OF THE AMERICAN SOCIETY FOR INFORMATION SCIENCE	USA	English
39	REVISTA ESPAÑOLA DE DOCUMENTACIÓN CIENTÍFICA	Spain	Spanish
36	INFORMATION PROCESSING & MANAGEMENT	Netherlands	English
29	LIBRARY SCIENCE WITH A SLANT TO DOCUMENTATION (and Information Studies)	India	English
25	INTERNATIONAL FORUM ON INFORMATION AND DOCUMENTATION**	Russia	English
23	ANNALS OF LIBRARY SCIENCE AND DOCUMENTATION	India	English
22	BULLETIN OF THE MEDICAL LIBRARY ASSOCIATION	USA	English
22	JOURNAL OF INFORMATION SCIENCE	UK	English
21	CIENCIA DA INFORMACAO	Portugal	Portuguese
21	DOCUMENTALISTE	France	French
17	RESEARCH POLICY	Netherlands	English
16	JOURNAL OF DOCUMENTATION	UK	English
15	IASLIC BULLETIN	India	English
15	LIBRARY AND INFORMATION SCIENCE RESEARCH	USA	English
15	LIBRI	Germany	English, French & German
13	CIENCIAS DE LA INFORMACION	Cuba	Spanish
12	LIBRARY QUARTERLY	USA	English
11	MALAYSIAN JOURNAL OF LIBRARY & INFORMATION SCIENCE	Malaysia	English
11	MEDICINA CLINICA	Spain	Spanish

*Based on searching the following truncated terms in the title and abstract fields of the DIALOG system: bibliometric? OR informetric?. Shows the distribution of journal article documents in the top 20 most productive journals over 11 databases: ERIC, INSPEC, Social SciSearch, LISA, British Education Index, Information Science Abstracts, Education Abstracts, Library Literature, SciSearch, PASCAL, and Arts & Humanities Search. The search yielded 1318 documents; of these 1170 were documents in journals. The 1170 documents were distributed over c.290 journals. The top 20 journals (about 7% of the total number of journals) account for over 64% of the total number of documents retrieved. The search used DIALOG's duplicate removal and rank algorithms for documents published from 1990 to 1999 inclusive. Journals with variant abbreviated names were merged (i.e., counted) with their corresponding full names. For each of the top journals, the country of publication and primary language(s) of the papers were obtained from Ulrich's International Periodicals Directory on the DIALOG system.
**English version of the Russian: MEZHDUNARODNYI FORUM PO INFORMATSII I DOKUMENTATSII.

bases, if at all, to attain fair representation. Even for English-language publications the survey is selective, but, it is hoped, representative of current research. It is of interest to compare this list with those of PERITZ (1990) on bibliometrics, which show the top 15 journals for the periods 1960 to 1978 and 1979 to 1983. Although perhaps not strictly comparable in compilation, the present list shows several important continuities. Eight of the top 15 journals in Table 1 occur in Peritz's later list of 15 journals. Four were also in her first list (*JASIS, Information Processing & Management, Annals of Library Science and Documentation,* and *Journal of Documentation*), while four began publishing only between 1977 and 1979 (*Scientometrics, Revista Española de Documentación Científica, Journal of Information Science,* and *Library and Information Science Research*). *JASIS* has held first, second, and second positions in succession, with 7%, 7%, and 6%, respectively, of papers published. *Scientometrics* has occupied first position in the two later periods, with 8% and 28%, respectively, of papers published. It is also of interest to briefly compare the list in Table 1 with the journals of the papers selected for the present review. The five most productive journals in this review occur in the top ten English-language journals of Table 1 (in order): *Scientometrics, JASIS, Information Processing & Management, Journal of Documentation,* and *Journal of Information Science.* The proportion of papers from these journals is higher, for example, 32% come from *Scientometrics* and 21% from *JASIS.*

A Model for the Content of Informetrics

Informetric research can be classified several ways, for example, by the types of data studied (e.g., citations, authors, indexing terms), by the methods of analysis used on the data obtained (e.g., frequency statistics, cluster analysis, multidimensional scaling), or by the types of goals sought and outcomes achieved (e.g., performance measures, structure and mapping, descriptive statistics). Often specific types of data, methods of analysis, and outcomes cluster into recognized subfields, which simplifies presentation; this approach is taken below. But not all research can be easily pigeonholed, so it is desirable to present initially a more detailed analysis of the research content of informetrics, with representative articles as examples. Therefore this review also takes an object-oriented approach, which I feel best captures the special content of the field.

Based on the definition of informetrics adopted above, the basic unit of analysis is a collection of publications, usually papers in journals or monographs or patents; and less commonly, journals, whole conference proceedings, or databases (i.e., without reference to the level of constituent publications). More correctly in informetrics, it is usually only surrogates that are studied, the bibliography of records. It is helpful to see each publication (record) as a repository of properties (bibliographic fields) with variable values, such as language, publication year, containing-journal, authors, and title. Each of these also has properties, such as the language's number of printed works, the journal's editor, the author's institution, the institution's address. An alternative and more complicated view places the document at a hub of relations or quasi-links (e.g., contained in, authored by) to property values or quasi-objects (e.g., journal X, author Y). Either way, the other main component of this model is a set of true links between publications, beginning as references/citations-from publications and terminating as citations-to publications, with the set of publications at the other link-end possibly expanding the initial collection. Importantly, since the publications at the end of each link are themselves repositories of properties, one can make indirect comparisons through the links, for example, from author(s) of a paper to author(s) of a cited patent, or from the publication year of a paper to the publication year of a cited monograph.

Four further remarks are necessary. First, the basic collection of publications is defined on selected values of some publication properties; for example, one may study publications on a subject, or produced by an institution, in some period of time. Second, each unique publication can be assigned, at least implicitly, an identifier property, typically some combination of elements of other properties, such as author-year-serial-first-page or simply an accession number in a collection. Third, publication properties may be intrinsic, in the sense that given a publication one can determine the value directly from its text elements; or extrinsic, such as library-use data, descriptors assigned by traditional abstracting and indexing (A&I) services, or sets of citations-to from citation indexes. This distinction is perhaps moot, given that informetric research is typically based on bibliographies of records, not directly on the publications per se. Fourth, many properties are nominally scaled, for example, language takes the values English, German, etc. (EGGHE & R. ROUSSEAU, 1990b, pp. 9-10). For informetric analyses, related numeric properties are typically created by variously forming subsets with the same nominal values, and then counting the elements (e.g., number of papers per journal, number of references per paper, number of papers with more than one author per paper). Informetric research can then, as noted, employ a range of statistical and mathematical techniques on these data for a variety of specific goals, within the broader goal of the field.

This model should accommodate the concerns of MCGRATH (1996) about a perceived inattention to basic units of analysis by informetricians. As an illustration of this concern, one might find that in a study based on the publications produced by a set of institutions or journals, the author tacitly changes the focus of analysis to a comparison of the institutions or journals themselves. This could arise in part from working directly with compact, even one-line, bibliographic records, rather than with the actual publications. (Of course, the initial focus of scientometric studies not based on printed publications would be different.) Care is also required when aggregating publication properties into higher object properties. For example, the annual impact factor of a journal is the number of citations from the ISI database in that year to all papers in the journal for the two previous years, divided by the number of those papers. To obtain an aggregate impact factor for a subject grouping of journals, it is inaccurate to use the arithmetic average of the journals involved. The geometric average better reflects the correct value, obtained by separately aggregating the total citations and the total publications of the subject grouping (EGGHE & R. ROUSSEAU, 1996a).

In what follows I refer mostly to scientific papers or documents, but my remarks are equally applicable to patents (see "Patent Bibliometrics" by NARIN). The same may be said for objects on the World Wide Web, to which the model is extended in the section below on new trends. The model differs mainly in emphasis from those of BORGMAN (1990a, pp. 15-16), LEYDESDORFF (1989), and NARIN & HAMILTON, but the differences are not trivial. Borgman's model for analyzing studies in scholarly communication recognizes three basic classes of variables: (1) producers of the communication (authors, research teams, institutions, fields, or countries); (2) artifacts, the formal product (individual article, conference paper, book, or aggregate levels such as journals or conferences); and (3) communication concepts (which cover the authors' use of terms in titles and other text, and motivations for citing). Leydesdorff draws a similar distinction: between scientists, texts, and cognitions. Although publications are clearly artifacts, and human producers have favored status in the real world, publications warrant central billing in informetrics. It should be emphasized that by publications I am not referring to physical objects per se, perhaps in the sense of Rawski (see OBERHOFER), but to a pattern of symbols, of necessity on some carrier. Whether there is value in giving them their own universe, perhaps a "world three" in the conception of Karl Popper (BROOKES, 1980), is best left to philosophers. The important matter of human interpretation of these publications, which embraces communication concepts and cognitions, is addressed below. Narin & Hamilton recognize three different types of informetric units: literature, patent, and linkage. As noted for present purposes, the first two are conflated, drawing the main contrast between publications and publication-publication links. Links have at the very least a co-star status in citation analysis and in studies on the World Wide Web.

Analysis of Examples

Five examples of general informetric research are now analyzed to illustrate the model and the nature of informetrics; some are not clearly representative of the subfields considered later. The examples have been placed in ascending order of complexity with respect to the model.

(1) NATH & JACKSON examined about 900 research papers on the subject of management information systems (MIS) published in ten MIS journals between 1975 and 1987. They showed that Lotka's classic (inverse-square) law, relating the number of authors of papers to the number of papers they published, did not fit their data, but the generalized Lotka's (inverse-power) law did. Analysis: the ten journals selected had previously been rated as the most desirable publication outlets for MIS research, and the papers chosen from these journals in the time span were evaluated to be on the subject separately by both authors.

(2) B.M. GUPTA & KARISIDDAPPA (1998) demonstrated that, while the number of funded and collaborative publications from 11 core journals in theoretical population genetics had not proportionally increased, either with the growth of all such publications or of the number of unique authors, from 1956 to 1980, the productivity of authors strongly correlated with both collaboration and funding. Analysis: the top journals were selected from a recognized subject bibliography, funding was determined from the acknowledgement field of documents, and collaborations, both institutional and international, were determined from the author/address fields of the documents.

(3) HART & SOMMERFELD determined the growth from 1970 to 1996 in the chemical engineering literature in five English-speaking countries, and showed that it related to the growth of the countries' gross domestic product (GDP). Analysis: the SCI database was used to obtain a listing of documents whose authors' corporate addresses were top-producing university chemical engineering departments in each of the five chosen countries, for the appropriate span of publication years, whereas annual GDP data for the five countries were obtained separately.

(4) OSAREH & WILSON identified the Third World Countries (TWCs) whose research was most strongly linked by citations in a five-year period, and analyzed this research with respect to national population sizes, gross national products (GNP), and so on. Citation linkages here are taken to represent information exchange between TWCs, or second-order collaboration on research. Analysis: TWCs were identified from an encyclopedia of TWCs; further, a large sample of documents with TWC geographical addresses was first obtained from the SCI geographical section; then all documents citing these documents were obtained from the SCI citation index, with the constraint that they have

a TWC as a geographical address component. In this example, countries of authors are substituted for documents on either side of citation links, and additional country information (population, GNP, etc.) is supplied from other reference sources.

(5) WORMELL determined the extent to which a set of top library and information science (LIS) journals are truly international. She looked at correlations between the geographical distribution patterns of the authors publishing in the journals, authors of works citing those publications, and subscribers to the journals, in two time periods. The correlation between authors' addresses and citers' addresses (aggregated to continental regions) was strongly positive; however, the correlation was weak or non-existent between the geographical distributions of either group and journal subscribers. That is, there is a strong writer-citer geographical nexus, either part of which can be used to define the international visibility and impact of the journals, whereas purchase of copies (which includes passive readership) is little related. Analysis: the further complexity of this study in terms of the model is apparent. The basic collection is a set of (journal-subsets of) documents, whose citing documents were determined via the SCI and the SSCI. For both sets of documents, on either side of the citation links, the countries of authors were substituted and analyzed. Also, for each journal, subscription lists were obtained and the countries of subscribers compared with those of their authors and citers.

When the (supposed) specific research goals in the above examples are considered, the studies of B.M. GUPTA & KARISIDDAPPA (1998), HART & SOMMERFELD, and OSAREH & WILSON qualify unambiguously as scientometric. The study of NATH & JACKSON with its focus on author productivity is more fully informetric in charting the specific subjects component, using informetric laws. The study of WORMELL is also clearly informetric, but because it suggests novel ways of measuring journal internationality, and perhaps moves beyond exclusive use of the journal impact factor, it can be seen as constructing a framework of indicators and laws. This highlights the following frequently heard complaint (e.g., in many comments on the state of informetrics in BRAUN (1994)) that too much informetric research is not directed toward a fundamental understanding of its domain of interest, but merely uses informetric devices to provide descriptive statistics for some other purpose, as in applied scientometrics. This complaint also pertains to many studies charting the specific subjects component of informetrics: they seem to be primarily expressions of interest in a specific subject matter in isolation, with little interest in the general goal of the field. An attendant concern with the proliferation of these diverse studies is the erosion of any possibility of standardizing units and methods of analysis, which limits their value even for comparisons. MCGRATH (1996) suggests that the lack of standardization has retarded the development of informetrics theory.

Form and Interpretation of Publications

To conclude this introductory survey of the content of informetrics, two further issues must be addressed. The first is the form-interpretation distinction. It is frequently noted that informetric research has a level of objectivity not seen in other analyses of literature, nor in other evaluations of scientific research performance (e.g., peer review) where it can be used at the very least to guide decisions (NARIN ET AL., p. 75). How is this objectivity attained? The first step is to obtain universal agreement on the existence and the equality/inequality of strings of symbols in text—units of form, which even simpler computers can evaluate (WILSON, 1998). The second and critical step lies in the interpretation of the strings. Usually one reads (at least a large part of) a text so as to interpret its message or content, a process of great complexity and high reader-dependence. In contrast, informetrics restricts its attention to a small number of specific types of short strings, and limits its interpretation of these strings to their general function in the communication process. These are, of course, the strings privileged with names like "title" and "reference," which provide the basis for the document properties or document-document links. Wide, or at least tacit, acceptance of the function(s) that these text units perform is essential. The third step is to construct measures to represent, say, the degree to which a function is performed, which requires similar agreement. For example, is a straight count of the number of certain text elements on a subject in a document a valid measure of the extent of treatment of the subject? At least the reliability of counts, and of most informetric measurements, should be high (BORGMAN, 1990a, p. 25). The fourth step is to choose a data analysis technique that is appropriate to what is being modeled.

Regarding the second step to objectivity, there has been a consensus on the functional interpretations of most of informetrics' privileged strings (titles, authors, etc.), probably due to long-established bibliographic convention. But dispute arises over more recent bibliographic elements such as references/citations, a matter addressed below. It is also at this second stage, but involving even more interpretation, that the previously bypassed elements of Borgman's (1990a) and LEYDESDORFF's (1989) models, viz. communication concepts and cognitions, appear in the present model. The notions of content and usage in the sense of Rawski (see, e.g., OBERHOFER) also belong here because they seem to relate to either commonly agreed-on and individual interpretations, or less likely, to separate author and reader interpretations. The possibility of a confusion of text form and text interpretation may also exist at the other end of the scale, in the assumption that public knowledge grows in exact relation to the number of relevant publications produced. Of course, an inexact, perhaps ordinal-level relation may be possible; see the studies of BRAUN ET AL. on analytical chemistry, and especially the study of WOLFRAM ET AL.

Single- and Multiple-Valued Variables

The second issue is the matter of multiple values, which relates to the evaluation of the properties of documents[1], especially those that are nominal-scaled. The relationships among the values take three forms. (1) A document may be assigned a unique identifier code, where the assignment is said to be one:one. (2) It may be assigned the name of the language of its text, the name of its containing journal, or its publication year. Each document takes one value but it may share it with other documents; the assignment is said to be many:one. (3) A document may be assigned a set of author names, descriptors, or title words. Each document may take more than one value (element) that may be shared with other documents; the assignment is said to be many:many. Exactly how this last case of nominal measurement should be regarded is not discussed here: one may prefer to treat authors (for example) as a single vector property, or as a set of quasi-linked quasi-objects in their own right. Or again, it may be useful to consider the first two types of assignment from document to property as binary functions, and the latter type of assignment as a more general binary relation.

It is important to look more closely at the issue of many:many mappings, for it is a recurrent problem in informetrics, and arises in other contexts later in this review. The following illustrations are restricted to documents and authors. There are four possible conventions for assignment (PRAVDIĆ & OLUIĆ-VUKOVIĆ): (1) Normal or full author count: the document is assigned fully to each of its authors, that is, each author is awarded one document. (2) Adjusted or fractional count: each author is assigned only a share of the document; specifically, if there are three authors, each is assigned only one-third of the document. (3) Straight or first-author count: only the first author is credited with the whole document, and other authors are excluded, that

---

[1]The problem of defining exactly what a document is may be avoided by adopting a strictly bibliographic position. But a case could be made that if the body of the text does not change and is reprinted, or printed with minimal change elsewhere (compare, e.g., KHURSHID & SAHAI (1991a; 1991b)), or appears in different languages, then correctly we have the same document. This would alter only the placement of some examples in what follows.

is, the simpler many:one case is regained to the detriment of equal or junior co-authors. (4) A modification of method 3 assigns the whole document not to the first author but to the author who is most productive in, say, the area under study—and presumably the dominant contributor or instigator of the document, although modesty prevents him/her from taking the first position. Quite apart from the issue of attribution of credit, or even of retrieval from A&I services that use only a first or a limited author registration system, these different assignment procedures may produce different informetric results, as in the study of Lotka's law. Of course, the problem is more general than authors and publications. It may occur even at higher aggregation levels in, say, the assignment of journals to databases. HOOD & WILSON consider this and additional assignment modes, and the consequences for the resulting distributions. Unfortunately, there is no informetric way of choosing the best of these procedures in any fundamental sense. One can only accept a suite of conventions interrelated through different weighting functions, as EGGHE & R. ROUSSEAU (1996b) discuss in their theoretical examination.

Of more immediate interest are the classes of analyses that the many:one and many:many assignments allow in informetrics. The simpler many:one case is considered first. If one constructs a matrix with document identifiers on the rows margin and the assigned journal names, publication years, etc. on the columns margin, and enters 1 in each cell where an assignment is made (and zero elsewhere), then the column totals provide a frequency distribution of documents over journals, years, etc. (the row totals are all 1s). The analysis of such univariate frequency distributions constitutes a major class of analyses in informetrics (MCGRATH, 1994). This type of analysis can be readily extended by substituting another property value for the marginal document identifier, (e.g., publication year), or by adding more dimensions to the conceptual matrix, (e.g., creating the matrix: document identifier × journal × year × language).

Next, the many:many case is considered. If one repeats the construction with component authors (or descriptors, or title elements) on the columns margin, then individual row and column totals frequently exceed 1 with the full count procedure, and one obtains two frequency distributions: documents over authors and authors over documents. Again, one may repeat the construction with identifiers of documents either cited by the left-margin documents, or citing them (an extrinsic property). This results in the interesting case of the cells marking document-document links, and, as before, the distributions of references or citations over documents. And, as before, the analysis may be extended by, for example, substituting another property value (e.g., publication year) for the document identifiers on both margins. (With appropriate subtraction one can, for example, obtain age curves for the references of a set of documents.) Of more interest, these many:many matrices motivate the construction of a matrix (or half-matrix) with the same variable on both margins, and the cells containing the count (full or fractional) of either documents or of links common to row-column pairs. These can be called "co-matrices" (e.g., co-word matrices, co-citation matrices) since the more informative "correlation matrices" is typically understood as containing but one transformation of the cell contents, using Pearson's correlation coefficient. The co-matrices display a network of binary relationships between like objects that may be variously interpreted; for example, the author-author matrix could show the degree of collaboration on documents. Where enough cells have a range of sufficiently large numbers, the co-matrices provide the basis for numerical taxonomic and related methods, which constitute a second major class of analyses in informetrics (McGrath, 1994). Most common here is the document-document matrix showing citation links. Once again, document identifiers may be substituted for property values, for example, with authors for identifiers (another multiple assignment) leading to author co-citation matrices, and so on.

CITATION ANALYSIS

Perhaps the largest subfield of informetrics is citation analysis or citation studies. In terms of the model introduced above, the more an informetric work focuses on the publication-publication (reference-citation) link, the more surely it may be classified in this subfield. More precisely, studies focusing on the reference-to end of the link can be placed in a separate reference analysis, but given some important differences, studies here parallel citation studies. One major difference between references and citations[2] is that the reference list for each document is fixed (the property is intrinsic). In contrast, the list of citations to a document is extrinsic in that it depends on the document set whose references are inverted, and this set extends indefinitely into the future from the time of publication of the document. For comparative analyses in informetrics, this extrinsic set must be standardized by both content and time frame. Accordingly, citation analysis is overwhelmingly based on the citation indexes produced by the Institute for Scientific Information (ISI). However, there are citation studies based

---

[2]There are various usages of "citation": a reference in the document of interest to a pre-existing document, the actual document or record of interest in a bibliography, or a reference in a later document to the document of interest (past, present, and future tenses?). The second usage is avoided here, and a strict distinction between reference and citation is made only if necessary to avoid confusion.

on national or subject-related citation databases (BHUSHAN & LAL; JIN & WANG; WILSON, 1995).

Citation analysis may be conveniently subdivided into three major areas of study: (1) the theory of citing, (2) citation performance and usage measures, and (3) co-citation analysis and literature mapping. Thus, it fully spans the major types of goals or outcomes of informetrics. If the analysis of frequency distributions of citation data is separated from the second category, citation analysis could represent all four of MCGRATH's (1994) subdivisions of informetric research. GARFIELD's (1998a) paper, "From Citation Indexes to Informetrics," provides a recent and brief synoptic review and history of citation indexes, including discussion of each of the three (or four) areas or subtopics. A selective annotated bibliography of citation analysis devoted to investigations in the humanities and social sciences is provided by HÉRUBEL & BUCHANAN.

Theory of Citing

As noted above, prerequisites for valid informetric analyses include wide agreement on the communication function of the text units employed and on the measures applied to them. In informetrics, this issue is raised most persistently with respect to citations, creating a special topic of research. A good introduction to the theory of citation is by GARFIELD (1998b), who acknowledges the central place of this more qualitative aspect of informetrics in the suggestion that "citationology" be used for the theory and practice of citation, as well as its "derivative" discipline, citation analysis. A recent review of citation studies by LIU deals with the complexities and the underlying norms of the citation process. The focus is on studies dealing with the different functions of citations, the quality of citations made, and the motivation for citing in general. A less conventional perspective on the theories of citation is provided by LEYDESDORFF & WOUTERS (1999).

Conventional basis for citation analysis. The conventional interpretation of citations that underlies citation analysis of research literature may be described as follows. A document is cited in another document because it provides information relevant to the performance and presentation of the research, such as positioning the research problem in a broader context, describing the methods used, or providing supporting data and arguments. It is not necessary for the citing to be exhaustive, of course, but only sufficient for the author's purpose. If it can be assumed that all citations are equal with respect to informing the research carried out and to its reporting, then several very useful conclusions can be drawn: (1) The more a document is cited from a subsequent body of literature, the more it has contributed information to, and the more influence it has had on, the research reported there. A measure of this influence or impact is the number of citations received. In Mertonian terms, the scientific author is publicly rewarded by these acknowledgments of intellectual debt. This motivates the development of performance measures. Needless to say, the content of extremely well-known works may eventually be simply assumed without explicit citing, a phenomenon termed "obliteration by incorporation." (2) A complementary perspective is that the number of times a document is cited, for example, over time, reflects how much it has been used in subsequent research. A declining rate suggests that the document's content is increasingly less relevant, that is, that the document is becoming obsolete. At least for research material, this is a more realistic measure of actual usage than a document's circulation in libraries. (3) Again, if two documents are jointly cited by another document, they jointly contribute to the performance and reporting of that research, and are associated by their role in that research and its presentation. Accordingly, the more the two documents are co-cited from a body of literature, the greater is the association of their content, in the opinion of the authors of that body of literature. A measure of this association and, for stable normal science, of similarity in subject content, is the number of co-citations the pair receives. This motivates co-citation analysis and its use in literature mapping.

Criticisms and counter-criticisms. If one does not accept that the above interpretation of citations is valid, at least in large part, then the conclusions do not follow, and citation analysis becomes a misguided enterprise. Various criticisms of the conventional view are raised from time to time and responded to, only to reappear and stimulate additional response. The key issues are the degree to which the central claim is correct or in error—perfect compliance is not essential—and how to validate/refute the competing interpretations. Criticisms of the above interpretation exist at a variety of levels; only the extremes and some recent representatives of them are considered here. One may accept the conventional view but find that the levels of citation error in formatting or content, even with improved editorial enforcement of reference standards, are much too high to justify citation analysis. For example, PANDIT found errors in 193 of 1094 references (a rate of 18%) in 131 articles in five core library science journals. The principal types of errors were: missing/wrong page numbers (28% of all errors), missing/incomplete/incorrect author/editor names (23%), and missing/incomplete/incorrect titles of articles (19%). Her review of a sample of references at the submitted manuscript stage for one of the journals found errors in 53% of references (most commonly in missing issue numbers and missing authors/editors), placing responsibility for citation errors on the document authors (regrettably, library and information scientists). This error rate was substantially reduced after editorial verification. It should be remarked that the error induced in citation studies of publication aggregates, such as journals and even authors, would not be as severe as these disturbing, but not atypical, figures imply. But further errors may arise in citation studies, for example, from different practices between journals in recording references. Even if reference variants are adequately correct and not appreciably different for the human reader, they may not be collated in computer analysis (see, e.g., cases listed in PERSSON).

One may partially relinquish the conventional view and attribute to citations a slightly different communicative intent, going beyond simply reporting research performed to actively convincing the reader of the conclusions reached and their value (see e.g., GILBERT). This seemingly more realistic view does not in itself affect the validity of the basis of citation analysis as described (see e.g., COZZENS). However, a more extreme version of this position, taking science to be principally a form of polemical writing, replete with rhetorical devices, appeal to authority, advancement of allies, etc., does undermine this basis. This more recent view of scientific writing has found favor principally in some nonscientific circles. Within the informetric community, it is most closely and persuasively represented by MACROBERTS & MACROBERTS. In this constructivist or non-Mertonian paradigm, a significant proportion of citations take on a different communicative function to that of information support or fair persuasion. Two examples dealing with issues raised by this new perspective are considered, although they do not support it.

First, with respect to gratuitous self-citing, that is, artificially inflating an author's citation count and performance rating, SNYDER & BONZI looked at self-citations and citations to other works in the physical sciences, social sciences, and arts and humanities. For each discipline, 25 journals were selected. For the physical and social sciences, the journals were the top-ranked by impact factor in the Journal Citation Reports, while for the Arts and Humanities, the journals were selected randomly from the categories of Asian studies and art history in the Arts and Humanities Citation Index. Overall, 9% of all citations were self-citations, with 15% in the physical sciences, 6% in the social sciences, and 3% in the humanities. The last two cases are acceptably low percentages, however one chooses to interpret their communicative function. But more convincingly, Snyder & Bonzi found no significant differences in the reasons (that is, in citer motivation) used to select self-citations and citations to other authors. Productive authors developing a theme naturally refer to their earlier work.

Second, with respect to citations for nonconventional purposes in general, BALDI measured characteristics of both potentially citing and potentially citable papers in a research area of astrophysics, and quantitatively related the probability of a citation occurring to these characteristics. For example, characteristics of papers in the potentially citable set included indicators of cognitive content and of quality, as well as indicators of the author's position in the scientific social structure and of his/her social ties to potentially citing authors. The possibility of a citation occurring was strongly influenced by indicators in the first group, but not by indicators in the second. It follows that astrophysicists are likely to cite in their work articles of relevance to intellectual content, etc., in accord with the conventional model, but not with respect to factors such as an author's prestige, as proposed by the constructivist model.

At present, and more generally, the nonconventional interpretation of the communication function of citations is being counterattacked with examples of validation studies of citation analysis: see H.D. WHITE and GARFIELD (1997). An issue of *Scientometrics* (BRAUN, 1998) contains a discussion of the critical paper, "Theories of Citation," by LEYDESDORFF (1998). Invited comments include, inter alia: an endorsement of the validity of citation analysis (KOSTOFF); the preoccupation of certain authors with deviant citation behavior (GARFIELD, 1998b); an attack on the ceremonial roles of citations and a criticism of the constructivist view of citation practice held by sociologists of science (VAN RAAN, 1998a); and the construction of a reference threshold model to show that citations, and indicators derived from citations for assessing publication performance, are valid measures in most of the fields of natural science (VINKLER, 1998a).

In addition to dispute over the correct communication function of citations, criticisms may also be directed specifically at the measures actually employed. For example, are simple straight counts ideal? Would a logarithmic transformation be more appropriate to eliminate multiplicative (bandwagon) effects, that is, citing highly cited authors simply because they are highly cited or have come to represent the general topic? For example, in a discussion of informetric laws, must the 70-year old discoveries of Lotka, Bradford, and Zipf be forever cited, or would a reference to a contemporary text such as EGGHE & R. ROUSSEAU (1990b) suffice? Again, even within the conventional framework, should citations be treated as equal or should there be a weighting for types of citations? An obvious case is that of citations highly critical of published work (negative citations) which seem to warrant negative weighting. This approach leads to citation-content and citation-context analysis where more text interpretation is required than the assignment of one typical communication function (see LIU; also PERITZ, 1992); further discussion of this issue follows later in this review. Nevertheless, it is interesting that even here, frequently occur-

ring individual citations tend toward standard higher-level interpretations, that is, the content of statements invoking the cited work becomes
rather similar over a wide range of citing authors (SMALL, 1978). The
weighting issue becomes more important with document aggregations
(e.g., journals or subjects), especially when citation counts are used to
evaluate performance. Another issue concerns the normalization of
references with respect to the total number of references in a document,
so that documents with an inordinate number of references do not
inordinately influence citation award. Fractional citations are now typically employed to counteract this effect (SMALL & SWEENEY).

Criticism may also be directed specifically at the assumptions of co-
citation analysis outlined above. These are most likely to arise when a
literature mapping produced by co-citation analysis for some domain
fails to satisfactorily agree with maps produced by other methods: co-
word analysis, or classical subject analysis (typically conventional wis-
dom). It must be remembered that, either with performance measures
or co-citation literature maps, the alternative methods (peer review,
subject expert opinion, etc.) do not have the status to unambiguously
validate or repudiate citation analysis techniques. Nevertheless, a limited repertoire of good alternatives does not allow citation analysis, and
co-citation mapping in particular, simply to be validated by default; see
for example the discussion by WOUTERS.

Citation Performance and Usage Measures

From the conventional interpretation of citation function, the frequency with which a document is cited can be taken as a measure of the
impact or influence of that document on the (research performed and
reported in the) citing literature. This premise may be extended to
aggregates of documents, for example, to an author's works or to a
specific journal. As producers of the only major citation index, ISI
developed and extensively employed this measure, especially with
respect to journals. It was named the "impact factor" by GARFIELD &
SHER in 1963. ISI defines the impact factor for a given journal in a given
year (e.g., 1998) as the number of citations from the ISI database in that
year (1998) to articles published in that journal in the previous two-year
period (1996 and 1997), divided by the total number of articles published in the journal in the two-year period. Yearly journal impact
factors are available for thousands of journals in the Journal Citation
Reports (JCR). More generally, the impact factor, especially from the ISI
citation indexes, has been used to evaluate scholarly contributions
produced by individual scholars, groups of scholars, departments, institutions, disciplines, and countries. Since a raison d'être for most of
these social units is the production of scholarly contributions, the im-

pact factor is a natural measure of their performance. The international journal *RESEARCH EVALUATION* publishes articles ranging from individual research projects up to intercountry comparisons of research performance using this measure. The reader's attention is also drawn to the *JASIS* issue edited by VAN RAAN (1998b) featuring seven articles from the Fourth International Conference on Science and Technology Indicators.

Criticisms of impact factors. Evaluations cannot be made with numbers in isolation if the basis (or unit) of comparison is uncertain. As already noted in comparing citation counts (assuming that unweighted, untransformed, and possibly unnormalized counts suffice), fair comparisons are possible only when the set of citing literature and the citing time frame are both appropriate and fixed. This problem is compounded when aggregations of documents are compared. Recent studies of these problems, which frequently lead to criticisms of the impact factor and suggestions for its modification (though not usually its abandonment) are now briefly discussed. VAN LEEUWEN ET AL. reviewed these problems and present data illustrating how they lead to inappropriate use of impact factors, for researchers in deciding their publication strategies, policy makers in evaluating research performance, and librarians in evaluating their journal collections.

A first issue is the problem of aggregating a set of documents, each with its linked set of (possibly zero) citing documents, into a larger unit, for example, a journal for which one suitable comparative performance measure is sought. The analysis by EGGHE & R. ROUSSEAU (1996a) of aggregating journal impact factors into one impact factor for a subject group of journals has already been noted. It is well-known that the distribution of citations over articles, and over journals, in the ISI database is highly skewed. Most journals have very low impact factors. For example, if one consults the 1997 JCR for SCI, one finds that 97% of journals have an impact factor of 5 or less, while 63% have an impact factor of 1 or less; the median journal impact factor is 0.73. Most papers are poorly cited, for example, SEGLEN (1992) found that for a random sample of articles from SCI, over 50% were completely uncited (from their third year after publication). When Seglen selected three different biochemical journals with temporally stable journal impact factors of 6.4, 3.8, and 2.4, and looked at the distribution of citations over their articles, he found that these distributions were also strongly skewed: for each of the three journals, 50% of all citations went to c.15% of articles, and 90% of all citations to c.50% of articles, whereas 30% of articles received no citations at all in the chosen time frame. Thus, mean journal impact factor is a somewhat deficient estimator for the performance of a typical paper in a journal; the median value would be a better estimator. With respect to other aggregations, Seglen found citedness to vary in the same manner over works by single authors. However, citedness can be a useful indicator of scientific impact at the national level once corrections are made for field effects. SEGLEN (1994) looked at the relationship between article citedness and journal impact and found poor correlations between them. He confirmed that the use of impact factors for journals as an evaluation parameter may give misleading results, unless the evaluated unit (author, research group, institution, or country) is equal to the world average. He reiterates that article citedness is unaffected by journal prestige, and that certain journals have high impact only because they publish a small proportion of high-impact articles.

A second issue concerns variation in citedness within a journal due to the inclusion of a variety of document types with inherently different attractiveness for citations. MOED ET AL. (1999) found that when documents in a number of biomedical articles for 1995 were sorted into types, and had separate impact factors calculated, articles, notes, and reviews obtained appreciably higher impact values than the respective total journal impact factor, whereas letters, editorials, etc. achieved appreciably lower impact factors. As a result of inclusion of the latter document types, journal impact factors may be 10% to 40% lower than would otherwise be expected, based on substantive articles. SCHWARTZ likewise contrasted different levels of citedness in different types of documents. For all sources in the physical sciences in ISI's databases up to 1990, 47% were uncited. However, when only articles were considered, and book reviews, conference abstracts, editorials, letters and obituaries were excluded, uncitedness dropped to 22%. A further restriction to only articles produced by U.S. authors cut the uncitedness rate to 14%. A similar drop in uncitedness was seen for the social sciences at the first two levels of disaggregation: fully 75% of all source items were uncited, but only 48% of articles. In the humanities, overall uncitedness was very high, 98%, and restriction to articles only caused a small reduction, to 93%.

The present problem of composing an impact factor for a journal would be simplified if no account were taken of the number of documents contained therein, that is, if the impact factor denominator were set to one. HARTER & NISONGER suggest restricting journal impact factor to ISI's numerator, and referring to the currently used journal impact factor as the (mean) "article impact factor." But no correction is made for the number of publications in a journal in the first case, and in the second case, the mean remains a poor estimator. It is also unlikely that the present use of "journal impact factor" could change so drastically; besides, the topic needs no more confusion.

The third issue naturally follows from results like those of SCHWARTZ above, concerning the appreciable difference in citedness even for the same document type between different disciplines. This is the comparability of different informetric units in terms of the number of citations received, and of their performance evaluation, whether they be aggregates (variously normalized or not) or simply individual publications. In other words, it is the citing set of documents, not the cited set of documents, that is now of interest. Should authors or journals publishing on a small subject be judged inferior to their counterparts in a larger subject simply because few citations are generated that could possibly go to them? SCHUBERT & BRAUN suggest three reference standards for citation-based assessments, with a balanced analysis of each. (1) For an individual publication, the basis for comparison could be the average citation rate of publications in its journal to obtain a relative citation rate (RCR). (2) Another basis of comparison could be the average citation rate of the set of records bibliographically coupled with the publication, and so judged by its author to be related; this is quickly obtainable from the CD-ROM edition of the citation indexes. (3) For an individual journal, the basis of comparison could be the average impact factor of those journals cited by the journal in question.

A fourth issue in the comparability of different units in terms of the number of citations received (and therefore of their measure of performance) again concerns the citing set of documents, but now the problem lies with the set's positioning and duration in time. MOED ET AL. (1999) review a number of their earlier studies on indicators reflecting scholarly journal impact. They find that the impact measure in the Journal Citation Reports (JCR) is inaccurate and biased toward journals with a rapid maturing of impact. Only for this limited number of journals is the maximum average impact reached two years after publication, or during their most citation-attractive years. But for most journals, the maximum period of impact is attained three to five (or even more) years after publication, a period excluded by the impact factor as currently defined. It can be argued that corrections are indicated by the parallel indicators of immediacy and half-lives reported in the JCR, but it is unlikely that evaluators would labor over composing their own suitable composite. The construction of any fair impact factor must directly take into account the time course of citations to journals. This leads to the closely related topic of literature obsolescence.

Obsolescence Studies

For monographs, usage profiles may be constructed for limited purposes from library circulation data, but for research articles especially, citations received are a better and more general measure of usage. This justifies placement of the topic in the present section. Of course, a high proportion of documents is never cited or receives insufficient citations to warrant charting their usage profiles in this way. For the remaining documents, or for aggregates of documents such as journals, the typical profile can be described thus: there is usually a lag from the time of publication until the first citations appear in print; then the number of citations grows with time to a maximum, in what has been variously termed an impulse or maturation phase; and finally the annual citation rate falls away to zero, in an obsolescence phase. In sum, the typical distribution is unimodal with a right skew. However, the first two phases, and especially the lag, may be very short relative to the length of the obsolescence phase, with the distribution being strongly skewed. A variety of measures has been proposed to capture features of the citation/reference age profile, the most immediately obvious being the median age of the distribution, termed its half-life. Another common measure is the Price index, the fraction of citations/references not older than a certain age, for example, two years. MCCAIN (1997) provides a summary of the more prominent measures, in a review that emphasizes the role of this work in serials management. As remarked, variation exists in the form of profiles, for example, some articles peak and decay early, while classics may maintain high levels seemingly indefinitely. Traditionally, it is the obsolescence of a work, its declining usage with time, that has been of interest to authors and librarians alike, but the speed of reception of a work, its quickness to attract citations and enhance performance measures (e.g., the impact factor), has received recent interest. The topic has drawn much attention; EGGHE (1994a) notes that some 3000 pieces of literature were produced from 1970 until his time of writing. Yet progress in understanding the fundamental processes has been slow. The review paper by LINE in 1993 found that significant issues raised by LINE & SANDISON in 1974, nearly 20 years before, remained open.

Part of the reason for slow progress may arise from aging profiles being determined by two different methods. More typical are studies using the synchronous approach where the age profile is that of the references in a set of documents published at the same time. Here the half-life is the median age of the reference set. This is not a strictly accurate use of the term "half-life," although it was accommodated for this context by BURTON & KEBLER, who first introduced the term into literature studies in 1960. (Incidentally, synchronous studies go back to GROSS & GROSS in 1927, well prior to the formation of a distinct field of bibliometrics.) Less common are studies using the diachronous approach where the number of citations to a set of documents, from an appropriate and fixed database, is followed through time. The half-life is the median age of the citation set. Use of this approach has grown since the advent of citation indexes, but it still accounts for only about one-fifth of studies on literature obsolescence (DIODATO & SMITH,

Table 1, p.102). Synchronous and diachronous studies tend to have slightly different emphases. The former can readily acquire large retrospective data sets and aim for precise mathematical description, whereas the latter typically select smaller numbers of older (subsequently well-cited) documents and seek reasons for major qualitative differences in profile types. Intermediate between the two approaches is the diasynchronous approach, a repetition of the synchronous approach at successive times (LINE). "Multisynchronous" also seems to be a suitable term for this intermediate approach, but unfortunately, each of these terms has also acquired slightly different meanings than described here (e.g., see Diodato & Smith).

Mathematical description of aging profiles. Recently there has been an increase of interest in the mathematical description of aging profiles, especially within the synchronous approach. This provides not only a summarization of data into comparable indices and for better prediction, but it also allows for logical exploration and, with well-understood models, the possibility of an explanation of underlying processes. On the negative side, a confusion of models, excessive curve fitting, and gratuitous mathematical manipulation may develop, and important qualitative aspects of the citation process may be overlooked. Early studies focused on a single negative exponential distribution as a suitable description, or on weighted sums or differences of exponential distributions, intermingling different rates. In the weighted approach, for example, the three-parameter model of AVRAMESCU (1979) could generate a variety of profile types. Where the reception phase (i.e., the time needed to start attracting growing numbers of citations) is very brief for a document or journal, and the number of citations received initially is high, a negative exponential function often adequately describes the data. This was true, for example, in the analysis of references of 15 leading physics journal for 1983 by U. GUPTA, or of one major biochemical journal for 1983 by BOTTLE & GONG. Otherwise, the full curve from the first citation can be better modeled by functions allowing for a mode.

EGGHE & RAVICHANDRA RAO (1992a) found that the lognormal distribution better fitted their data sets (references from three monographs) than other candidate distributions, viz. the exponential, the negative binomial, and the Weibull. Their approach was novel in calculating for each candidate the ratio of the number of references in a year to that in the preceding year (the aging or obsolescence function), and then checking which function best matched the appropriately transformed data. For the exponential distribution, for example, the aging function is of course constant; for the lognormal distribution the value falls to a minimum a little later than the profile mode. Further, EGGHE (1997b) demonstrated that, whereas the commonly used Price index bore fixed relations to both the median and mean reference age when the reference age profile matched a negative exponential distribution, this would not be the case for lognormally distributed reference age profiles. B.M. GUPTA (1998) also found, using the Kolmogorov-Smirnov statistic, that the lognormal distribution well-fitted the age profile of over 7000 references in eight of nine annual sets of articles on population genetics between 1931 and 1979. SANGAM carried out a similar study on c.18,000 references in five psychology journals, including a number of annual reference sets for some journals from 1972 to 1996; he found 23 were best-fitted with the lognormal distribution, and 24 with the negative binomial distribution. TAHAI & RIGSBY analyzed the age profile of c.12,000 references from articles in eight accounting journals in the period 1982-1984. They found that a three-parameter Generalized Gamma distribution better fitted the data, using maximum likelihood fit estimation, than either the exponential or Weibull distributions (which are one- and two-parameter special cases of it, respectively), or the lognormal distribution (a two-parameter limiting case of it). The authors then used the General Gamma distribution to describe the references in c.50 social science journals to fix the mode (generally at c.3 years with c.27% of references), the median (generally at c.7 years), and the projected full lifetime. They showed that if the journal impact factor were calculated using these different time windows, different rank orderings of the journal would be obtained. Clearly, with respect to synchronous studies at least, the General Gamma distribution seems to be the best model to date, perhaps unsurprising given its three parameters, two of which are determiners of shape.

In the largest study using the diachronous approach, GLÄNZEL & SCHOEPFLIN (1995) followed some 5000 articles from seven journals for 1980-1981 in the SCI-SSCI databases for ten years. They fitted a negative binomial distribution to the obsolescence phase of the profile (for prior theoretical reasons), and obtained a number of comparative indicators. Other studies used far fewer data. HURT & BUDD tracked one highly cited 1982 paper, the first major summary of superstring theory in physics, in the SCI database over five years, and found a Weibull distribution best fitted the profile. CANO & LIND tracked the citation careers of 20 articles (10 highly cited and 10 scarcely cited) in medicine and biochemistry; they described the two classes of curves obtained in terms of the normalized cumulative number of citations received, and fitted two intersecting straight lines and a single straight line, respectively, to the two different data classes. As noted, the principal focus of diachronous studies has not been model construction and curve fitting to date, but such a development would be beneficial for comparisons with synchronous studies.

Regarding the initial time lag, R. ROUSSEAU (1994b) developed two forms of double exponential models for the time to the first citation, of which one equates to the Gompertz growth function. One model better fits data with very short delay times, in the order of months, and the other with longer delay times, in the order of a year or more. A critical issue with respect to reception times in general is exactly what date should be used as time zero for the cited document (and for that matter, the date of appearance of citing articles also): the date of submission, the date of acceptance, the date given on the publishing journal, the date when the journal was actually published, or the date of its notification in *Current Contents*. LUWEL & MOED found that the length of time between submission and publication of an article, its publication delay, affected its subsequent citation profile. The half-lives of the age distribution of references in journals with long publication delays were longer than for journals that publish submitted materials rapidly. The delays are discipline-dependent (e.g., they tend to be longer for mathematics and engineering/technical journals), but are also dependent on the journal's editorial policy (e.g., the proportion and extent of revision required). Apropos of the structure of the present review, an analysis of the small document field providing a chronology of its submission/revision/acceptance with respect to its journal of publication makes its only appearance here. With more such studies, this document field might warrant separate placement, perhaps in a section on journal-related analyses.

The synchronous-diachronous problem. A question that has dogged obsolescence studies since the 1970s is whether synchronous and diachronous methods yield strictly comparable results. Even for the complete literature of a homogeneous subject—an ideal—the retrospective profile from the present (via the synchronous approach) would not necessarily closely match the subsequent profile for past documents (via the diachronous approach) unless stability prevailed through the intermediate time interval. One obvious disruptant is literature growth. If the literature on a subject grows rapidly, then more documents are available at later times to cite earlier works; but then, there are also more documents available in the immediate past to cite. Again, a rapidly growing field with a quick turnover of ideas might have more reason to cite a greater proportion of newer documents. A growth in the number of references per document with time, perhaps associated with longer articles, would add a second order of confusion. What frequency distributions for citations/references show, then, may not reflect real document obsolescence, but rather an apparent obsolescence, a real aging confounded with literature size changes (see MOTYLEV and LINE).

Theoretical work does suggest that such a disparity can arise between these approaches. Adopting the simplest models for growth and real obsolescence in a homogenous literature—positive and negative exponential distributions, respectively—EGGHE (1993b) found that synchronous studies would demonstrate an increase in apparent obsolescence, and diachronous studies the opposite. EGGHE (1994a) modified the methods used here to the continuous case; these were applied by EGGHE ET AL. (1995) to more simply confirm the earlier results, and extend them to the case of negative exponential growth, that is, to a declining homogenous literature: the opposite results would then occur. It might be argued, as the authors recognized, that these exponential models were chosen for their relative tractability and not strict realism, but the important point is that the two commonly used approaches produce opposite results.

Clearly, the interplay of factors here is complex and further investigation will surely produce contradictions in the short term. For example, in a massive empirical study of the whole SCI database between 1961 and 1982, NAKAMOTO found a high coincidence between synchronous and diachronous frequency distributions: the decline in the proportion of citations to 1961 publications through the database to 1982 mirrored the decline in the proportion of the age of references in the 1982 publications back to 1961. A contrasting result was found by DIODATO & SMITH. In their study, citations to articles in six music journals from 1975 were followed through the Arts & Humanities Citation Index (A&HCI) until 1989, and the resulting profile was compared with that of the references in the same journals for 1989. Since a proportion of references was to very old material, the median reference age was c.26 years while the citation half-life was only 7 years; however, even when adjustments were made to align and normalize the two profiles, and despite their broad qualitative similarity, they proved not to be equivalent statistically.

Factors affecting obsolescence. Earlier work identified some factors that affect the aging profile of documents and document aggregates, especially journals and subjects. For example, papers in the hard sciences appeared to age more quickly than those in the social sciences. These findings are summarized and updated in a list of synchronous median citation ages for various scholarly fields in CUNNINGHAM & BOCOCK (Table 2, p. 259). There is a trend toward more slowly aging literatures running from the natural sciences through the social sciences to the humanities, with values ranging from c.4 years for metallurgical engineering (and computer science, from the authors' own study) to c.22 years for Biblical criticism. But the location of the major fields over this range is neither systematic nor obvious, for example, the median reference age for geology is c.12 years, and for archeology is c.9.5 years. This suggests that if there is anything fundamental in this hard-soft spectrum, at the very least it is obscured by other factors such as differences in the (ages of the) publication types of documents cited, or in the sampling of journal types made from fields, or in the speed of development of the field when surveyed.

LINDHOLM-ROMANTSCHUK & WARNER investigated the proportion of citations from SSCI and A&HCI made to monographs versus articles for the authors of outstanding academic books (from 1973 to 1990) in 30 social science and humanities fields. They found the ratio for philosophy to be nearly 8:1, and for sociology and economics to be c.2.5:1. Would a preference for citing enduring monographs as opposed to ephemeral articles lead to the slower discipline-based aging suggested? (Worthy articles in the humanities, especially, might be fairly speedily gathered into monographic collections anyway). GLÄNZEL & SCHOEPFLIN (1994a) asked whether referencing a high proportion of nonserial works (books, monographs, etc.) might lead to slower obsolescence in the natural and applied sciences. In a study of c.8 million references in over 2000 journals in the 1993 SCI database, they found this was not the case, despite the proportion of nonserial references ranging from practically zero, in the life sciences, to over 50% in some engineering fields. GLÄNZEL & SCHOEPFLIN (1995) investigated the aging profiles of documents in journals from five diverse disciplines for 1980-1981 over a ten-year period in the SCI-SSCI databases. They found that aging was faster for the single chemical and medical journals than for the pairs of journals for sociology and psychology, but that for the single mathematical journal was as slow as that of the social sciences. This slow aging of mathematical journals was earlier noted by R. ROUSSEAU (1988a). Glänzel & Schoepflin found that fast aging did not necessarily imply fast reception, supporting a potential four-fold classification of profiles (slow/fast reception × slow/fast aging) that extends to the previous fast/fast versus slow/slow pattern proposed by AVERSA. In contrast, in a study analyzing more than 3000 journals across all subfields in the SCI database from 1981 to 1995, MOED ET AL. (1998) attributed the aging characteristics of individual journals to the journals themselves. However, different subfields had different proportions of journals from the four different classes. Glänzel & Schoepflin's conclusions are then explicable not in terms of subject fields per se, but simply in how they selected journals from the fields. To achieve some standardization in such studies, it might be best to select only core journals from the different fields (DIODATO & SMITH).

GLÄNZEL & SCHOEPFLIN (1995) also noted that, where appreciable, self-citations tended to be high initially in a journal's age profile. This observation was taken up by R. ROUSSEAU (1999) who studied data in the 1995 JCR on two self-citation measures for a set of highly cited journals, and for a comparison set of randomly selected moderately cited journals. One measure is the self-cited rate, the proportion of citations going to a journal from itself versus to the journal from the whole set of sources in the database (for 1995). The other measure is the self-citing rate, the proportion of citations going to a journal versus to all journals from the journal itself (in 1995). The first measure includes external citations to the journal; if low, the journal draws more of these. From the ratio of these two measures, R. Rousseau found that the self-citation profile did indeed peak earlier than the profile for citations from other journals, both for the highly cited journals (excluding annual reviews) and to a much lesser degree for the comparison set. This study underlines yet another aspect of the complexity of citation profiles, and, incidentally, for constructing journal impact factors.

Finally, obsolescence may be considered at the level of types of document and of reference-citation linkages, which follows from earlier discussion in this review on citing theory and leads to later discussion of highly interpreted word analyses. BOTTLE & GONG analyzed the age profiles of seven different types of references identified in the nearly 5000 references of one annual volume of the major biochemistry journal *Cell*. The type of reference with the minimum median age, c.3 years, was predominant (with c.53% of all references) and dealt with properties of substances, whereas the type with the maximum median age, c.9 years, had near-minimum occurrence (c.3%) and dealt with whole-organism biochemistry. A comparable diachronous study is that of MCCAIN & TURNER. Following AVERSA, the authors traced the citation profiles of 11 highly cited articles in molecular genetics, which were published in 1979-1980, for the succeeding seven years through the SCI database. Two classes of profile were observed: four papers peaked at c.5-6 years with a slow subsequent decline, and seven papers peaked at c.2-3 years with a rapid decline. McCain & Turner sought reasons for the class differences by studying text pieces in a sample from the c.3000 citing documents, interpreting the context from which the relevant citations were made and the content of the citation statements per se. The staying power of the slow-aging articles derived from either theoretical or technical contributions that proved most useful to subsequent authors, for example, in inspiring new work or in offering superior analytical methods. The fast agers were highly cited for experimental results, or for theoretical analysis of apparently limited and immediate application. These two studies remind us that at a fine level of detail, citation links are content channels. They also reopen the issue of the nature of real obsolescence. In what sense has the content of a document become obsolete when it ceases to be cited? Is it still used in the wider sense of having been learned, or has it become irredeemably outdated (except to historians), even with results now known to be flawed or invalid? Citation counts may broadly measure document usage, but higher interpretation is needed to probe this issue more deeply (see, e.g., OBERHOFER). The problem of differences between synchronous and diachronous approaches is broader than that of simple literature growth or decline. There is also the matter of a literature diversifying into subtopics, with hidden adjustments to the sizes of potential cited and citing sets. The delineation of full homogenous or subject-steady literature sets, holding one variable constant, seems a necessary prerequisite for more quantitative analyses. The need for a rigorous definition of such literature sets has been emphasized by PERITZ (1992).

Co-Citation Analysis and Literature Mapping

Information exchange and interdisciplinarity. A prior section discusses the construction of co-matrices, which establish binary (or pairwise) relationships between document identifiers, or of properties substituted for them. Of particular interest is the pairwise citation link. If one aggregates identical values of properties such as journals, subject groupings of journals, institutions, countries, and so on, then these more compact co-matrices can be interpreted as displaying a measure of the exchange of information between these units through the literature, in a sense, a secondary or indirect collaboration. For example, for different subjects, this approach may be used to construct their degrees of interdisciplinarity (mutual information exchange); there is an almost certain asymmetry of the co-matrix in this case. Again, the spread of influence from one subject to other subjects may be studied, especially if a time series of such co-matrices is constructed. ACKERSON studied the cross-citation activity of 59 core journals in six disciplines of the physical and biochemical sciences. She used a citation-counting method to assess subject dispersion and core journals to define disciplines. From measurements on the rate of diffusion among the disciplines, and data on their half-lives, judgments about weeding and storage of materials could be made for library and information environments. TOMOV & MUTAFOV studied the relationship between citing and cited biomedical journals, with journals further grouped by their principal subjects into two fields, reproduction and andrology. They developed a set of informetric indicators to measure the interdisciplinarity between these two fields, using journal citing and cited behavior and journal impact factors, and assigned indexes of interdisciplinarity to each of the 20 journals involved. ZITT & BASSECOULARD (1998) developed a method for determining the degree of the internationalization of science through its journals, based on the distribution of relationships between cited and citing countries. They compared distributions for the journals from the SCI that were broadly classified in the earth and space sciences and in applied biology. MORRIS & MCCAIN studied interdisciplinary exchange in medical informatics; their study is discussed in the section on journal co-citation mapping.

Literature classification and mapping: introductory remarks. A different perspective on co-citation matrices is introduced in the earlier discussion of the conventional basis for citation analysis. The pairwise relationships between document identifiers, or their substituted properties, or their aggregates, may be interpreted as a measure of similarity of relevance or similarity of subject content, when appropriately normalized or transformed to ensure a symmetric matrix. The techniques of numerical taxonomy may then be applied to extract a hierarchical classification of the marginal units (documents, authors, journals) based on their degree of similarity with respect to the appropriately interpreted citation linkages. But more still can be done to display these interrelationships visually as maps, an area of promise to be addressed shortly. The just-described approach to co-citation analysis originates with SMALL (1973) and with MARSHAKOVA. A more restricted version applied to document references, bibliographic coupling, was advanced earlier; it is discussed below. This co-citation technique was extended to authors using the primary author, rather than the document, as the aggregated unit of analysis by H.D. WHITE & GRIFFITH. In 1990, a *JASIS* Perspectives issue (LUNIN & H.D. WHITE) featured four papers on author co-citation analysis, including a methodological paper by MCCAIN (1990). In 1991, MCCAIN used essentially the same technique on journals as the aggregate unit of analysis and carried out a journal co-citation analysis to map the field of economics through its journal literature. Studies on the mapping of literatures through co-citation analysis are discussed extensively in two *ARIST* reviews by H.D. WHITE & MCCAIN (1989; 1997a), allowing substantial abbreviation in the following discussion.

Numerical taxonomic methods and co-citation-based classification. To transform the matrix of co-citation links between pairs of units (documents, and especially authors and journals) into an hierarchical classification of units based on their degree of similarity with respect to the links, requires a sequence of decisions about appropriate measures and techniques. That the distribution of citations over documents is highly skewed has already been noted; a high proportion is uncited or negligibly cited, and consequently will not attain sufficient levels of co-citation to be of use in the present analysis. A first decision, then, is the selection of citation and co-citation thresholds necessary to ensure that an adequate similarity structure will be extracted from the raw data matrix (see BRAAM ET AL., 1988). A second decision is the choice of indices to measure degree of similarity from the raw co-citation data; different indices may differ in properties, affecting the resulting hierarchical classification to varying degrees, and especially any later mapping. Braam et al. (1988) recommend employing two indices in parallel analysis of a data set: the Jaccard Index (SOKAL & ROHLF) and Salton's cosine formula (SALTON & BERGMARK). A third decision is the choice of procedure for clustering the transformed data, that is, of cluster analysis (see MCCAIN, 1990). A useful summary here may be to outline the procedure used by ISI (see e.g., SMALL & GARFIELD; VAN RAAN, 1991). For example, in the 1984 SCI database there were c.6×10^6 unique source documents, and c.10^7 citations. Setting a threshold of 1.5 (fractional) citation counts per document reduced clusterable source documents to c.7×10^4. From these, a single linkage clustering algorithm produced some 10^4 clusters, with c.2×10^4 documents being excluded. These first-level (C1) clusters represented the core papers in small research specialties, with an average of five papers each. The C1 clusters were then clustered in the same manner to produce c.1400 C2 clusters (major fields?). These in turn produced c.180 C3 clusters (sub-disciplines?), and these in turn produced c.20 C4 clusters (disciplines?). Thus a taxonomic structure of four levels was constructed on about one-hundredth of the database on the most influential documents.

Problems for the above approach reside in the validity of the resulting classification—in the sense that it may be less an expression of the data than of the methods employed—and, relatedly, in the comparison of different classifications (cluster patterns) in a quantitative/statistical sense. SHAW investigated the statistical validity of co-citation graphs on citation data from the first quarter of SCI for 1972. He states, "The results suggest that as the co-citation threshold increases, meaningful pairwise associations are broken, related documents appear in different components, and the partition becomes statistically invalid. And, as the co-citation threshold decreases, meaningless pairwise associations are created, unrelated documents appear in the same component, and the partition becomes statistically invalid" (p. 42). A definitive analysis that tests the validity of co-citation graphs as a function of both citation frequency and co-citation strength is still to be done. A criticism of co-citation studies relates to the uncitedness/negligible citedness of most documents; it is apparent that only highly cited and co-cited documents will play a role in establishing the classification. It might be argued, of course, that it is these documents of proven influence that matter in laying out the classification structure; and further, that other documents are not really excluded, but may be connected into the structure, to an appropriate core, by using citation links. To counteract such criticisms especially as they relate to the use of science policy indicators based on co-citation analysis, ZITT & BASSECOULARD (1996) suggest two methods for improving "recall": using clustering methods that limit the number of singletons, and limiting the threshold rate to allow less-cited papers into the co-cited cores. In micro studies, they found a dramatic increase in recall; however, they caution that attention should be paid to the balance of extension and relevance of recall. Their suggestions may lead to a "reassessment of the performance of the co-citation approach for structuring scientific fields and providing related indicators not limited to the 'leading edge'. It also opens new opportunities for comparison/combination with other relational methods such as co-word analysis" (p. 223).

At this juncture, a digression from an emphasis on methods to an interesting theoretical consequence of this work may be appreciated, specifically to VAN RAAN's (1991) paper on the fractal geometry of information space as shown by co-citation clustering. The author used the online version of SCI, clustering the 1984 core papers by the 1986 citing papers. Associated with each small core of influential papers was a set of many more influenced and citing papers, in a specific research front. Above it was noted that influential cores can be aggregated into successively more inclusive higher-level cores. For example, some 10^4 specialties (correctly C1-level groups) clustered into some 1400 major fields (C2-level groups) and further into some 180 subdisciplines (C3-level groups). The corresponding (successively aggregated) research fronts can be expected to grow as the taxonomic level rises, but, considering the fractality of many natural and social phenomena, one may ask how. Van Raan looked at the rank-frequency (Zipf-type) distribution of the number of documents in research fronts for the taxonomic levels C2 and C3, and interpreted the results in terms of fractal theory. He found that the distribution for level C2 was more equitable/less concentrated, with a higher fractal dimension of 1.4, than the distribution for level C3, with fractal dimension 1.1. That is, the research fronts at the major field level were relatively more diverse in terms of their document numbers. VAN RAAN (1990) reports that the equivalent distribution for the tiny specialties (at the C1 level) was even more equitable, with a fractal dimension of 2.0; that diversity here was still greater. Stating these results in another way, as one places the whole taxonomic structure of scientific literature under a microscope, and successively increases the magnification, one repeatedly sees roughly the same pattern of numerous distinct subsets of papers appearing within existing sets of papers, but the diversity of sizes in the appearing subsets grows.

Mapping of the literature. Returning to the co-matrix of similarity/dissimilarity measures based on co-citation links for documents, authors, or journals, an alternative interpretation might be recalled: if certain conditions are met, the binary relation of dissimilarity between objects may be mapped into the binary relation of distance between objects, thereby allowing the relations in the matrix to be displayed in physical space. To achieve this, the matrix of objects and distances between them need to be placed into a dimensional framework. (This process is the converse of the procedure of plotting points on a framework of axes, e.g., finding cities on a two-dimensional map, and then finding distances between them.) In these techniques of display or visualization a central problem is the reduction in the number of dimensions necessary to accommodate all the object-object distances. The aim is to obtain one or a few two-dimensional displays without misleading distortion of the pattern in the matrix. The most common two-dimensional visualization technique employed here is multidimensional scaling or MDS (see e.g., BORG & GROENEN; TIJSSEN). Other techniques to obtain a minimal set of dimensions that accommodate the data include factor analysis and principal components analysis. The *ARIST* review by H.D. WHITE & MCCAIN (1997) on visualization of literatures covers aspects of MDS as it relates to applied informetrics in the section titled "Offline Visualizations." Future reviews on informetrics will likely include more on the visualization of literatures, either through connections to large databases of information services such as DIALOG or through front ends that manipulate downloaded textual data. The discussion below covers representative works on document, author and journal co-citation analysis, some of which are too recent to have been included in the review by H.D. White & McCain (1997). The reader should notice particularly the problems of interpretation and validation that attend numerical (objective) methods of classification. For purposes of interpretation, factor analysis is helpful, as is a good subject knowledge, of course. Ultimately one needs to study (a sample of) the documents in a cluster, ideally assigning the cluster a minimal list of title or descriptor words/phrases. Validation or rejection decisions typically involve seeking subject-expert evaluation, demonstrating conformity (or otherwise) to interpreted review articles, or comparing results with those from different methods, such as co-word analysis.

Document co-citation mapping. SCHWECHHEIMER & WINTERHAGER note that this method is especially useful in interdisciplinary areas, which tend to be poorly served by traditional classification systems. They used co-cited pairs of documents to map such highly dynamic specialties in climate research. In a typical next step, the authors plan to have their results evaluated by peer review; acceptance here is a significant step to validation. MILMAN & GAVRILOVA analyzed the citations to and co-citations between documents in chemical engineering to provide a "geography of research fronts." The results showed that the USSR had a low proportion of research front papers due to frequent citations to books and to a small number of highly cited papers. SMALL (1999) provides a brief historical review of science mapping used by ISI on its citation databases. Of relevance here are the

ISI-pioneered two-dimensional MDS maps of science using co-cited documents, and the more recent PC-based science-mapping program (SCI-Map) which allows the user to build a network of clusters of nodes from a seed document, that is, to construct a map of his/her own intellectual, or at least literature, neighborhood.

Author co-citation mapping. EOM (1998; 1999) extends his earlier works on the intellectual structure of the decision-support systems (DSS) field using author co-citation over two successive time periods, 1971-1990 and 1991-1995. From an analysis of the relevant authors' works, he interprets changes in the resulting maps as showing that DSS research had shifted from foundation studies to group DSS, model management, and design and implementation studies. ROWLANDS used 21 leading authors in the field of information policy for an author co-citation study; he combined the resulting two-dimensional MDS map with non-informetric evidence to validate his theme-based clusters of authors. He notes that the "social, collaborative and intellectual structure[s] of information policy scholarship are highly convergent" (p. 533). ELLIS ET AL. looked at the relationship between information science and information systems research through author co-citation analysis of highly cited researchers in each field. Authors with high productivity in smaller areas, such as information retrieval and user studies in information science, were aggregated into these broad areas. Unfortunately, the authors do not present their analysis visually through literature mapping techniques. H.D. WHITE & MCCAIN (1998) studied the structure of information science for three consecutive periods 1972-1979, 1980-1987, and 1988-1995, using author co-citation techniques. They mapped the entry and departure of 120 highly cited authors in the field over this time span, as well as changes in their interrelationships. Two major specialties were identified: experimental information retrieval and citation analysis. DING ET AL. performed a similar study on 39 highly cited IR researchers for two time periods, 1987-1991 and 1992-1997. They discuss difficulties with this approach; for example, in the interpretation and labeling of clusters, and in the loss of co-author collaborative relationships when only first authors are considered (as was the case with the IS databases used).

Journal co-citation mapping. Applying similar techniques in her earlier author co-citation analysis papers, MCCAIN (1998) used 36 journals (and other publications) to look at research in interdisciplinary neural networks over three consecutive periods from 1990 to 1997. She considers that the MDS maps based on journal co-citation analysis adequately reflect the field as described in the literature. MORRIS & MCCAIN performed another journal co-citation analysis, using ISI's science and social science citation databases, on medical informatics. Twenty-seven core journals in medical informatics research were identified using an appropriate subject search for medical informatics in seven DIALOG databases covering the field. The authors found evidence of interdisciplinarity; they say medical informatics "extends across hard and soft science boundaries, and its literature is used differently by authors in those arenas—the former emphasizing engineering versus information management and education issues; the latter emphasizing issues of theory versus clinical practice" (p. 465).

Map navigation. With the explosive growth of PC technology, perhaps the most exciting aspect of the construction of these literature maps is their potential for virtual navigation through the literature. SMALL's 1999 historical review of science mapping used by ISI on their citation databases discusses the SCI-Viz PC interface for navigating nested maps (SMALL, 1998). C. CHEN uses the spatial metaphor to search and navigate within a three-dimensional virtual world, such as a digital library. A number of author co-citation maps (consisting of 367 authors over three periods) were assembled to reveal the structure of the hypertext links. C. Chen also generates a document-document similarity matrix to show the semantic structure of documents in space. Of course, such exploration is not exclusively for the general user, but also for the informetrician interested in the underlying knowledge structure. In this case, there is always the problem of studying the map rather than studying the terrain, compounded by the absence of an actual validating terrain. This should not be a deterrent, but a challenge.

Criticisms of static literature mapping. According to LEYDESDORFF & WOUTERS (1999), MDS maps, even when presented as a connected sequence of temporal snapshots (perhaps in the manner of ISI's historiographs: see SMALL, 1999), still do not adequately capture what is truly essential in the study of scientific literature: its dynamic and self-developing aspect. There are several interesting issues to be explored here, but the step from one position to the other, perhaps conceptually profound, will probably be quickly accomplished by additional software. With respect to the self-developing aspect (a notion found in the work of SALTON & MCGILL but blocked from development by computational limitations), NOYONS & VAN RAAN developed a methodology of self-organized structuring of scientific fields. A data set continually reclassifies itself (self-organizes) as new data are added in time, that is, iteratively with each input set. Prospects of developing dynamic rules across iterative stages (each like an MDS snapshot) seem imminent. Mention should also be made here of KOHONEN's feature map algorithm, a nonsupervised learning method within the family of artificial neural networks for displaying documents based on weighted subject terms. LIN's paper illustrates the creation of Kohonen self-organizing feature maps in real time based on collections of up to 660 documents. With respect to the dynamic aspect,

EGGHE (1998) discusses the dynamic (time evolutionary) aspects of citation theory as reflected in the evolution of source journals and the evolution of the rankings of journals according to their impact factors. It is but a short step to view the literature (knowledge?) landscapes in ecological and evolutionary terms, perhaps lending substance to Ranganathan's maxim that the library (collection) is a living organism. Thus SCHARNHORST treats scientific communication networks as an evolving system, using the notion of "fitness landscapes," a concept from the fields of organic evolution, evolutionary algorithms, and complex optimization.

Co-Reference Analysis or Bibliographic Coupling

As stated in the introductory remarks on citation analysis, the more an informetric work focuses on the publication-publication (reference-citation) link, the more surely it may be classified in this subfield; and the more it focuses on the reference-to end of the publication link, the more it can be placed in the partially separate compartment of reference analysis. To parallel the term "co-citation analysis," "co-reference analysis" could be used; however, it would introduce terminological confusion because "coreference" is an established term in linguistics, to which informetrics will surely draw closer with time. Besides, "bibliographic coupling" is the term introduced by KESSLER in 1963 to refer to the strength of links between references in physics articles. Basically, bibliographic coupling is a technique for clustering (citing) documents according to their number of shared references. Co-citation analysis, on the other hand, is a technique for clustering (cited) documents according to their number of co-occurrences in subsequent documents' reference lists. Relative to co-citation analysis, studies using bibliographic coupling are rare. Recently however, two papers by GLÄNZEL & CZERWON used bibliographic coupling on the same data set: in 1995, to locate core documents (see below); and in 1996, to investigate the research profile of countries that had published at least 20 core documents vis-à-vis their international collaboration patterns and their citation impact. Their data set was a selection of c.4500 articles, notes, and reviews in the 1992 annual cumulation of Science Citation Index, having at least ten related papers each. These articles were termed the "core documents," counterparts of highly co-cited (and cited) documents in co-citation analysis. The core documents represent recent research-front topics. Not unexpectedly, the core documents are mostly from highly-developed countries, published in high-impact journals, and hold a key position in science communication.

Mixed co-reference and co-citation analyses. PERSSON analyzed the references of a set of 209 papers published in *JASIS* between 1986 and

1990 (via the CD-ROM version of SSCI) using both co-citation and bibliographic coupling techniques. With the co-citation technique, references were initially aggregated into same-authored works, and a map prepared of highly cited authors based on their strength of co-citation in order to outline the core literatures, or intellectual base, of the research reported. The core authors' papers were mostly post-1970, but a few classic works were included. Results accord with the original author co-citation analysis of the field of information science by H.D. WHITE & GRIFFITH, who found that information science works can be broadly divided into an informetrics group and an information retrieval group. With the bibliographic coupling technique, papers were mapped according to the number of shared authors in the references: 25% of papers shared five or more authors, and were thematically identified by title elements; these constitute the principal research fronts in the papers analyzed. This work is of additional interest in demonstrating the feasibility and value of micro-approach studies: absence of vast computer power is compensated for by personal knowledge of the literature studied. STERN used the same techniques as Persson: author co-citation analysis and bibliographic coupling on a set of documents bibliographically coupled to a single piece of work by an individual researcher, a Swedish sociologist. The reference list of this article was used to retrieve c.100 documents from 1986 to 1990 in the SSCI that shared at least three references with the initial article.

Citation-Like Fields: Acknowledgements

The acknowledgement field of publications has at least one feature in common with the citation field: identification of individuals and institutions to whom the author owes some debt. It suffers in comparison by treating a wide variety of debts (or having different communication functions) and from the absence of even a rudimentary standardization. However, one might add that on close scrutiny of citations, or to a constructivist, the first caveat may not be quite as strong, and that not too long ago (pre-ISI), citations were poorly standardized. Acknowledgements also do not appear in bibliographic records and so require analysis of the actual document: this area belongs not to bibliometrics but to informetrics. Thus the field has only recently been studied in its own right. CRONIN ET AL. (1992) classified more than 2000 acknowledgements in four top-ranked LIS journals from 1971 to 1990 into six types. They found a positive correlation between ranked acknowledged individuals and ranked cited authors for a specific domain. The authors conclude that the acknowledgement field might well be useful in performance evaluation studies. CRONIN & WEAVER-WOZNIAK discuss the development of an online acknowledgement index as a logical extension to ISI's family of citation-based products, as well as an addition to the informetrician's toolbox. They suggest the term "influmetrics" for the study of the author-acknowledgement-citation nexus of research collaborations, a term they say was coined by Elisabeth Davenport. HARSANYI suggests that the acknowledgement field, or its equivalent footnotes, can be used to reveal "subauthorship" collaboration. She notes that there are no clear criteria distinguishing co-authorship from technical assistance and that a subauthor in the natural sciences is more likely to be a co-author in the social sciences. LEWISON ET AL. analyzed another type of acknowledgement, of organizations and agencies that funded the research reported. Using the Wellcome Trust's Research Outputs Database (ROD), which records funding acknowledgements made by some 122,000 UK biomedical papers published from 1988 to 1992, the authors report the results of two questionnaire-based surveys. They found that 39% of the papers in ROD had no acknowledgements; however, most of these were supported by university and health service internal funds rather than by external funding bodies.

WORD-RELATED ANALYSES

Under this heading a number of usually separate informetric studies are gathered. In the sense that documents are long folded ribbons of words, the whole content of informetric analysis as presented might be subsumed under this heading. However, the sense of word (or phrase) may be restricted to symbol strings that are typically and immediately interpreted beyond a recognition of their function in communication so as to obtain (at least a hint of) the underlying message of the document. With appropriate knowledge, of course, something of a document's subject may be learned from reading its journal title, author's name, or reference list (HJØRLAND). But for present purposes it is not essential to develop this idea with greater precision. The first bibliographic field discussed is the language in which the document is written, because this determines the principal repertoire of symbols used, and interpretation of them to the degree required here. Then the title, descriptors, and classification codes are considered. The title is fully intrinsic to the document, while the latter two are usually extrinsic document properties, assigned from thesauri or classification schemes for bibliographic purposes. (The abstract, and indeed the full body of the document, could be included here as well, but as yet these have been little studied by informetricians.) The title receives brief attention in its own right, but the major purpose of analyses is literature classification and mapping, via co-matrices. For this purpose, the title and uncontrolled descriptor phrases will first have to be parsed into suitable units. It may be necessary to convert these units into a canonical form using techniques such as phrase permutation, collation of inflections and stemming, or even controlled substitution. The linguistic basis of this work is apparent. The present set of analyses is extended to include content analysis, a technique that has not yet achieved any prominence in informetrics and one that requires even more specialist knowledge in the interpretation of symbol strings. Needless to say, all these analyses are quantitative, even if preceded by a purely qualitative stage, and the overlap with information retrieval theory can be appreciable. It should be noted that the topic of the distribution of the frequency of word or phrase occurrence in text passages (Zipf's law) is discussed in the separate section on informetric laws.

Languages

There appear to be few informetric studies on language, at least in the period reviewed. YITZHAKI (1998) claims that between one-third to one-half of the world's social sciences research literature is published in languages other than English. To measure the relative own-language preference of researchers among U.S., UK, German, and French scholars, he selected c.50 research papers from 1990s volumes of nine sociological journals from different countries of publication, and determined the language of their c.12,000 references. Author self-citations were ignored and repeated references were counted only once. He used the measure "language self-citation" to determine the proportion of references written in the same language as the citing source, a measure analogous to journal self-citation. His results showed that in drawing on sources for their own works, the German sociologists had the strongest bias toward their own language, followed by the French, whereas UK and U.S. sociologists displayed the lowest preference for their own language. A review of suitable measures for own-language preference has recently been undertaken by EGGHE ET AL. (1999). MIGON & SKALSKA-ZLAT looked at the publication links between informetric and bibliolinguistic research, using the LISA database from 1974 to 1990. The authors found that about 25% of c.2800 publications on informetrics or bibliometrics dealt with bibliolinguistics, either directly (that is, had "language" or its derivatives in the titles) or indirectly (that is, based on a content analysis of a sample of publications). They also analyzed translated books from Index Translationum to determine which languages were most prominent in both the supply of publications for translation and in the translation from foreign languages into native languages. The authors propose the name "metrical bibliolinguistics" for such studies using informetric techniques on languages, although perhaps "metrical infolinguistics" or "linguistical informetrics" is more timely. A final comment: in the section on informetric laws below, it is noted that the frequency distribution of publications on scientific topics over languages seems to be little studied. Yet the standardly quoted example from Valentine Reilly, reported in BROOKES (1977, p. 193), displays an unusually strong convex distribution in the Bradford form of presentation, and this does seem to agree intuitively with expectations. More work is required here.

Titles

The document title appears to have received little attention, either in bibliometrics or informetrics, other than as a source of words or phrases for co-word analyses and literature mapping. An important theme among the small set of studies that qualify here concerns title length (total number of words in the title) and title informativeness or information value (number of substantive/indexable/significant-content words). Pioneer works on this topic include TOCATLIAN and BIRD & KNIGHT. BUXTON updated an earlier work by BUXTON & MEADOWS that found an appreciable increase in the title length of articles in 11 English-language journals on a range of subjects over the period 1947-1973. Adding a sample of titles from the same journals from 1984 confirmed that this trend had subsequently ceased, along with a similar trend for substantive words. In contrast, LIPETZ found that, for a single journal, *JASIS*, both the total number of words and the number of substantive words had increased slightly over the whole period, 1955 to 1995, the total words from a median value of 7 to 9 and the substantive words from a median value of 4 to 5; that is, the titles had become wordier and more informative. The ratio of substantive words to total words, however, showed moderate decline, suggesting a rise in author verbosity. A. WHITE & HERNANDEZ compared the titles of articles in old established journals in the social sciences with those in journals in the new field of counseling. In the older group they found an increase in both title lengths and title complexity over time. Title complexity was measured by an empirical formula based on the number of words and characters, somewhat like the Flesch Readability Index for text; the temporal increase in title complexity resulted more from a greater use of longer words than from the increase in title length per se. No such trends were (yet?) apparent in the titles of articles in the new field. Each of the authors reviewed leaned toward the suggestion of Bird & Knight that in rapidly expanding fields or disciplines, progressively longer titles are needed to distinguish one article from another, although beyond a certain limit, of course, more words are superfluous for this purpose. Buxton notes that this limit may even be reduced by the creation of new words to replace initial word groups.

LIPETZ also noted a parallel increase in the use of colons in *JASIS* titles: from no use at all in 1955 to use in c.46% of titles in 1995. Such a rise in "titular colonicity" has been proposed as an indicator of a rise in article scholarliness (PERRY), but is regarded as a triviality by others. However, the addition of a colon does allow for the addition of a clause to a title, a way of lengthening it without shifting to grammatical complexity or an abstract-like multiple sentence structure. Lipetz demonstrated that in *JASIS* titles, the clause following the colon adds few if any substantive words to the whole title. Some might see a correlation here between verbosity and scholarliness.

In a study of 18 English-language journals from 1940 to 1990, YITZHAKI (1997) found appreciable differences in the number of substantive words in the titles of articles from the humanities vis-à-vis articles from the natural and social sciences. Articles from the humanities did not display the general trend to more substantive words over time in the latter two groups. YITZHAKI (1994) also found a moderate positive correlation between title lengths and number of authors for articles in four fields of the natural sciences (excluding mathematics), but negligible or even negative correlation for articles from the social sciences and the humanities. He suggests that this trend may have been better expressed in the natural sciences because of higher levels of multiple authorship. If there is a causal relationship here, one wonders whether it is due to the need for a more precise specification of titles in collaborative works or to some concession to the different interests of the collaborators.

The title of an article in a scientific journal is typically regarded as an indicator of the central content of the article in the opinion of the author, somewhere between an extreme summary and a positioning of the article in the current research framework. An interesting question is how well the title of the article accurately reflects its content, or alternatively, in which segments of the article the substantive title words are most likely to occur. DIODATO (1982) examined the occurrence of title words in a number of text segments for research papers in five diverse disciplines of scholarship for the period 1960 to 1980. He noted differences between disciplines, but in general, the best reflection of title word occurrence was found in the abstract, followed in order by the first paragraph of the article, the second paragraph, and the titles of cited articles. Apart from implications for indexing, this study—along with other works reviewed above—has bearing on a general theory of titling, parallel with a theory of citing. Within the scholarly literature, there may be uniformity in titling due to long established bibliographic practice. But a perusal of titles in the wider LIS literature clearly suggests that titles may perform quite different communicative functions, a matter surely warranting quantitative analysis.

Addendum on words and full text. DIODATO (1982) discusses the types of symbol strings that qualify as words in scholarly studies in English text. In practice the issue is more complicated than selecting any set of symbols between spaces. At the basic orthographic level, see BROOKS (1998); more generally, see, for example, DI SCIULLO & WILLIAMS. There is an urgency for standardizing analytic practice before studies on full text become commonplace. As yet informetric studies on full text are few, and those now reviewed have sufficient similarities to the above studies to warrant their placement here. Of common interest are the lengths of articles (total number of words in the article) and the number of references per article. LITTLE ET AL. studied a random sample of articles from 30 journals in three natural science disciplines in 1980 and 1987. They found that the mean length of articles increased c.12% and the mean number of references per article by 18%; however, the text-reference ratio showed no significant change. An interesting finding was that single-authored papers tended to be longer than multi-authored papers, though with the same text-reference ratio. YITZHAKI & BEN-TAMAR found increases in both the length and number of references of research papers in 20 English-language journals from various fields over the period 1940 to 1990. In the same set of journals, YITZHAKI (1995) found a moderate positive correlation between the number of references and the length of articles, which held equally for the sciences, social sciences, and humanities.

Co-Word Analysis

In addition to co-citation analysis and bibliographic coupling, the structure of subject interrelationships in a set of documents may be mapped by another technique, co-word analysis. This technique uses the co-occurrence of the same words or phrases in a chosen field in two documents to measure the relationship between the two documents. Once a measure for the strength of the relationship between all pairs of documents has been established, then the techniques used in co-citation analysis (e.g., cluster analysis, factor analysis, multidimensional scaling) can be applied to determine and map the required structure. Given that the chosen word-related field is universally present, co-word analysis treats all articles, unlike co-citation analysis which excludes at a minimum the uncited articles, and is therefore more inclusive of its data. Co-word analysis was largely developed by French researchers, but the technique is now used worldwide. A useful guide is LEYDESDORFF's (1994) review in English of *La Scientométrie* (CALLON ET AL.), a volume of the French monographic series *Que sais-je?* The volume devotes a chapter to the discussion of the co-word technique used as an indicator or measure of the scientific communication process. COURTIAL, one of the authors of the monograph, demonstrates the use of co-word analysis on the field of scientometrics itself. Because the review by H.D. WHITE & MCCAIN (1997) presents numerous examples of literature mapping using co-word analysis (see also TIJSSEN), and of combined co-word and co-citation analyses, the following discussion includes only representative works, especially those too recent to appear in the review by H.D. White & McCain.

Analysis of title words. COURTIAL ET AL. applied co-word analysis to normalized titles in a family of patents in the DERWENT database. The clusters that resulted from the use of LEXIMAPPE, a dedicated package for co-word analysis, were easily identifiable technological themes. Co-word analysis gave both qualitative information (themes and their word change over time) and quantitative information (importance of the themes).

Combined analyses of title words and classification codes. BHATTACHARYA ET AL. constructed co-matrices of both title words and classification codes for c.14,000 articles from 22 journals classified by the SCI as on Condensed Matter Physics (CMP). The articles for a specified time period were downloaded from the INSPEC database. Classification codes were based on the *Physics and Astronomy Classification Scheme* used in the INSPEC database. Fifty high-frequency title keywords and 50 classification (theme) codes were selected for the co-word analysis and co-classification analysis, respectively. Seventeen structurally equivalent blocks based on similarity of positions were determined for title keywords and eight for the classification codes. The authors showed that the macro-level features helped in understanding the micro-level structure of the discipline of CMP.

Analysis of descriptors. AMUDHAVALLI & RAGHAVAN used LEXIMAPPE to map the literature of information retrieval (IR), using five-year samples downloaded from the LISA database from 1975 to 1990. Co-word analysis was performed on high-frequency keywords taken from the descriptor field. The major IR clusters were identified and their movements over time were tracked. Results suggest that IR has not appreciably changed in overall structure since 1975, since most of the clusters persisted through the period and remained in the same map quadrants. GRIVEL ET AL. (1995) used the SDOC system (similar to the LEXIMAPPE system) to map the literature of social history in the German bibliographical database, SOLIS. Co-word analysis was carried out on descriptor terms to produce a classification and a mapping of research themes, that is, keyword clusters. RUIZ-BAÑOS ET AL. (1999a; 1999b) used a data set for the field of archeology over the period 1980 to 1993, from the Francis database. The articles were divided into 12 time periods and, using co-word analysis via the LEXIMAPPE system on the descriptor field, an archeological network map was produced. COULTER

ET AL. mapped publications on software engineering using co-word analysis on descriptor terms from the *ACM Computing Classification System*. Their mapping system, Content Analysis and Information Retrieval (CAIR), can also be used on a corpus of textual data that contains descriptors or index terms such as those used in their study; it can also generate descriptor terms from a text corpus.

Combined analyses of several word fields. NOYONS & VAN RAAN used informetric mapping techniques to develop a new methodology to accommodate the self-organizing of scientific fields, that is, allowing variables such as journal categories or document titles to generate a subject structure that establishes meaningful subfields. Their approach involved four major steps: (1) using the co-occurrence of INSPEC classification codes in documents from the field of neural network research for establishing a coarse overview map, then using the co-occurrence of keywords (from titles, abstracts, controlled terms in the descriptor field, and uncontrolled terms in the identifier field) to make detailed maps of the different subfields; (2) determining the interrelations between the different clusters (subfields) based on the similarities of the keywords and classification codes; (3) using co-word techniques to construct separate maps of each subfield; and (4) using the overall structure of the field and the detailed subfield maps to monitor the dynamic features of the entire research field over time.

NOYONS ET AL. provide an example of the combination of several types of co-analyses to establish literature structures, supplemented with additional informetric measures of performance. They studied the research scope and performance of the University Centre for Micro-Electronics in Leuven, Belgium. Mapping the literature produced by the Centre was accomplished using the co-occurrences of classification codes, as used by the INSPEC database. This produced a map of 18 subdomains. A more detailed map was obtained by zooming in on the 18 subdomains through the creation of co-word maps. A range of informetric performance indicators was then established for the "map objects": number and percentage of publications published in a year or range of years, number and percentage of citations received by all publications during a time period, average number of citations for publications from all institutes, etc. One can easily imagine informetric maps becoming not only dynamic, but also information-rich—complex weather maps, as it were, for guiding S&T policy.

KOSTOFF ET AL. used the Database Tomography (DT) textual analysis system to extract multiword phrases, and to give frequencies and phrase proximities, from large textual databases. They applied this to the field of hypersonic/supersonic flow (HSF), deriving their dataset from the Science Citation Index and Engineering Index A&I services. Informetric analyses of authors, journals, institutions, and citation data supplemented the DT results to derive "technical intelligence" from the HSF literature (p. 445). The DT system goes beyond the classical co-word analysis approach of CALLON ET AL. by allowing semantic relationships in full text to be exploited. In addition, DT can be used on nonformal (e.g., nonjournal) literature where citing is irregular or absent and co-citation analysis is not suitable. However, the full capability of DT was not exploited because only words from the title and abstract were used in this study.

Analysis of words in full text. LEYDESDORFF (1997) analyzed the full texts of 17 articles in biochemistry using co-word analysis. Extensive grammatical and other rules were invoked to limit the number of words and their occurrences for co-analysis, for example, by equating singulars and plurals, replacing comparatives and superlatives by the basic form of the adjective, and excluding words occurring fewer than three times. The resulting data set of c.28,500 word occurrences over c.1300 words was further processed to provide a matrix (for each of the 17 articles) of four sections typically found in research papers: introduction, materials and methods, results, and conclusion. These matrices were factor-analyzed into three factors: observational, theoretical, and methodological. Using the distribution of words over the three factors (or dimensions) for all but one article worked at the individual article level; at the level of the data set, the structure was no longer present. Words changed position as well as meaning among the three dimensions from one text to the another, even within the narrow subject area of the data set; hence, Leydesdorff's title, "Why Words and Co-Words Cannot Map the Development of the Sciences."

Combined co-word and co-citation analyses. BRAAM ET AL. (1991a) mapped scientific and technological R&D specialties, using citation data from SciSearch for co-citation analysis, and subject indexing terms from Chemical Abstracts and Biological Abstracts for co-word analysis. The latter included terms from both the descriptor and identifier fields, and subject classification codes. Their study shows that co-citation analysis does map research specialties where a consensus exists among researchers; however, where a consensus is lacking, specialties may fragment into several different clusters in such maps. The use of co-word analysis, in combination, does improve the identification of the subject content of the clusters. In a later study, again combining co-word and co-citation analysis, BRAAM ET AL. (1991b) focused on dynamic aspects of scientific research. Their data set consisted of publications on the Rydberg specialty from the INSPEC A&I service. They used the title, abstract, classification code, descriptor, and identifier terms for co-word analyses, and citations (to nearly all of the publications) from SciSearch for co-citation analysis. To show the dynamics of research topics, they charted the temporal evolution of individual words.

This showed which words emerged, persisted, or disappeared over the chosen period, 1974-1986. Again, by combining the two techniques, they were able to obtain a more complete picture of the dynamics of the research, including judgments about topics of research from both authors' and indexers' points of view.

Highly Interpreted Word Analyses: Content Analysis

In measuring and displaying the similarity of documents by the various co-matrix techniques, the common possession of identical strings of symbols (intrinsic or assigned) determines the outcome. The only interpretation required is a recognition of the strings' communicative function, and possibly a parsing for suitable subunits, which relies on general grammatical knowledge. It is after the analysis that higher-level interpretation is made, with factors and clusters assigned symbol strings that are read for subject content; in the case of co-word analysis, of course, the reading may be made directly. (In the other component of informetrics not concerned with charting specific subjects, this step is not necessary.) The attractive objectivity of informetric methods starts to be lost when specific knowledge is applied before the mechanical analysis, as for example, in (quantitative) content analysis. Here symbol strings are either initially privileged for analysis from their subject content alone, or worse, specialist subject knowledge justifies the substitution of one string with another: identical strings (homographs) are mapped to different strings, or different strings (synonyms) are mapped into the same strings, so the mapping may be highly context-dependent. The problem is that analysts with different prior knowledge are likely to make different judgments here: unless analysts (coders, indexers, classifiers) are very similar with respect to prior knowledge, then despite voluminous rationales and guidelines, the reliability of evaluations may be low. The problem can be at least bypassed by separating the analyst from the coder/indexer/classifier, and assuming the latter to perfectly represent the consensus view of the specialist community and of the author—as for example, when one reads descriptors for their subject content (e.g., BIERBAUM ET AL.) or substitutes journal titles with subject codes (e.g., KATZ & HICKS, 1995). In an interesting variant on the latter for multidisciplinary journals, subject codes are substituted for the journals in the reference lists of papers (GLÄNZEL ET AL.). This problem is important in quantitative content analysis, as is illustrated by the four studies below, selected because of their use of other conventional informetric measures.

CRONIN ET AL. (1997), in a study of journals dealing with women's studies, performed a content analysis of 135 editorial statements in three journals. They recognized six principal dimensions (e.g., collectivism, legitimation) in pieces of text within the editorials and considered their distribution across the three journals. Of present interest is not the minimal quantitative analysis, but the extensive explication (quasi-definition, examples) necessary to support the assignment of the six labels—which is probably still inadequate for all but the subject special-ist. Needless to say, even this level of objectivity is a significant gain for a rather polemical topic, and is the justification for content analysis in the pioneering studies of KRIPPENDORFF (see also WEBER). MAR-TENS & SARETZKI analyzed textual data associated with more than 5500 conferences on biotechnology into some 70 codes, which were then grouped into five dimensions (e.g., fields of knowledge, areas of applications). In contrast to the previous study, little information is given about the coding or dimension assignment procedures; however, an extensive quantitative analysis was made (using a co-dimension correlation matrix, principal components analysis, and a correspon-dence analysis mapping) to determine the main themes of these confer-ences, and their relationships to variables such as organizing institu-tions, year, etc. PERITZ (1995) selected a group of c.70 papers dealing with the correlation between job satisfaction and job performance and assigned them to three content dimensions. She conducted a set of correlation analyses that established appreciable differences in the-matic content between groups of papers. The goal of this work was to establish homogeneous sets of papers for a better analysis of citer motivation, a goal that emphasizes the connection between the present topic and citation-content and citation-context analyses. In the former case, the statement invoking the citation link is interpreted, especially to identify the concepts for which the paper is cited; in the latter case, the wider context of the citation link is interpreted, with the aim of understanding broadly how the cited paper is used in this text (e.g., whether it supports an argument, offers additional data). Peritz notes that there is an "element of subjectivity" in the assignment of variables here, but found full agreement between the independent evaluations of the two experts in her study (typically agreements of even 75% are considered acceptable). DAVIS & LIPSON analyzed c.240 articles in the first ten volumes of a journal on family therapy to establish the main themes and topics of the journal. In addition to using indexer-provided subject terms from a relevant database, and other informetric indica-tors, they described a linguistic-analytical procedure for the content analysis of title words and phrases, which moves toward levels of replicability typical of informetric analyses. Only in the final assign-ment of terms to broad themes did they again adopt the (consensus) evaluation of subject experts.

What may be considered undue attention to a type of analysis not typically regarded as informetric is justified by reminding the reader of the ultimate importance of subject content in document analysis, of the growth of full-text databases, and of continuing gains in both computer power and computational linguistics. The impediments to a fully algorithmized content analysis may be appreciable, but they are not prohibitive. Gains here would allow informetrics to make progress in a number of areas, for example, in explaining the subject-related informetric laws of Bradford and Zipf. More generally, such an analysis could, for example, enhance the approach of SWANSON & SMALHEISER in detecting isolated but potentially complementary research areas and thereby promoting scientific discovery.

AUTHOR-RELATED ANALYSES

Apects of the analysis of the author field of documents are discussed in the separate section on informetric laws, viz. the frequency distribution of publications over authors (Lotka's law), and of authors over publications. But through the author field of publications, additional properties can be brought into focus for informetric analysis, either by direct use of information in the document, or by use of information from other sources. Most prominent of the intrinsic properties are institutional affiliation and regional and country addresses, and in some cases, data pertaining to an author's temporary, previous, or new location. Among extrinsic properties are gender, professional training, and research prizes. Of course, gender information is often apparent if authors' full names are listed, and some serials provide author profiles. By substituting any of these properties for author names, and aggregating documents by like values, frequency distributions can be obtained and treated in the same manner as authors. The output of publications from institutions and from geographic regions can be used as measures of research performance, along with the aggregated citations received. Much of this work in S&T fields has an applied scientometric orientation and is not reviewed here.

More exclusively informetric studies often arise from analyses of the publications of single journals. A recent representative is LIPETZ's analysis of authorship of the journal *JASIS* (and its predecessor) for its 50th anniversary. Using basic author-field data, he found that the number of authors in *JASIS* grew slightly faster than the number of papers published because multiple authorship had become more common. In addition, individual authors were increasingly likely to produce multiple papers. Using institutional and geographic address information, he found that academic affiliation of authors shifted from c.25% in 1955 to c.90% in 1995; in 1955, the nonprofit corporation had the greatest author affiliation (c.32%). In 1995, some 40% of authors with academic affiliation belonged to LIS schools and some 40% to other academic departments, but only 10% had academic library affiliations. Further, representation of authors from different countries increased substantially. Finally, using first or minor name listings, and/or additional external sources, he showed that in 1995 the percentage of female authors was 34%, up from c.10% in 1965; the proportion of papers that had any female authors at all was c.43%; and collaborative male-and-female authorship had risen to c.19%.

The many:many mapping between documents and authors leads to the construction of co-author matrices, which display the degree of collaboration of authors on a set of documents. (The same matrices could be extended to measure and map the degree of author similarity through their publications, a development that seems better suited to aggregating of authors into institutions or geographic regions.) HARSANYI reviews the literature on collaborative authorship on scholarly documents. Some 70 empirical studies are listed in tabular form, with information on the environment of each study, the additional variables studied, and the type of analysis undertaken. She also discusses the persistent issue of how best to apportion authorship credit. Because of the complex relationship between productivity and collaboration, Harsanyi suggests coupling informetric measures with other techniques. A brief account of more recent studies on author collaboration than those reviewed by Harsanyi follows.

In the first three studies, data sets are large, of the order of tens of thousands of papers, and are of at least a decade's duration; data sets are taken either from SCI or from large subject bibliographies. KATZ & HICKS (1997) found that collaboration with an author from the same or another domestic institution resulted in an increase in the average impact (i.e., the average number of citations received per paper) of about 0.75 citations, while collaborating with an author from a foreign institution resulted in an increase in the average impact of about 1.6 citations. Further increases in citation rates were found with an additional (third) author from either a home or a foreign institution, to average increases of 1.6 and 3.2 citations, respectively. KRETSCHMER proposed a model of scientific collaboration based on a single nonlinear function for both two- and three-dimensional collaborative network patterns. The latter pattern was used successfully to model co-authorship (collaboration) networks in both the international and Indian medical literature (KUNDRA & KRETSCHMER), leading the authors to ask whether their model has more general validity. A fourth study by MELIN & PERSSON used c.23,000 papers from the 1993 SCI to examine the co-authorship patterns of 22 Nordic universities. The authors found no major differences between the 22 universities of various sizes with respect to internal, national, or international co-authorships; however, over one-half of all the papers did have external collaborators (national or international). In a further study on research collaboration in universities, MELIN compared the collaboration patterns of 49 northern European and American universities. He found that American universities had more national and less international co-authorship than northern European universities. Within the selected European universities, there was no appreciable difference with respect to the national and scientific size. BORDONS ET AL. used both SCI and SSCI from 1990 to 1996 to determine interdisciplinary collaboration among nine schools in one Spanish university; the study also showed an increase in collaboration over this period at all levels: intra-university, extra-university, and international. In this study, intra-university collaboration was established by extrinsic data on 68 funded research projects associating the authors (project leaders) and the publications.

TIME AND GROWTH STUDIES

The importance of time as a determinant of the features of science and of its literature was recognized in the earliest precursor studies of bibliometrics (e.g., COLE & EALES). Perhaps the most obviously affected feature is the size of the literature produced in a subject area, which is the main focus of this section. However, since it is the description, and especially the mathematical description of the time curves that is of interest, the discussion has applicability to other size measures, such as the number of scientists, authors, or journals. The very rapid growth in the size of the scientific literature up until the 1970s (see e.g., PRICE, 1986) has now substantially slowed. In a study of 190 journals founded before/in 1950, ARCHIBALD & LINE found not only reduced growth in the annual output of articles through the late 1970s, but also an even lower growth rate and possible decline thereafter. The total number of journals was still increasing in the late 1980s but at a much slower rate. This effect has not been universal, however. For example, LIPETZ found the number of articles in *JASIS* to have grown exponentially from 1955 to 1995. There has been a widespread interest in the growth of the literature for many years, and B. M. GUPTA ET AL. (1997) remark that as many as 18 different research fields in the social sciences have produced works on the topic. Yet apparently few researchers have studied the growth of scientific specialties from the point of view of precise description and mathematical modeling (B.M. GUPTA ET AL., 1995), the approach addressed here.

It is convenient to divide current studies into those using simpler standard models, and those developing and/or using more complex models. In the first group, early candidates for describing the cumulative literature profile with time were the linear model and, not suprisingly given early growth rates, the exponential model (see TABAH). Again, unsurprisingly, models to accommodate an S-shaped profile were soon added to the list. The model commonly adopted is the logistic curve, which is backed by intuitively appealing premises, wide occurrence, and/or convention. However, as often pointed out, many functions can produce S-shaped curves, and the logistic curve has disadvantages (see e.g., B.M. GUPTA ET AL., 1995; HALL; WOL-FRAM ET AL.), such as convergence problems in the estimation of parameters. In addition, the inflection point is fixed midway between the initial and final asymptotes, which is often unrealistic; for the latter case, the Gompertz curve is a more suitable model. These and other common models, the Ware function and the power curve, were studied by EGGHE & RAVICHANDRA RAO (1992b). The power curve places an exponent on the variable time; when this is unity, the linear model results. EGGHE (1994a) offers a slightly improved analysis. Egghe & Ravichandra Rao (1992b) investigated the forms of two types of rate functions for each of the curves, and examined 20 different data sets to find the best match to the qualitatively distinct rate function profiles. They found that the power model with a positive exponent, generating a concave but subexponential curve, best fitted their scientific and technical data sets, and that the Gompertz curve, generating an S-shaped curve, best fitted their social science and humanities data sets. HOOD found that the power model provided a good description of the growth of the literature in the rapidly growing field of fuzzy set theory from its inception in 1965 until 1993. HALL found growth rates in the cumulative literatures for two recent and rapidly growing areas in the geosciences from c.1960 to 1980 to be overall concave. With reference to Egghe & Ravichandra Rao (1992b), these are probably best described by the power model; however, Hall chose to express each in terms of their annual production (growth rates), with the best description being pairs of overlapping logistic curves. Wolfram et al. looked at growth rates in 20 subject-specific databases covering science and technology, the social sciences, and the arts and humanities, for the period 1968 to 1987. They tested data against the linear, exponential, and power models, but the logistic model was not tested because of fitting difficulties. The power model (which was introduced in this paper) gave the best fits, and the exponential the worst. The authors comment that the phase of general exponential growth in science and scholarship is clearly over. SU & HAN suggest that the substitution of different time-dependent functions for the positive growth rate constant in the exponential equation would generate a variety of commonly used growth curves. They propose using a polynomial function whose parameters could be obtained by multilinear regression to give good fits to different types of data set; however, the model remains to be tested on actual data sets.

Growth models based on more sophisticated premises have been developed, tested, and investigated. One class of models derives from work in the field of diffusion of innovations, and includes the earlier models of Bass and Mansfield. JAIN & GARG and GARG ET AL. found the Bass model gave good fits to the S-shape cumulative production of papers on Indian laser research from 1968 to 1988, and of papers on Indian solar power research from 1970 to 1990. Based on similar premises, SHARMA ET AL. developed a new model, an exponential-logistical equation, which B. M. GUPTA ET AL. (1997) compared to the two previous models for sets of publication data from four scientific and technical fields over a 70- to 90-year span. A variant of the model, with two parameters and an additional weighting factor, was found to give superior matching in all cases.

A second class of models derives from work in population ecology and epidemic theory. The Lotka-Volterra equations are a set of differential equations that chart the time course of the size of populations of different animal species, subject to number changes from birth, death, immigration, and so on. Most importantly, the equations are coupled to include the effects of competition, predation, etc. between species. BRUCKNER ET AL. adapted these equations, substituting subject fields for species, and scientists for animals in order to accommodate, for example, competition between subjects for scientists, interfield mobility, and recruitment of new workers. Further, they allowed for the formation of new fields (rapid evolutionary diversification in the ecological model?) and for a stochastic element in their model. The model can simulate a wide variety of growth and decline profiles for the numbers of scientists in (interacting) research fields, but its application to real data remains to be tested. There has also been renewed interest in the related epidemic model of scientific dynamics, developed by both GOFFMAN & NEWILL and NOWAKOWSKA. In this development, animal predators and prey change guise to disease infectives and susceptibles, and then again, to practicing scientists/authors and (inspired) recruits/readers. An additional category of immunes or removals, those uninspired to join or even to depart, completes the cast. The set of differential equations for this model satisfactorily described several literatures in medicine and in mathematics in Goffman's early work (KRÖBER). A consequence of the coupling between key variables in this class of models, expressed as difference equations, introduces a nonlinearity, which suggests the possibility of deterministic chaos in the growth of numbers of papers and scientists. TABAH looked first at the broad cumulative pattern of the literature on superconductivity; it displayed slow linear growth from its inception in 1966 until a seminal article in 1986, after which growth was exponential to the early 1990s when the first signs of a slowing appeared. However, on a week-by-week basis, the output was quite erratic, with growth occurring in fits and starts; at this level Tabah found the literature growth to display typical chaotic behavior.

Two comments serve as a summary for the above brief review. First, and more generally, the purpose of the modeling and data-fitting exercise must be kept in mind: whether a model (equations) should simply fit the data closely, perhaps for summarization or prediction, or whether it should also uncover/explain the principal underlying mechanisms (the goal of the latter group of models above). Second, the dynamic nature of information systems is emphasized; TABAH notes the relative absence of studies in information science where time is treated as a key variable. Whether in the study of obsolescence, or of informetric laws, or in the above studies—which in a sense supplement the other two—a feature of current informetric research has been an interest in the key role of time.

INFORMETRIC LAWS

An important subfield of informetrics, of long standing and of considerable sophistication, is the study of the informetric laws. In terms of the content-of-informetrics model adopted above, the principal properties of interest are the publication author(s), the publication journal, and the text words themselves; but, as noted below, the laws apply also to other informetric properties. Here the subfield is treated as a pure science, in the constructing-a-framework-of-indicators-and-laws component of informetrics, whereas applications are largely ignored. However, mindful of retaining a wider readership, mathematical symbolism has been minimized. An introduction is provided that the moderately informed reader may bypass. Earlier reviews include LOCKETT, sections of H.D. WHITE & MCCAIN (1989, pp. 124-137) and TAGUE-SUTCLIFFE (1994, pp. 152-168), and selected sections from EGGHE & R. ROUSSEAU (1990b, pp. 291-384). A very brief contemporary course might consist of R. ROUSSEAU & S. ROUSSEAU (1993), followed by OLUIĆ-VUKOVIĆ (1995), and closing with the comments of BURRELL (1994).

Background

The informetric laws originate with the discoveries of LOTKA, BRADFORD, and ZIPF (1936; 1949). Lotka, a biomathematician, investigated the literature output of a sample of chemists, and found that the number of authors who had published a specific number of papers was approximately equal to the inverse square of that number multiplied by the number of authors who had published one paper only, that is, setting $f(y)$ as the number of authors publishing y papers, he found that $f(y) \approx 1/y^2 \times f(1)$. (A purely illustrative example: if 1000 authors published one paper each on a subject, then c.250 published two papers each, c.111 published three papers each, and so on.) Bradford, a chemist turned librarian, was interested in the problem of the scatter of papers on a scientific subject through the scientific journals. He found that if the journals were first ranked in order of their numbers of papers on a subject, and then divided into, say, three groups with an equal number of papers, the numbers of journals in successive groups grew in the ratio of $1 : k : k^2$. (A purely illustrative example: if 3000 papers on a subject were found in 800 journals, then the ratio of (ranked) journals, in successive groups of 1000 papers, was 42 : 158 : 600, or approximately $1 : 3.8 : 3.8^2$.) Bradford also supported this statement with his two sets of tabulated data plotted as the cumulative number of papers versus the cumulative number of ranked journals. Zipf, a philologist with a wide interest in J-shaped distributions, developed an observation made earlier by ESTOUP and others on word occurrences. He found that if words are ranked in decreasing order of their number of occurrences in a sufficiently long stretch of text, then the number of occurrences $y(r)$ of a word of rank r is proportional to its rank r, or $y(r) \propto 1/r$. (Again, illustrating: if the word of rank 1, for example "the," has 1000 occurrences in a stretch of text, then the word of rank 2, for example "of," occurs c.500 times, the word of rank 3, for example "and," occurs c.330 times, and so on.)

A first question is: what do these three findings have in common? Let us first recast them into standard modern terminology, that of a collection of sources (authors, journals, or word-types) producing items (papers, papers again, or occurrences). What they have in common is the form of the distribution of numbers of items over number of sources, which, when appropriately displayed, is variously described as extremely right-skewed, reversed-J-shaped, or quasi-hyperbolic. This is clearly shown in the sequences of steadily falling or rising numbers in the illustrations above. This shape contrasts strongly with the bell-shaped, normal or Gaussian distribution, seemingly so prevalent and on which so much of contemporary statistics, or at least of its application, is based (MICCERI). This reversed-J frequency distribution occurs in additional informetric phenomena, for example, in the distribution of citations (items) awarded to authors (sources), which is typically even more right-skewed than the publications of authors (STEPHAN & LEVIN). It also commonly appears in other sociological phenomena (see the Haitun-Kunz debate: HAITUN, 1982b, 1982c; KUNZ), and even more widely (see, e.g., FOLINSBEE; HARA & OKAYAMA; WALTERS), with connections to fractal theory (SCHROEDER). Why, then, does the title "informetric laws"—or even the slightly better "informetric law" (BOOKSTEIN, 1990a)—persist? After all, other mathematically described regularities occur in informetrics (see, e.g., ZUNDE). Furthermore, it is moot whether Zipf's law is strictly informetric, or at least bibliometric under the adopted definition (BROADUS). Items can translate to publications or citation-links, and sources to the values of publication properties (or quasi-objects) such as the-contained-in-journal or the-author for the other two laws; but this can be done for Zipf's law only with title words or descriptors as sources. The answer is partly an accident of history sustained by convention, and partly because each demonstrates a specific form of presentation of the underlying distribution, a matter addressed shortly.

Regularities and laws. A next question concerns the use of the term "law(s)." It is best to first introduce the concept of a regularity, a typically occurring and apparently invariant pattern in natural (including social) phenomena (when appropriately displayed). Once recognized, it may be described in words, albeit inadequately, or described mathematically, with at least better precision. Later this description may be improved still further, especially as more is learned about the regularity. The term "law" typically refers to a mathematical (or quasi-mathematical) description of a regularity, especially if it also involves some deductive steps from plausible postulates. A possible danger is that the description thereby acquires a status superior to that of the regularity that provides its raison-d'être. Thus, Lotka, Bradford, and Zipf discovered (instances of) significant regularities. Lotka gave an acceptably modern, albeit approximate, mathematical description of his regularity that remains today as (the classic) Lotka's law (although the use of "law" did not originate until 1949, according to POTTER). Bradford described his regularity in a somewhat unusual manner, subsequently developed into a more conventional mathematical form by LEIMKUHLER. Bradford also presented his data in the form of (pictorial) graphs, which were subsequently translated into conventional mathematical form by BROOKES (1968). Unfortunately, the two descriptions and their derivations differ slightly, with Leimkuhler taking Bradford's groups to be "successive" sets of papers, and Brookes as "successively more inclusive" sets of papers (see EGGHE, 1991a). Consequently, the same regularity acquires two pairs of descriptions, Bradford's verbal law (sequence of ratios) and the classic Leimkuhler law (equation), and Bradford's graphical law (plotted graphs) and Brookes's law (equation). Finally, Zipf's broad description of his regularity, Zipf's law, proved to be unacceptably inaccurate too often, and the regularity is now more typically described by a better equation derived by MANDELBROT (1954), known as (the classic) Mandelbrot law. The important point here is that in the period under review, an awareness has developed that too much attention has been given to the laws, and insufficient attention has been given to the regularities. It is the regularities that researchers are trying to understand, and their mathematical descriptions are more correctly hypotheses—likely incomplete, hopefully improving—toward this end (e.g., BASU, 1995; BOOKSTEIN, 1990a; BURRELL, 1988a; SAAM & REITER).

Presentation forms. It has often been noted (e.g., most recently by OLUIĆ-VUKOVIĆ, 1995) that a general slowness to accept and exploit the underlying unity of the informetric laws, at least in empirical studies, derives in part from differences in the way data, and consequently mathematical descriptions, have been presented. It is important to outline these forms of presentation. They apply to more than the informetric distributions, of course, but within this context it is often simpler to refer to them by the name of their originator (see WILSON, 1995).

(a) The *size-frequency form:* in this form of presentation the number of items produced by a source, y (for yield of items), is placed on the abscissa (X-axis), and the number of sources producing a specific yield of items, f (for frequency), is placed on the ordinate (Y-axis). Lotka developed his law in this presentation form: f vs. y.

(b) The *size-cumulative-frequency form* of presentation is obtained by summation (or integration) of f(y) over successive y values from maximum to minimum yield; this gives F(y), the number of sources that produce at least the yield value y. This form of presentation is: F vs. y. A brief name for this form of presentation might be Pareto, after the Italian economist who was the discoverer of another J-shaped regularity (PARETO); however, this is not typical practice in informetrics (but see WAGNER-DÖBLER, 1997). The principal use of this presentation form in informetrics normally resides in equating the rank of a source with respect to item production, r(y), with F(y). For example, if 10 sources produce a yield ≥ 5 items, then the rank(s) of the sources producing 5 items each is 10.

(c) The *rank-frequency form* can be immediately obtained from the above by transposing the axes, that is, r vs. y becomes y vs. r. It is in this form that Zipf presented his data, and Zipf's law and Mandelbrot's law are both stated. The initial part of this statement is not strictly correct historically. ZIPF (1936, p.vi, pp.40-44, Plates I-III) first presented his word-occurrence data in size-frequency form, though with transposed axes; only thereafter (pp.44-47, Plate IV) did he acknowledge the rank-frequency form. This presentation attained prominence in ZIPF (1949). A more detailed account is provided in R. ROUSSEAU & ZHANG.

(d) The *rank-cumulative-frequency form* of presentation may be obtained, for example, by summation (or integration) of the yield per rank, y(r), over successive r values, from maximum (i.e., top) to minimum (i.e., bottom) rank, alternatively and confusingly, from low r values to high r values; this gives Y(r) vs. r. On the ordinate is placed Y, the cumulative number of items from the most prolific source to and including the source with rank r (alternatively, from the r most productive sources). This form of presentation is: Y vs. r. Bradford presented his data graphically in this form of presentation, and Brookes' law and Leimkuhler's law are both stated in this form.

(e) The *equal-production-groups form* of presentation follows from the above. This accommodates Bradford's verbal law. On the ordinate Y, g equal groups of items are marked off, that is, with Y_T/g items each where Y_T is the total yield. Given a function $Y(r)$, or correctly its transpose $r(Y)$, the number of ranks (sources) producing the successive equal-production groups is obtained. As noted above, this may be in terms of distinct successive intervals, as Bradford's verbal law states, or in terms of overlapping successive intervals. This final form of presentation is unusual in that one reads from the ordinate to the abscissa, the reverse of the approach used above.

Four additional comments are essential. First, one or both axes may be expressed as a proportion of the relevant total variable (i.e., normalized or relativized or fractionalized). For example, in the size-frequency case, where F_T is the total number of sources, the ordinate becomes f/F_T; this can also be interpreted as the probability of obtaining a specific yield. (The size-frequency presentation of a continuous probability distribution is termed the density function, and of its discrete counterpart, the probability function.) Second, the size-cumulative-frequency form typically employed in statistics is constructed in the reverse order to that used in informetrics to obtain ranks. (In this case, the size-cumulative-frequency presentation of a continuous function normalized and read as probability is termed the distribution function, and of its discrete counterpart, the cumulative function.) When this reverse ranking approach is carried through to the rank-cumulative frequency (Bradford) form of presentation, and the axes are doubly normalized, the well-known Lorenz form of presentation is produced. Third, rank numbers do not have to equate to the cumulative sum of the numbers of ordered sources, but only preserve the ordering. Without a standarized method of assignment, however, little of interest can be done mathematically in the rank-frequency forms of presentation. Fourth, for the informetric distributions in particular, one or both axes may be logarithmically transformed to better display the data and/or for parameter estimation. Both axes are transformed with presentations (a)-(c), and the abscissa only with (d). This is due to the shape of the informetric regularities, which are now considered.

The informetric distribution. The key features of the form of the informetric regularities known prior to this review are now briefly summarized. To some degree, an unfamiliarity with how to handle their underlying distribution may have contributed to the multitude of presentation forms just surveyed. First, the broad outline of the distribution is considered:

(a) In the Lotka, Pareto, and Zipf presentations, the form of the distribution is extremely skewed, almost hyperbolic in appearance with very long tails along the axes.

(b) Logarithmically transforming both axes converts the quasi-hyperbola into something like a straight line, of which the (negative) slope provides the exponent of the hyperbola. For example, for Lotka's law, $f(y) \propto 1/y^2 = y^{-2}$, and so, $\ln f(y) \propto -2 \ln y$.

(c) Also, recalling the summation (integration) $\rightarrow$ transposition $\rightarrow$ summation (integration) approach adopted across the forms of presentation above, with minimal calculus one can immediately obtain crude approximations for the Pareto form: $r(y) = F(y) \propto y^{-1}$; for the Zipf form: $y(r) \propto r^{-1}$; and for the Bradford form: $Y(r) \propto \ln r$. The rationale for logarithmically transforming only the abscissa in the last case, plotting against $\ln r$, is clear.

(d) Specifying the equations in detail, however, raises the issue of what correctly constitutes equivalence between the different presentation forms, a matter discussed in BOOKSTEIN (1990a), R. ROUSSEAU (1990b), and EGGHE (1991a), and returned to below.

(e) A surprising feature of the informetric regularities is that for commonly found values of the Lotka exponent, as the (absolute value of the) exponent decreases, the second and even the first moments of the distribution become infinite. This means that the variance, and even the mean, of a sample grows with the sample size, and cannot converge to population parameters. That is, the central limit theorem is not followed, and familiar statistical thinking must be abandoned (HAITUN, 1982b; YABLONSKY, 1985).

(f) The distribution appears to be broadly stable with time; consequently this factor was rather neglected until the late 1980s.

Second, the tails of the distribution are considered:

(a) In contrast to most uses of the normal distribution, it is the tails of this distribution that contain the data of most interest. Lotka was interested in the high proportions of a population of chemists who produced only one or a few publications. Typically, it is the top-producing sources that are of interest, promoting a Zipf form of presentation. Likewise in compiling subject collections, the interest is in high producers, but the Bradford form of presentation is more useful.

(b) Unfortunately, the data in the distribution tails are troublesome. In the Lotka form, the high-producing region (right tail) contains yield values with no sources, and with equal numbers of sources, making continuous approximations difficult, and in the former case producing negative infinities in the log-log plot. In the Zipf form, the low-producing region (right tail) is populated with tied ranks, viz. the large equal-production classes on the left of the Lotka form. In fact, NELSON & TAGUE even suggest that, in order to satisfactorily display and treat such data, it may be necessary to split data sets into separate Lotka and Zipf presentations, respectively emphasizing each tail.

(c) The double summation (integration) that produces the Bradford form of presentation smooths away difficulties with gaps and ties, but their effect lingers in the distribution shape. With a log-transformed abscissa, one clearly sees the tripartite nature of the informetric distribution. Typically there is a concave region or core of a few high producers, a central linear region most closely following the broad outline discussed earlier, and often a falling-off from the projection of the central line in the low-producing tail, termed a Groos droop (GROOS). Economists have characterized this tripartite shape as the "vital few," the "middle class," and the "trivial many."

This introduction may be concluded by noting—as though the informetric regularity itself were not sufficiently challenging—that there are often considerable difficulties with disparate nomenclature in the literature on the subject, not to mention a chaos of symbol systems. For example, "Zipf's law " may simply indicate the word-occurrence regularity, or even then, it may be eclipsed or concatenated with the prior discoverer of the word-occurrence regularity, Estoup. Or it may indicate use of the rank-frequency form of presentation of the distribution to, say, journal-article data. Or again, it may refer to Zipf's mathematical equation, or to Mandlebrot's law; but even here, for continuous data, "Zipf" may be replaced by "Pareto." Clearly, communication on this topic would benefit from a little effort spent on clarification with respect to data sets, forms of presentation, and named equations.

The Inverse Power Law

An important advancement in the study of the informetric regularities in the first half of the period under review has been a clarification of the exact status of the various forms of the inverse power law typically used to describe them. This has been in the making since the earliest

days of bibliometrics (FAIRTHORNE), but progress, or at least acceptance, has been slow. In part this may be due to the use of two different
mathematical traditions, the continuous and the discrete, with preference being given to the former despite informetric data being overwhelmingly discrete in form. This in turn may have fostered a perception that the topic consisted of quite distinct theoretical (mathematical
or formal) and empirical (data-oriented) studies (DROTT). The continuous tradition is considered first.

The continuous approach. A central problem for the continuous approach is how best to approximate discrete and erratic data by a continuous smooth curve, most importantly in the size-frequency form,
given that the remaining presentation forms are at least theoretically
derived by (successive) integration from it. Different approximations in
different studies lead to different results, perhaps trivial mathematically, but irritating to the data-focused reader already facing a medley
of homographic and synonymous symbols. The issue remains an open
one (R. ROUSSEAU, 1990b), and it is briefly considered before turning
to the significant gains it has allowed.

One may plot typical size-frequency data as a sequence of vertical
integral-valued line intervals or spikes, initially of decreasing length at
successive and adjacent integral values of yield, but thereafter as a
sequence of shorter often equal-length, including unit-length, spikes,
separated by gaps in the yield values. A first problem is as follows. Any
continuous curve describing these data must attempt to meet three
requirements: to conform to the chosen family of (power-law) functions; to coincide with the tops of the spikes initially; and thereafter, to
average over them, in the sense that the sum of the spike lengths over
an interval of the abscissa equals the area under the curve over that
interval. Alternatively, each spike may be replaced by a unit-width bar
(yield value $\pm 1/2$), and one seeks that curve from the appropriate
family bounding an area equal to that of the full histogram. A second
problem is this: to integrate the curve (equivalent to summing the
spikes), upper and lower bounds must be fixed. The lower bound is
typically taken as 1 (or 1 - 1/2) for informetric regularities. The upper
bound was typically left open (at infinity) early on, but later taken as the
maximum yield value (with or without + 1/2), but R. Rousseau (1990b)
suggests more flexibility is needed with respect to fixing this bound on
the continuous curve. A third problem relates to the assignment of
ranks from the now-obtained size-cumulative-frequency curve when it
is transposed into the rank-frequency (Zipf) presentation form: what
rank will the maximum yield take? One naturally prefers this rank to
equal 1 (as it would in the case of summation), but this does not follow
with the integration of the continuous curve; for example, with an
upper bound at the maximum yield spike, the initial rank (without

correction) is zero. The problem of fitting continuous smooth curves to discrete, erratic, and highly skewed data is compounded when one takes a satisfactorily fitting curve in one form of presentation, converts it by continuous methods without care into another form, and expects a literal match to the converted discrete data. Nevertheless, as data sets grow in size, the assumption of continuity becomes increasingly plausible; testament to this fact is the highly profitable analysis of continuous bibliographies (Information Production Processes or IPPs) by Egghe (EGGHE & R. ROUSSEAU, 1990b, pp. 292-384), whose results will shortly be considered.

Before proceeding, however, an additional problem with the treatment of ranks, of concern to both continuous and discrete approaches, must be addressed: how should each source with the same yield (i.e., tied sources) be ranked, and additionally be plotted or used in parameter estimation? Summation of spikes simply produces jumps in the rank count, and integration of the matching curve mimics this effect. HEINE reviews five different methods of ranking, and notes that the shape of the rank-cumulative-frequency (Bradford) presentation or bibliograph—where an additional integration emphasizes shape over gaps and ties—may be affected by the choice of method made. Furthermore, he notes often unstated differences in the method employed in different studies, making comparisons suspect. R. ROUSSEAU (1988b) recommends plotting all sources in an equal-productivity class as one datum with the same maximum (outer or last-in-line) rank. This saves the low-producing region of the (semi-logarithmic) bibliograph from the exponential hooks that arise when all sources are plotted as successive ranks (breaking-ties-at-random method) and that obscure the broad pattern. However, at least in establishing curve parameters, there may be an advantage to introducing a selection of such individually ranked sources as a low-producing-tail weighting device. (R. ROUSSEAU, 1994a). Also, in the rank-frequency (Zipf) presentation, displaying all sources at successive ranks and producing equal-productivity-class "step-treads" can be instructive in some cases (SMITH & DEVINE). R. Rousseau (1988b) also suggests that a (rounded-down) median rank assignment (mid-rank method) may more accurately fix the commencement of a Groos droop. It should be noted that the last-in-line method leads to an unintuitive ranking when there is more than one maximum producing source; luckily, this is rare in informetric studies.

Interrelationships of the forms of the law. The interrelationships of the different forms of the inverse power law in describing the informetric regularities are now briefly summarized. The pre-eminent contributor to, and motivator of, this clarification has been Egghe (EGGHE, 1985, 1990a, 1991a; EGGHE & R. ROUSSEAU, 1990b, pp. 292-384). Also significant are R. ROUSSEAU (1988b; 1990b), BOOKSTEIN (1990a), TAGUE

& NICHOLLS, and, from an earlier period, YABLONSKY (1980) and
HAITUN (1982a). With respect to these sources: first, the overall classification into three families follows from Egghe (1985), but R. Rousseau's
(1990b) notion of exact equivalence between presentation forms is
adopted (see also Egghe, 1991a). Second, different workers have used
slightly different approaches, especially with respect to integration
bounds, and so have obtained slightly different interrelationships between some non-exponent parameters and the top rank value assigned.
Thus, the equations are stated only in a general way, with the original
sources recommended for details of parameter interconversion. For
example, with respect to integrations, see R. Rousseau (1988b), though
noting the generalization of R. Rousseau (1990b); and with respect to
the treatment of equal-production (Bradford) groups, see Egghe (1991a).
Third, there is no common symbolism in this area, but it is hoped that
the system used here combines intuitive appeal, sufficient compatibility with existing studies, and the need for systematic presentation.
Regarding the latter, it should be noted that identically labeled parameters do not necessarily equate across the different families in the same
presentation form. Fourth, the practice is adopted of naming the accepted mathematical descriptions of the specific regularities (laws) after their originators, rather than using the name of the discoverers of the
specific regularities per se. One might prefer to use "Bradford" for
"Leimkuhler," or "Zipf" for "Mandelbrot" (Bookstein, 1990a), or these
names paired. It should also be remarked that a case can be made for
labeling the size-cumulative-frequency form of the law with "Pareto,"
rather than using this name to label a continuous analog of Zipf's law.

Three families of laws are recognized. These are considered here
from the most general and encompassing to the most specific.

(1) The *General three-parameter law,* which applies when the exponent,
     α, of the size-frequency (Lotka) presentation takes the values: $\alpha > 1$,
     $\alpha \neq 2$. Generally $\alpha \leq 3$, but higher values have been reported (PAO,
     1986). For $\alpha = 1$ a family of functions is obtained which is not
     regarded as informetric: see R. ROUSSEAU (1988b) and TAGUE &
     NICHOLLS. Treating each form of presentation:

     (a) *Size-frequency (Lotka) form.* Lotka's Law:

$$f(y) = A_1/y^\alpha \qquad [1]$$

where f = the number (or frequency) of sources each producing a yield
of y items, where y = 1, 2, . . . , A_2. The three parameters are: α, the
exponent; A_1, the frequency of sources with unit yield, that is, $f(1)$; and
A_2, the continuous equivalent of the maximum yield. A_2 has been taken

as infinite, and more recently as the maximum yield value y_{max}; see R. ROUSSEAU (1988b; 1990b). Incidentally, with A_2 taken as infinite, the total number of sources F_T is estimated from the curve as $A_1 \varsigma(\alpha)$, where $\varsigma(-)$ is Riemann's Zeta function.

(b) *Size-cumulative-frequency (Pareto) form.*

$$F(y) = [B_1/y^\beta] - B_2 \qquad [2]$$

where F = the number of sources producing at least y items each. This is obtained by integrating the Lotka law down-yield from A_2. The three parameters are: $B = (\alpha - 1)$, the exponent; B_1; and B_2. Then setting:

$$r(y) = F(y) \qquad [3]$$

gives r, the rank of the source(s) producing y items. R. Rousseau (1988b) fixes the rank of the source with yield A_2 as 1.

(c) *Rank-frequency (Zipf) form.* Mandelbrot's Law:

$$y(r) = C_1/[1 + C_2\, r]^\gamma \qquad [4]$$

where y = the number of items produced by the source of rank r. This is obtained by transposing rank and yield in the previous presentation form. The three parameters are: $\gamma = 1/(\alpha - 1)$, the exponent; C_1; and C_2.

(d) *Rank-cumulative-frequency (Bradford) form.* Leimkuhler's Law:

$$Y(r) = \{D_1/\delta\} \times \{D_2^\delta - [D_2^{\delta-1} - (\delta-1)\, r/D_1]^{\delta/(\delta-1)}\} \qquad [5]$$

where Y = the total number of items produced by sources of at least rank r. One way of obtaining this is by integrating the Mandelbrot's Law down-rank. Alternatively, the Lotka law may first be converted to a distribution of the total number of items produced per yield value, in symbols from f(y) to yf(y), and the latter integrated with respect to y to obtain Y(y); r can then be substituted for y from the r(y) size-cumulative-frequency relation (see, e.g., BOOKSTEIN, 1990a). The general equation above was proposed by R. Rousseau (1988b); its three parameters are: $\delta = (2 - \alpha)$, the exponent; D_1; and D_2. It may be consoling to note at this stage in the multiplicity of parameters used that $D_1 = A_1$ and $D_2 = A_2$.

(e) *Equal-production groups form* is of limited interest for the general law, and comment is delayed until the section "The shape of the distribution: theoretical investigations."

(2) The *classic or exact two-parameter law*, with a = 2. Although the original discoverers regarded this inverse-square law only as an

approximation to the regularity of their data, it dominated early work in the field, perhaps due to its simplicity of form.

(a) *Size-frequency (Lotka) form.* Lotka's Law:

$$f(y) = A_1 / y^2 \qquad \text{[1a]}$$

where f = the number of sources each producing y items, where y = 1, 2, . . . , A_2. The two parameters are as before: A_1 = f(1); and A_2, the continuous equivalent of the maximum yield, variously infinity or y_{max}. With A_2 taken as infinite, the total number of sources F_T is estimated from the curve as $A_1 \varsigma(2) = A_1 (\pi^2/6) = f(1) \times 1.65$, so that $f(1)/F_T \approx 61\%$.

(b) *Size-cumulative-frequency form.* This may be obtained from equation [2] by setting β = 1. Ranks may be obtained as in equation [3].

(c) *Rank-frequency (Zipf) form.* Mandelbrot's Law:

$$y(r) = C_1 / [1 + C_2 r] \qquad \text{[4a]}$$

where y = the number of items produced by the source of rank r. This has the same form as equation [4] with γ =1. A common variant form is:

$$y(r) = C_3 / [C_4 + r] \qquad \text{[4b]}$$

where $C_3 = C_1/C_2$ and $C_4 = 1/C_2$.

(d) *Rank-cumulative-frequency (Bradford) form.* Leimkuhler's Law:

$$Y(r) = D_1 \ln [1 + D_2 r] \qquad \text{[5a]}$$

where Y = the total number of items produced by sources of at least rank r. A common variant form of this equation is:

$$X(x) = [\ln (1 + D_3 x)] / [\ln (1 + D_3)] \qquad \text{[5b]}$$

where X = the fraction of the total number of items produced by the fraction x of the total number of ranks. If one symbolizes the total number of ranks (or sources) as R_T (or F_T), and the total number of items as Y_T, then X = Y(r)/Y_T and x = r/R_T. Here $D_3 = D_2 R_T$.

(e) *Equal-production groups form.* If sources are placed in rank order, with all sources ranked in the breaking-ties-at-random method (HEINE), and the collection divided into g groups with the same number of items each, viz. Y_G =Y_T/g , then Bradford's original statement of his law, Bradford's Verbal Law, can be written:

if $R_{G0}(i)/R_{G0}(1) = k_0^{(i-1)})$, when i = 1,. . . ., g, then k_0 = constant.   [6a]

Here $R_{G0}(i)$ = the number of ranks (sources) in the i-th group; i is the group index, with i = 1 representing the core group; and k_0 > 1, is the Bradford multiplier. It should be noted that the value of k_0 depends on the number of groups chosen. The subscript G symbolizes Group and the 0 is a reminder that the groups are taken successively, so that, for example, the total number of ranks equals the sum of the ranks in each of the separate groups, that is, $R_T = \Sigma R_{G0}(i)$ from i = 1 to g. Generally, this is the interpretation used, so that the subscript 0 can be dropped. The classic Leimkuhler law was initially derived from Bradford's Verbal Law.

(3) A *special family* of simplified rank-related variants of the classical law is obtained by rank-shifting.

    (a) *Rank-frequency (Zipf) form.* Zipf's Law:

$$y(r) = C_1/r \qquad \text{[4c]}$$

where y = the number of items produced by the source of rank r. This may be obtained from equation [4a] with $C_2 = 1$, and r set equal to (1+r). This is sometimes generalized by readmitting an exponent $\gamma \neq 1$.

    (b) *Rank-cumulative-frequency (Bradford) form.* Brookes' or the Weber-Fechner Law:

$$Y(r) = D_1 \ln r \qquad \text{[5c]}$$

where Y = the total number of items produced by sources of at least rank r. This may be obtained from equation [5a] with $D_2 = 1$, and r set equal to (1+r).

    (c) *Equal-production groups form.* If equal-production groups are constructed as before, but now the number of sources in successively more inclusive groups is considered, that is, the number of sources in group i = 1 with Y_G items, in group i = 2 with $2Y_G$ items, and so on, then a similar treatment can be made to produce what is called Bradford's Graphical Law:

if $R_{G1}(i)/R_{G1}(1) = k_1^{(i-1)}$, when i = 1, . . . , g, then k_1 = constant. [6b]

Here $R_{G1}(i)$ = the number of ranks (sources) in the i-th group; i is the group index, with i = 1 representing the core group; and k_1 > 1, is the appropriate Bradford multiplier; k_1 depends on the number of groups chosen. The 1 on the subscript G is a reminder that these groups are successively more inclusive, for example, the total number of ranks now equals that in the final group, that is, $R_T = R_{G1}(g)$. Brookes' Law was derived from this interpretation of Bradford's results.

Three additional remarks conclude this outline. First, interest in the group form of the informetric laws has waned in recent years, as more data sets are found that insufficiently comply with the classical model. In fact, this approach to the description of regularities is rather atypical, a consequence of Bradford's unusual formulation of his law. Nevertheless, several interesting results deserve mention. Noting the dependence of the Bradford multiplier k on the number of equal-production groups, g, formed in an informetric data set, BROOKS (1990b) asked if there was an optimum value for g in the sense of producing groups with a high uniformity of concentration across groups, and with no sources excluded in partitioning. He developed a computer program to determine this optimum for real bibliographies by exhaustive partitioning from 2 to (total number of items)/2 groups, and concluded that 3 or 4 groups typically gave the best results and a minimum "perfect Bradford multiplier." Noting that earlier researchers had surmised that for typically partitioned collections, Bradford multipliers were roughly equal to average production (total number of items/total number of sources), EGGHE (1990a) explored theoretically the relationship between the value of k and g, and established that with 4 to 5 groups, the surmise was quite accurate. He extended this approach to construct for continuous bibliographies a "group-free multiplier," that is, a constant whose value depended on two parameters of the bibliography, for example, the total number of items and the maximum yield, or alternatively, k and g. Note that it is the two-parameter classic model that is dealt with here. See also EGGHE (1990b; 1991a).

Second, the relationship was noted earlier between the rank-cumulative-frequency form of presentation with relativized linear axes (see, for example, the variant classic Leimkuhler equation [5b] above) and the reversed form of the Lorenz diagram. A natural step is to display the present model(s) in Lorenz form, and explore/use connections to the Gini Index which, measuring the area between the resulting curve and the diagonal line (uniform distribution), is a measure of concentration (DAGUM). Discussion is limited to a simple mention of recent and various studies on the theme (BURRELL, 1991, 1992b, 1993; EGGHE, 1992; RAVICHANDRA RAO, 1988; WAGNER-DÖBLER, 1997), and its connection to the broader study of concentration measures (Y.-S. CHEN ET AL., 1993; EGGHE & R. ROUSSEAU, 1990b, pp. 361-370).

Third, inverse power models with more than three parameters have been proposed. A four-model family developed from the behavior of equal-production groups when $\alpha \neq 2$ was suggested by EGGHE (1985). R. ROUSSEAU & ZHANG proposed a third additive constant to the classic Leimkuhler law to accommodate an aberrantly high top-producing source. FANG & FANG proposed a fourth constant substracted from the right-hand side in the general Lotka law to facilitate parameter estimation. TAGUE & NICHOLLS mention the possibility of a fourth constant added to the denominator of the general Lotka law prior to exponentiation, but consider its effect on curve shapes to be adequately absorbed into a slightly lower value of the exponent.

The discrete approach. Next to be considered are recent advances in the discrete mathematical approach to the description of informetric regularities. In contrast to the continuous approach, this works exclusively with the discrete data, i.e., in terms of the earlier description, only with the integrally valued vertical-line intervals or spikes, sited at integral abscissa values, and summing spike lengths to produce other forms of presentation of the data. Thus, there is complete agreement with the data in each presentation form, but there is a loss in amenability, and most often transparency, of analysis, and in the richness of available techniques. For example, the exploration of the shape of a smooth continuous curve by two orders of differentiation is replaced by less transparent manipulations in difference equations. Consequently this approach has not produced a comparable body of work on the topic—paradoxically, given that the data are discrete. Earlier studies include HUBERT (1978), MORSE & LEIMKUHLER, and MORSE. A more recent introduction to discrete methods in the present context is PEARSON.

Of prime interest is the index method of Y.-S. CHEN & LEIMKUHLER (1986; 1987a; 1987b); further developments in this work are introduced in later sections. In outline, each equal-production class or spike in the Lotka form is assigned an index ($i = 1, 2, \ldots, m$) from unit yield upward. Thus the data are converted into a sequence of m ordered triples, each containing the class index, the class representative yield, and the number of sources in the class, symbolically $\{(i, y_i, f(y_i))\}$, which bypasses gaps in the higher yield values, a nuisance for the continuous case. Formulas can be simply constructed for these triples to provide analogs of the previously discussed continuous operations. A summation of $f(y_i)$ over i yields $F(y_i)$, where F vs. y_i is the size-cumulative-frequency representation (somewhat confusingly labeled Lotka's law by the authors). Rules linking r_i to $F(y_i)$, and $y(r_i)$ to y_i are analogous to the transposition of axes that produce the rank-frequency or Zipf-form of presentation: y vs. r_i, where the rank assigned to each class is the outer or maximal rank. The index values of course do not transpose, producing an initially disconcerting inversion in the tabulated data. The total yield produced at each rank is obtained from the representative yield $y(r_i)$ × the number of sources taking that rank, from which summation over i provides the Bradford presentation: Y vs. r_i. In summary, the set of equations produced is the discrete analog of the continuous general model discussed above. Except in the Bradford form of presentation, where the equation has not been simplified to exclude the summation sign, these equations have the same general form as those for the continuous three-parameter model.

The shape of the distribution: theoretical investigations. The shape of the inverse power law in its different presentation forms has been typically treated as tripartite since recognition of the Groos droop. There is a central region which is well-behaved in the sense of being linear on log-log-transformed axes, or in the rank-cumulative-frequency form, with a log-transformed abscissa. At either end the tails may continue the central line, or curve up (concave) or down (convex); in the extreme the central region may vanish. Theoretical work on the shape of the inverse power law using the continuous approach is considered first. In translating between the appropriately transformed forms of presentation, it is useful to reiterate two perhaps obvious points: (1) that increase in collection size (in general) shifts the Lotka- and Zipf-form curves northeastward, and in the Bradford-form raises and rotates the curve to the northwest; (2) that a steep Lotka-form curve entails low concentration (proportionally more sources are low producers), whereas a steep Zipf-form curve entails the opposite. Discussion is limited to the Bradford-form or bibliograph, and following R. ROUSSEAU (1988b), the shape of the general Leimkuhler law is investigated. This is governed by the value of the Lotka exponent α: (a) When $\alpha > 2$, the bibliograph is fully concave, that is, the low-producing tail displays a continuous rise. An example is provided in R. ROUSSEAU (1994a) in the data set labeled STAT, with $\alpha = 2.14$. (b) When $\alpha = 2$, the bibliograph takes the familiar J-shape of the classical Leimkuhler curve, approaching an oblique asymptote. Again, see R. Rousseau for the data set labeled DOLBY, with $\alpha \approx 2$. (c) When $1 < \alpha < 2$, the bibliograph is S-shaped, that is with a droop, and without an asymptote. Again, see R. Rousseau for the data set labeled SACHS, with $\alpha = 1.4$.

Two comments are in order. First, for the equal-production-groups presentation, the behavior of the Bradford multiplier is clear: for $\alpha > 2$ cumulative production increases more rapidly with rank, or alternatively the ranks increase more slowly, than for $\alpha = 2$; that is, the group multiplier k declines. For $1 < \alpha < 2$, the reverse applies. Second, with $\alpha > 1$ and being typically informetric, the model cannot produce a convex core. Such data sets do appear to be rare; indeed the standardly quoted example is that of Valentine Reilly, reported in BROOKES (1977, p. 193). Nevertheless one suspects that, as with Reilly's data set, the distribution of papers on a topic over the language in which they are written should conform to this bibliograph shape: there is most frequently a very high top-producing source, English, then a rapid decline to a rather small class of low or singleton sources. Perhaps the model needs to be extended to $\alpha < 1$, or further generalized.

Theoretical work on the shape of the inverse power law using the discrete, and specifically index, approach, has been undertaken by Y.-S. CHEN & LEIMKUHLER (1987a; 1987b) and Y.-S. CHEN (1989), for the Bradford-, Zipf-, and Lotka-forms of presentation, respectively. The tripartite division is now characterized via the index. In the low-producing tail the value of the index equals that of the representative yield (there are no gaps), while in the high-producing head, the value of the index remains close to or equals the index sum (equal production classes typically have one source each). With regard to the Bradford-form of presentation, the shape of the low-producing tail is determined by the Lotka exponent as in the continuous tradition; however, a coefficient to fix the concavity/linearity/convexity of the high-productivity head, constructed from local slope data, is also provided.

The shape of the distribution: empirical explanations. It is now appropriate to survey some recent empirical studies and suggestions as to why the informetric regularities depart in their extremities from linearity on log-transformed axes (or axis). Again, focus is on the Bradford presentation, particularly on the low-productivity region and the Groos droop. Brookes' original suggestion was that the droop may result from collection incompleteness, an always plausible and (in practice) irrefutable explanation. However, recent studies have shifted opinion away from this position. An important tool in many of these studies has been the decomposition and/or merger of distributions. A slowly evolving consensus is presented in four parts:

- *Sampling effects.* QIU & TAGUE set up a database with a classic Leimkuhler- or J-shaped distribution and sampled it by journal in two ways: with a weighted sampling, biasing selection toward the core journals (the typical collection development procedure), and with an unweighted sampling, giving even the low-producing journals an equal chance of selection. Small droops could be detected in the small samples, but the J-shape was retained in larger samples of either class. OLUIĆ-VUKOVIĆ (1995) contrasts this with O'NEILL's study where larger samples displayed greater droops; however, it should be remarked that O'Neill's population was the Keenan-Atherton physics data, and this displayed an S-shaped distribution.
- *Subject homogeneity.* EGGHE & R. ROUSSEAU (1988b) found that merging two J-shaped distributions of similar-sized collections could result in an S-shaped distribution. They suggest that as the component literatures were on

separate and homogeneous subjects, a merger would result in a heterogeneous composite, so that an S-shaped
distribution may well be a consequence of the
interdisciplinarity of a collection. AIYEPEKU compounded the periodical literatures on the geography of a
number of countries, of different sizes but with S-shaped
distributions, and produced what he claims is a J-shaped
distribution (though a careful inspection of Aiyepeku's
curve does suggest a small droop). Is this a case of heterogeneous literatures merging to achieve (more) homogeneity?

- *Subject maturation.* ETO presented a data set on the new
field of expert systems that showed not a droop but a rise
in the low-productivity region, that is, the Leimkuhler-J-
shape curve becomes fully concave upward, in terms of
the theoretical model, $\alpha > 2$. The author suggested that
this rise resulted from a very rapid diffusion of papers on
the subject into many journals, and that in due course, a
proportion of those with one or two papers would acquire
more, and the rise would subside. Eto also assembled
data sets displaying the variety of bibliograph shapes
discussed in the previous theoretical section, and extended
his maturation explanation to cover all cases. R.
ROUSSEAU (1990a) investigated the literature of another
new subject, microcomputer software, and found a J-shape
bibliograph with no Eto rise.

- *Core-droop reciprocity.* OLUIĆ-VUKOVIĆ (1992) separated
the literature produced by Croatian chemists in a ten-year
period into that appearing in domestic and in international journals and found that the former had an S-shaped
distribution like the full collection, and the latter a J-
shaped distribution. The author noted that the core of the
domestic group and of the full collection was dominated
by four journals. When these were "fragmented" into low-
producing journals, a J-shaped distribution resulted, of
identical shape to the collection without the four-journal
core at all. Of special interest here is the correlation of a
large core with a large droop; in a sense, the middle of the
collection remains like an inert fulcrum in a distribution
seesaw. This notion is also developed by the author with
respect to temporal changes (see below).

In summary, what has emerged from these studies is an acceptance
of the full variety of distribution shapes allowed for in the tripartite
division as an intrinsic collection feature, and not necessarily as artifacts

of its compilation; and further, a recognition of the importance of time in the determination of the distribution shape.

Fitting equations to data. In early studies, the determination of how well different mathematical models/equations fitted data sets was carried out through a variety of procedures, making cross-study comparisons difficult, and sometimes producing conflicting results. Beginning with the work of PAO (1985), procedures for fitting the Lotka presentation have been systematized, and to that extent standardized, mainly by PAO (1986), NICHOLLS (1986; 1987; 1989), and TAGUE & NICHOLLS; the 1987 paper by Nicholls is a useful brief introduction. Fixing the fitting procedure requires a sequence of decisions that is not necessarily strictly linear. The decisions are presented in five steps.

(1) Establish the nature of the data set. To conform to statistical practice, this should be a random sample from a population whose (equation) parameters are estimated from sample statistics. In the present analyses, data sets rarely qualify, recent exceptions being those of HUBER (1998a; 1998b), and an early approximate exception, that of LOTKA. Largely as a consequence of how subject collections are formed, the data sets may be more akin to (incomplete) censuses, and parameter estimates may be more correctly approximations (Tague & Nicholls). How this bears on the validity of statistical methods (discussed below) remains to be analyzed (Nicholls, 1989). WILSON (1999) found that a thorough search of all online databases of the DIALOG system returned c.60% of documents measured to be at least moderately about a specific subject in an exhaustively compiled collection. This bad census/giant sample gave good estimates of size-invariant properties of the exhaustively compiled collection typically studied in informetric analyses.

(2) Measure, tabulate, and visually display the data. At this stage one must decide, for example, whether to use straight, complete or fractional counts for the assignment of authors to items. Nicholls (1989) notes that about two-thirds of prior studies on author productivity employed the complete count method only, and recommends this method.

(3) Choose an equation(s) appropriate for the content to be captured in the form of the plotted data. Here Lotka's three-parameter equation is considered, but the discussion is more widely applicable.

(4) Estimate the equation parameters in turn from the data. It is valuable to survey the variety of methods that have been employed here. Lotka's exponent may be determined:

   (a) By *a priori assignment.* NICHOLLS (1989) notes that about one-half of studies on author productivity to that time assumed an exponent $\alpha = 2$. This may have been for convenience, or from a too-literal interpretation of Lotka's statements. Better grounds for the a priori fixing of parameter values are shown in Sichel's initial application of his GIGP distribution below (SICHEL, 1985, 1986). EGGHE & R. ROUSSEAU (1990b, p. 343) recommend estimation of parameters in Leimkuhler's function through a preliminary equal-production group analysis of the data, that is, on theoretical grounds.

(b) From *graphical inspection* of the plotted data (in log-log form).

(c) From *empirical estimates*, for example, based on the ratio of the number of sources with one item to the number of sources with two items (see TAGUE & NICHOLLS).

(d) By the *method of moments*, for example, by directly equating the mean production calculated from the data with the equation-based expression, and solving for the exponent by, for example, iterative means (Tague & Nicholls). For exponents ≤ 2, the first moment of the population is infinite.

(e) By *linear least squares* (LLS) in the log-log plot. This is the first of several optimization methods, selecting the line that minimizes/maximizes some residual function; in the present case, minimizing the sum of the squares of deviations, or alternatively maximizing the coefficient of determination r^2 (where r is the correlation coefficient). This method was initially recommended by PAO (1985). The method may be sensitive to problems with moment determination. A serious problem here is where to exclude the erratic data for high producers. Recommendations are to exclude them based on visual inspection, from the point where tied data ends, at the square root of the total number of sources (VLACHY), or based on trial and error to produce (optimistically) a fairly stable exponent. (A similar problem occurs in the Bradford presentation as to where to truncate the Groos droop data in order to estimate parameters for the Leimkuhler function (EGGHE & R. ROUSSEAU, 1990b)). Truncation, even when explicitly located, may be criticized for throwing away data. But without truncation of the data before tied data ceases and before gaps in yield values appear in the high-productivity tail, the researcher using log-transformed axes is faced with a sequence of zeros and negatively infinite values through which to fit the regression line. FANG & FANG suggest the subtraction of a constant from the right-hand side of the Lotka equation, as a computational device to allow LLS to be employed without truncation or the equating of negative infinities to zero.

(f) By *nonlinear least squares* (NLS) on the data without the log-log transformation. This avoids the problems just discussed, especially for very large data sets (see e.g., GRIFFITH). NLS may be used in other cases, for example, to fit the bibliograph curve in a semi-log plot (R. ROUSSEAU, 1994a).

(g) By χ^2 *minimization*: finding an exponent (or line) that minimizes the sum of the squared differences between the observed and the expected frequencies.

(h) By the method of *maximum likelihood* (ML), that is, maximizing the likelihood (the total probability of occurrence of the observed data given the line) that the fitted line generates the observed data points. This is now the recommended method for determining the Lotka exponent (NICHOLLS, 1989). It is also favored for parameter estimation in general, although the mathematical difficulties of solving likelihood equations for more complex distributions are often prohibitive, and numerical methods are required. In the present case, determining the ML estimator of the Lotka exponent requires the employment of tables based on the Riemann Zeta function (see R. ROUSSEAU, 1993).

Once the exponent is estimated, the parameter A_1 may be determined by a similar suite of methods:

(a) By *a priori assignment*: if the exponent $\alpha \approx 2$, then $A_1 = (6/\pi^2) \times$ number of sources, where $(6/\pi^2) = 0.608$.

(b) By *empirical estimation*: NICHOLLS (1989) reports that up to his time of writing, more than one-third of studies on author productivity estimated A_1 from the actual proportion of single contributions.

(c) By directly calculating the *LLS intercept* on the ordinate of the log-log plot, or equivalent direct calculations using NLS.

(d) By an *infinite Riemann series*, approximated by the Pao-Singer formula (PAO, 1985). This is the method recommended by NELSON (1989).

(e) By a *finite Riemann series*, calculated to the maximum yield. Discussion of the estimation of the third parameter of the equation, A_2, is held until later; suffice it to say that in (d), this is taken to be infinite, and in (e) $A_2 = y_{max}$.

(5) Once the parameters are estimated so that the best-fitting equation of its type is obtained and plotted, evaluate how good the fit to the data actually is. Again, a variety of methods have been employed. Prior to the 1970s, evaluations were primarily based on inspection of the plotted line through the data, or on parallel rows of numbers. At least as a heuristic, this impressionistic method should not be discounted. It could profitably be widened into a proper analysis of

residuals, for example, see Y.-S. CHEN (1989) in a different context. The r^2 measure of linearity in LLS methods is sometimes used, but is found to only weakly correlate with other goodness-of-fit measures (NICHOLLS, 1989). TAGUE-SUTCLIFFE's (1992b) preliminary investigation of Bayesian methods of goodness-of-fit deserves mention here. The two nonparametric methods currently employed are the χ^2 test and the Kolmogorov-Smirnov (K-S) test; but in neither case do typical informetric data sets always meet all test prerequisites or conform to the conditions for optimal employment. The well known χ^2 statistic, for example, is suitable for discrete variables; however it can tolerate few cell frequencies with small values, so that either the high producers must be excluded or be variously pooled. Also, the value of the test statistic is affected by sample size: given a large enough random sample, data will depart significantly from the expected values (that is, from the fitted line). The K-S test, introduced into the present context by COILE, is based on the probability of finding a specified absolute maximum deviation between the cumulations of the observed (data points) and expected (fitted line) frequencies. It is based on an assumption of continuity, but is regarded as a valid albeit more conservative test for discrete variables. The value of the test statistic is also affected by sample size, although less so than χ^2; again, given a large enough random sample, rejection will occur. On balance, Nicholls (1989) recommends the use of the K-S statistic, although he notes a greater usage of χ^2 to that time, but suggests that it be employed only in a comparative way. (Using his recommended procedures, Nicholls (1989) found that of 70 data sets, 90% were adequately fitted by Lotka's two-parameter equation, with a median exponent = 2.6 and a median $A_1 = 77\%$ number of sources.) In contrast, SICHEL (1992a) concludes that the K-S statistic is superior to the χ^2 statistic only for sample sizes ≤ 30, a rare case with informetric data sets, and recommends χ^2. He finds that for such sets this statistic typically rejects many models that the K-S statistic accepts.

One matter needing attention is the estimation of the third Lotka parameter A_2, typically now taken as y_{max}. This leads to the subjects of order statistics and the statistics of extreme values (NELSON, 1992; TAGUE & NICHOLLS). It also leads to the statistics of exceedances: estimating the probabilities of obtaining values in excess of some threshold, for example, of the earth being hit by a meteor in excess of a 20-kilometer radius (HUBER, 1998a). (A timely reminder: it is the extreme values in the Lotka presentation that achieve high rank from another perspective.) The best ML estimate of a population y_{max} is, needless to say, the sample y_{max} (Tague & Nicholls). A recent study is of interest here. KINNUCAN & WOLFRAM present a method of directly comparing more general (e.g., three-parameter) with less general (e.g., two-parameter) models of the same type (e.g., the Lotka equation). While the model with more parameters must give a better fit, the authors ask whether the gain is sufficient to warrant a more complex model. The Lotka exponent in either model was obtained from ML estimation. In the two-parameter model A_1 was obtained from the Pao-Singer formula and in the three-parameter model A_1 was obtained by a finite Riemann series calculation, with the population y_{max} equal to that of the actual data. Goodness-of-fit was tested with the ML χ^2, or G^2, which is well-suited for the comparison of nested models because minimizing G^2 is equivalent to maximizing the likelihood function. Kinnucan & Wolfram found that whereas the two-parameter model fitted only five of ten data sets, the three-parameter model fitted eight of ten. Preconceptions aside, the three-parameter model is clearly warranted here.

In summary, I return to the matter of current tests-of-fit, χ^2 and K-S, which can only be employed in a comparative or qualitative way. Studies on the fit of equations to data sets often appraise the equations by using the statistics simply as measures-of-fit, an unfortunate state of affairs for a procedure whose objective is precise decision making, especially precise rejection. It can only promote the proliferation and longevity of models. A somewhat more stringent procedure appraises equations by the proportion of tested databases in which a nonrejectable value of the goodness-of-fit statistic was obtained. One hopes to see progress here.

Recent surveys of the fit of equations to data. A review of recent surveys of models proposed for the informetric regularities follows. These variously classify models and/or compare them to data sets, with the intent of reducing the number of candidates to a single best. An earlier study of note is that of ASAI.

QIU looks at 22 equations, broadly of the inverse power law type, and first classifies them according to the form of presentation. Given the attention to presentation forms above, it may be of interest to note some numbers here. Twelve are of the rank-cumulative-frequency form (with five being normalized); three are of the rank-frequency form; one is of the size-cumulative-frequency form (and normalized); and two are of the size-frequency form (with one normalized). Of the four described as miscellaneous, two relate to equal-production groupings; one is a part-normalized size-cumulative-frequency form; and one is a part-normalized rank-cumulative-frequency form. Conversion to the same form of Bradford presentation, and other manipulations, reduces this number to 14 distinct models. Likewise, 30 bibliographies were screened for conformity to Brookes' conditions (well-defined, apparently complete, and of limited time span), and reduced to 19. Using nonlinear least squares (NLS) and the K-S goodness-of-fit test, Qiu nominates several distributions as giving superior data fits. Not surprisingly, Egghe's four-parameter model performed best overall, passing (at the 5% significance level) on 11 of the 19 data sets. However, in estimating parameters of the model by numerical methods, convergence to the final solution was influenced by the initial values chosen. This apparently results from two parameters being strongly inversely correlated, leading Qiu to question the "reality" of the model. Several discrete models fitted best in the three-parameter class. Yet, surprisingly, none of the models afforded good fits to those data sets with pronounced Groos droops.

In a sequel to Qiu's paper, R. ROUSSEAU (1994a) demonstrated that the General three-parameter Leimkuhler function, not tested by Qiu, gave good fits to 28 of 30 informetric data sets, including those with marked Groos droops. (The Lotka exponents equivalent to the best-fitting General Leimkuhler function were in the range 1.9–2.4.) As in Qiu's study, R. Rousseau used an NLS method to estimate equation parameters in some cases, as noted earlier, employing a weighting scheme for singleton sources, and the K-S goodness-of-fit test. The two data sets that were rejected even at the 10% significance level were very large sets of word-occurrence data (see previous comments on the K-S statistic), and in one case had a very high-occurring first-ranked word. Apropos of KINNUCAN & WOLFRAM, it may be noted that a two-parameter Leimkuhler function gave good fits to only 19 of the 30 data sets. With respect to fitting the inverse power laws to informetric regularities, R. Rousseau's procedure warrants consideration as a standard, along with that of NICHOLLS (1989) discussed earlier.

BASU (1995) classified the eight unique models in rank-cumulative-frequency form in QIU, along with the parameterless and two-parameter General Hierarchical models of BASU (1992), by the form of their first differential, that is, of their rate of change of slope with rank, or effectively by their form in Zipf presentation. Three classes of model were found, of which it is argued that only one (with both hierarchical models) can accommodate the Groos droop. This is confirmed with respect to one data set: neither Egghe's four-parameter model nor Leimkuhler's exact function matched as well in this case. RAVICHANDRA RAO (1998) analyzed how well a wide variety of 25 different two- and three-parameter models fitted 12 different data sets in Bradford presentation. Parameters were estimated by regression analysis, and goodness-of-fit estimated by r^2. The lognormal distribution gave the best fits to seven of the data sets and the second best fits to the remainder. Other equations found to best fit one or two data sets include the reciprocal hyperbola and the modified Hoel function. WANG & WANG contrast the findings of Yang (in 1984 and 1985, in Chinese) where seven models, including those of Lotka and of Mitsevich, were tested against eight data sets, with the findings of QIU. They then compared the best-fitting model in either case, Smolkov's four-parameter model and Egghe's four-parameter model, respectively, on their fits to Bradford's original two data sets, with the K-S statistic. They found Smolkov's models gave acceptable fits whereas Egghe's model was rejected. Again, problems were encountered in estimating the parameter values of the latter model using the LS method.

In summary, one wonders whether candidate models can only increase in number and variety, and never decrease. After all, a great many distributions can have similar shapes in a restricted range of values and with appropriate parameters, and selecting the "correct" underlying distribution(s) in a medley of data sets of diverse compilation and with random variation is not trivial. Nevertheless, few give reasonable fits to more than a few data sets, and even fewer have any obvious explanatory value, so there is little incentive to abandon the General three-parameter inverse power models discussed above. With that said, a different class of three-parameter models should be considered. These have recently entered the description of informetric regularities, and some afford very good fits indeed to data sets.

Stochastic Compound Distributions

Models derived from the probabilities of occurrence of different classes of events have been proposed periodically to describe the informetric regularities (e.g., see VLACHY, Table II, p. 176). Mention could be made, for example, of an early interest in fitting the Negative Binomial (NB) distribution (ALLISON; RAVICHANDRA RAO, 1980), an interest that remains (B.M. GUPTA ET AL., 1998); while in the study just described above, RAVICHANDRA RAO (1998) recommends the lognormal distribution as the overall best-fitting distribution. In fact, given that the regularities are considered to arise largely from probabilistic processes, the degree to which the purely deterministic inverse power law has dominated descriptions may seem surprising. Of the two types of probabilistic models currently receiving (renewed) attention, compound distributions or mixture models are considered here. Discussion of their overtly temporal aspects, as well as discussion of the other type, stochastic birth-and-death models, is postponed until the section on dynamics. Variants of mixture models were proposed earlier for the informetric regularities (see the description of a model of Brookes in HUBERT, 1981), and they have prior application in librametrics (e.g., BURRELL, 1985).

A clear introduction to these models is provided by BURRELL (1988b), supplemented by NELSON (1989) and LAND ET AL.; see also Table 1 and the accompanying discussion by OLUIĆ-VUKOVIĆ (1997, pp. 838-839). However, some preliminary remarks are needed here. The first of two steps in the construction of a mixture model is to represent each source as a random generator of a sequence of instantaneous and independent item-production-events. The simplest, but not the only, model for such a generator of counts (non-negative integer values) is a stationary Poisson process. This has one parameter equal to the average rate of production of the process over time; stationary (or homogeneous) means that the parameter does not vary with the passage of time. Though there is no surety as to exactly when the next item will be produced, the Poisson equation does give the probability that a specified number of items (counts) will have been generated after a certain time has elapsed. The second step is to construct a population of such generators, that is, to allow the Poisson parameter (the mean item-production rate) of individuals to distribute like that of the actual population one wishes to describe. To describe the informetric regularities, a key requirement for the distribution is a strong positive skew, and further, there must be sufficient flexibility to accommodate the very long tails without an excess of parameters. Having selected a suitable mixing distribution, one combines or compounds it with the unit counting processes (Poisson generators) to produce the required population description. One can then, for example, determine the most probable size of the class of sources producing a specific yield of items after a certain time. The essential point is that random variation has been built into the (stochastic) model; the deterministic component resides in the (choice of) mixing distribution, and to a lesser degree the counting process. This should result in better fits to data. However, unless empirically confirmed, the two components are only plausible postulates riding on the success of the compound distribution in fitting the data, and even then, the mixing distribution eventually needs something stronger than plausibility. Furthermore, the compounding (or convoluting) of counting processes with mixture distributions, and the estimation of the resulting parameters, are not casual mathematical exercises. A primer on convolutions for information scientists is provided by R. ROUSSEAU (1998). Ideally, the resulting distribution will turn out to be one already known, or related to it in some way, for example, by having fewer (or more) parameters or tending toward its form as the variable tends to infinity.

The Generalized Inverse Gaussian Poisson distribution. The most impressive of the stochastic compound distributions used in the study of the informetric regularities, and certainly a challenger to the General Inverse Power family, is the Generalized Inverse Gaussian Poisson (GIGP) distribution of SICHEL (1985; 1986; 1992a). The counting process is Poisson, and the mixing distribution is the Generalized Inverse

Gaussian distribution, producing a very flexible three-parameter family of discrete distributions for modeling informetric data in the Lotka presentation. In special or limiting cases, the GIGP variously becomes the Negative Binomial, the Geometric, and other distributions well-known to informetricians. The GIGP has been zero-truncated (that is, had zero-producing sources deleted) to more realistically model informetric regularities. Sichel (1992a) considers that simply shifting the distribution rightward is ill-advised, for example, as in AJIFERUKE, despite the fact that Ajiferuke found that the shifted IGP distribution (GIGP with two parameters) still gave the best fit of 16 distributions to 94 sets of author-productivity data. Zero-truncation makes the parameter estimation more difficult. Initially Sichel used an ad-hoc variety of methods (a priori assignment to one or two parameters, graphical inspection, empirical estimates, a novel form of χ^2 minimization, ML estimation), but more recently BURRELL & FENTON provided a numerical ML method for estimating all three parameters. Using the χ^2 method, Sichel obtained excellent fits to word-occurrence data (SICHEL, 1975), and journal-publication and author- or institution-publication data (Sichel, 1985; 1986; 1992a). Further, exploiting the flexibility of the model to accommodate a mode, Sichel (1992a) obtained an excellent fit even to the number of references in papers, and he also suggests a method for treating a second mode at zero references.

Of special note is the fact that the shape of the GIGP distribution is affected by all three parameters with (to simplify somewhat) each part of the tripartite division determined by a single parameter (SICHEL, 1992b). The dominant single time-invariant parameter affects overall shape, particularly the slope of the linear central portion (on log-transformed axes). Of interest are values less than zero, for example, values between –0.5 and –2.0 producing typical Lotka exponents of (minus) 1.5 to 3.0. A second parameter affects the low-producing tail, allowing for a Groos droop and an Eto rise. The third parameter affects the high-producing tail: fractional positive values produce a core zone (concave region of the classical Leimkuhler J), but this straightens as the parameter value approaches one, at which moments become infinite and the distribution becomes stable Paretian. However, all informetric data tested can be well-fitted with values of this parameter below 1, that is, by a distribution with all moments finite—a considerable surprise to workers accustomed to thinking of the regularities as irredeemably non-Gaussian. Indeed, one reservation as to the present use of the GIGP concerns the legitimacy of fitting such a distribution to regularities that correctly (?) have infinite moments (HAITUN, 1990). A second reservation, expressed by COCKS & BROOKES, essentially concerns estimating key parameters of an informetric distribution from the Lotka form, where the least-certain elements in the data set (the numbers in the lowest producing classes) are the most influential. Other reservations concern the opacity/complexity of the GIGP equation, which familiarity and better explanation should dispel; and, critically and typically, the absence of any satisfying informetric interpretation of the GIGP distribution.

The Lotka-Bradford distribution. Another stochastic compound distribution that has been of value in the recent study of informetric regularities is the Generalized Waring distribution. This fits the long tail of informetric regularities only at the cost of taking infinite moments, and in that sense is inferior to the GIGP (BURRELL & FENTON). However, it deserves attention here, in part because of its use by BURRELL (1988a; 1989) in exploring the time evolution of bibliographies, discussed in the next section. Returning to the homogenous Poisson generator in an earlier paragraph, it can be seen that the probability of obtaining a specific count is time-dependent in the sense that the cumulative output of the process increases, on average linearly, with time. Also, following Burrell (1988a), the Poisson parameter (the mean productivity rate) need not be constant. For example, if the parameter itself is taken as a random process varying with time, the generator can then be characterized as a doubly stochastic Poisson process and described by a two-parameter Negative Binomial function. One parameter contains a factor of elapsed time in the sense described, and the other can be varied over the sources in the population as before. Using a flexible Beta distribution as the mixing distribution produces the three-parameter Generalized Waring distribution. One parameter is fixed to make the distribution conform to the very long tails of the informetric regularities, rendering the moments infinite; in the limit (yield tending to infinity), this distribution takes the form of Lotka's Inverse Square law. Burrell (1988a) refers to the distribution when zero-truncated as the Lotka-Bradford (LB) distribution and uses ML or χ^2 to estimate the two parameters. Fits to several data sets are at least comparable to those of the three-parameter GIGP. The change in the form of the distribution with time can be followed by varying the time-dependent parameter. Again, a shortcoming of the model is a lack of a satisfactory explanation as to why the appropriate source parameter distributes as a Beta distribution.

The Poisson Lognormal distribution. A third distribution where the mixing distribution does have explanatory underpinnings is the Poisson Lognormal (PL) model (STEWART). Here the counting process is the homogeneous Poisson, and the mixture distribution is the (continuous) Lognormal distribution; alternatively, the log of the Poisson parameter can be taken to distribute normally over the population. The parameters are estimated by ML numerically. The model gives good to excellent fits (by either χ^2 or K-S) to informetric data sets, sometimes better than the GIGP, and better than the Generalized Lotka function. Stewart notes that the selection of the Lognormal distribution is justified where the propensity of a source to produce an item (e.g., an author to produce a paper) is a multiplicative function of normally distributed and uncorrelated capabilities (e.g., intelligence, training, motivation, resources). An alternative justification perhaps better relatable to the Bradford regularity derives the Lognormal distribution from a randomly disturbed adherence to the law of proportionate effect.

In summary, the recently proposed stochastic mixture models, especially the GIGP, give very good descriptions of the informetric regularities, in part because random variation has been built into the model, and in part from the choice of very flexible mixing distributions. As is discussed in the following section, they also can incorporate time-dependence. However, in general, they must be equipped with stronger justification than satisfactorily representing the broad shape of the observed data.

Dynamics

Some empirical studies. A notable recent trend in informetrics is a renewed interest in time as a variable in the form of the informetric regularities. One aspect of this interest is in the time-dependency of the shape of the Bradford form of the regularity, that is, in the bibliograph. Interest here was revived by the computational modeling of BURRELL (1988a) and of Y.-S. CHEN (1989), discussed below, and by the empirical studies of OLUIĆ-VUKOVIĆ (1989). It is also appropriate to note the earlier empirical work of DIKEMAN and of BRAGA. The empirical results may perhaps be crudely divided with respect to the order of the time frame of interest, relative to the lifetime of the subject studied: first, for orders equivalent to subject lifetimes (of many decades), and second, for the short term (of years to decades) when the basic nature of the field and its growth is relatively steady. Considering the shorter time frame first, results indicate that, although the incremental (for example, annual) bibliographs appear to maintain the same form, the resulting cumulative bibliographs show a shift in relative concentration of items to the more productive sources, and a relative decline in the proportion of low-, especially single-, item sources. That is, the tendency is for the cumulative bibliographs to shift with time from a linear-or-J shape to an S-shape, despite an increasing number of sources (GARG ET AL.; OLUIĆ-VUKOVIĆ, 1989; WAGNER-DÖBLER, 1997). Over the longer time frame, this same pattern shift may be sustained for many decades (Braga), but may be complicated by the phases of growth and stability in the overall field (see e.g., SEN & CHATTERJEE), which in turn may depend on the phases of growth and decline of composite subfields

(Wagner-Döbler, 1997). For example, a new addition to the field of mathematical logic is the theory of fuzzy sets. After an initial latency phase from 1966 to 1975, it underwent explosive growth from 1976 to 1985, displaying an Eto rise in the proportion of low-producing journals, while the overall field of mathematical logic continued to display its century-long trend of increasing core concentration and increasing Groos droop. However, the pattern may be more complex than one of an epidemic growth phase in a subfield correlating with a simple influx of authors and journals. Distinct subclasses of pioneers and later immigrants may be recognized. This is demonstrated in a parallel study of author productivity by WAGNER-DÖBLER & BERG for branches of mathematical logic. Whereas over the whole expansion phase an influx of short-term authors leads to a rise in the Lotka exponent and the proportion of low-producing authors, the initial stage of the expansion may display the exact opposite due to the efforts of the productive pioneers. A study in German by Reiter and others (reported in SAAM & REITER) on the frequency distribution of authors in a set of psychotherapy journals over time complicates the analysis further. Here the concentrations of authors fell continuously from the journals' inception to eventual stable values, suggesting that while a small group of authors sustains a journal initially, its ultimate success depends on its ability to attract a wide and persistent pool of nonfounding authors.

In summary, recent empirical studies clearly demonstrate the important role of time as a variable in determining the form of the informetric regularities. They also point to the need for broadening informetric law studies to include simultaneous life-cycle analyses of major component subfields, and a finer, more microscopic view of the interrelationships of papers, journals, and authors at each stage in the temporal evolution of collections. One final comment: there may be value in revisiting the data in DIKEMAN's pioneering 1974 thesis.

Stochastic compound models. It is perhaps more accurate to credit revival of interest in the underlying role of time in the informetric laws not to empirical studies but to further developments of stochastic mixture models. Of course, studies concerned with fitting stochastic models to informetric law data without explicit time variables were often motivated by recognition of the importance of the time span in establishing characteristics of distributions, such as RAVICHANDRA RAO's (1980) use of the Negative Binomial distribution for author productivity. BURRELL's (1988a) derivation of the two-parameter Lotka-Bradford distribution has been previously discussed. One parameter is time-dependent, and by substitution of values (arbitrary or unscaled time) into a computer model of the Lotka-Bradford process, Burrell could simulate time-dependent cumulative bibliographies and demonstrate the importance of elapsed time on the bibliograph shape, prior to

OLUIĆ-VUKOVIĆ's (1989) empirical study. Regrettably, Burrell's simulations were graphically presented in a form not typical for informetric studies, though typical for the field of statistics, cumulating the relative frequencies of the Lotka plot from low- to high-producing values. Burrell (1989) extended the Lotka-Bradford process to accommodate a varying-sized population of sources, and investigated the number of new sources entering the collection with each increment of time. His model confirmed BRADFORD's original suggestion in 1934 that as an established field grows, new journals enter but at a declining rate. BURRELL (1992a) further extended this approach from the Generalized Waring process (the Lotka-Bradford parent) to the Gamma-Poisson process, and introduced time-dependent factors into the Leimkuhler function and the Gini index. Another previously discussed stochastic mixture model, the GIGP distribution of SICHEL (1985; 1992a) has two time-dependent parameters, each affecting the shape of the alternate tails of the distribution, while the third, determining the broad overall shape, is time-invariant. An exploration of the temporal evolution of this distribution would be especially interesting in the light of the following discussion.

Simon's model.   A different type of stochastic computer model of informetric regularities was introduced by Y.-S. CHEN ET AL. (1994). This is based on Simon's model for the whole family of quasi-hyperbolic regularities, in which the value for modeling bibliometric processes had already been suggested by KENDALL. Simon's basic model rests on two assumptions, and the focus of recent work has been on analyzing and refining these assumptions to make the model more realistic. Because the model has great promise for future investigation of the informetric regularities, it is desirable to first devote some space to outlining its intuitive appeal. Simon's model pertains to a set of sources that may be ordered into a sequence of equal-productivity classes, for example, into a large class of journals each with one paper, a smaller class each with two papers, and so on—in other words, a Lotka presentation. Of interest are the rules that will produce the distribution of items over sources at some later time, or stated otherwise, the rules by which each next item is assigned. Simon makes two assumptions: (1) that the next item has a fixed probability of going to a new source for the system (for example, a journal that has yet no papers on the subject of interest), and (2) that otherwise it goes into an existing source in a productivity class with a probability proportional to the number of items already in that class. A simple way to envisage these assignment probabilities is to equate them to lengths on a line interval, of unit length since the total probability equals one. Then for the case where the probability of entry of a new journal is 0.2, and where, say, there are already two productivity classes, ten journals with one paper each, and three journals with two papers each, the unit line interval can be divided into contiguous intervals of lengths of 0.2, $0.5 = (10/16) \times 0.8$, and $0.3 = (6/16) \times 0.8$. The assignment fate of the next paper is determined by where on the unit line interval the value of a randomly generated fraction falls. Between 0 and 0.2 a (new) source adds to the singleton class; from above 0.2 to 0.7, a source is deleted from the singleton class and added to the class of two's; above 0.7 a source is deleted from the pairs class and added to a new class of three items per journal. The probability of any source with two items $(0.3/3 = 0.1)$ gaining the new item exceeds that of any singleton journal $(0.5/10 = 0.05)$. Generally, advantage accrues to the journals already possessing more items, an effect variously termed success-breeds-success (SBS), cumulative advantage (CA), or the Matthew effect, but this advantage is tempered by the probability of the birth of new sources, the one variable the model allows. The process may be continued repeatedly, with time measured in iterations (item assignments), and the evolution of the distribution of items over sources monitored.

Chen's development of the Simon model. SIMON derived a solution for his model, which is considered below. Y.-S. CHEN (1989) found that sets of actual author-productivity data systematically deviated from this solution when expressed in his indexed-based approach. Accordingly, in constructing their algorithm for Simon's model, Y.-S. CHEN ET AL. (1994) modified one basic assumption: they allowed for the probability of entry of new sources to decrease with time, that is, with the number of iterations, symbolized here as p_{new}, although α seems to be the typical symbol. It may be remarked that Simon also considered a time-varying p_{new}. By selecting both a range of constant entry probabilities, from 0.01 to 0.99, and entry probabilities with different rates of decline with time, a wide variety of shapes seen in the Lotka, Zipf, and Bradford presentations of informetric regularities could be generated. Notably, lower p_{new} produced higher concentration in the higher productivity sources, and time-declining p_{new} shifted the distribution toward the top producers. Prior to their detailed analysis of the variety of Bradford presentations (bibliographs), Y.-S. CHEN ET AL. (1995) also modified the other assumption: journals that failed to add to their production of items in any time interval were penalized with a reduction in their assignment probabilities (their attractiveness for items) and this reduction grew with the time that elapsed since last publication. This was termed the autocorrelation rate of old journals, symbolized here as w_{old}, although Y.-S. Chen et al. use γ. A unit value for w_{old} returns the unmodified assumption. With both variables constant, the bibliographs tended to maintain constant form as the collection size grew. However, varying p_{new} and w_{old} had opposite effects on the bibliograph shape, though to different degrees; generally a lowering of p$_{new}$ shifted the bibliograph from the southeast (straight- or J-shaped, and with high p$_{new}$, concave with an Eto rise) to the northwest (S-shaped or convex). An analysis of the statistical variation in the distribution would require repeated runs for any case. The important point, however, is that the interplay of these two variables could at least qualitatively generate all known bibliograph shapes.

An exchange of letters between OLUIĆ-VUKOVIĆ (1995) and Y.-S. CHEN (1995) helpfully summarizes previous empirical results in relation to the Simon model, and concurs as to its possible modeling value, but also acknowledges the critical need for establishing the validity of the underlying assumptions and the interrelationships of the two variables used. After a careful analysis of real-time transitions in paper-journal distributions in her 1992 data, OLUIĆ-VUKOVIĆ (1998) reiterates doubt about the closeness of the Simon model to real situations. In particular, it does not appear that at least the high-producing journals gained items by a cumulative advantage principle at all, but rather at an approximately constant, albeit high, innate rate. Again, the matter of journals dropping out of the system, from cessation of publication or from splitting or merger, also needs to be addressed; Simon's original third assumption of sources exiting with a probability proportional to the number of sources in their equal-production class may not be realistic here. Another issue to be explored is the matter of the stability of the form of the distribution over time. In summary, it is apparent that a more detailed and extensive analysis of real data sets is required to provide the basis for a richer and more realistic Simon, or post-Simon, model. The value of this general approach, however, seems assured.

The Generalized Source Item Production Scheme. In his 1955 paper, SIMON derived a mathematical solution for his basic model, which he termed the Yule distribution, and which in the limit (that is, as item yield tends to infinity) has the required Lotka form of the inverse power law. EGGHE & R. ROUSSEAU (1995) extended this derivation to include both the declining probability of new source entries, and a more generalized conception of the SBS principle for assignment to old sources. By using the notion of a quasi-steady state, that is, the system is not required to run to a limit where the influx of new sources ceases, they were able to derive an exact time-dependent Lotka function, and potentially duplicate the algorithmically derived results of Y.-S. CHEN ET AL. (1994; 1995). This approach was further developed in EGGHE & R. ROUSSEAU (1996b) to provide exact functions for the expected total number of sources, total average production per source, and number of sources with a specified number of items, at any iteration time in the system evolution; and extended further by EGGHE (1996) to allow for an item to be assigned not to a single source, as in the case of journals, but to multiple sources, as in the case of authors. Egghe names this most

developed model a Generalized Source Item Production Scheme (GSIPS).
It must be remarked that, although understandable in outline, the level
of mathematical manipulation in these papers appears prohibitively
difficult for most informetricians; at certain stages, plausible approximations are necessary to carry the combinatorial analysis forward.
Therefore, it seems likely that the majority of informetricians will be
obliged to use computer modeling approaches in their further exploration of the informetric regularities.

Schubert and Glänzel's model. A possibly more amenable approach to
the dynamic modeling of informetric regularities, which in a sense is a
continuous version of the Simon-based models, is the 1984 model of
SCHUBERT & GLÄNZEL. The model is used in BOXENBAUM ET AL.
and developed further in GLÄNZEL & SCHUBERT. The approach is
based on the transfer of a chemical substance between contiguous
compartments or cells in, say, an industrial process or the body of an
organism. An immediate connection with the introduction above to the
Simon model can be made by visualizing each of the aforementioned
equal-productivity classes of sources as a (linear) sequence of cells, with
the representative class production value ((0),1,2,...) as a cell index, and
the number of sources per class as the cell variable, or its amount of
substance. The distribution of the relative frequency, or probability of
occurrence, of sources over the indexed cells provides a linear Lotka
presentation. The time rate of change of the number of sources in each
cell is governed only by the rate of entry from the lower-indexed cell,
the rate of exit to the higher-indexed cell, and the rate of leakage from
the cell out of the system. If one fixes the rate of source entry into the
system through the lowest-indexed cell (source birth), ensures that the
transfer rate increases from lower to higher cells according to their
number of items, that is, cell index × cell value (SBS principle), and
allows cell leakage to be proportional to the number of sources per cell
(Simon's assumption three), one has an analog of Simon's model that is
governed by a system of differential equations. Under certain constraints, the system reaches a steady-change regime described by a two-
parameter Waring distribution. Further constraints result in the Yule
distribution, and letting the cell index tend to infinity produces Lotka's
law. This model may be programmed on a computer, and has the
advantage of directly allowing for real time. Schubert & Glänzel demonstrate that it gives good agreement with the Lotka presentation of
sets of author-productivity data. Further, the model has been modified
by Glänzel & Schubert to describe the temporal evolution of the distribution of citations (items) over a fixed set of papers (sources). As
constructed, however, the model is not explicitly discrete or stochastic,
although presumably this could be accommodated, and as with prior

models, the problem remains of adjusting it to better approximate what it purports to model.

Further empirical studies. One reservation with the assumptions of the Simon model discussed above concerns the degree of validity of the cumulative advantage assumption. This is an issue of concern in recent empirical studies on the effect of time on the form of the Lotka law. Some aspects of these effects have already been examined; these were of the order of phases in a subject's life cycle. Here, relatively shorter time frames are considered. The studies of WAGNER-DÖBLER & BERG and WAGNER-DÖBLER (1995), and of B.M. GUPTA & KARISIDDAPPA (1997), deal with the production of papers by authors in the fields of mathematical logic and of genetics, respectively. The studies of HUBER (1998a; 1998b) deal with random samples of U.S. inventors and their awarding of patents, but the conventional article-production terminology is used here as well. These studies recast an individual author's total contribution to the appropriate literature as a product of two factors: the duration that the author publishes on the subject, and his/her rate of publication production. The distribution of each factor over the population or sample of authors used in the study is then determined. With respect to duration, the caveat of Wagner-Döbler & Berg should be noted: that the time slice of subject collections typically used in author productivity studies includes the entire duration of the output of some authors, and, especially at each end of the time slice, only fractions of the durations of other authors' outputs; this caveat does not apply to Huber's random samples. To eliminate these fractional effects, the correct unit of comparison should be the equal-duration cohort. Wagner-Döbler (1995), Huber (1998b), and B.M. Gupta & Karisiddappa (1997) all found a negative exponential distribution of author frequencies over durations in their respective populations or samples. They also found duration to be uncorrelated with productivity rate, a result that at first sight seems surprising, viz. that the productivity distributions in cohorts of authors with (fully-spanned) equal durations declines rapidly from a Lotka skew to near uniformity as the duration length increases (and as, of course, the numbers of included authors sharply decline). As expected and in contrast, random samples of the same low to medium durations extracted from the full populations retain Lotkian skewness. Alternatively stated, in each subset of authors spanning the range from short to long durations are authors spanning the range from low to high productivity rates (although, with the latter groups, productivity-rate distributions are displaced to somewhat higher values).

This finding motivates the next analytical step. In a careful study of the production (patent award) time profile of inventors with proven five-or-more-year durations, HUBER (1998a) established that an individual author's production is well-modeled as a Poisson process. Like WAGNER-DÖBLER (1995), he finds no significant evidence of individual cumulative advantage, that is, of authors' productivity increasing as their total production grows. Further, the Poisson coefficient (mean productivity rate) of inventors is found to distribute unevenly across the population. Huber refers to this as non-uniform giftedness and in his 1998a study models it as a Gamma distribution. Using this as a mixing distribution for the Poisson processes produced a typical Lotka skew distribution with an exponent of c.2 for the time period under consideration. In the following study HUBER (1998b) incorporated duration of item production into the mixing distribution as follows. The distributions of the actual rates of invention and duration-of-invention lifetimes were established over the sample. Both proved to be negative exponential distributions, and were uncorrelated, and could then be combined by means of a Melin transformation to produce the required mixing distribution. When the mixing distribution was applied to the individual-inventor Poisson parameter, now interpreted as expressing innate creative potential rather than actual annual output as in the previous case, a correction factor to produce the overall Lotka distribution for productivity was needed. This factor disfavors inventors with high potential and needs to be further explored.

In summary, what has been achieved in these studies is the partitioning of the Lotka law into a set of individually explorable factors: a source productivity rate that appears to be innate or only minimally affected by cumulative advantage; a source duration-of-production lifetime that is uncorrelated with productivity rate; and a distribution for each that appears to be extremely concentrated over the population or sample studied. Huber draws on his 1998b study to propose a general explanation for the form of Lotka's law, and for the informetric laws in general; this deserves to be considered in the next section. To conclude, it might be remarked that no mention has been made here of the quality or impact of the publications or patents produced, and that the inclusion of such factors would require additional complications and analytical techniques and model complexity; for example, the model of SAAM & REITER has eight variables and eleven parameters.

General Explanations of the Regularities

It may be helpful to draw together here the three major families of models, or their most impressive representatives, that have been proposed as accurate descriptions of the informetric regularities: (1) the General three-parameter Inverse Power law, (2) the Generalized Inverse Gaussian Poisson (GIGP) model, and (3) the Generalized Source

Item Production Scheme (GSIPS). The first may be regarded as a time-invariant, limiting case of the other two. Further investigation of these models is clearly needed, but ultimately acceptance will depend on how satisfactorily they explain the regularities.

Aspects of general explanations for the informetric laws are discussed in BOOKSTEIN (1979), EGGHE & R. ROUSSEAU (1990b, pp. 297-312), HUBERT (1981), RAPOPORT, and STEINDL. General explanations are of two broad types. The first may be variously termed mechanistic, bottom-up, microscopic, or diachronic, and be likened to, for example, statistical mechanical explanations in thermodynamics. In the Simon model, for instance, rules need only be specified for the (probabilities of) interactions at the unit level of a population, and the regularity emerges as a system property from the persistent interaction of the units of the population. In this case, the rules specify the probabilities for the birth of one type of entity, sources, in terms of the birth of another type of entity, items; this is an example of the family of birth-and-death processes. The rules also specify the probabilities that items will be added to (or deleted from) sources. For this case, the assignment probabilities of items to the established equal-production classes of sources are proportional to the previous number of items in a class, the SBS principle. Different heuristics to those in the present introduction or in Y.-S. CHEN (1989) may be used to generate the assignment probabilities, for example, urn models (PRICE, 1976; TAGUE, 1981). Again, the system may be recast as a set of all possible states, and its temporal evolution governed by the repeated application of a transition probability matrix of appropriate order (see e.g., MORSE; PAO & MCCREERY). Also, selected restrictions on, or different interpretations of, the above general process appear to underwrite a variety of seemingly dissimilar models (see e.g., IJIRI). These include the recent models of SEN, employing Bose-Einstein statistics (see also, e.g., FEDOROWICZ and WOODROOFE & HILL), and of BASU (1992; 1995), developing the broken-stick or hierarchical-division model (see also, e.g., BULMER; STEWART). Intuitively, Basu's model also appears to have affinity to fractal theory. The relationship of the exponent of the inverse power law to the fractal dimension of a system is shown in, for example, EGGHE & R. ROUSSEAU (1990b, pp. 308-312) and VAN RAAN (1991). Three comments are in order here. First, a general integrative survey of these various models would be exceptionally helpful. Second, the introduction of real time into the item-birth rule would be profitable, allowing connection to be made to growth phases in a subject area (see the previous section, "Some empirical studies" under "Dynamics") to the epidemic theory of growth in general (see "TIME AND GROWTH STUDIES"). Third, a reassessment and widening of the rules of assignment are called for. For example, how much previous history determines the current productivity rate of a source? Or, discounting a possible start-up period, is the productivity rate innate, independent of the system as constructed? And, what are the consequences of dispro-portionate growth (i.e., elevating (bandwagon) or decaying (burnout)) in (a few) sources on the form of the regularities?

To some, the above type of explanation may seem unsatisfactory, in a sense writing into its rules that which it is trying to explain. One or more of the second broad type of explanations might be preferable: explanations that may be called top-down, synchronic, or, perhaps again in parallel to thermodynamics, phenomenological. Here one speci-fies, or recognizes, a broad constraint on the operation of the system as constructed that logically necessitates the observed form of the regular-ity. An early example is Zipf's Principle of Least Effort which today is not endorsed, perhaps unfairly (R. ROUSSEAU & ZHANG). Again, from the assumption that words, that is, short strings of symbols, are selected so as to optimize the maximum number of bits of information (in the sense of SHANNON & WEAVER) that are transmitted per symbol, MANDELBROT (1954) derived his rank equation for word distribution (see also EGGHE & R. ROUSSEAU, 1990b, pp. 306-308, for a fractal-based interpretation).

A more general approach was suggested by MANDELBROT (1960; 1961). To many, informetric regularities seem to be best described, at least in their long tails, by a family of stable distributions with infinite variance. That is, when suitably located and scaled, the data compose into distributions of the same type, or alternatively, factor into distribu-tions of the same type. To reproduce the same form through time, very highly skewed (with infinite variance) informetric distributions of ne-cessity belong to this stable non-Gaussian, Paretian, or Pareto-Levy family. In a series of papers, BOOKSTEIN (1977; 1979; 1988; 1990b; 1995; 1997) significantly expanded this approach. BOOKSTEIN & WRIGHT is a good introduction to this series. Not only is the inverse power distribution self-reproducing of self-maintaining in time ("resilient to time interval ambiguity" in Bookstein's terms) but it is also resilient (or robust or indifferent) to exactly how one defines the other components of the regularity, that is, the sources (e.g., the journals), the items (e.g., the papers) and the system (e.g., the subject collection). According to Bookstein, ambiguity in the definition of these informetric concepts is distinct from random error in measurement through which the regu-larities are displayed. In fact, Bookstein (1995) suggests that this error also has the same form as the underlying process and is itself resilient to ambiguity. Ambiguity is also distinct from the fuzzy-set notions of degree-of-membership in a well-defined concept. Rather, it is inherent in the way such concepts are constructed out of a background of primi-tive properties; without a certain resilience to typical variation in definition, such concepts would be unemployable in a real world. Reservations about this hypothesis, which do not bear on its possible general validity, might include: (1) While it is true that the distributions reproduce in time in a broad way, recent work indicates that there may be appreciable changes in shape. (2) It appears that the notion of concept resiliency may require more effort to clarify and validate than what it purports to explain. (3) It is not essential for the notion of ambiguity to be restricted to sociological concepts as contrasted to physical concepts, reminiscent of the earlier Haitun dichotomy (HAITUN, 1982b, 1982c; KUNZ). (4) A misuse of this hypothesis could lead to a toleration of poor standards in the initial treatment of data in informetric studies, which is not as simple a procedure as clean rows of numbers might suggest (HEINE).

A final and more recent candidate explanation of this type is proposed by HUBER (1998b), following his separation of inventor-patent conformity to Lotka's law into two components, productivity rate and duration of production (see the section "Further empirical studies" under "Dynamics"). Incidentally, BOOKSTEIN's (1995) thinking shows parallels to this analysis. Huber considers these components to distribute over a population in the manner of statistics of exceedances, that is, as values beyond some (high) threshold; whatever the underlying probability distribution of the variable of interest, exceedances distribute as a Generalized Pareto distribution. In effect, the informetric laws must take the form they do because they involve extreme value sets.

These two types of explanation, of constraints on objects in a system as opposed to constraints on a system of objects, may not be as different as first appears. For example, it may be that for any such system to have long-term viability in typically disruptive environments, its recruitment of new sources vis-à-vis concentration in, and death of, old sources must lie in some optimal range. This could be labeled the concentrate-but-diversify principle, but it would be specified in bottom-up rules. It is not impossible that explanations of both types will in due course be seen as different perspectives of a single explanation, leaving open which element should be the most basic. In the meantime, new insights may perhaps be gained from a closer inspection of the different particular informetric regularities, especially of Bradford's discovery.

The Individual Informetric Regularities

Lotka and Zipf. Ultimately, any fully satisfactory explanation of Lotka's author-productivity regularity must be given in psychological terms. This is not pursued here beyond suggesting a useful introductory article by SIMONTON. The inequality in the author-productivity distribution must at some stage also simultaneously incorporate measures of document importance, for example, of citedness (STEPHAN & LEVIN). Again, a similar level of explanation for Zipf's word-occurrence regularity will involve deeper linguistic analyses that span syntax, text linguistics, semantics, and the pragmatics of scientific writing. Attention is again drawn to content analysis, treated elsewhere in this review, and also to qualitative work on the construction of scientific prose in a somewhat different research tradition (SELZER). This kind of investigation will induce stronger ties with information retrieval theory, as well as database and software engineering (see comments in EGGHE, 1998). With respect to the former, see WOLFRAM. With respect to the latter, and to the field of software metrics, there appears to be growing interest in Zipf's law (KOKOL & KOKOL; PRATHER) and in the Simon modeling approach (Y.-S. CHEN, 1991, 1992). Finally, because words and phrases define subjects, the investigation of Zipf's regularity has strong bearing on that of Bradford's regularity. In summary, it is apparent that in the further exploration of the regularities, more (relevant) data must supplement simple source-item counts, even when time is included (see concluding comments in HEINE).

A common problem in the analysis of these two regularities, but of very limited interest for Bradford studies, is that of the possible multiple assignment of items to sources. This topic was introduced earlier, but here it is considered in relation to the informetric regularities, as seen in recent studies. PRAVDIĆ & OLUIĆ-VUKOVIĆ looked at changes to the shape of the author-productivity distribution (presented in Bradford form) when the different conventions for the assignment of publications to authors were employed in the data set. Appreciable changes in shape and in the relative rankings of individual authors were found. The best correlation was obtained between straight or normal counting (each author is assigned the full paper) and fractional counting (each author is assigned the fraction 1/(number of authors) of the paper). R. ROUSSEAU (1992) found that the distribution of author productivity when expressed in terms of fractional authors produced a somewhat erratic display in Lotka presentation, but that this could be modeled with a lognormal function with a mode between 1/2 (as from two-authored papers) and 1. With the other usual integral author assignments, typical Lotka distributions are obtained. R. Rousseau suggested this to be an instance of the breakdown of the robustness property of informetric regularities proposed by Bookstein (discussed earlier). EGGHE (1993a) argued that this was not necessarily the case, because the aberrant unimodal profile of the fractional count could be interpreted as the union of a typical integer count Lotka distribution (decreasing from unit yield) with a reversed Lotka distribution decreasing (from the mode, or correctly the cusp) toward zero yield. Egghe extended this duality approach to consider the interaction of the distributions number-of-papers-per-author and number-of-authors-per-paper, and the form of weighting functions necessary to interconvert the different procedures for the assignment of authors (see also EGGHE & R. ROUSSEAU, 1996b). EGGHE (1994b) then investigated the matter of how the form of the Lotka distribution typical for single-author assignments could be extended for multiple assignments while retaining its robustness. EGGHE's 1996 accommodation of Simon's model for the multiple assignment of items to sources has been noted. With respect to the frequency distribution of the number-of-authors-per-paper, two recent empirical studies may be mentioned. AJIFERUKE considered the fit of a large number of mainly probability distributions to a larger number of such data sets, and found the best agreement was with a shifted Inverse Gaussian-Poisson distribution (see the earlier discussion of the GIGP). R. ROUSSEAU (1994c) found, at least for data sets from information science where single authors are still predominant, that simple one-parameter Geometric or zero-truncated Poisson distributions gave equally good fits to the data.

Finally, somewhat related to the present theme, is the question of whether the Mandelbrot law, which is valid for the occurrence of single words, correctly describes the occurrence of multiple-word phrases. SMITH & DEVINE suggest that it does, at least for larger rank values when the additive parameter in the denominator can be ignored, because as the number of phrase components increases from one word, the absolute value of the exponent falls, approximately as 1, 2/3, 2/5. . . . Using Mandelbrot's combinatorial/fractal approach to word-occurrence (discussed earlier), EGGHE (1998) concludes that strictly multiple-word phrases only approximate the Mandelbrot law, with an exponent decreasing from the single word case according to a function of the ranks of the component individual words.

Bradford. Of the three historical informetric regularities, Bradford's remains the most central to those interested in the broader levels of knowledge organization. Its discovery was motivated by the need for a better understanding of literature control, and it has been used intermittently to suggest improved collection development techniques— though with little apparent impact on practicing librarians. R. ROUSSEAU (1987) updated Brookes' technique for delineating a core set of journals from his discontinuous bibliograph to the continuous Leimkuhler function, and EGGHE (1990b) updated Brookes' technique for determining the size of completed bibliographies by using Leimkuhler's function and an equal-production-groups approach. It is worthwhile to recall that a set of core journals for a subject is the set that gives the highest average return of documents, indexed as on a subject, per journal. For a subject insufficiently large to have its own set of unique journals, no attention is given to the numbers of papers in the core that are not on the subject matter that must be scanned, or, for the librarian, that must also be purchased (see HAWKINS). Again, no attention is given to the quality, importance, or citedness of the core papers. If account is also taken of the mean impact factor of journals, the composition of the core journals for a subject may alter appreciably (BROOKS, 1990a). Needless to say, further adjustments would likely arise if documents were gauged as to their publication type (review article, letter, etc.), length, amount of discussion on the subject of interest, and informativeness.

In bibliometrics' early days there was an interest in characterizing different types of subject literatures by the parameters of equations (such as Brookes' law) fitted to their Bradford presentation or bibliographs, for example, in distinguishing between hard and soft sciences. This interest remains, albeit more carefully expressed (COLEMAN, 1993, 1994). Following studies such as that by DROTT & GRIFFITH, however, it has been accepted that the study of informetric laws investigates what might be termed structural or literature-intrinsic characteristics (see, e.g., the review of OLUIĆ-VUKOVIĆ, 1995). Any study of differences in subject content is indirect, through such factors as growth, subfield composition, journal attractiveness, and author inflow. That said, it is appropriate to introduce an approach more cognizant of content. As with the other informetric regularities, it is difficult to see how a fully satisfactory understanding is possible without more types of data on collections, sources, and items, especially when researchers now have the advantage of developing more complex hypotheses through computer modeling. The essential requirement is that the subject content must be expressed in formal terms, and be measured at least up to the level of quantitative display; co-word and co-citation maps immediately come to mind. This suggests that the Simonesque population of sources and items interacting in time might be allowed to operate in subject spatial dimensions. This would provide a credible spatial framework and possible real explanatory value to AVRAMESCU's (1980) diffusion-based explanation for the Bradford regularity, as well as closer links to the cross-disciplinary spread of significant terms (e.g., HOOD; LOSEE, 1995) and the related field of the diffusion of innovations (e.g., REID). One wonders whether the development of subject literatures has parallels to diffusion-limited-aggregation (DLA) models, generators of fractal structures in chemistry (SCHROEDER, pp. 194-200). A connection between the spatially enhanced Simonesque model and competitive/evolutionary models in ecology is also suggested. After all, the assignment of papers to journals is in fact an emergent property of a complex of subject-located author-submission/editor-selection decisions. Two articles with bearing on this theme are the discussion by BOOKSTEIN (1994) of the competitive nature of paper-journal interaction against a multisubject background and the analysis by CRONIN & MCKENZIE of the fate of papers submitted to one journal. There are also interesting parallels between information seeking and use, and foraging behavior in ecology (SANDSTROM) which may be more than merely metaphorical.

In summary, the addition of a subject-based spatial framework from other branches of informetrics into current dynamics approaches, with an exploration of approaches used in other disciplines, should presage a highly fruitful phase for the study of the Bradford regularity.

NEW TRENDS IN INFORMETRICS

The literature reviewed above may belie the fact that informetrics, although building on an established base, is a new field in the process of definition. How might informetrics develop until its next *ARIST* review? Previous sections review the current status of continuing developments of (1) more general dynamic models for the informetric laws, with greater explanatory appeal; (2) visual displays of knowledge landscapes with attendant exploratory capacity; and (3) an understanding of the form-interpretation mapping of text (e.g., of citation function) by authors and readers. Further progress in, and an intermixing of, these trends may be expected. In this section novel developments are introduced. First, attention is drawn to what may be regarded as two corrections, or at least two improvements, to first-generation informetrics, that is, to bibliometrics. Second, developments in truly second-generation informetrics are briefly considered.

Improvements to Bibliometrics

Analysis of full text. One problem for bibliometrics is that, in mainly studying bibliographies, it has been limited to a small subset of document properties. Now, with full-text documents increasingly available in electronic format, informetrics can study collections of whole documents, without sacrificing the convenience that bibliographies have afforded. The benefits should be considerable. As already noted, the addition of citation indexes to traditional bibliographic publications greatly expanded bibliometrics, and the further addition of even a small document field such as the acknowledgements is proving fruitful (CRONIN & WEAVER-WOZNIAK). One immediate minor benefit would be a resolution of the status of Zipf's Law of word occurrence. As mentioned earlier (see also BROADUS), this law pertains primarily to full text, and thus under the definition of bibliometrics adopted here, barely qualifies as a central bibliometric law, whereas within the broader scope of informetrics its position is both legitimized and enhanced.

More generally, some guidance is provided by scholars who already attribute a very broad scope to bibliometrics, as that of statistical analysis of text that focuses on formal characteristics rather than on simply extracting meaning. Thus, PAISLEY (pp. 282-285) recognizes a first generation of bibliometrics to include Mendenhall's 1887 study of word lengths, Zipf and Yule's statistical studies of vocabulary, and the analysis of the *Federalist Papers* by Mosteller and Wallace in 1963—perhaps more typically described as a mix of statistical linguistics and stylometrics (see TWEEDIE ET AL). Following a second generation of bibliometrics, essentially citation analysis, Paisley sees a third generation developing along the lines of the formal orientation of content analysis and of coverage analysis in media studies (e.g. MILLER & STEBENNE). This perspective is more accurate when transferred to informetrics. Thus, one should be optimistic about informetrics becoming a quantitative history of (scientific) ideas, and of developing what is suggested in the introduction to this review as bibliometrics' second component. It would be more readily attainable with an informetrics toolbox that could directly parse full text in electronic format, from sentence level to document level, and statistically analyze the results obtained. Finally, a shift to full-document analysis should blend informetrics more with information retrieval theory, which, incidentally, has analyzed databases of full text since the early 1990s (HARTER & HERT). Full-document analysis is also drawing computational linguistics closer to informetrics in the areas of subject (or content) analysis and the mapping of scientific fields, for example, through the use of an integrated Linguistic-Informetric system (POLANCO ET AL.) and the use of the Technology Opportunities Analysis System (TOAS) (WATTS ET AL.).

Measurement. A second problem concerns the "metrics" of bibliometrics. Assuming the suitability of "biblios," the field might have been labeled more accurately as (normal quantitative) "biblioscience." Attention to measurement per se (e.g., to issues like the conversion of promising notions into quantitative variables, a central issue in psychometrics), was relatively neglected. Perhaps the basic numbers analyzed in bibliometrics were too easily procured (by counting the elements in sets, or by simply transcribing the publication year). A shift to full-document analyses, and more generally to the study of cyberspace, should promote the metric component of informetrics. TAGUE-SUTCLIFFE (1994) optimistically designated a category called "measurement of information" for papers on quantitative methods in documentation in the *Journal of Documentation*, but at the time of writing, no papers qualified. An exemplar of the psychometrics approach is TAGUE-SUTCLIFFE's (1995) construction of a measure for the informativeness of documents to readers; see also additional comments by FRICKÉ. Equally important document properties, with more bearing on the formation of literature collections for informetric analyses, are the (degrees of) subject relevance and aboutness. Both notions need clarification and formalization prior to any satisfactory quantification, and validation in user studies. On the notion of relevance, see SCHAMBER, SARACEVIC, and MIZZARO; on the notion of subject, see HJØRLAND and WILSON (1995). The value of even a simple measure of subject aboutness in the compilation of literature collections for informetric analysis was demonstrated by WILSON (1998), who used a content-analysis approach, validated by A&I services' judgments. SEGLEN's (1996) measurement of the information content of documents based on formal components of tables and figures provides an interesting variation of the content-analysis approach. But these properties scarcely exhaust the list of basic document notions needing quantification, either in informetrics (e.g., citer-motivation thresholds, as in VINKLER, 1998a) or in information science generally (BOYCE ET AL.; LOSEE, 1990). Nor does the measurement of basic document properties exhaust the metric component of informetrics. Other important issues include the clarification of desirable and necessary properties for a whole class of measures, for example, measures of concentration (EGGHE & R. ROUSSEAU, 1990b, pp. 361-370), and of collaboration (EGGHE, 1991b); and the analysis and construction of (better) derived measures, for example, with respect to the impact factor (MOED ET AL, 1999) and with respect to composite indices of research institute performance (VINKLER, 1998b). Derived measures have received more attention in scientometrics. Further import of techniques from other metric fields, such as latent trait models for the measurement of publication impact (ALVAREZ & PULGARÍN), can be expected. Finally, one wonders what meta-metrical role BOOKSTEIN's (1990a; 1990b; 1997) hypothesis on concept ambiguity could play here.

Informetrics on the World Wide Web

The development of Informetrics will be shaped considerably by the continuing technological revolution, with its shift from paper to the electronic medium. In this new realm, traditional bibliometric research continues on electronic documents in electronic journals (HARTER), using enhanced analytical power, and better facilitated by digital libraries (CUNNINGHAM). But currently receiving more attention are new objects for study, and new methods for their analysis, on the World Wide Web. These are introduced by drawing analogies with the basic first-generation informetric objects of the model proposed at the outset of this review. Equivalent to the document or patent is the Web site/page of one or more screens, identified by its Universal Resource Locator (URL), whose elements (domains) provide the geographic address and institution of the Web site's server, and possibly its author(s). In much the same way as a bibliography of suitable document surrogates or records may be compiled by a search for keywords in secondary sources, a bibliography of suitable hits or visits may be compiled by use of a search engine on the Web. Equivalent to document-document (reference-citation) links are site-site links established through the Web's hypertext system: a link made to a site indicates that the site is an information source to the generator of the link (at the clickable point on the page), and that the number of such links is a measure of the influence or the authority of the site. Also the parallels between "co-sitation" and co-citation networks are obvious (for "sitation," see R. ROUSSEAU, 1997). However, some differences of degree or emphasis must be noted. First, Web sites are not carefully filtered scholarly publications or patents, but a potpourri of papers, journals, mailing lists, bulletin boards, virtual conferencing, self-advertising—any message of any quality from anyone with access to the Web. Therefore, as CRONIN ET AL. (1998) note, links include not only citations, but also acknowledgements and more; they include whole "genres of invocation." Second, informetric research focuses more on links than on sites—on the "Web," not on the "nodes"; that is, traditional roles have changed places. In a sense, hyperlinks maintained in the hypertext system of the Web are less virtual than the reference-citation links that are only implicit in document subtext. In addition, hyperlinks may explicitly link context to context.

The following are representative studies. With respect to the measurement of performance, INGWERSEN calculated Web impact factors (Web-IF) for domains or sites on the basis of the number of Web sites linked to that domain or site. The measure was satisfactory for national domains but weak for institutions. CHAKRABARTI ET AL., members of the IBM Clever project, developed a search engine that effects citation searching, and similarly measures impact factors of Web sites and electronic documents. With respect to knowledge mapping, LARSON carried out an exploratory analysis of the intellectual structure of cyberspace using co-sitation analysis on a set of highly sited earth-sciences-related web sites. GRIVEL ET AL. (1997) extended the methodologies of clustering and mapping of bibliographic data to the Web in order to provide complementary types of navigation for information analysis. With respect to informetric-oriented content analysis, BAR-ILAN used content analysis to classify c.800 suitable Web pages (with unique URLs) that were obtained from a search for the term(s) "informetric(s)" on six major search engines. About 40% of the Web pages could be broadly classified as "bibliographic references," with other common categories including ISSI, virtual library, and cybermetrics. With respect to informetric laws and modeling, R.

ROUSSEAU (1997) reports that Lotka's Law adequately describes the distribution of hits over URL domains. EGGHE (1997a) draws on the analysis of strings of text as fractal phenomena and the concept of duality of site and link to calculate fractal features of hypertext systems.

Not unexpectedly, new subfields of informetrics have been proposed for such studies. In 1995 BOSSY introduced the term *"Netometrics"* to describe Internet-mediated scientific interaction, which she sees as becoming the main source of data for studies of science in action. In 1997 ALMIND & INGWERSEN suggested *"Webometrics"* for the study of the World Wide Web, and all network-based communication, by informetric methods. A similar, but not necessarily identical, subfield is suggested by the title of the new journal *CYBERMETRICS*, established in 1997 by the Centro de Información y Documentación Científica (CINDOC) in Madrid, under the editorship of Isidoro Aguillo. The journal, appropriately electronic-only, covers research in scientometrics, informetrics, and bibliometrics—a regrettable triumvirate—with special emphasis on their interrelations with the Internet, on the evaluation of electronic journals on the Web, and on the application of informetric techniques to cyberspace communication in general.

CONCLUSION

Projecting these developments, can the extensive definition of informetrics given in the Introduction be improved? An intensive definition in the spirit of FAIRTHORNE, but using the definition of bibliometrics by H.D. WHITE & MCCAIN (1989) as a template, is: informetrics is the quantitative study of collections of moderate-sized units of potentially informative text, directed to the scientific understanding of informing processes at the social level. However, in explicating the elements in this definition—no simple task—distinctions that already appear arbitrary must be made. For example, how might one exclude: notice-boards, software, (digitized) pictures, spoken words, pheromones, DNA, etc.? And yet if these distinctions are not made, informetrics might appear to have imperial designs on other fields, whose researchers come from other traditions and who may be indifferent or ill-disposed to such ambitions. The most likely fields are statistical/quantitative linguistics, software metrics, stylometrics, (and quantitative aspects of) reader studies, media studies, and semiotics. Therefore it is prudent to leave the boundaries ill-defined at present. How the field defines itself will depend in part on the competition for ideas and for researchers with these and other fields, a process best described with techniques from informetrics itself. Informetrics may indeed absorb these fields to become an area of very general quantitative study. By then, perhaps, one should not be surprised to see another change of title. As "information" supplanted "books," might "knowledge," for example, supplant "information?" Will "informetrics" by then be "epistometrics?"

BIBLIOGRAPHY

ACKERSON, LINDA G. 1999. Visualizing the Configuration of Scientific Literature. Reference & User Services Quarterly. 1999 Fall; 39(1): 43-52. ISSN: 1094-9054.

AIYEPEKU, WILSON O. 1977. The Bradford Distribution Theory: The Compounding of Bradford Periodical Literatures in Geography. Journal of Documentation. 1977 September; 33(3): 210-219. ISSN: 0022-0418; CODEN: JDOCAS.

AJIFERUKE, ISOLA. 1991. A Probabilistic Model for the Distribution of Authorships. Journal of the American Society for Information Science. 1991 May; 42(4): 279-289. ISSN: 0002-8231; CODEN: AISJB6.

AJIFERUKE, ISOLA; TAGUE, JEAN. 1990. A Model for the Full Circulation Data. See reference: EGGHE, LEO; ROUSSEAU, RONALD, eds. 1990a. 1-16.

ALLISON, PAUL D. 1980. Inequality and Scientific Productivity. Social Studies of Science. 1980 May; 10(2): 163-179. ISSN: 0306-3127; CODEN: SSTSD2.

ALMIND, TOMAS C.; INGWERSEN, PETER. 1997. Informetric Analyses on the World Wide Web: Methodological Approaches to "Webometrics". Journal of Documentation. 1997 September; 53(4): 404-426. ISSN: 0022-0418; CODEN: JDOCAS.

ALVAREZ, PEDRO; PULGARÍN, ANTONIO. 1997. The Diffusion of Scientific Journals Analyzed through Citations. Journal of the American Society for Information Science. 1997 October; 48(10): 953-958. ISSN: 0002-8231; CODEN: AISJB6.

AMUDHAVALLI, A. 1997. Informetrics. In: Feather, John; Sturges, Paul, eds. International Encyclopedia of Information and Library Science. London, England: Routledge; 1997. 227-228. ISBN: 0-41-509860-2.

AMUDHAVALLI, A.; RAGHAVAN, K. S. 1995. Co-Word Analysis of Literature on Information Retrieval. See reference: KOENIG, MICHAEL E. D.; BOOKSTEIN, ABRAHAM, eds. 23-32.

ARCHIBALD, G.; LINE, MAURICE B. 1991. The Size and Growth of Serial Literature 1950-1987, in Terms of the Number of Articles per Serial. Scientometrics. 1991 January; 20(1): 173-196. ISSN: 0138-9130; CODEN: SCNTDX.

ASAI, ISAO. 1981. A General Formulation of Bradford's Distribution: The Graph-Oriented Approach. Journal of the American Society for Information Science. 1981 March; 32(2): 113-119. ISSN: 0002-8231; CODEN: AISJB6.

AVERSA, ELIZABETH S. 1985. Citation Patterns of Highly Cited Papers and Their Relationships to Literature Aging: A Study of the Working Literature. Scientometrics. 1985; 7(3-6): 383-389. ISSN: 0138-9130; CODEN: SCNTDX.

AVRAMESCU, AUREL. 1979. Actuality and Obsolescence of Scientific Litera-ture. Journal of the American Society for Information Science. 1979 September; 30(5): 296-303. ISSN: 0002-8231; CODEN: AISJB6.

AVRAMESCU, AUREL. 1980. Theoretical Foundation of Bradford's Law. International Forum on Information and Documentation. 1980; 5(1): 15-22. ISSN: 0304-9701; CODEN: IFIDD7.

BALDI, STEPHANIE. 1998. Normative versus Social Constructivism Processes in the Allocation of Citations: A Network-Analytic Model. American Sociological Review. 1998 December; 63(6): 829-846. ISSN: 0003-1224; CODEN: ASREAL.

BAR-ILAN, JUDIT. 2000. The Web as an Information Source on Informetrics? A Content Analysis. Journal of the American Society for Information Science. 2000 March 15; 51(5): 432-443. ISSN: 0002-8231; CODEN: AISJB6.

BASU, APARNA. 1992. Hierarchical Distributions and Bradford's Law. Jour-nal of the American Society for Information Science. 1992 August; 43(7): 494-500. ISSN: 0002-8231; CODEN: AISJB6.

BASU, APARNA. 1995. Models of Bradford's Law as Solutions of Differential Equations. See reference: KOENIG, MICHAEL E. D.; BOOKSTEIN, ABRAHAM, eds. 53-62.

BHATTACHARYA, SUJIT; SUKHEEJA, GAGAN; BASU, PRAJIT. 1999. Map-ping the Knowledge Domain of a Research Field through Scientometric Indicators. In: Macías-Chapula, César A., ed. 7th Conference of the International Society for Scientometrics and Informetrics; 1999 July 5-8; Colima, México. Colima, México: Universidad de Colima, México; 1999. 37-49. ISBN: 968-6190-91-0.

BHUSHAN, BHARAT; LAL, BANWARI. 1991. Indian Science Citation Index: A Strategy. Program. 1991 January; 25(1): 59-67. ISSN: 0033-0337; CODEN: PRGMBD.

BIERBAUM, ESTHER GREEN; BROOKS, TERRENCE A.; BROOKS, ROBERT M. 1992. Subject Control of the Literature of Acquired Immunodeficiency Syndrome (AIDS). Information Processing & Management. 1992; 28(1): 89-98. ISSN: 0306-4573; CODEN: IPMADK.

BIRD, P. R.; KNIGHT, M. A. 1975. Word Count Statistics of the Titles of Scientific Papers. Information Scientist. 1975 June; 9(2): 67-69. ISSN: 0020-0263.

BLACKERT, L.; SIEGEL, K. 1979. Ist in der Wissenschaftlich-Technischen Information Platz für die INFORMETRIE? [Is There a Place for Informetrie in Scientific and Technical Information?]. Wissenschaftliche Zeitschrift der Technischen Hochschule Ilmenau. 1979; 25(6): 187-199. (In German). ISSN: 0043-6917.

BOOKSTEIN, ABRAHAM. 1977. Patterns of Scientific Productivity and Social Change: A Discussion of Lotka's Law and Bibliometric Symmetry. Journal of the American Society for Information Science. 1977 July; 28(4): 206-210. ISSN: 0002-8231; CODEN: AISJB6.

BOOKSTEIN, ABRAHAM. 1979. Explanations of the Bibliometric Laws. Col-lection Management. 1979 Summer-Fall; 3(2-3): 151-162. ISSN: 0146-2679; CODEN: COMADF.

BOOKSTEIN, ABRAHAM. 1988. Applications of the Bibliometric Distributions. See reference: EGGHE, LEO; ROUSSEAU, RONALD, eds. 1988a. 5-13.

BOOKSTEIN, ABRAHAM. 1990a. Informetric Distributions, Part I: Unified Overview. Journal of the American Society for Information Science. 1990 July; 41(5): 368-375. ISSN: 0002-8231; CODEN: AISJB6.

BOOKSTEIN, ABRAHAM. 1990b. Informetric Distributions, Part II: Resilience to Ambiguity. Journal of the American Society for Information Science. 1990 July; 41(5): 376-386. ISSN: 0002-8231; CODEN: AISJB6.

BOOKSTEIN, ABRAHAM. 1994. Towards a Multi-Disciplinary Bradford Law. Scientometrics. 1994 May; 30(1): 353-361. ISSN: 0138-9130; CODEN: SCNTDX.

BOOKSTEIN, ABRAHAM. 1995. Ambiguity in Measurement of Social Science Phenomena. See reference: KOENIG, MICHAEL E. D.; BOOKSTEIN, ABRAHAM, eds. 73-82.

BOOKSTEIN, ABRAHAM. 1997. Informetric Distributions. III. Ambiguity and Randomness. Journal of the American Society for Information Science. 1997 January; 48(1): 2-10. ISSN: 0002-8231; CODEN: AISJB6.

BOOKSTEIN, ABRAHAM; O'NEILL, EDWARD; DILLON, MARTIN; STEPHENS, DAVID. 1990. Loglinear Model of Library Acquisitions. See reference: EGGHE, LEO; ROUSSEAU, RONALD, eds. 1990a. 17-29.

BOOKSTEIN, ABRAHAM; WRIGHT, B. 1997. Ambiguity in Measurement. Scientometrics. 1997 November-December; 40(3): 369-384. ISSN: 0138-9130; CODEN: SCNTDX.

BORDONS, MARIA; ZULUETA, M. A.; ROMERO, F.; BARRIGÓN, S. 1999. Measuring Interdisciplinary Collaboration within a University: The Effects of the Multidisciplinary Research Programme. Scientometrics. 1999 November-December; 46(3): 383-398. ISSN: 0138-9130; CODEN: SCNTDX.

BORG, INGWER; GROENEN, PATRICK. 1997. Modern Multidimensional Scaling: Theory and Applications. New York, NY: Springer-Verlag; 1997. 471p. ISBN: 0-387-94845-7.

BORGMAN, CHRISTINE L. 1990a. Editor's Introduction. In: Borgman, Christine L., ed. Scholarly Communication and Bibliometrics. Newbury Park, CA: Sage Publications; 1990. 10-27. ISBN: 0-8039-3879-9.

BORGMAN, CHRISTINE L., ed. 1990b. Scholarly Communication and Bibliometrics. Newbury Park, CA: Sage Publications; 1990. 363p. ISBN: 0-8039-3879-9.

BOSSY, MARCIA J. 1995. The Last of the Litter: "Netometrics". Solaris Information Communication. 1995; (2): 245-250. ISSN: 1265-4876. Available WWW: http://www.info.unicaen.fr/bnum/jelec/Solaris/d02/2bossy.html.

BOTTLE, ROBERT T. 1997. Information Science. In: Feather, John; Sturges, Paul, eds. International Encyclopedia of Information and Library Science. London, England: Routledge; 1997. 212-216. ISBN: 0-41-509860-2.

BOTTLE, ROBERT T.; GONG, Y. T. 1987. A Bibliometric Study on the Ageing and Content Typology Relationship of the Biochemical Literature. Journal of Information Science. 1987; 13(1): 59-63. ISSN: 0165-5515; CODEN: JISCDI.

BOXENBAUM, HAROLD; PIVINSKI, FRANCINE; RUBERG, STEPHEN J. 1987. Publication Rates of Pharmaceutical Scientists: Application of the Waring Distribution. Drug Metabolism Reviews. 1987; 18(4): 553-571. ISSN: 0360-2532; CODEN: DMTRAR.

BOYCE, BERT R.; KRAFT, DONALD H. 1985. Principles and Theories in Information Science. In: Williams, Martha E., ed. Annual Review of Information Science and Technology: Volume 20. White Plains, NY: Knowledge Industry Publications, Inc. for the American Society for Information Science; 1985. 153-178. ISSN: 0066-4200; ISBN: 0-86729-175-3.

BOYCE, BERT R.; MEADOW, CHARLES T.; KRAFT, DONALD H. 1994. Measurement in Information Science. San Diego, CA: Academic Press; 1994. 283p. ISBN: 0-12-121450-8.

BRAAM, ROBERT R.; MOED, HENK F.; VAN RAAN, ANTHONY F. J. 1988. Mapping of Science: Critical Elaboration and New Approaches, A Case Study in Agricultural Biochemistry. See reference: EGGHE, LEO; ROUSSEAU, RONALD, eds. 1988a. 15-28.

BRAAM, ROBERT R.; MOED, HENK F.; VAN RAAN, ANTHONY F. J. 1991a. Mapping of Science by Combined Co-Citation and Word Analysis. I. Structural Aspects. Journal of the American Society for Information Science. 1991 May; 42(4): 233-251. ISSN: 0002-8231; CODEN: AISJB6.

BRAAM, ROBERT R.; MOED, HENK F.; VAN RAAN, ANTHONY F. J. 1991b. Mapping of Science by Combined Co-Citation and Word Analysis. II. Dynamical Aspects. Journal of the American Society for Information Science. 1991 May; 42(4): 252-266. ISSN: 0002-8231; CODEN: AISJB6.

BRADFORD, SAMUEL C. 1934. Sources of Information on Specific Subjects. Engineering. 1934 January 26; 137(3550): 85-86. ISSN: 0013-7782; CODEN: ENGNA2.

BRAGA, GILDA MARIA. 1978. Some Aspects of the Bradford's Distribution. In: Brenner, E. H., comp. Proceedings of the American Society for Information Science (ASIS) 41st Annual Meeting; Volume 15; 1978 November 13-17; New York, NY. White Plains, NY: Knowledge Industry Publications, Inc. for ASIS; 1978. 51-54. ISSN: 0044-7870; CODEN: PAISDQ.

BRAUN, TIBOR, ed. 1994. Little Scientometrics, Big Scientometrics . . . and Beyond? Scientometrics. 1994 June-August; 30(2-3): 373-537. (Issue on Little Scientometrics, Big Scientometrics . . . and Beyond?). ISSN: 0138-9130; CODEN: SCNTDX.

BRAUN, TIBOR, ed. 1998. Theories of Citation. Scientometrics. 1998 September; 43(1): 3-148. (Issue on the Theories of Citation). ISSN: 0138-9130; CODEN: SCNTDX.

BRAUN, TIBOR; BUJDOSO, ERNO; SCHUBERT, ANDRAS. 1987. Literature of Analytical Chemistry: A Scientometric Evaluation. Boca Raton, FL: CRC Press, Inc.; 1987. 259p. ISBN: 0-8493-6591-0.

BROADUS, ROBERT N. 1987. Toward a Definition of "Bibliometrics". Scientometrics. 1987 November; 12(5-6): 373-379. ISSN: 0138-9130; CODEN: SCNTDX.

BROOKES, BERTRAM C. 1968. The Derivation and Application of the Bradford-Zipf Distribution. Journal of Documentation. 1968 December; 24(4): 247-265. ISSN: 0022-0418; CODEN: JDOCAS.

BROOKES, BERTRAM C. 1977. Theory of the Bradford Law. Journal of Documentation. 1977 September; 33(3): 180-209. ISSN: 0022-0418; CODEN: JDOCAS.

BROOKES, BERTRAM C. 1980. The Foundations of Information Science. Part I. Philosophical Aspects. Journal of Information Science. 1980; 2(3-4): 125-133. ISSN: 0165-5515; CODEN: JISCDI.

BROOKES, BERTRAM C. 1988. Comments on the Scope of Bibliometrics. See reference: EGGHE, LEO; ROUSSEAU, RONALD, eds. 1988a. 29-41.

BROOKES, BERTRAM C. 1990. Biblio-, Sciento-, Infor-Metrics??? What Are We Talking About? See reference: EGGHE, LEO; ROUSSEAU, RONALD, eds. 1990a. 31-43.

BROOKS, TERRENCE A. 1990a. Literature Core Zones Adjusted by Impact Factors. Journal of Information Science. 1990; 16(1): 51-57. ISSN: 0165-5515; CODEN: JISCDI.

BROOKS, TERRENCE A. 1990b. Perfect Bradford Multipliers: A Definition and Empirical Investigation. See reference: EGGHE, LEO; ROUSSEAU, RONALD, eds. 1990a. 45-55.

BROOKS, TERRENCE A. 1998. Orthography as a Fundamental Impediment to Online Information Retrieval. Journal of the American Society for Information Science. 1998 June; 49(8): 731-741. ISSN: 0002-8231; CODEN: AISJB6.

BRUCKNER, E.; EBELING, W.; SCHARNHORST, A. 1990. The Application of Evolution Models in Scientometrics. Scientometrics. 1990 January; 18(1-2): 21-41. ISSN: 0138-9130; CODEN: SCNTDX.

BUCKLAND, MICHAEL K.; LIU, ZIMING. 1995. History of Information Science. In: Williams, Martha E., ed. Annual Review of Information Science and Technology: Volume 30. Medford, NJ: Information Today, Inc. for the American Society for Information Science; 1995. 385-416. ISSN: 0066-4200; ISBN: 1-57387-019-6; CODEN: ARISBC; LC: 66-25096.

BULMER, M. G. 1974. On Fitting the Poisson Lognormal Distribution to Species-Abundance Data. Biometrics. 1974 March; 30(1): 101-110. ISSN: 0006-341X; CODEN: BIOMB6.

BURRELL, QUENTIN L. 1985. A Note on Ageing in a Library Circulation Model. Journal of Documentation. 1985 June; 41(2): 100-115. ISSN: 0022-0418; CODEN: JDOCAS.

BURRELL, QUENTIN L. 1988a. Modelling the Bradford Phenomenon. Journal of Documentation. 1988 March; 44(1): 1-18. ISSN: 0022-0418; CODEN: JDOCAS.

BURRELL, QUENTIN L. 1988b. Predictive Aspects of Some Bibliometric Processes. See reference: EGGHE, LEO; ROUSSEAU, RONALD, eds. 1988a. 43-63.

BURRELL, QUENTIN L. 1989. On the Growth of Bibliographies with Time: An Exercise in Bibliometric Prediction. Journal of Documentation. 1989 December; 45(4): 302-317. ISSN: 0022-0418; CODEN: JDOCAS.

BURRELL, QUENTIN L. 1990. Empirical Prediction of Library Circulations Based on Negative Binomial Processes. See reference: EGGHE, LEO; ROUSSEAU, RONALD, eds. 1990a. 57-64.

BURRELL, QUENTIN L. 1991. The Bradford Distribution and the Gini Index. Scientometrics. 1991 June; 21(2): 181-194. ISSN: 0138-9130; CODEN: SCNTDX.

BURRELL, QUENTIN L. 1992a. The Dynamic Nature of Bibliometric Processes: A Case Study. In: Ravichandra Rao, I. K., ed. Informetrics 91: Selected Papers from the 3rd International Conference on Informetrics; 1991 August 9-12; Bangalore, India. Bangalore, India: Sarada Ranganathan Endowment for Library Science; 1992. 97-129b. OCLC: 34314067.

BURRELL, QUENTIN L. 1992b. The Gini Index and the Leimkuhler Curve for Bibliometric Processes. Information Processing & Management. 1992; 28(1): 19-33. ISSN: 0306-4573; CODEN: IPMADK.

BURRELL, QUENTIN L. 1993. A Remark on the Geometry of Egghe's Dual IPPS. Information Processing & Management. 1993 July-August; 29(4): 515-521. ISSN: 0306-4573; CODEN: IPMADK.

BURRELL, QUENTIN L. 1994. Scientostochastics? Scientometrics. 1994 June-August; 30(2-3): 505-509. ISSN: 0138-9130; CODEN: SCNTDX.

BURRELL, QUENTIN L.; FENTON, MICHAEL R. 1993. Yes, the GIGP Really Does Work—and Is Workable. Journal of the American Society for Information Science. 1993 March; 44(2): 61-69. ISSN: 0002-8231; CODEN: AISJB6.

BURTON, R. E.; KEBLER, R. W. 1960. The "Half-Life" of Some Scientific and Technical Literatures. American Documentation. 1960 January; 11(1): 18-22. ISSN: 0096-946X.

BUXTON, A. B. 1987. Titles Revisited. Journal of Documentation. 1987 March; 43(1): 65-68. ISSN: 0022-0418; CODEN: JDOCAS.

BUXTON, A. B.; MEADOWS, A. J. 1977. The Variation in the Information Content of Titles of Research Papers with Time and Discipline. Journal of Documentation. 1977 March; 33(1): 46-52. ISSN: 0022-0418; CODEN: JDOCAS.

CALLON, MICHEL; COURTIAL, JEAN-PIERRE; PENAN, HERVÉ. 1993. La Scientométrie [Scientometrics]. Paris, France: Presses Universitaires de France; 1993. 126p. (Que sais-je?; Volume 2727; in French). ISBN: 2-13-045249-3.

CANO, V.; LIND, N.C. 1991. Citation Life Cycles of Ten Citation Classics. Scientometrics. 1991 October; 22(2): 297-312. ISSN: 0138-9130; CODEN: SCNTDX.

CHAKRABARTI, SOUMEN; DOM, BYRON; GIBSON, DAVID; KLEINBERG, JON M.; KUMAR, S. RAVI; RAGHAVAN, PRABHAKAR; RAJAGOPALAN, SRIDHAR; TOMKINS, ANDREW. 1999. Hypersearching the Web. Scientific American. 1999 June; 280(6): 54-60. ISSN: 0036-8733; CODEN: SCAMAC. Also available WWW: http://www.sciam.com/1999/0699issue/0699raghavan.html.

CHEN, CHAOMEI. 1999. Visualising Semantic Spaces and Author Co-Citation Networks in Digital Libraries. Information Processing & Management. 1999 May; 35(3): 401-420. ISSN: 0306-4573; CODEN: IPMADK.

CHEN, YE-SHO. 1989. Analysis of Lotka's Law: The Simon-Yule Approach. Information Processing & Management. 1989; 25(5): 527-544. ISSN: 0306-4573; CODEN: IPMADK.

CHEN, YE-SHO. 1991. Zipf's Law in Natural Languages, Programming Languages, and Command Languages: The Simon-Yule Approach. International Journal of Systems Science. 1991 November; 22(11): 2299-2312. ISSN: 0020-7721; CODEN: IJSYA9.

CHEN, YE-SHO. 1992. Zipf-Halstead Theory of Software Metrication. International Journal of Computer Mathematics. 1992; 41(3-4): 125-138. ISSN: 0020-7160; CODEN: IJCMAT.

CHEN, YE-SHO. 1995. On the Dynamic Behavior of Bradford's Law—Response. Journal of the American Society for Information Science. 1995 December; 46(10): 799-800. ISSN: 0002-8231; CODEN: AISJB6.

CHEN, YE-SHO; CHONG, P. PETE; TONG, MORGAN Y. 1993. Theoretical Foundation of the 80/20 Rule. Scientometrics. 1993 October; 28(2): 183-204. ISSN: 0138-9130; CODEN: SCNTDX.

CHEN, YE-SHO; CHONG, P. PETE; TONG, MORGAN Y. 1994. The Simon-Yule Approach to Bibliometric Modeling. Information Processing & Management. 1994 July-August; 30(4): 535-556. ISSN: 0306-4573; CODEN: IPMADK.

CHEN, YE-SHO; CHONG, P. PETE; TONG, MORGAN Y. 1995. Dynamic Behavior of Bradford's Law. Journal of the American Society for Information Science. 1995 June; 46(5): 370-383. ISSN: 0002-8231; CODEN: AISJB6.

CHEN, YE-SHO; LEIMKUHLER, FERDINAND F. 1986. A Relationship between Lotka's Law, Bradford's Law, and Zipf's Law. Journal of the American Society for Information Science. 1986 September; 37(5): 307-314. ISSN: 0002-8231; CODEN: AISJB6.

CHEN, YE-SHO; LEIMKUHLER, FERDINAND F. 1987a. Analysis of Zipf's Law: An Index Approach. Information Processing & Management. 1987; 23(3): 171-182. ISSN: 0306-4573; CODEN: IPMADK.

CHEN, YE-SHO; LEIMKUHLER, FERDINAND F. 1987b. Bradford's Law: An Index Approach. Scientometrics. 1987 March; 11(3-4): 183-198. ISSN: 0138-9130; CODEN: SCNTDX.

COCKS, T. M.; BROOKES, BERTRAM C. 1986. Sichel's Unification of Bibliometric Frequency Distributions. Journal of Information Science. 1986; 12(1/2): 45-51. ISSN: 0165-5515; CODEN: JISCDI.

COILE, RUSSELL C. 1977. Lotka's Frequency Distribution of Scientific Productivity. Journal of the American Society for Information Science. 1977 November; 28(6): 366-370. ISSN: 0002-8231; CODEN: AISJB6.

COLE, F. J.; EALES, NELLIE B. 1917. The History of Comparative Anatomy, Part I. A Statistical Analysis of the Literature. Science Progress. 1917 April; 11(44): 578-596. ISSN: 0036-8504; CODEN: SCPRAY.

COLEMAN, S. R. 1993. Bradford Distributions of Social-Science Bibliographies Varying in Definitional Homogeneity. Scientometrics. 1993 May; 27(1): 75-91. ISSN: 0138-9130; CODEN: SCNTDX.

COLEMAN, S. R. 1994. Disciplinary Variables That Affect the Shape of Bradford's Bibliograph. Scientometrics. 1994 January; 29(1): 59-81. ISSN: 0138-9130; CODEN: SCNTDX.

COULTER, NEAL; MONARCH, IRA; KONDA, SURESH. 1998. Software Engineering As Seen through Its Research Literature: A Study in Co-Word

Analysis. Journal of the American Society for Information Science. 1998 November; 49(13): 1206-1223. ISSN: 0002-8231; CODEN: AISJB6.

COURTIAL, JEAN-PIERRE. 1994. A Coword Analysis of Scientometrics. Scientometrics. 1994 November-December; 31(3): 251-260. ISSN: 0138-9130; CODEN: SCNTDX.

COURTIAL, JEAN-PIERRE; CALLON, MICHEL; SIGOGNEAU, A. 1993. The Use of Patent Titles for Identifying the Topics of Invention and Forecasting Trends. Scientometrics. 1993 February; 26(2): 231-242. ISSN: 0138-9130; CODEN: SCNTDX.

COZZENS, SUSAN E. 1989. What Do Citations Count? The Rhetoric-First Model. Scientometrics. 1989 May; 15(5-6): 437-447. ISSN: 0138-9130; CODEN: SCNTDX.

CRONIN, BLAISE; DAVENPORT, ELISABETH; MARTINSON, ANNA. 1997. Women's Studies: Bibliometric and Content Analysis of the Formative Years. Journal of Documentation. 1997 March; 53(2): 123-138. ISSN: 0022-0418; CODEN: JDOCAS.

CRONIN, BLAISE; MCKENZIE, GAIL. 1992. The Trajectory of Rejection. Journal of Documentation. 1992 September; 48(3): 310-317. ISSN: 0022-0418; CODEN: JDOCAS.

CRONIN, BLAISE; MCKENZIE, GAIL; STIFFLER, MICHAEL. 1992. Patterns of Acknowledgement. Journal of Documentation. 1992 June; 48(2): 107-122. ISSN: 0022-0418; CODEN: JDOCAS.

CRONIN, BLAISE; SNYDER, HERBERT W.; ROSENBAUM, HOWARD; MARTINSON, ANNA; CALLAHAN, EWA. 1998. Invoked on the Web. Journal of the American Society for Information Science. 1998 December; 49(14): 1319-1328. ISSN: 0002-8231; CODEN: AISJB6.

CRONIN, BLAISE; WEAVER-WOZNIAK, S. 1995. The Praxis of Acknowledgement: From Bibliometrics to Influmetrics. Revista Española de Documentación Científica. 1995 April; 18(2): 172-177. (In English). ISSN: 0210-0614; CODEN: REDCD3.

CUNNINGHAM, SALLY JO. 1998. Applications for Bibliometric Research in the Emerging Digital Libraries. Scientometrics. 1998 October; 43(2): 161-175. ISSN: 0138-9130; CODEN: SCNTDX.

CUNNINGHAM, SALLY JO; BOCOCK, D. 1995. Obsolescence of Computing Literature. Scientometrics. 1995 October; 34(2): 255-262. ISSN: 0138-9130; CODEN: SCNTDX.

CYBERMETRICS: International Journal of Scientometrics, Informetrics and Bibliometrics. 1997-. Aguillo, Isidro F., ed. ISSN: 1137-5019. Available WWW: http://www.cindoc.csic.es/cybermetrics/editors.html.

DAGUM, CAMILO. 1987. Gini Ratio. In: Eatwell, John; Milgate, Murray; Newman, Peter, eds. The New Palgrave: A Dictionary of Economics: Volume 2. London, England: MacMillan Press; 1987. 529-532. ISBN: 0-935859-10-1.

DAVIS, MARI; LIPSON, LORRAINE. 1995. Interdisciplinarity and the Emergence of a New Specialism: A Bibliometric Analysis of the First Decade of the Australian and New Zealand Journal of Family Therapy. See reference: KOENIG, MICHAEL E. D.; BOOKSTEIN, ABRAHAM, eds. 123-135.

DE GLAS, FRANK. 1986. Fiction and Bibliometrics: Analyzing a Publishing House's Stocklist. Libri. 1986 March; 36(1): 40-64. ISSN: 0024-2667; CODEN: IBMNAQ.

DI SCIULLO, ANNE-MARIE; WILLIAMS, EDWIN. 1987. On the Definition of Word. Cambridge, MA: MIT Press; 1987. 118p. ISBN: 0-262-54047-9.

DIKEMAN, ROBERT KENNETH. 1974. On the Relationship between the Epidemic Theory and the Bradford Law of Dispersion. Cleveland, OH: Case Western Reserve University; 1974 August. 175p. (Ph.D. dissertation). Available from: UMI, Ann Arbor, MI. (UMI order no. AAD 75-05059).

DING, YING. 1998a. Scholarly Communication and Bibliometrics. Part 1: The Scholarly Communication Model—Literature Review. International Forum on Information and Documentation. 1998 April-June; 23(2): 20-29. ISSN: 0304-9701; CODEN: IFIDD7.

DING, YING. 1998b. Scholarly Communication and Bibliometrics. Part 2: The Scholarly Communication Process—Literature Review. International Forum on Information and Documentation. 1998 July-September; 23(3): 3-19. ISSN: 0304-9701; CODEN: IFIDD7.

DING, YING; CHOWDHURY, GOBINDA G.; FOO, SCHUBERT. 1999. Mapping the Intellectual Structure of Information Retrieval Studies: An Author Co-Citation Analysis 1987-1997. Journal of Information Science. 1999; 25(1): 67-78. ISSN: 0165-5515; CODEN: JISCDI.

DIODATO, VIRGIL P. 1982. The Occurrence of Title Words in Parts of Research Papers: Variations among Disciplines. Journal of Documentation. 1982 September; 28(3): 192-206. ISSN: 0022-0418; CODEN: JDOCAS.

DIODATO, VIRGIL P. 1994. Dictionary of Bibliometrics. New York, NY: Haworth Press; 1994. 185p. ISBN: 1-56024-852-1.

DIODATO, VIRGIL P.; SMITH, FRAN. 1993. Obsolescence of Music Literature. Journal of the American Society for Information Science. 1993 March; 44(2): 101-112. ISSN: 0002-8231; CODEN: AISJB6.

DROTT, M. CARL. 1981. Bradford's Law: Theory, Empiricism and the Gaps Between. Library Trends. 1981 Summer; 30(1): 41-52. ISSN: 0024-2594; CODEN: LIBTA3.

DROTT, M. CARL; GRIFFITH, BELVER C. 1978. An Empirical Examination of Bradford's Law and the Scattering of Scientific Literature. Journal of the American Society for Information Science. 1978 September; 29(5): 238-246. ISSN: 0002-8231; CODEN: AISJB6.

EGGHE, LEO. 1985. Consequences of Lotka's Law for the Law of Bradford. Journal of Documentation. 1985 September; 41(3): 173-189. ISSN: 0022-0418; CODEN: JDOCAS.

EGGHE, LEO. 1988. Methodological Aspects of Bibliometrics. Library Science with a Slant to Documentation. 1988 September; 25(3): 179-191. ISSN: 0024-2543; CODEN: LSSDA8.

EGGHE, LEO. 1990a. A Note on Different Bradford Multipliers. Journal of the American Society for Information Science. 1990 April; 41(3): 204-209. ISSN: 0002-8231; CODEN: AISJB6.

EGGHE, LEO. 1990b. Applications of the Theory of Bradford's Law to the Calculation of Leimkuhler's Law and the Completion of Bibliographies.

Journal of the American Society for Information Science. 1990 October; 41(7): 469-492. ISSN: 0002-8231; CODEN: AISJB6.

EGGHE, LEO. 1991a. The Exact Place of Zipf's and Pareto's Law amongst the Classical Information Laws. Scientometrics. 1991 January; 20(1): 93-106. ISSN: 0138-9130; CODEN: SCNTDX.

EGGHE, LEO. 1991b. Theory of Collaboration and Collaborative Measures. Information Processing & Management. 1991; 27(2-3): 177-202. ISSN: 0306-4573; CODEN: IPMADK.

EGGHE, LEO. 1992. Duality Aspects of the Gini Index for General Information Production Processes. Information Processing & Management. 1992; 28(1): 35-44. ISSN: 0306-4573; CODEN: IPMADK.

EGGHE, LEO. 1993a. Consequences of Lotka's Law in the Case of Fractional Counting of Authorship and of First Author Counts. Mathematical and Computer Modelling. 1993 November; 18(9): 63-77. ISSN: 0895-7177; CODEN: MCMOEG.

EGGHE, LEO. 1993b. On the Influence of Growth on Obsolescence. Scientometrics. 1993 June; 27(2): 195-214. ISSN: 0138-9130; CODEN: SCNTDX.

EGGHE, LEO. 1994a. A Theory of Continuous Rates and Applications to the Theory of Growth and Obsolescence Rates. Information Processing & Management. 1994; 30(2): 279-292. ISSN: 0306-4573; CODEN: IPMADK.

EGGHE, LEO. 1994b. Special Features of the Author-Publication Relationship and a New Explanation of Lotka's Law Based on Convolution Theory. Journal of the American Society for Information Science. 1994 July; 45(6): 422-427. ISSN: 0002-8231; CODEN: AISJB6.

EGGHE, LEO. 1996. Source-Item Production Laws for the Case That Items Have Multiple Sources with Fractional Counting of Credits. Journal of the American Society for Information Science. 1996 October; 47(10): 730-748. ISSN: 0002-8231; CODEN: AISJB6.

EGGHE, LEO. 1997a. Fractal and Informetric Aspects of Hypertext Systems. Scientometrics. 1997 November-December; 40(3): 455-464. ISSN: 0138-9130; CODEN: SCNTDX.

EGGHE, LEO. 1997b. Price Index and Its Relation to the Mean and Median Reference Age. Journal of the American Society for Information Science. 1997 June; 48(6): 564-573. ISSN: 0002-8231; CODEN: AISJB6.

EGGHE, LEO. 1998. On the Law of Zipf-Mandelbrot for Multi-Word Phrases. Journal of the American Society for Information Science. 1998 March; 50(3): 233-241. ISSN: 0002-8231; CODEN: AISJB6.

EGGHE, LEO. 1999. A Model for Measuring the Congestion in Library Shelves. Scientometrics. 1999 November; 46(3): 417-430. ISSN: 0138-9130; CODEN: SCNTDX.

EGGHE, LEO; RAVICHANDRA RAO, I. K. 1992a. Citation Age Data and the Obsolescence Function: Fits and Explanations. Information Processing & Management. 1992; 28(2): 201-217. ISSN: 0306-4573; CODEN: IPMADK.

EGGHE, LEO; RAVICHANDRA RAO, I. K. 1992b. Classification of Growth Models Based on Growth Rates and Its Applications. Scientometrics. 1992 September; 25(1): 5-46. ISSN: 0138-9130; CODEN: SCNTDX.

EGGHE, LEO; RAVICHANDRA RAO, I. K.; ROUSSEAU, RONALD. 1995. On the Influence of Production on Utilization Functions: Obsolescence or Increased Use? Scientometrics. 1995 October; 34(2): 285-315. ISSN: 0138-9130; CODEN: SCNTDX.

EGGHE, LEO; ROUSSEAU, RONALD, eds. 1988a. Informetrics 87/88: Select Proceedings of the 1st International Conference on Bibliometrics and Theoretical Aspects of Information Retrieval; 1987 August 25-28; Diepenbeek, Belgium. Amsterdam, The Netherlands: Elsevier; 1988. 329p. ISBN: 0-444-70425-6.

EGGHE, LEO; ROUSSEAU, RONALD. 1988b. Reflections on a Deflection: A Note on Different Causes of the Groos Droop. Scientometrics. 1988 November; 14(5-6): 493-511. ISSN: 0138-9130; CODEN: SCNTDX.

EGGHE, LEO; ROUSSEAU, RONALD, eds. 1990a. Informetrics 89/90: Selection of Papers Submitted for the 2nd International Conference on Bibliometrics, Scientometrics and Informetrics; 1989 July 5-7; London, Ontario, Canada. Amsterdam, The Netherlands: Elsevier; 1990. 401p. ISBN: 0-444-88460-2.

EGGHE, LEO; ROUSSEAU, RONALD. 1990b. Introduction to Informetrics: Quantitative Methods in Library, Documentation and Information Science. Amsterdam, The Netherlands: Elsevier Science Publishers; 1990. 450p. ISBN: 0-444-88493-9.

EGGHE, LEO; ROUSSEAU, RONALD. 1995. Generalized Success-Breeds-Success Principle Leading to Time-Dependent Informetric Distributions. Journal of the American Society for Information Science. 1995 July; 46(6): 426-445. ISSN: 0002-8231; CODEN: AISJB6.

EGGHE, LEO; ROUSSEAU, RONALD. 1996a. Averaging and Globalising Quotients of Informetric and Scientometric Data. Journal of Information Science. 1996; 22(3): 165-170. ISSN: 0165-5515; CODEN: JISCDI.

EGGHE, LEO; ROUSSEAU, RONALD. 1996b. Modelling Multi-Relational Data with Special Attention to the Average Number of Collaborators as a Variable in Informetric Distributions. Information Processing & Management. 1996; 32(5): 563-571. ISSN: 0306-4573; CODEN: IPMADK.

EGGHE, LEO; ROUSSEAU, RONALD; YITZHAKI, MOSHE. 1999. The "Own-Language Preference": Measures of Relative Language Self-Citation. Scientometrics. 1999 June; 45(2): 217-232. ISSN: 0138-9130; CODEN: SCNTDX.

ELLIS, DAVID; ALLEN, DAVID; WILSON, THOMAS D. 1999. Information Science and Information Systems: Conjunct Subjects Disjunct Disciplines. Journal of the American Society for Information Science. 1999 October; 50(12): 1095-1107. ISSN: 0002-8231; CODEN: AISJB6.

EOM, SEAN B. 1998. The Intellectual Development and Structure of Decision Support Systems (1991-1995). OMEGA: International Journal of Management Science. 1998 October; 26(5): 639-657. ISSN: 0305-0483; CODEN: OMEGA6.

EOM, SEAN B. 1999. Decision Support Systems Research: Current State and Trends. Industrial Management & Data Systems. 1999; 99(5): 213-220. ISSN: 0263-5577; CODEN: IMDSD8.

ESTOUP, J. B. 1916. Les Gammes Stenographiques. [Stenographic Exercise]. 4th ed. Paris, France: Institut Stenographique; 1916. (In French).

ETO, HAJIME. 1988. Rising Tail in Bradford Distribution: Its Interpretation and Application. Scientometrics. 1988 May; 13(5-6): 271-287. ISSN: 0138-9130; CODEN: SCNTDX.

FAIRTHORNE, ROBERT A. 1969. Empirical Hyperbolic Distributions (Bradford, Zipf, Mandelbrot) for Bibliometric Description and Prediction. Journal of Documentation. 1969 December; 25(4): 319-343. ISSN: 0022-0418; CODEN: JDOCAS.

FANG, P. H.; FANG, JOHN M. 1995. A Modification of Lotka's Function for Scientific Productivity. Information Processing & Management. 1995; 31(1): 133-137. ISSN: 0306-4573; CODEN: IPMADK.

FARRADANE, JASON E. L. 1953. Information Service in Industry. Research. 1953; 6: 327-330. ISSN: 0034-5113.

FARRADANE, JASON E. L. 1955. Professional Education of the Information Scientist. In: Congrès International des Bibliothèques et des Centres de Documentation: Volume 2B; 1955 September 11-18; Brussels, Belgium. The Hague, The Netherlands: Martinus Nijhoff; 1955. 76-81. OCLC: 31035893.

FEDOROWICZ, JANE. 1982. The Theoretical Foundation of Zipf's Law and Its Application to the Bibliographic Database Environment. Journal of the American Society for Information Science. 1982 September; 33(5): 285-293. ISSN: 0002-8231; CODEN: AISJB6.

FOLINSBEE, R. E. 1977. World's View—from Alph to Zipf. Geological Society of America Bulletin. 1977; 88: 897-907. ISSN: 0016-7606; CODEN: BUGMAF.

FOX, CHRISTOPHER JOHN. 1983. Information and Misinformation: An Investigation of the Notions of Information, Misinformation, Informing, and Misinforming. Westport, CT: Greenwood Press; 1983. 223p. ISBN: 0-313-23928-2.

FRICKÉ, MARTIN. 1998. Jean Tague-Sutcliffe on Measuring Information. Information Processing & Management. 1998; 34(4): 385-394. ISSN: 0306-4573; CODEN: IPMADK.

GARFIELD, EUGENE. 1979. Citation Indexing: Its Theory and Application in Science, Technology, and Humanities. New York, NY: Wiley; 1979. 274p. ISBN: 0-471-02559-3.

GARFIELD, EUGENE. 1997. Validation of Citation Analysis. Journal of the American Society for Information Science. 1997 October; 48(10): 962. ISSN: 0002-8231; CODEN: AISJB6.

GARFIELD, EUGENE. 1998a. From Citation Indexes to Informetrics: Is the Tail Now Wagging the Dog? Libri. 1998 June; 48(2): 67-80. ISSN: 0024-2667; CODEN: IBMNAQ.

GARFIELD, EUGENE. 1998b. Random Thoughts on Citationology: Its Theory and Practice (Comments on Theories of Citation?). Scientometrics. 1998 September; 43(1): 69-76. ISSN: 0138-9130; CODEN: SCNTDX.

GARFIELD, EUGENE. 2000. From 1950s Documentalists to 20th Century Information Scientists—and Beyond: ASIS Enters the Year 2000 Facing Remarkable Advances and Challenges in Harnessing the Information Technology Revolution. Bulletin of the American Society for Information Science. 2000 December-January; 26(2): 26-29. ISSN: 0095-4403; CODEN: BASICR.

GARFIELD, EUGENE; SHER, IRVING H. 1963. New Factors in the Evaluation of Scientific Literature through Citation Indexing. American Documentation. 1963; 14(3): 195-201. ISSN: 0096-946X.

GARG, K. C.; SHARMA, PRAVEEN; SHARMA, LALITA. 1993. Bradford's Law in Relation to the Evolution of a Field: A Case Study of Solar Power Research. Scientometrics. 1993 June; 27(2): 145-156. ISSN: 0138-9130; CODEN: SCNTDX.

GILBERT, G. NIGEL. 1977. Referencing as Persuasion. Social Studies of Science. 1977 March; 7(1): 113-122. ISSN: 0306-3127; CODEN: SSTSD2.

GILLETT, R. 1991. Pitfalls in Assessing Research Performance by Grant Income. Scientometrics. 1991 October; 22(2): 253-263. ISSN: 0138-9130; CODEN: SCNTDX.

GLÄNZEL, WOLFGANG; CZERWON, HANS-JÜRGEN. 1995. A New Methodological Approach to Bibliographic Coupling and Its Application to Research-Front and Other Core Documents. See reference: KOENIG, MICHAEL E. D.; BOOKSTEIN, ABRAHAM, eds. 167-176.

GLÄNZEL, WOLFGANG; CZERWON, HANS-JÜRGEN. 1996. A New Methodological Approach to Bibliographic Coupling and Its Application to the National, Regional and Institutional Level. Scientometrics. 1996 October; 37(2): 195-221. ISSN: 0138-9130; CODEN: SCNTDX.

GLÄNZEL, WOLFGANG; KRETSCHMER, HILDRUN, eds. 1992. Selected Papers Presented at the 4th International Conference on Bibliometrics, Informetrics and Scientometrics; 1993 September 11-15; Berlin, Germany. Research Evaluation. 1992 December; 2(3): 121-188. ISSN: 0958-2029; CODEN: REEVEW.

GLÄNZEL, WOLFGANG; KRETSCHMER, HILDRUN, eds. 1994a. Selected Papers Presented at the 4th International Conference on Bibliometrics, Informetrics and Scientometrics; 1993 September 11-15; Berlin, Germany. Scientometrics. 1994 May; 30(1): 1-372p. ISSN: 0138-9130; CODEN: SCNTDX.

GLÄNZEL, WOLFGANG; KRETSCHMER, HILDRUN, eds. 1994b. Selected Papers Presented at the 4th International Conference on Bibliometrics, Informetrics and Scientometrics; 1993 September 11-15; Berlin, Germany. Science and Science of Science. 1994; 3(5): 166p.

GLÄNZEL, WOLFGANG; SCHOEPFLIN, URS. 1994a. A Stochastic Model for the Ageing of Scientific Literature. Scientometrics. 1994 May; 30(1): 49-64. ISSN: 0138-9130; CODEN: SCNTDX.

GLÄNZEL, WOLFGANG; SCHOEPFLIN, URS. 1994b. Little Scientometrics, Big Scientometrics ... and Beyond? Scientometrics. 1994 June-August; 30(2-3): 375-384. ISSN: 0138-9130; CODEN: SCNTDX.

GLÄNZEL, WOLFGANG; SCHOEPFLIN, URS. 1995. A Bibliometric Study on Ageing and Reception Processes of Scientific Literature. Journal of Information Science. 1995; 21(1): 37-53. ISSN: 0165-5515; CODEN: JISCDI.

GLÄNZEL, WOLFGANG; SCHUBERT, ANDRAS. 1995. Predictive Aspects of a Stochastic Model for Citation Processes. Information Processing & Management. 1995 January-February; 31(1): 69-80. ISSN: 0306-4573; CODEN: IPMADK.

GLÄNZEL, WOLFGANG; SCHUBERT, ANDRAS; CZERWON, HANS-JÜRGEN. 1999. An Item-by-Item Subject Classification of Papers Published in Multidisciplinary and General Journals Using Reference Analysis. Scientometrics. 1999 March-April; 44(3): 427-439. ISSN: 0138-9130; CODEN: SCNTDX.

GOFFMAN, WILLIAM; NEWILL, VAUN A. 1964. Generalization of Epidemic Theory: An Application to the Transmission of Ideas. Nature. 1964 October 17; 204(4955): 225-228. ISSN: 0028-0836; CODEN: NATUAS.

GOPINATH, M.A. 1992. Shiyali Ramamrita Ranganathan: A Profile in Relation to Librametry. In: Ravichandra Rao, I. K., ed. Informetrics 91: Selected Papers from the 3rd International Conference on Informetrics; 1991 August 9-12; Bangalore, India. Bangalore, India: Sarada Ranganathan Endowment for Library Science; 1992. 9-16. OCLC: 34314067.

GOR'KOVA, VALENTINA I. 1988. Informetriya [Informetrics]. Moscow, Russia: VINITI; 1988. 325p. (Itogi Nauki I Tekhniki series, 10 [Results in Science and Technology]; in Russian).

GRIFFITH, BELVER C. 1988. Exact Fits in Bibliometrics: Some Tools and Results. See reference: EGGHE, LEO; ROUSSEAU, RONALD, eds. 1988a. 85-95.

GRIVEL, LUC; MUTSCHKE, PETER; POLANCO, XAVIER. 1995. Thematic Mapping on Bibliographic Databases by Cluster Analysis: A Description of the SDOC Environment with SOLIS. Knowledge Organization. 1995; 22(2): 70-77. ISSN: 0943-7444.

GRIVEL, LUC; POLANCO, XAVIER; KAPLAN, ANDRÉ. 1997. A Computer System for Big Scientometrics at the Age of the World Wide Web. Scientometrics. 1997 November-December; 40(3): 493-506. ISSN: 0138-9130; CODEN: SCNTDX.

GROOS, OLE V. 1967. Bradford's Law and the Keenan-Atherton Data. American Documentation. 1967 January; 18(1): 46. ISSN: 0096-946X.

GROSS, PAUL L. K.; GROSS, E. M. 1927. College Libraries and Chemical Education. Science. 1927 October; 66(1713): 385-389. ISSN: 0036-8075; CODEN: SCIEAS.

GUPTA, B. M. 1998. Growth and Obsolescence of Literature in Theoretical Population Genetics. Scientometrics. 1998 July-August; 42(3): 335-347. ISSN: 0138-9130; CODEN: SCNTDX.

GUPTA, B. M.; KARISIDDAPPA, C. R. 1997. Productivity of Authors as Reflected by Duration of Their Scientific Participation and Speed of Publication. Scientometrics. 1997 July-August; 39(3): 281-291. ISSN: 0138-9130; CODEN: SCNTDX.

GUPTA, B. M.; KARISIDDAPPA, C. R. 1998. Collaboration in Theoretical Population Genetics Specialty. Scientometrics. 1998 July; 42(3): 349-376. ISSN: 0138-9130; CODEN: SCNTDX.

GUPTA, B. M.; SHARMA, LALITA; KARISIDDAPPA, C. R. 1995. Modelling the Growth of Papers in a Scientific Specialty. Scientometrics. 1995 June; 33(2): 187-201. ISSN: 0138-9130; CODEN: SCNTDX.

GUPTA, B. M.; SHARMA, PRAVEEN; KARISIDDAPPA, C .R. 1997. Growth of Research Literature in Scientific Specialities: A Modelling Perspective. Scientometrics. 1997 November-December; 40(3): 507-528. ISSN: 0138-9130; CODEN: SCNTDX.

GUPTA, B. M.; SHARMA, LALITA; KUMAR, SURESH. 1998. Literature Growth and Author Productivity Patterns in Indian Physics. Information Processing & Management. 1998 January; 34(1): 121-131. ISSN: 0306-4573; CODEN: IPMADK.

GUPTA, USHA. 1990. Obsolescence of Physics Literature: Exponential Decrease of the Density of Citations to Physical Review Articles with Age. Journal of the American Society for Information Science. 1990 June; 41(4): 282-287. ISSN: 0002-8231; CODEN: AISJB6.

HAITUN, S. D. 1982a. Stationary Scientometric Distributions. Part I. Different Approximations. Scientometrics. 1982 January; 4(1): 5-25. ISSN: 0138-9130; CODEN: SCNTDX.

HAITUN, S. D. 1982b. Stationary Scientometric Distributions. Part II. Non-Gaussian Nature of Scientific Activities. Scientometrics. 1982 March; 4(2): 89-104. ISSN: 0138-9130; CODEN: SCNTDX.

HAITUN, S. D. 1982c. Stationary Scientometric Distributions. Part III. The Role of the Zipf Distribution. Scientometrics. 1982; 4(3): 181-194. ISSN: 0138-9130; CODEN: SCNTDX.

HAITUN, S. D. 1990. Criteria of Gaussian/Non-Gaussian Nature of Distributions and Populations. See reference: EGGHE, LEO; ROUSSEAU, RONALD, eds. 1990a. 149-161.

HALL, DONALD H. 1990. Growth and Citation Selection Rates in Rapidly Growing Sciences from Date Stacking and Bibliographic Databases. See reference: EGGHE, LEO; ROUSSEAU, RONALD, eds. 1990a. 163-192.

HARA, H.; OKAYAMA, S. 1988. Fractal Dimension and Scaling Behavior of Cracks in a Random Medium: 'Frequency-Rank' Distribution Described by Generalized Random Walks. Physical Review B: Condensed Matter. 1988; 37(16): 9504-9511. ISSN: 0163-1829; CODEN: PHRVAO.

HARSANYI, MARTHA A. 1993. Multiple Authors, Multiple Problems— Bibliometrics and the Study of Scholarly Collaboration: A Literature Review. Library & Information Science Research. 1993 Fall; 15(4): 325-354. ISSN: 0740-8188; CODEN: LISRDH.

HART, P. W.; SOMMERFELD, J. T. 1998. Relationship between Growth in Gross Domestic Product (GDP) and Growth in the Chemical Engineering Literature in Five Different Countries. Scientometrics. 1998 July; 42(3): 299-311. ISSN: 0138-9130; CODEN: SCNTDX.

HARTER, STEPHEN P. 1996. The Impact of Electronic Journals on Scholarly Communication: A Citation Analysis. The Public-Access Computer Systems Review. 1996; 7(5): 5-34. ISSN: 1048-6542. Available WWW: http://info.lib.uh.edu/pr/v7/n5/hart7n5.html

HARTER, STEPHEN P.; HERT, CAROL A. 1997. Evaluation of Information Retrieval Systems: Approaches, Issues and Methods. In: Williams, Martha E., ed. Annual Review of Information Science and Technology: Volume 32. Medford, NJ: Information Today, Inc. for the American Society for Information Science; 1997. 3-94. ISSN: 0066-4200; ISBN: 1-57387-047-1; CODEN: ARISBC; LC: 66-25096.

HARTER, STEPHEN P.; NISONGER, THOMAS E. 1997. ISI's Impact Factor as Misnomer: A Proposed New Measure to Assess Journal Impact. Journal of the American Society for Information Science. 1997 December; 48(12): 1146-1148. ISSN: 0002-8231; CODEN: AISJB6.

HAWKINS, DONALD T. 1979. The Percentage Distribution: A Method of Ranking Journals. In: Tally, R. D.; Deultgen, R. R., eds. Information Choices and Policies: Proceedings of the American Society for Information Science (ASIS) 42nd Annual Meeting: Volume 16; 1979 October 14-18; Minneapolis, MN. White Plains, NY: Knowledge Industry Publications, Inc. for ASIS; 1979. 229-235. ISBN: 0-914236-47-4.

HEINE, MICHAEL H. 1998. Bradford Ranking Conventions and Their Application to a Growing Literature. Journal of Documentation. 1998 June; 54(3): 303-331. ISSN: 0022-0418; CODEN: JDOCAS.

HERTZEL, DOROTHY H. 1987. History of the Development of Ideas in Bibliometrics. In: Encyclopedia of Library and Information Science: Volume 42 (Supplement 7). New York, NY: Dekker; 1987. 144-218. ISBN: 0-8247-2042-3.

HÉRUBEL, JEAN-PIERRE V. M.; BUCHANAN, ANNE L. 1994. Citation Studies in the Humanities and Social Sciences: A Selective and Annotated Bibliography. Collection Management. 1994; 18(3/4): 89-137. ISSN: 0146-2679; CODEN: COMADF.

HJERPPE, ROLAND. 1980. A Bibliography of Bibliometrics and Citation Indexing and Analysis. Stockholm, Sweden: The Royal Institute of Technology Library; 1980. 166p. (Report TRITA-LIB-2013). OCLC: 7865568.

HJERPPE, ROLAND. 1982. Supplement to "A Bibliography of Bibliometrics and Citation Indexing and Analysis" (TRITA-LIB-2013). Scientometrics. 1982; 4(3): 241-281. ISSN: 0138-9130; CODEN: SCNTDX.

HJØRLAND, BIRGER. 1992. The Concept of "Subject'" in Information Science. Journal of Documentation. 1992 June; 48(2): 172-200. ISSN: 0022-0418; CODEN: JDOCAS.

HOOD, WILLIAM W. 1998. An Informetric Study of the Distribution of Bibliographic Records in Online Databases: A Case Study Using the Literature of Fuzzy Set Theory (1965-1993). Sydney, Australia: The University of New South Wales; 1998. 617p. (Ph.D. dissertation). Available WWW: http://adt.caul.edu.au.

HOOD, WILLIAM W.; WILSON, CONCEPCIÓN S. 1999. The Distribution of Bibliographic Records in Databases Using Different Counting Methods for Duplicate Records. Scientometrics. 1999 December; 46(3): 473-486. ISSN: 0138-9130; CODEN: SCNTDX.

HUBER, JOHN C. 1998a. Cumulative Advantage and Success-Breeds-Success: The Value of Time Pattern Analysis. Journal of the American Society for Information Science. 1998 April 15; 49(5): 471-476. ISSN: 0002-8231; CODEN: AISJB6.

HUBER, JOHN C. 1998b. The Underlying Process Generating Lotka's Law and the Statistics of Exceedances. Information Processing & Management. 1998 July; 34(4): 471-487. ISSN: 0306-4573; CODEN: IPMADK.

HUBERT, JOHN J. 1978. A Relationship between Two Forms of Bradford's Law. Journal of the American Society for Information Science. 1978 May; 29(3): 159-161. ISSN: 0002-8231; CODEN: AISJB6.

HUBERT, JOHN J. 1981. General Bibliometric Models. Library Trends. 1981 Summer; 30(1): 65-81. ISSN: 0024-2594; CODEN: LIBTA3.

HULME, EDWARD WYNDHAM. 1923. Statistical Bibliography in Relation to the Growth of Modern Civilization: Two Lectures Delivered in the University of Cambridge in May 1922. London, England: Butler and Tanner, Grafton; 1923. 44p. OCLC: 1513732.

HURT, CHARLIE D.; BUDD, JOHN M. 1992. Modeling the Literature of Superstring Theory: A Case of Fast Literature. Scientometrics. 1992 July-August; 24(3): 471-480. ISSN: 0138-9130; CODEN: SCNTDX.

IJIRI, YUJI. 1987. Birth-and-Death Processes. In: Eatwell, John; Milgate, Murray; Newman, Peter, eds. The New Palgrave: A Dictionary of Economics: Volume 1. London, England: MacMillan Press; 1987. 249-250. ISBN: 0-935859-10-1.

INGWERSEN, PETER. 1998. The Calculation of Web Impact Factors. Journal of Documentation. 1998 March; 54(2): 236-243. ISSN: 0022-0418; CODEN: JDOCAS.

INGWERSEN, PETER; CHRISTENSEN, FINN HJORTGAARD. 1997. Data Set Isolation for Bibliometric Online Analyses of Research Publications: Fundamental Methodological Issues. Journal of the American Society for Information Science. 1997 March; 48(3): 205-217. ISSN: 0002-8231; CODEN: AISJB6.

JAIN, ASHOK; GARG, K. C. 1992. Laser Research in India: Scientometric Study and Model Projections. Scientometrics. 1992 March-April; 23(3): 395-415. ISSN: 0138-9130; CODEN: SCNTDX.

JIN, BIHUI; WANG, BING. 1999. Chinese Science Citation Database: Its Construction and Application. Scientometrics. 1999 June; 45(2): 325-332. ISSN: 0138-9130; CODEN: SCNTDX.

KATZ, J. SYLVAN; HICKS, DIANA. 1995. The Classification of Interdisciplinary Journals: A New Approach. See reference: KOENIG, MICHAEL E. D.; BOOKSTEIN, ABRAHAM, eds. 245-254.

KATZ, J. SYLVAN; HICKS, DIANA. 1997. How Much Is a Collaboration Worth? A Calibrated Bibliometric Model. Scientometrics. 1997 November-December; 40(3): 541-554. ISSN: 0138-9130; CODEN: SCNTDX.

KEENAN, STELLA. 1996. Concise Dictionary of Library and Information Science. London, England: Bowker-Saur; 1996. 214p. ISBN: 1-85739-022-9.

KENDALL, M. G. 1960. The Bibliography of Operational Research. Operational Research Quarterly. 1960 March-June; 11(1-2): 31-35. ISSN: 0030-3623.

KESSLER, M. M. 1963. Bibliographic Coupling between Scientific Papers. American Documentation. 1963; 14(1): 10-25. ISSN: 0096-946X.

KHURSHID, ANWER; SAHAI, HARDEO. 1991a. Bibliometric Distributions and Laws: Some Comments and a Selected Bibliography. Journal of Educational Media and Library Sciences. 1991; 28(4): 433-459. ISSN: 1013-090X; CODEN: CYTHD5.

KHURSHID, ANWER; SAHAI, HARDEO. 1991b. Bibliometric, Scientometric and Informetric Distributions and Laws: A Selected Bibliography. International Forum on Information and Documentation. 1991 April; 16(2): 18-29. ISSN: 0304-9701; CODEN: IFIDD7.

KINNUCAN, MARK T.; WOLFRAM, DIETMAR. 1990. Direct Comparison of Bibliometric Models. Information Processing & Management. 1990; 26(6): 777-790. ISSN: 0306-4573; CODEN: IPMADK.

KOENIG, MICHAEL E. D.; BOOKSTEIN, ABRAHAM, eds. 1995. 5th Biennial Conference of the International Society for Scientometrics and Informetrics; 1995 June 7-10; River Forest, IL. Medford, NJ: Learned Information, Inc.; 1995. 703p. ISBN: 1-57387-010-2; OCLC: 34144742.

KOHONEN, TEUVO. 1989. Self-Organization and Associative Memory. 3rd edition. New York, NY: Springer-Verlag; 1989. 328p. ISBN: 0-387-51387-6; LC: 89-19681; OCLC: 20015322.

KOKOL, PETER; KOKOL, TATJANA. 1996. Linguistic Laws and Computer Programs. Journal of the American Society for Information Science. 1996 October; 41(10): 781-785. ISSN: 0002-8231; CODEN: AISJB6.

KOSTOFF, RONALD N. 1998. The Use and Misuse of Citation Analysis in Research Evaluation. Scientometrics. 1998 September; 43(1): 27-43. ISSN: 0138-9130; CODEN: SCNTDX.

KOSTOFF, RONALD N.; EBERHART, HENRY J.; TOOTHMAN, DARRELL RAY. 1999. Hypersonic and Supersonic Flow Roadmaps Using Bibliometrics and Database Tomography. Journal of the American Society for Information Science. 1999 April 15; 50(5): 427-447. ISSN: 0002-8231; CODEN: AISJB6.

KRETSCHMER, HILDRUN. 1999. A New Model of Scientific Collaboration Part 1. Theoretical Approach. Scientometrics. 1999 November-December; 46(3): 501-518. ISSN: 0138-9130; CODEN: SCNTDX.

KRIPPENDORFF, KLAUS. 1980. Content Analysis. An Introduction to Its Methodology. Beverly Hills, CA: Sage Publications; 1980. 191p. ISBN: 0-8039-1497-0.

KRÖBER, GÜNTER. 1994. Remembering the Epidemic Model. Science and Science of Science. 1994; 3(5): 41-44.

KUNDRA, RAMESH; KRETSCHMER, HILDRUN. 1999. A New Model of Scientific Collaboration Part 2: Collaboration Patterns in Indian Medicine. Scientometrics. 1999 November-December; 46(3): 519-528. ISSN: 0138-9130; CODEN: SCNTDX.

KUNZ, M. 1988. A Case Study against Haitun's Conjectures. Scientometrics. 1988 January; 13(1-2): 25-33. ISSN: 0138-9130; CODEN: SCNTDX.

LAND, KENNETH C.; MCCALL, PATRICIA L.; NAGIN, DANIEL S. 1996. A Comparison of Poisson, Negative Binomial, and Semiparametric Mixed Poisson Regression Models with Empirical Applications to Criminal Careers Data. Sociological Methods & Research. 1996 May; 24(4): 387-442. ISSN: 0049-1241.

LARSON, RAY R. 1996. Bibliometrics of the World-Wide-Web—An Exploratory Analysis of the Intellectual Structure of Cyberspace. In: Hardin, Steve, ed. Proceedings of the American Society for Information Science

(ASIS) 59th Annual Meeting; 1996 October 21-24; Baltimore, MD. Medford, NJ: Information Today, Inc. for ASIS; 1996. 71-78. ISSN: 0044-7870; ISBN: 1-57387-037-4; LC: 64-8303; CODEN: PAISDQ. Also available WWW: http://sherlock.berkeley.edu/asis96/asis96.html.

LEIMKUHLER, FERDINAND F. 1967. The Bradford Distribution. Journal of Documentation. 1967 September; 23(3): 197-207. ISSN: 0022-0418; CODEN: JDOCAS.

LEWISON, GRANT; DAWSON, GRAHAM; ANDERSON, JOE. 1995. The Behaviour of Biomedical Scientific Authors in Acknowledging Their Funding Sources. See reference: KOENIG, MICHAEL E. D.; BOOKSTEIN, ABRAHAM, eds. 255-263.

LEYDESDORFF, LOET. 1989. The Relations between Qualitative Theory and Scientometric Methods in Science and Technology Studies. Scientometrics. 1989 May; 15(5-6): 333-347. ISSN: 0138-9130; CODEN: SCNTDX.

LEYDESDORFF, LOET. 1994. La Scientométrie. Scientometrics. 1994 June-August; 30(2-3): 539-541. (Book review of Callon, Courtial & Penan, 1993). ISSN: 0138-9130; CODEN: SCNTDX.

LEYDESDORFF, LOET. 1997. Why Words and Co-Words Cannot Map the Development of the Sciences. Journal of the American Society for Information Science. 1997 May; 48(5): 418-427. ISSN: 0002-8231; CODEN: AISJB6.

LEYDESDORFF, LOET. 1998. Theories of Citation? Scientometrics. 1998 September; 43(1): 5-25. ISSN: 0138-9130; CODEN: SCNTDX.

LEYDESDORFF, LOET; WOUTERS, PAUL. 1996. Quantitative Measuring or Qualitative Understanding: Is It Possible to Bridge the Divide in STS? EASST Review (The quarterly journal of The European Association for the Study of Science and Technology). 1996 September; 15(3): 6p. Available WWW: http://www.chem.uva.nl/easst/easst963_3.html.

LEYDESDORFF, LOET; WOUTERS, PAUL. 1999. Between Texts and Contexts: Advances in Theories of Citation? (A Rejoinder). Scientometrics. 1999 February; 44(2): 169-182. ISSN: 0138-9130; CODEN: SCNTDX. Also available WWW: http://www.chem.uva.nl/sts/loet/citation/rejoin.htm.

LIEVROUW, LEAH A. 1990. Reconciling Structure and Process in the Study of Scholarly Communication. In: Borgman, Christine L., ed. Scholarly Communication and Bibliometrics. Newbury Park, CA: Sage Publications; 1990. 59-69. ISBN: 0-8039-3879-9.

LIN, XIA. 1997. Map Displays for Information Retrieval. Journal of the American Society for Information Science. 1997 January; 48(1): 40-54. ISSN: 0002-8231; CODEN: AISJB6.

LINDHOLM-ROMANTSCHUK, YLVA; WARNER, JULIAN. 1996. The Role of Monographs in Scholarly Communication: An Empirical Study of Philosophy, Sociology and Economics. Journal of Documentation. 1996 December; 52(4): 389-404. ISSN: 0022-0418; CODEN: JDOCAS.

LINE, MAURICE B. 1993. Changes in the Use of Literature with Time—Obsolescence Revisited. Library Trends. 1993 Spring; 41(4): 665-683. ISSN: 0024-2594; CODEN: LIBTA3.

LINE, MAURICE B.; SANDISON, ALEXANDER. 1974. Progress in Documentation: "Obsolescence" and Changes in the Use of Literature with Time. Journal of Documentation. 1974 September; 30(3): 283-350. ISSN: 0022-0418; CODEN: JDOCAS.

LIPETZ, BEN-AMI. 1999. Aspects of JASIS Authorship through Five Decades. Journal of the American Society for Information Science. 1999 September; 50(11): 994-1003. ISSN: 0002-8231; CODEN: AISJB6.

LITTLE, ANNE E.; HARRIS, ROMA M.; NICHOLLS, PAUL T. 1990. Text to Reference Ratios in Scientific Journals. See reference: EGGHE, LEO; ROUSSEAU, RONALD, eds. 1990a. 211-216.

LIU, MENGXIONG. 1993. Progress in Documentation: The Complexities of Citation Practice—A Review of Citation Studies. Journal of Documentation. 1993 December; 49(4): 370-408. ISSN: 0022-0418; CODEN: JDOCAS.

LOCKETT, MARY W. 1989. The Bradford Distribution—A Review of the Literature, 1934-1987. Library & Information Science Research. 1989; 11(1): 21-36. ISSN: 0740-8188; CODEN: LISRDH.

LOSEE, ROBERT M. 1990. The Science of Information: Measurement and Applications. San Diego, CA: Academic Press; 1990. 293p. ISBN: 0-12-455771-6.

LOSEE, ROBERT M. 1995. The Development and Migration of Concepts from Donor to Borrower Disciplines: Sublanguage Term Use in Hard & Soft Sciences. See reference: KOENIG, MICHAEL E. D.; BOOKSTEIN, ABRAHAM, eds. 265-273.

LOTKA, ALFRED J. 1926. The Frequency Distribution of Scientific Productivity. Journal of the Washington Academy of Sciences. 1926; 16(12): 317-323. ISSN: 0043-0439.

LUNIN, LOIS F.; WHITE, HOWARD D., eds. 1990. Perspectives on Author Cocitation Analysis. Journal of the American Society for Information Science. 1990 September; 41(6): 429-468. ISSN: 0002-8231; CODEN: AISJB6.

LUWEL, M.; MOED, HENK F. 1998. Publication Delays in the Science Field and Their Relationship to the Ageing of Scientific Literature. Scientometrics. 1998 January-February; 41(1-2): 29-40. ISSN: 0138-9130; CODEN: SCNTDX.

MACÍAS-CHAPULA, CÉSAR A., ed. 1999. 7th Conference of the International Society for Scientometrics and Informetrics; 1999 July 5-8; Colima, México. Colima, México: Universidad de Colima, México; 1999. 606p. ISBN: 968-6190-91-0.

MACROBERTS, MICHAEL H.; MACROBERTS, BARBARA R. 1996. Problems of Citation Analysis. Scientometrics. 1996 July-August; 36(3): 435-444. ISSN: 0138-9130; CODEN: SCNTDX.

MANDELBROT, BENOIT B. 1954. Structure Formelle des Textes et Communication: Deux Études [Formal Structure of Writing and Communication: Two Studies]. Word. 1954; 10: 1-27. (In French). ISSN: 0043-7956.

MANDELBROT, BENOIT B. 1960. The Pareto-Lévy Law and the Distribution of Income. International Economic Review. 1960 May; 1(2): 79-106. ISSN: 0020-6598; CODEN: INERAE.

MANDELBROT, BENOIT B. 1961. Stable Paretian Random Functions and the Multiplicative Variation of Income. Econometrica. 1961 October; 29(4): 517-543. ISSN: 0012-9682; CODEN: ECMTA7.

MARSHAKOVA, I. V. 1973. A System of Document Connections Based on References. Nauchno-Tekhnicheskaia Informatsiia. Seriia 2. 1973; 6: 3-8. (In Russian). ISSN: 0548-0027.

MARTENS, B.; SARETZKI, T. 1994. Quantitative Analysis of Thematic Structures in the Field of Biotechnology: A Study on the Basis of Conference

Data. Scientometrics. 1994 May; 30(1): 117-128. ISSN: 0138-9130; CODEN: SCNTDX.

MCCAIN, KATHERINE W. 1990. Mapping Authors in Intellectual Space: A Technical Overview. Journal of the American Society for Information Science. 1990 September; 41(6): 433-443. ISSN: 0002-8231; CODEN: AISJB6.

MCCAIN, KATHERINE W. 1991. Mapping Economics through the Journal Literature: An Experiment in Journal Cocitation Analysis. Journal of the American Society for Information Science. 1991 May; 42(4): 290-296. ISSN: 0002-8231; CODEN: AISJB6.

MCCAIN, KATHERINE W. 1997. Bibliometric Tools for Serials Collection Management in Academic Libraries. In: Hepfer, Cindy; Malinowski, Teresa; Gammon, Julia, eds. Advances in Serials Management: Volume 6. Greenwich, CT: JAI Press; 1997. 105-146. ISSN: 1040-4384.

MCCAIN, KATHERINE W. 1998. Neural Networks Research in Context: A Longitudinal Journal Cocitation Analysis of an Emerging Interdisciplinary Field. Scientometrics. 1998 March-April; 41(3): 389-410. ISSN: 0138-9130; CODEN: SCNTDX.

MCCAIN, KATHERINE W.; TURNER, KATHLEEN. 1989. Citation Context Analysis and Aging Patterns of Journal Articles in Molecular Genetics. Scientometrics. 1989 July; 17(1-2): 127-163. ISSN: 0138-9130; CODEN: SCNTDX.

MCGRATH, WILLIAM E. 1988. Parameters for Cluster Analysis of Library Overlap. See reference: EGGHE, LEO; ROUSSEAU, RONALD, eds. 1988a. 121-132.

MCGRATH, WILLIAM E. 1994. Little Scientometrics, Big Scientometrics: and Beyond. Scientometrics. 1994 June-August; 30(2-3): 439-442. ISSN: 0138-9130; CODEN: SCNTDX.

MCGRATH, WILLIAM E. 1996. The Unit of Analysis (Objects of Study) in Bibliometrics and Scientometrics. Scientometrics. 1996 February; 35(2): 257-264. ISSN: 0138-9130; CODEN: SCNTDX.

MELIN, GÖRAN. 1999. Impact of National Size on Research Collaboration: A Comparison between Northern European and American Universities. Scientometrics. 1999 September; 46(1): 161-170. ISSN: 0138-9130; CODEN: SCNTDX.

MELIN, GÖRAN; PERSSON, OLLE. 1998. Hotel Cosmopolitan: A Bibliometric Study of Collaboration at Some European Universities. Journal of the American Society for Information Science. 1998 January; 49(1): 43-48. ISSN: 0002-8231; CODEN: AISJB6.

MICCERI, THEODORE. 1989. The Unicorn, the Normal Curve, and Other Improbable Creatures. Psychological Bulletin. 1989; 105(1): 156-166. ISSN: 0033-2909; CODEN: PSBUAI.

MIGON, KRZYSZTOF; SKALSKA-ZLAT, MARTA. 1995. Bibliolinguistics and Bibliometrics—Connections and Interdependence: Theoretical and Quantitative Analysis. See reference: KOENIG, MICHAEL E. D.; BOOKSTEIN, ABRAHAM, eds. 331-347.

MILLER, T.; STEBENNE, D. 1988. The Bibliometrics of Politics. Gannett Center Journal. 1988; 2(4): 24-30. ISSN: 0893-8342.

MILMAN, B. L.; GAVRILOVA, YU. A. 1993. Analysis of Citations and Co-citation in Chemical Engineering. Scientometrics. 1993 May; 27(1): 53-74. ISSN: 0138-9130; CODEN: SCNTDX.

MIZZARO, STEFANO. 1997. Relevance: The Whole History. Journal of the American Society for Information Science. 1997 September; 48(9): 810-832. ISSN: 0002-8231; CODEN: AISJB6.

MOED, HENK F.; VAN LEEUWEN, THED N.; REEDIJK, J. 1998. A New Classification System to Describe the Ageing of Scientific Journals and Their Impact Factors. Journal of Documentation. 1998 September; 54(4): 387-419. ISSN: 0022-0418; CODEN: JDOCAS.

MOED, HENK F.; VAN LEEUWEN, THED N.; REEDIJK, J. 1999. Towards Appropriate Indicators of Journal Impact. Scientometrics. 1999 November; 46(3): 575-589. ISSN: 0138-9130; CODEN: SCNTDX.

MORRIS, THEODORE A.; MCCAIN, KATHERINE W. 1998. The Structure of Medical Informatics Journal Literature. Journal of the American Medical Informatics Association. 1998 September-October; 5(5): 448-466. ISSN: 1067-5027; CODEN: JAMAFU.

MORSE, PHILIP M. 1981. The Underlying Characteristics of the Bradford Distribution. Scientometrics. 1981 November; 3(6): 415-436. ISSN: 0138-9130; CODEN: SCNTDX.

MORSE, PHILIP M.; LEIMKUHLER, FERDINAND F. 1979. Exact Solution for the Bradford Distribution and Its Use in Modeling Informational Data. Operations Research. 1979; 27(1): 187-198. ISSN: 0030-364X; CODEN: OPREA1.

MOTYLEV, V. M. 1989. The Main Problems of Studying Literature Aging. Scientometrics. 1989 January; 15(1-2): 97-109. ISSN: 0138-9130; CODEN: SCNTDX.

NACKE, OTTO. 1979. Informetrie: Ein Neuer Name für Eine Neue Disziplin [Informetrics: a New Name for a New Discipline]. Nachrichten für Dokumentation. 1979 December; 30(6): 212-226. (In German). ISSN: 0027-7436; CODEN: NADOAW.

NACKE, OTTO; WEHMEIER, R.; EISENHARDT, OTTO H. 1980. Informetrie und Scientometrie: Cui Bono? Ein Dialog, Eine Liste und Ein Programm [Informetrics and Scientometrics: Cui Bono? A Dialogue, a List and a Programme]. Nachrichten für Dokumentation. 1980 June; 31(3): 100-106. (In German). ISSN: 0027-7436; CODEN: NADOAW.

NAKAMOTO, HIDESHIRO. 1988. Synchronous and Diachronous Citation Distributions. See reference: EGGHE, LEO; ROUSSEAU, RONALD, eds. 1988a. 157-163.

NALIMOV, V. V.; MUL'CHENKO, Z. M. 1969. Naukometriya: Izuchenie Razvitiya Nauki kak Informatsionnogo Protsessa [Scientometrics: Study of the Development of Science as an Information Process]. Moscow, Russia: Nauka; 1969. 169p. (In Russian). OCLC: 18430924. English translation: 1971. Washington, DC: Foreign Technology Division, U.S. Air Force Systems Command, Wright-Patterson AFB, Ohio; 1971. 196p. NTIS: AD735-634.

NARIN, FRANCIS. 1994. Patent Bibliometrics. Scientometrics. 1994 May; 30(1): 147-155. ISSN: 0138-9130; CODEN: SCNTDX.

NARIN, FRANCIS; HAMILTON, KIMBERLY S. 1996. Bibliometric Performance Measures. Scientometrics. 1996 July-August; 36(3): 293-310. ISSN: 0138-9130; CODEN: SCNTDX.

NARIN, FRANCIS; MOLL, JOY K. 1977. Bibliometrics. In: Williams, Martha E., ed. Annual Review of Information Science and Technology: Volume 12. White Plains, NY: Knowledge Industry Publications, Inc. for the American Society for Information Science; 1977. 35-58. ISSN: 0066-4200; ISBN: 0-914236-11-3.

NARIN, FRANCIS; OLIVASTRO, DOMINIC; STEVENS, KIMBERLY A. 1994. Bibliometrics Theory, Practice and Problems. Evaluation Review. 1994 February; 18(1): 65-76. ISSN: 0193-841X.

NATH, RAVINDER; JACKSON, WADE M. 1991. Productivity of Management Information Systems Researchers: Does Lotka's Law Apply? Information Processing & Management. 1991; 27(2/3): 203-209. ISSN: 0306-4573; CODEN: IPMADK.

NELSON, MICHAEL J. 1989. Stochastic Models for the Distribution of Index Terms. Journal of Documentation. 1989 September; 45(3): 227-237. ISSN: 0022-0418; CODEN: JDOCAS.

NELSON, MICHAEL J. 1992. Modelling the Tail of Bibliometric Distributions. In: Ravichandra Rao, I. K., ed. Informetrics 91: Selected Papers from the 3rd International Conference on Informetrics; 1991 August 9-12; Bangalore, India. Bangalore, India: Sarada Ranganathan Endowment for Library Science; 1992. 343-357. OCLC: 34314067.

NELSON, MICHAEL J.; TAGUE, JEAN M. 1985. Split Size-Rank Models for the Distribution of Index Terms. Journal of the American Society for Information Science. 1985 September; 36(5): 283-296. ISSN: 0002-8231; CODEN: AISJB6.

NICHOLLS, PAUL TRAVIS. 1986. Empirical Validation of Lotka's Law. Information Processing & Management. 1986; 22(5): 417-419. ISSN: 0306-4573; CODEN: IPMADK.

NICHOLLS, PAUL TRAVIS. 1987. Estimation of Zipf Parameters. Journal of the American Society for Information Science. 1987 November; 38(6): 443-445. ISSN: 0002-8231; CODEN: AISJB6.

NICHOLLS, PAUL TRAVIS. 1989. Bibliometric Modeling Processes and the Empirical Validity of Lotka's Law. Journal of the American Society for Information Science. 1989 November; 40(6): 379-385. ISSN: 0002-8231; CODEN: AISJB6.

NOWAKOWSKA, MARIA. 1984. Theories of Research. Seaside, CA: Intersystems Publications; 1984. 2 volumes. ISBN: 0-914105-20-5.

NOYONS, E. C. M.; MOED, HENK F.; LUWEL, M. 1999. Combining Mapping and Citation Analysis for Evaluative Bibliometric Purposes: A Bibliometric Study. Journal of the American Society for Information Science. 1999 February; 50(2): 115-131. ISSN: 0002-8231; CODEN: AISJB6.

NOYONS, E. C. M.; VAN RAAN, ANTHONY F. J. 1998. Monitoring Scientific Developments from a Dynamic Perspective: Self-Organized Structuring to Map Neural Network Research. Journal of the American Society for Information Science. 1998 January; 49(1): 68-81. ISSN: 0002-8231; CODEN: AISJB6.

O'CONNOR, DANIEL O.; VOOS, HENRY. 1981. Empirical Laws, Theory Construction and Bibliometrics. Library Trends. 1981 Summer; 30(1): 9-20. ISSN: 0024-2594; CODEN: LIBTA3.

O'NEILL, EDWARD T. 1973. Limitations of the Bradford Distributions. In: Waldron, Helen J.; Long, F. R., eds. Innovative Developments in Information Systems: Their Benefits and Costs: Proceedings of the American Society for Information Science (ASIS) 36th Annual Meeting: Volume 10; 1973 October 21-25; Los Angeles, CA. Westport, CT: Greenwood Press for ASIS; 1973. 177-178. ISBN: 0-87715-410-4.

OBERHOFER, CECILIA M. A. 1993. Information Use Value: A Test on the Perception of Utility and Validity. Information Processing & Management. 1993; 29(5): 587-600. ISSN: 0306-4573; CODEN: IPMADK.

OLUIĆ-VUKOVIĆ, VESNA. 1989. Impact of Productivity Increase on the Distribution Pattern of Journals. Scientometrics. 1989 July; 17(1-2): 97-109. ISSN: 0138-9130; CODEN: SCNTDX.

OLUIĆ-VUKOVIĆ, VESNA. 1992. Journal Productivity Distribution: Quantitative Study of Dynamic Behavior. Journal of the American Society for Information Science. 1992 July; 43(6): 412-421. ISSN: 0002-8231; CODEN: AISJB6.

OLUIĆ-VUKOVIĆ, VESNA. 1995. On the Dynamic Behavior of Bradford's Law. Journal of the American Society for Information Science. 1995 December; 46(10): 790-799. ISSN: 0002-8231; CODEN: AISJB6.

OLUIĆ-VUKOVIĆ, VESNA. 1997. Bradford's Distribution: From the Classical Bibliometric "Law" to the More General Stochastic Models. Journal of the American Society for Information Science. 1997 September; 48(9): 833-842. ISSN: 0002-8231; CODEN: AISJB6.

OLUIĆ-VUKOVIĆ, VESNA. 1998. Simon's Generating Mechanism: Consequences and Their Correspondence to Empirical Facts. Journal of the American Society for Information Science. 1998 August; 49(10): 867-880. ISSN: 0002-8231; CODEN: AISJB6.

OSAREH, FARIDEH. 1996a. Bibliometrics, Citation Analysis and Co-Citation Analysis: A Review of the Literature I. Libri. 1996 September; 46(3): 149-158. ISSN: 0024-2667; CODEN: IBMNAQ.

OSAREH, FARIDEH. 1996b. Bibliometrics, Citation Analysis and Co-Citation Analysis: A Review of the Literature II. Libri. 1996 December; 46(4): 217-225. ISSN: 0024-2667; CODEN: IBMNAQ.

OSAREH, FARIDEH; WILSON, CONCEPCIÓN S. 1997. Third World Countries (TWC) Research Publications by Disciplines: A Country-by-Country Citation Analysis. Scientometrics. 1997 July-August; 39(3): 253-266. ISSN: 0138-9130 ; CODEN: SCNTDX.

OTLET, PAUL. 1934. Traité de Documentation, Le Livre sur le Livre: Theorie et Pratique [Treatise on Documentation, The Book on the Book: Theory and Practice]. Brussels, Belgium: Editiones Mundaneum; 1934. 431p. OCLC: 2294082.

PAISLEY, WILLIAM. 1990. The Future of Bibliometrics. In: Borgman, Christine L., ed. Scholarly Communication and Bibliometrics. Newbury Park, CA: Sage Publications; 1990. 281-299. ISBN: 0-8039-3879-9.

PANDIT, IDRISA. 1993. Citation Errors in Library Literature: A Study of Five Library Science Journals. Library & Information Science Research. 1993 Spring; 15(2): 185-198. ISSN: 0740-8188; CODEN: LISRDH.

PAO, MIRANDA LEE. 1985. Lotka's Law: A Testing Procedure. Information Processing & Management. 1985; 21(4): 305-320. ISSN: 0306-4573; CODEN: IPMADK.

PAO, MIRANDA LEE. 1986. An Empirical Examination of Lotka's Law. Journal of the American Society for Information Science. 1986 January; 37(1): 26-33. ISSN: 0002-8231; CODEN: AISJB6.

PAO, MIRANDA LEE; MCCREERY, LAURIE. 1986. Bibliometric Application of Markov Chains. Information Processing & Management. 1986; 22(1): 7-17. ISSN: 0306-4573; CODEN: IPMADK.

PARETO, VILFREDO. 1897. Cours d'Economie Politique [Course of Political Economics]. Paris, France: Rouge and Cie; 1897. 2 volumes. (In French). OCLC: 2569315.

PEARSON, CHARLS. 1987. Application of the Finite Difference Calculus to the Observation of Symbol Processes. Reference Librarian. 1987 Summer; (18): 173-198. ISSN: 0276-3877; CODEN: RELBD6.

PERITZ, BLUMA C. 1984. On the Careers of Terminologies. The Case of Bibliometrics. Libri. 1984 September; 34(3): 233-242. ISSN: 0024-2667; CODEN: IBMNAQ.

PERITZ, BLUMA C. 1990. A Bradford Distribution for Bibliometrics. Scientometrics. 1990 May; 18(5-6): 323-329. ISSN: 0138-9130; CODEN: SCNTDX.

PERITZ, BLUMA C. 1992. On the Objectives of Citation Analysis: Problems of Theory and Method. Journal of the American Society for Information Science. 1992 July; 43(4): 448-451. ISSN: 0002-8231; CODEN: AISJB6.

PERITZ, BLUMA C. 1995. Some Themes in a Behavioral Science: Lessons from a Citation-and-Content-Analysis. See reference: KOENIG, MICHAEL E. D.; BOOKSTEIN, ABRAHAM, eds. 413-423.

PERITZ, BLUMA C.; EGGHE, LEO, eds. 1997. Proceedings of the 6th Conference of the International Society for Scientometrics and Informetrics; 1997 June 16-19; Jerusalem, Israel. Jerusalem, Israel: The School of Library, Archive and Information Studies of the Hebrew University of Jerusalem; 1997. 539p. ISBN: 965-222-793-5.

PERRY, J. A. 1985. The Dillion Hypothesis of Titular Colonicity: An Empirical Test from the Ecological Sciences. Journal of the American Society for Information Science. 1985 July; 36(4): 251-258. ISSN: 0002-8231; CODEN: AISJB6.

PERSSON, OLLE. 1994. The Intellectual Base and Research Fronts of JASIS 1986-1990. Journal of the American Society for Information Science. 1994 January; 45(1): 31-38. ISSN: 0002-8231; CODEN: AISJB6.

POLANCO, XAVIER; GRIVEL, LUC; ROYAUTÉ, JEAN. 1995. How to Do Things with Terms in Informetrics: Terminological Variation and Stabilization as Science Watch Indicators. See reference: KOENIG, MICHAEL E. D.; BOOKSTEIN, ABRAHAM, eds. 435-444.

POTTER, WILLIAM GRAY. 1981. Lotka's Law Revisited. Library Trends. 1981 Summer; 30(1): 21-39. ISSN: 0024-2594; CODEN: LIBTA3.

PRATHER, R. E. 1988. Comparison and Extension of Theories of Zipf and Halstead. The Computer Journal. 1988 June; 31(3): 248-252. ISSN: 0010-4620; CODEN: CMPJA6.

PRAVDIĆ, NEVENKA; OLUIĆ-VUKOVIĆ, VESNA. 1991. Distribution of Scientific Productivity: Ambiguities in the Assignment of Author Rank. Scientometrics. 1991 January; 20(1): 131-144. ISSN: 0138-9130; CODEN: SCNTDX.

PRICE, DEREK J. DE SOLLA. 1965. Networks of Scientific Papers. Science. 1965 July 30; 149(3683): 510-515. ISSN: 0036-8075; CODEN: SCIEAS.

PRICE, DEREK J. DE SOLLA. 1976. A General Theory of Bibliometric and Other Cumulative Advantage Processes. Journal of the American Society for Information Science. 1976 September-October; 27(5): 292-306. ISSN: 0002-8231; CODEN: AISJB6.

PRICE, DEREK J. DE SOLLA. 1986. Little Science, Big Science—and Beyond. New York, NY: Columbia University Press; 1986. 301p. ISBN: 0-231-04956-0.

PRITCHARD, ALAN. 1969. Statistical Bibliography or Bibliometrics? Journal of Documentation. 1969 December; 25(4): 348-349. ISSN: 0022-0418; CODEN: JDOCAS.

PRITCHARD, ALAN; WITTIG, G. R. 1981. Bibliometrics: A Bibliography and Index. Volume 1: 1874-1959. Watford, Hertfordshire, England: ALLM Books; 1981. 144p. ISBN: 0-9506784-0-6.

QIU, LIWEN. 1990. An Empirical Examination of the Existing Models for Bradford's Law. Information Processing & Management. 1990; 26(5): 655-672. ISSN: 0306-4573; CODEN: IPMADK.

QIU, LIWEN; TAGUE, JEAN M. 1990. Complete or Incomplete Data Sets: The Groos Droop Investigated. Scientometrics. 1990 September; 19(3-4): 223-237. ISSN: 0138-9130; CODEN: SCNTDX.

RAISIG, L. MILES. 1962. Statistical Bibliography in the Health Sciences. Bulletin of the Medical Library Association. 1962 July; 50(3): 450-461. ISSN: 0025-7338; CODEN: BMLAAG.

RAPOPORT, A. 1957. The Stochastic and "Teleological" Rationales of Certain Distributions and the So-Called Principle of Least Effort. Behavioral Science. 1957; 2(2): 147-161. ISSN: 0005-7940; CODEN: BEHSAS.

RAVICHANDRA RAO, I. K. 1980. The Distribution of Scientific Productivity and Social Change. Journal of the American Society for Information Science. 1980 March; 31(2): 111-122. ISSN: 0002-8231; CODEN: AISJB6.

RAVICHANDRA RAO, I. K. 1988. Probability Distributions and Inequality Measures for Analyses of Circulation Data. See reference: EGGHE, LEO; ROUSSEAU, RONALD, eds. 1988a. 231-248.

RAVICHANDRA RAO, I. K., ed. 1992. Informetrics 91: Selected Papers from the 3rd International Conference on Informetrics; 1991 August 9-12; Bangalore, India. Bangalore, India: Sarada Ranganathan Endowment for Library Science; 1992. 577p. OCLC: 34314067.

RAVICHANDRA RAO, I. K. 1998. An Analysis of Bradford Multipliers and a Model to Explain Law of Scattering. Scientometrics. 1998 January-February; 41(1-2): 93-100. ISSN: 0138-9130; CODEN: SCNTDX.

RAYWARD, W. BOYD. 1997. The Origins of Information Science and the International Institute of Bibliography/International Federation for Information and Documentation (FID). Journal of the American Society for Information Science. 1997 April; 48(4): 289-300. ISSN: 0002-8231; CODEN: AISJB6.

REID, EDNA O. F. 1997. Evolution of a Body of Knowledge: An Analysis of Terrorism Research. Information Processing & Management. 1997 January; 33(1): 91-106. ISSN: 0306-4573; CODEN: IPMADK.

RESEARCH EVALUATION. 1991-. Van Raan, Tony, ed. Guildford, Surrey, UK: Beech Tree Publishing. ISSN: 0958-2029; CODEN: REEVEW.

ROUSSEAU, RONALD. 1987. The Nuclear Zone of a Leimkuhler Curve. Journal of Documentation. 1987 December; 43(4): 322-333. ISSN: 0022-0418; CODEN: JDOCAS.

ROUSSEAU, RONALD. 1988a. Citation Distribution of Pure Mathematics Journals. See reference: EGGHE, LEO; ROUSSEAU, RONALD, eds. 1988a. 249-260.

ROUSSEAU, RONALD. 1988b. Lotka's Law and Its Leimkuhler Representation. Library Science with a Slant to Documentation. 1988 September; 25(3): 150-178. ISSN: 0024-2543; CODEN: LSSDA8.

ROUSSEAU, RONALD. 1990a. A Bibliometric Study of Nieuwenhuysen's Bibliography of Microcomputer Software for Online Information and Documentation Work. Journal of Information Science. 1990; 16(1): 45-50. ISSN: 0165-5515; CODEN: JISCDI.

ROUSSEAU, RONALD. 1990b. Relations between Continuous Versions of Bibliometric Laws. Journal of the American Society for Information Science. 1990 April; 41(3): 197-203. ISSN: 0002-8231; CODEN: AISJB6.

ROUSSEAU, RONALD. 1992. Breakdown of the Robustness Property of Lotka's Law: The Case of Adjusted Counts for Multiauthorship Attribution. Journal of the American Society for Information Science. 1992 December; 43(10): 645-647. ISSN: 0002-8231; CODEN: AISJB6.

ROUSSEAU, RONALD. 1993. A Table for Estimating the Exponent in Lotka's Law. Journal of Documentation. 1993 December; 49(4): 409-412. ISSN: 0022-0418; CODEN: JDOCAS.

ROUSSEAU, RONALD. 1994a. Bradford Curves. Information Processing & Management. 1994 March-April; 30(2): 267-277. ISSN: 0306-4573; CODEN: IPMADK.

ROUSSEAU, RONALD. 1994b. Double Exponential Models for First-Citation Processes. Scientometrics. 1994 May; 30(1): 213-227. ISSN: 0138-9130; CODEN: SCNTDX.

ROUSSEAU, RONALD. 1994c. The Number of Authors per Article in Library and Information Science Can Often Be Described by a Simple Probability Distribution. Journal of Documentation. 1994 June; 50(2): 134-141. ISSN: 0022-0418; CODEN: JDOCAS.

ROUSSEAU, RONALD. 1997. Sitations: An Exploratory Study. Cybermetrics: International Journal of Scientometrics, Informetrics and Bibliometrics. 1997; 1(1). ISSN: 1137-5019. Available WWW: http://www.cindoc.csic.es/cybermetrics/articles/v1i1p1.html.

ROUSSEAU, RONALD. 1998. Convolutions and Their Applications in Information Science. Canadian Journal of Information and Library Science. 1998 September; 23(3): 29-47. ISSN: 1195-096X; CODEN: CJISDE.

ROUSSEAU, RONALD. 1999. Temporal Differences in Self-Citation Rates of Scientific Journals. Scientometrics. 1999 March-April; 44(3): 521-531. ISSN: 0138-9130; CODEN: SCNTDX.

ROUSSEAU, RONALD; ROUSSEAU, SANDRA. 1993. Informetric Distributions: A Tutorial Review. Canadian Journal of Information and Library Science. 1993 July; 18(2): 51-63. ISSN: 1195-096X; CODEN: CJISEF.

ROUSSEAU, RONALD; ZHANG, QIAOQIAO. 1992. Zipf's Data on the Frequency of Chinese Words Revisited. Scientometrics. 1992 June; 24(2): 201-220. ISSN: 0138-9130; CODEN: SCNTDX.

ROUSSEAU, SANDRA; ROUSSEAU, RONALD. 1999. Optimal Fines in Libraries and Documentation Centers. In: Macías-Chapula, César A., ed. 7th Conference of the International Society for Scientometrics and Informetrics; 1999 July 5-8; Colima, México. Colima, México: Universidad de Colima, México; 1999. 431-440. ISBN: 968-6190-91-0.

ROWLANDS, IAN. 1999. Patterns of Author Cocitation in Information Policy: Evidence of Social, Collaborative and Cognitive Structure. Scientometrics. 1999 March-April; 44(3): 533-546. ISSN: 0138-9130; CODEN: SCNTDX.

RUIZ-BAÑOS, R.; BAILÓN-MORENO, R.; JIMÉNEZ-CONTRERAS, W.; COURTIAL, JEAN-PIERRE. 1999a. Structure and Dynamics of Scientific Networks. Part I. Fundamentals of the Quantitative Model of Translation. Scientometrics. 1999 February; 44(2): 217-234. ISSN: 0138-9130; CODEN: SCNTDX.

RUIZ-BAÑOS, R.; BAILÓN-MORENO, R.; JIMÉNEZ-CONTRERAS, W.; COURTIAL, JEAN-PIERRE. 1999b. Structure and Dynamics of Scientific Networks. Part II. The New Zipf's Law, the Clusters of Co-Citations and the Model of the Descriptor Presence. Scientometrics. 1999 February; 44(2): 235-265. ISSN: 0138-9130; CODEN: SCNTDX.

SAAM, NICOLE J.; REITER, L. 1999. Lotka's Law Reconsidered: The Evolution of Publication and Citation Distributions in Scientific Fields. Scientometrics. 1999 February; 44(2): 135-155. ISSN: 0138-9130; CODEN: SCNTDX.

SALTON, GERARD; BERGMARK, D. 1979. Citation Study of Computer Science Literature. IEEE Transactions on Professional Communication. 1979; 22(3): 146-158. ISSN: 0361-1434; CODEN: IEPCBU.

SALTON, GERARD; MCGILL, MICHAEL J. 1983. Introduction to Modern Information Retrieval. New York, NY: McGraw-Hill; 1983. 448p. ISBN: 0-07-066526-5.

SANDSTROM, PAMELA EFFREIN. 1994. An Optimal Foraging Approach to Information Seeking and Use. Library Quarterly. 1994 October; 64(4): 414-449. ISSN: 0024-2519; CODEN: LIBQAS.

SANGAM, S. L. 1999. Obsolescence of Literature in the Field of Psychology. Scientometrics. 1999 January; 44(1): 33-46. ISSN: 0138-9130; CODEN: SCNTDX.

SARACEVIC, TEFKO. 1996. Relevance Reconsidered '96. In: Ingwersen, Peter; Pors, Niels Ole, eds. CoLIS 2: 2nd International Conference on Conceptions of Library and Information Science: Integration in Perspective; 1996 October 13-16; Copenhagen, Denmark. Copenhagen, Denmark: Royal School of Librarianship; 1996. 201-218. ISBN: 87-7415-260-2.

SCHAMBER, LINDA. 1994. Relevance and Information Behavior. In: Williams, Martha E., ed. Annual Review of Information Science and Technology: Volume 29. Medford, NJ: Learned Information, Inc. for the American Society for Information Science; 1994. 3-48. ISSN: 0066-4200; ISBN: 0-938734-91-1; CODEN: ARISBC; LC: 66-25096.

SCHARNHORST, ANDREA. 1998. Citation Networks, Science Landscapes and Evolutionary Strategies. Scientometrics. 1998 September; 43(1): 95-106. ISSN: 0138-9130; CODEN: SCNTDX.

SCHROEDER, MANFRED R. 1991. Fractals, Chaos, Power Laws: Minutes from an Infinite Paradise. New York, NY: W.H. Freeman; 1991. 429p. ISBN: 0-7167-2357-3.

SCHUBERT, ANDRAS. 1996a. Scientometrics: A Citation Based Bibliography, 1990. Scientometrics. 1996 January; 35(1): 155-163. ISSN: 0138-9130; CODEN: SCNTDX.

SCHUBERT, ANDRAS. 1996b. Scientometrics: A Citation Based Bibliography, 1991. Scientometrics. 1996 March-April; 35(3): 393-399. ISSN: 0138-9130; CODEN: SCNTDX.

SCHUBERT, ANDRAS. 1996c. Scientometrics: A Citation Based Bibliography, 1992. Scientometrics. 1996 May; 36(1): 131-140. ISSN: 0138-9130; CODEN: SCNTDX.

SCHUBERT, ANDRAS. 1996d. Scientometrics: A Citation Based Bibliography, 1993. Scientometrics. 1996 June; 36(2): 273-280. ISSN: 0138-9130; CODEN: SCNTDX.

SCHUBERT, ANDRAS. 1999. Scientometrics: A Citation Based Bibliography, 1994-1996. Scientometrics. 1999 February; 44(2): 267-315. ISSN: 0138-9130; CODEN: SCNTDX.

SCHUBERT, ANDRAS; BRAUN, TIBOR. 1993. Reference Standards for Citation Based Assessments. Scientometrics. 1993 January; 26(1): 21-35. ISSN: 0138-9130; CODEN: SCNTDX.

SCHUBERT, ANDRAS; GLÄNZEL, WOLFGANG. 1984. A Dynamic Look at a Class of Skew Distributions: A Model with Scientometric Applications. Scientometrics. 1984 May; 6(3): 149-167. ISSN: 0138-9130; CODEN: SCNTDX.

SCHWARTZ, CHARLES A. 1997. The Rise and Fall of Uncitedness. College & Research Libraries. 1997 January; 58(1): 19-29. ISSN: 0010-0870.

SCHWECHHEIMER, H.; WINTERHAGER, M. 1999. Highly Dynamic Specialities in Climate Research. Scientometrics. 1999 March; 44(3): 547-560. ISSN: 0138-9130; CODEN: SCNTDX.

SCIENTOMETRICS: An International Journal for All Quantitative Aspects of Science of Science, Communication in Science and Science Policy. 1979-. Braun, Tibor, ed. Amsterdam, The Netherlands: Elsevier Science Publishers. ISSN: 0138-9130; CODEN: SCNTDX.

SEGLEN, PER O. 1992. The Skewness of Science. Journal of the American Society for Information Science. 1992 October; 43(9): 628-638. ISSN: 0002-8231; CODEN: AISJB6.

SEGLEN, PER O. 1994. Causal Relationship between Article Citedness and Journal Impact. Journal of the American Society for Information Science. 1994 January; 45(1): 1-11. ISSN: 0002-8231; CODEN: AISJB6.

SEGLEN, PER O. 1996. Quantification of Scientific Article Contents. Scientometrics. 1996 March-April; 35(3): 355-366. ISSN: 0138-9130; CODEN: SCNTDX.

SELLEN, MARY K. 1993. Bibliometrics: An Annotated Bibliography, 1970-1990. New York, NY: G. K. Hall & Co.; 1993. 169p. ISBN: 0-8161-1954-6.

SELZER, JACK, ed. 1993. Understanding Scientific Prose. Madison, WI: University of Wisconsin Press; 1993. 388p. ISBN: 0-299-13900-X.

SEN, SUBIR K. 1989. Bibliographic Scattering: A Generalised Source Approach. Scientometrics. 1989 September; 17(3-4): 197-204. ISSN: 0138-9130; CODEN: SCNTDX.

SEN, SUBIR K.; CHATTERJEE, SUNIL K. 1998. Bibliographic Scattering and Time: An Empirical Study through Temporal Partitioning of Bibliographies. Scientometrics. 1998 January-February; 41(1-2): 135-154. ISSN: 0138-9130; CODEN: SCNTDX.

SENGUPTA, I. N. 1992. Bibliometrics, Informetrics, Scientometrics and Librametrics: An Overview. Libri. 1992 April-June; 42(2): 75-98. ISSN: 0024-2667; CODEN: IBMNAQ.

SHANNON, CLAUDE ELWOOD; WEAVER, WARREN. 1949. The Mathematical Theory of Communication. Urbana, IL: University of Illinois Press; 1949. 117p. OCLC: 1561841.

SHAPIRO, FRED R. 1992. Origins of Bibliometrics, Citation Indexing, and Citation Analysis: The Neglected Legal Literature. Journal of the American Society for Information Science. 1992 June; 43(5): 337-339. ISSN: 0002-8231; CODEN: AISJB6.

SHAPIRO, FRED R. 1995. Coinage of the Term Information Science. Journal of the American Society for Information Science. 1995 June; 46(5): 384-385. ISSN: 0002-8231; CODEN: AISJB6.

SHARMA, LALITA; BASU, APARNA; BHARGAVA, S. C. 1993. A New Model of Innovation Diffusion. Journal of Scientific & Industrial Research. 1993 March; 52: 151-158. ISSN: 0022-4456; CODEN: JSIRAC.

SHAW, WILLIAM M., JR. 1985. Critical Thresholds in Co-Citation Graphs. Journal of the American Society for Information Science. 1985 January; 36(1): 38-43. ISSN: 0002-8231; CODEN: AISJB6.

SICHEL, HERBERT S. 1975. On a Distribution Law for Word Frequencies. Journal of the American Statistical Association. 1975 September; 70(351): 542-547. ISSN: 0162-1459; CODEN: JSTNAL.

SICHEL, HERBERT S. 1985. A Bibliometric Distribution Which Really Works. Journal of the American Society for Information Science. 1985 September; 36(5): 314-321. ISSN: 0002-8231; CODEN: AISJB6.

SICHEL, HERBERT S. 1986. The GIGP Distribution Model with Applications to Physics Literature. Czechoslovak Journal of Physics. 1986; B36(1): 133-137. ISSN: 0011-4626; CODEN: CZYPAO.

SICHEL, HERBERT S. 1992a. Anatomy of the Generalized Inverse Gaussian-Poisson Distribution with Special Applications to Bibliometric Studies.

Information Processing & Management. 1992; 28(1): 5-17. ISSN: 0306-4573; CODEN: IPMADK.

SICHEL, HERBERT S. 1992b. Note on a Strongly Unimodal Bibliometric Size Frequency Distribution. Journal of the American Society for Information Science. 1992 May; 43(4): 299-303. ISSN: 0002-8231; CODEN: AISJB6.

SIMON, HERBERT A. 1955. On a Class of Skew Distribution Functions. Biometrika. 1955; 42(Pts. 3-4): 425-440. ISSN: 0006-3444; CODEN: BIOKAX.

SIMONTON, DEAN KEITH. 1997. Creative Productivity: A Predictive and Explanatory Model of Career Trajectories and Landmarks. Psychological Review. 1997 January; 104(1): 66-89. ISSN: 0033-295X; CODEN: PSRVAX.

SMALL, HENRY. 1973. Co-citation in the Scientific Literature: A New Measure of the Relationship between Two Documents. Journal of the American Society for Information Science. 1973 July-August; 24(4): 265-269. ISSN: 0002-8231; CODEN: AISJB6.

SMALL, HENRY. 1978. Cited Documents as Concept Symbols. Social Studies of Science. 1978 August; 8(3): 327-340. ISSN: 0306-3127; CODEN: SSTSD2.

SMALL, HENRY. 1998. A General Framework for Creating Large-Scale Maps of Science in Two or Three Dimensions: The SciViz System. Scientometrics. 1998 January-February; 41(1-2): 125-133. ISSN: 0138-9130; CODEN: SCNTDX.

SMALL, HENRY. 1999. Visualizing Science by Citation Mapping. Journal of the American Society for Information Science. 1999 July; 50(9): 799-813. ISSN: 0002-8231; CODEN: AISJB6.

SMALL, HENRY; GARFIELD, EUGENE. 1985. The Geography of Science: Disciplinary and National Mappings. Journal of Information Science. 1985; 11(4): 147-159. ISSN: 0165-5515; CODEN: JISCDI.

SMALL, HENRY; SWEENEY, E. 1985. Clustering the Science Citation Index Using Co-Citations, I: A Comparison of Methods. Scientometrics. 1985 March; 7(3-6): 391-409. ISSN: 0138-9130; CODEN: SCNTDX.

SMITH, F. J.; DEVINE, K. 1985. Storing and Retrieving Word Phrases. Information Processing & Management. 1985; 21(3): 215-224. ISSN: 0306-4573; CODEN: IPMADK.

SNYDER, HERBERT; BONZI, SUSAN. 1998. Patterns of Self-Citation across Disciplines (1980-1989). Journal of Information Science. 1998; 24(6): 431-435. ISSN: 0165-5515; CODEN: JISCDI.

SOKAL, ROBERT R.; ROHLF, F. JAMES. 1995. Biometry: The Principles and Practice of Statistics in Biological Research. 3rd edition. New York, NY: W. H. Freeman; 1995. 887p. ISBN: 0-7167-2411-1.

STEINDL, JOSEF. 1987. Pareto Distribution. In: Eatwell, John; Milgate, Murray; Newman, Peter, eds. The New Palgrave: A Dictionary of Economics: Volume 3. London, England: MacMillan Press; 1987. 809-810. ISBN: 0-935859-10-1.

STEPHAN, PAULA E.; LEVIN, SHARON G. 1991. Inequality in Scientific Performance: Adjustment for Attribution and Journal Impact. Social Studies of Science. 1991 May; 21(2): 351-368. ISSN: 0306-3127; CODEN: SSTSD2.

STERN, PETER. 1995. Bibliometric Maps as Valid Representations of Scientific Practice: Controversies and Closure in the Social Sciences. See reference: KOENIG, MICHAEL E. D.; BOOKSTEIN, ABRAHAM, eds. 533-544.

STEWART, JOHN A. 1994. The Poisson-Lognormal Model for Bibliometric/ Scientometric Distributions. Information Processing & Management. 1994 March-April; 30(2): 239-251. ISSN: 0306-4573; CODEN: IPMADK.

SU, YI; HAN, LI-FENG. 1998. A New Literature Growth Model: Variable Exponential Growth Law of Literature. Scientometrics. 1998 June; 42(2): 259-265. ISSN: 0138-9130; CODEN: SCNTDX.

SWANSON, DON R.; SMALHEISER, NEIL R. 1999. Implicit Text Linkages between Medline Records: Using Arrowsmith as an Aid to Scientific Discovery. Library Trends. 1999 Summer; 48(1): 48-59. ISSN: 0024-2594; CODEN: LIBTA3.

TABAH, ALBERT N. 1992. Nonlinear Dynamics and the Growth of Literature. Information Processing & Management. 1992; 28(1): 61-73. ISSN: 0306-4573; CODEN: IPMADK.

TAGUE, JEAN M. 1981. The Success-Breeds-Success Phenomenon and Bibliometric Processes. Journal of the American Society for Information Science. 1981 July; 32(4): 280-286. ISSN: 0002-8231; CODEN: AISJB6.

TAGUE, JEAN M. 1988. What's the Use of Bibliometrics? See reference: EGGHE, LEO; ROUSSEAU, RONALD, eds. 1988a. 271-278.

TAGUE, JEAN; NICHOLLS, PAUL TRAVIS. 1987. The Maximal Value of Zipf Size Variable: Sampling Properties and Relationship to Other Parameters. Information Processing & Management. 1987; 23(3): 155-170. ISSN: 0306-4573; CODEN: IPMADK.

TAGUE-SUTCLIFFE, JEAN M. 1992a. An Introduction to Informetrics. Information Processing & Management. 1992; 28(1): 1-3. ISSN: 0306-4573; CODEN: IPMADK.

TAGUE-SUTCLIFFE, JEAN M. 1992b. How Good Is a Model? Explicativity as a Goodness-of-Fit Measure. In: Ravichandra Rao, I. K., ed. Informetrics 91: Selected Papers from the 3rd International Conference on Informetrics; 1991 August 9-12; Bangalore, India. Bangalore, India: Sarada Ranganathan Endowment for Library Science; 1992. 484-505. OCLC: 34314067.

TAGUE-SUTCLIFFE, JEAN M., ed. 1992c. Special Issue: Informetrics. Information Processing & Management. 1992; 28(1): 1-151. ISSN: 0306-4573; CODEN: IPMADK.

TAGUE-SUTCLIFFE, JEAN M. 1994. Quantitative Methods in Documentation. In: Vickery, Brian C., ed. Fifty Years of Information Progress: A Journal of Documentation Review. London, England: Aslib; 1994. 147-188. ISBN: 0-85142-327-2.

TAGUE-SUTCLIFFE, JEAN M. 1995. Measuring Information: An Information Services Perspective. San Diego, CA: Academic Press; 1995. 206p. ISBN: 0-12-682660-9.

TAHAI, ALIREZA; RIGSBY, JOHN T. 1998. Information Processing Using Citations to Investigate Journal Influence in Accounting. Information Processing & Management. 1998 March-May; 34(2-3): 341-359. ISSN: 0306-4573; CODEN: IPMADK.

TECHNOMETRICS: A Journal of Statistics for the Physical, Chemical, and Engineering Sciences. 1959-. Kafadar, Karen, ed. Alexandria, VA: American Society for Quality and the American Statistical Association. ISSN: 0040-1706; CODEN: TCMTA2.

TIJSSEN, ROBERT J. W. 1992. Cartography of Science: Scientometric Mapping with Multidimensional Scaling Methods. Leiden, The Netherlands: DSWO Press; 1992. 307p. ISBN: 90-6695-061-7.

TOCATLIAN, J. 1970. Are Titles of Chemical Papers Becoming More Informative? Journal of the American Society for Information Science. 1970 September-October; 21(5): 345-350. ISSN: 0002-8231; CODEN: AISJB6.

TOMOV, DIMITER T.; MUTAFOV, H. G. 1996. Comparative Indicators of Interdisciplinarity in Modern Science. Scientometrics. 1996 October; 37(2): 267-278. ISSN: 0138-9130; CODEN: SCNTDX.

TWEEDIE, F. J.; SINGH, S.; HOLMES, D. I. 1996. Neural-Network Applications in Stylometry: The Federalist Papers. Computers and the Humanities. 1996; 30(1): 1-10. ISSN: 0010-4817; CODEN: COHUAD.

VAN LEEUWEN, THED N.; MOED, HENK F.; REEDIJK, J. 1999. Critical Comments on Institute for Scientific Information Impact Factors: A Sample of Inorganic Molecular Chemistry Journals. Journal of Information Science. 1999; 25(6): 489-498. ISSN: 0165-5515; CODEN: JISCDI.

VAN RAAN, ANTHONY F. J. 1990. Fractal Dimension of Co-Citations. Nature. 1990 October 18; 347(6294): 626. ISSN: 0028-0836; CODEN: NATUAS.

VAN RAAN, ANTHONY F. J. 1991. Fractal Geometry of Information Space as Represented by Co-Citation Clustering. Scientometrics. 1991 March-April; 20(3): 439-449. ISSN: 0138-9130; CODEN: SCNTDX.

VAN RAAN, ANTHONY F. J. 1997. Scientometrics: State-of-the-Art. Scientometrics. 1997; 38(1): 205-218. ISSN: 0138-9130; CODEN: SCNTDX.

VAN RAAN, ANTHONY F. J. 1998a. In Matters of Quantitative Studies of Science the Fault of Theorists Is Offering Too Little and Asking Too Much. Scientometrics. 1998 September; 43(1): 129-139. ISSN: 0138-9130; CODEN: SCNTDX.

VAN RAAN, ANTHONY F. J., ed. 1998b. Special Topic Issue: Science and Technology Indicators. Journal of the American Society for Information Science. 1998 January; 49(1): 3-81. ISSN: 0002-8231; CODEN: AISJB6.

VINKLER, PETER. 1998a. Comparative Investigation of Frequency and Strength of Motives toward Referencing: The Reference Threshold Model. Scientometrics. 1998 September; 43(1): 107-127. ISSN: 0138-9130; CODEN: SCNTDX.

VINKLER, PETER. 1998b. General Performance Indexes Calculated for Research Institutes of the Hungarian Academy of Sciences Based on Scientometric Indicators. Scientometrics. 1998 January-February; 41(1-2): 185-200. ISSN: 0138-9130; CODEN: SCNTDX.

VLACHY, JAN. 1980. Evaluating the Distribution of Individual Performance. Scientia Yugoslavica. 1980; 6(1-4): 155-189. ISSN: 0350-686X.

WAGNER-DÖBLER, ROLAND. 1995. Where Has the Cumulative Advantage Gone? Some Observations about the Frequency Distribution of Scientific Productivity, of Duration of Scientific Participation, and of Speed of Publication. Scientometrics. 1995 February; 32(2): 123-132. ISSN: 0138-9130; CODEN: SCNTDX.

WAGNER-DÖBLER, ROLAND. 1997. Time Dependencies of Bradford Distributions: Structure of Journal Output in 20th-Century Logic and 19th-

Century Mathematics. Scientometrics. 1997 June; 39(3): 231-252. ISSN: 0138-9130; CODEN: SCNTDX.

WAGNER-DÖBLER, ROLAND; BERG, JAN. 1995. The Dependence of Lotka's Law on the Selection of Time Periods in the Development of Scientific Areas and Authors. Journal of Documentation. 1995 March; 51(1): 28-43. ISSN: 0022-0418; CODEN: JDOCAS.

WALLACE, DANNY P. 1987. A Solution in Search of a Problem: Bibliometrics & Libraries. Library Journal. 1987 May 1; 112(8): 43-47. ISSN: 0363-0277; CODEN: LIBJA7.

WALTERS, S. M. 1986. The Name of the Rose: A Review of Ideas on the European Bias in Angiosperm Classification. New Phytologist. 1986; 104(4): 527-546. ISSN: 0028-646X; CODEN: NEPHAV.

WANG, CHONGDE; WANG, ZHE. 1998. Evaluation of the Models for Bradford's Law. Scientometrics. 1998 May; 42(1): 89-95. ISSN: 0138-9130; CODEN: SCNTDX.

WATTS, ROBERT J.; PORTER, ALAN L.; CUNNINGHAM, S.; ZHU, DONGHUA. 1997. TOAS Intelligence Mining; Analysis of Natural Language Processing and Computational Linguistics. In: Komorowski, J.; Zytkow, J., eds. 1st European Symposium, PKDD '97: Principles of Data Mining and Knowledge Discovery; 1997 June 24-27; Trondheim, Norway. Berlin, Germany: Springer-Verlag; 1997. 323-334. ISBN: 3-540-63223-9.

WEBER, ROBERT PHILIP. 1990. Basic Content Analysis. 2nd edition. Newbury Park, CA: Sage Publications; 1990. 96p. ISBN: 0-8039-3863-2.

WHITE, ARDEN; HERNANDEZ, NELDA RAE. 1991. Increasing Field Complexity Revealed through Article Title Analyses. Journal of the American Society for Information Science. 1991 December; 42(10): 731-734. ISSN: 0002-8231; CODEN: AISJB6.

WHITE, HOWARD D. 1990. Author Co-Citation Analysis: Overview and Defense. In: Borgman, Christine L., ed. Scholarly Communication and Bibliometrics. Newbury Park, CA: Sage Publications; 1990. 84-106. ISBN: 0-8039-3879-9.

WHITE, HOWARD D.; GRIFFITH, BELVER C. 1981. Author Cocitation: A Literature Measure of Intellectual Structure. Journal of the American Society for Information Science. 1981 May; 32(3): 163-171. ISSN: 0002-8231; CODEN: AISJB6.

WHITE, HOWARD D.; MCCAIN, KATHERINE W. 1989. Bibliometrics. In: Williams, Martha E., ed. Annual Review of Information Science and Technology: Volume 24. Amsterdam, The Netherlands: Elsevier Science Publishers B.V. for the American Society for Information Science; 1989. 119-186. ISSN: 0066-4200; ISBN: 0-444-87418-6; CODEN: ARISBC; LC: 66-25096.

WHITE, HOWARD D.; MCCAIN, KATHERINE W. 1997. Visualization of Literatures. In: Williams, Martha E., ed. Annual Review of Information Science and Technology: Volume 32. Medford, NJ: Information Today, Inc. for the American Society for Information Science; 1997. 99-168. ISSN: 0066-4200; ISBN: 1-57387-047-1; CODEN: ARISBC; LC: 66-25096.

WHITE, HOWARD D.; MCCAIN, KATHERINE W. 1998. Visualizing a Discipline: An Author Co-Citation Analysis of Information Science, 1972-1995.

Journal of the American Society for Information Science. 1998 April 1; 49(4): 327-355. ISSN: 0002-8231; CODEN: AISJB6.

WIENER, NORBERT. 1948. Cybernetics: or, Control and Communication in the Animal and the Machine. New York, NY: Wiley; 1948. 194p. OCLC: 1022297.

WILSON, CONCEPCIÓN S. 1995. The Formation of Subject Literature Collections for Bibliometric Analysis: The Case of the Topic of Bradford's Law of Scattering. Sydney, Australia: The University of New South Wales; 1995. 533p. (Ph.D. dissertation). Available WWW: http://adt.caul.edu.au.

WILSON, CONCEPCIÓN S. 1998. Defining Subject Collections for Informetric Analyses: The Effect of Varying the Subject Aboutness Level. Scientometrics. 1998 January-February; 41(1-2): 209-223. ISSN: 0138-9130; CODEN: SCNTDX.

WILSON, CONCEPCIÓN S. 1999. Using Online Databases to Form Subject Collections for Informetric Analyses. Scientometrics. 1999 December; 46(3): 647-667. ISSN: 0138-9130; CODEN: SCNTDX.

WOLFRAM, DIETMAR. 1992. Applying Informetric Characteristics of Databases to IR System File Design, Part I: Informetric Models. Information Processing & Management. 1992; 28(1): 121-133. ISSN: 0306-4573; CODEN: IPMADK.

WOLFRAM, DIETMAR; CHU, CLARA M.; LU, XIN. 1990. Growth of Knowledge: Bibliometric Analysis Using Online Database Data. See reference: EGGHE, LEO; ROUSSEAU, RONALD, eds. 1990a. 355-372.

WOODROOFE, MICHAEL; HILL, BRUCE. 1975. On Zipf's Law. Journal of Applied Probability. 1975 September; 12(3): 425-434. ISSN: 0021-9002; CODEN: JPRBAM.

WORMELL, IRENE. 1998. Informetric Analysis of the International Impact of Scientific Journals: How "International" Are the International Journals? Journal of Documentation. 1998 December; 54(5): 584-605. ISSN: 0022-0418; CODEN: JDOCAS.

WOUTERS, PAUL. 1999. The Citation Culture. Amsterdam, The Netherlands: University of Amsterdam; 1999. 278p. (Ph.D. dissertation). Forthcoming from Stanford University Press.

YABLONSKY, A. I. 1980. On Fundamental Regularities of the Distribution of Scientific Productivity. Scientometrics. 1980 January; 2(1): 3-34. ISSN: 0138-9130; CODEN: SCNTDX.

YABLONSKY, A. I. 1985. Stable Non-Gaussian Distributions in Scientometrics. Scientometrics. 1985 March; 7(3-6): 459-470. ISSN: 0138-9130; CODEN: SCNTDX.

YITZHAKI, MOSHE. 1994. Relation of Title Length of Journal Articles to Number of Authors. Scientometrics. 1994 May; 30(1): 321-332. ISSN: 0138-9130; CODEN: SCNTDX.

YITZHAKI, MOSHE. 1995. Relation between Number of References and Length of Journal Article. See reference: KOENIG, MICHAEL E. D.; BOOKSTEIN, ABRAHAM, eds. 647-657.

YITZHAKI, MOSHE. 1997. Variation in Informativity of Titles of Research Papers in Selected Humanities Journals: A Comparative Study.

Scientometrics. 1997 February; 38(2): 219-229. ISSN: 0138-9130; CODEN: SCNTDX.

YITZHAKI, MOSHE. 1998. The "Language Preference" in Sociology: Measures of "Language Self-Citation", "Relative Own-Language Preference Indicator", and "Mutual Use of Languages". Scientometrics. 1998 January-February; 41(1-2): 243-254. ISSN: 0138-9130; CODEN: SCNTDX.

YITZHAKI, MOSHE; BEN-TAMAR, D. 1991. Number of References in Biochemistry and Other Fields: A Case Study of the Journal of Biological Chemistry throughout 1910-1985. Scientometrics. 1991; 21(1): 3-22. ISSN: 0138-9130; CODEN: SCNTDX.

ZIPF, GEORGE KINGSLEY. 1936. The Psycho-Biology of Language. An Introduction to Dynamic Philology. London, England: George Routledge & Sons Ltd.; 1936. 336p. OCLC: 359717.

ZIPF, GEORGE KINGSLEY. 1949. Human Behavior and the Principle of Least Effort: An Introduction to Human Ecology. Cambridge, MA: Addison-Wesley; 1949. 573p. OCLC: 268582.

ZITT, MICHEL; BASSECOULARD, ELISE. 1996. Reassessment of Cocitation Methods for Science Indicators: Effect of Method Improving Recall Rates. Scientometrics. 1996 October; 37(2): 223-244. ISSN: 0138-9130; CODEN: SCNTDX.

ZITT, MICHEL; BASSECOULARD, ELISE. 1998. Internationalization of Scientific Journals: A Measurement Based on Publication and Citation Scope. Scientometrics. 1998 January-February; 41(1-2): 255-271. ISSN: 0138-9130; CODEN: SCNTDX.

ZUNDE, PRANAS. 1984. Empirical Laws and Theories of Information and Software Sciences. Information Processing & Management. 1984; 20(1-2): 5-18. ISSN: 0306-4573; CODEN: IPMADK.

4 Literature Dynamics: Studies on Growth, Diffusion, and Epidemics

ALBERT N. TABAH
Université de Montréal

INTRODUCTION

The growth and evolution of a subject area is central to understanding its place in the history of knowledge claims. The dynamics of its literature allows one to follow the evolution of that area. There are several approaches to the study of literature dynamics. The historical approach is to follow the movement of ideas and people in the relatively distant past, concentrating on the internal development of specific fields. One example is HOLTON's (1988) *Thematic Origins of Scientific Thought*. The sociological approach is to follow the social processes associated with the activities of scientists and to concentrate more on the structural and networking aspects within given fields. The works of MERTON, LEMAINE ET AL., and KNORR-CETINA & MULKAY belong to this category. Merton, notably, has made significant contributions to institutional theory building and to our understanding of science as a social institution. The philosophical approach is to follow the truth claims of scientific knowledge and obtain insights into the process of scientific discovery. Recent significant examples include works by POPPER, KUHN (1970), and RESCHER. The information science approach is to follow the published literature and infer from the growth of the literature the movement of ideas and associations between scientists. The best known proponent of this line of work is PRICE (1961; 1963). Those trying to obtain a deeper and more holistic picture of the development of a field of interest may want to somehow combine all four approaches in the hope of arriving at more reliable conclusions. However, such an undertaking would be impractical. The richness of the data would be more than offset by the volume and complexity of interpretative possibilities. The strategy in this review involves follow-

Annual Review of Information Science and Technology (ARIST), Volume 34, 1999
Martha E. Williams, Editor
Published for the American Society for Information Science (ASIS)
By Information Today, Inc., Medford, NJ

ing the process started by Price and using publication indicators to obtain a deeper understanding of literature dynamics of scientific literatures. Most work involving dynamics so far has used the literatures of sciences for sources of data.

The subject of literature dynamics belongs to the specialty of bibliometrics, one component of informetrics (WILSON). One of the first to use the term "literature dynamics" was KOCHEN in 1969. Bibliometrics has previously been covered in *ARIST* by NARIN & MOLL and by WHITE & MCCAIN (1989). However, they did not cover literature dynamics nor studies on the growth of literatures. Growth is closely related to the process of aging. Since the subject has already been adequately covered by White & McCain, aging and obsolescence are not specifically covered in this review. A seminal reference on obsolescence is that of LINE & SANDISON. Aging is a subjective phenomenon and reflects the decreasing interest shown in a given literature with time. Growth refers to the increase in productivity of an area of interest and is the concrete manifestation of output. Obsolescence is related to a group of users, whereas growth is a universal measure. The measurement of obsolescence is dependent on local data, whereas growth can be measured with publicly available data. Therefore, the emphasis in this chapter is on the output, or the growth dynamics of literatures, as reflected in the work of those active in a research area.

There is a certain amount of discussion in the literature on how growth affects aging and obsolescence (EGGHE & RAVICHANDRA RAO, 1992a; 1992b). A number of authors have shown that the rate of growth affects obsolescence (BROOKES; EGGHE). Brookes showed that the rate of obsolescence is linked to both a specific literature and the use of that literature. Specifically, the faster a literature or even a given journal grows (in terms of number of articles published per year), the more rapidly it ages. Growth influences aging but it does not cause aging (EGGHE & ROUSSEAU). So far, no one has claimed the contrary—that the aging process of a literature affects its growth.

The approach adopted here starts from the principal assumption that growth patterns in the formal literature of a scientific field fully parallel the advances and the conceptual developments of that field (PRICE, 1969). This premise has in fact been accepted for a number of years. Most current research in scientometrics (i.e., bibliometrics applied to the sciences) is largely based on the use of publications to measure the growth of a field. This has to be differentiated from the growth of knowledge, which is a more abstract concept and cannot be measured directly.

A related aspect of literature dynamics and one that is attracting new interest is that of information visualization. Using techniques in bibliometrics, such as co-citation analyses, it is now possible to see moving images (and the dynamics) of how authors and fields of interest move over time—how they grow, fragment, and disappear. A chapter entitled "Visualization of Literatures" by WHITE & MCCAIN (1997) recently covered this topic in *ARIST*.

This review is organized as follows. The first section discusses the literature of growth, diffusion, and epidemics. It also addresses the phenomenon of fast-growing literatures. The second section deals with methodological issues. It discusses problems related to publication counts and considerations of the time factor in studies of literature dynamics. A third section deals with structural problems, such as the link between paradigm shifts and literature growth, and the growth and development of scientific specialties. The chapter concludes with the implications of the World Wide Web for studies on the growth of literatures and the impact of recent work in complexity on the study of literature dynamics in information science. In each section terms such as growth, diffusion, and epidemics are defined.

EMPIRICAL ASPECTS OF LITERATURE DYNAMICS

Growth of Literature

The impetus for recent studies on the growth of literature originated with PRICE. In 1951 he proposed that science in general grows exponentially, doubling its size every ten to fifteen years. He popularized his ideas in 1961. In 1963 he added that the exponential rate could not be sustained for a long time, that the growth of science was about to slow down and enter a steady-state level, and that most exponential growth is part of a logistic curve.

Price's popularity extends beyond the realm of information science and the history of science, and it is now a generally accepted thesis that science (as reflected in the annual production of publications) grows exponentially. The literature contains a large number of instances where his ideas have been tested. Only a small number of the results can be reported here.

Supporting Price, MAY examined the mathematical literature between 1868 and 1965. He found exponential growth but at half the rate stated by Price: an annual increase of 1.5% and a doubling rate every 28 years. He reasoned that had Price started his data series in the 1900s and gone back to the middle of the nineteenth century, he would have obtained significantly slower growth rates.

On the other side of the argument, OLIVER compared the number of contributing scientists and the number of papers in semiconductor physics for the years 1963 and 1968 and found no significant differences between the two years. KING ET AL. based their analysis on the growth of scientists and engineers and on the number of journals published between 1960 and 1977 and extrapolated their curves to 1985. They found a constant (linear) growth rate rather than an exponential one, especially when they took into consideration the growth of scientific manpower during the same time period.

MENARD found differing growth rates in different literatures. He found linear growth in optics and acoustics between 1900 and 1960. However, in two subfields of physics (nuclear and solid state) he found exponential growth, though at different rates. He classified subfields according to three patterns of growth: (1) slowly growing: old and large fields that grow constantly but relatively slowly (e.g., economic geology, geomorphology), (2) rapidly growing: showing consistent growth trends with doubling in only five to ten years (e.g., continental drift, geochemistry); and (3) cyclical subfields where support or interest appear to fluctuate (e.g., petroleum geology, structural geology).

Throughout the 1960s several Soviet workers took exception to the exponential model but their work scarcely received any mention in the Western literature (BECK). In the West, MORAVCSIK (1975) attempted to link exponential growth to research fronts growing at the epidermis of science. Some others, such as BOTTLE & REES, found a zigzag pattern in the literature on liquid crystals. After an initial peak early in the twentieth century and a pause in the 1930s and 1940s, growth resumed its exponential phase in the 1960s. In their survey, which spanned 1910-1972, they also found that the core journals changed considerably between periods of growth. The late nineteenth century literature was dominated by German scientists, and the most productive journals carried German and French titles. The post-World War II literature was dominated by American scientists, and the most productive journals carried English titles. HALL found a similar zigzag mechanism in the geoscience literature for 1940-1980, where overall the literature doubled every eight years.

HAWKINS (1978), in part influenced by the work of GOFFMAN (1971), examined the literature of noble gas compounds. He found patterns of sudden start and rapid growth as well as movements of large numbers of investigators in and out of subspecialties. Most investigators remained active in the field for only short periods of time. He characterized the overall growth of the literature of noble gas compounds as "a sudden spurt of interest following initial discovery, followed by a decline, and then a moderate growth" (p. 199).

Despite extensions and disagreements over the last three decades, the exponential paradigm has nevertheless remained the best known and most publicized model to describe literature growth (TAGUE ET AL.).

More recent work on growth features either curve-fitting exercises with available data or development of informetric models to simulate mechanisms of growth. WOLFRAM ET AL. used 20 years of bibliographic data from some 20 databases and tried to fit three growth models to the data: linear, exponential, and their own power model. They found that the linear and power models fit the data well, whereas the exponential model showed the poorest fit. They concluded that "the breakdown in exponential growth is well underway and is giving way to linear growth" (p. 362), thus supporting Price's earlier claim.

EGGHE & RAVICHANDRA RAO (1992b) re-examined Wolfram's data and found that the exponential growth never occurred and that only power models and Gompertz models applied to the data. Power models fit scientific and technical online databases better, whereas the Gompertz distribution better fit social sciences and humanities online databases.

CZERWON examined publication and citation indicators in the growth of a new specialty, that of Monte Carlo methods in lattice field theory. He analyzed factors such as publication counts, impact factor, relative citation rate, aging, and scattering among 668 articles indexed by International Nuclear Information System (INIS) Atomindex between 1979 and 1984. Among his conclusions was the idea that the specialty provides a characteristic example of the growth of a new science subfield from a core body of seminal literature. While his work is valuable and provides a useful model for future scientometric investigations of growth areas, his findings were based on a time-series of six points of annual data, which is clearly insufficient. He did not compare the growth of the one specialty to growth of other specialties in physics, nor to growth in previous years.

TABAH (1996) recently examined the growth of physics literature by taking account of the monthly growth patterns of each of the chapters in Physics Abstracts between 1977 and 1987. He found that Physics Abstracts went through three major phases of growth. From its start in 1903 until World War II the index showed little growth, an average rate of 2.2% per year. Between 1948 and 1970 it grew much faster, 13.8% per year. After 1970 the growth slowed down to 3.4% per year. For the focus period of this study, 1977-1987, the physics literature grew at a compound rate of 4.1% per year. When compared to the previous 80 years, the last 20 years displayed rather linear growth. As for the 58 individual chapters, between 1977 and 1987, 40 (69%) showed growth, 17 (29%) showed no growth, and only one (2%) showed a downward trend. The conclusion was that the trend of a growth pattern is often dependent on the scale of measure and the volume of data. Many models that use yearly data impose a smoothing process that may skew the results. Growth does not proceed in an uninterrupted manner; it is characterized by discontinuities related to discoveries, crises, and revolutions in the progress of science.

Recent work on growth increasingly takes into account large sets of data over a much longer time period. GUPTA ET AL. examined the growth of literature in theoretical population genetics between 1896 and 1979 from the point of view of a diffusion model. The growth pattern followed an exponential curve and fit rather well with a Gompertz distribution.

SCHUMMER made the interesting point that "cognitive units allowing a cumulative measure of scientific knowledge are difficult to ascertain in many disciplines" (p.108). However, the task is facilitated in sciences where a major index has been organized around a classification system (such as in physics, chemistry, computer science, and zoology). Schummer's purpose was to demonstrate the growth of chemistry based on the growth of the number of chemical substances discovered in the last 200 years. Starting with 1800 in chemistry, he found a stable exponential growth of 5.5% with a doubling time of 12.9 years, in conformity with PRICE's (1961) assertion of a 15-year doubling time. However, he found no sign of saturation for the late twentieth century that Price predicted. The small deviations in the growth curve that occurred during war years soon returned to the normal pattern. Schummer tried to find the reason for the stability of the pattern and proposed two possibilities: externalist reasons linked to socio-economic factors and internalist reasons linked to methodological factors surrounding chemical research. He proposed that methodological factors linked to older innovations that continue to spawn new innovations could be a source for exponential growth. Thus, a positive feedback process, where each new substance can be combined with older substances, could account for an initial linear growth in research yielding to an exponential growth for chemical substances.

Recently VAN RAAN found exponential growth in a synchronous study of 1998 papers citing works going back to 1800. He described the dynamics as super-exponential growth, fitting a Gompertz distribution. The slowdown after the 1960s predicted by PRICE (1963) was not visible in his data.

Thus, while exponential growth is still the dominant model for describing the growth of scientific literature over the last two centuries, it is not necessarily valid in all cases. The growth of a given scientific literature depends on the specialty, the time period, and on the scale of measurement, and may at different times exhibit different mechanisms. As DE MEY pointed out, "despite important practical considerations and suggestions implied by this growth model of science, its importance for our understanding of paradigms lies not so much in the characteristics of the growth of science on a global scale as in the analysis of the detailed mechanisms of this growth" (p. 114).

The advent of the Internet era and the increasing availability of published research on the World Wide Web has prompted several researchers to examine the growth dynamics of the Web and to test whether it follows bibliometric distributions. BAR-ILAN has analyzed the growth of Usenet messages during the eruption of mad-cow disease and identified core newsgroups dealing with the subject. BAR-ILAN & PERITZ searched "informetric or informetrics" on the Web for six months between January 3, 1998 and June 7, 1998 and found that some documents had disappeared, some new ones had been added, and some had undergone changes. While the word "informetric" remained relatively stable, most changes were ascribed to the particularities of the search engines used. In other words, it becomes difficult to track changes in the literature due to the confounding effects in the indexing strategies of the Internet search engines. One would expect even more changes to occur for hotter topics.

Support for the concern about the use of Web search engines for bibliometric analysis is provided by ROUSSEAU. He used two Internet engines to search for three words on the Internet with the purpose of identifying irregularities in the indexing of the search engines. The data he obtained from AltaVista were irregular and noisy and had to be subjected to median filtering. The results from NorthernLight were more stable. Similar concerns were expressed by SNYDER & ROSENBAUM and by OPPENHEIM ET AL.

Another finding of interest for studies in the growth of electronic literature comes from the physics and nonlinear dynamics community. A number of groups recently reported that the growth of complex systems, including the Internet, follows scaling laws, that is, exponential distributions (AMARAL ET AL.; HUBERMAN & ADAMIC; LEE ET AL.). The significance of these results is that the growth patterns of complex self-organizing systems (including science and its publications) follow a universal form that is independent of the size or any other detail of the system. Instead, the mechanisms of growth depend on the interplay of the units composing the system, and patterns arise out of the random interactions of these lower-level units. This result has the potential for providing long-sought explanations for the bibliometric laws that have so far eluded information scientists.

Diffusion

Diffusion refers to a process of dispersal. It is akin to a random walk (a stochastic process), either geographically or through a gradient, and over a whole population. It does not change individuals, but affects the characteristics of the whole population. In the case of literature growth, the influence of a work or an idea is diffused randomly through a population of actors. The growth of literature thus constitutes a form of social diffusion.

Most recent work on diffusion comes from the literature on diffusion of innovations. The literature of social diffusion and the diffusion of innovations was reviewed by KUMAR & KUMAR and by MAHAJAN & WIND. Most of these models are variations on the logistic model (the S-curve) of population growth. These models assume that an innovation spreads through a population of potential adopters when it comes into contact with adopters.

ROGERS reviewed diffusion from a nonmathematical point of view. In *Diffusion of Innovations* he defined diffusion as: "The process by which (1) an innovation (2) is communicated through certain channels (3) over time (4) among members of a social system. The four elements . . . are identifiable in every diffusion research study, and in every diffusion campaign or program" (p.10). BARTHOLOMEW suggested that the difference between models is that if the diffusion is modeled as being propagated by an external source, the growth looks like an inverted J-curve. If the model includes interpersonal contact, the growth looks like an S-curve. However, more recent work in the area of telecommunications innovations demonstrated that patterns of diffusion almost always take the form of modified logistic (S) curves, the differences being a function of the environment (presumably the subject area) and the target group and whether the speed of diffusion is slow or rapid (EASINGWOOD & LUNN). Thus, it may be difficult to develop a mathematical diffusion model that takes the myriad possibilities into consideration at the same time.

In information science, discussions on information diffusion are limited. AVRAMESCU (1975; 1980) likened the mechanics of information dissemination in science and technology to a heat diffusion process. His approach remains singular in information science. LE COADIC (1974; 1987) started from the notion that the diffusion of scientific ideas in society is a dynamic process and followed the same logistic curve as the diffusion of innovations and of rumors. He thus aligned himself with GOFFMAN's (1966) epidemic model.

KORTELAINEN recently applied the principles of diffusion research to the development of the audience of the journal *Annales Zoologici Fennici*. She analyzed authorship and citation patterns and compared them to changes in the stated scope of the journal between 1974 and 1995. In its early years the journal's contents were largely of Scandinavian origin. After its inclusion in the Science Citation Index in 1979, outside participation increased and the number of foreign citations rose. As the journal redefined its scope in the late 1980s and broadened its geographical coverage, it became increasingly relevant to a larger international audience. The author concluded that this case study can be used to further examine the relevance of compatibility and other variables associated with diffusion research (such as relative advantage, complexity, trialability, and observability) and their importance to information science.

One model that is related to diffusion but has received almost no attention from information science is that of percolation. Percolation refers to the random flow of a fluid through a gradient. This gradient can be visualized as a lattice network of cells. The degree of association between the cells determines how rapidly the fluid will travel through the system. The rapidity of the flow is a function of the degree of interconnectivity between the different subunits in the system. The goal is to find the minimum number of objects in the system so information will travel unimpeded. The minimum number of objects necessary for this to take place is called the percolation threshold. Below the threshold, the slow diffusion of information at different locations in the lattice forms individual subunits of various sizes within which information travels efficiently.

BOGAERT ET AL. applied these principles to the environmental problem of land masses breaking into smaller parcels. Their purpose was to identify the smallest fragment that can support a population successfully, without that population becoming extinct. The authors simulated a set of 99 percolation maps and converted the patch-area data into rank distributions. The distributions fit a BRADFORD curve. They also found a threshold value (p_c=0.5928, the critical Bernouilli probability) just above which the smallest clusters coalesced into one large cluster. The authors likened the process to the "success breeds success" (SBS) principle where cells that coalesce with each other have a greater chance to form patches and will eventually cross the threshold to form a large patch. This is akin to the number of authors publishing and being cited by others. Once they are cited, the probability that they will be cited again grows considerably. Such simulations have the potential for new insights into how fields of interest grow and how diverse areas of interest join to form an important discipline. They also provide a new understanding of epidemic processes and network formation models (WATTS). Work on percolation is mathematically challenging, but the potential rewards for information science are significant.

Epidemics

The difference between a diffusion model and an epidemic process is that diffusion has no vector of communication, whereas an epidemic is an entirely time-dependent model with a contagion vector. In other words, both involve time but an epidemic has a carrier agent and proceeds more rapidly.

Contrary to a diffusion process, an epidemic changes the behavior of certain individuals in the population and it is not random. It is a rapid phenomenon, and it is a directed process. In diffusion, the rate between events is constant, whereas in epidemics it accelerates in the exponential phase and slows down at the saturation phase of a logistic curve. Propagation rates in epidemic models increase monotonically with time, whereas in diffusion models they are globally constant over time (STRANG).

It should be pointed out that the literature reflects a general state of confusion over appropriate terminology, and several authors talk about epidemic models when they mean diffusion and vice versa. Some use the two terms interchangeably and some even use the term an epidemic model of diffusion.

Comparisons between the transmission of ideas and epidemic processes date back to the mid-nineteenth century. In 1855 BRODIE was the first to state that "there are epidemics of opinion as well as disease" (p. 26). ROSS developed the first generalized algebraic formulation of epidemics adaptable to the description of a variety of situations and coined the phrase, a theory of happenings. He pointed out that his results can also be applied to fields such as economics and sociology. LOTKA (1923) revised Ross's work and, expressing his model in differential terms, obtained a logistic equation to describe population growth.

A similar approach was used by KERMACK & MCKENDRICK to develop a mathematical epidemic theory. They devised a set of three coupled differential equations to reflect the relationships between the number of susceptibles, the infection rate, the recovery rate, and the removal (death) rate. In the basic model of the spread of an epidemic three variables are used: (1) the number of people who are susceptible to a disease (S), (2) the number of people infected (I), and (3) the number of people removed from the population after having been infected (R). A susceptible person becomes infected through contact with an infective person. Once infected, a person becomes immediately capable of infecting others. After a period of time in the infected category, a person is removed, due to either death or isolation, and is then immune to the infection; once removed, a person can no longer infect anyone again or become infected again. Generally speaking, the total population in these models is regarded as constant. In other words, $N = S + I + R$ is constant.

These models make important assumptions. First, the larger the possibility that people are infectious, the more people they will infect. This is true for most diseases (ANDERSON & MAY). Second, the more susceptibles there are, the more contacts an infective person will have.

This can be seen in the rapid spread of an epidemic in a city and the general lack of epidemics in the countryside where populations are smaller and more dispersed. Bringing the analogy closer to information science, a paper in a hot field with a large output will be cited more often than one in which productivity is languid.

KERMACK & MCKENDRICK also derived a threshold level for an epidemic, which essentially is the ratio of the removal rate divided by the contact rate between susceptibles and infectives. Thus, the higher the contact rate, the lower the threshold will be and the more rapidly an epidemic will spread. The initial population of infectives does not influence the likelihood of an epidemic. A lower initial population of infectives only takes longer to start an epidemic. Once past the threshold, the epidemic first grows at an exponential rate, then eventually slows down and dies out. It usually dies out not for lack of susceptibles but for lack of infectives. Once most of the infectives are removed and their total falls below the threshold, their number is insufficient to further infect the susceptibles, and the epidemic dies out.

Goffman used this model in the 1960s to develop his own epidemic theory on the diffusion of ideas and the growth of scientific specialties (GOFFMAN, 1966; GOFFMAN & NEWILL, 1967). Goffman regarded the transmission of a scientific idea within a population as being analogous to the spread of a communicable disease in society. He took the published article as the agency of transmission (vector) and characterized the transmission as an idea moving from an infective (author of a paper) to a susceptible (reader of a paper who will be infected given effective contact) (GOFFMAN & NEWILL, 1964). The analogy to the standard model of disease spread indicates that a susceptible person may become infected as a result of contact with an infected person. The newly infected individual then passes through a latency period (publication lag time) and then through an infectious time (time during which the work is cited) before becoming removed by no longer being active in the field. Thus, the spread of ideas within a scientific community can be seen as a variation of an infection process (SIEGFRIED).

Goffman tried to apply the theory of epidemics to the problem of growth in science. By using mast cell research and the growth of symbolic logic in mathematics as case studies, he demonstrated that it was possible to see growth and development as sequences of overlapping epidemics (GOFFMAN, 1966). He also demonstrated that once a producer left a given subspecialty in science, he/she was never expected to return to it (GOFFMAN, 1970). He summarized his work by stating that "this approach makes it possible to establish, quantitatively, the relative importance of past lines of inquiry within a given area of scientific activity and to predict the future behavior of existing lines of investigation as well as the emergence of new ones within the area" (GOFFMAN,

1971, p. 173). The difficulty with Goffman's model of three simultaneous differential equations is that they involve a number of simplify-
ing assumptions and parameters that are difficult to estimate or derive
empirically.

After two decades of neglect, Goffman's model has been updated,
and data for 1974-1990 have been added by WAGNER-DÖBLER &
BERG (1994). They used data on the literature of mathematical logic to
forecast epidemics in five subfields, but could not support Goffman's
epidemic theory. They also tested the data for their adherence to the
LOTKA (1926) and the BRADFORD distributions. They found in both
cases that the shapes of the distributions were largely dependent on the
stage of the epidemic and the time interval chosen for the analysis
(WAGNER-DÖBLER, 1997; WAGNER-DÖBLER & BERG,1995).
WAGNER-DÖBLER (1999) also tested the predictions of GOFFMAN
(1971) concerning the next epidemic in mathematical logic. He sought
the connection between waves of mathematical discovery and economic cycles. He confirmed Goffman's prediction and concluded that
"the growth of waves of scientific literature are connected with growth
waves of important ideas, at least in [mathematical] logic. And they are
pulsating in the same rhythm" (WAGNER-DÖBLER, 1999, p. 641).

It should be pointed out that generalized mathematical treatments of
epidemics have been developed not only for contagious diseases but
also for the spread of rumors (DIETZ), the spread of riots (BURBECK
ET AL.), the diffusion of innovations (ROGERS), the propagation of
consumer goods (MAHAJAN & WIND), and the dynamics of technological progress (GIRIFALCO). All of these social phenomena belong to
the same family of collective action that can be described qualitatively
by the same mathematical models. The time courses of the behaviors
are similar and indicate the similarity of the dynamics among them.

Similarly, for information science, the thesis can be advanced that the
dynamics of spread in society involves the diffusion of information and
that this diffusion works by a self-consistent mechanism. The mechanism may show slight variations depending on whether the spread
involves a rumor, the growth of knowledge, or the spread of action in a
given population. The epidemic growth of literatures also belongs to
this category, with the special characteristic that it is a dramatic event
that occurs within a short period of time.

This approach is reflected in the work of FAN (1985a; 1985b), who
advocated shifting the emphasis away from infectives and susceptibles
and instead paying more attention to the content of messages transmitted between people. According to him, "such a structure permits predictions about the rate of change of ideas in society based solely on the
information available to the population" (FAN, 1985b, p.1). Increasingly, with the availability of electronic forms of communication, it is

becoming possible to attend to the messages transmitted and to their change over time in order to gain insight into the evolution of ideas. Fan termed this process ideodynamics and stated that it is possible to codify information content into units he called infons, although he offered no information on the units of measurement. The advantage of ideodynamics is that it emphasizes the time course in the spread of an idea regardless of the inherent values of the messages transmitted. Fan claimed his version of differential equations can be used to predict the time course in the development of an idea or a habit based on the information content transmitted in a population.

The veracity of Fan's claims has yet to be demonstrated. The difficulty is that ideodynamics remains a theoretical concept. While Fan developed the tools to do ideodynamic analysis, he did not operationalize and quantify the concept of an infon nor develop a metric for an idea. In other words, there is no satisfactory way to define an idea unit and to measure it, and much is built on questionable premises. To date, the most practical measuring unit of an idea remains, despite all its imperfections, the published article—the same unit used to measure the spread of information and its growth in science as well as the epidemic growth of an idea and its ramifications.

From a sociological point of view, epidemic theory closely resembles MENZEL & KATZ's contagion theory. Menzel and Katz examined the transmission of ideas in a medical community with the purpose of finding out what influenced the diffusion of an idea or an innovation. Their results indicated that the closer an individual was to the medical community and the more integrated he/she was into it, the sooner that person was likely to adopt a given product. This is not very different from established epidemic models in that the more often a susceptible individual is exposed to a disease, the faster that person will become an infective. WORTHEN pointed out that GOFFMAN's (1996) is a mathematical model whereas Menzel and Katz's is a sociometric model; otherwise they are equivalent in terms of modeling an information process. Menzel and Katz's model is influenced by a two-step communication model and reflects changes in a network of potential adopters. Goffman's model is influenced by a mathematical model which, when it can be applied, attaches a numeric value to the evolution of an epidemic and tries to predict the number of people who will be infected with a given idea. In sum, epidemic theory provides a model (and explanation) for the rapid spread of a given collective behavior in a given population. As such, it conveniently summarizes a large amount of data and provides insight into the mechanisms of spread.

One of the challenges in information science is to identify the causative agents in the genesis and formation of epidemics. One attempt toward an understanding of the mechanism was made by TABAH

(1996), who hypothesized that some epidemics start as a result of surprising and significant publications that attract scientists to approach a given problem, to work on it, and to contribute to the field. The resulting increase in publications forms an epidemic process that can be followed in the abstracting literature. He termed these information epidemics. If the work is not successful and the initial spurt of interest fades, the rapid increase and decrease of publications looks like a spike on a time-series chart. If the work is successful and the initial work becomes seminal and ends up giving rise to a significant body of work and the formation of a new specialty, then the process can be called a knowledge epidemic. Two recent examples come from cold fusion and high-temperature superconductivity (HTSC) literature. In cold fusion the initial claims of two chemists drew world-wide attention, but their results could not be replicated. Interest in the phenomenon waned rapidly and the publication output fell significantly. This is an example of an information epidemic. On the other hand, the publication of a surprising paper on HTSC in late 1986 caused a large number of physicists to switch their work to HTSC and to contribute heavily. The success of the work transformed much of physics research. Within two years the monthly output of articles increased four-fold, a number of new journals in the specialty were started, and many physics departments were able to recruit new doctoral students to work on HTSC-related problems. The rapid rise in the number of publications in HTSC is an example of a knowledge epidemic. TABAH (1996) attempted a systematic search for information epidemics in Physics Abstracts between 1977 and 1987 and found only four. The large number of spikes on time-series charts were due to the indexing of conference publications and special journal issues.

The interesting consequence of sudden discoveries or surprising publications is that they may influence many people to see old facts and rework old theories in a new light and thus offer surprising solutions to old problems (a classic case of Kuhnian paradigm shift). The rush to rework and to publicize may in fact result in information epidemics. Given this framework, the discovery of further information epidemics in other scientific specialties should not be surprising.

It should be pointed out, however, that there are two kinds of epidemics and two separate models. The difference depends on the presence or absence of a vector of transmission. The first can be called a contagion model. It is vector-based and follows the transmission of an infectious agent in a population. It is largely grounded in the Kermack-McKendrick equations. This is the approach that largely influenced models of communication and diffusion of ideas. The second approach can be called a catalyst model. It is not vector-based. It involves factors affecting the incidence of noncommunicable diseases in a population and the cumulation of a number of results in the outbreak of disease. The specific causes of the epidemic are unknown or questionable.

Both types of models are applicable to information science. The ability of an influential work to infect researchers with an important idea or result clearly belongs to the contagion model. However, if it is assumed—as a working approach—that information epidemics occur frequently in science, and if one is looking for factors that bring on such epidemics, one also needs to take the catalyst model into consideration. The medical equivalents of these two are measles and heart disease, respectively. Measles is transmitted by a carrier, a virus. Heart disease, although devoid of an identifiable carrier, is nevertheless present in epidemic proportions in society due to the confluence of a number of factors (e.g., smoking, high-cholesterol diet) that, when present simultaneously in an individual, often result in the onset of heart disease. Similarly for physics, the transformation of superconductivity research in the late 1980s clearly belongs to the contagion model (TABAH, 1995). On the other hand, work performed in cluster physics in the late 1970s expanded as a result of advances in instrumentation and the increasing potential for economic benefits, rose rapidly in the 1980s, and lost steam in the late 1990s. The model explaining the epidemic growth of cluster physics suits the catalyst model better. The challenge with the contagion model is to identify the vector, which is relatively easy to recognize by growth in publication numbers and with citation analyses. The challenge with the catalyst model is to understand the catalytic process; to recognize the factors that are present in a nascent area of interest and that carry the potential to give rise to an information epidemic.

Fast-Growing Literatures

The discussion of epidemic theory and the epidemic growth of literatures has led some to propose fast-growing literatures as a special kind of scientific literature. Generally, the origins of fast-growing literatures can be traced to a specific work or a group of influential (sometimes seminal) articles that attract a new group of workers and induce them to publish extensively. Fast-growing literatures are special in that their growth reaches exponential proportions within a few months of the publication (or impact) of the first influential paper. They show explosive characteristics that attract the attention of a large number of workers both within and outside the field.

The characteristics of a fast growing area of science were described by DE MEY. He said that articles are short and enjoy a low rejection rate by journals; that references in articles are recent, predominantly cite journal articles, and are low in number but high in self-citations; that representation in secondary literature (indexes) is low; and generally that "information disseminates fast and efficiently" (p. 123).

Another recent work directly focused on rapidly growing literatures is that of BUDD & HURT, who counted the number of citations obtained by an influential paper on superstring theory over five years and tested the distribution against growth models suggested by PRICE (1965) and by KUHN (1970). They concluded that the distribution does not fit theoretical models and suggested that a different mechanism is at work for what they call fast literature (BUDD & HURT, 1991, p. 97). HURT & BUDD defined a fast literature as "denoted by its very rapid citation impact, citation frequency, and its concomitant swift diffusion into the literature of the specialty" (p. 472).

Further support for fast-growing literatures comes from the work of TABAH (1996), characterizing information epidemics as fast-growing literatures where influential works give rise to rapidly expanding scientific activity. In sum, a general model for a fast-growing literature is one where journal articles grow exponentially over a number of months, led by a group of highly influential works that obtain several hundred citations within a year of publication, and the doubling of the output in the field takes place within a year.

METHODOLOGICAL ISSUES

Publication Counts

The cornerstone of the methodology examining literature growth is the use of publication counts. Popularized by PRICE (1951; 1969), bibliometric studies of growth based on publication counts have become the standard approach. On the one hand, publication counts can be regarded as an unrefined measure because of the complexities of the communication system in science and the filtering process that precedes the printing of a work. On the other hand, their simplicity and ease of comparison with past activities make them impossible to ignore. Especially in the pure sciences, a publication represents the primary product of a scientist's work and is at the heart of the reward system.

Although counting publications is simple and relatively straightforward, interpretation of the data can create difficulties that have in the past led to severe criticisms of bibliometric methodology (EDGE; MORAVCSIK, 1973). The main problems concern the least publishable unit (LPU), disciplinary variance, variance in quality of work, and variance in journal quality (BROAD; COZZENS). LPUs are instances where authors fragment their research results into small units and publish them as multiple works rather than one unified work. The problems with LPUs are serious because they inflate publication counts by fragmenting the presentation of data and increasing the number of co-authorships. Particularly with the evaluation or comparison of small publishing entities (such as individuals or research groups), the results can be misleading.

There is evidence that variance in quality of works or journals may not be a serious problem. Several studies have found a high correlation between quality and quantity. In other words, a large number of publications is paralleled by high quality of the work. In the 1950s CLARK found a high correlation between a person's publication volume and his/her eminence in the field of psychology. Eminence was measured as a function of the author having held high offices in the American Psychological Association, the National Academy of Sciences of the United States, an entry in *Who's Who in America* or *American Men of Science*, and citations in Psychological Abstracts or *Annual Review of Psychology*. PRICE in *Little Science, Big Science* claimed that "flagrant violations there may be, but on the whole there is, whether we like it or not, a reasonably good correlation between the eminence of a scientist and his productivity of papers. It takes persistence and perseverance to be a good scientist, and these are frequently reflected in a sustained production of scholarly writing" (PRICE, 1963, p. 40).

ZUCKERMAN showed that Nobel laureates (who clearly produce outstanding work) publish more than other scientists at every stage of their working lives. GARFIELD (1979a) found that works by Nobel prizewinners are cited thirty times more often than the average for their fields. J.R. COLE & S. COLE reported a high positive relationship between quality and quantity for 120 university physicists (J.R. COLE & S. COLE; S. COLE & J.R. COLE). More recently, COLE supported this finding by making a connection between the quantity of works published by scientists in the past, their high citation patterns, and their eminence in their fields (p. 142).

Similarly, LAWANI (1977; 1982) found a high correlation between the number of papers published and the citations obtained by the authors in Nigerian entomological literature. He also found a positive correlation between the quantity and the quality of publications for a given country. STAHL & STEGER found a high correlation between innovation and productivity in 154 U.S. Air Force scientists and engineers. They argued that innovation is a measure of quality and one of original and useful contribution, whereas productivity is one of quantity or output, without regard to innovativeness. This statement should be qualified. MARTIN & IRVINE found that although the correlation between quality and quantity for any given person over a short period of time is tenuous, over longer time periods and for larger functional units (such as research groups, departments, or institutes) there is some correlation between peer judgments and the quantity of output.

WALLACE & BONZI provided evidence for the hypothesis that journals that constitute the nucleus in a BRADFORD distribution will be more frequently cited than nonnucleus journals. Thus, nucleus journals that publish the majority of studies in a given area were shown to be of superior quality. STEPHAN & LEVIN showed that prolific scientists write in the more prestigious journals and that they do not trade quality for quantity by publishing in journals that have a lower impact. FRUMAU found a high correlation between the number of U.S. patents, the number of international published articles (identified in the INSPEC database), and R&D expenditures. Given that patents are an accepted measure of quality, the finding adds support to the link between quality and quantity.

In addition, there is a high degree of correlation between publication counts and other measures of scientific excellence such as funding and peer ranking. MCALLISTER & NARIN found a 0.95 correlation between the amount of National Institutes of Health (NIH) funds received and the number of biomedical publications from 120 medical schools. ANDERSON ET AL. reported a high degree of correlation between a university's size (by the number of papers it produces) and the citation quality of its publications (influence per paper). Recently FEIST found a strong correlation between the quantity of publications and other variables such as prestige, eminence, and professional visibility. A high quantity of publications was related to high impact and membership in the National Academy of Sciences of the United States. Given this evidence that has been building consistently over the last four decades, one can comfortably state that there is in fact a close parallel between quality and quantity in publication.

The best way to avoid criticisms of publication counts is to refrain from comparing disciplines (such as mathematics versus biological sciences) and to use reliable data sources (e.g., major international indexes such as Physics Abstracts). If comparison is necessary, it should be possible to choose groups publishing papers in the same universe of journals. These can be works produced in the same specialty or in closely knit specialties that tend to publish in a narrow group of journals.

It can be argued that the use of some of the other science indicators is even more faulty. Patents mostly apply to technology and manufacturing. Reliable funding and manpower statistics (such as the number of Ph.D.s graduating) are difficult to obtain and have a big time lag. Researchers often obtain support from many different sources at the same time, and it is difficult for the analyst to apportion funding to specific research projects. Indicators based on funding present an additional circular argument in that scientists need money in order to work, but to get money they must demonstrate adequate work (COHN).

When exciting news hits an area of interest, researchers immediately switch and work on a problem irrespective of funding considerations. For example, many researchers in superconductivity, once they learned of the news on high-temperature superconductivity (HTSC) in late 1986, transformed their laboratories overnight without first applying for new funding.

One way to sidestep the problems above is to limit the inquiry to one discipline, such as physics or chemistry, then use publication counts to follow short-term changes in a given specialty. This way, changes in publication numbers are driven by the dynamic characteristics of the fields of study themselves. The statistics are obtained for the work of many groups of authors, not for individuals. Thus, the influence of any one person with unusual publication patterns is lessened.

The current availability of a large number of bibliographic databases has considerably eased the acquisition of publication information. Several studies have established an adequate methodology for online bibliometric studies. Among them, LANCASTER & LEE used online databases to track the growth of acid-rain literature and to follow the diffusion of the topic through databases of various kinds. The same approach was used by several authors to uncover new specialties in a number of fields of science (DOU ET AL.; HAWKINS, 1977; MOED; PERSSON).

It is always possible that an indexing service for some reason or another (changes in indexers, or holidays) may publish materials from several issues of a journal at the same time, thus artificially inflating publication counts. It is also possible to find duplicate citations during the course of an online search. However, such events are unusual and represent a negligible part of a scientific database.

Changes in fast-growing literatures and information epidemics occur too rapidly for any one new journal or special issue to affect the picture significantly. It is outside the potential of any one serial or monographic publication to bring about a change of such a magnitude unless one is dealing with a subspecialty where the monthly productivity is so low (one to five items) that the publication of a special journal issue will significantly affect the results.

The Time Factor

The very notion of growth is synonymous with change, and change can only be understood in dynamic terms, with the help of concepts and models that make time an explicit variable. While the literature on growth is voluminous, there are comparatively few studies in information science in which the time element is taken as the key variable. For most, it is peripheral to the focus of interest and is usually expressed in periods of years. The most recent review of the time factor dates back to 1977 (NEELAMEGHAN). A review by ZUNDE briefly summarizes equations in information science, including some involving time-related growth phenomena.

So far no one has addressed the problem of an adequate metric for time and what the proper period of duration should be in scientometric studies. The general attitude has been that it is easier to work with annual publication data because they smooth over large monthly variations and that the longer time period somehow removes concerns about the submission date of articles versus the cover date of publications versus the indexing lag time of the data sources.

With regard to the growth of scientific fields over time, the notion of research fronts was introduced by PRICE (1965) to describe the dynamic aspects of literature growth. However, he did not mention time specifically. Another well-known study that lacks the time variable is GOFFMAN's (1966) epidemic model mentioned above. GRIFFITH ET AL. provided maps of scientific literatures showing literatures central to a subject area along with peripheral subject clusters. Instructive as they were, the maps were developed by static techniques, with no explanations of causes and no place for a time factor. The concept of coherent social groups described by GRIFFITH & MULLINS suffered from the same lack.

During the 1980s and early 1990s, growth processes in various subfields received attention from a variety of researchers, both theoretical and applied (BRUCKNER ET AL.; BURRELL; HAITUN; KUNZ; MOED ET AL.; SICHEL; SMALL; TROFIMENKO). The majority of the theoretical studies involved probabilistic distributions where growth occurs randomly and (with the exception of Burrell) the time element is considered to be linear. BRUCKNER ET AL. adopted a theoretical evolutionary model to demonstrate growth, but their applications of the simulation models to growth trends in subfields remain to be shown empirically. Discipline-oriented studies have typically adopted an approach to counting publications by the year. The majority of the disciplines under study have indeed shown relatively slow and steady rates of growth that can safely be represented in yearly terms. However, even papers dealing with fast-growing literatures have adopted yearly counts for their studies and as such have missed much of the dynamics available with monthly approaches (BUILOVA ET AL.; HURT & BUDD; REBROVA & KOMAROV).

SEN & CHATTERJEE recently examined the time-dependence of bibliographic scattering. They examined three bibliographies of differing sizes and subjects and their growth and bibliographic scattering patterns. They could not find any stable patterns of scattering associated with a given stage of growth. They concluded that the patterns were entirely dependent on the states of growth of a given subject field over time and on the inherent characteristics of the subject field.

The best known study of monthly (as opposed to yearly) changes in a subfield remains that by SULLIVAN ET AL. They followed the month-by-month changes in the development of electroweak theory by means of co-citation studies and were able to demonstrate the evolution of thinking and the relative success of opposing theories as reflected in the co-citation of star publications. Their studies have so far not been replicated, probably because such a study would require a specialized database and be expensive to conduct.

With the exception of Sullivan et al., the approaches mentioned above can be seen as reflections of an equilibrium process and represent the growing world of communication (publications) only in very crude terms. They better portray slow-moving closed-system models and do not at all portray the world of fast-growing literatures. The growth of knowledge is a dynamic process, and time-dependent phenomena need to be explained in terms of time-dependent models. Fast-growing literatures can be tracked on a short-term basis and results can be obtained quickly with the help of high-performance computers and simulation programs. Although such methods have been used to model dynamic changes in a number of natural phenomena (such as weather patterns), they have not yet been applied in information science.

Converging Indicators

Given some of the above-mentioned criticisms of using publication counts alone to obtain a reliable understanding of the evolution of a specialty, it is valuable to use supporting indicators to add certainty to the interpretation of the findings. Most researchers use single indicators to operationalize research variables. In other words, even complex social variables until recently have been measured by one indicator at a time.

In the 1980s, decreasing budgets for basic research, the concentration of resources into a small number of central facilities, and continuing doubts about the effectiveness and objectivity of the peer-review system gave rise to the search for new methods of evaluating research performance (CHUBIN & HACKETT). One of the more influential teams, MARTIN & IRVINE at the University of Sussex, developed a set of converging partial indicators that are based on the number of publications and citations obtained as a portion of the group total for various research groups and major research centers. Martin & Irvine concentrated on large research centers and major research facilities such as the Centre européen de recherche nucleaire (CERN) and astronomy observatories rather than on specialties and they combined peer review with bibliometric measures of productivity and impact. In this way, they developed measures to evaluate the relative performances of different research centers.

Studies by Martin & Irvine and many similar studies were inspired by approaches to triangulation used in sociology and communication. Triangulation refers to the comparison of several types of data gathered about a single social phenomenon. When the same conclusions can be reached by using a variety of measures, the researcher's certainty in the interpretation of the phenomenon is considerably strengthened (WEBB ET AL.).

In the case of fast-growing literatures, the increase in output can be traced to an influential work that is cited by a large number of scientists and to the increasing number of authors participating in the growth of the specialty. If all three indicators point in the same direction, that is, the growth of literature is paralleled by an increase in the number of authors and a concentration of citations in the same influential work(s), then that sudden increase can be called an information epidemic and signifies an important growth point in that scientific specialty.

Thus, the influence of a paper can be quantified by three factors: (1) output, an increased number of papers following the publication of the influential work; (2) spread, an increased number of research groups or institutions working on the same specialty area and citing the influential paper; and (3) impact, an increased number of citations obtained by the influential work immediately after publication. Citation frequency is an accepted indicator of the importance of a work as judged by those working in the same field (GARFIELD, 1979b; VIRGO). The usefulness of a certain publication can be traced by its citation patterns, whereas increased rates of collaboration can be traced by counting authors. In the beginning of a new specialty area, there will be a higher proportion of self-citations (due to the small number of workers in the field), which tapers off as the field gets crowded. The intensity of spread and impact reflects the facts that a certain cohesion exists in the field under study and that workers are not turning out trivial and disconnected works.

In the initial stages of a new growth area, only a few research groups are likely to participate in the work. However, as the field grows and new scientists are attracted to the area, one can expect the proportion of the new literature due to any one group to decrease, the diversity of the groups to increase, and the rate of collaborative publication to increase. As a field evolves, it draws more cooperation, and the number of co-authorships increases concomitantly. Within the strict limits of examining the growth of literature, the productivity of individual scientists or countries is not that important; it is more relevant to follow the productivity of specific groups of scientists. MOED & VAN RAAN stated that groups of researchers form the basis of progress and are the most interesting and most policy-relevant entities to evaluate. Different groups tend to work on different problems. However, when one finds several dissimilar groups working and publishing on the same problem, this convergence confers added importance to the field, especially when compared to single disconnected efforts coming from a variety of sources.

COLE & ZUCKERMAN discussed the emergence of a cognitive consensus: "A growing consensus among specialists on the usefulness of certain publications is a prime indicator that a specialty is developing distinctive problematics and thus a cognitive identity. The extent of convergence of citations to particular papers and to the work of particular authors is a rough measure of such consensus .... Converging citations do not mean that all agree on the significance of cited research or that all highly cited authors have a common orientation but only that the cited work is influential in some respect" (p. 146).

A more satisfactory approach to obtaining proof of the degree and orientation of influence is to use qualitative methodology and interview techniques, and ask each author why a particular piece of work was cited. While such an approach may look promising at first, qualitative methodology is a cumbersome and lengthy process and has its own drawbacks. Nevertheless, if a large majority of authors gives the same (or similar) reasons, then that should be considered conclusive.

The contention here is that if a strong burst of publications is accompanied by a growth in the number of authors and if a large number of authors cite the same publications, then that constitutes sufficient evidence that a consensus exists on the influence of a given work or group of works and that this influence is giving rise to an information epidemic. Citation behavior is somewhat akin to territorial claims between competing species in ecology: each author or group of authors tries to expand its territory at the expense of others. In the work undertaken here, this is the concept of acceptance, measured by citation counts and the number of research groups working on the side of one approach to problem solving or another. In that respect, bibliometric methodology depicts the ongoing struggle and provides valuable insights into the conflicts.

All the foregoing is not intended to dismiss potential problems with citations and citation analysis, which have been well summarized (GARFIELD, 1979a; MACROBERTS & MACROBERTS; SMITH). One set of criticisms comes from the perceived weaknesses of the Science Citation Index itself. Its coverage, especially of non-English literatures, is limited, its citation indexing covers first authors only, and there are large numbers of errors in the data with respect to spelling, publication names, and citations. The second set of criticisms deals with authors' citation practices. It is not always clear why an author cites a work. Not all citations are made in a positive light. Some works are cited so often as to lose their relative merit. Others are so well integrated into their disciplines that authors no longer feel the need to cite them (obliteration by incorporation). The problem of the least publishable unit (LPU) is liable to inflate citation counts for some authors. Others go to second-hand sources rather than cite original documents. These criticisms are largely valid, and citation analysis must be approached with consider-able prudence. On the other hand, if an author or a work obtains hundreds of citations within a short period of time (such as a year or two), then that author or work must have been awarded considerable endorsement, approbation, and recognition no matter what the prob-lems may be with citation analysis. Overall, with sufficient volumes of data, quite reliable indications can be obtained on the direction and the impact of a given research specialty.

Despite their simplicity, publication numbers provide the most rapid and practical indicators available to signal growth. One cannot trace funding alone: superconductivity research was developed with very cheap materials. One cannot trace researchers and authors alone, be-cause at times great ideas come from small laboratories with limited staff and money. Co-citation maps are expensive to chart and require voluminous data that may not be available or may be beyond many researchers' financial means to obtain. One also needs a considerable lag time before undertaking a co-citation study. In contrast, the triangu-lation approach mentioned above provides a clear, direct method to obtain essentially the same information at less cost and effort. The three measures of publication counts, authorship, and citation counts are simple to obtain and simple to interpret. When used together, they provide powerful indicators of intensive areas of growth in scientific specialties.

PRACTICAL ASPECTS

Paradigm Shifts and Literature Growth

The expression paradigm shift owes its prominence to the influence of KUHN and his *The Structure of Scientific Revolutions* (1970). Kuhn challenged the then prevalent view of the accumulative mechanism of scientific growth where development comes as a slow, piecemeal pro-cess. Instead, he suggested, progress follows the steady pace of normal science, occasionally interrupted by a revolutionary process where an accepted set of views (a paradigm) is challenged by a new set of data and observations and undergoes a reformation. During the revolution-ary period, there is an increased level of activity (cogitation) and the scientific community is divided into various camps of theories and explanations. The different camps lack communication and a full understanding of each other's work, and thus are said to be incommensurable (KUHN, 1974). During this time the literature is expected to show an increased level of growth, some of which comes from influential work that is highly cited.

It should be pointed out that during times of normal science, the stage of steady accumulation of knowledge, one expects to find a steady population of researchers active in the specialty domain. It is when a breakthrough occurs and a significant piece of work is published that many more resarchers, including outsiders from other specialties, are attracted to it. This is when the literature is expected to show concomitant growth and exhibit spikes of growth on a time-series chart.

The implications of KUHN's (1970) ideas for information science, on whether paradigm shifts at the micro-level are reflected in the literature, were tested by several researchers. MORAVCSIK & MURUGESAN examined the implications of paradigm shifts on citation patterns in two cases of the physics literature: superconductivity and nonconservation of parity. They were able to substantiate Kuhn's claims, but added that the idea of a simple paradigm shift was too unsophisticated to account for all the citation patterns observed.

CRANE (1980) explored how the elements of a paradigm shift, as defined by Kuhn, fit past experience in theoretical high-energy physics. She found the presence of the different elements but not always in constant conjunction with one another (as posited by the idea of cogitation), meaning that established and successful fields are not always characterized by normal science. She also added that, rather than following Kuhn's theories of revolutionary growth, some fields came closer to HOLTON's (1962) idea of branching in science and growth by leapfrogging. Similarly, NADEL found that Kuhn is only partially right; that during times of theory competition, the degree of incommensurability varies over time.

Growth and Development of Scientific Specialties

The growth of scientific literatures and literature dynamics are closely connected to the growth and development of scientific specialties. KUHN's *The Structure of Scientific Revolutions* (1970) models revolutionary changes in the sciences with the idea of new perspectives (paradigms) bringing about sudden shifts from normal science to revolutionary science. PRICE, in *Science since Babylon* (1961), popularized the notion of invisible colleges, the informal network of researchers at the core of a specialty, and their influence on the growth of a scientific specialty. GRIFFITH & MULLINS pointed to the importance of coherent social groups in the development and success of a scientific discipline. COLE & ZUCKERMAN outlined three aspects of focus in the development of specialties: growth in authorship and literature, cognitive development, and the development of organizational infrastructures. Although variable in their extent and influence, all three are interrelated and play a role in studies of specializations. Recently, MURRAY depicted the rise of theory groups in American sociolinguistics.

MEADOWS & O'CONNOR approached the subject from an information science point of view and examined publications at different growth points in the development of a specialty. They started their article with a simple question: "Is [it possible], purely from a statistical analysis of scientific research papers, to identify the appearance of a new growth area and, if so, how soon after its first appearance can such an area be identified?" (p. 95) and concluded with a wish: "It would obviously be of value if a growth area could itself be discovered purely by a statistical analysis of the literature in the general field" (p. 99). Thus, the analysis of the growth of literatures in information science touches on the sociology of science by the fact that both use the same unit of measurement—a unit that remains within the purview of information science.

Several sociologists have outlined and defined detailed stages in the growth of a scientific specialty. CRANE, in *Invisible Colleges* (1972), proposed a four-stage model of the development of knowledge. MULLINS described four stages in the development of a theory group. MULKAY ET AL. outlined a three-stage model. Yet another four-stage classification of the life cycle of scientific specialties was proposed by DE MEY. Whatever the approach, an understanding of how new research areas come into being is central to the study of literature dynamics. From the vantage point of information science, an integrated model reads as follows:

1. *Birth of a notion.* A discovery is announced in the literature. It is usually generated by an individual or a limited group and is transmitted very rapidly. If the work is influential, it brings a rapid reaction from the scientific community.

2. *Spread.* The scientific community reacts to the announcement by an increase in participation, collaboration, and diversity of publications. Citations of the first work increase. The number of self-citations, at first high due to a vacuum created by the first work, decreases, and is accompanied by a shortening half-life of citations.

3. *Widespread acceptance.* As the field grows, it gains new adherents and starts fragmenting into subspecialties. Efforts toward popularization increase.

4. *Codification and institutionalization.* At this stage, new knowledge is reorganized into a coherent whole. The field is absorbed into the knowledge base of society.

Information epidemics exist during the first two stages and knowledge epidemics during the second and third stages. In the case of fast-growing literatures, the influential work that brings on a burst of activity refocuses scientists and catalyzes a coordinated effort to look at problems from a new angle. Those who accept this new point of view form a separate group that, if successful, breaks off and forms a new subspecialty. This is what constitutes the dynamic of a scientific literature.

CONCLUSIONS

This review provides a summary of the main theoretical arguments and empirical results available in literature dynamics. The discussion centers on studies of growth, the diffusion of information, epidemic theory, and fast-growing literatures. It also deals with the methodological problems of publication counts, the time factor, and converging indicators. Finally, it discusses two important considerations for literature dynamics, paradigm shifts, and the development of scientific specialties.

Some of the principal questions are: Do publication counts adequately measure scientific progress? Are the quantity and the quality of publications related? Can information science contribute to a better understanding of scientific progress? While these questions are not formulated in this way at the outset, the evidence presented in this review should allow one to answer all three in the affirmative.

The evolution of the Internet has created new challenges to understand the dynamics of a freely evolving communication medium and to seek to apply bibliometric methodology to the communication patterns of the World Wide Web. That phase is just beginning and the field is wide open for new discoveries.

The agenda for future research in literature dynamics will largely depend on new methodological tools available in the scientific world. One set of tools will come from efforts to better understand the dynamics of growth on the Web. There is now growing interest on the part of bibliometricians to find out whether the basic laws of the field also apply to publications on the World Wide Web. Another set of tools will necessarily have to come from new approaches in nonlinear dynamics and complexity theory developed over the last two decades. Many of these approaches are mathematically challenging and have not been standardized for the study of social phenomena. Social occurrences are complex phenomena and most of their interesting effects come from the interactions and the co-evolution of their subunits. However, the study of dynamics in society is no longer in the purview of social scientists, but has recently benefited from significant contributions from physicists, especially in matters pertaining to the dynamics of the Internet and to the analysis of social networks. Contributions from outside the field, far from being regarded as encroachments, should be welcomed for their potential to invigorate the field and to provide fresh new theoretical insights into literature dynamics.

BIBLIOGRAPHY

AMARAL, LUIS A. NUNES; BULDYREV, SERGEY V.; HAVLIN, SHLOMO; SALINGER, MICHAEL A.; STANLEY, H. EUGENE. 1998. Power Law Scaling for a System of Interacting Units with Complex Internal Structure. Physical Review Letters. 1998; 80(7): 1385-1388. ISSN: 0031-9007.

ANDERSON, RICHARD C.; NARIN, FRANCIS; MCALLISTER, PAUL. 1978. Publication Ratings versus Peer Ratings of Universities. Journal of the American Society for Information Science. 1978; 29(2): 91-103. ISSN: 0002-8231.

ANDERSON, ROY M.; MAY, ROBERT M. 1991. Infectious Diseases in Humans: Dynamics and Control. Oxford, England: Oxford University Press.; 1991. 757p. ISBN: 0-19-854599-1; LC: 90-014312.

AVRAMESCU, AUREL. 1975. Modelling Scientific Information Transfer. International Forum on Information and Documentation. 1975; 1(4): 13-19. ISSN: 0304-9701.

AVRAMESCU, AUREL. 1980. Coherent Informational Energy and Entropy. Journal of Documentation. 1980; 36(1): 293-312. ISSN: 0022-0418.

BAR-ILAN, JUDIT. 1997. The "Mad Cow Disease", Usenet Newsgroups and Bibliometric Laws. Scientometrics. 1997; 39(1): 29-55. ISSN: 0138-9130.

BAR-ILAN, JUDIT; PERITZ, BLUMA C. 1999. The Life Span of a Specific Topic on the Web: The Case of "Informetrics": A Quantitative Analysis. Scientometrics. 1999; 46(3): 371-382. ISSN: 0138-9130.

BARTHOLOMEW, DAVID J. 1976. Continuous Time Diffusion Models with Random Duration of Interest. Journal of Mathematical Sociology. 1976; 4(2): 187-199. ISSN: 0022-250X.

BECK, LEONARD N. 1970. Soviet Discussion of the Exponential Growth of Scientific Publications. In: North, Jeanne B., ed. The Information Conscious Society: Proceedings of the American Society for Information Science (ASIS) 33rd Annual Meeting: Volume 7; 1970 October 11-15; Philadelphia, PA. Washington, DC: American Society for Information Science; 1970. 5-17. OCLC: 2009339.

BOGAERT, JAN; ROUSSEAU, RONALD; VAN HECKE, PIET. 2000. Percolation as a Model for Informetric Distributions: Fragment Size Distribution Characterised by Bradford Curves. Scientometrics. 2000; 47(2): 195-205. ISSN: 0138-9130.

BOTTLE, ROBERT T.; REES, M. K. 1979. Liquid Crystal Literature: A Novel Growth Pattern. Journal of Information Science. 1979; 1(2): 117-119. ISSN: 0165-5515.

BRADFORD, SAMUEL C. 1934. Sources of Information on Specific Subjects. Engineering. 1934; 137: 85-86. ISSN: 0013-7782.

BROAD, WILLIAM J. 1981. The Publishing Game: Getting More for Less. Science. 1981; 211(4487): 1137-1139. ISSN: 0036-8075.

BRODIE, BENJAMIN C. 1855. Psychological Inquiries: In a Series of Essays, Intended to Illustrate the Mutual Relations of the Physical Organization and the Mental Faculties. 2nd edition. London, England: Longman, Brown, Green, and Longmans; 1855. 275p. OCLC: 1661421.

BROOKES, BERTRAM C. 1970. The Growth, Utility, and Obsolescence of Scientific Periodical Literature. Journal of Documentation. 1970; 26: 283-294. ISSN: 0022-0418.

BRUCKNER, E.; EBELING, W.; SCHARNHORST, A. 1990. The Application of Evolution Models in Scientometrics. Scientometrics. 1990; 18(1-2): 21-41. ISSN: 0138-9130.

BUDD, JOHN M.; HURT, CHARLIE D. 1991. Superstring Theory: Information Transfer in an Emerging Field. Scientometrics. 1991; 21(1): 87-98. ISSN: 0138-9130.

BUILOVA, N. M.; ZAKHAROVA, E. K.; AKSHINSKAYA, N. V. 1990. How Information Publications Reflect Studies on High-Temperature Superconductivity. Nauchno-Tekhnicheskaya Informatsiya, Ser. 1. 1990; 17(8): 22-28. ISSN: 0548-0019.

BURBECK, STEPHEN L.; RAINE, WALTER J.; STARK, M. J. ABUDU. 1978. The Dynamics of Riot Growth: An Epidemiological Approach. Journal of Mathematical Sociology. 1978; 6(1): 1-22. ISSN: 0022-250X.

BURRELL, QUENTIN L. 1988. Predictive Aspects of Some Bibliometric Processes. In: Egghe, Leo; Rousseau, Ronald, eds. Informetrics 87/88: Select Proceedings of the 1st International Conference on Bibliometrics and Theoretical Aspects of Information Retrieval; 1987 August 25-28; Diepenbeek, Belgium. Amsterdam, The Netherlands: Elsevier; 1988. 43-63. ISBN: 0-444-70425-6; LC: 88-9628.

CHUBIN, DARYL E.; HACKETT, EDWARD J. 1990. Peerless Science: Peer Review and U.S. Science Policy. Albany, NY: SUNY Press; 1990. 267p. ISBN: 0-7914-0309-2; LC: 89-21855.

CLARK, KENNETH E. 1957. America's Psychologists: A Survey of a Growing Profession. Washington, DC: American Psychological Association; 1957. 247p. LC: 56-012942.

COHN, S. 1986. The Effect of Funding Changes upon the Rate of Knowledge Growth in Algebraic Topology, 1955-75. Social Studies of Science. 1986; 16(1): 23-59. ISSN: 0306-3127.

COLE, JONATHAN R.; COLE, STEPHEN. 1971. Measuring the Quality of Sociological Research: Problems in the Use of the Science Citation Index. American Sociologist. 1971; 6(1): 23-29. ISSN: 0003-1232.

COLE, JONATHAN R.; ZUCKERMAN, HARRIET A. 1975. The Emergence of a Scientific Specialty: The Self-Exemplifying Case of the Sociology of Science. In: Coser, Lewis A., ed. The Idea of Social Structure: Papers in Honor of Robert K. Merton. New York, NY: Harcourt-Brace-Jovanovich; 1975. 139-174. ISBN: 0-15-540548-9; LC: 75-013881.

COLE, STEPHEN. 1992. Making Science: Between Nature and Society. Cambridge, MA: Harvard University Press; 1992. 290p. ISBN: 0-674-54347-5; LC: 91-42192.

COLE, STEPHEN; COLE, JONATHAN R. 1967. Scientific Output and Recognition: A Study in the Operation of the Reward System in Science. American Sociological Review. 1967; 32(3): 377-390. ISSN: 0003-1224.

COZZENS, SUSAN E. 1990. Literature Based Data in Research Evaluation: A Manager's Guide to Bibliometrics. London, England: Science Policy Support Group; 1990. 19p. (SPSG Concept Paper No. 11). ISBN: 1-87323-000-1.

CRANE, DIANA. 1972. Invisible Colleges: Diffusion of Knowledge in Scientific Communities. Chicago, IL: University of Chicago Press; 1972. 213p. ISBN: 0-226-11857-6; LC: 72-182088.

CRANE, DIANA. 1980. An Exploratory Study of Kuhnian Paradigms in Theoretical High Energy Physics. Social Studies of Science. 1980; 10(1): 23-54. ISSN: 0306-3127.

CZERWON, H. J. 1990. Scientometric Indicators for a Specialty in Theoretical High-Energy Physics: Monte Carlo Methods in Lattice Field Theory. Scientometrics. 1990; 18(1-2): 5-20. ISSN: 0138-9130.

DE MEY, MARC. 1992. The Cognitive Paradigm: An Integrated Understanding of Scientific Development. Chicago, IL: University of Chicago Press; 1992. 314p. ISBN: 0-226-14259-0; LC: 92-15297.

DIETZ, KLAUS. 1967. Epidemics and Rumours: A Survey. Journal of the Royal Statistical Society, Ser. A. 1967; 130(4): 505-528. ISSN: 0035-9238.

DOU, HENRI; HASSANALY, PARINA; QUONIAM, LUC. 1989. Infographic Analytical Tools for Decision Makers: Analysis of the Research Production of the Sciences. Scientometrics. 1989; 17(1-2): 61-70. ISSN: 0138-9130.

EASINGWOOD, CHRISTOPHER J.; LUNN, SIMON O. 1992. Diffusion Paths in a High-Tech Environment: Clusters and Commonalities. R&D Management. 1992; 22(1): 69-80. ISSN: 0033-6807.

EDGE, DAVID. 1979. Quantitative Measures of Communication in Science: A Critical Review. History of Science. 1979; 17(36): 102-134. ISSN: 0073-2753.

EGGHE, LEO. 1993. On the Influence of Growth on Obsolescence. Scientometrics. 1993; 27: 195-214. ISSN: 0138-9130.

EGGHE, LEO; RAVICHANDRA RAO, I. K. 1992a. Citation Age Data and the Obsolescence Function: Fits and Explanations. Information Processing & Management. 1992; 28(2): 201-217. ISSN: 0306-4573.

EGGHE, LEO; RAVICHANDRA RAO, I. K. 1992b. Classification of Growth Models Based on Growth Rates and Its Applications. Scientometrics. 1992; 25(1): 5-46. ISSN: 0138-9130.

EGGHE, LEO; ROUSSEAU, RONALD. 2000. Aging, Obsolescence, Impact, Growth, and Utilization: Definitions and Relations. Journal of the American Society for Information Science. 2000; 51(11): 1004-1017. ISSN: 0002-8231.

FAN, DAVID B. 1985a. Ideodynamic Predictions for the Evolution of Habits. Journal of Mathematical Sociology. 1985; 11(3): 265-281. ISSN: 0022-250X.

FAN, DAVID B. 1985b. Ideodynamics: The Kinetics of the Evolution of Ideas. Journal of Mathematical Sociology. 1985; 11(1): 1-23. ISSN: 0022-250X.

FEIST, GREGORY J. 1997. Quantity, Quality, and Depth of Research as Influences on Scientific Eminence: Is Quantity Most Important? Creativity Research Journal. 1997; 10(4): 325-335. ISSN: 1040-0419.

FRUMAU, COEN C. F. 1992. Choices in R&D and Business Portfolio in the Electronics Industry: What the Bibliometric Data Show. Research Policy. 1992; 21(1): 97-124. ISSN: 0048-7333.

GARFIELD, EUGENE. 1979a. Citation Indexing: Its Theory and Application in Science, Technology and Humanities. New York, NY: Wiley; 1979. 274p. (Information Sciences Series). ISBN: 0-471-02559-3; LC: 78-9713.

GARFIELD, EUGENE. 1979b. Is Citation Analysis a Legitimate Evaluation Tool? Scientometrics. 1979; 1: 359-375. ISSN: 0138-9130.

GIRIFALCO, LOUIS A. 1991. Dynamics of Technological Change. New York, NY: Van Nostrand Reinhold; 1991. 524p. ISBN: 0-442-00563-6; LC: 90-45717.

GOFFMAN, WILLIAM. 1966. Mathematical Approach to the Spread of Scientific Ideas: The History of Mast Cell Research. Nature. 1966; 212(5061): 449-452. ISSN: 0028-0836.

GOFFMAN, WILLIAM. 1970. An Application of Epidemic Theory to the Growth of Science: Symbolic Logic from Boole to Godel. In: Rose, John, ed. Progress of Cybernetics: Proceedings of the 1st International Congress of Cybernetics; 1969; London, England. New York, NY: Gordon and Breach; 1970. 971-984. (Progress of Cybernetics; v. 3). LC: 73-111944.

GOFFMAN, WILLIAM. 1971. A Mathematical Method for Analyzing the Growth of a Scientific Discipline. Journal of the Association for Computing Machinery. 1971; 18(2): 173-185. ISSN: 0004-5411.

GOFFMAN, WILLIAM; NEWILL, VAUN A. 1964. Generalization of Epidemic Theory: An Application to the Transmission of Ideas. Nature. 1964; 204(4955): 225-228. ISSN: 0028-0836.

GOFFMAN, WILLIAM; NEWILL, VAUN A. 1967. Communication and Epidemic Processes. Proceedings of the Royal Society of London, Series A. 1967; 298: 316-334. ISSN: 0080-4630.

GRIFFITH, BELVER C.; MULLINS, NICHOLAS C. 1972. Coherent Social Groups in Scientific Change. Science. 1972; 177(4053): 959-964. ISSN: 0036-8075.

GRIFFITH, BELVER C.; SMALL, HENRY; STONEHILL, JUDITH A.; DEY, SANDRA. 1974. The Structure of Scientific Literatures II: Toward a Macro- and Microstructure for Science. Science Studies. 1974; 4(4): 339-365. ISSN: 0036-8539.

GUPTA, B. M.; SHARMA, LALITA; KARISIDDAPPA, C. R. 1995. Modelling the Growth of Papers in a Scientific Specialty. Scientometrics. 1995; 33(2): 187-201. ISSN: 0138-9130.

HAITUN, S. D. 1982. Stationary Scientometric Distributions, Part II: Non-Gaussian Nature of Scientific Activities. Scientometrics. 1982; 4(2): 89-94. ISSN: 0138-9130.

HALL, DONALD H. 1989. Rate of Growth of Literature in Geoscience from Computerized Databases. Scientometrics. 1989; 17(1-2): 15-38. ISSN: 0138-9130.

HAWKINS, DONALD T. 1977. Unconventional Uses of On-line Information Retrieval Systems: On-line Bibliometric Studies. Journal of the American Society for Information Science. 1977; 28(1): 13-18. ISSN: 0002-8231.

HAWKINS, DONALD T. 1978. The Literature of Noble Gas Compounds. Journal of Chemical Information and Computer Sciences. 1978; 18(4): 190-199. ISSN: 0095-2338.

HOLTON, GERALD. 1962. Models for Understanding the Growth of Research. Daedalus. 1962; 91: 94-131. ISSN: 0011-5266.

HOLTON, GERALD. 1988. Thematic Origins of Scientific Thought: Kepler to Einstein. Revised edition. Cambridge, MA: Harvard University Press; 1988. 499p. ISBN: 0-674-87747-0.

HUBERMAN, BERNARDO A.; ADAMIC, LADA A. 1999. Growth Dynamics of the World Wide Web. Nature. 1999; 401(6749): 131. ISSN: 0028-0836.

HURT, CHARLIE D.; BUDD, JOHN M. 1992. Modelling the Literature of Superstring Theory: A Case of Fast Literature. Scientometrics. 1992; 24(3): 471-480. ISSN: 0138-9130.

KERMACK, W. O.; MCKENDRICK, A. G. 1927. A Contribution to the Mathematical Theory of Epidemics. Proceedings of the Royal Society A. 1927; 115: 700-721. ISSN: 0080-4630.

KING, DONALD W.; MCDONALD, DENNIS D.; RODERER, NANCY K. 1981. Scientific Journals in the United States: Their Production, Use and Economics. Stroudsburg, PA: Hutchinson Ross Publication Co.; 1981. 319p. ISBN: 0-87933-380-4; LC: 80-25945.

KNORR-CETINA, KARIN D.; MULKAY, MICHAEL J. 1983. Science Observed: Perspectives on the Social Study of Science. London, England: Sage Publications; 1983. 272p. ISBN: 0-8039-9782-5; LC: 82-042701.

KOCHEN, MANFRED. 1969. Stability in the Growth of Knowledge. American Documentation. 1969; 18: 186-197. ISSN: 0096-946X.

KORTELAINEN, TERTTU. 1996. Compatibility and Audience: Applying a Concept of Diffusion Research in Bibliometrics. In: Ingwersen, Peter; Pors, Niels Ole, eds. Information Science: Integration in Perspective; 1996 October 13-16; Copenhagen, Denmark. Copenhagen, Denmark: Royal School of Librarianship; 1996. 171-184. ISBN: 8-774-15260-2.

KUHN, THOMAS S. 1970. The Structure of Scientific Revolutions. 2nd edition. Chicago, IL: University of Chicago Press; 1970. 210p. ISBN: 0-226-45804-0; LC: 79-107472.

KUHN, THOMAS S. 1974. Second Thoughts on Paradigms. In: Suppe, Frederick, ed. The Structure of Scientific Theories. Urbana, IL: University of Illinois Press; 1974. 589-612. ISBN: 0-252-00318-7; LC: 72-089604.

KUMAR, V; KUMAR, U. 1992. Innovation Diffusion: Some New Technological Substitution Models. Journal of Mathematical Sociology. 1992; 17(3): 175-194. ISSN: 0022-250X.

KUNZ, M. 1987. Time Spectra of Patent Information. Scientometrics. 1987; 11(3-4): 163-173. ISSN: 0138-9130.

LANCASTER, F. W.; LEE, JA-LIH. 1985. Bibliometric Techniques Applied to Issues Management: A Case Study. Journal of the American Society for Information Science. 1985; 36(6): 389-397. ISSN: 0002-8231.

LAWANI, STEPHEN M. 1977. Citation Analysis and the Quality of Scientific Productivity. BioScience. 1977; 27(1): 26-31. ISSN: 0006-3568.

LAWANI, STEPHEN M. 1982. On the Relationship between Quantity and Quality of a Country's Research Productivity. Journal of Information Science. 1982; 5: 143-145. ISSN: 0165-5515.

LE COADIC, YVES F. 1974. Information Systems and the Spread of Scientific Ideas. R&D Management. 1974; 4(2): 97-111. ISSN: 0033-6807.

LE COADIC, YVES F. 1987. Modelling the Communication, Distribution, Transmission or Transfer of Scientific Information. Journal of Information Science. 1987; 13(3): 143-148. ISSN: 0165-5515.

LEE, YOUNGKI; AMARAL, LUIS A. NUNES; CANNING, DAVID; MEYER, MARTIN; STANLEY, H. EUGENE. 1998. Universal Features in the Growth Dynamics of Complex Systems. Physical Review Letters. 1998; 81(15): 3275-3278. ISSN: 0031-9007.

LEMAINE, GERARD; MACLEOD, ROY; MULKAY, MICHAEL; WEINGART, PETER. 1976. Perspectives on the Emergence of Scientific Disciplines. The Hague, The Netherlands: Mouton & Co.; 1976. 281p. ISBN: 90-279-7743-7.

LINE, MAURICE B.; SANDISON, ALEXANDER. 1974. "Obsolescence" and Changes in the Use of Literature with Time. Journal of Documentation. 1974; 30(3): 283-350. ISSN: 0022-0418.

LOTKA, ALFRED J. 1923. Contributions to the Analysis of Malaria Epidemiology. American Journal of Hygiene. 1923; 3(Suppl. 1): 1-121. ISSN: 0096-5294.

LOTKA, ALFRED J. 1926. Thre Frequency Distribution of Scientific Productivity. Journal of the Washington Academy of Sciences. 1926; 16(12): 317-323. ISSN: 0043-0439.

MACROBERTS, MICHAEL H.; MACROBERTS, BARBARA R. 1989. Problems of Citation Analysis: A Critical Review. Journal of the American Society for Information Science. 1989; 40(5): 342-349. ISSN: 0002-8231.

MAHAJAN, VIJAY; WIND, YORAM. 1986. Innovation Diffusion Models of New Product Acceptance. Cambridge, MA: Ballinger Publishing Co.; 1986. 318p. ISBN: 0-88730-076-6; LC: 85-023300.

MARTIN, BEN R.; IRVINE, JOHN. 1983. Assessing Basic Research: Some Partial Indicators of Scientific Progress in Radio Astronomy. Research Policy. 1983; 12(1): 61-90. ISSN: 0048-7333.

MAY, K. O. 1966. Quantitative Growth of the Mathematical Literature. Science. 1966; 154(3757): 1672-1673. ISSN: 0036-8075.

MCALLISTER, PAUL R.; NARIN, FRANCIS. 1983. Characterization of the Research Papers of U.S. Medical Schools. Journal of the American Society for Information Science. 1983; 34(2): 123-131. ISSN: 0002-8231.

MEADOWS, A. J.; O'CONNOR, J. G. 1971. Bibliographical Statistics as a Guide to Growth Points in Science. Science Studies. 1971; 1(1): 95-99. ISSN: 0036-8539.

MENARD, HENRY W. 1971. Science: Growth and Change. Cambridge, MA: Harvard University Press; 1971. 215p. ISBN: 0-674-79280-7; LC: 77-156138.

MENZEL, HERBERT; KATZ, ELIHU. 1955. Social Relations and Innovation in the Medical Profession: The Epidemiology of a New Drug. Public Opinion Quarterly. 1955; 19: 337-352. ISSN: 0033-362X.

MERTON, ROBERT K. 1973. The Sociology of Science. Chicago, IL: University of Chicago Press; 1973. 605p. ISBN: 0-226-52091-9; LC: 72-97623.

MOED, HENK F. 1988. The Use of Online Databases for Bibliometric Analysis. In: Egghe, Leo; Rousseau, Ronald, eds. Informetrics 87/88: Select Proceedings of the 1st International Conference on Bibliometrics and Theoretical Aspects of Information Retrieval; 1987 August 25-28; Diepenbeek, Belgium. Amsterdam, The Netherlands: Elsevier; 1988. 133-146. ISBN: 0-444-70425-6; LC: 88-9628.

MOED, HENK F.; BURGER, W. J. M.; FRANKFORT, J. G.; VAN RAAN, ANTHONY F. J. 1985. The Application of Bibliometric Indicators: Important Field- and Time-Dependent Factors to Be Considered. Scientometrics. 1985; 8(3-4): 177-203. ISSN: 0138-9130.

MOED, HENK F.; VAN RAAN, ANTHONY F. J. 1985. Critical Remarks on Irvine and Martin's Methodology for Evaluating Scientific Performance. Social Studies of Science. 1985; 15(3): 539-547. ISSN: 0306-3127.

MORAVCSIK, MICHAEL J. 1973. Measures of Scientific Growth. Research Policy. 1973; 2(3): 266-275. ISSN: 0048-7333.

MORAVCSIK, MICHAEL J. 1975. Phenomenology and Models of the Growth of Science. Research Policy. 1975; 4(1): 80-86. ISSN: 0048-7333.

MORAVCSIK, MICHAEL J.; MURUGESAN, POOVANALINGAM. 1979. Citation Patterns in Scientific Revolutions. Scientometrics. 1979; 1: 161-169. ISSN: 0138-9130.

MULKAY, MICHAEL J.; GILBERT, G. NIGEL; WOOLGAR, STEVE. 1975. Problem Areas and Research Networks in Science. Sociology: the Journal of the British Sociological Association. 1975; 9(2): 187-203. ISSN: 0038-0385.

MULLINS, NICHOLAS C. 1973. Model for the Development of Sociological Theories. In: Mullins, Nicholas C., ed. Theories and Theory Groups in Contemporary American Sociology. New York, NY: Harper & Row; 1973. 17-35. ISBN: 0-06-044649-8; LC: 73-6229.

MURRAY, STEPHEN O. 1998. American Sociolinguistics: Theorists and Theory Groups. Philadelphia, PA : John Benjamin Publishing Co.; 1998. 339p. ISBN: 1-55619-532-X.

NADEL, EDWARD. 1983. Commitment and Co-citation: An Indicator of Incommensurability in Patterns of Formal Communication. Social Studies of Science. 1983; 13(2): 255-282. ISSN: 0306-3127.

NARIN, FRANCIS; MOLL, JOY K. 1977. Bibliometrics. In: Williams, Martha E., ed. Annual Review of Information Science and Technology: Volume 12. White Plains, NY: Knowledge Industry Publications, Inc. for the American Society for Information Science; 1977. 35-58. ISSN: 0066-4200; ISBN: 0-914236-11-3.

NEELAMEGHAN, A. 1977. Expressions of Time in Information Science and Their Implications: An Overview. Annals of Library Science and Documentation. 1977; 24(1): 13-33. ISSN: 0003-4835.

OLIVER, M. R. 1971. The Effect of Growth on the Obsolescence of Semiconductor Physics Literature. Journal of Documentation. 1971; 27(1): 11-17. ISSN: 0022-0418.

OPPENHEIM, CHARLES; MORRIS, ANNE; MCKNIGHT, CLIFF. 2000. The Evaluation of WWW Search Engines. Journal of Documentation. 2000; 56(2): 190-211. ISSN: 0022-0418.

PERSSON, OLLE. 1988. Measuring Scientific Output by Online Techniques. In: Van Raan, Anthony F. J., ed. Handbook of Quantitative Studies of Science and Technology. Amsterdam, The Netherlands: North-Holland; 1988. 229-252. ISBN: 0-444-70537-6; LC: 88-025979.

POPPER, KARL R. 1963. Conjectures and Refutations: The Growth of Scientific Knowledge. London, England: Routledge & Kegan Paul; 1963. 412p. OCLC: 3959022.

PRICE, DEREK J. DE SOLLA. 1951. Quantitative Measures of the Development of Science. Archives Internationales d'Histoire des Sciences. 1951; 14: 85-93. ISSN: 0003-9810.

PRICE, DEREK J. DE SOLLA. 1961. Science since Babylon. New Haven, CT: Yale University Press; 1961. 149p. LC: 61-10186.

PRICE, DEREK J. DE SOLLA. 1963. Little Science, Big Science. New York, NY: Columbia University Press; 1963. 118p. ISBN: 0-231-08562-1.

PRICE, DEREK J. DE SOLLA. 1965. Networks of Scientific Papers. Science. 1965; 149: 510-515. ISSN: 0036-8075.

PRICE, DEREK J. DE SOLLA. 1969. Measuring the Size of Science. Proceedings of the Israel Academy of Sciences and Humanities. 1969; 4: 98-111. ISSN: 0578-9230.

REBROVA, MARIIA PAVLOVNA; KOMAROV, VASILII VLADIMIROVICH. 1989. Some Aspects of the Scientometric Analysis of the Development of Research in the Area of Superconductivity. Nauchno-Tekhnicheskaya Informatsiya, Ser. 1. 1989; 16: 23-27. ISSN: 0548-0019.

RESCHER, NICHOLAS. 1978. Scientific Progress: A Philosophical Essay on the Economics of Research in Natural Science. Pittsburgh, PA: University of Pittsburgh Press; 1978. 278p. ISBN: 0-8229-1128-0; LC: 77-74544.

ROGERS, EVERETT M. 1983. Diffusion of Innovations. 3rd edition. New York, NY: Free Press; 1983. 453p. ISBN: 0-02-926650-5; LC: 82-70998.

ROSS, RONALD. 1915. Some a Priori Pathometric Equations. British Medical Journal. 1915; (March 27): 546-547. ISSN: 0959-8146.

ROUSSEAU, RONALD. 1999. Daily Time Series of Common Single Word Searches in AltaVista and NorthernLight. CyberMetrics. 1999; 2/3(1): paper 2. ISSN: 1137-5019. Available WWW: http://www.cindoc.csic.es/cybermetrics/articles/v2i1p2.html.

SCHUMMER, J. 1997. Scientometric Studies on Chemistry I: The Exponential Growth of Chemical Substances, 1800-1995. Scientometrics. 1997; 39: 107-123. ISSN: 0138-9130.

SEN, SUBIR K.; CHATTERJEE, SUNIL K. 1997. Bibliographic Scattering and Time: An Empirical Study through Temporal Partitioning of Bibliographies. In: Peritz, Bluma; Egghe, Leo, eds. Proceedings of the 6th Conference of the International Society for Scientometrics and Informetrics; 1997 June 16-19; Jerusalem, Israel. Jerusalem, Israel: The School of Library,

Archive and Information Studies, Hebrew University of Jerusalem; 1997. 391-399. ISBN: 965-222-793-5.

SICHEL, HERBERT S. 1986. The GIGP Distribution Model with Applications to Physics Literature. Czechoslovak Journal of Physics B. 1986; 36: 133-137. ISSN: 0011-4626.

SIEGFRIED, ANDRE. 1965. Germs and Ideas. London, England: Oliver and Boyd; 1965. 98p. LC: 65-2950.

SMALL, HENRY. 1993. Macro-Level Changes in the Structure of Co-Citation Clusters: 1983-1989. Scientometrics. 1993; 26(1): 5-20. ISSN: 0138-9130.

SMITH, LINDA C. 1981. Citation Analysis. Library Trends. 1981; 30(1): 83-106. ISSN: 0024-2594.

SNYDER, HERBERT; ROSENBAUM, HOWARD. 1999. Can Search Engines Be Used as Tools for Web-Link Analysis? A Critical View. Journal of Documentation. 1999; 55(4): 375-384. ISSN: 0022-0418.

STAHL, MICHAEL J.; STEGER, JOSEPH A. 1977. Measuring Innovation and Productivity—A Peer Rating Approach. Research Management. 1977; 20(1): 35-38. ISSN: 0034-5334.

STEPHAN, PAULA E.; LEVIN, SHARON G. 1991. Inequality in Scientific Performance: Adjustment for Attribution and Journal Impact. Social Studies of Science. 1991; 21(2): 351-368. ISSN: 0306-3127.

STRANG, DAVID. 1991. Adding Social Structure to Diffusion Models: An Event History Framework. Sociological Methods & Research. 1991; 19(3): 324-353. ISSN: 0049-1241.

SULLIVAN, DANIEL; KOESTER, DAVID; WHITE, D. HYWEL; KERN, RAINER. 1979. Understanding Rapid Theoretical Change in Particle Physics: A Month-by-Month Co-citation Analysis. In: Tally, Roy D.; Deultgen, Ronald R., eds. Information Choices and Policies: Proceedings of the American Society for Information Science (ASIS) 42nd Annual Meeting: Volume 16; 1979 October 14-18; Minneapolis, MN. White Plains, NY: Knowledge Industry Publications, Inc. for ASIS; 1979. 276-285. ISBN: 0-914236-47-4.

TABAH, ALBERT N. 1995. Knowledge Epidemics in the Growth of Physics. In: Koenig, Michael E.D.; Bookstein, Abraham, eds. Proceedings of the 5th Biennial Conference of the International Society for Scientometrics and Informetrics; 1995 June 7-10; Chicago, IL. Medford, NJ: Learned Information; 1995. 555-564. ISBN: 1-57387-010-2.

TABAH, ALBERT N. 1996. Information Epidemics and the Growth of Physics. Montreal, Quebec: McGill University; 1996. 273, 90p. (Ph.D. dissertation). Available from: University Microfilms, Ann Arbor, MI.

TAGUE, JEAN M.; BEHESHTI, JAMSHID; REES-POTTER, LORNA K. 1981. The Law of Exponential Growth: Evidence, Implications and Forecasts. Library Trends. 1981; 30(1): 125-150. ISSN: 0024-2594.

TROFIMENKO, A. P. 1987. Scientometric Analysis of the Development of Nuclear Physics during the Last 50 Years. Scientometrics. 1987; 11(3-4): 231-250. ISSN: 0138-9130.

VAN RAAN, ANTHONY F.J. 2000. On Growth, Aging and Fractal Differentiation of Science. Scientometrics. 2000; 47(2): 347-362. ISSN: 0138-9130.

VIRGO, JULIE. 1977. A Statistical Procedure for Evaluating the Importance of Scientific Papers. Library Quarterly. 1977; 47(4): 257-267. ISSN: 0024-2519.

WAGNER-DÖBLER, ROLAND. 1997. Time Dependencies of Bradford Distributions: Structures of Journal Output in 20th Century Logic and 19th Century Mathematics. Scientometrics. 1997; 39(3): 231-252. ISSN: 0138-9130.

WAGNER-DÖBLER, ROLAND. 1999. William Goffman's "Mathematical Approach to the Prediction of Scientific Discovery" and Its Application to Logic, Revisited. Scientometrics. 1999; 46(3): 635-645. ISSN: 0138-9130.

WAGNER-DÖBLER, ROLAND; BERG, JAN. 1994. Regularity and Irregularity in the Development of Scientific Disciplines: The Case of Mathematical Logic. Scientometrics. 1994; 30(1): 303-319. ISSN: 0138-9130.

WAGNER-DÖBLER, ROLAND; BERG, JAN. 1995. The Dependence of Lotka's Law on the Selection of Time Periods in the Development of Scientific Areas and Authors. Journal of Documentation. 1995; 51(1): 28-43. ISSN: 0022-0418.

WALLACE, DANNY P.; BONZI, SUSAN. 1985. The Relationship between Journal Productivity and Quality. In: Parkhurst, Carol A., ed. ASIS '85: Proceedings of the American Society for Information Science (ASIS) 48th Annual Meeting: Volume 22; 1985 October 20-24; Las Vegas, NV. White Plains, NY: Knowledge Industry Publications, Inc. for the American Society for Information Science; 1985. 193-196. ISBN: 0-86729-176-1.

WATTS, DUNCAN J. 1999. Small Worlds. Princeton, NJ: Princeton University Press; 1999. 262p. ISBN: 0-691-00541-9; LC: 98-56088.

WEBB, EUGENE T.; CAMPBELL, DONALD T.; SCHWARTZ, RICHARD D.; SECHREST, LEE; GROVE, J. B. 1981. Nonreactive Measures in the Social Sciences. 2nd edition. Boston, MA: Houghton Mifflin Company; 1981. 394p. ISBN: 0-395-30767-8.

WHITE, HOWARD D.; MCCAIN, KATHERINE W. 1989. Bibliometrics. In: Williams, Martha E., ed. Annual Review of Information Science and Technology: Volume 24. Amsterdam, The Netherlands: Elsevier Science Publishers B.V. for the American Society for Information Science; 1989. 119-186. ISSN: 0066-4200; ISBN: 0-444-87418-6; CODEN ARISBC.

WHITE, HOWARD D.; MCCAIN, KATHERINE W. 1997. Visualization of Literatures. In: Williams, Martha E., ed. Annual Review of Information Science and Technology: Volume 32. Medford, NJ: Information Today, Inc. for the American Society for Information Science; 1997. 99-168. ISSN: 0066-4200; ISBN: 1-57387-047-1.

WILSON, CONCEPCIÓN S. 1999. Informetrics. In: Williams, Martha E., ed. Annual Review of Information Science and Technology: Volume 34. Medford, NJ: Information Today, Inc. for the American Society for Information Science; 1999. 107-247. ISSN: 0066-4200; ISBN: 1-57387-093-5.

WOLFRAM, DIETMAR; CHU, CLARA M.; LU, XIN. 1990. Growth of Knowledge: Bibliometric Analysis Using Online Database Data. In: Egghe, Leo; Rousseau, Ronald, eds. Informetrics 89/90: Selection of Papers Submitted for the 2nd International Conference on Bibliometrics, Scientometrics and Informetrics; 1989 July 5-7; London, Ontario. Amsterdam, The Netherlands: Elsevier; 1990. 355-364. ISBN: 0-444-88460-2; LC: 90-38114.

WORTHEN, DENNIS B. 1973. The Epidemic Process and the Contagion Model. Journal of the American Society for Information Science. 1973; 24(5): 343-346. ISSN: 0002-8231.

ZUCKERMAN, HARRIET. A. 1967. Nobel Laureates in Science: Patterns of
    Productivity, Collaboration, and Authorship. American Sociological Re-
    view. 1967; 32(3): 391-403. ISSN: 0003-1224.
ZUNDE, PRANAS. 1981. On Empirical Foundations of Information Science.
    Atlanta, GA: School of Information and Computer Science, Georgia Insti-
    tute of Technology; 1981. 646p. NTIS: PB82-125998.

5   Measuring the Internet

ROBERT E. MOLYNEUX and
ROBERT V. WILLIAMS
University of South Carolina

INTRODUCTION

This review reports on an examination of the literature that measures characteristics of the Internet. This topic has not been covered in previous *ARIST* volumes, though specific aspects have been dealt with in recent years. In her 1996 review of efforts to catalog and classify the Internet, WOODWARD briefly discusses measurement issues, but does not go into any detail. HARTER & HERT also briefly discuss early efforts at evaluating Internet search engines in their 1997 review of information retrieval evaluation.

The purpose of this essay is to assess the literature of Internet measurement, provide a broad outline of the scope of current Internet measurement issues, and make recommendations for the future of this measurement (and its literature). Studies considered appropriate to this review are those that attempt to systematically count, describe, or characterize the Internet—particularly its publicly available parts—and the users and uses of it.

The importance of measurement is clear. As CERF observes in Internet Request For Comment (RFC) 1262, "Measurement of the Internet is critical for future development, evolution and deployment planning."

Organization of This Review

General subjects that affect all the topics discussed here are dealt with first. The next four sections discuss:

- Conclusions about the Internet measurement literature
- Definition of the Internet from a technical standpoint
- The history of Internet measurement
- The nature of the Internet data environment

Annual Review of Information Science and Technology (ARIST), Volume 34, 1999
Martha E. Williams, Editor
Published for the American Society for Information Science (ASIS)
By Information Today, Inc., Medford, NJ

Subsequent sections cover the measurement of specific characteristics:

- Internet technical characteristics
- Information measurement and the Internet
- Internet user and use demographics
- Internet commerce

This review covers the measurement literature that is related only to the Internet and excludes coverage of computer networks that do not use the Internet networking protocols. This review is preliminary because many of the topics here are of sufficient scope to be subjects of *ARIST* chapters themselves. Topics not covered for reasons of space, time, or limits on available information are intranets, extranets, and electronic data interchange. Current information concentrates on United States sources, although it is probable that in the future the increasing universalization of the Internet will result in more measurement activities outside the U.S.

THE INTERNET MEASUREMENT LITERATURE

The literature of Internet measurement is dispersed, fragmentary, fugitive, and rarely scholarly. These characteristics have significant impact on the nature of this review: they necessitate discussion of sources that have not been subjected to critical review, require attention to issues and programs that are currently more business-focused than research-focused, and lead to the treatment of issues that are only in the formative stages and may have disappeared by the time this review appears. A significant portion of the literature cited here is on the Internet and thus is subject to the advantages of the Internet (currency) and the disadvantages (impermanence of the text and addresses) that impede scholarship. A related matter is the lack of scholarly indexing of Internet data and reports on measurement studies. With traditional indexing, the general characteristics and coverage of sources are known so that one can be reasonably confident of finding the major literature on a subject with a careful search. With the lack of such indexing on the Internet, the bounds of any literature, including scholarly materials, are difficult to define with any confidence. In fact, the indexing on commercial sources is often amateurish and feckless; an article printed today with an author and title might not be retrievable with either of these items tomorrow after being moved. Even a known-item search is a perilous activity on many sites. The Internet by its very nature is creating problems for humanity amid its prospects for human advancement. It is sad to note that problems that already have been addressed or solved are being rediscovered on the Internet. For example, the *WIRED* and ZDNET Web sites are basic sources of current information but are not organized by principles that have worked for millennia.

In addition to these difficulties, if a cited source moves or disappears, the reader cannot examine the data, text, or characterization and compare it to this review. If the source has not moved, the text may not be the same as was examined for this review. The problem of impermanence of sources and references and indexing must be solved if the Internet is to be a tool of scholarship. An example of this problem occurred when we tried to estimate the number of Usenet newsgroups for Table 1. Depending on when we consulted the recognized source, DEJA.COM, we found justification for 15,000, 60,000, or 80,000 newsgroups and none of these numbers is likely to be on the Web site when this review appears.

In spite of its fragmented nature, sources used here can be roughly classed in four types: factoids, for-profit sources, systematic studies, and scholarly literature. This simple classification seems to subsume a large part of the literature examined for this study.

Factoids are facts, often interesting, as in the Internet Index (TREESE), but usually are stray facts whose purpose is to support a contention, not illuminate a subject. These kinds of data are ubiquitous in press accounts and ordinary conversation and largely ignored for this study because of the reader's inability to examine methodology, methods of collection, related literature, or the bodies that report the data. However, in a few areas, notably the discussion of Internet advertising measurement, this type of information predominates.

For-profit studies are sold by the companies that conduct them. Except for the press releases that announce them (and the factoids generated from them for publicity purposes), the studies are invisible to the world at large because details are known only to those paying for them. Only rarely is there a hint of the methodology used or the extent of the connection to existing literature on the problem or topic. When these studies enter the public domain for a reasonable price—usually long after they are useful to other researchers—they generally appear to be well done and most would easily qualify as systematic. Unfortunately, they contribute little to scholarly study of a problem area.

Systematic studies report information collected in a systematic fashion and with methodological sophistication, but without citations or other attempts to acknowledge relevant literature. *BOARDWATCH MAGAZINE*, which reports information of interest to Internet service providers, publishes a *Directory of Internet Service Providers* that provides useful statistics, such as download times for 39 national backbone companies. This directory has archetypical systematic measurement

Table 1. Estimated Sizes of Internet Areas in Terabytes (1999)

Area	Source	Date	Size
World Wide Web			
Publicly available	Kahle	1996	.6
	Alexa Internet[1]	1997	2.0
	Lawrence & Giles (1998c); Sullivan[2]	1998	19.5
	Forrester Research[3]	1999	34.0
Restricted access			?
Total World Wide Web			?
Databases			
Publicly available			?
Restricted access			?
Total databases[4]	Williams[5]	1998	4.8
FTP sites	Kahle	1996	5.0
Gopher sites	Kahle[6]	1996	.1
Usenet	Kahle	1996	.2
	Kahle; Dern[7]	1999	.3
Total[8]		1999	30-44

[1] *LIBRARY OF CONGRESS INFORMATION BULLETIN.*

[2] Based on LAWRENCE & GILES' (1998c) lower-bound estimate of number of pages times T. SULLIVAN's estimated average size of a Web page at 61 kilobytes (KB). Does not include publicly accessible Web databases.

[3] Based on Forrester Research's May 1999 estimate of 550 million Web pages, as quoted in Search Engine Watch site 5/11/99 (D. SULLIVAN).

[4] Does not take into account overlap of databases.

[5] Based on the following calculation: 5000 databases in TURECKI-LUCZYCKA multiplied by WILLIAMS' average of 1.063 million records per database multiplied by Williams' middle-range estimate of 900KB average record size.

[6] Estimate is high because Gopherspace has contracted as the Web has expanded.

[7] Based on the following calculation: KAHLE's 1996 estimate of 240 gigabytes for 20,000 newsgroups, at an average of 12 megabytes per newsgroup. At that average, the 25,000+ newsgroups estimated in 1999 by DERN would equal 300 gigabytes. This calculation assumes that newsgroup files are like other kinds of files that move about the Internet, when they are not. In addition, the size of newsgroup files has increased.

[8] The extensive range in the May 1999 total size is given because the two estimates most affecting it, LAWRENCE & GILES (1998c) and Forrester Research (SEARCHENGINEWATCH.COM), are considered lower-bound and upper-bound estimates.

Note: This table does not attempt to measure traffic flow, so email and newsgroup traffic is not considered unless the resulting files are stored somewhere.

information. It is well thought out and contains a discussion of its methodology, but lacks universality: it exists on an intellectual island without indexing or citations connecting it to other literatures. A more narrowly focused article by RICKARD in 1998, "Backbone Performance Measurements," appeared in *Boardwatch* itself. This study is clearly of value to that magazine's constituency, and could be valuable to someone else who managed to discover it. Moreover, it has a Web site that essentially updates the printed article, but the article does not connect with other studies in a matrix that characterizes a scholarly literature.

Scholarly literature, in addition to being careful and systematic in methodology, focuses on a coherent set of questions, is additive as each study builds on others, discusses methodology, cites related sources, is cited in scholarly indexes, and is archived for access by others. It exists in an open, critical atmosphere where other researchers may freely make critical comments and thus is part of a self-correcting system. It is the original open source movement. It seeks to generalize results from data analyses and to arrive at explanations for observed phenomena. In short, the purpose of scholarship is to analyze its subject correctly and generalize appropriately. For example, it characterizes distributions of data with well-known names such as Zipf and Poisson. Unlike systematic studies that have no history, scholarly literatures can be said to exist in a body. Three topics comprise such literature here: retrospective Internet traffic studies, analysis of Internet search engines, and a nascent topic, Web characterization activities.

The purpose of scholarship is to arrive at correct conclusions to the questions addressed in spite of human foibles or difficulties in handling evidence. In order to accomplish this goal, disciplined practices, such as citing sources, have been established. Web pages and news stories about Internet data typically do not follow these scholarly norms, a fact that does not reflect on the accuracy of observations or data in such sources, but does reflect on their use for scholarly purposes where such norms can be critical. In this review, the purpose is to tread carefully between the various pitfalls in the literature of Internet measurement and to provide judgments of the state of that literature and what it reveals about the Internet today.

Despite the fact that the fragmentary, dispersed, and nonscholarly literature on Internet measurement is currently dominant, the topic is sufficiently important to deserve attention at this time, when it is still in its formative phase. A leitmotiv of this discussion, then, is that scholarly norms should be observed, that data presented without them are inherently less trustworthy than data presented with them, and that data should be archived as much as possible so that historical studies done in the future will have the data themselves, not just reports on them.

DEFINING THE INTERNET

The Internet is a network of computers running the Transmission Control Protocol/Internet Protocol (TCP/IP) packet transmission protocol suite. Protocols are the standards networks use to allow computers to communicate with each other. The term TCP/IP is a metonymy for a large number of interrelated protocols such as hypertext transfer protocol (HTTP), the underlying protocol of the World Wide Web, and many others that form this suite. There are other networking protocol suites (for example, Banyan Vines IP, Novell Netware), but TCP/IP is the standard for the Internet. In addition to the Internet, there are intranets, which are usually defined as private TCP/IP networks, which are used by a company to communicate information within that company, such as rules, forms, and competitive intelligence; and extranets, which are networks with private content that are sent over public networks through secure means. All three use TCP/IP as their network protocol. As noted above, intranets and extranets are excluded from this review.

The Internet now has millions of computers and networks connected to it. Each of these networks is connected to a data transmission system using the TCP/IP suite. As a result, each computer using HTTP can search for, retrieve, access, and use multimedia information stored on servers running the server portion of HTTP. The computers may also access information or communicate with other computers on the network by using other protocols in the suite such as the Simple Mail Transfer Protocol (SMTP), File Transfer Protocol (FTP), Telnet, Gopher, and applications running on those or compatible protocols such as video conferencing, Usenet newsgroups, games, and scheduling software. New applications for deployment on the Internet are in the process of being developed. As of early 1999, various bodies, such as the INTERNET ARCHITECTURE BOARD, the INTERNET SOCIETY, the WORLD WIDE WEB CONSORTIUM (W3C), the INTERNET ENGINEERING TASK FORCE, and the INTERNET RESEARCH TASK FORCE are the principal organizations involved in developing and establishing standards for the Internet.

BRIEF HISTORY OF INTERNET MEASUREMENT

Among general histories of the Internet are the INTERNET SOCIETY's Web site of histories by a number of people involved in Internet development, and books such as *Where Wizards Stay Up Late* (HAFNER & LYON), which found a popular market because of general interest in the Internet. Data from the early days are sketchy, however.

Most would accept the beginning date for the Internet as 1969, when Bolt, Beranek, and Newman delivered to the U.S. Department of

Defense's Advanced Research Projects Agency a small experimental packet-switched network known as ARPANET. The ARPANET was designed both to prove the concept of packet switching as a means of handling network traffic and to test the network as a means of resource sharing for defense contractors scattered around the country. From the beginning, one of the major concerns of ARPANET was the technical operation of the network so that maximum efficiency could be maintained. KLEINROCK & NAYLOR say in 1974 that the ARPANET began as an experiment with a major emphasis on measurement: "Early on, during the days when the ARPANET was still a concept rather than a reality, we were careful to include in every specification of the network design the ability to monitor network behavior with the use of specific measurement tools" (p. 767).

This early concern led to the measurement of operational characteristics, such as packet flow, lost packets, most efficient routes for transmission, and so forth. These aspects were reported to a limited extent in the Requests For Comments (RFCs), which, in effect, are the statute law of the Internet and a major means of communication within the Internet community. The first RFC was issued in April 1969. The beginnings of a measurement literature can be seen in 1971 in RFC 96 (WATSON) on the network as an interactive experiment and RFC 113 (HARSLEM ET AL.) on network activity, which discusses measurement topics but with few data points. In his 1976 book on queuing theory, KLEINROCK uses ARPANET data in his examples.

Data on the early days of the Internet can be found most easily through secondary sources. GRAY's Internet Statistics is a compilation of data from various sources, most beginning in 1993, but Gray stopped collecting data in 1996. Hobbes' Internet Timeline (ZAKON), however, continues to be updated. Hobbes' Web site is usually the first place to look for anyone interested in the history of the Internet, particularly in its data. In addition to the chronological timeline, a summary section presents data on Internet growth and numerous links provide access to other sources. COFFMAN & ODLYZKO in 1998 use estimates of growth to arrive at a prediction that around 2002 data traffic in the U.S. will overtake voice traffic. Notable in this article are the lengths to which the authors had to go to get their data.

MERIT NETWORK INCORPORATED is a consortium that contracted with the National Science Foundation to build and manage NSFNET. Statistics of this partnership are available beginning in various months (depending on the series) of 1988 through April 1995.

Although QUARTERMAN's book, *The Matrix: Computer Networks and Conferencing Systems Worldwide*, a 1990 survey of information on networking across the globe, is not primarily a source of data, it nonetheless gives data but, more usefully, has numerous bibliographic references. Quarterman continues his work at Matrix Information and Directory Services (MIDS), which is discussed further below.

Measurement in a more systematic fashion appears later. In 1991 RFC 1262 (CERF) outlines guidelines for measurement and in 1992 RFC 1296 (LOTTOR) analyzes Internet growth. It appears at this writing, though, that while measurement is acknowledged to be critical, a broad-based, scholarly measurement literature has been slow to develop.

THE INTERNET DATA ENVIRONMENT
Nature of Internet Data

Internet data collection efforts face the same two problems of all data collection: reliability and validity. Anomalies appear, values are missing, definitions used are ambiguous, and different collection techniques yield different results when measuring the same phonomena at the same or different times. Consider that estimates of the size of the Internet and related matters—even when made at the same time—may vary for many reasons. One reason is different operational definitions. For instance, in estimating how many people use the Internet, what constitutes use? Is someone who only gets and receives email through an account at work on the Internet? Is someone on the Internet if his or her access is only email and not Web access? Another reason is difficulty in gathering the data, which, without good sampling techniques, involves estimating a large moving target with few places to observe its movement.

The popularity of the Internet and the attention it attracts creates a demand for data about its scope and growth. The Internet is said to be growing "exponentially" without consideration of what that term means. The quest for Internet data has resulted in a great deal of careless and exaggerated prose, and arriving at accurate understandings of underlying reality is tricky. In general, the data seen in the press are factoids dragged in to support certain views rather than to clarify the subject.

Another complication of Internet data comes from the design of the Internet itself. For example, in order to conserve scarce bandwidth and increase speed, software and hardware on the Internet save copies of requested files in caches. As a result, a server log (a file that saves information on that server's transactions) may not show all uses of a Web site it contains—particularly popular sites—because files are cached where they are used throughout the Internet. Thus, a request for a Web site can be supplied not only by the Web server but also by a cache on the other side of the globe. How can a Web company accurately bill an advertiser or a Webmaster assess the use of his or her Web page under these circumstances?

The dynamic nature of the Internet also complicates its measurement for at least two reasons. First, what is true today may not be true tomorrow and will probably be obsolete the day after. An attempt was made for this review (see Table 1 earlier in this chapter) to estimate the size of Gopherspace but Gopher, as beguiling as it once was, is essentially not used anymore because it has been replaced by the Web. Files are still available via Gopher, but with many broken links and no literature on its current state. The second complication is that, if the results of two studies on a given phenomenon disagree, it is not clear whether the disagreement is a function of dynamic changes in the Internet, poor analysis, different techniques based on different assumptions, different software, or examination of different sectors of the Internet that have different properties.

Quantities and Size of Internet Data

Extraordinary amounts of data are generated as a result of Internet processes. As mentioned, servers generate transaction or log files that can be quite large. This fact is particularly true of traffic measurement. Traffic data indicate flows of traffic and sessions, the behavior of packets and their underlying protocols, and the implementation of protocols by various vendors. The amount of data requires increasingly specialized equipment to keep up with the increasing speed of data generation, increasing traffic, and extraordinary storage requirements of these large datasets.

Some data are lost because of the impracticality of storage, especially when server log files—even on moderate-sized servers—can grow to hundreds of megabytes a day. One of the authors wrote a large number of newspapers, Internet service providers (ISPs), and backbone companies involved with distribution of the Starr Report (U.S. OFFICE OF THE INDEPENDENT COUNSEL) in order to obtain data from this most interesting day in the history of government publication and of the Internet. There were few useful responses. There were reports in the press about this event. For example, a *Wall Street Journal* story says, "In the first 24 hours, a file containing an exact duplicate of the entire report was downloaded fully 750,000 times" (ZIEGLER ET AL., p B1). No source is cited. How does one know that number is correct? Is it the sum of all the sites that distributed the *Starr Report* or a guess? Other questions that would be useful to know for planning purposes are not addressed. What about the download history over the next month? What did the decay curve look like? Is there any way to estimate the number of copies made available from caches? These questions, of course, are outside the scope of the newspaper article but would be within the scope of scholarship if the data were available.

Similarly, a federal government agency was contacted by phone and asked for the log files to see how many copies of the *Starr Report* were reviewed by employees in the agency. The daily log files were 100 megabytes and incomplete because of a characteristic of the protocol used. It was estimated that the log files, if complete, would have been 200 megabytes. Even if the obvious privacy problems were dealt with, how could this file be delivered and examined, in addition to all the other potential log files? What if the log files were a gigabyte or more each day?

These questions are not trivial. The next time an Internet event like distribution of the *Starr Report* occurs, if it is to be measured, the infrastructure must be in place to capture data, and the cooperation of the various parties assured. Meanwhile, articles about the broad impact of the *Starr Report* on the Internet are intriguing but the sources of data and their accuracy are unclear. As is seen in the discussion of retrospective traffic measurement below, data-collecting testbeds are being built in order to capture more accurate data in the future. It may be useful to consider cooperative projects to use these testbeds to measure signal Internet events.

A crucial sidelight to the quantities of data is the issue of sampling methodology. Sampling in research is used when it is impossible or difficult to collect data on all possible objects (the population) that are the subject of investigation. While Internet samples are large, they may not accurately represent the underlying population of all Internet packets, traffic, or links. Internet data collection largely precludes probability sampling where any one item is equally likely to be sampled. Rather, nonprobability samples, for example, samples of convenience, have been used. Without probability samples, it is difficult to assess many aspects of the Internet based on inferential statistics. In spite of the difficulties, inferential methods have been used and are discussed below where appropriate.

Another problem occurs in distributing data on the Web characterization activities discussed below. Data are collected by bulk data providers such as ISPs and distributed after manipulation (to protect privacy, for example) to "reduced data consumers," including scholars. Here the distribution method obscures the raw data and data-collection techniques.

Internet Data Ownership

A final important aspect of the data environment is the fact that while the Internet is based on open protocols (that is, anyone can implement them freely), these protocols increasingly are executed by proprietary entities: corporations with profit-making or intellectual-property interests. These entities are reluctant to share competitive information or disclose trade secrets. Hence, the data are often lost to the scholarly community.

The Internet data environment will improve as resources and people are committed to the study of the various subsets of the Internet measurement problem outlined here. Corporations spending millions of dollars want to track their dollars and the effects of their products and services. Academics find this new world intriguing and will redirect their resources from other research activities. Corporations generally have more resources than scholars but may not wish to share their data and techniques with competitors. The scholarly world, by sharing information publicly and by its self-correcting mechanisms, can provide additional data and techniques upon which to build an understanding of the Internet. Certain observable trends (discussed below) suggest opportunities and benefits for cooperative enterprises between the commercial and scholarly worlds.

Meanwhile, commercial entities reinvent data manipulation. It is interesting to read of their difficulties, for example, with counting hits to measure Web page use. Web page hits are a proxy measure for Web page use, which cannot be measured. Libraries employ similar variables, such as number of volumes as a proxy for the impact of a library on its community. However, as BALBI pointed out in 1835, number of volumes does not measure a library's quality. The commercial world would probably benefit by hiring people who have actually compiled and manipulated such data and dealt with these kinds of knotty problems.

The previous sections review Internet measurement issues that affect discussion of all the topics reviewed below. We now turn to discussion of these topics, beginning with measuring technical characteristics of the Internet.

MEASURING INTERNET TECHNICAL CHARACTERISTICS

This section discusses three major technical aspects of the Internet: measurement of Internet clients and servers, measurement of Internet traffic, and Web characterization activities. The copious early literature analyzing packet-switching networks—including those using TCP/IP—is not covered here both because of its size and because the themes that are current now in traffic studies began to take shape in the 1990s.

Clients and Servers

The Internet is designed as a client-server network. The terminology can be slightly confusing because both clients and servers can be either hardware or software, and both client and server software can run concurrently on one machine. Nonetheless, the server (or client) software runs on the server (or client) platform. With these facts in mind, servers are generally powerful machines that process and send files to client software that usually runs on less powerful machines. Netscape is HTTP client software that can exchange information with HTTP server software written by Apache, Microsoft, Netscape, or any manufacturer that develops a server using this open protocol. Network protocols establish the rules for such communications.

Clients and servers are available both commercially and free. The Netcraft Web Server Survey (NETCRAFT, 1999a), which has been conducted since August 1995, is a model for analysis and description of Web servers on the Internet. The site reports which server software is running on Internet sites. It includes historical data, a discussion of survey methodology (NETCRAFT, 1999b), and a number of data subsets, for example, Web servers by top-level domain. The February 1999 survey received replies from more than 4 million Web servers. Of those, 2,351,000 (or 54.7%) are from the Apache Server Project, an open source supplier of Web servers. Microsoft server products run on 1,000,000 hosts (23%), while Netscape servers account for 178,027 (4%) of Web hosts. A host is a computer connected to the Internet, and a Web host is a host running HTTP server software.

Similar data for Europe are available from RÉSEAUX IP EUROPÉENS (RIPE) (1999a). In October 1990, when its data begins, RÉSEAUX IP EUROPÉENS (1999b) reports 31,724 domains; in January 1999 it reports 8,200,000. The largest domains in Europe are .de for Germany (18%) and .uk for the United Kingdom (17.9%). No other European domain has more than 1 million hosts. The ASIA PACIFIC NETWORK INFORMATION CENTRE is not a source of similar data.

Data on Web clients are readily available (searches of browser statistics on AltaVista, for instance, find about 500 to 1000 pages), but these pages as well as pages found by other search engines are a motley collection of the worst of Internet data. Pages may be outdated, cover odd time frames, for instance a month three years ago, and lack methodological discussions. Determining who is winning the "browser wars" is a difficult sampling problem. A site for this information is BROWSERWATCH, which gives statistics of browsers used by its own visitors. This strategy is practical. Dave Garaffa, who maintains the site, argues that because this site is visited by people who wish to be informed about current developments, the data reflect the browsers used by those whose interest in browsers is greatest. Methodology of the data collection is discussed on the page. Historical data are not available.

Other sources include data on Usenet through 1995 summarized in Hobbes' Internet Timeline (ZAKON) and reports on growing numbers of security incidents by COMPUTER EMERGENCY RESPONSE TEAM.

Internet Traffic Measurement

Internet traffic measurement consists of tracking Internet activity on a physical level by observing the packets and flows of transferred files. Two bodies of literature are dealt with here. The first is current studies, which monitor traffic in real time in order to assess the current state of the network. The second is retrospective studies, which report the results of later data analyses in order to assess accurately, to predict, to improve use of available and future bandwidth, and to plan for the future intelligently.

Traffic data collection and traffic monitoring are an explicit part of the Internet protocol suite. The suite includes, for example, the Simple Network Management Protocol used by network managers, plus an increasing array of software to analyze not only log files but also real-time traffic. Internet traffic is largely self-regulating because its routers are capable of dynamically directing traffic. Network managers take this information on traffic flows into account in allocating load and monitoring the state of servers, routers, and links and use it to detect and assess failures rapidly.

Current traffic studies. Information on current Internet traffic is available on public Web sites. Their purpose is to provide information on the state of connections to all or parts of the Internet to customers and others with a serious interest. For a fuller survey of this class of monitors, see the Internet Information Presentation Web page maintained by the COOPERATIVE ASSOCIATION FOR INTERNET DATA ANALYSIS (CAIDA) (1999a) under Real-Time Operational Statistics. The major backbone operators also support Web sites that provide current traffic information and are linked to the CAIDA site.

There are also sites for more general users. NetCopter (CLEAR INK) attempts to provide a picture of network connections from the perspective of its own connection to primary name servers of large ISPs. Thus, if the network connection is slow at a specific personal computer, this is not a place to look for information. The program pings (queries a server to find out if it exists and is online) the largest ISPs and measures return times and packet loss. Traceroutes (a program, like ping, that tests servers but gives more information on the route to the queried server) are also available to the name servers.

Probably the best general Web source is *The Internet Weather Report* maintained by MATRIX INFORMATION AND DIRECTORY SER-

VICES INCORPORATED (MIDS) because of the historical data it archives. It maintains four servers on the Internet and measures aspects of signals between them. In addition, it has a discussion of methodology (QUARTERMAN, 1998). Like NETWORK WIZARDS and NETCRAFT (1999a), MIDS makes data available and sells derivatives from the raw data.

Retrospective traffic studies. These studies, based on data collected over time, are concerned with observing the phenomena that move the packets, protocols, and flows along the Internet and achieving generalized understandings of how the network actually works. For the most part, the authors are network engineers whose focus is on making the Internet and TCP/IP more efficient. Unlike most of the topics discussed here, the retrospective studies are older than the Internet and they inherited techniques from and built on the foundations of earlier network traffic analysis. The retrospective literature, which appears in print sources and on the Internet, is, in fact, a full-fledged scholarly literature reflecting a systematic investigation of Internet traffic. A study of this literature, including its history, would be useful; only a hint of its richness can be given here.

PAXSON (1994) examined data from a single site over three years (1991-1994) using eight one-month traces of TCP connections. The study shows the nature of the growth of various protocols and their relationship to each other over the period. For example, the growth of Gopher and HTTP traffic relative to other protocols is clearly illustrated in the data from this site. Paxson also discusses other studies that show exponential growth, such as 1984-1994 Usenet traffic volume. Growth, the article concludes, is fueled by new people discovering the Internet and others using it more. While Paxson's study was of a single site, K. THOMPSON ET AL. used a traffic monitor (a specialized computer on the network to measure traffic) on the MCI Internet backbone and the NSF-sponsored vBNS network. Many of the results, such as daily fluctuations in traffic volume, are consistent with common experience.

The studies by Paxson and Thompson et al. use passive methods: they capture traffic data in the normal working of the Internet. Other studies use active methods: they introduce traffic in order to test network behavior. For instance, CLAFFY ET AL. tested packet latency (how long it takes a packet to move between hosts) by pinging selected sites and concluded that round-trip times (between ping and response) are poor measures of latency. Prior to this study, round-trip times had been seen as relatively straightforward proxies for latency. This contribution to the literature subsequently resulted in more careful studies of latency.

In experiments using active methods, PAXSON (1996; 1997) used TCP between sites set up with testbeds to provide an estimate of packet dynamics, that is, to get more information than merely packet latency and loss. Packets get lost for a variety of reasons; one purpose of TCP is to ensure delivery of packets, including retransmission of lost packets. The Network Probe Daemon (NPD) was employed between 37 sites in the first study and 35 in the second in an attempt to measure traffic in a systematic fashion. NPDs were programs that ran on sites spread over the Internet and were used to test routing behavior. PAXSON (1997) arrives at estimates of packet loss but discovers a much richer vein of packet behavior. Both PAXSON (1997) and CLAFFY ET AL. report flaws or pathologies in the implementation of the Internet protocols. In their study of Internet routing instability, LABOVITZ ET AL. point out the importance of the loss of Internet bandwidth owing to these poor implementations, so these are also worthy of study to determine the amount of such loss and correct it.

In spite of the difficulties in sampling the Internet as mentioned above, many results are readily understandable and believable. Nonetheless, the future of these traffic studies appears to lie in efforts to develop better procedures to run systematic tests on the Internet using sampling. "A Framework for IP Performance Metrics," released in 1998 as RFC 2330 (PAXSON ET AL.) from the Internet Engineering Task Force, discusses measurement issues. There are several efforts to position machines at various places on the Internet. A source of these efforts and others is found in the Measurement Tool Taxonomy section of COOPERATIVE ASSOCIATION FOR INTERNET DATA ANALYSIS (1999b). A sample of the tools listed there is discussed here. An introduction to new efforts from a 1998 workshop can also be found in the *Internet Statistics and Metrics Analysis: Engineering Data and Analysis, Workshop Report* (COOPERATIVE ASSOCIATION FOR INTERNET DATA ANALYSIS, 1998).

The active measures are elaborate in design in order to take into account the latest knowledge about measuring Internet traffic and arriving at well-constructed samples. By using a number of sites, researchers can test a greater number of connections, thus mitigating problems with sampling Internet traffic described above. The INTERNET PERFORMANCE MEASUREMENT AND ANALYSIS PROJECT, NATIONAL INTERNET MEASUREMENT INFRASTRUCTURE (NIMI), PROJECT FELIX, and SKITTER, among others, are in various stages of startup and operation and are likely to produce much data in the future. In addition, if studies of events such as the release of the *Starr Report* could be accommodated in these traffic monitors, their value would be increased and be of use in a more general context.

Analyzing retrospective data. One goal in these traffic studies is discovery of traffic invariants: observations, generalizations, and conclusions that appear to be true under varying network conditions. The quest for invariants has been a source of frustration until recently because results of one study are often not repeated in the next: studies take time to complete and publish, the network changes rapidly, studies may examine different parts of the network, and the quality of studies may vary. However, several invariants are now being discussed in the literature. The big three are that network traffic exhibits heavy tails, is long-range dependent, and is self-similar.

Heavy tails refers to the fact that, while most traffic on the Internet consists of data flows through small connections, there are episodes of substantial data flows through large connections. A histogram of such a distribution shows high frequencies of the minor flows (low byte counts) and low frequencies of the major flows (high byte counts) in the upper tail. These are the heavy tails which typically have more bytes than the rest of the distribution. Current literature on heavy tails seems to indicate that this phenomenon is a function of the sizes of files being requested (CROVELLA ET AL.; WOODRUFF ET AL.). It should be noted that generalizations about the distributions of file sizes are not fully established. For example, in the Woodruff et al. paper, the fourth graph in Figure 1 (logarithmic scale of file sizes) seems to show that the file sizes in the sample are roughly lognormal, although the authors make no such claim.

Dependence as used in traffic studies is a correlation between events in one time and events in a previous time. Long-range dependence occurs when the correlations are calculated over long periods of time. As of this writing, there appears to be no theory to explain this relationship of traffic over time.

Self-similarity refers to recurring patterns across varying scales of measurement. For instance, network traffic is not smooth but often shows bursts across all time periods. The concept is derived from fractal geometry; the phenomenon has also been termed fractal in network traffic analysis.

At least two schools of thought on heavy-tailed distributions are forming. These received explicit voice in 1997, beginning with RESNICK's article, "Heavy Tail Modeling and Teletraffic Data." Resnick, who comes from an operations research background, considers network traffic in the context of previous literature. Two criticisms of this article are worthy of note.

ADLER's approach is different and he criticizes Resnick's analysis on statistical grounds. Roughly put, he argues that Resnick's approach does not have explanatory power and asks why traditional methods, such as transforming the distributions, are not used first.

The criticism by WILLINGER & PAXSON must be understood in a different context both because of their backgrounds as network engineers and because each has done studies that have contributed to this literature. They draw a distinction between structural analysis and black-box methods. They conducted structural analysis, where traffic streams are examined in detail and packets are analyzed by protocols or by the connections of which they are a part. Resnick used black-box methods, where packets are treated as black boxes that need not be analyzed internally. Willinger & Paxson are skeptical that studies that do not examine the internal structures of packets can provide a useful understanding of network traffic. Others echo this view.

It seems clear that this exchange between Resnick and the others is the beginning of this discussion, not the end. In 1998 ADLER ET AL. edited a compilation that discusses heavy-tailed distributions from the perspectives of authors from several fields. For example, WILLINGER ET AL. further develop the idea of structural models originally posed by WILLINGER & PAXSON. The fact that the network world has found traffic characteristics that can be described using terminology from other fields suggests that more sophisticated understanding of network traffic is at hand, particularly with the prospect of better data appearing soon.

As strong as this literature is, it is young. As a result, there is enough unknown about traffic behavior that the literature does not yet deal with the problem of prediction of future traffic in anything but the grossest terms. We know that traffic will increase over the next year and we know that there are patterns in network use through the week and through the year. But how can traffic be predicted on a more granular level? That is, how can traffic that will arrive a second or minute from now be predicted? Prediction of future traffic on this level would be a profoundly useful ability.

Web Characterization Studies

Studies of Web characteristics are intended to "Characterize the Web and provide information and test scenarios for the Web community about the Web and how it is being used now and in the near future. Better understanding [of] the Web is crucial in order to . . . ensure its long term interoperability and robustness" (WORLD WIDE WEB CON-SORTIUM, 1999a). The WORLD WIDE WEB CONSORTIUM (1999b) initially sponsored these studies as part of revamping HTTP 1.0. The literature on this area is less mature than that of retrospective studies, but is approaching the level of a coherent scholarly literature.

Retrospective studies by CROVELLA ET AL. and WOODRUFF ET AL. overlap these studies because they are concerned with Web characteristics as they relate to traffic. Woodruff et al. are concerned not only with file sizes but also with general characteristics of Web pages based on their study of 2.6 million Web pages. BRAY in 1995 studied 1.5

million textual objects retrieved from the Web. He reports average Web page size, number of images, links to other pages, and internal formatting. PITKOW's 1998 summary is a concise review of the previous literature on the Web, its use, and characteristics of Web pages. He reports on percent of domains found, style, HTML tags used, and other characteristics. KOEHLER similarly investigates Web-page characteristics including their permanence. He examines 344 Web sites over a year and estimates the permanence of Web site URLs (17.7% die in that year) and Web pages (31.8% die in that year). O'NEILL ET AL. examine the question of sampling the Web and present statistics from a June 1998 survey (OCLC ONLINE COMPUTER LIBRARY CENTER, INCORPORATED). A second survey is to be done in June 1999.

No studies examining the history of one site seem to have been done. Such a study would give a picture of a site's growth in terms of hits, bytes held, and bytes served. If the study were done well, it would also explore methodologies to overcome the changes in data that result from changes in server log software as sites grow and move to larger servers. Additionally, it would be useful to develop methods to bridge the comparability gap between different server log programs.

Two useful archives of information on these activities are the INTERNET TRAFFIC ARCHIVE, last updated in 1997, and the WEB CHARACTERIZATION REPOSITORY at Virginia Tech, which includes materials from the Archive.

INFORMATION MEASUREMENT AND THE INTERNET

The Internet has been called a vast library of information resources, but LYNCH has objected to this characterization because of the lack of the kind of organization typical of libraries. Doubtless, a wide variety of analogs (archives, records centers, publishers, etc.) could easily be argued. It is obvious that there is a tremendous quantity and variety of information available via the Internet and a lot of people worldwide who are using it for many different reasons and with varying degrees of satisfaction. This section addresses these issues as they relate to efforts to measure the information aspects of the Internet (including digital libraries connected to it).

How Much Information Is on the Internet?

Despite the obviousness of the question, there appears to be no serious attempt to determine how much information is on the Internet. This may be because any answer would immediately be out of date. More likely it is because of the difficulties involved in definition, for example, the definition of information. There is no unit of information to measure except a proxy: the number of bytes on the Internet. Another problem is determining what and when information (like users, above) is on the Internet. Proprietary information is accessible only on a membership/subscription basis. The contents of Web-accessible databases do not actually exist as Web pages until search results are displayed.

Despite these problems, it should be possible to make a rough estimate. The estimate in Table 1 (earlier in this chapter) of the size of the Internet in early 1999 as somewhere between 30 and 44 terabytes (trillions of bytes) is based on precarious but defensible assumptions from the best available data. Areas where no estimates exist are indicated. The table categories are discussed in the sections that follow.

The World Wide Web. Estimates of publicly accessible Web sites and those accessible only by subscription or membership are sparse. (Intranets are excluded here because of their clearly proprietary nature.) No studies were located that attempt to measure the size of subscription/membership Web sites, though these are addressed to an extent in the discussion below on databases on the Internet. In their study of Web search engines, LAWRENCE & GILES (1998c) limit their analysis to publicly available/indexable information on the Web and estimate the lower-bound number of indexable pages to be 320 million. They claim their estimate is a lower bound because they focus on scientific information and not more popular information, which search engines tend to overindex. The study received considerable publicity in the press, particularly because of their reports on search engines; they compiled this coverage for easy consultation (LAWRENCE & GILES, 1998a).

SearchEngineWatch (D. SULLIVAN) notes that Forrester Research reported in early May 1999 that there were 550 million Web pages. A search of the Forrester Web site did not, however, reveal the source of this estimate (an instance of the problem of factoids in Internet measurement).

The problem of measuring Web page size and links was studied by T. SULLIVAN, who used a spider to search and retrieve pages containing 45 randomly selected nouns and 45 randomly selected adjectives on the AltaVista search engine. He found that average page size for this May 1998 survey was 61KB and that 23% of the pages contained dead links. In comparison, LAWRENCE & GILES (1998c) found in December 1997 that the percentage of invalid links in pages retrieved by several major search engines varied from about 2% to 5%. Their followup study in September 1998 (LAWRENCE & GILES, 1998b) found that the invalid links problem had increased, with a range from 2% to 9%.

SEARCHENGINEWATCH.COM has become a popular and easily accessible site for monitoring both size estimates of the Web and search engine performance. This site regularly updates and publishes search engine ratings in the areas of audience reach, number of Web pages indexed, percent of the Web indexed, and freshness or currency of indexing. An interesting measure developed by this site is its Search Engine EKG, which is a measure of comprehensiveness and freshness of the major search engines. It is based on placing test pages on the Web and determining the extent to which each search engine has indexed the information and kept the index up to date (D. SULLIVAN). Several links to statistics kept by other people and organizations are also available on the searchenginewatch.com site. One of the latest and best, particularly in terms of good explanation of his methodology for estimating size of search engines and databases, is maintained by NOTESS.

Databases on the Internet. As noted, the major measurement issues here are definition of a database on the Internet, how to measure database size and characteristics when most databases do not technically exist as Web pages until search results are generated, and how to measure subscription/membership databases. The *Gale Guide to Internet Databases* (TURECKI-LUCZYCKA), the most comprehensive listing, cuts through these problems by simply listing the types of databases included and noting the types of information not included (mailing lists, discussion groups, Usenet newsgroups, and library online public-access catalogs).

As of early 1999, it is clearly evident that the Internet is—and will increasingly become—the preferred user access venue for both free and fee-based database publishers. (Scholarly journal publishers are apparently not far behind, according to a late 1998 article by PEEK ET AL.). It is not clear how this movement will impact Internet measurement issues such as size, use, users, access, and quality. For non-Internet databases these issues have been the focus of considerable, long-term work by WILLIAMS, whose latest analysis appears in the 1998 edition of the *Gale Directory of Databases.* However, no comparable work specifically concentrating on Internet-based databases was located, although information appears in the *Gale Guide to Internet Databases* in 1999.

The library community has begun to address measurement issues related to databases and other full-text resources through the INTERNATIONAL COALITION OF LIBRARY CONSORTIA (ICOLC), which in late 1998 issued a set of guidelines for statistical measures of the use of Web-based resources. The thrust of the document, however, is to place responsibility for collection and maintenance of use/user data on the vendors and not on the participating libraries or library consortia. The guidelines do include a description of the minimum statistical elements to be included in reports to subscribing libraries, restrictions regarding privacy and user confidentiality, and allowable practices for analytical use for comparison purposes among participating institutions. No mention is made of provisions for use by other researchers.

FTP, Gopher, and Usenet files on the Internet. Locating recent and reliable information on these aspects of the Internet has been difficult. While all three continue to be active aspects of the Internet (with Gopher steadily declining), few studies of their size and characteristics were located. KAHLE's 1996 estimates of FTP and Gopher sizes (which are not documented) are used in Table 1; there appear to be no other recent estimates. References to Gopher mostly cease by 1995 or 1996. Kahle in 1996 estimates 20,000 newsgroups and DERN in 1999 estimates more than 25,000 newsgroups.

How "Good" Is the Information on the Internet?

The question of the quality of information encompasses a number of subsidiary questions, such as subject characteristics of the information, information seeking behavior, retrieval effectiveness, and quality of content. Partial efforts have been made to address these issues but no comprehensive studies were identified. The DIGITAL LIBRARIES WORKING GROUP ON DIGITAL LIBRARY METRICS addresses topics relating to digital libraries specifically and the Internet generally, including information seeking behavior and problems of use (such as the effects of speed, backup servers, amount of network traffic, characteristics of users, and effort versus effect). Thus far this group has not gotten beyond specification of the issues involved and possible ways to address them. Of particular interest to the group are questions about appropriate use of the long-established information retrieval measures of recall and precision and whether concepts such as ORR's "goodness" of library service can be applied in the digital library environment.

Subject characteristics. DILLON ET AL. studied subject characteristics of the Internet by sampling FTP sites with an eye to creating MARC records of FTP documents. The report was issued in 1993, before the invention of the Web, so a replication of this study would be useful. In 1994 MAULDIN & LEAVITT used the Lycos Web crawler to collect information on the contents of Web sites and report on a number of different subject characteristics based on titles and headings within the documents found. This study led to a 1995 report by MAULDIN, developer of the Lycos search engine, on his attempt to construct a global map of the Web as reflected through the search engine. Also in 1996, the Inktomi Project at the University of California, Berkeley reports descriptive statistics on the analysis of more than 2.6 million Web pages (WOODRUFF ET AL.). LARSON reports in 1996 his attempt to map the intellectual structure of the Web using cocitation analysis techniques that have been applied in mapping the core literature of traditional sources. Using the AltaVista search engine, he identified available core materials in a limited set of subject areas, applied cocitation techniques, and produced useful disciplinary maps. The maps provide good evidence that using hyptertext links within Web documents is a valid subject-searching technique on the Web. This finding contrasts with the common accusation that the Web is a wasteland in which retrieval is dependent on chance browsing. The possibilities and benefits of citation analysis in a Web environment are discussed in 1998 by LAWRENCE ET AL., who also developed a pilot citation indexing site, Research Index (formerly CiteSeer), of Web documents in computer science.

Information seeking behavior. Studies of Internet use with a focus on information seeking behavior are now well advanced. More than 10 papers were presented at the 1998 American Society for Information Science (ASIS) annual meeting (PRESTON). These papers reflect a variety of methodologies and groups of users. Because of space limitations, only those that focus specifically on measurement issues are discussed here. A number of researchers addressed multiple complex aspects of behavior. BILAL and HIRSH examined the information seeking behavior of children using the Web, with particular focus on search process and relevance determination. CHOO ET AL. used questionnaires and interviews to collect data on the information seeking behavior of managers and information technology specialists using the Web. The authors propose a specific behavioral model that takes into account motivations (strategies and reasons for viewing and searching) and moves (tactics used to find and use information). HERT & MARCHIONINI studied users (internal and external) of U.S. federal statistical Web sites using a combination of methods that included literature and Web-site reviews, expert critiques of the Web sites, site mapping, document analysis, interviews, questionnaires, focus groups, transaction log analysis, question analysis, and usability tests. Although their central purpose was to make recommendations for improving the Web sites studied, the authors emphasize the importance of using multiple methods for Web-site evaluation. RIEH & BELKIN studied a small group of faculty and doctoral students to determine how they made judgments about the quality of information on the Web. They concluded that source credibility and authority were paramount considerations, the same as for print resources. WANG ET AL. conducted an exploratory study of user searching on the Web using a holistic approach that attempted to look at the entire search process, including accuracy of finding factual information, behaviors, needs, cognitive style, and feelings. They considered the entire interaction process of searching and used both quantitative and qualitative measurement instruments.

Other researchers addressed behavior from a more technical perspective. ABRAMSON examined use of the Web on 43 public terminals at American University Library during four weeks in fall 1997 to determine which sites were most frequently used along with other characteristics of Web surfing at these terminals. Of the six four-hour blocks she measured, she found peak use between 12 to 4 p.m., followed by 4 to 8 p.m. Use was highest on Monday, declined through Saturday, and began to rise again on Sunday. This study was preceded by BERTOT ET AL., who in 1997 report Web use statistics of a number of U.S. federal agencies and propose specific evaluation techniques, particularly use of server-generated log files.

Information retrieval effectiveness. While there is a long and rich tradition of information retrieval evaluation (reviewed by HARTER & HERT in *ARIST* in 1997), only in the last few years has systematic attention been given to Internet-based information retrieval effectiveness. The relative recency of development of the Web and Web search engines is likely the primary reason. However, the issues of rapid change in Web-site content, duplicate records, uneven indexing of Web sites, differences in information quality, and lack of satisfactory relevance measures add to the problem of determining retrieval effectiveness. Description and evaluation of user browsing strategies dominated early work in this area (BERGHEL; CATLEDGE & PITKOW), but the dominant focus in the last three years has been on Web search engines. In an overview of early performance evaluation studies of search engines, SCHWARTZ notes the difference in the quality of assessments provided in such ratings as ZDNet's annual "search engine showdown" and those conducted by the information retrieval research community. CHU & ROSENTHAL, who evaluated Lycos, Excite, and AltaVista, review early search-engine evaluation studies and propose a specific comparative study and evaluation methodology. Their measures cover composition of the Web search engine, search capabilities, retrieval performance (precision, recall, and response time), output options, and user effort. DING & MARCHIONINI report on a similar study of Lycos, InfoSeek, and Open Text. SU ET AL. did a pilot study of retrieval performance in four search engines and derived specific measures for relevance, efficiency, utility, and user satisfaction. They ranked the search engines according to how each performed on these criteria and overall.

While these studies are important to the developing measurement literature on Internet search-engine performance, none has received the kind of attention given to the LAWRENCE & GILES (1998b; 1998c) studies of late 1997 to late 1998, a time of intensive attention to financial investment in search-engine stocks. In the first study, they used 575 science-oriented questions posed by employees of the NEC Research Institute, and dealt with issues of relevance and overlap by analyzing each page retrieved from each search engine. They appear to treat relevance casually however, defining it as an exact match between terms in retrieved documents and queries. They examined the quality of Web search engines, noting that no engine indexes more than 30% of the indexable Web and that search effectiveness can be greatly improved by using several search engines. They conclude that in choosing search engines, searchers may have to make tradeoffs in recency and comprehensiveness. Their September 1998 followup study (LAWRENCE & GILES, 1998b) concludes that the comprehensiveness of search engines is not keeping up with Web growth.

Web search-engine evaluation will doubtless continue to be a hot topic in the next few years because of their economic value as Internet portals and advertising venues (see discussion below). In most cases the central purpose of the studies is to determine the search engines with the best overall performance. However, search engines change features so frequently that long-term comparisons may be impossible and, as SU points out, researchers have not been consistent in how to measure performance, thus compounding the measurement problem. It remains to be seen whether the evaluation efforts will employ the Cranfield experimental techniques developed in the information science literature (see HARTER & HERT) or whether they will follow other approaches. MACCALL questions whether the traditional measures of recall and precision are appropriate to Internet retrieval because of the dynamic nature of Internet documents and proposes what he terms a relativity theory to deal with this issue.

Fortunately, Web retrieval effectiveness may get additional attention in the near future since the TEXT RETRIEVAL CONFERENCE (TREC), noted for its work in information retrieval research on large text databases, has added a new Web track to its various problem areas of study for 1999. According to the task description, researchers choosing this track will analyze about 2 gigabytes of data from a snapshot of the Web to determine whether links can be used to enhance retrieval.

Quality of content. A good deal of anecdotal information has appeared in the popular press on the problems of separating good information from bad and of dealing with the thousands of items obtained through a Web search. However, no systematic studies of these problems have yet appeared. They have received some attention in the critical area of health information on the Web (IMPICCIATORE ET AL.), and specific criteria for evaluating health information have been proposed (BONATI ET AL.; KIM ET AL.), but empirical measurement approaches to quality were not located. Surprisingly, no studies were located on the quality of legal information on the Internet. This entire area of quality of information seems ripe for systematic study.

INTERNET DEMOGRAPHICS: USERS AND USE

According to a January 1999 study by NUA LIMITED, which was based on a variety of sources using various methodologies, there are 153.25 million Internet users worldwide. By comparison, COMPUTER INDUSTRY ALMANAC INCORPORATED estimates 150 million users worldwide as of the end of 1998 and projects that by the end of the year 2000 there will be 320 million.

All statements of the size, growth rate, and number of users of the Internet worldwide are just estimates, and these estimates vary greatly from source to source, with each source using a different measurement methodology. Like most macroeconomic statistical measures, the quality of the estimates is directly related to the level of economic development in the country/region and to market demands for valid and reliable measures. Multiple estimates exist for North America, Europe, and certain parts of the Far East, and the producers of these estimates continually compare results and methodologies. Fewer choices are available for less-developed parts of the world and these usually contain considerable errors. However, an interesting new index has been developed by INTERNATIONAL DATA CORPORATION (IDC) to deal with problems of data availability. The IDC/World Times Information Society Index is a measure of the abilities of 55 countries, including some less developed countries, to participate in high-technology activities. It includes more than 23 variables on various types of infrastructure development, including computers, the Internet, telecommunications, and social issues.

A number of different organizations have begun to provide estimates that describe various aspects of the Internet, particularly those relating to users and use. The GEORGIA INSTITUTE OF TECHNOLOGY. GRAPHICS, VISUALIZATION, & USABILITY CENTER (GVU) WWW User Survey provides details on user characteristics worldwide. Surveys are done approximately twice each year and are endorsed by the World Wide Web Consortium (W3C) and the Institut National de Recherche en Informatique et en Automatique (INRIA). The Center's tenth survey results (based on data collected October-December 1998) were released in February 1999 on its Web site. Survey results include a wide variety of demographic variables as well as questions on experience using computers and the Internet, attitudes toward censorship, and access methods. The GVU methodology (details available on the Web site) is based on nonprobabilistic sampling methods using respondent self-selection. The Center cautions users of the data (which are freely released on the Web site but subject to limitations on use) that the results are biased toward the experienced user. KEHOE & PITKOW summarize the results of the first five surveys and discuss problems related to the methodology. GUPTA's Hermes Project, which cooperated with early GVU surveys in 1994, no longer appears to be operating, even though results of the fourth Hermes user survey in 1995 are still available on the project Web site.

MATRIX INFORMATION AND DIRECTORY SERVICES INCORPORATED (MIDS), under the direction of John Quarterman, provides demographic and related information on Internet use, users, and activities worldwide. MIDS issues a variety of products to paying subscribers, including *MATRIX MAPS QUARTERLY (MMQ)*, and *MATRIX NEWS*, while *The Internet Weather Report (IWR)* (MATRIX INFORMATION AND DIRECTORY SERVICES INCORPORATED), is freely available. Most of the demographic information appears in *MMQ* special reports and is based on at least annual surveys conducted by MIDS as well as a cooperative survey done by NETWORK WIZARDS since 1987. Recent surveys are sponsored by the INTERNET SOFTWARE CONSORTIUM (ISC) and some methodological details are available on its site.

Sources for other worldwide demographic data on the Internet are difficult to locate and tend to be nationally or regionally focused. The most comprehensive data exist for the U.S. and Canada. Most of the reporting services are marketing-oriented but include considerable demographic information. MEDIA METRIX INCORPORATED (1999), COMMERCENET, and NIELSEN//NETRATINGS appear to be the leaders in doing regular surveys of use and users.

Relevant Knowledge and Media Metrix, formerly two separate companies, merged in 1998 to form an Internet measurement service, MEDIA METRIX INCORPORATED (1999), in the areas of audience measurement, use, and user characteristics for the U.S. market. Media Metrix is probably best known for its hotly debated monthly report of the top rankings of Web site visits. The company uses a combination of interviews, respondent-downloaded software for capturing Internet use data, and other methods to produce a wide variety of products. At the core of its approach is a representative sample of more than 40,000 respondents selected via random-digit dialing to represent use at home and work. Exact details of the study methodologies are proprietary, but some information has been reported in two recent articles on the Web site (IVINS; MEDIA METRIX INCORPORATED, 1998). The company currently issues a variety of routine (monthly, weekly, and real-time) and specialized (to customer demand) products. The major product is the *Web Report* on all reportable U.S. Web sites with data on use, visits, minutes per visit, and demographics such as age and gender. It is available monthly to subscribers (as the *Key Measures Report*) and every six months (as the *Trend Report*) via the company Web site. Other reports of the company include: *Digital Media Report, Local Market Re-*

port, *Ad Network Report, Life Graphics* (based on Claritas social group segmentation measurements, which have particularly good lifestyle data), *Technology Measurement Services* (mostly hardware ownership characteristics), and the *Top 500 Web Sites Report*. Other services and products are likely to be offered by the time this volume appears.

The CommerceNet/Nielsen Internet Demographic Survey is performed approximately annually and provides extensive demographic data to subscribers (COMMERCENET RESEARCH CENTER). A major feature of the CommerceNet data system is the Gateway to Internet Demographics Online (GIDEON) software, where subscribers enter their individual choices of demographic variables and can manipulate the data to suit their needs. The methodology for the survey is available to subscribers.

In March 1999, Nielsen Media Research, Inc. and NetRatings, Inc. began a combined service called NIELSEN//NETRATINGS that closely rivals Media Metrix for providing a wide variety of demographic data on both home and work Internet users. Statistically representative samples of the U.S. population are drawn through random-digit dialing. The home-based users sample consists of more than 9,000 households. Respondents selected for tracking install supplied software that captures use data, including advertising response. All participants are then interviewed by phone or email to obtain detailed demographic data. Considerable detail on the methodologies for sample selection and audience measurement is available on the Web site. A wide variety of demographic statistics and advertising-oriented products are available to subscribers. The venture has just begun publishing lists of top Web sites (unique audience and reach percentages), top advertisers, and basic user statistics.

While Media Metrix, CommerceNet/Nielsen, and Nielsen// NetRatings currently (as of early 1999) appear to be the leaders in the area of Internet demography, the other organizations that collect demographic data are ZIFF-DAVIS, Roper Starch, CYBER DIALOGUE, and VANDERBILT UNIVERSITY OWEN GRADUATE SCHOOL OF MANAGEMENT. Each of these is discussed briefly.

ZIFF-DAVIS and Roper Starch have combined to produce Internet-Trak, a monthly telephone survey of users selected to be representative of the entire U.S. While the focus of the survey is on product purchasing by users, a considerable variety of demographic information is available in the published results. Minimal information about methodology is available on the Web site, but a summary of results of the latest survey is available there. CYBER DIALOGUE, which purchased the rights to the American Internet User Survey formerly conducted by FIND/SVP, continues the survey and has added additional surveys based on focus groups. The American Internet Survey included more than 20,000 users and nonusers in its sampling frame and asked more than 150 demographic and use questions. Summary, or tease, results are available on its Web page. VANDERBILT UNIVERSITY OWEN GRADUATE SCHOOL OF MANAGEMENT has a research program on Internet commerce called Project 2000, and issued several reports in the last two years that contain extensive demographic information. The principal investigators of this project, NOVAK & HOFFMAN, issued a report in 1997 on Web measurement standards.

The demand for Internet marketing surveys continues to increase so rapidly that it is almost impossible to keep up. Several regularly updated sources, however, provide entree to both the data and those involved in doing surveys. The *Internet Industry Almanac*, published annually, provides statistical data on all aspects of the Internet worldwide with particularly good breakdowns by country of demographic variables (JULIVSSEN & PETSKA-JULIVSSEN). The NUA Internet Surveys Web site identifies both general and specialized (particularly marketing-oriented) surveys and provides links to an electronic newsletter about surveys that are available on the Web (NUA LIMITED). YAHOO's (Internet) Statistics and Demographics Web page simply links to sites that maintain statistical data. The Internet Index Home Page by TREESE of Open Market is an occasional collection of miscellaneous factoids on the Internet useful for those trying to get rough demographic data. CYBERATLAS is similar in format to Treese's page, but more extensive in its collection and presentation of data.

Whether Internet demographic statistics are becoming more reliable and valid remains to be seen. The title of a November 1997 article in *Wired News* by COURT, "Truths about Net Use Remain Elusive" still appears to apply despite the vast increase in the number of surveys, studies, and companies involved in collecting data. Methodologies still vary greatly and are often proprietary, results are usually available only for a fee, geographical coverage is spotty, and the orientation toward data for marketing purposes is forcing surveyors to narrow their samples and audiences for results. This last reason should eventually lead to improved and open methodologies that could result in vast amounts of data on a wide variety of demographic variables, as it did for mass communications marketing surveys in the 1950s and 1960s. The development of industry standards and the forging of alliances in the electronic commerce arena, as discussed below, should enhance these developments.

INTERNET COMMERCE

Defining Internet commerce is not a simple task. Efforts by both government agencies and private companies are only beginning to come to some agreement about terminology and measurement approaches. This review takes a broad-based approach by including coverage of all identified measurement issues that relate to Internet commerce (I-commerce), now increasingly referred to as electronic commerce (e-commerce).

Government Interest

The amount of e-commerce continues to grow at an astonishing pace, estimated by ACTIVMEDIA, INCORPORATED in early 1998 to exceed $1,522 billion by the year 2000; equivalent to 2% of global GDP and 5% of GDP in the top 25 economies. Governments are beginning to take a keen interest in promoting and measuring it, as well as monitoring it for taxation purposes. According to a February 1999 press release by U.S. Secretary of Commerce William M. Daley, U.S.-based e-commerce ranges from $7.4 billion to $13 billion, with an average of $9 billion in 1998. He estimates that by the year 2000, U.S.-based retailing on the Internet will be a $30-billion business (DALEY, 1999b).

The *Sacher Report*, issued by the ORGANIZATION FOR ECONOMIC COOPERATION AND DEVELOPMENT (OECD) in 1997, was the first major study of e-commerce by an international government organization. The report recommends government support of an open-ended infrastructure for the Internet, government encouragement of the convergence of technologies for connecting to the Internet, and government partnerships with industry to raise the visibility of e-commerce. The report also addresses the critical issue of taxation and e-commerce with a firm recommendation against any type of data exchange tax (sometimes called a bit tax), but suggests that the question of the taxation of goods and services be worked out in consensual agreements between product source and destination. These recommendations are unlikely to be satisfactory to any of the parties. Since the publication of the *Sacher Report,* the OECD has continued to sponsor conferences on the topic of e-commerce and worked to deal with related problems such as cryptography, consumer protection, access issues, and law enforcement (FERNÉ).

While the U.S. government has had a long history of funding, promoting, and coordinating activities related to the Internet, most of these efforts have focused on its use for defense and educational purposes, with much less attention to e-commerce possibilities. This focus is clearly changing. Secretary of Commerce Daley announced in February 1999 that the department would begin to publish separate Internet sales data (formerly maintained as part of catalog sales data in retail trade reports) on a regular basis. He notes that 39% of retailers are now selling on the Internet and 86% of Internet users express concern about security and privacy of transactions (DALEY, 1999a).

Even when these two focal points of defense and education dominated, issues related to e-commerce were not entirely neglected in
previous work by such groups as the President's INFORMATION IN-
FRASTRUCTURE TASK FORCE (IITF), chaired by Vice President Al
Gore, the COUNCIL ON COMPETITIVENESS, the National Institute
for Standards and Technology (NIST) and others. A quick overview of
the IITF Web page shows more than 100 government-related reports on
the Internet from 1990 to 1997. Many of these relate directly to economic
and e-commerce issues. The major reports that require specific mention
in order to provide a good chronological overview of U.S. government
developments and recommendations related to e-commerce are: *Breaking the Barriers to the National Information Infrastructure* (COUNCIL ON
COMPETITIVENESS); *A Nation of Opportunity: Realizing the Promise of
the Information Superhighway* (U.S. ADVISORY COUNCIL ON THE
NATIONAL INFORMATION INFRASTRUCTURE); *A Framework for
Global Electronic Commerce* (CLINTON & GORE); *The Emerging Digital
Economy* (U.S. GOVERNMENT WORKING GROUP ON ELECTRONIC
COMMERCE); and *Electronic Commerce and the Global Marketplace*
(JOHNSON, 1998a).

Major Measurement Issues

While none of the basic activities of Internet commerce is new, the
facts that they are taking place almost entirely within an electronic
environment and that this environment is growing so fast, generate a
variety of questions that have greatly troubled those involved, whether
they are already heavily invested or just beginning to invest. The situation has worsened somewhat because the companies that traditionally
track sales figures, ad effectiveness, consumer familiarity with product
names, audience viewing/participation, and related data have been
relatively slow in developing new data-collection techniques and other
methodologies for the Internet. Only in the last year or so have these
organizations become active in the area of e-commerce. Similar problems have occurred in measuring electronic data interchange (EDI)
transactions. EDIs now appear to be migrating rapidly to Internet-
based extranets, but without clear-cut measurement methods that capture (and distinguish) business-to-business transactions of all types of
goods. Related problems of measurement occur in efforts by the U.S.
federal government in reporting wholesale and retail data, growth of
the economy, labor-force productivity, and economic value-added issues (U.S. GOVERNMENT WORKING GROUP ON ELECTRONIC
COMMERCE, pp. 120-140).

Two kinds of issues dominate the measurement literature about
Internet commerce: the nature and size of Internet commerce and the

marketing/advertising of goods and services over the Internet. These themes pervade the following sections.

Business-to-business e-commerce. An indication of the speed at which this level of commerce on the Internet is growing can be seen in two separate forecasts by the same company. In July 1997, as reported in *The Emerging Digital Economy* (U.S. GOVERNMENT WORKING GROUP ON ELECTRONIC COMMERCE), Forrester Research estimates that business-to-business commerce will be $377 billion for U.S. companies by 2002; in a December 1998 forecast, FORRESTER RESEARCH estimates $1.3 trillion by 2003. Similarly, an October 1998 study by ZIFF-DAVIS MARKET INTELLIGENCE reports that total corporate local area network (LAN) traffic now consists of 21% Internet traffic, indicating that companies are making extensive use of the Internet for business-related purposes, such as competitive intelligence, purchases, and Internet email.

Despite an obvious rapid rate of change in this aspect of e-commerce, there is ample evidence that executives of some companies are still feeling their way toward understanding how to maximize their own Internet presence and to justify the cost of their investment. A late 1998 study by MAINSPRING COMMUNICATIONS INCORPORATED shows that financial institutions do not know, even when they are purposefully beginning Web ventures vital to the company, how or when to measure site use or customer satisfaction and have only vague ideas about overall costs. WHITE ET AL. studied Web adoption practices of 20 business publishers and developed a typology of innovation that may be applicable to other types of business.

Measurement studies of business-to-business commerce do not appear to go beyond simple surveys of types of activities involving use of the Internet and estimates of total goods and services exchanged. The technical appendices on methodology in *The Emerging Digital Economy* (U.S. GOVERNMENT WORKING GROUP ON ELECTRONIC COMMERCE) on this type of e-commerce are only simple descriptions or case studies conducted in selected companies. If companies are to get a holistic view of all of their Internet/Web site use in order to maximize business potential, they must develop or adopt more specific methodologies.

Business-to-consumer e-commerce. As noted earlier, the Secretary of Commerce announced in February 1999 (DALEY, 1999a) that Internet retail sales exceeded $9 billion in 1998, or triple the 1997 figures. However, little is known about the sources and methods behind this figure; the announcement says Internet sales are included with catalog sales. A separate e-commerce number system will be developed for 1998 and 1999 retail sales, with the information to be made available by mid-

2000. Presumably, the sources and methods for the sales figures will be reported at the same time.

According to a study done by SHELLEY TAYLOR & ASSOCIATES, the success of Web retailing is closely related to the ability of the company to construct a Web site that is well designed to respond to the way humans process purchasing decisions. Their Click-Here Commerce 1999 study of 50 U.S. and European online stores in several different industries shows that e-commerce is an evolution, not a revolution, in retailing practice and that many companies make basic mistakes in Web-site construction and navigation. They used 175 evaluation criteria for the study and present a company-by-company analysis of results. Unfortunately, only an abstract of the report is available on the Web site, so methodology details are not available.

If the stock valuation numbers of Internet-based companies such as Amazon.com, eBay, and uBid are any indication of the potential importance of the Internet to retail sales, then the future is very bright for this area. An April 1999 paper by SIBULKIN & SOSVILLE of Mainspring, Inc. details the rapidly changing numbers in all areas usually considered important to retail marketing (demographics, attitudes toward buying on the Internet, etc.) and outlines the advantages and disadvantages for different types of retailers in using the Internet. Their typology of business models (commerce destination, gateway, context provider, and online exchange) is particularly useful in helping retailers identify how their business fits into e-commerce.

Site visits and traffic analysis.   Two key questions asked by any potential Internet advertiser concern the number of visitors to a site and what visitors do on a site. Variations on these questions are often referred to as site analysis, the stickiness (retention rate) of a site, and clickstream (activity pattern) analysis. A large number of commercial organizations exist to answer these questions, and each has its own method for collecting the data. The intensity of the debate over methods—and the survival of the companies doing the ratings—was highlighted in a conference news report by FESTA on CNET News in June 1998. Festa provides a brief review of the measurement problems involved and how each company represented at this "Web ratings debate" sponsored by Infoseek does its work. Companies represented at the conference were Nielsen Media, Media Metrix, Relevant Knowledge, and NetRatings. Specific measurement issues discussed were sampling frame selection, home versus work respondent selection, installation of proprietary measurement software on computers at work, caching of frequently visited sites (particularly in workplace situations) and what this does to server log data, and the reliability and validity of specific methods (such as interviews, installed software, and diaries) for collecting data.

The literature (print and Web-based) on these methods is only now beginning to gain coherence, and it is still difficult to obtain details on the use of various methods, most of which are proprietary. The previously mentioned study by NOVAK & HOFFMAN is a useful beginning point for understanding the issues and possible standards. The primary organizations involved are discussed under Internet demographics above, but new organizations enter the market on a regular basis. As of early 1999, the best sites for companies doing this type of work are CYBERATLAS, NUA LIMITED's surveys, and WEB COMMERCE TODAY.

Advertising revenue and ad effectiveness. Internet advertising revenue in 1998 was expected to exceed $2 billion, according to a 1999 report by the INTERNET ADVERTISING BUREAU (IAB). The size of the market and the long-standing worry of advertisers about their effectiveness (HAMILTON) have inspired a number of systematic efforts in the past two years to bring order out of the chaos. The issues involved in advertiser-supported Web-site activities have been discussed in a number of papers, beginning in 1995 by HOFFMAN ET AL., HOFFMAN & NOVAK, and NOVAK & HOFFMAN. In 1997, Novak & Hoffman categorize types of advertiser Web sites (sponsored content sites, sponsored search agents and directories, sponsored entry portal sites), discuss the need to understand what makes a successful sponsored site, draft a common terminology for measurement, compare Web advertising to other forms of media advertising, and categorize the various organizations (profit and nonprofit) working on developing metrics for this new area of advertising. They also discuss critical measurement issues related to banner ads (considered passive advertising exposure) and target ads (considered active advertising exposure) and how these link to various pricing models such as cost-per-thousand (CPM) exposures, flat fee, and click throughs (for greater exposure to the ad message). They recognize that Web advertising is interactive and note that it may be the "first commercial medium in which it is actually possible to measure consumer response, not just assume it" (NOVAK & HOFFMAN, p. 216).

The potential of the Internet and the size of the revenue that it can generate have led advertising industry associations to take a keen interest. Through various profit and nonprofit organizations, action is being taken to provide independent audits of traffic and site analyses. The central organizations involved in setting standards are the AUDIT BUREAU OF CIRCULATIONS' subsidiary ABC Interactive and Audit Bureau of Verification Services (ABVS), Inc.; BPA Interactive, a subsidiary of BPA INTERNATIONAL; the COALITION FOR ADVERTISING SUPPORTED INFORMATION AND ENTERTAINMENT (CASIE), a joint project of the Association of National Advertisers and the

American Association of Advertising Agencies; the Future of Advertising Stakeholders Summit (FAST) Forward Steering Committee, a combined group of executives from both sides (clients and ad agencies) of the advertising industry and host sites; and the IAB. In addition, scholarly attention is beginning to be paid to this area, particularly in trying to model clickstream data (CHATTERJEE ET AL.).

The third edition of the "CASIE Guiding Principles of Interactive Media Audience Measurement" (COALITION FOR ADVERTISING SUPPORTED INFORMATION AND ENTERTAINMENT) in 1999 is the latest and most complete detailing of the basic principles adopted by the Internet advertising industry and encompasses all advertiser-subsidized content to be delivered over television or personal computers. It proposes 13 specific principles regarding measurement practices and terminology that cause problems of reliability and validity in interactive media measurement. While the principles are too extensive to list here, their focus is on guaranteeing accurate measures that match the level of accountability provided by other advertising-supported media. The principles include auditing by objective third-party research entities and call for full disclosure of data and methods (though only to subscribers). If these principles are firmly accepted by the industry—as appears likely—this should spur progress toward standardization of terminology and measurement approaches. However, because agreement and implementation of the CASIE guidelines is not yet assured, the work of other industry groups also deserves mention.

The IAB issued its own paper, "Metrics and Methodology" (INTERNET ADVERTISING BUREAU. MEDIA MEASUREMENT TASK FORCE) in 1997. It proposes voluntary guidelines for the measurement of comparable data for online advertising and stresses that its central purpose is to begin the process of establishing a viable and useful advertising currency. Thus, it is more focused on the nature of the problem and establishing procedures and terminology than it is on specific measurement methods. The IAB continues its earlier work in a variety of areas with particular focus on ad effectiveness. It commissioned a 1998 study on online ad effectiveness using 12 leading Web sites and more than 16,000 respondents. Methodology and results are summarized on the MILLWARD BROWN INTERACTIVE Web site.

BPA Interactive, with a history of serving traditional publishers, considers itself the only nonprofit Web auditing firm (BPA INTERNATIONAL) and endorses the CASIE principles. It conducts audits of any subscribing Web site internationally and bases its analysis on a complete census of a site's log files using a page-view approach rather than hits. Complete details on methodology used in the audit do not appear on the BPA site but are available on request to subscribers.

The Audit Bureau of Circulations' (also with a long tradition of auditing for traditional publishers) subsidiaries, ABC Interactive and ABVS, perform functions similar to BPA Interactive for Web publishers. In 1999 BENNETT, at the request of CASIE, issued a white paper on delivery of interactive ad measurement that describes different approaches to observing online advertisement banners and some technologies that have been developed to deal with measurement problems caused by caching. Caching is a critical area of advertising research that is not yet covered by CASIE standards. The Audit Bureau of Circulations is the U.S. representative to the International Federation of Audit Bureaux, which also has a keen interest in international developments in Internet advertising issues.

The FAST Forward Steering Committee, chaired by Rich LeFurgy of the IAB, is attempting to deal with all of these issues as well as the future of interactive advertising. The Committee held several meetings in 1998 and was supposed to issue a general report in early 1999 (GARDNER), although none had appeared as of late 1999.

One of the major measurement problems with Internet advertising is that the pricing models are still fluid and both Web site operators and advertisers are not at all certain which models are to their advantage. As of early 1999, the major pricing models are exposure (usually CPM ad views or a flat fee for a set period of time for the ad to appear on a Web site), click throughs (where pricing is based on the number of times a user clicks on an ad), interactivity (the user has some level of activity with the advertisers' host site), and advertiser-specified outcomes (usually a purchase but it may also be awareness or attitude change). Each model has advantages and disadvantages from a measurement perspective, for the host site and the advertiser. These models are currently the subject of intense debate among the various parties discussed here (NOVAK & HOFFMAN).

The issue of ad effectiveness is closely tied to the question of CPM ad views or exposures. The general feeling of many advertisers is that CPM ad costs on the Web exceed costs for other media. However, BOYCE, of Wired Digital, Inc., argues that all comparisons across media are difficult and that CPM arguments about Web advertising must take into account the higher level of education and income of Web users, the active viewing of this audience compared with passive TV viewing, and the much lower ad-to-edit ratio on the Web (meaning the proportion of editorial content is much higher than in other media). These factors, he concludes, should and do lead to greater ad effectiveness on the Internet (BOYCE). Boyce's contentions about active viewing and ad effectiveness are supported in a 1999 study by Ipsos-ASI which found that 40% of viewers remember a Web banner ad compared to

41% of viewers of a 30-second TV commercial (FOLEY). This finding and the methodology used by Ipsos-ASI in the study have been the subject of criticism from NIELSEN (1999), a well-known author on Web design and frequent critic of Web-based advertising practices through his useit.com Alertbox site. Nielsen maintains that the Ipsos-ASI methodology comparing TV viewing with Web viewing was not only inappropriate but also biased, making the results unrealistic as a prediction of real-world Web viewing.

NIELSEN's (1997) larger view on Web advertising is that Web viewing is a cognitive process using a "cold" medium while TV viewing is an emotional process using a "warm" medium. Thus, in various columns on his Web site, he is not optimistic about the effectiveness of advertising on the Web, noting that click throughs have steadily declined from about 1% in 1997 to about 0.25% in early 1999. NIELSEN (1998b) analyzes the revenue generated by the top Web site in 1998, Yahoo, and notes that it earned only 0.4 cents per page view. While Yahoo, with its tremendous number of page views, may be able to survive on this, most sites will not be able to do so and must find other sources of revenue. Using the Yahoo traffic data, Nielsen developed an interesting measure of Web traffic rankings that can be used by anyone to calculate a site ranking (NIELSEN, 1998a).

Nielsen's views on the ineffectiveness of Web banner ads and the declining value of Web advertising for most Internet companies appear to be in the minority as of early 1999. The general trend is toward increased use of advertising, on which most Internet companies depend for generating revenue. It seems certain, however, that the issues will not go away and advertisers will continue to seek proof that they are getting the best use of their money. Thus, one can expect to see the continuing establishment and growth of sites such as the WebConnect Site Price Index (WEBCONNECT) that report Web ad rates, ad effectiveness, and return on investment for ad campaigns. One can also expect that the major industry groups will continue to monitor both prices and effectiveness and advertisers will insist on independent audits of Web sites with advertising. An interesting and potentially useful model for studying reach and frequency issues, based on the Beta Binomial Distribution, has been proposed by LECKENBY & HONG.

Despite the likelihood that independent auditors of Internet use will eventually win the day, both sides of the Internet market (advertisers and host sites) have several choices of how to collect the data needed by the other side. Essentially, these are (1) contracting with a full-service marketing research company to provide as detailed an analysis of use and users as needed to sell a site or decide which site to use for ad placement; (2) purchasing a site analysis software tool to generate the reports needed for selling a site and provide detailed demographic and use data for internal decision making; or (3) combinations of the first two approaches, which could include verification by independent auditing as well as maintaining in-house data on how well a site's use and users match broad industry benchmarks and user characteristics. As of early 1999, the combination approach appears to be gaining favor because it takes advantage of the experience that companies have gained in measuring other media use, provides multiple options for internal measurement, and could meet the increasing demand of advertisers for independent auditing.

INTERNET PROFILES CORPORATION (I/PRO) is an example of a company that does a comprehensive job of the combined approach. The company has also separately contracted with Nielsen Media to provide demographic and benchmark data to supplement its own analyses of Web site use and users. For in-house analysis, a number of sophisticated software products have become available in the last year at modest prices. Currently the leading developers appear to be AdKnowledge, Inc., Andromedia, Inc., MediaHouse Software, Inc., net.Genesis Corp., Sane Solutions LLC, and Webmanage Technologies, Inc. Principal analytical features of most of these products appear to be page views, browser detection, and customer information based on the use of plugins and cookies (HANNON; M. J. THOMPSON, 1999a). One of the best sources for keeping up with developments in this area is the print- and Web-based magazine, *The Industry Standard.*

Some systems, however, promote themselves as complete ad management systems, from design advice to determining return on investment (ROI) for specific ads placed at specific sites. ADKNOWLEDGE, INCORPORATED's AdKnowledge System analytical software, released in late 1998, and ANDROMEDIA INCORPORATED's, Smart e-Marketing Platform, released in early 1999, are each being touted as a complete package for the ad campaign, with automated analyses of post-click consumer actions, ad placement, and so forth, all correlated to the ads that generated the consumer response. An independent review of these products was not available at the time of writing, but these specific products are mentioned as examples of the likely focus of advertisers as they attempt to deal with questions of ad effectiveness that are not answered by independent auditing processes.

Consumer behavior in an online environment. By no means has consumer behavior been ignored in the work on advertising effectiveness; it is the heart of that work. However, rigorous studies of specific behavioral theories in the context of an online environment do not appear to be common, or at least are not appearing to any great extent in the open literature. One exception is the work of NOVAK ET AL. of Vanderbilt University's Project 2000. Using data collected in the GVU surveys, they have able been to test and refine a flow construct of consumer behavior that they believe has potential for marketing approaches in the online environment.

All of the key issues and questions about survey research methods come to the forefront when dealing with consumer behavior: sampling representativeness, self-selection of respondents, weighting of the sample, and validity and reliability of the survey instruments. In addition, the newness of online research methods arouses suspicion about the results, particularly if they do not match results from traditional methods such as phone or in-person interviews. Despite these misgivings, there is considerable optimism that online research is getting better, as evidenced by the summaries of the January 1999 conference, "The Future of Research: Online," sponsored by the ADVERTISING RESEARCH FOUNDATION.

Privacy and e-commerce. While advertisers and Web portal operators work vigorously to learn more about the characteristics of users, the users are equally concerned about invasion and protection of their privacy. Measurement issues obviously apply here, but they are not so easily identified because of the variable nature of this concern among users and the slow legislative progress being made in establishing specific legal protection. (The U.S. Congress did pass the Children's Online Privacy Act in 1998, which has alleviated many concerns about the protection of children using the Internet.)

The principal action on privacy has been the establishment of TRUSTE, a nonprofit organization dedicated to developing a standardized third-party oversight privacy program. TRUSTe licenses sites that meet its guidelines and authorizes them to display its trustmark seal. Precise details of this standardized testing program are not available on the Web site but the following are listed: initial and periodic review of licensees for posting of privacy guidelines, seeding of licensee Web sites with unique user identifier information and verifying how they handle this information, and collecting reports from the general Internet community regarding violations by licensees of privacy guidelines. TRUSTe regularly reports progress and developments to the U.S. Federal Trade Commission, the U.S. Department of Commerce, and the White House. A May 1999 survey found that 93% of the .com sites it surveyed collected at least one type of personal information and 57% collected demographic information (CULNAN). The survey is the subject of controversy in part because of its funding by industry sources (GLAVE).

CONCLUSIONS

This review has briefly covered the history, current status, and likely future of efforts to measure characteristics of the Internet. Because it is written at a time of rapid change (January-May 1999) in the Internet and in activities that measure it, many of the issues raised here may well have been settled or have taken different directions by the time the review is published. Some of the sources cited here, particularly those on the Web, will undoubtedly disappear by the time this review is published. In fact, some have already changed, moved, or disappeared since we completed the first draft. As discussed earlier, this is, and will continue to be, a problem of scholarship on Internet-related areas of study.

Only two areas with a body of mature, scholarly literature were identified: retrospective traffic studies and analysis of Internet search engines and their use. Web characterization studies, which overlap with retrospective traffic studies, are in the process of forming such a literature.

Internet researchers fall into groups with different questions in search of the same answers. In e-commerce, research done by the business community and by the academic community proceed from different assumptions and have different impacts because information is not shared by one community but is shared by the other. A similar divergence of interests occurs in the analysis of Internet traffic, which has been pioneered by network engineers but now may benefit from analysis from other fields. It seems likely that in these areas and others where the necessity for answers is great, the various communities will converge as they work toward the answers, whether through cooperation or competition. It can be hoped that in this convergence, researchers can avoid wasting time by borrowing successful techniques instead of reinventing them.

Generally, however, the Internet data environment is not friendly toward scholarship. As MANLEY & SELTZER observe: "New Web tools make money, statistical analyses of the Web do not."

It is of central importance that scholarly activity find a hospitable home on the Internet. To that end, it is necessary to:

- Foster such efforts as NATIONAL INTERNET MEASUREMENT INFRASTRUCTURE (NIMI), SKITTER, and PROJECT FELIX, which promise to bring scientific sampling to the study of network traffic and perhaps to other areas, such as episodic events like distribution of the *Starr Report*.
- Create a means for early release of data to the public either directly or through central archiving sources (similar, perhaps, to the Inter-University Consortium for Political and Social Research) so that data are available

to researchers at a reasonable cost. Perhaps the
INTERNET TRAFFIC ARCHIVE and the WEB CHAR-
ACTERIZATION REPOSITORY could be subsidized.

- Increase attention by researchers to the potential value
  of Internet-generated data for a wide range of social,
  behavioral, and demographic questions.
- Improve funding by the major funding agencies to measurement issues as they apply to topics raised here.
- Develop scholarly indexing of Internet resources, including the literature of measurement.
- Create a means of ensuring that studies and data are
  permanently archived and that their Internet addresses
  do not change.

BIBLIOGRAPHY

ABRAMSON, ALICIA D. 1998. Monitoring and Evaluating Use of the World
Wide Web in an Academic Library. See reference: PRESTON, CECILIA,
ed. 315-326.
ACTIVMEDIA, INCORPORATED. 1998. Press Releases. Available WWW:
http://www.activmedia.com/.
ADKNOWLEDGE INCORPORATED. 1998. The Advisor from AdKnowledge.
Available WWW: http://www.adknowledge.com/aksystem/
advisor.html.
ADLER, ROBERT J. 1997. Discussion. Annals of Statistics. 1997 October; 25(5):
1849-1852. ISSN: 0090-5364.
ADLER, ROBERT J.; FELDMAN, RAISA E.; TAQQU, MURAD S., eds. 1998. A
Practical Guide to Heavy Tails: Statistical Techniques and Applications.
Boston, MA: Birkhauser; 1998. 533p. ISBN: 0-8176-3951-9.
ADVERTISING RESEARCH FOUNDATION. 1999. Top 10 Insights about the
Validity of Conducting Research Online. Available WWW: http://
www.arfsite.org/Webpages/onlineresearch99/LA_99_top10.htm.
ALEXA INTERNET. 1997. Alexa: Navigate the Web Smarter & Easier. Avail-
able WWW: http://www.alexa.com/.
ALTAVISTA. Available WWW: http://altavista.digital.com/.
ANDROMEDIA INCORPORATED. 1999. Smart e-marketing Software. Avail-
able WWW: http://andromedia.com/products/.
ASIA PACIFIC NETWORK INFORMATION CENTRE. Available WWW: http:/
/www.apnic.org/.
AUDIT BUREAU OF CIRCULATIONS. 1999. ABC Mission Statement. Avail-
able WWW: http://www.accessabc.com/main/mission.htm.
BALBI, ADRIANO. 1986. A Statistical Essay on the Libraries of Vienna and the
World. Translation of Essai Statistique sur Les Bibliothèques de Viènne
(1835). Jefferson, NC: McFarland & Co.; 1986. 162p. ISBN: 0-89950-149-4.
[See particularly pages 30-42 in the chapter entitled "Difficulties Encoun-
tered in the Statistical Comparison of Libraries."]

BENNETT, RICHARD. 1999. White Paper: How Interactive Ads Are Delivered and Measurement Implication. Available WWW: http://www.abcinteractiveaudits.com/admeasurement.html.

BERGHEL, HAL. 1996. The Client's Side of the World Wide-Web. Communications of the ACM. 1996; 39(1): 30-40. ISSN: 0001-0782.

BERTOT, JOHN C.; MCCLURE, CHARLES R.; MOEN, WILLIAM E.; RUBIN, JOHN. 1997. Web Usage Statistics: Measurement Issues and Analytical Techniques. Government Information Quarterly. 1997; 14(4): 373-395. ISSN: 0740-624X.

BILAL, DANIA. 1998. Children's Search Processes in Using World Wide Web Search Engines: An Exploratory Study. See reference: PRESTON, CECILIA, ed. 45-53.

BOARDWATCH MAGAZINE. 1998-1999. Boardwatch Magazine's Directory of Internet Service Providers: Guide to Internet Access and the World Wide Web: Volume 3(2). Golden, CO: Mecklermedia; 1998 Winter-1999 Spring. OCLC: 34562081.

BONATI, MAURIZIO; IMPICCIATORE, PIERO; PANDOLFINI, CHIARA. 1998. Quality on the Internet. British Medical Journal. 1998 November 28; 317(7171): 1501. ISSN: 0959-8138.

BOYCE, RICK. 1998. Exploding the Web CPM Myth. Available WWW: http://www.iab.net/advertise/content/web_cpm.html.

BPA INTERNATIONAL. 1999. Just the Facts: BPA Interactive: Where Web Hype Becomes Web Facts. Available WWW: http://www.bpai.com/interactive/.

BRAY, TIM. 1996. Measuring the Web. In: 5th International World Wide Web Conference; 1996 May 6-10; Paris, France. Available WWW: http://www5conf.inria.fr/fich_html/papers/P9/Overview.html.

BROWSERWATCH. 1999. Available WWW: http://browserwatch.internet.com/. [Statistics can be found at: http://browserwatch.internet.com/stats/stats.html.]

CATLEDGE, LARA D.; PITKOW, JAMES E. 1995. Characterizing Browsing Strategies in the World Wide Web. In: Proceedings of the 3rd International World Wide Web Conference; 1995 April 10-14; Damstadt, Germany. Available WWW: http://www.igd.fhg.de/archive/www95/proceedings/papers/80/userpatterns/UserPatterns.Paper4.formatted.html.

CERF, VINTON G. 1991. Guidelines for Internet Measurement Activities. 1991 October 1. (RFC 1262). Available FTP: ftp://ftp.isi.edu/in-notes/rfc1262.txt.

CHATTERJEE, PATRALI; HOFFMAN, DONNA L.; NOVAK, THOMAS P. 1998. Modeling the Clickstream: Implications for Web-Based Advertising Efforts. Available WWW: http://www2000.ogsm.vanderbilt.edu/papers/clickstream/clickstream.html.

CHOO, CHUN WEI; DETLOR, BRIAN; TURNBULL, DON. 1998. A Behavioral Model of Information Seeking on the Web—Preliminary Results of a Study of How Managers and IT Specialists Use the Web. See reference: PRESTON, CECILIA, ed. 290-302.

CHU, HETING; ROSENTHAL, MARILYN. 1996. Search Engines for the World Wide Web: A Comparative Study and Evaluation Methodology. In: Hardin,

Steve, ed. Global Complexity: Information, Chaos and Control: Proceedings of the American Society for Information Science (ASIS) 59th Annual Meeting: Volume 33; 1996 October 21-24; Baltimore, MD. Medford, NJ: Information Today, Inc. for ASIS; 1996. 127-135. ISSN: 0044-7870; ISBN: 1-57387-037-4.

CLAFFY, KIMBERLY C.; POLYZOS, GEORGE; BRAUN, HANS-WERNER. 1993. Measurement Considerations for Assessing Unidirectional Latencies. Internetworking: Research and Experience. 1993 September; 4(3): 121-132. ISSN: 1049-8915.

CLEAR INK. 1999. NetCopter. Available WWW: http://www.netcopter.com/.

CLINTON, WILLIAM J.; GORE, ALBERT, JR. 1997. A Framework for Global Electronic Commerce. Washington, DC: The White House; 1997. 30p. (Prex 1.2:F 84). Available WWW: http://www.iitf.nist.gov/eleccomm/ecomm.htm.

COALITION FOR ADVERTISING SUPPORTED INFORMATION AND ENTERTAINMENT (CASIE). 1999. CASIE Guiding Principles of Interactive Media Audience Measurement. 3rd edition. Available WWW: http://www.casie.org/guidel/.

COFFMAN, K. G.; ODLYZKO, ANDREW. 1998. The Size and Growth Rate of the Internet. First Monday. 1998 October 5; 3(10). ISSN: 1396-0466. Available WWW: http://www.firstmonday.dk/issues/issue3_10/coffman/.

COMMERCENET. 1999. About CommerceNet. Available WWW: http://www.commerce.net/about/.

COMMERCENET RESEARCH CENTER. 1999. CommerceNet Research Center. Available WWW: http://www.commerce.net/research/.

COMPUTER EMERGENCY RESPONSE TEAM. 1999. CERT Statistics. Available WWW: http://www.cert.org/stats/.

COMPUTER INDUSTRY ALMANAC INCORPORATED. 1999. Press Release: Over 150 Million Internet Users Worldwide at Year-End 1998. 1999 April 30. Available WWW: http://www.c-i-a.com/199904iu.htm.

COOPERATIVE ASSOCIATION FOR INTERNET DATA ANALYSIS (CAIDA). 1998. Internet Statistics and Metrics Analysis: Engineering Data and Analysis Workshop Report; 1998 August 31-September 1; San Diego, CA. Available WWW: http://www.caida.org/outreach/isma/9808/.

COOPERATIVE ASSOCIATION FOR INTERNET DATA ANALYSIS (CAIDA). 1999a. Internet Information Presentation. Available WWW: http://www.caida.org/outreach/info.

COOPERATIVE ASSOCIATION FOR INTERNET DATA ANALYSIS (CAIDA). 1999b. Internet Tools Taxonomy. Available WWW: http://www.caida.org/tools/taxonomy/.

COUNCIL ON COMPETITIVENESS. 1995. Breaking the Barriers to the National Information Infrastructure: A Conference Report. Available WWW: http://nii.nist.gov/pubs/barriers/cover1.html.

COURT, RANDOLPH. 1997. Truths about Net Use Remain Elusive. Wired News. Available WWW: http://www.wired.com/news/news/business/story/8745.html.

CROVELLA, MARK E.; TAQQU, MURAD S.; BESTAVROS, AZER. 1998. Heavy-Tailed Probability Distributions in the World Wide Web. In: Adler, Robert J.; Feldman, Raisa E.; Taqqu, Murad S., eds. A Practical Guide to Heavy Tails: Statistical Techniques and Applications. Boston, MA: Birkhauser; 1998. 3-25. ISBN: 0-8176-3951-9.

CULNAN, MARY J. 1999. Georgetown Internet Privacy Policy Survey. Available WWW: http://www.msb.edu/faculty/culnanm/gippshome.html.

CYBER DIALOGUE. 1999. American Internet User Survey. Available WWW: http://www.cyberdialogue.com/products/isglaius/index.html.

CYBERATLAS. 1998. About CyberAtlas. Available WWW: http://cyberatlas.internet.com/resources/about/article.

DALEY, WILLIAM M. 1999a. Press Conference on E-Commerce. 1999 February 5. Available WWW: http://osecnt13.osec.doc.gov/public.nsf/docs/commerce-ftc-online-shopping-briefing.

DALEY, WILLIAM M. 1999b. Press Release: Commerce Department to Use Internet Sales to Measure Retail Activity Impact on Economy. 1999 February 5. Available WWW: http://osecnt13.osec.doc.gov/public.nsf/docs/commerce-ftc-press-release.

DEJA.COM. Available WWW: http://www.deja.com/.

DERN, DANIEL P. 1999. Usenet—Still Useful after All These Years. Byte. 1999 April 5. Available WWW: http://www.byte.com/features/1999/04/0405newsgroups.html.

DIGITAL LIBRARIES WORKING GROUP ON DIGITAL LIBRARY METRICS. 1998. D-Lib Working Group on Digital Library Metrics: Other Documents. Available WWW: http://www.dlib.org/metrics/public/metrics-documents.html.

DILLON, MARTIN; JUL, ERIK; BURGE, MARK; HICKEY, CAROL. 1993. Assessing Information on the Internet toward Providing Library Services for Computer-Mediated Communication. Dublin, OH: OCLC; 1993. Available WWW: http://www.oclc.org/oclc/research/9194res/front.htm.

DING, WEI; MARCHIONINI, GARY. 1996. A Comparative Study of Web Search Service Performance. In: Hardin, Steve, ed. Global Complexity: Information, Chaos and Control: Proceedings of the American Society for Information Science (ASIS) 59th Annual Meeting: Volume 33; 1996 October 21-24; Baltimore, MD. Medford, NJ: Information Today, Inc. for ASIS; 1996. 136-142. ISSN: 0044-7870; ISBN: 1-57387-037-4.

ERNST & YOUNG LLP. 1999. Second Annual Internet Shopping Study. Available WWW: http://www.ey.com/industry/consumer/internetshopping/overview.asp.

FERNÉ, GEORGES. 1997. Electronic Commerce: A New Economic and Policy Area. Journal of Internet Banking and Commerce, 1997 September; 2(4). ISSN: 1204-5357. Available WWW: http://www.arraydev.com/commerce/jibc/9704-08.htm.

FESTA, PAUL. 1998. Net Traffic Ratings Debated. CNET: News: Enterprise Computing. 1998 June 12. Available WWW: http:///www.news.com/News/Item/0,4,23124,00.html.

FIND/SVP. 1998. American Internet User Survey. Available WWW: http://etrg.findsvp.com/internet/findf.html.

FOLEY, MARIANNE. 1999. Online Banner Ads as Effective as Television Ads in Building Brand Awareness, New Ipsos-ASI Research Confirms. Available WWW: http://www.businesswire.com/webbox/bw.021799/1010484.htm.

FORRESTER RESEARCH. 1998. Available WWW: http://www.forrester.com/er/intro/.

GARDNER, ELIZABETH. 1998. Meeting of Big Advertisers Points Up Web's Problems. Internet World. 1998 August 24. Available WWW: http://www.internetworld.com/print/1998/08/24/news/19980824-fastsummit.html.

GEORGIA INSTITUTE OF TECHNOLOGY. GRAPHICS, VISUALIZATION, & USABILITY CENTER. 1999. GVU's 10th WWW User Survey. Available WWW: http://www.gvu.gatech.edu/user_surveys/survey-1998-10/.

GLAVE, JAMES. 1999. Who's Taking Privacy's Pulse? Wired News. 1999 March 8. Available WWW: http://www.wired.com/news/news/politics/story/18314.html.

GRAY, MATTHEW. 1996. Internet Statistics: Growth and Usage of the Web and the Internet. Available WWW: http://www.mit.edu/people/mkgray/net/.

GUPTA, SUNIL. 1995. Hermes: Consumer Survey of WWW Users: Preliminary Results from the 4th Survey. Available WWW: http://www-personal.umich.edu/~sgupta/hermes/survey4/survey4.pdf.

HAFNER, KATIE; LYON, MATTHEW. 1996. Where Wizards Stay Up Late: The Origins of the Internet. New York, NY: Simon and Schuster; 1996. 304p. ISBN: 0-684-81201-0.

HAMILTON, ANNETTE. 1997. Why Web Advertising Is Unreliable. 1997 December. Available WWW: http://www.zdnet.com/anchordesk/story/story_1497.html.

HANNON, BRIAN. 1998. Site Analysis Tools Driving Web Strategy. PC Week Online. 1998 August 10. Available WWW: http://www.zdnet.com/pcweek/news/0810/10web.html.

HARSLEM, E. F.; HEAFNER, J. F.; WHITE, J. E. 1971. Network Activity Report: UCSB‹ - ›RAND. 1971 April 5. (RFC 113). Available FTP: ftp://ftp.isi.edu/in-notes/rfc113.txt.

HARTER, STEPHEN A.; HERT, CAROL A. 1997. Evaluation of Information Retrieval Systems: Approaches, Issues, and Methods. In: Williams, Martha E., ed. Annual Review of Information Science and Technology: Volume 32. Medford, NJ: Information Today, Inc. for the American Society for Information Science; 1997. 3-93. ISSN: 0066-4200; ISBN: 1-57387-047-1.

HERT, CAROL A.; MARCHIONINI, GARY. 1998. Information Seeking Behavior on Statistical Websites: Theoretical and Design Implications. See reference: PRESTON, CECILIA, ed. 303-314.

HIRSH, SANDRA. 1998. Relevance Determinations in Children's Use of Electronic Resources: A Case Study. See reference: PRESTON, CECILIA, ed. 63-72.

HOFFMAN, DONNA L.; NOVAK, THOMAS P. 1997. A New Marketing Paradigm for Electronic Commerce. The Information Society. 1997; 13(1): 43-54. ISSN: 0197-2243.

HOFFMAN, DONNA L.; NOVAK, THOMAS P.; CHATTERJEE, PATRALI. 1995. Commercial Scenarios for the Web: Opportunities and Challenges. Journal of Computer-Mediated Communication. 1995 December; 1(3). ISSN: 1083-6101. Available WWW: http://www.ascusc.org/jcmc/vol1/issue3/hoffman.html.

IMPICCIATORE, PIERO; PANDOLFINI, CHIARA; CASELLA, NICOLA; BONATI, MAURIZIO. 1997. Reliability of Health Information for the Public on the World Wide Web: Systematic Survey of Advice on Managing Fever in Children at Home. British Medical Journal. 1997 June 28; 314(7098): 1875-1879. ISSN: 0959-8138.

INFORMATION INFRASTRUCTURE TASK FORCE (IITF). 1997. The President's Information Infrastructure Task Force Home Page. Available WWW: http://iitf.doc.gov/.

INTERNATIONAL COALITION OF LIBRARY CONSORTIA (ICOLC). 1998. Guidelines for Statistical Measures of Usage of Web-Based Indexed, Abstracted, and Full Text Resources. 1998 November. Available WWW: http://www.library.yale.edu/consortia/webstats.html.

INTERNATIONAL DATA CORPORATION. 1999. Information Society Index. Available WWW: http://www.idc.com/ITOver/isi.htm.

INTERNET ADVERTISING BUREAU. 1999. Internet Advertising Revenues Exceed $1 Billion for the First Time. Available WWW: http://www.iab.net/news/content/billion.html.

INTERNET ADVERTISING BUREAU. MEDIA MEASUREMENT TASK FORCE. 1997. Metrics and Methodology. 1997 September 15. Available WWW: http://www.iab.net/advertise/adsource.html.

INTERNET ARCHITECTURE BOARD. Available WWW: http://www.iab.org/.

INTERNET ENGINEERING TASK FORCE. Available WWW: http://www.ietf.org/.

INTERNET PERFORMANCE MEASUREMENT AND ANALYSIS PROJECT. 1999. IPMA Project Home Page. Available WWW: http://www.merit.edu/ipma/.

INTERNET PROFILES CORPORATION. 1998. About I/PRO. Available WWW: http://www.ipro.com/about.

INTERNET RESEARCH TASK FORCE. Available WWW: http://www.irtf.org/.

INTERNET SOCIETY. 1999. Internet Histories. Available WWW: http://www.isoc.org/internet/history/.

INTERNET SOFTWARE CONSORTIUM. 1999. Internet Domain Survey. Available WWW: http://www.isc.org/ds/.

INTERNET TRAFFIC ARCHIVE. Available: http://ita.ee.lbl.gov/.

IVINS, BOB. 1999. Reconciling Audience Measurement Data to Server Logs. Available WWW: http://www.rkinc.com/Methodology/convergence.html. Note: This page is no longer available to the general public on this site; it is limited to subscribers only.

JOHNSON, JAMES. 1998a. Electronic Commerce and the Global Marketplace: Report on International Organizations Activities. 1998 March. Available WWW: http://nii.nist.gov/pubs/ecgm-jj.htm.

JOHNSON, JAMES. 1998b. Informatics 2000: Electronic Commerce and Trade Information Task Force Framework for Action. 1998 April. Available WWW: http://nii.nist.gov/pubs/info-jj.htm.

JULIVSSEN, EGIL; PETSKA-JULIVSSEN, KAREN, eds. 1998. Internet Industry Almanac. San Jose, CA: Computer Industry Almanac, Inc.; 1998. 387p. ISBN: 0-942107-13-6.

KAHLE, BREWSTER. 1996. Archiving the Internet. Available WWW: http://www.archive.org/sciam_article.html. Revised version appears: 1997. Preserving the Internet. Scientific American. 1997 March; 276(3): 82-84. ISSN: 0036-8733. Also available WWW: http://www.sciam.com/0397issue/0397kahle.html.

KEHOE, COLLEEN M.; PITKOW, JAMES E. 1996. Surveying the Territory: GVU's Five WWW User Surveys. The World Wide Web Journal. 1996; 1(3): 77-84. ISSN: 1085-2298. Available WWW: http://www.gvu.gatech.edu/gvu/user_surveys/papers/w3j.html.

KIM, PAUL; ENG, THOMAS R.; DEERING, MARY JO; MAXFIELD, ANDREW. 1999. Published Criteria for Evaluating Health Related Web Sites: Review. British Medical Journal. 1999 March 6; 318(7184): 647-649. ISSN: 0959-8138.

KLEINROCK, LEONARD. 1976. Chapter 6: Computer-Communication Networks: Measurement, Flow Control, and ARPANET Traps. In: Kleinrock, Leonard. Queueing Systems. Volume II: Computer Applications. New York, NY: Wiley; 1976. 422-515. ISBN: 0-471-49111-X.

KLEINROCK, LEONARD; NAYLOR, WILLIAM. 1974. On Measured Behavior of the ARPA Network. In: American Federation of Information Processing Societies (AFIPS) Conference Proceedings: National Computer Conference and Exposition: Volume 43; 1974 May 6-10; Chicago, IL. Montvale, NJ: AFIPS Press; 1974. 767-780. OCLC: 35375333.

KOEHLER, WALLACE. 1999. An Analysis of Web Page and Web Site Constancy and Permanence. Journal of the American Society for Information Science. 1999 February; 50(2): 162-180. ISSN: 0002-8231.

LABOVITZ, CRAIG; MALAN, G. ROBERT; JAHANIAN, FARNAM. 1997. Internet Routing Instability. In: Proceedings of ACM SIGCOMM'97; 1997 September 14-18; Cannes, France. Computer Communication Review. 1997 October; 27(4): 115-126. ISSN: 0146-4833; ISBN: 0-89791-905-X. Also available via two formats at WWW: http://www.acm.org/sigcomm/sigcomm97/papers/p109.html.

LARSON, RAY R. 1996. Bibliometrics of the World Wide Web: An Exploratory Analysis of the Intellectual Structure of Cyberspace. In: Hardin, Steve, ed. Global Complexity: Information, Chaos and Control: Proceedings of the American Society for Information Science (ASIS) 59th Annual Meeting: Volume 33; 1996 October 21-24; Baltimore, MD. Medford, NJ: Information Today, Inc. for ASIS; 1996. 71-78. ISSN: 0044-7870; ISBN: 1-57387-037-4.

LAWRENCE, STEVE; GILES, C. LEE. 1998a. Press Coverage of Science Article. Available WWW: http://www.neci.nj.nec.com/homepages/lawrence/papers/search-science98/feedback.html.

LAWRENCE, STEVE; GILES, C. LEE. 1998b. Search Engine Coverage Update. 1998 September. Available WWW: http://www.neci.nj.nec.com/homepages/lawrence/websize98.html.

LAWRENCE, STEVE; GILES, C. LEE. 1998c. Searching the World Wide Web. Science. 1998 April 3; 280: 98-100. ISSN: 0036-8075. Available in summary at WWW: http://www.neci.nj.nec.com/homepages/lawrence/websize.html.

LAWRENCE, STEVE; GILES, C. LEE; BOLLACKER, KURT. 1998. CiteSeer: Autonomous Citation Indexing. Available WWW: http://www.neci.nj.nec.com/homepages/lawrence/citeseer.html.

LECKENBY, JOHN D.; HONG, JONGPIL. 1998. User Reach/Frequency for Web Media Planning. Journal of Advertising Research. 1998 January-February; 38(1): 7-20. ISSN: 0021-8499.

LIBRARY OF CONGRESS INFORMATION BULLETIN. 1998. A Snapshot of Cyberspace: Alexa Internet Donates Web Archive. Library of Congress Information Bulletin. 1998 November; 57(11): 266. Also available WWW: http://lcweb.loc.gov/loc/lcib/9811/alexa.html.

LOTTOR, MARK. 1992. Internet Growth (1981-1991). 1992 January. (RFC 1296). Available FTP: ftp://ftp.isi.edu/in-notes/rfc1296.txt.

LYNCH, CLIFFORD. 1997. Searching the Internet. Scientific American. 1997 March; 276(3): 52-56. ISSN: 0036-8733. Also available WWW: http://www.sciam.com/0397issue/0397lynch.html.

MACCALL, STEVEN L. 1998. Relevance Reliability in Cyberspace: Towards Measurement Theory for Internet Information Retrieval. See reference: PRESTON, CECILIA, ed. 13-22.

MADDOX, KATE. 1998. FAST Forward Committee Readies Ad Guidelines. Advertising Age. 1998 November 16; 69(46): 44-46. ISSN: 0001-8899.

MAINSPRING COMMUNICATIONS INCORPORATED. 1998. Online Brokerage Business Model Dictates Which Metrics Are Employed. 1998 November 12. Available WWW: http://www.mainspring.com/analysis/ld/1,2146,doc-138-Abstract,00.html.

MANLEY, STEPHEN; SELTZER, MARGO. 1997. Web Facts and Fantasy. In: Proceedings of the 1997 USENIX Symposium on Internet Technologies and Systems; 1997 December 8-11; Monterey, CA. Available WWW: http://www.eecs.harvard.edu/~vino/web/sits.97.html.

MATRIX INFORMATION AND DIRECTORY SERVICES INCORPORATED. 1999. The Internet Weather Report. Available WWW: http://www.mids.org/weather/.

MATRIX MAPS QUARTERLY (MMQ). 1993-. Austin, TX: Matrix, Inc. ISSN: 1073-0958. Available WWW as Matrix Maps: http://www.matrix.net/publications/mmq/index.html.

MATRIX NEWS. 1991-. Austin, TX: Matrix, Inc. ISSN: 1059-0749. Available WWW: http://www.matrix.net/publications/mn.

MAULDIN, MICHAEL L. 1995. Measuring the Web with Lycos. Available WWW: http://www.lazytd.com/lti/pub/lycos-websize-9510.html.

MAULDIN, MICHAEL L.; LEAVITT, JOHN R. R. 1994. Web Agent Related Research at the Center for Machine Translation. In: 1994 Meeting of the ACM Special Interest Group on Networked Information Discovery and Retrieval. Available WWW: http://www.lazytd.com/lti/pub/signidr94.html.

MEDIA METRIX INCORPORATED. 1998. A Comparison of World Wide Web Audience Estimates Utilizing Two Different Approaches. 1998 October 13.

Available WWW: http://us.mediametrix.com/products/methodologies.jsp.

MEDIA METRIX INCORPORATED. 1999. About Media Metrix. Available WWW: http://us.mediametrix.com/aboutus/index.jsp.

MERIT NETWORK INCORPORATED. Available WWW: http://www.merit.edu/.

MILLWARD BROWN INTERACTIVE. 1998. IAB Advertising Effectiveness Study Executive Summary. Available WWW: http://www.mbinteractive.com/site/iab/exec.html.

NATIONAL INSTITUTE FOR STANDARDS AND TECHNOLOGY. 1999. ITL Programs. Available WWW: http://www.itl.nist.gov/.

NATIONAL INTERNET MEASUREMENT INFRASTRUCTURE (NIMI). Available WWW: http://www.psc.edu/networking/nimi/. NIMI is based on Paxson's Network Probe Daemon as discussed in PAXSON (1996; 1997).

NETCRAFT. 1999a. The Netcraft Web Server Survey. Available WWW: http://www.netcraft.com/Survey/.

NETCRAFT. 1999b. Survey Mechanics. Available WWW: http://www.netcraft.com/Survey/mechanics.html.

NETRATINGS, INCORPORATED. 1998. Panel Methodology. Available WWW: http://www.netratings.com/products_panel.htm.

NETRATINGS, INCORPORATED. 1999. Products and Services. Available WWW: http://www.netratings.com/products.htm.

NETWORK WIZARDS. 1999. Internet Domain Survey. Available WWW: http://www.nw.com/.

NIELSEN, JAKOB. 1997. Why Advertising Doesn't Work on the Web. Alertbox. 1997 September 1. Available WWW: http://www.useit.com/alertbox/9709a.html.

NIELSEN, JAKOB. 1998a. Compute Your Own Web Traffic Rank. Alertbox. 1998 November 1. Available WWW: http://www.useit.com/alertbox/relativeranking.html.

NIELSEN, JAKOB. 1998b. Why Yahoo Is Good (But May Get Worse). Alertbox. 1998 November 1. Available WWW: http://www.useit.com/alertbox/981101.html.

NIELSEN, JAKOB. 1999. Details in Study Methodology Can Give Misleading Results. Alertbox. 1999 February 21. Available WWW: http://www.useit.com/alertbox/990221.html.

NIELSEN MEDIA RESEARCH INCORPORATED. 1999. Who We Are and What We Do. Available WWW: http://www.nielsenmedia.com/.

NIELSEN//NETRATINGS. 1999. Products: IQ. Available WWW: http://www.nielsen-netratings.com/products_IQ.htm.

NOTESS, GREG R. 1999. Search Engine Statistics. Available WWW: http://www.notess.com/search/stats/.

NOVAK, THOMAS P.; HOFFMAN, DONNA L. 1997. New Metrics for New Media: Towards the Development of Web Measurement Standards. World Wide Web Journal. 1997; 2(1): 213-246. ISSN: 1085-2298. Draft version available WWW: http://www2000.ogsm.vanderbilt.edu/novak/web.standards/webstand.html.

NOVAK, THOMAS P.; HOFFMAN, DONNA L.; YUNG, YIU-FAI. 1998. Measuring the Flow Construct in Online Environments: A Structural Modeling Approach. 1998 May. Available WWW: http://www2000.ogsm.vanderbilt.edu/papers/flow.construct/measuring_flow_construct.html.

NUA LIMITED. 1999. How Many Online? Available WWW: http://www.nua.ie/surveys/how_many_online/index.html.

O'NEILL, EDWARD T.; MCCLAIN, PATRICK D.; LAVOIE, BRIAN F. 1998. A Methodology for Sampling the World Wide Web. Available WWW: http://www.oclc.org/oclc/research/publications/review97/oneill/o'neillar980213.htm.

OCLC ONLINE COMPUTER LIBRARY CENTER, INCORPORATED. 1998. Statistics. Available WWW: http://wcp.oclc.org.

ONLINE PRIVACY ALLIANCE. 1999. OPA Top 100 Survey. Available WWW: http://www.privacyalliance.org/resources/100_summary.shtml.

ORGANIZATION FOR ECONOMIC COOPERATION AND DEVELOPMENT (OECD). 1997. Electronic Commerce: Opportunities and Challenges for Government. Paris, France: OECD; 1997. 83p. ISBN: 92-641-5512-0. Also available WWW: http://www.oecd.org/dsti/sti/it/ec/act/sacher.htm.

ORR, RICHARD. 1973. Measuring the Goodness of Library Services: A General Framework for Considering Quantitative Measures. Journal of Documentation. 1973 September; 29: 315-332. ISSN: 0022-0418.

PAXSON, VERN. 1994. Growth Trends in Wide-Area TCP Connections. IEEE Network. 1994 July/August; 8(4): 8-17. ISSN: 0890-8044.

PAXSON, VERN. 1996. End-to-End Routing Behavior in the Internet. In: Proceedings of ACM SIGCOMM'96 (Special Interest Group on Data Communication); 1996 August 26-30; Stanford University, Stanford, CA. Computer Communication Review. 1996 October; 26(4): 25-38. ISSN: 0146-4833; ISBN: 0-89791-790-1. Also available via two formats at WWW: http://www.acm.org/sigcomm/ccr/archive/1996/conf/paxson.html.

PAXSON, VERN. 1997. End-to-End Internet Packet Dynamics. In: Proceedings of ACM SIGCOMM'97; 1997 September 14-18; Cannes, France. Computer Communication Review. 1997 October; 27(4): 139-152. ISSN: 0146-4833; ISBN: 0-89791-905-X. Also available via two formats at WWW: http://www.acm.org/sigcomm/sigcomm97/papers/p086.html.

PAXSON, VERN; ALMES, G.; MAHDAVI, J.; MATHIS, M. 1998. Framework for IP Performance Metrics. 1998 May. (RFC 2330). Available FTP: ftp://ftp.isi.edu/in-notes/rfc2330.txt.

PEEK, ROBIN; POMERANTZ, JEFFREY; PALING, STEPHEN. 1998. The Traditional Scholarly Journal Publishers Legitimize the Web. Journal of the American Society for Information Science. 1998 September; 49(11): 983-989. ISSN: 0002-8231.

PITKOW, JAMES E. 1998. Summary of WWW Characterizations. In: Proceedings of the 7th International World Wide Web Conference; 1998 April 14-18; Brisbane, Australia. Available WWW: http://www7.scu.edu.au/programme/fullpapers/1877/com1877.htm.

PRESTON, CECILIA, ed. 1998. Information Access in the Global Information Economy: Proceedings of the American Society for Information Science (ASIS) 61st Annual Meeting: Volume 35; 1998 October 24-29; Pittsburgh, PA. Medford, NJ: Information Today, Inc. for ASIS; 1998. 604p. ISSN: 0044-7870; ISBN: 1-57387-066-8.

PROJECT FELIX. 1999. Independent Monitoring for Network Survivability. Available WWW: http://govt.argreenhouse.com/felix/.

QUARTERMAN, JOHN S. 1990. The Matrix: Computer Networks and Conferencing Systems Worldwide. Newton, MA: Butterworth-Heinemann; 1997. 719p. ISBN: 1-55558-033-5.

QUARTERMAN, JOHN S. 1998. Statistics about the MIDS IWR. Available WWW: http://www.mids.org/weather/pingstats/index.html.

RÉSEAUX IP EUROPÉENS (RIPE). 1999a. RIPE Network Coordination Centre. Available WWW: http://www.ripe.net/.

RÉSEAUX IP EUROPÉENS (RIPE). 1999b. RIPE Region Hostcount. Available WWW: http://www.ripe.net/ripencc/pub-services/stats/hostcount/index.html.

RESNICK, SIDNEY. 1997. Heavy Tail Modeling and Teletraffic Data. Annals of Statistics. 1997 October; 25(5): 1805-1869. ISSN: 0090-5364.

RICKARD, JACK. 1998. Backbone Performance Measurements. Boardwatch. 1998 September. Available WWW: http://boardwatch.internet.com/mag/98/sep/bwm50.html. See also: http://boardwatch.internet.com/traceroute.html for continuing information on this subject.

RIEH, SOO YOUNG; BELKIN, NICHOLAS J. 1998. Understanding Judgment of Information Quality and Cognitive Authority in the WWW. See reference: PRESTON, CECILIA, ed. 279-289.

SCHWARTZ, CANDY. 1998. Web Search Engines. Journal of the American Society for Information Science. 1998; 49(11): 973-982. ISSN: 0002-8231.

SEARCHENGINEWATCH.COM. 1999. Fast Aims for Largest Index. Available WWW: http://searchenginewatch.internet.com/sereport/99/05-fast.html.

SHELLEY TAYLOR & ASSOCIATES. 1999. Click-Here Commerce. 1999 February. Available WWW: http://infofarm.com/html/chc_overview.html.

SIBULKIN, STEVEN; SOSVILLE, GREG. 1999. Creating Value in the Online Consumer Marketplace. 1999 April 20. Available WWW: http://www.mainspring.com/analysis/ld/1,2146,doc-1027-Full,00.html.

SKITTER. Available WWW: http://www.caida.org/tools/measurement/skitter/.

SU, LOUISE T. 1997. Developing a Comprehensive and Systematic Model of User Evaluation of Web-Based Search Engines. In: Williams, Martha E., ed. Proceedings of the 18th National Online Meeting; 1997 May 13-15; New York, NY. Medford, NJ: Information Today, Inc.; 1997. 335-345. ISBN: 1-57387-043-9.

SU, LOUISE T.; CHEN, HSIN-LIANG; DONG, XIAOYING. 1998. Evaluation of Web-Based Search Engines from the User's Perspective. See reference: PRESTON, CECILIA, ed. 348-361.

SULLIVAN, DANNY. 1999. Search Engine Status Reports. Available WWW: http://searchenginewatch.com/reports/index.html.

SULLIVAN, TERRY. 1998. State of the Web (SOWS) II: How Much Is Too Much? Available WWW: http://www.pantos.org/atw/.

TEXT RETRIEVAL CONFERENCE (TREC). 1999. Overview. Available WWW: http://trec.nist.gov/overview.html.

THOMPSON, KEVIN; MILLER, GREGORY J.; WILDER, RICK. 1997. Wide-Area Internet Traffic Patterns and Characteristics. IEEE Network. 1997; 11(6): 10-23. ISSN: 0890-8044.

THOMPSON, MARYANN JONES. 1999a. The Measures of Web Success. The Industry Standard. 1999 February 15. Available WWW: http://www.thestandard.com/articles/special/display/0,2168,3501,00.html.

THOMPSON, MARYANN JONES. 1999b. Spotlight: The Demographics of Who's Online. The Industry Standard. 1999 March 8. Available WWW: http://www.thestandard.com/metrics/display/0,1283,856.html.

THOMPSON, MARYANN JONES. 1999c. Spotlight: Why E-Commerce Forecasters Don't Get It Right. The Industry Standard. 1999 March 1. Available WWW: http://www.thestandard.com/metrics/display/0,1283,850.html.

TOMAIUOLO, NICHOLAS G.; PACKER, JOAN G. 1996. An Analysis of Internet Search Engines: Assessment of Over 200 Search Queries. Computers in Libraries. 1996 June; 16(6): 58-62. ISSN: 1041-7915.

TREESE, WIN. 1999. The Internet Index Home Page. Available WWW: http://www.openmarket.com/intindex/index.cfm.

TRUSTE. 1999. TRUSTe. Available WWW: http://www.truste.org/.

TURECKI-LUCZYCKA, GWEN, ed. 1998. Gale Guide to Internet Databases. Detroit, MI: Gale; 1998. 1019p. ISBN: 0-7876-1189-1.

U.S. ADVISORY COUNCIL ON THE NATIONAL INFORMATION INFRASTRUCTURE. 1996. A Nation of Opportunity: Realizing the Promise of the Information Superhighway. Washington, DC: U.S. Advisory Council on the National Information Infrastructure; for sale by the Superintendent of Documents, U.S. Government Printing Office; 1996. 107p. Also available WWW: http://www.benton.org/Library/KickStart/nation.home.html.

U.S. GOVERNMENT WORKING GROUP ON ELECTRONIC COMMERCE. 1998. The Emerging Digital Economy. Washington, DC: National Technical Information Service; 1998. 1 volume. (NTIS order number PB-98-137029). Available WWW: http://www.ecommerce.gov/emerging.htm.

U.S. OFFICE OF THE INDEPENDENT COUNSEL. 1998. Referral to the United States House of Representatives Pursuant to Title 28, United States Code, §595(c). 1998 September 9. (The Starr Report). Available WWW: http://www.house.gov/icreport/1cover.htm.

VANDERBILT UNIVERSITY. OWEN GRADUATE SCHOOL OF MANAGEMENT. 1999. Project 2000. Available WWW: http://www2000.ogsm.vanderbilt.edu/.

WANG, PEILING; TENOPIR, CAROL; LAYMAN, ELIZABETH; PENNIMAN, DAVID; COLLINS, SHAWN. 1998. An Exploratory Study of User Searching of the World Wide Web: A Holistic Approach. See reference: PRESTON, CECILIA, ed. 389-399.

WATSON, RICHARD W. 1971. An Interactive Network Experiment to Study Modes of Access to the Network Information Center. 1971 February 12. (RFC 96). Available FTP: ftp://ftp.isi.edu/in-notes/rfc96.txt.

WEB CHARACTERIZATION REPOSITORY. Available WWW: http://purl.org/net/repository/.

WEB COMMERCE TODAY. 1999. Web Commerce Today Research Room. Available WWW: http://www.webcommercetoday.com/research/.

WEBCONNECT. 1999. WebConnect Site Price Index. Available WWW: http://sitepriceindex.com/.

WHITE, MARILYN DOMAS; ABELS, EILEEN G.; GORDON-MURNANE, LAURA. 1998. What Constitutes Adoption on the Web: A Methodological Problem in Assessing Adoption of the World Wide Web for Electronic Commerce. See reference: PRESTON, CECILIA, ed. 217-226.

WILLIAMS, MARTHA E. 1998. The State of Databases Today: 1999. In: Gale Directory of Databases: Volume 1. Detroit, MI: Gale; 1998. xvii-xxviii. ISSN: 1066-8934; ISBN: 0-7876-2299-0.

WILLINGER, WALTER; PAXSON, VERN. 1997. Discussion: Annals of Statistics. 1997 October; 25(5): 1856-1866. ISSN: 0090-5364.

WILLINGER, WALTER; PAXSON, VERN; TAQQU, MURAD. 1998. Self-Similarity and Heavy Tails: Structural Modeling of Network Traffic. In: Adler, Robert J.; Feldman, Raisa E.; Taqqu, Murad S., eds. A Practical Guide to Heavy Tails: Statistical Techniques and Applications. Boston, MA: Birkhauser; 1998. 27-54. ISBN: 0-8176-3951-9.

WIRED. Available WWW: http://www.wired.com/.

WOODRUFF, ALLISON; AOKI, PAUL M.; BREWER, ERIC; GAUTHIER, PAUL; ROWE, LAWRENCE A. 1996. An Investigation of Documents from the World Wide Web. In: 5th International World Wide Web Conference; 1996 May 6-10; Paris, France. Available WWW: http://www5conf.inria.fr/fich_html/papers/P7/Overview.html.

WOODWARD, JEANETTE. 1996. Cataloging and Classifying Information Resources on the Internet. In: Williams, Martha E., ed. Annual Review of Information Science and Technology: Volume 31. Medford, NJ: Information Today, Inc. for the American Society for Information Science; 1996. 189-220. ISSN: 0066-4200; ISBN: 1-57387-033-1.

WORLD WIDE WEB CONSORTIUM. 1999a. The Architecture Domain. Available WWW: http://www.w3.org/Architecture/.

WORLD WIDE WEB CONSORTIUM. 1999b. The Architecture Domain: Web Characterization Activity. Available WWW: http://www.w3.org/WCA/.

YAHOO. 1999. (Internet) Statistics and Demographics. Available WWW: http://dir.yahoo.com/Computers_and_Internet/Internet/Statistics_and_Demographics/.

ZAKON, ROBERT H. 1999. Hobbes' Internet Timeline v4.1. Available WWW: http://www.isoc.org/zakon/Internet/History/HIT.html.

ZDNET. 1999. This site is the portal for Ziff-Davis publications Web pages. Available WWW: http://www.zdnet.com/.

ZIEGLER, BART; WEBER, THOMAS E.; MILLER, MICHAEL W. 1998. A Wildfire Transforms the Global Village. Wall Street Journal. 1998 September 14; B1, B11. ISSN: 0099-9660; 0043-0080.

ZIFF-DAVIS. 1998. InternetTrack. Available WWW: http://www.ziffdavis.com/marketresearch/IT2Q.htm.

ZIFF-DAVIS MARKET INTELLIGENCE. 1999. News Release: The Internet is becoming a Major Portion of Overall Corporate WAN Traffic According to a Study by Ziff-Davis. Available WWW: http://www.ziffdavis.com/news/docs98/1020.htm.

Applications of Machine Learning in Information Retrieval

6

SALLY JO CUNNINGHAM,
IAN H. WITTEN, and
JAMES LITTIN
University of Waikato

INTRODUCTION

Much of the work in information retrieval (IR) can be automated. Processes such as index construction and simple query expansion are usually accomplished by computer, while document classification and thesaurus-term selection are more often performed manually. However, manual development and maintenance of document databases is time-consuming, tedious, and error-prone. Algorithms that mine documents for indexing information, and model user interests to help them formulate queries, reduce the workload and can ensure more consistent retrieval. Such algorithms are based in machine learning, a dynamic, burgeoning area of computer science that is finding application in domains ranging from expert systems, where learning algorithms supplement (or even supplant) domain experts for generating rules and explanations (LANGLEY & SIMON), to intelligent agents, which learn to play particular, highly specialized, support roles for individual people and are seen by some to herald a new renaissance of artificial intelligence in information technology (HENDLER). Machine learning algorithms discover patterns in large quantities of data—literally "learning" from existing examples. The patterns can then be used in domain applications to change a system's behavior, so as to make the system behave "better" in some sense (for example, improving the precision of a user's search results) (WITTEN & FRANK).

IR has many characteristics that are suitable for machine learning. Key IR processes are classification tasks that are well-suited to machine learning. In many cases, these are tasks that until recently had to be accomplished manually, if at all. Learning algorithms use examples,

Annual Review of Information Science and Technology (ARIST), Volume 34, 1999
Martha E. Williams, Editor
Published for the American Society for Information Science (ASIS)
By Information Today, Inc., Medford, NJ

attributes, and values, which information retrieval systems can supply in abundance. Most such systems have thousands of documents (examples), and the plethora of natural-language features that can be extracted from documents provide a wealth of attributes. Thus much data is available; indeed, it is apparent that there are too many features and examples in most systems for machine learning schemes to process satisfactorily.

The next section introduces the basic ideas that underpin applications of machine learning to IR: different machine learning paradigms, different ways of representing text, different ways of extracting features from text, and problems posed by multiple collections. The third section describes applications of machine learning to text categorization, a process that is expensive and time-consuming when performed manually. The fourth section considers how machine learning can be applied to the query-formulation process: the automatic creation of user models that provide a context within which to interpret users' queries, and the use of relevance feedback to support the query-refinement process. The fifth section examines methods of document filtering, where the user specifies a query that is to be applied to an ever-changing set of documents. The final section summarizes the area and presents some conclusions.

It is important to note that in sections two through five we discuss only machine learning applications in these areas of IR—it is beyond the scope of this paper to present a complete review of all significant approaches to each problem. The discussion of a machine learning application does not imply that the machine learning approach is the best or the only applicable technique in that context.

Finally, evaluation is required to determine the effect—positive or negative—of machine learning techniques on specific information retrieval system architectures, document collections, and user groups. Where appropriate, a brief discussion of the relative effectiveness of a machine learning application is presented with the description of the application itself. A discussion of effective evaluation and evaluation techniques is also beyond the scope of this paper; HARTER & HERT offer a substantive examination of these issues. One particularly influential evaluation effort for many of the techniques described in this paper is TREC (Text REtrieval Conference), an ongoing series of conferences centered on the comparative evaluation of IR systems over a common, and large, set of documents, queries, and relevance assessments. While the TREC contributions have not been singled out, many of the techniques described in this paper have appeared—in some form—in a TREC trial.

INFORMATION RETRIEVAL

IR has been automated for decades, but only since the late 1980s has machine learning been applied to this area. The IR process can be divided into four distinct phases: indexing, query formulation, comparison, and feedback (LEWIS). All of these provide opportunities for learning. Researchers tend to focus on one of these subprocesses when trying to improve the performance of their retrieval systems. For example, clustering techniques (MARTIN) build links between related documents so that indexing becomes more effective, and user-modeling techniques attempt to extract as much information as possible from user queries (BHATIA ET AL.; KRULWICH, 1995a).

This section explores the basic ideas that underpin the application of machine learning to IR. First, we briefly discuss the major machine learning paradigms. Next we discuss the paramount importance of the language model used to represent text, and describe several different representations. Following this, we present methods for extracting valuable features from the text. Finally, we describe the problems of retrieval in multiple-collection systems and present two learning algorithms designed to overcome them.

Machine Learning Paradigms

One aim of machine learning is to devise algorithms that can supplement, or supplant, domain experts in knowledge-engineering situations. Using learning algorithms to automate IR processes such as document classification and user modeling can alleviate the workload of information workers and reduce inconsistency. General texts on machine learning paradigms and techniques include LANGLEY, PIATETSKY-SHAPIRO & FRAWLEY, and WITTEN & FRANK.

LANGLEY & SIMON identify five major paradigms in machine learning research, four of which have been applied in IR studies. The paradigms are (1) rule induction, (2) instance-based learning, (3) neural networks, (4) genetic algorithms, and (5) analytic learning. The first four learn from information with very simple structure: examples of the concept being learned, often described by lists of symbolic or numeric attributes. Heuristics are applied to generate structures that represent relationships implicit in the data. These four paradigms are used in so-called intelligent IR systems where the examples (documents) are described by simple features such as word-frequency measures.

The fifth paradigm, analytic learning, is typically employed to learn proofs or explanations for example situations using background knowledge. By compiling groups of explanations, a system may be able to reduce the amount of searching required to solve similar problems in the future. The background knowledge and complex structure necessary to store explanations make analytic learning systems infeasible for large-scale IR. These algorithms learn much from rigorous expert explanations and require few examples—in some ways the antithesis of the usual IR scenario.

Genetic algorithms are the least frequently applied of the other four paradigms. As the name suggests, they mimic the behavior of biological genetic systems. Examples are represented as a string of values similar to genes in a chromosome. A population of examples is stored, and at each iteration operators such as mutation and crossover are applied. Mutation changes some of the values in an example randomly, whereas crossover combines different values from pairs of examples into a new instance. The population of examples is prevented from growing indefinitely by retaining only the strongest examples as determined by some fitness measure. Evolution is terminated when the user is satisfied with the strength of the surviving examples. In IR, the values in each example might represent the presence or absence of words in documents: a vector of binary terms. The evolutionary process is halted when an example emerges that is representative of the documents being classified.

Why genetic algorithms have been largely ignored by IR researchers is unclear. The random nature of the genetic operators, and the resulting nondeterministic behavior of the algorithms, may be a reason. Also, it can be difficult to set control parameters, such as the probabilities of crossover and mutation, to ensure good performance.

Decision-tree and rule-induction schemes are the most-studied and best-developed machine learning technique. They generate an explicit description of the concept represented by the input data. As with all learning algorithms, the accuracy and appropriateness of the concept description reflect the quality of the data supplied. The algorithms have only the information present in the input to learn from, and choose the most potent regularities to create the concept description. If strong patterns appear by chance, or the data are irrelevant to the classification task, the concept description will be inadequate. Algorithms use different techniques to determine which patterns in the data are appropriate for incorporating in the concept description, but they generally can be classed as either covering or divide-and-conquer algorithms. A divide-and-conquer algorithm, C4.5 (QUINLAN, 1993), has become the benchmark for inductive machine learning.

Instance-based learning algorithms do not create explicit concept descriptions that can be used to classify new examples. Instead, they store training examples and classify new examples by comparison. The representation of stored examples and the mechanisms for comparison differ between algorithms. The simplest is the nearest-neighbor technique, where training examples are stored verbatim in an n-dimensional space, n being the number of attributes describing the concept. Examples are compared using Euclidean distance, all attributes being given equal importance. Instance-based methods are, computationally, among the simplest learning schemes, and variations are often considered as models of human learning. Many theories from cognitive psychology are implemented as instance-based learners for evaluation purposes. Case-based reasoning systems are essentially instance-based algorithms, but typically offer more structured document or situation (case) representations, and may include more sophisticated distance measurements (for example, weighting certain attributes more heavily than others). In the past, case-based reasoning has been applied most frequently to recommendation systems (for example, to support help desk operation); applications in IR are emerging that similarly offer recommendations based on previously observed examples—e.g., to suggest a subject classification for a new document (HEARST, 1993).

Neural networks also lack explicit concept descriptions. They represent knowledge as weighted links between nodes in a multilayer network, with activation spreading from input to output nodes during the classification process. Learning involves altering the weights on the links until the output nodes give the correct response to the inputs. The literature on neural network applications in IR is sizable in its own right, and is beyond the scope of this review. The topic is covered in 1990 by DOSZKOCS ET AL. in their *ARIST* chapter and in 1998 by CUNNINGHAM ET AL. in their review of the use of neural network and other network-based learning techniques in text retrieval.

All these approaches to machine learning have been successfully applied to real-world problems. The choice of method in each case seems to be based largely on the experience and preference of the researchers involved. This success is also apparent in IR applications, with the different paradigms being used in similar proportions to other domains.

Models of Text and Text Representation

For a retrieval system to categorize documents effectively, it must extract enough information from them to discriminate examples of each category. The system must create a model of the documents' text that somehow captures the essence of what they are about. Natural language has myriad properties that can be used to create such a model, but most are intangible, and without a reasonably solid working knowledge of the language in question, a processor (human or computer) cannot take advantage of them. Moreover, speed of processing is an important factor in large-scale IR, so in reality only a small set of easily extracted features can be used by any practical system. In this section, we describe the text models most commonly used in applications of machine learning to IR—that is, the primary processing applied to the text of documents in a collection. The extracted document text generally includes either the full text of a given document, or substantive/significant portions of the document (for example, document abstracts). The text models are considered from the point of view of the machine learning features that can be derived from each type of model.

Term-vector models. The most popular text representations are based on the "bag of words" or term-vector model, where a document is represented by a set of terms (LEWIS; WITTEN ET AL.). Documents that contain a given set of terms each correspond to a certain point in n-dimensional space, where n is the number of terms. Terms are usually words, and a term vector is either a Boolean vector representing a set of words that appear in the document, or a numeric vector whose values are derived from the number of occurrences of each term in a document. The latter is based on the common-sense understanding that the more often a term is mentioned, the more likely it is to be central to the subject matter. When document vectors reflect the frequencies with which terms appear, documents are considered similar if their term vectors lie close together in vector space. The components of the term vector are commonly weighted, for example, by dividing term frequencies by the number of documents in which that term appears. This particular weighting scheme is called term-frequency times inverse document frequency weighting, or $tf \bullet idf$. All other information implicit in the text, such as the meaning and order of words, is omitted from the document's vector representation. However, the simplicity of this model makes it one of the most popular in IR.

Most IR systems that use symbolic-learning algorithms are based on the term-vector model of text because it provides a finite set of attributes (APTÉ ET AL., 1994a, 1994b; COHEN, 1995b). The attributes have very simple structure: either a binary value indicating term appearance (e.g., CRAWFORD ET AL.), or a term-frequency measure (APTÉ ET AL., 1994a). A set of term vectors representing the contents of a retrieval system's database is no more than a table of numbers.

Many weighting schemes and similarity measures have been proposed (for a survey see JONES & FURNAS). In practice, it appears that no single ranking function is superior for all users and all queries. BARTELL ET AL. (1994; 1998) address the problem of function selection by providing a general similarity measure whose parameters are optimized to a particular user over several queries. Initial tests appear promising. In a small-scale experiment using 51 training queries and 25 test queries, the learned similarity measure performed at least as well as several classic ranking functions, and within 1% of an estimated optimal similarity measure.

Latent semantic indexing. The term-vector model suffers from many well-known problems. For example, there are different ways to refer to the same object or concept, which do not necessarily have words in common: the problem of synonymy. Conversely, many words mean quite different things in different contexts: the problem of polysemy. Finally, the term-vector model assumes that words are independent, whereas many words occur in key phrases so that the appearance of one in conjunction with the other should not be taken as independent evidence of the similarity between query and document.

In an attempt to circumvent these problems, some researchers remap the term vectors into a different space. One way of doing this is latent semantic indexing (DEERWESTER ET AL.). This representation maps terms, queries, and documents into vectors of k factor weights, where k is the dimensionality of the new concept matrix. An advantage of this approach is that the newly constructed space has so-called semantic qualities: terms that are used in similar contexts are associated, and a document may be located near relevant terms that do not actually appear in its text. A query is processed by representing its terms as a vector in the space, and then ranking documents by their proximity to the query vector. The representation can be used to compare documents with documents (document clustering) and queries with queries (query clustering). This seems to form an ideal basis for the application of machine learning, although to date it has only appeared in a few machine learning applications (HULL ET AL.; MOULINIER; SCHÜTZE ET AL.). Its principal disadvantage is its cost: it is not clear whether it can be applied to large-scale document collections.

Sequential models. Compressed algorithms can be used to categorize documents in a very simple manner that invokes the principle of minimum description length (RISSANEN). A sample of text from each category is used to train the compression algorithm. The document to be classified is added to each training sample in turn and the sample that compresses the document into the fewest bits is judged to have the same category as the document. The relative degrees of compression achieved by each sample can also be used to rank the categories. Intuitively, one would expect a better compression algorithm to achieve greater classification accuracy, because the algorithm is able to use stronger patterns in the sample text to compress the unlabeled document (LANG).

Feature Extraction

The text model adopted by an IR system defines the features, or types of information, to extract from the text. It is these features that the learning component uses to find regularities from which it can create classifiers. The better a system is at selecting auspicious features, the better its chance of generating an accurate concept description. IR applications generally suffer from an overabundance of features and a relatively small number of training examples, a situation that leads to high computational costs for model creation and a tendency to overfit the training data. Pruning the feature set to a manageable size can increase the accuracy and stability of the induced model (KOLLER & SAHAMI, 1996). It is commonly accepted that feature extraction is the most critical stage of the learning process in almost any domain (KRULWICH, 1995a; LEWIS & RINGUETTE).

Problems in feature extraction arise for several reasons (LEWIS & CROFT; MARTIN). First, the large number of synonyms in English (or any other natural language) allow a similar idea to be expressed by different words in different documents. With any of the text models described in the previous section, except those based on latent semantic indexing, related documents would have to use enough of the same words for the similarity to be recognized. Second, many words may appear in both documents simply because they are in the same language; such words are distributed throughout most documents and have no discriminatory power. Third, due to polysemy the same words can appear in different documents with quite different meanings.

Two documents may even be considered similar because they both omit a number of important words. This is necessarily the case in two-class categorization situations where the documents in the negative class are similar only in that they are not related to documents in the positive class. In multiclass clustering situations, however, it is necessary to further differentiate the documents, and then the significance of missing words is not so plain. Usually this issue is ignored, but MARTIN's text-clustering system deals with it in the following way. When comparing documents, the absence of a keyword from both term vectors indicates that the documents could both contain the word, but the information is not available. If, however, one vector contains the word but the other does not, the documents are assumed to differ with respect to that word.

Weighting terms. One common technique for indicating the degree to which a document is about a term is to weight the term. This is generally done by multiplying the term frequency, the number of times that the term appears in the document, by the inverse document frequency, the number of documents in which it appears—in other words, $tf \bullet idf$. Machine learning approaches can be applied to the creation and tuning of term weights. For example, FUHR & BUCKLEY adopt a probabilistic approach to assigning weights to index terms. They view the result of processing a set of queries as a space of query-document pairs with attached relevance judgments (relevant or nonrelevant). Given an experimental sampling of this space, the probability of relevance of a document given each index term can be estimated. This estimate is then used predictively in retrieval to estimate a document's relevance to a new query. The probability estimates can be revised in the light of additional relevance data. An interesting feature of this approach is that the system can refine its retrieval capability incrementally, based on use.

Another consideration in determining a term's weight may be the position of that term in the document. For example, words appearing in a title or abstract are more likely to express a concept central to the document than terms buried in a middle section. Documents encoded in a markup language such as HTML or SGML provide a particularly rich source of structural information that can be used to fine-tune a weighting, and the link structure of Web documents can be similarly useful in indicating significant terms, for example, those that appear in the anchor phrase for a link (BOYAN ET AL.).

Using a thesaurus. Another standard technique is to employ a thesaurus to match synonymous or otherwise related terms (MARTIN). The thesaurus can be constructed automatically, most commonly by detecting related terms through their coincidence in document pairs (SALTON & MCGILL). GREFENSTETTE uses sophisticated, but practical and robust, techniques of natural-language processing to derive appropriate semantic context from free text. FURNAS presents an adaptive indexing scheme that learns semantic connections between individual terms by monitoring user interactions. The user is assumed to issue a series of queries in a single session that are related to the same information need. Once a relevant document is located, the system updates the weights for terms in earlier, unsuccessful queries, on the basis that these terms are useful synonyms.

Fully automated thesaurus construction techniques produce term-relationship networks that can be used to augment queries automatically, but the networks themselves generally cannot be interpreted by people. GÜNTZER ET AL. use a semiautomated technique for constructing a semantically meaningful thesaurus. User interactions are monitored, and a knowledge acquisition subsystem attempts to infer concept relationships between query terms by matching query structures to previously defined production rules. In most cases these relationships are somewhat uncertain and must be confirmed by the user before being committed to the thesaurus.

Identifying phrases. Other approaches to extracting the most distinctive parts of documents transcend the use of single words. KRULWICH's (1995a) system, operating in a bulletin board environment, identifies semantically significant phrases in documents. Phrases can consist of words in the keyword, name, title, and subject fields, and certain patterns in the text fields of documents. For example, a single word that is fully capitalized, or a short phrase in a different format (e.g., bullets, diagram labels, or section headings) is usually regarded as significant. Each document is rechecked for the complete set of phrases, and the system learns a subset of phrases that best describes the category. The induction algorithm used by KRULWICH (1995a) is simple, because the purpose of the study was to develop more sophisticated feature-extraction heuristics. Comparison of a number of different learning algorithms, from neural networks to standard decision tree learners, underscored the point that feature selection is the most critical part of the learning process.

CONRAD & UTT use a similar technique to extract names of companies and people from *Wall Street Journal* articles. Company names are recognizable when they include words such as "Corporation" and "Inc." and personal names are capitalized and may be preceded by a title such as "Ms." Tables of common personal names, titles, and so on, are stored by the system and used to identify important objects in the articles. The system is being extended to recognize synonyms and abbreviations such as "Digital Equipment Corporation/DEC." Although these techniques are very simple, the researchers show figures of 89% for precision and 79% for recall on a test database of 139 articles.

These systems use formatting information to determine the extent of phrases, as well as their relative importance. If a system has access only to the plain text of documents, the problem arises of determining the appropriate granularity with which to divide the text. The standard grain size is the word. Words are relatively easy to distill from text, and are obvious distinct units of meaning, although even here the question of word boundaries, and stemming or affix stripping, is a nontrivial issue. But the difficulties inherent in language outlined above have led researchers to examine larger sections of text such as phrases, sentences, paragraphs, and groups of paragraphs.

A number of studies have shown that simple template- and parser-based methods, and statistical phrase-formation algorithms, are able to find important phrases. In a study of phrase clustering, LEWIS & CROFT used a simple syntactic method. They defined a phrase to be any pair of nonfunction words that headed a syntactic structure connected by a grammatical relation. For example, a verb and the first noun of the following noun phrase form a phrase. Extracted phrases are clustered into small groups containing a seed, along with the phrases most similar to it. They showed that the use of phrases instead of single words slightly improved both recall and precision.

More recently, COHEN & SINGER (1996a) investigated the use of sparse phrases consisting of a small subset of nearby, though not necessarily consecutive, terms in a fixed order. The sparse phrases present in any of the training documents are extracted and used as simple classifiers or experts, each one assigning a single class if its associated sparse phrase appears in a document. Initial weights are assigned to these experts and adjusted during a training phase by comparing the experts' predictions to the "true" classification value for each training document. When categorizing an unknown document, the predictions of these experts are combined by using the weights. In general, most of the experts may be "sleeping," in the sense that the phrases they represent do not occur in the document and therefore cannot participate in prediction; hence this method is dubbed the sleeping experts algorithm. The key, of course, is to decide which sparse phrases to use. COHEN & SINGER (1996a) chose all possible phrases of a certain length (four words)—an enormous set. They claim that the resources required to do this are quite modest because an overwhelming majority (over 99%) of phrases appear just once in the corpus and information is retained only on experts that appear at least twice.

Detecting subtopics. HEARST's (1994) text tiling system uses linguistic analysis to determine where subtopic changes occur in lengthy texts. These boundaries, which generally occur at paragraph breaks, are used to divide the text into subsections. Each subsection has its own vocabulary of words relevant to its topic, and the distribution of these words is skewed toward related sections. A global word-based approach to comparing two documents might miss relationships between individual sections because the distribution of the relevant words across the whole document is relatively sparse. SALTON ET AL. also match sections of full text to determine document similarity.

Collection Fusion

IR systems generally have a single text database that is consistent in terms of indexing and content. However, some systems are required to search a number of databases to satisfy a user's query (TOWELL ET AL.). For example, separate collections might be used for documents about football and motor racing, and a query about world champions would find relevant documents in both collections. Problems arise because the individual collections inevitably have different term distributions. If the same document were in both collections, it would receive different scores for the same query; therefore scores from different collections cannot be directly compared. The effect is exacerbated when collections have their own servers, and use different ranking and retrieval strategies.

A typical query to a multiple-collection system asks for a certain number of documents, N, selected from C collections, and ranked in order of relevance. The problem of merging the documents in a valid order is called collection fusion (VOORHEES ET AL.). Simple solutions such as selecting the top N/C documents from each collection, or assuming that relevance scores are compatible across collections and selecting the N highest-scoring documents overall, perform poorly. TOWELL ET AL. introduce a collection fusion scheme that uses the document distributions of training queries to learn the appropriate number of relevant documents from each collection to retrieve for a new query. The algorithm models the distribution of a query by averaging the distributions of its k nearest neighbors in the training data. The number of documents to retrieve from each collection is calculated using a maximization procedure (not described in the article), and the order of presentation is determined by a random process biased toward collections with the greatest number of articles remaining.

A second learning scheme described by TOWELL ET AL. clusters training queries that retrieve several common documents from each collection. The average of the query vectors in each cluster is the system's representation of the topic covered by those queries. For each collection, each cluster is given a weighting proportional to the number of relevant documents retrieved from that collection. After training, new queries are matched with the most similar cluster and that cluster's weighting model is used to determine the proportion of documents to retrieve from each collection.

In terms of precision given a fixed recall figure, both these learning algorithms perform significantly better than simple nonadaptive schemes such as that described above. Of the two, the first comes closest to the results obtained by combining the collections and using a single server, achieving precision figures within 10% for recall of 10 to 200 documents.

YAGER & RYBALOV present a simple, parametarized approach to describe how documents from different collections can be interleaved. They present a simple technique for learning this parameter from the result lists returned for a given query.

TEXT CATEGORIZATION

Text categorization is the process of classifying documents into one of a number of categories. Document classification is required at several stages of the information retrieval process. A user's queries must be classified to determine which documents in the collection are relevant. A query may be treated as a document in its own right, or as a description of the desired concept. The category represented by the query may not be represented explicitly in the database; the system's indexing mechanism determines how documents that fit the category description are located.

There is an extensive literature on unsupervised document clustering. Generally, nearest-neighbor techniques are used to categorize documents into naturally occurring groups that may or may not represent semantically meaningful categories. Many algorithms force a document to belong to only one cluster, which is unduly Procrustean given that in practice most pieces of text can be usefully described by several different classification headings. Unsupervised document clustering lies outside the scope of this article; the reader is directed to WILLETT for a survey of document-clustering methods.

Many machine learning techniques have been applied to text-categorization problems. The next section describes algorithms that have been used and the concept descriptions they create. Although no particularly striking successes have been claimed, perhaps because absolute measures of performance are lacking, none of the systems discussed is considered ineffective by its developers.

Algorithms, Concept Descriptions, and Data Structures

The use of learning systems in IR typically involves either applying an existing off-the-shelf algorithm in some manner, or developing a new learning algorithm specifically for this problem. The choice of approach depends on the intended use of the system, and on the experience and interests of the developers.

Standard algorithms. Many standard machine learning algorithms have been used in IR systems. In general, simple, robust rule induction techniques like ID3 (QUINLAN, 1986) are used for text-classification problems, such as identifying text features that catalyze learning (KRULWICH, 1995a; LEHNERT ET AL.; SODERLAND & LEHNERT). CHEN used ID3 as a control for an experiment with ID5R (UTGOFF), an incremental extension of ID3. Somewhat more elaborate rule induction algorithms such as ID5R, C4.5 (QUINLAN, 1993), (First Order Inductive Learing) and FOIL (QUINLAN, 1990) are usually relegated to feasibility experiments (e.g., BLOEDORN ET AL.; CHEN; COHEN, 1995b; CUNNINGHAM & SUMMERS). Few studies have conducted systematic comparisons of learning schemes using document collections of any significant size. MOULINIER analyzes the relative performance of ID3 (QUINLAN, 1986), the rule learners CHARADE (GANASCIA) and SWAP-1 (APTÉ ET AL., 1994a), the instance-based scheme IB (AHA), and neural networks, using a document collection of Reuters news articles. LEWIS & RINGUETTE compare Bayesian rule induction (based on Bayes' rule of conditional probability) with the decision-tree learner DT-min10 (BUNTINE) on two collections, one of which was the Reuters collection.

One defining feature of a learning algorithm is the form in which it represents the concepts it learns. In IR this concept description is used to classify documents, or to explain the existing labels of documents. Inductive learning schemes, such as ID3, FOIL, and INDUCT (GAINES), are useful for these tasks because they produce simple, easily understood rules or decision trees (LEWIS & RINGUETTE). A human supervisor can evaluate and augment these structures for classification purposes, or use them to gain insight into human-categorized databases.

Production rules are the most common form for concept descriptions in document categorization applications. Categorization has been undertaken with propositional rules such as those generated by INDUCT (CUNNINGHAM & SUMMERS), SWAP-1 (APTÉ ET AL., 1994a), and other symbolic machine learning algorithms; with rules refined from decision trees (BLOEDORN ET AL.; CRAWFORD ET AL.; CUNNINGHAM & SUMMERS); and with relational rules generated by first-order learners like FOIL (COHEN, 1995b). An example of propositional rules generated from 730 Reuters news articles appears in Figure 1. Synthesized from a decision tree created by CART (BREIMAN ET AL.), these rules test the presence or absence of a particular word in a document in order to predict whether articles are about terrorism. Other algorithms use rules involving numerical thresholds on the number of occurrences of words.

---

if article contains word "bomb"
      then if article contains words "injure" or "kill"
        then **terrorism** article
      else ~ **terrorism** article
    else if article contains word "kidnapping"

Figure 1. Rules representing a decision tree generated by CART

Relational terms add an extra dimension to a rule set. Most applications of machine learning to IR, other than those using compression algorithms directly, discard the ordering of words in the text. One exception is COHEN (1995b) who, using the relational learning algorithm FOIL (QUINLAN, 1990), was able to generate rules to specify the relationships between words in a document. Figure 2 shows rules intended to classify documents about machine learning. Instead of merely appearing in the same document, the words "decision" and "tree" in the second rule of Figure 2 must also satisfy the successor relation, that is "tree" must directly follow "decision" at some point in the document.

The use of term context in the formation of decision rules has also been investigated in an order-independent manner. The RIPPER rule generation system (COHEN, 1995a), which was originally designed to deal effectively with situations in which there are a very large number

machine_learning_article(S):-learning(S,P).
machine_learning_article(S):-decision(S,P), tree(S,Q),
    successor(P,Q).

Figure 2. Relational rules generated by FOIL for document classification

of features, can also accommodate set-valued features (COHEN, 1996b). This allows a terms's context to be represented as a set of other terms that co-occur in the document, with no indication of term ordering or proximity (COHEN & SINGER, 1996a).

Classifiers based on the Support Vector Machine (SVM) represent subject classes as a vector of learned feature weights (DUMAIS ET AL.; JOACHIMS, 1998, 1999). For example, the Reuters category for financial interest might be learned as:

confidence ("interest" category) = 0.3* interest + 0.4* rate +
0.7* quarterly

One significant advantage of the SVM approach is its training speed: Dumais et al. found that construction of an SVM-based classifier for the Reuters-21578 collection was roughly 30 times faster than model construction times reported for the popular chunking algorithm on this dataset. Classification accuracy for the SVM model was slightly better than for classifiers constructed using Naïve Bayes (a Bayesian classifier that "naïvely" assumes feature independence) and Bayes nets (Bayesian models that do not assume independence). The SVM model attained significantly better classification accuracy than was obtained with Rocchio-style query expansion.

When human comprehension of the concept description is not important, other methods are often applied. Versions of the nearest-neighbor instance-based technique are used when clusters of documents or queries are generated and compared (TOWELL ET AL.). Distance metrics are usually very simple, such as the sum of the differences of term counts (SALTON ET AL.). Bayesian probabilistic algorithms also have no readily comprehensible concept description. LEWIS & RINGUETTE used Bayes' rule to estimate $P(C_j = 1 \mid D)$, the probability that a category Cj should be assigned to a document D given the category's prior probability and the conditional probabilities of particular words occurring in a document given that it belongs in the category. Each category is assigned to its top-scoring documents in proportion to the number of times it was assigned to the training data. Lewis & Ringuette compared the precision and recall of their Bayesian algorithm with a decision-tree learning algorithm and found little difference between the two. The Bayesian classifier was able to handle ten times as many features as the decision-tree learner, although both algorithms peaked in performance between ten and one hundred features. This was a comparatively small feature set, given that documents in the training set are typically represented by term vectors containing hundreds of elements. For hierarchic classification systems, the feature set for the model can be minimized by inducing a hierarchy of classifiers, rather than a single classifier for the entire classification scheme. Each split in the classification hierarchy is represented with a distinct classifier to categorize documents into the subtopics at that level. Each individual classifier tends to be small, and each contains a subject-specific subset of the overall feature set (KOLLER & SAHAMI, 1997).

The creation of a correctly (usually manually) classified training set is a bottleneck in the induction of a text categorizer. While a large training set can be expensive to construct, most algorithms tend to overfit or produce low-accuracy models on small training sets. If the set of categories forms a hierarchy, then information implicit in this structure can be incorporated into the learning algorithm. MCCALLUM ET AL. (1998; 1999) demonstrated that, when using small training sets, classification accuracy can be significantly improved by the application of shrinkage, a statistical technique that learns better estimates of the probability that a particular keyword describes a given class by combining information about that keyword along the entire branch of the classification hierarchy that contains that class. For learning tasks involving a flat set of categories, the Transductive Support Vector Machine (TSVM) algorithm (a variant of SVM) performs well when training sets are small (JOACHIMS, 1999). Experiments indicate that TSVMs can require only one-twentieth of the training examples needed by a Bayesian learner. However, these experiments were based on classification schemes containing relatively few categories (five to ten); it is not clear that TSVMs can maintain this advantage in a realistically sized scheme requiring the learner to distinguish between hundreds or thousands of categories.

Another method for overcoming a small training set for classification is to combine manual and automated classification. This is particularly effective when the classification topics are expected to be highly idiosyncratic and based on the needs of a single user, for example, in organizing personal World Wide Web bookmarks. MAAREK & BEN-SHAUL describe a system that permits the user to suggest categories, and to flexibly determine which portions of the data should be automatically categorized.

HEARST (1993) proposes a case-based reasoning approach to represent the main topics and subtopics in full-text documents. A subtopic structure outline is an abstract representation of a document, and can be used as an example for case-based reasoning. Document cases are placed in a network, positioned according to which cases they resemble. To specify which features may differ without materially affecting the topic, a term vector is associated with each section of a document. Cases are organized first by their main topic, and then grouped according to which and how many of their section term vectors are similar.

Unsupervised learning schemes have seen relatively little application in document classification. While attractive in that they do not require training data to be preclassified, the algorithms themselves are generally far more computation-intensive than supervised schemes. The added processing time is particularly significant in a domain such as text classification, in which instances may be described by hundreds or thousands of attributes. Trials of unsupervised schemes include those by AONE ET AL., who use the conceptual clustering scheme COBWEB (FISHER) to induce the natural groupings of close-captioned text associated with video newsfeeds; LIERE & TADEPALLI, who explore the effectiveness of AutoClass (CHEESEMAN ET AL.) in producing a classification model for a portion of the Reuters corpus; and GREEN & EDWARDS, who use AutoClass to cluster news items gathered from several sources into what they call stories, which are groupings of documents covering similar topics.

Specialized algorithms. A number of learning algorithms have been developed strictly for text classification. In a 1961 paper MARON describes his use of a probabilistic model to match words appearing in a document to a set of indexing terms. A training set of documents is classified manually, and a statistical model is constructed of the correlation between clue words (nouns, hyphenated words, and other terms felt to convey subject information) and the classifications associated with documents containing those terms. The statistical model can then be used to classify new documents probabilistically, and the model can be refined by basing it on very large training sets. Maron (overoptimistically) states that this technique essentially solves the problem of automated classification: "No real intellectual breakthroughs are required before a machine will be able to index rather well. Just as in the case of machine translation of natural language, the road is gradual but, by and large, straightforward" (MARON, p. 415).

BHUYAN & RAGHAVAN developed a probabilistic scheme that builds document relationship clusters based on user feedback. To store information about pairs of documents, three graphs are generated from a series of queries. If both documents in a pair are relevant to a query, weight is added to the corresponding edge in the POS_POS graph to reflect the similarity of the documents. If the first document is relevant and the second is not, the edge of the POS_NEG graph is similarly updated; and conversely for the third graph, NEG_POS. A new graph G is generated by summing the weights of the POS_NEG and NEG_POS graphs and subtracting those of the POS_POS graph. The graph G indicates the similarity between documents, with lower weighted edges denoting greater similarity.

In an extension to the OKAPI system, GOKER & MCCLUSKEY define concepts with a set of concept term structures. Initially the concept description is bound to the set of all terms that appear in more than one document. Then more highly weighted terms are added until all relevant documents are covered. This set is called the active set; the remaining terms make up the passive set. After each user session, new terms are merged into each set and existing terms are transferred between sets as their weights change. The active set is limited to 32 terms by moving the terms with lowest strength back into the passive set. After each query, the concept description can be used to refine the ranking between documents that were initially given the same weight. A document's new weight is the sum of the words that appear in both the concept description and the document.

The learning system in NewsWeeder (LANG) is based on the principle of minimum description length. The minimum description length trades model complexity for error rate, and is used in this domain to determine how to weight each term, and how to decide which terms have so little discriminatory power that they can be omitted. NewsWeeder's term-distribution model assumes that the probabilities of occurrence of any two terms in a document are independent. However, the probabilities are allowed to depend on the length of the document. Distributions of each term are computed for each category, and across all categories. To create a model for each category, a choice is made between the category-specific distribution and the overall distribution of each term. If the difference between the probabilities for a term is larger than a threshold, the category-specific distribution is used for that term; otherwise the overall distribution is used. The threshold value represents the cost of including parameters that specify the category. Finally, linear regression is used to produce a continuous prediction of the user's ratings for new documents.

The multiple-cause mixture model (SAHAMI ET AL., 1996) is novel in that it supports unsupervised as well as supervised learning of classification categories. In unsupervised mode it does not require preclassified training examples, and induces a set of ostensible naturally occurring categories for the document set. Unlike many earlier clustering schemes, this method can classify documents into multiple categories. Unfortunately, the unsupervised mode is extremely expensive computationally.

The category-discrimination method algorithm for text categorization is based on the concept of cue validity in cognitive psychology (GOLDBERG). Features are selected for inclusion in the categorization model based on how each feature distinguishes documents belonging to a given category from documents assigned to similar categories. The features whose cue validity exceeds a set threshold are then considered as candidates for a rule-based text categorizer. The categorizer is constructed by conducting a multistage search to determine the optimal parameter settings and to eliminate unnecessary features.

Existing document subject classifications can be adapted for better retrieval performance by using genetic algorithms (GORDON, 1991). Genetic algorithms modify document descriptions so as to improve their ability to match relevant queries and to fail to match nonrelevant queries. As a result of this process, the relative density of document clusters increases so that descriptively similar documents are grouped together. These groups can then be identified by traditional clustering techniques.

Uncertainty Feedback

Most retrieval systems store vast amounts of text, and it is impractical to use it all to train a classification system. Any sample selected as a training set should include documents that are good discriminators for the categories represented in the collection. Random sampling is usually unsuitable, particularly when the distribution of categories is skewed and the sample size is relatively small. Relevance feedback (discussed below) performs a kind of sampling by selecting documents that are representative of a given category, but as the learning system improves, many of these documents provide no new information from which the system can learn.

LEWIS & GALE present an algorithm for sequentially selecting a subset of training documents based on uncertainty feedback, which identifies documents for which the system is most unsure of the appropriate category. By labeling these documents, the human supervisor creates a training set of example documents that are more disparate than those selected by random sampling. The system starts with a small set of examples, selected either randomly or as being particularly representative of some categories, and creates a classifier for these documents. It then proceeds through a classification—feedback—create a new classifier loop until the supervisor judges the current concept description accurate enough. Experiments show that this point can be reached with as much as a 500-fold decrease in the number of examples required by random sampling.

QUERY FORMULATION

The user's input to an IR system is the query. Queries are most often Boolean combinations of terms/keywords that may be found in whole or partial documents. Some systems accept simple lists of query terms or query phrases; conceptually, these terms/phrases are generally treated as an OR-ed Boolean query. However, Boolean queries are far from ideal for representing users' information needs (HEARST, 1994; SALTON ET AL.). Inexperienced users often find them difficult to structure effectively, and they provide no way to indicate the relative importance of individual terms. To overcome these problems, many systems allow the query process to be iterative. The system uses the original query as an initial representation of the user's information need and progressively refines it until the user is satisfied with the set of documents retrieved.

This section shows how machine learning techniques can be applied to three important aspects of systems to support users in the query formulation process. The first is user modeling, applied in machine learning as an activity that occurs over a series of interactions with the system as it builds a profile of the user's interests. The second is relevance feedback, a standard technique for query refinement in which the system gains information from the user about the pertinence of selected matching documents. The third is information filtering, where a user specifies a query that is to be applied to a changing set of documents. This is appropriate when the user's interests remain constant and the document database is continually expanding.

Modeling User Concepts

Machine learning has primarily been applied to long-term user modeling, an activity that occurs over a series of interactions with the system as it builds a profile of each user. Machine learning is most useful where a user's requirements remain constant, for in these situations it is the user's interests that the system tries to identify. Consideration of how a retrieval system can model user interests by analyzing queries is deferred to the section on modeling user interests below. Here we describe a system which directly solicits information from users to form user models.

BHATIA ET AL. introduce a model that describes concepts in the user's vocabulary and can serve to interpret and refine queries in a manner appropriate for the individual user. First, the system interviews the user to determine objects, and relationships between them, that are important in the user's universe of discourse. The interviewing process is based on personal construct theory (KELLY). Objects named by the user (called entities in personal construct theory) are stored in a table, and presented back to the user in randomly selected triples. The user must come up with a perceived bipolar property of the entities (called a construct) that serves to differentiate one of the entities from the other two. The construct becomes a row of the table, and the user is asked to enter a value from a predetermined scale that indicates the relevance of the construct to each entity. The user may spontaneously add new entities and constructs throughout the interview. Constructs provide the basis for understanding the entities, and may not necessarily reflect their actual differential groupings. Therefore the system develops a different structure for each user's world view.

The user profile is employed by the system to map concepts important to the user to keywords occurring in documents in the database. The user selects a small set of familiar documents, with at least one document containing an example of each concept to be used during querying. The system maps each concept to a set of index terms obtained from the appropriate example documents. Documents are represented in term-vector format, with terms weighted using the $tf{\bullet}idf$ method. Terms with weights above an empirically determined threshold are selected as representative of the document. The user enters queries using his or her own vocabulary and concepts, and the system maps these to production rules and keywords to search the remainder of the database.

Relevance Feedback

Because of the general nature of initial queries, which often have only a few terms, and the system's imperfect representation of the content of documents, a user's query to an IR system usually returns only a few interesting documents, diluted by many nonrelevant documents that match only weakly (LEWIS). Even if the documents are ranked, the user still must scan through the list to determine the cutoff point for nonrelevant documents. Often users accept a short, incomplete list of documents, or a single reference, and the results of their initial query will suffice. However, when a more complete list of relevant documents is required, the initial query must be modified. Users may do this themselves, but often find it difficult to make effective refinements, having stated their requirements to the best of their ability in the first place.

The relevance feedback technique employs user feedback on query results to refine a user's query. Typically, the user is presented with a result set from a query. The user indicates the relevance/irrelevance of items in the result set, and the system then adds significant terms from relevant documents and subtracts significant terms from irrelevant documents (HARMAN). The expanded query is then processed, and the user is again offered the opportunity to refine the query over the new set of retrieved documents. In this case, the user may not be aware of the terms added to or deleted from the original query. Alternatively, the user may be presented with a list of suggested significant terms extracted from documents matching the user's query; here, the user directly selects the additional terms to add to/subtract from the evolving query (TSENG).

A learning system can use terms or documents indicated to be relevant as positive examples, and those deemed nonrelevant as negative examples (LEWIS). The user's first query becomes the initial concept description, and the system attempts to refine this as the relevance feedback process continues. The small size of the initial query limits the number of features to learn from, inadvertently combating the dimensionality problem. The feature set is expanded as new terms are found to be important to relevant documents, but it generally does not approach the number of terms present in the documents. The terms of the initial query can also be given more emphasis than positive examples introduced later, so that they always have more weight during the learning process.

The restrictively small size of the initial feature set can be overcome by requiring the user to provide a sample set of relevant documents, called inductive query by example (CHEN ET AL., 1998b). Learning algorithms induce the keywords from these initial documents, and the relevance feedback process then refines this term set as described above.

The amount of training data available to a learning system via relevance feedback is relatively small, with a bias toward positive examples. Bias occurs because the system is trying to find positive examples of the user's desired concept, and presents the user with items that best match the concept so far developed. LEWIS suggests that bias is probably appropriate in this situation.

BHUYAN & RAGHAVAN store relevance feedback information from several users in three graphs denoting different relationships between pairs of documents. When enough information has been stored, the graphs are combined and used to form clusters. The system tries to obtain a consistent classification for documents over a number of user interactions. Documents considered jointly relevant by a number of users are placed in the same group, and the clusters are used in later searches to retrieve related documents more efficiently.

GOKER & MCCLUSKEY, KRULWICH (1995a), and LANG all use relevance feedback as part of the learning cycle. The technique is used to inform the system which documents or terms are useful as discriminators of documents that interest the user. These terms are used as features for the learning algorithm. SAVOY extends this technique to hypertext retrieval by using relevance feedback to update and construct links between documents according to their co-appearance in sets of documents relevant to queries. GORDON (1988) uses a genetic algorithm to combine information from several different descriptions of the same document with user relevance judgments. Each document description is assumed to be relevant to a different set of users, and the genetic algorithm attempts to differentially move descriptions closer to relevant queries. THOMPSON presents a method for using the statistical technique of combination of expert opinion (CEO) to merge indexers' classifications and relevance feedback from searchers.

CHEN uses relevance feedback in an iterative text-categorization scheme using the ID5R as an iterative decision-tree learner that rearranged the structure of the tree to accommodate new examples as they are presented. Chen initially presents the algorithm with a set of keyword groups representing positive examples of the desired concept. A similar set of negative examples is also supplied, as ID5R requires both positive and negative examples to learn a concept description. The resulting decision tree is used to search the remainder of the database, and the set of new documents retrieved is presented to the user for the relevance feedback step. The user classifies them as positive or negative, and this information is used to update the decision tree. This process is repeated until the entire database is classified correctly. Later CHEN ET AL. (1998b) compare the effectiveness of three learning algorithms—genetic algorithms, ID3, and simulated annealing—to relevance feedback in identifying additional relevant documents. Although all three algorithms were found to have some advantage over conventional relevance feedback, genetic algorithms were found to be particularly effective in improving recall and precision. The executive speed of the genetic algorithm was not found to be problematic; however, the experiment used relatively small test sets (fewer than 50 documents), so it is not known whether the performance would be acceptable under more realistic conditions.

YANG & KORFHAGE note that previous research has shown that including term weightings in queries can improve retrieval performance in a system based on the vector-space model; however, it is also well-known that users find it difficult to assign correct weights. A genetic algorithm is used to test the fitness of a variety of queries containing different weightings for query terms, where fitness is measured by relevance feedback based on the document sets retrieved by each weighted form of the query. Tests using the Cranfield collection (a standard set of documents, queries, and known relevances between documents and queries (CLEVERDON ET AL.)) show that this technique achieves higher precision than both the original unmodified queries and previously reported results from other relevance-feedback techniques on the Cranfield document set.

BOYAN ET AL. use a range of machine learning methods, including reinforcement-learning techniques that propagate rewards through a graph, to improve the rankings returned by a Web search engine based on feedback collected unobtrusively from users. The system is similar to a regular search engine. Users do not give explicit feedback; instead, the system records which hits they follow. The system uses the $tf \bullet idf$ retrieval metric but also takes account whether the word appears in a title or heading, is bold, italicized, or underlined, and so on. These features appear as weights, and are optimized using simulated annealing (a general optimization method that stochastically simulates the cooling of a physical system).

INFORMATION FILTERING

In most IR domains a user's interactions with the system occur over an extended period of time. In some cases interaction is a discrete event unrelated to previous interactions, whereas other domains involve continuous interaction involving the same topic. For example, a search for books about functional programming languages might be a single exercise with a library's computerized cataloging system, whereas following a thread in a USENET newsgroup would be an ongoing procedure with interactions occurring daily or even hourly. In the former case the user is probably willing to endure an extended dialogue in order to locate the desired material. The outcome may be several books on the subject in question, and the user may not need to return for some time.

In situations where users' interests remain constant and the documents that satisfy those interests are continually changing, it is necessary to model their interests to filter the continuous stream of information for articles of interest. A user should not have to search the entire USENET feed to find a handful of articles that are probably only of passing interest. The effort required to find these articles is often more than users are willing to expend. In this situation it is necessary to keep track of interesting articles and separate them from the morass of uninteresting text.

Modeling User Interests

The most effective kind of user modeling occurs during a series of interactions with the system as it builds a profile of each user, a technique that is most applicable when a user's requirements remain constant. In these situations it is the user's interests that the system tries to identify.

Most news-reading systems allow users to keep a hotlist of relevant newsgroups, but force the user to rummage through these groups to determine which articles are of interest, usually on the strength of titles or a keyword search. As the number of groups and the range of topics increase, the user's task becomes overwhelming. A trade-off is necessary between looking through fewer articles about a range of interests, and finding postings that are truly interesting (LANG).

To lessen the strain on the user, some systems build a profile of the user's interests during interactive sessions and present articles that match that profile. This user model may be generated collaboratively with the user (KRULWICH, 1995a; LANG) or from logs of user sessions (GOKER & MCCLUSKEY), and is continually updated to reflect changes in the user's interests and the content of the text database.

HULL ET AL. and SCHÜTZE ET AL. analyze the performance of three learning schemes—linear discriminant analysis, logistic regression, and neural networks—in improving the accuracy of relevant/nonrelevant ratings. Their work is unusual in that the document base for their experiments, the Tipster corpus, is of significant size: 3.2 gigabytes of text in more than 1 million documents, against which they processed 100 topics corresponding to the routing tasks of TREC-2 and TREC-3. Their results indicate that the classifiers achieve 10% to 15% higher accuracy (combined recall and precision) than Rocchio-style expansion relevance feedback (BUCKLEY ET AL.), which works from a linear combination of the query vector, the centroid of relevant documents, and sometimes the centroid of nonrelevant documents.

BLOEDORN ET AL. attempt to improve the comprehensibility of user profiles by using a generalization hierarchy. They note that a user interested in documents on scuba, whitewater rafting, and kayaking is more generally described as having an interest in water sports, and that this broader term can then be used to suggest additional topics of interest (such as snorkeling), as well as to more naturally communicate the profile to the user. In practical use of new filtering agents, user comprehension of profiles can be important because the user may need to edit or validate the model learned by the system (MITCHELL ET AL.). In the Bloedorn et al. scheme, the term vector for a document is augmented by subject categories (generated by an automated text classifier) and tags describing organization, person, and place names (also automatically extracted). The user marks a sample set of documents as relevant (positive examples) or nonrelevant (negative examples), and the profile is induced from this training set by a decision-tree learner such as C4.5 (QUINLAN, 1993).

Web-based systems can also take advantage of available information about a user's actions while using a document collection, to further refine the user profile. WebACE (BOLEY ET AL.; HAN ET AL.) constructs a profile of user Web browsing. Documents viewed by the user are rated for their degree of interest to that user, based on interaction characteristics such as the length of time spent viewing that page and the number of times that the user visited that page. After a sufficient number of documents have been categorized by interest level, the document-term vectors are processed by a clustering algorithm. A comprehensible profile of user interests is created by generating a label for each cluster. Interestingly, the label is not simply a set of frequently occurring terms in the cluster, but instead includes terms most useful in distinguishing one cluster from another. WebACE can also autonomously search for new documents likely to be of interest to the user: document terms from a cluster are combined to generate a Web query, and new documents retrieved by this query are ranked for relevance by their similarity to the cluster.

The OKAPI system provides retrieval services for three databases at City University in London. OKAPI ranks retrieved documents by the probability that they are relevant to the user's query. The system also uses standard relevance-feedback techniques to expand the user's initial query. GOKER & MCCLUSKEY describe an incremental learning algorithm that, when used with OKAPI, forms a model of the user's areas of interest. The algorithm learns from logs of user sessions that contain details of search terms, search and response time, number of references examined, and other information. The resulting concept descriptions can be used the next time a user carries out a search on a similar subject, with emphasis on alleviating weight-block problems.

The ideas discussed above can also be applied to user group models. Instead of building a profile of a single person, the system models a number of users and employs the information to select documents relevant to individuals and to the group as a whole.

Information-Filtering Applications

Machine learning has been applied to information filtering in several different domains: USENET news reading, Web browsing, and email filtering.

News reading. Krulwich's system (KRULWICH, 1995a, 1995b; KRULWICH & BURKEY) filters information from a number of sources in a Lotus Notes environment, using a term-vector approach. Documents constitute four groups, ranging from general discussion to memos and bulletins. The number of documents relevant to the average user is estimated at fewer than a dozen of the 3000 that appear daily. By presenting documents that are predicted to be relevant to the user, and obtaining information on which are relevant and why, the system is able to fine-tune each user's filter. During each nightly search of the database, several articles are collected that match the current profile. These documents are presented to the user, who scans them for items of interest. As articles are selected, the user is asked to indicate why they are interesting, be it the subject area, author, or whatever. These reasons become categories for the system to learn.

LANG describes a similar system, NewsWeeder, that learns user models for identifying interesting USENET news articles. In addition to providing the services of a traditional newsreader, NewsWeeder generates virtual newsgroups tailored to individual users' preferences. Each user's personalized list is ranked according to a predicted interest rating for each article. The user selects any articles from the list that appear interesting, reads them, and rates them from 1 (essential) to 5 (never want to see anything like it again). All other articles are marked "skip," indicating that the user does not even want to read them. Ratings are collected, and overnight the system learns a new model, based on linear regression, that is used to predict the ratings the user will give to the next set of articles appearing in his or her personalized newsgroup.

IAN (GREEN & EDWARDS) also filters USENET articles, using either C4.5 (QUINLAN, 1993) or the Instance-Based Prototypical Learning (IBPL) algorithm (PAYNE & EDWARDS) to refine its model of user interest. Tests of both algorithms indicate that they are better suited to predicting coarse-grained interest classifications (such as interesting/not interesting) than fine-grained ones (such as level of interest on a graduated scale).

The GroupLens architecture provides collaborative filtering for USENET newsgroups (RESNICK ET AL.). The algorithm that predicts a user's interest in an unseen newsgroup posting is based on the common-sense heuristic that people who have agreed on postings in the past are likely to continue to agree in the future, at least for articles in the same newsgroup. Several techniques have been tested for correlating user ratings, including reinforcement learning and multivariate regression.

Web browsing and searching. The type of profile development above is also readily applicable to Web browsing. LAW (EDWARDS ET AL.) interactively identifies links of potential interest on a page that the user is browsing, and also autonomously searches for Web pages matching the user profile. The profile-updating algorithm is based on the user's response to suggestions: if the user saves as a bookmark, prints, or frequently visits a link or Web page, then it is classified as a positive example; otherwise it is a negative example. Experiments with profile-updating schemes indicate that rule-induction techniques such as C4.5 (QUINLAN, 1993) and instance-based learning algorithms such as IBPLI (PAYNE & EDWARDS) can achieve acceptable predictive accuracy. The AARON system (GREEN & EDWARDS) uses a similar profile construction approach to construct a personalized newspaper from news items previously gathered from a variety of sites.

The Web page recommendation system of PAZZANI ET AL. (1995; 1996) also learns from both positive and negative examples, taken from a user-constructed hotlist and coldlist (set of URLs for Web pages that the user visited, but did not like). It learns separate profiles for each user topic, under the assumption that multiple profiles will be more accurate for each interest than a single conglomerate user model. A genetic algorithm-based spider (a program that semi-autonomously crawls across links in the Web) developed by CHEN ET AL. (1998a) is given a set of URLs for Web pages that characterize the user's interests, and the spider locates related pages. This spider searched significantly more slowly than a spider based on a simple breadth-first search, and did not achieve a higher relevance rating for returned documents; however, the genetic algorithm did return documents that would not have been reached by the breadth-first search, suggesting that genetic algorithms may be useful in augmenting the results of simpler and faster search agents.

WebWatcher (ARMSTRONG ET AL.; JOACHIMS ET AL.) learns user preferences for link traversal across the Web, and employs this model to suggest hyperlinks for the user to follow. The user first briefly describes the goals of an information search to WebWatcher: the types of information needed (for example, a paper or a description of software), a subject area, the name of a relevant author, etc. As the user explores a set of connected pages, WebWatcher highlights links that appear to be relevant to the search, where relevance is measured by similarity between keywords in the user's description of the search goals and keywords that relate to the available hyperlinks. The latter are terms in the link itself, in the sentence containing the link, and in the heading of the document associated with the link. WebWatcher's recommendations are refined offline by induction over a set of user interactions. Limited testing with three techniques—a Boolean concept learner, the compression algorithm Wordstat, and $tf \bullet idf$—indicates that all three can potentially improve WebWatcher's accuracy in predicting the user's link traversal preferences.

The Letizia Web-browsing agent browses the Web in parallel with a user (LIEBERMAN; LIEBERMAN & MAULSBY). As the user visits Web pages, Letizia incrementally builds a user model and uses the model to autonomously locate potentially interesting pages. These pages are presented to the user only at the user's request. The user model is based on the content of the documents that the user manually selects (using a similarity measure based on $tf \bullet idf$), and on heuristics related to the user's actions. For example, a page from which the user has selected several links is treated as a positive example of an interesting document, while a page that the user scans quickly without searching one of its links is treated as a negative example.

The Fab Web page recommendation system (BALABANOVIC; BALABANOVIC & SHOHAM, 1997) is based on a collaborative filtering architecture that also includes adaptive collection agents that locate and retrieve documents in the system's recommendations database. Like users, these agents have profiles. Search agents use a best-first or beam-search strategy to scan the Web directly for documents that match the agent's profile, while index agents automatically construct queries to Web indexers to locate new pages. A user's relevance rating is used to update the profile of the agent that originally located that page. The Fab developers hypothesize that this type of feedback will eventually result in agent specialization, with each agent's profile evolving to represent a particular concept or document type. The process is accelerated by periodically eliminating collection agents whose retrieved documents prove unpopular with Fab's users.

In an interesting twist on Web monitors, the Do-I-Care agent (ACKERMAN ET AL.; STARR ET AL.) monitors a set of Web pages for interesting changes. Where a URL-minder notifies users of any modification to preselected pages, Do-I-Care uses machine learning techniques (in this version, Bayesian classification) to learn regularities in the types of change that the user finds interesting (for example, a significant increase in the document size or the addition of heavily weighted terms). Another imaginative approach is the application of Artificial Life to the Web (MENCZER ET AL.). A population of agents, evolved using density-dependent selection, locate information for the user. Agents compete for relevant documents and gain the energy necessary for survival as a reward for presenting the user with appropriate information.

Finally, COHEN & SINGER (1996b) address the problem of maintaining a Web resource directory page: a list of pointers to documents on a given topic. Keeping these directories current is difficult, given the exponential growth of the Web. Their system begins with an existing directory, which is treated as a list of positive examples for the directory's topic. The documents linked to this directory are retrieved and fed into a rule-learning system (in this case, RIPPER, by COHEN (1995a), or the sleeping experts algorithm by COHEN & SINGER (1996a)). The rules are then translated into search engine queries that are periodically run to search for new documents to include in the directory.

Email filtering. Several systems have been developed to filter personal email. COHEN (1996a) uses the RIPPER algorithm (COHEN, 1995a) to induce mailbox classification rules from the contents of a user's personal mail files. Rules are based on the presence of a term in a given field of a message, for example, "classify an incoming message in the call-for-papers mailbox if it contains 'cfp' and '95' in the subject field." The Maxims email agent learns more complex tasks: it can prioritize, delete, forward, and archive messages as well as categorize them (LASHKARI ET AL.). Maxims is based on the programming-by-demonstration paradigm: it observes the user dealing with email, stores situation/action pairs describing these observations, and predicts future actions based on matches to stored situations. In addition to predicting the next action, Maxims also generates an estimate of its confidence in that prediction. This confidence level is based on intuitively important factors: the number of examples that the agent has seen, the user's consistency in handling the most closely matching prior situations, and the degree of similarity between the new situation and previous ones. Obviously, the longer Maxims observes a user and the more consistent that user is in dealing with email, the better the predictions.

Few classification or filtering algorithms discussed in this chapter consider the cost of misclassification when constructing a model. For applications such as email filtering, where the cost of misclassifying a legitimate message as junk is much higher than the cost of classifying junk mail as interesting, the addition of cost information to a model can greatly increase its utility. A simple technique for incorporating this type of misclassification cost is to set thresholds for classification acceptance within a probabilistic model (SAHAMI ET AL., 1998).

Augmenting Models from Other Information Sources

A significant problem for information filtering is the time that it takes to learn a model of each user's interests by monitoring his or her interactions. DE KROON ET AL. reduce the model construction period by priming the model with information garnered from the user's home page, bookmarks, and responses to a brief questionnaire. AutoClass (CHEESEMAN ET AL.), a Bayesian clustering algorithm, was used to produce the initial user-interest model. This algorithm appears particularly appropriate for the task, as the number of subclasses (the different, potentially diverse and numerous, areas of interest that comprise a given user's model) does not have to be specified in advance.

In many filtering systems each user's filtering profile is developed (learned) in isolation. The Webhunter Web document recommendation system (LASHKARI) uses an alternative retrieval technique: collaborative filtering. Rather than starting by correlating an individual user with a document, collaborative filtering bases its recommendations on correlations between users. Webhunter presents a user with a set of Web pages to evaluate, and the user's personal agent records which Web pages he or she likes or dislikes. The agent then compares itself with other agents, looking for agents with similar values for similar items. Highly correlated agents accept recommendations from one another.

As a further refinement, Webhunter includes limited content analysis of documents to partition the document space. The idea is that while two users may both find one type of resource interesting, they may vehemently disagree on the usefulness of a different resource. Reliance on a simple user correlation may mask these differences and lead to less reliable Web-page suggestions. Further, the set of Web pages known to Webhunter is large in comparison with the number of pages that any individual user has the patience to evaluate. This makes it less likely that any two users have examined a large proportion of the same pages, which affects the ability of the agents to notice similarities between users. The use of content analysis to group the Web pages into clusters makes it easier to find correlations between user tastes.

The browsing advisor (JACZYNSKI; JACZYNSKI & TROUSSE, 1998a, 1998b) uses a case-based reasoning framework to learn correlations between the browsing patterns of two or more users. The idea is that if a current user is traversing a similar sequence of documents/links as a past user, then the two users are likely to be attempting to satisfy the same information need. The relevant documents retrieved by the past user can then be suggested to the present user for retrieval.

The filtering systems described above assume that the user's interest profile remains stable over time. In reality, of course, the user's interests undergo concept drift as his or her information needs change gradually (or suddenly). Drift can be monitored by using a time window on the training data, and a change in concept detected by noting significant changes in the classifier's accuracy or the dataset's value. KLINKENBERG & RENZ demonstrate the efficacy of windowing techniques in detecting concept drift using an artificial dataset.

CONCLUSIONS

Machine learning is becoming an important source of tools for automating IR tasks. All phases of IR can be (and are) performed manually, but automation has many benefits, for example, larger document collections can be processed more quickly and consistently, and new techniques can be easily implemented and tested. Human ability at these tasks provides a benchmark performance threshold that many systems are approaching. However, perfect performance is probably unattainable in the foreseeable future because the models of natural languages used are necessarily very restricted.

The most important phase of the IR process is feature selection, which we discuss at length in the sections on machine learning and models of text and text representation above. This is particularly significant when learning algorithms are employed at some point in the process. Although machine learning schemes perform feature selection themselves, they work best when given a small number of distinctive features to learn from. Limiting the feature set reduces the space and time consumed by the algorithm, and lessens the risk that weak features appear in concept descriptions by chance.

Simple techniques for eliminating potentially weak features often work well once the nature of the features to be used is determined. Most systems use the word as the basic unit of content, and stoplists, stemmers, and thesauri help to reduce the number of possible words a system has to cope with. When objects larger than words, such as phrases and headings, are used as features, the need for selection is even more critical. It is possible to determine the extent of such features using syntactic analysis, and even formatting information. Coarser-grained features do not suffer from problems such as synonymy, so the co-occurrence of a phrase in two documents is a better indication of similarity than the appearance of individual words.

The term-frequency-times-inverse-document-frequency ($tf \bullet idf$) measure is one of the simplest and most effective automatic methods of classifying text. The fact that it uses the term-vector representation for documents suggests that information about the distribution of important words is often all that is necessary for effective retrieval. The measure is resistant to the effects of stopwords and document length. Standard machine learning schemes using the same form of text representation are less resilient, requiring the data to be prefiltered to reduce the number of features. To keep space and time consumption to practical levels, the feature space must be limited to several hundred words. That is generally a minute fraction of the total vocabulary of a text collection, so a good feature-selection mechanism is necessary. When the number of classes and the number of features are suitably limited, machine learning algorithms generate concise and intuitive concept descriptions.

Four main phases of the IR process are identified by LEWIS, and learning techniques have been applied to all of them. The first, indexing, incorporates feature extraction, document clustering, and text classification. Feature selection has already been noted as the most vital part of the process, and most researchers expend considerable effort in this area. Document clustering assists in retrieval by creating links between similar documents. This allows related documents to be retrieved once one of the documents has been deemed relevant to a query. Links can be made at any level, from common keywords to similar paragraph subtopics. By following links to an arbitrary level, the system can retrieve documents with a given degree of similarity, and rank them accordingly.

The remaining three phases, querying, comparison, and feedback, usually form a loop that is repeated until the user is satisfied with the retrieved documents. Most users find it difficult to formulate their information needs in terms of keywords, and selection of effective words is a stressful task. Systems that use feedback about the relevance of retrieved documents help the user by strengthening the weight of discriminatory terms present in the query, and introducing new terms garnered from relevant documents.

The ease with which an effective query can be entered is enhanced by modeling the user. Creating a representation of the user's information needs reduces the user's effort in selecting relevant documents in a changing information environment. Continual updating of the model, by means of user feedback, lets the system track shifts in interest and information need. By creating a model of each user's background and experience, the system can interpret individual users' queries appropriately.

Machine learning technology has been successfully applied in many IR systems, both experimental and operational. The learning techniques currently employed are simple, and some remaining problems may be overcome using more advanced technology. Machine learning is a rapidly growing area, and new algorithms and techniques are continually pushing the limits of performance higher. But the force really driving the applications of machine learning to IR is not so much developments in machine learning technology as changes in the information environment that demand new ways of working. The instant availability of enormous amounts of textual information on the Internet and in digital libraries has provoked a new interest in software agents that act on behalf of users, sifting through the information to identify documents that may be relevant to users' individual needs. The application of machine learning to IR is only just beginning.

BIBLIOGRAPHY

ACKERMAN, MARK S.; STARR, BRIAN; PAZZANI, MICHAEL. 1997. The Do-I-Care Agent: Effective Social Discovery and Filtering on the Web. In: RIAO '97 Conference Proceedings: Computer Assisted Searching on Internet; 1997 June 25-27; Montreal, Canada. Paris, France: CID; 1997. 17-31. ISBN: 2-905450-06-1.

AHA, DAVID. 1992. Tolerating Noisy, Irrelevant and Novel Attributes in Instance-Based Learning Algorithms. International Journal of Man-Machine Studies. 1992; 36: 267-287. ISSN: 0020-7373.

ALLAN, JAMES. 1995. Relevance Feedback with Too Much Data. In: Fox, Edward A.; Ingwersen, Peter; Fidel, Raya, eds. SIGIR '95: Proceedings of the Association for Computing Machinery Special Interest Group on Information Retrieval (ACM/SIGIR) 18th Annual International Conference on Research and Development in Information Retrieval; 1995 July 9-13; Seattle, WA. New York, NY: ACM Press; 1995. 337-343. ISBN: 0-89791-714-6.

AONE, CHINATSO; BENNETT, SCOTT WILLIAM; GORLINSKY, JIM. 1996. Multi-Media Fusion through Application of Machine Learning and NLP. In: Machine Learning in Information Access: Papers from the 1996 AAAI Spring Symposium; Stanford, CA. Menlo Park, CA: AAAI Press; 1996. 96-99. ISBN: 1-57735-007-3.

APTÉ, CHIDANAND; DAMERAU, FRED; WEISS, SHOLOM M. 1994a. Automated Learning of Decision Rules for Text Categorization. ACM Transactions on Information Systems. 1994; 12(3): 233-250. ISSN: 1046-8188.

APTÉ, CHIDANAND; DAMERAU, FRED; WEISS, SHOLOM M. 1994b. Towards Language Independent Automated Learning of Text Categorization Models. In: Croft, W. Bruce; van Rijsbergen, C. J., eds. SIGIR '94: Proceedings of the Association for Computing Machinery Special Interest Group on Information Retrieval (ACM/SIGIR) 17th Annual International Conference on Research and Development in Information Retrieval; 1994 July 3-6; Dublin, Ireland. Berlin, Germany: Springer-Verlag; 1994. 23-30. ISBN: 3-540-19889-X.

ARMSTRONG, ROBERT; FREITAG, DAYNE; JOACHIMS, THORSTEN; MITCHELL, TOM. 1995. WebWatcher: A Learning Apprentice for the World Wide Web. In: Proceedings of the AAAI Spring Symposium on Information Gathering from Heterogeneous, Distributed Environments; 1995 March 27-29; Stanford, CA. Menlo Park, CA: AAAI Press; 1995. 6-12. (AAAI SS-95-08). ISBN: 0-929280-91-1.

BAEZA-YATES, RICARDO A. 1992. Introduction to Data Structures and Algorithms Related to Information Retrieval. In: Frakes, William B.; Baeza-Yates, Ricardo A., eds. Information Retrieval: Data Structures and Algorithms. Englewood Cliffs, NJ: Prentice-Hall; 1992. 13-27. ISBN: 0-13-463837-9.

BALABANOVIC, MARKO. 1997. An Adaptive Web Page Recommendation Service. In: Proceedings of the International Conference on Autonomous Agents (Agents '97); 1997 February 5-8; Marina del Ray, CA. New York, NY: ACM Press; 1997. 378-385. ISBN: 0-89791-877-0.

BALABANOVIC, MARKO; SHOHAM, YOAV. 1995. Learning Information Retrieval Agents: Experiments with Automated Web Browsing. In: Proceedings of the AAAI Spring Symposium on Information Gathering from Heterogeneous, Distributed Environments; 1995 March 27-29; Stanford, CA. Menlo Park, CA: AAAI Press; 1995. 13-18. (AAAI SS-95-08). ISBN: 0-929280-91-1.

BALABANOVIC, MARKO; SHOHAM, YOAV. 1997. Combining Content-Based and Collaborative Recommendation. Communications of the ACM. 1997 March; 40(3): 66-73. ISSN: 0001-0782.

BARTELL, BRIAN T.; COTTRELL, GARRISON W.; BELEW, RICHARD K. 1994. Learning the Optimal Parameters in a Ranked Retrieval System Using Multi-Query Relevance Feedback. In: Proceedings of the 3rd Annual Symposium on Document Analysis and Information Retrieval; 1994 April 15-17; Las Vegas, NV. Available WWW: http://www-cse.ucsd.edu/users/gary/pubs/dair94.ps.

BARTELL, BRIAN T.; COTTRELL, GARRISON W.; BELEW, RICHARD K. 1998. Optimizing Similarity Using Multi-Query Relevance Feedback. Journal of the American Society for Information Science. 1998; 49(8): 742-761. ISSN: 0002-8231.

BHATIA, SANJIV K.; DEOGUN, JITENDER S.; RAGHAVAN, VIJAY V. 1995. Conceptual Query Formulation and Retrieval. Journal of Intelligent Information Systems. 1995; 5(3): 183-209. ISSN: 0925-9902.

BHUYAN, JAY N.; RAGHAVAN, VIJAY V. 1991. A Probabilistic Retrieval Scheme for Cluster-Based Adaptive Information Retrieval. In: Proceedings of the 8th International Workshop on Machine Learning: 1991 June; Evanston, IL. San Mateo, CA: Morgan Kaufmann; 1991. 240-244. ISBN: 1-55860-200-3.

BLOEDORN, ERIC; MANI, INDERJEET; MACMILLAN, T. RICHARD. 1996. Representational Issues in Machine Learning of User Profiles. In: Machine Learning in Information Access: Papers from the 1996 AAAI Spring Symposium; Stanford, CA. Menlo Park, CA: AAAI Press; 1996. 9-17. ISBN: 1-57735-007-3.

BLOSSEVILLE, M. J.; HÉBRAIL, G.; MONTEIL, M. G.; PÉNOT, N. 1992. Automatic Document Classification: Natural Language Processing, Statistical Analysis, and Expert System Techniques Used Together. In: Belkin, Nicholas; Ingwersen, Peter; Pejtersen, Annelise Mark, eds. SIGIR '92: Proceedings of the Association for Computing Machinery Special Interest Group on Information Retrieval (ACM/SIGIR) 15th Annual International Conference on Research and Development in Information Retrieval; 1992 June 21-24; Copenhagen, Denmark. New York, NY: ACM Press; 1992. 51-57. ISBN: 0-89791-523-2.

BOLEY, DANIEL; GINI, MARIA; MOORE, JERRY. 1998. A Client-Side Web Agent for Document Categorization. Internet Research: Electronic Networking Applications and Policy. 1998; 8(5): 387-399. ISSN: 1066-2243.

BOYAN, JUSTIN A.; FREITAG, DAYNE; JOACHIMS, THORSTEN. 1996. A Machine Learning Architecture for Optimizing Web Search Engines. In: Proceedings of the AAAI Workshop on Internet-Based Information Systems; 1996 August 5; Portland, OR. Menlo Park, CA: AAAI Press; 1996. 1-8. ISBN: 1-57735-017-0.

BREIMAN, LEO; FRIEDMAN, JEROME H.; OLSHEN, RICHARD A.; STONE, C. J. 1984. Classification and Regression Trees. Belmont, CA: Wadsworth, Inc.; 1984. 358p. ISBN: 0-534-98054-6.

BUCKLEY, CHRIS; SALTON, GERARD; ALLAN, JAMES. 1994. The Effect of Adding Relevance Information in a Relevance Feedback Environment. In: Croft, W. Bruce; van Rijsbergen, C.J., eds. SIGIR '94: Proceedings of the Association for Computing Machinery Special Interest Group on Information Retrieval (ACM/SIGIR) 17th Annual International Conference on Research and Development in Information Retrieval; 1994 July 3-6; Dublin, Ireland. Berlin, Germany: Springer-Verlag; 1994. 292-300. ISBN: 3-540-19889-X.

BUNTINE, WRAY. 1990. A Theory of Learning Classification Rules. Sydney, Australia: School of Computing Science, University of Technology; 1990. 172p. (Ph.D. dissertation). Available from: University of Technology, Sydney, Australia.

CHEESEMAN, PETER; KELLY, J.; SELF, M.; STUTZ, J.; TAYLOR, W.; FREEMAN, D. 1988. AUTOCLASS: A Bayesian Classification System. In:

Proceedings of the 5th International Conference on Machine Learning; 1988 June 12-15; Ann Arbor, MI. San Mateo, CA: Morgan Kaufmann; 1988. 54-64. ISBN: 0-934613-64-8.

CHEN, HSINCHUN. 1995. Machine Learning for Information Retrieval: Neural Networks, Symbolic Learning, and Genetic Algorithms. Journal of the American Society for Information Science. 1995; 46(3): 194-216. ISSN: 0002-8231.

CHEN, HSINCHUN; CHUNG, YI-MING; RAMSEY, MARSHALL; YANG, CHRISTOPHER C. 1998a. An Intelligent Personal Spider (Agent) for Dynamic Internet/Intranet Searching. Decision Support Systems. 1998; 23: 41-58. ISSN: 0167-9236.

CHEN, HSINCHUN; SHANKARANARAYANAN, GANESAN; SHE, LINLIN; IYER, ANAND. 1998b. A Machine Learning Approach to Inductive Query by Examples: An Experiment Using Relevance Feedback, ID3, Genetic Algorithms, and Simulated Annealing. Journal of the American Society for Information Science. 1998; 49(8): 693-705. ISSN: 0002-8231.

CLEVERDON, CYRIL W.; MILLS, JACK; KEEN, MICHAEL. 1966. Factors Determining the Performance of Indexing Systems. Volume I: Design. Cranfield, England: ASLIB Cranfield Research Project; 1966. 377p. OCLC: 3911240.

COHEN, WILLIAM W. 1995a. Fast Effective Rule Induction. In: Proceedings of the 12th International Conference on Machine Learning; 1995 July 9-12; Tahoe City, CA. San Francisco, CA: Morgan Kaufmann; 1995. 115-123. ISBN: 1-55860-377-8.

COHEN, WILLIAM W. 1995b. Text Categorization and Relational Learning. In: Proceedings of the 12th International Conference on Machine Learning; 1995 July 9-12; Tahoe City, CA. San Francisco, CA: Morgan Kaufmann; 1995. 124-132. ISBN: 1-55860-377-8.

COHEN, WILLIAM M. 1996a. Learning Rules That Classify E-mail. In: Machine Learning in Information Access: Papers from the 1996 AAAI Spring Symposium; Stanford, CA. Menlo Park, CA: AAAI Press; 1996. 18-25. ISBN: 1-57735-007-3.

COHEN, WILLIAM W. 1996b. Learning with Trees and Rules with Set-Valued Features. In: Proceedings of the 13th National Conference on Artificial Intelligence (AAAI '96); 1996 August 4-8; Portland, OR. Menlo Park, CA: AAAI Press; 1996. 709-716. ISBN: 0-262-51091-X.

COHEN, WILLIAM W.; SINGER, YORAM. 1996a. Context-Sensitive Learning Methods for Text Categorization. In: Frei, Hans-Peter; Harman, Donna; Schäuble, Peter; Wilkinson, Ross, eds. SIGIR '96: Proceedings of the Association for Computing Machinery Special Interest Group on Information Retrieval (ACM/SIGIR) 19th Annual International Conference on Research and Development in Information Retrieval; 1996 August 18-22; Zurich, Switzerland. New York, NY: ACM Press; 1996. 307-316. ISBN: 0-89791-792-8.

COHEN, WILLIAM W.; SINGER, YORAM. 1996b. Learning to Query the Web. In: Proceedings of the AAAI Workshop on Internet-Based Information Systems; 1996 August 5; Portland, OR. Menlo Park, CA: AAAI Press; 1996. 16-25. ISBN: 1-57735-017-0.

CONRAD, JACK G.; UTT, MARY HUNTER. 1994. A System for Discovering Relationships by Feature Extraction from Text Databases. In: Croft, W. Bruce; van Rijsbergen, C. J., eds. SIGIR '94: Proceedings of the Association for Computing Machinery Special Interest Group on Information Retrieval (ACM/SIGIR) 17th Annual International Conference on Research and Development in Information Retrieval; 1994 July 3-6; Dublin, Ireland. Berlin, Germany: Springer-Verlag; 1994. 260-270. ISBN: 3-540-19889-X.

CRAWFORD, S. L.; FUNG, R. M.; APPELBAUM, L. A.; TONG, R. M. 1991. Classification Trees for Information Retrieval. In: Proceedings of the 8th International Workshop on Machine Learning; 1991 June; Evanston, IL. San Mateo, CA: Morgan Kaufmann; 1991. 245-249. ISBN: 1-55860-200-3.

CUNNINGHAM, SALLY JO; HOLMES, GEOFFREY; LITTIN, JAMIE; BEALE, RUSSELL; WITTEN, IAN H. 1998. Applying Connectionist Models to Information Retrieval. In: Amari, Shun-ichi; Kasabov, Nikola, eds. Brain-like Computing and Intelligent Information Systems. Singapore: Springer Verlag; 1998. 435-460. ISBN: 98-13-08358-1.

CUNNINGHAM, SALLY JO; SUMMERS, BRENT. 1995. Applying Machine Learning to Subject Classification and Subject Description for Information Retrieval. In: Proceedings of the 2nd New Zealand International Two-Stream Conference on Artificial Neural Networks and Expert Systems (ANNES '95); 1995 November 20-23; Dunedin, New Zealand. Los Alamitos, CA: IEEE Computer Society Press; 1995. 243-246. ISBN: 0-8186-7174-2.

DE KROON, H. C. M.; MITCHELL, TOM M.; KERCKHOFFS, EUGENE J. H. 1996. Improving Learning Accuracy in Information Filtering. In: Proceedings of the ICML Workshop on Machine Learning Meets Human Computer Interaction; 1996 July 3; Bari, Italy. 41-50. Available: http://www.cs.cmu.edu/afs/cs/project/theo-11/www/publications.html.

DEERWESTER, SCOTT; DUMAIS, SUSAN T.; LANDAUER, THOMAS K.; FURNAS, GEORGE W.; HARSHMAN, RICHARD A. 1990. Indexing by Latent Semantic Analysis. Journal of the American Society for Information Science. 1990; 41(6): 391-407. ISSN: 0002-8231.

DOSZKOCS, TAMAS E.; REGGIA, JAMES A.; LIN, XIA. 1990. Connectionist Models and Information Retrieval. In: Williams, Martha E., ed. Annual Review of Information Science and Technology: Volume 25. Amsterdam, The Netherlands: Elsevier Science Publishers for the American Society for Information Science; 1990. 209-260. ISBN: 0-444-88531-5.

DUMAIS, SUSAN T.; PLATT, JOHN; HECKERMAN, DAVID; SAHAMI, MEHRAN. 1998. Inductive Learning Algorithms and Representations for Text Categorization. In: Proceedings of the 7th International Conference on Information and Knowledge Management (CIKM '98); 1998 November 3-7; Bethesda, MD. New York, NY: ACM Press; 1998. 148-155. ISBN: 1-58113-061-9.

EDWARDS, PETER; BAYER, DAVID; GREEN, CLAIRE; PAYNE, TERRY R. 1996. Experience with Learning Agents Which Manage Internet-Based Information. In: Machine Learning in Information Access: Papers from the 1996 AAAI Spring Symposium; Stanford, CA. Menlo Park, CA: AAAI Press; 1996. 31-40. ISBN: 1-57735-007-3.

FISHER, DOUGLAS. 1987. Knowledge Acquisition Via Incremental Conceptual Clustering. Machine Learning. 1987; 2: 139-172. ISSN: 0885-6125.

FUHR, NORBERT; BUCKLEY, CHRIS. 1991. A Probabilistic Learning Approach for Document Indexing. ACM Transactions on Information Systems. 1991; 9(3): 223-248. ISSN: 1046-8188.

FURNAS, GEORGE W. 1985. Experience with an Adaptive Indexing Scheme. In: Proceedings of the Association for Computing Machinery Special Interest Group on Computer-Human Interaction (ACM/SIGCHI) Conference on Human Factors in Computing Systems; 1985 April 14-18; San Francisco, CA. New York, NY: ACM Press; 1985. 131-135. ISBN: 0-89791-149-0.

GAINES, BRIAN R. 1991. The Tradeoff between Knowledge and Data in Knowledge Acquisition. In: Piatetsky-Shapiro, Gregory; Frawley, William J., eds. Knowledge Discovery in Databases. Menlo Park, CA: AAAI Press; 1991. 491-505. ISBN: 0-262-66070-9.

GANASCIA, JEAN-GABRIEL. 1991. Deriving the Learning Bias from Rule Properties. In: Hayes, Jean E.; Michie, Donald; Tyugu, E., eds. Machine Intelligence: Volume 12. Oxford, England: Clarendon Press; 1991. 151-167. ISBN: 0-19-853823-5.

GOKER, A.; MCCLUSKEY, T. L. 1991. Incremental Learning in a Probabilistic Information Retrieval System. In: Proceedings of the 8th International Workshop on Machine Learning; 1991 June; Evanston, IL. San Mateo, CA: Morgan Kaufmann; 1991. 255-259. ISBN: 1-55860-200-3.

GOLDBERG, JEFFREY L. 1995. CDM: An Approach to Learning in Text Categorization. In: Proceedings of the 7th International Conference on Tools with Artificial Intelligence; 1995 November 5-8; Herndon, VA. Los Alamitos, CA: IEEE Computer Society Press; 1995. 258-265. ISBN: 0-8186-7313-3.

GORDON, MICHAEL D. 1988. Probabilistic and Genetic Algorithms for Document Retrieval. Communications of the ACM. 1988; 31(10): 1208-1218. ISSN: 0001-0782.

GORDON, MICHAEL D. 1991. User-Based Document Clustering by Redescribing Subject Descriptions with a Genetic Algorithm. Journal of the American Society for Information Science. 1991; 42(5): 311-322. ISSN: 0002-8231.

GREEN, CLAIRE L.; EDWARDS, PETER. 1996. Using Machine Learning to Enhance Software Tools for Internet Information Management. In: Proceedings of the AAAI Workshop on Internet-Based Information Systems; 1996 August 5; Portland, OR. Menlo Park, CA: AAAI Press; 1996. 48-56. (WS-96-06). ISBN: 1-57735-017-0.

GREFENSTETTE, GREGORY. 1994. Explorations in Automatic Thesaurus Discovery. Boston, MA: Kluwer; 1994. 305p. ISBN: 0-792-39468-2.

GÜNTZER, U.; JÜTTNER, G.; SEEGMÜLLER, G.; SARRE, F. 1989. Automatic Thesaurus Construction by Machine Learning from Retrieval Sessions. Information Processing & Management. 1989; 25(3): 265-273. ISSN: 0306-4573.

HAN, EUI-HONG; BOLEY, DANIEL; GINI, MARIA; GROSS, ROBERT; HASTINGS, KYLE; KARYPIS, GEORGE; KUMAR, VIPID; MOBASHER, BAMSHAD; MOORE, JERRY. 1998. WebACE: A Web Agent for Document Categorization and Exploration. In: Proceedings of the 2nd International Conference on Autonomous Agents (Agents '98); 1998 May 9-13;

Minneapolis, MN. New York, NY: ACM Press; 1998. 408-415. ISBN: 0-89791-983-1.

HARMAN, DONNA. 1992. Relevance Feedback and Other Query Modification Techniques. In: Frakes, William B.; Baeza-Yates, Ricardo A., eds. Information Retrieval: Data Structures and Algorithms. Englewood Cliffs, NJ: Prentice Hall; 1992. 241-263. ISBN: 0-13-463837-9.

HARTER, STEPHEN P.; HERT, CAROL A. 1997. Evaluation of Information Retrieval Systems: Approaches, Issues, and Methods. In: Williams, Martha E., ed. Annual Review of Information Science and Technology: Volume 32. Medford, NJ: Information Today, Inc. for the American Society for Information Science; 1997. 3-94. ISSN: 0066-4200; ISBN: 1-57387-047-1.

HEARST, MARTI A. 1993. Cases as Structured Indexes for Full-Length Documents. In: Proceedings of the Symposium on Case-Based Reasoning and Information Retrieval; 1993 March 23-25; Stanford, CA. Menlo Park, CA: AAAI Press; 1993. 140-145. ISBN: 0-929280-45-8.

HEARST, MARTI A. 1994. Context and Structure in Automated Full-Text Information Access. Berkeley, CA: Computer Science Division (EECS), University of California; 1994. 128p. (Report no. UCB/CSD-94/836). OCLC: 31784982.

HENDLER, JAMES A. 1997. Intelligent Agents: Where AI Meets Information Technology. IEEE Expert. 1997; 11(6): 20-23. ISSN: 0885-9000.

HULL, DAVID; PEDERSEN, JAN; SCHÜTZE, HINRICH. 1996. Document Routing as Statistical Classification. In: Machine Learning in Information Access: Papers from the 1996 AAAI Spring Symposium; Stanford, CA. Menlo Park, CA: AAAI Press; 1996. 49-53. ISBN: 1-57735-007-3.

JACZYNSKI, MICHEL. 1997. A Framework for the Management of Past Experiences with Time-Extended Situations. In: Proceedings of the 6th International Conference on Information and Knowledge Management (CIKM'97); 1997 November 10-14; Las Vegas, NV. New York, NY: ACM Press; 1997. 32-39. ISBN: 0-89791-970-X.

JACZYNSKI, MICHEL; TROUSSE, BRIGITTE. 1998a. Broadway, a Case-Based Browsing Advisor for the Web or How to Support Browsing on the Web by Reusing Past Navigations of a Group of Users. In: Nikolous, Christos; Stephanidis, Constantine, eds. Research and Advanced Technology for Digital Libraries. Berlin, Germany: Springer-Verlag; 1998. 697-698. (Lecture Notes in Computer Science 1513). ISBN: 3-540-65101-2.

JACZYNSKI, MICHEL; TROUSSE, BRIGITTE. 1998b. WWW Assisted Browsing by Reusing Past Navigations from a Group of Users. In: Advances in Case-Based Reasoning: Proceedings of the 4th European Workshop on Case-Based Reasoning; 1998 September 23-25; Dublin, Ireland. Berlin, Germany: Springer-Verlag; 1998. 160-171. (Lecture Notes in Artificial Intelligence 1488). ISBN: 3-540-64990-5.

JOACHIMS, THORSTEN. 1998. Text Categorization with Support Vector Machines: Learning with Many Relevant Features. In: Proceedings of the 10th European Conference on Machine Learning (ECML-98); 1998 April 21-24; Chemnitz, Germany. Berlin, Germany: Springer-Verlag; 1998. 137-142. (Lecture Notes in Computer Science 1398). ISBN: 3-540-64417-2.

JOACHIMS, THORSTEN. 1999. Transductive Inference for Text Classification Using Support Vector Machines. In: Proceedings of the 16th International

Conference on Machine Learning (ICML); 1999 June 27-30; Bled, Slovenia. Available WWW: http://www-ai.cs.uni-dortmund.de/PERSONAL/joachims.html.

JOACHIMS, THORSTEN; FREITAG, DAYNE; MITCHELL, TOM. 1997. WebWatcher: A Tour Guide for the World Wide Web. In: Proceedings of the 15th International Joint Conference on Artificial Intelligence (IJCAI); 1997 August 23-27; Nagoya, Japan. San Francisco, CA: Morgan Kaufmann; 1997. 770-777. ISBN: 1-55860-480-4.

JONES, WILLIAM P.; FURNAS, GEORGE W. 1987. Pictures of Relevance: A Geometric Analysis of Similarity Measures. Journal of the American Society for Information Science. 1987; 38(6): 420-442. ISSN: 0002-8231.

KELLY, GEORGE ALEXANDER. 1963. A Theory of Personality: The Psychology of Personal Constructs. New York, NY: W. W. Norton; 1963. 190p. OCLC: 445715.

KLINKENBERG, RALF; RENZ, INGRID. 1998. Adaptive Information Filtering: Learning in the Presence of Concept Drifts. In: Learning for Text Categorization: Papers from the 1998 Workshop; 1998 July 27; Madison, WI. Menlo Park, CA: AAAI Press; 1998. 33-40. ISBN: 1-57735-058-8.

KOLLER, DAPHNE; SAHAMI, MEHRAN. 1996. Toward Optimal Feature Selection. In: Proceedings of the 13th International Conference on Machine Learning (ICML-96); 1996 July 3-6; Bari, Italy. San Francisco, CA: Morgan Kaufmann; 1996. 284-292. ISBN: 1-55860-419-7.

KOLLER, DAPHNE; SAHAMI, MEHRAN. 1997. Hierarchically Classifying Documents Using Very Few Words. In: Proceedings of the 14th International Conference on Machine Learning (ICML-97); 1997 July 8-12; Nashville, TN. San Francisco, CA: Morgan Kaufmann; 1997. 170-178. ISBN: 1-55860-486-3.

KRULWICH, BRUCE. 1995a. Learning Document Category Descriptions through the Extraction of Semantically Significant Phrases. In: Proceedings of the IJCAI Workshop on Data Engineering for Inductive Learning; 1995 August 20; Montreal, Canada. Available WWW: http://ai.iit.nrc.ca/DEIL/krulwich.ps.Z.

KRULWICH, BRUCE. 1995b. Learning User Interests across Heterogeneous Document Databases. In: Proceedings of the AAAI Spring Symposium on Information Gathering from Heterogeneous, Distributed Environments; 1995 March 27-29; Stanford, CA. Menlo Park, CA: AAAI Press; 1995. 106-110. ISBN: 0-929280-91-1.

KRULWICH, BRUCE; BURKEY, CHAD. 1996. Learning User Information Interests through the Extraction of Semantically Significant Phrases. In: Machine Learning in Information Access: Papers from the 1996 AAAI Spring Symposium; Stanford, CA. Menlo Park, CA: AAAI Press; 1996. 110-112. ISBN: 1-57735-007-3.

LANG, KEN. 1995. NewsWeeder: Learning to Filter Netnews. In: Proceedings of the 12th International Conference on Machine Learning; 1995 July 9-12; Tahoe City, CA. San Francisco, CA: Morgan Kaufman; 1995. 331-339. ISBN: 1-55860-377-8.

LANGLEY, PAT. 1996. Elements of Machine Learning. San Francisco, CA: Morgan Kaufmann; 1996. 419p. ISBN: 1-55860-301-8.

LANGLEY, PAT; SIMON, HERBERT A. 1995. Applications of Machine Learning and Rule Induction. Communications of the ACM. 1995; 38(11): 55-64. ISSN: 0001-0782.

LASHKARI, YEZDI. 1995. The Webhunter Personalized Document Filtering System. Available WWW: http://agents.www.media.mit.edu/groups/agents/projects.

LASHKARI, YEZDI; METRAL, MAX; MAES, PATTIE. 1994. Collaborative Interface Agents. In: Proceedings of the 12th National Conference on Artificial Intelligence: Volume 1; 1994 August 1-4; Seattle, WA. Menlo Park, CA: AAAI Press; 1994. 444-449. ISBN: 0-262-61102-3.

LEHNERT, WENDY; SODERLAND, STEPHEN; ARONOW, D.; FENG, FANGFANG; SHMUELI, A. 1995. Inductive Text Classification for Medical Applications. Journal of Experimental and Theoretical Artificial Intelligence. 1995; 7: 49-80. ISSN: 0952-813X.

LEWIS, DAVID D. 1991. Learning in Intelligent Information Retrieval. In: Proceedings of the 8th International Workshop on Machine Learning; 1991 June; Evanston, IL. San Mateo, CA: Morgan Kaufmann; 1991. 235-239. ISBN: 1-55860-200-3.

LEWIS, DAVID D.; CROFT, W. BRUCE. 1990. Term Clustering of Syntactic Phrases. In: SIGIR '90: Proceedings of the Association for Computing Machinery Special Interest Group on Information Retrieval (ACM/SIGIR) 13th Annual International Conference on Research and Development in Information Retrieval; 1990 September 5-7; Brussels, Belgium. New York, NY: ACM Press; 1990. 385-404. ISBN: 0-89791-408-2.

LEWIS, DAVID D.; GALE, WILLIAM A. 1994. A Sequential Algorithm for Training Text Classifiers. In: Croft, W. Bruce; van Rijsbergen, C. J., eds. SIGIR '94: Proceedings of the Association for Computing Machinery Special Interest Group on Information Retrieval (ACM/SIGIR) 17th Annual International Conference on Research and Development in Information Retrieval; 1994 July 3-6; Dublin, Ireland. Berlin, Germany: Springer-Verlag; 1994. 3-12. ISBN: 3-540-19889-X.

LEWIS, DAVID D.; RINGUETTE, MARC. 1994. A Comparison of Two Learning Algorithms for Text Categorization. In: Proceedings of the 3rd Annual Symposium on Document Analysis and Information Retrieval; 1994 April 11-13; Las Vegas, NV. 81-93. Available WWW: http://www.research.att.com/~lewis/chronobib.html.

LIEBERMAN, HENRY. 1995. Letizia: An Agent That Assists Web Browsing. In: IJCAI-95: Proceedings of the 14th International Joint Conference on Artificial Intelligence; 1995 August 20-25; Montreal, Canada. San Mateo, CA: Morgan Kaufmann; 1995. 924-929. ISBN: 1-55860-363-8.

LIEBERMAN, HENRY; MAULSBY, DAVID. 1996. Instructible Agents: Software That Just Keeps Getting Better. IBM Systems Journal. 1996; 35(3/4): 539-556. ISSN: 0018-8670.

LIERE, RAY; TADEPALLI, PRASAD. 1996. The Use of Active Learning in Text Categorization. In: Machine Learning in Information Access: Papers from the 1996 AAAI Spring Symposium; Stanford, CA. Menlo Park, CA: AAAI Press; 1996. 113-115. ISBN: 1-57735-007-3.

MAAREK, YOELLE S.; BEN-SHAUL, ISRAEL Z. 1996. Automatically Organizing Bookmarks per Contents. Computer Networks and ISDN Systems. 1996; 28: 1321-1333. ISSN: 0169-7552.

MARON, M. E. 1961. Automatic Indexing: An Experimental Inquiry. Journal of the ACM. 1961; 8: 404-417. ISSN: 0004-5411.

MARTIN, JOEL D. 1995. Clustering Full Text Documents. In: Proceedings of the IJCAI Workshop on Data Engineering for Inductive Learning; 1995 August 20; Montreal, Canada. Available WWW: http://ai.iit.nrc.ca/DEIL.

MCCALLUM, ANDREW; NIGAM, KAMAL; RENNIE, JASON; SEYMORE, KRISTIE. 1999. Building Domain-Specific Search Engines with Machine Learning Techniques. In: Proceedings of the AAAI-99 Spring Symposium on Intelligent Agents in Cyberspace. Available WWW: http://www.cs.cmu.edu/~mccallum/papers/cora-aaaiss99.ps.gz.

MCCALLUM, ANDREW; ROSENFELD, RONALD; MITCHELL, TOM; NG, ANDREW Y. 1998. Improving Text Classification by Shrinkage in a Hierarchy of Classes. In: Proceedings of the 15th International Conference on Machine Learning (ICML-98); 1998 July 24-26; Madison, WI. San Francisco, CA: Morgan Kaufmann; 1998. 359-367. ISBN: 1-55860-556-8.

MENCZER, FILIPPO; BELEW, RICHARD K.; WILLUHN, WOLFRAM. 1995. Artificial Life Applied to Adaptive Information Agents. In: Proceedings of the AAAI Spring Symposium on Information Gathering from Heterogeneous, Distributed Environments; 1995 March 27-29; Stanford, CA. Menlo Park, CA: AAAI Press; 1995. 128-132. (AAAI SS-95-08). ISBN: 0-929280-91-1.

MITCHELL, TOM; CARAHUANA, RICH; FREITAG, DAYNE; MCDERMOTT, JOHN; ZABOWSKI, DAVID. 1994. Experience with a Learning Personal Assistant. Communications of the ACM. 1994; 37(7): 81-91. ISSN: 0001-0782.

MOULINIER, ISABEL. 1996. A Framework for Comparing Text Categorization Approaches. In: Machine Learning in Information Access: Papers from the 1996 AAAI Spring Symposium; Stanford, CA. Menlo Park, CA: AAAI Press; 1996. 61-68. ISBN: 1-57735-007-3.

PAYNE, TERRY R.; EDWARDS, PETER. 1997. Interface Agents That Learn: An Investigation of Learning Issues in a Mail Agent Interface. Applied Artificial Intelligence. 1997; 11(1): 1-32. ISSN: 0883-9514.

PAZZANI, MICHAEL; MURAMATSU, JACK; BILSUS, DANIEL. 1996. Syskill & Webert: Identifying Interesting Web Sites. In: Machine Learning in Information Access: Papers from the 1996 AAAI Spring Symposium; Stanford, CA. Menlo Park, CA: AAAI Press; 1996. 69-78. ISBN: 0-262-51091-X.

PAZZANI, MICHAEL; NGUYEN, LARRY; MANTIK, STEFANUS. 1995. Learning from Hotlists and Coldlists: Towards a WWW Information Filtering and Seeking Agent. In: Proceedings of the 7th International Conference on Tools with Artificial Intelligence; 1995 November 5-8; Herndon, VA. Los Alamitos, CA: IEEE Computer Society Press; 1995. 492-495. ISBN: 0-8186-7313-3.

PIATETSKY-SHAPIRO, GREGORY; FRAWLEY, WILLIAM J., eds. 1991. Knowledge Discovery in Databases. Menlo Park, CA: AAAI Press/MIT Press; 1991. 525p. ISBN: 0-262-66070-9.

QUINLAN, JOHN ROSS. 1986. Induction of Decision Trees. Machine Learning. 1986; 1: 81-106. ISSN: 0885-6125.

QUINLAN, JOHN ROSS. 1990. Learning Logical Definitions from Relations. Machine Learning. 1990; 5: 239-266. ISSN: 0885-6125.

QUINLAN, JOHN ROSS. 1993. C4.5: Programs for Machine Learning. San Mateo, CA: Morgan Kaufmann; 1993. 302p. ISBN: 1-55860-238-0.

RESNICK, PAUL; IACOVOU, NEOPHYTOS; SUCHAK, MITESH; BERGSTROM, PETER; RIEDL, JOHN. 1994. GroupLens: An Open Architecture for Collaborative Filtering of Netnews. In: Proceedings of the Association for Computing Machinery (ACM) Conference on Computer Supported Cooperative Work; 1994 October 22-26; Chapel Hill, NC. New York, NY: ACM Press; 1994. 175-186. ISBN: 0-89791-689-1.

RISSANEN, JORMA. 1985. Minimum Description Length Principle. In: Kotz, Samuel; Johnson, Norman Lloyd, eds. Encyclopedia of the Statistical Sciences: Volume 5. New York, NY: Wiley; 1985. 523-527. ISBN: 0-471-05552-2.

SAHAMI, MEHRAN; DUMAIS, SUSAN T.; HECKERMAN, DAVID; HORVITZ, ERIC. 1998. A Bayesian Approach to Filtering Junk E-Mail. In: Learning for Text Categorization: Papers from the 1998 Workshop; 1998 July 27; Madison, WI. Menlo Park, CA: AAAI Press; 1998. 55-62. (AAAI WS-98-05). ISBN: 1-57735-058-8.

SAHAMI, MEHRAN; HEARST, MARTI; SAUND, ERIC. 1996. Applying the Multiple Cause Mixture Model to Text Categorization. In: Machine Learning in Information Access: Papers from the 1996 AAAI Spring Symposium; Stanford, CA. Menlo Park, CA: AAAI Press; 1996. 78-87. ISBN: 1-57735-007-3.

SALTON, GERARD; ALLAN, JAMES; BUCKLEY, CHRIS. 1994. Automatic Structuring and Retrieval of Large Text Files. Communications of the ACM. 1994; 37(2): 97-108. ISSN: 0001-0782.

SALTON, GERARD; MCGILL, MICHAEL J. 1983. Introduction to Modern Information Retrieval. New York, NY: McGraw-Hill; 1983. 448p. ISBN: 0-07-054484-0.

SAVOY, JACQUES. 1994. A Learning Scheme for Information Retrieval in Hypertext. Information Processing & Management. 1994; 30(4): 515-533. ISSN: 0306-4573.

SCHÜTZE, HINRICH; HULL, DAVID; PEDERSEN, JAN. 1995. A Comparison of Classifiers and Document Representations for the Routing Problem. In: Fox, Edward A.; Ingwersen, Peter; Fidel, Raya, eds. SIGIR '95: Proceedings of the Association for Computing Machinery Special Interest Group on Information Retrieval (ACM/SIGIR) 18th Annual International Conference on Research and Development in Information Retrieval; 1995 July 9-13; Seattle, WA. New York, NY: ACM Press; 1995. 229-237. ISBN: 0-89791-714-6.

SESHADRI, V.; WEISS, SHOLOM M.; SASISEKHARAN, RAGURAM. 1995. Feature Extraction for Massive Data Mining. In: Proceedings of the International Conference on Knowledge Discovery and Data Mining (KDD-95); 1995 August 20-21; Montreal, Canada. Menlo Park, CA: AAAI Press; 1995. 258-262. ISBN: 0-929280-82-2.

SODERLAND, STEPHEN; LEHNERT, WENDY. 1995. Learning Domain-Specific Discourse Rules for Information Extraction. In: Empirical Methods in Discourse Interpretation and Generation: Papers from the 1995 AAAI Spring Symposium; 1995 March; Palo Alto, CA. Menlo Park, CA: AAAI Press; 1995. 143-148. ISBN: 0-929280-89-X.

STARR, BRIAN; ACKERMAN, MARK S.; PAZZANI, MICHAEL. 1996. Do I Care?—Tell Me What's Changed on the Web. In: Machine Learning in Information Access: Papers from the 1996 AAAI Spring Symposium; Stanford, CA. Menlo Park, CA: AAAI Press; 1996. 119-121. ISBN: 1-57735-007-3.

THOMPSON, P. 1991. Machine Learning in the Combination of Expert Opinion Approach to IR. In: Proceedings of the 8th International Workshop on Machine Learning; 1991 June; Evanston, IL. San Mateo, CA: Morgan Kaufmann; 1991. 270-274. ISBN: 1-55860-200-3.

TOWELL, G.; VOORHEES, ELLEN M.; GUPTA, NARENDRA K.; JOHNSON-LAIRD, BEN. 1995. Learning Collection Fusion Strategies for Information Retrieval. In: Proceedings of the 12th International Conference on Machine Learning; 1995 July 9-12; Tahoe City, CA. San Francisco, CA: Morgan Kaufmann; 1995. 540-548. ISBN: 1-55860-377-8.

TSENG, YUEN-HSIEN. 1998. Solving Vocabulary Problems with Interactive Query Expansion. Journal of Library & Information Science. 1998 April; 24(1): 1-18. ISSN: 0363-3640.

UTGOFF, PAUL E. 1989. Incremental Induction of Decision Trees. Machine Learning. 1989; 4: 161-186. ISSN: 0885-6125.

VOORHEES, ELLEN M.; GUPTA, NARENDRA K.; JOHNSON-LAIRD, BEN. 1995. Learning Collection Fusion Strategies. In: Fox, Edward A.; Ingwersen, Peter; Fidel, Raya, eds. SIGIR '95: Proceedings of the Association for Computing Machinery Special Interest Group on Information Retrieval (ACM/SIGIR) 18th Annual International Conference on Research and Development in Information Retrieval; 1995 July 9-13; Seattle, WA. New York, NY: ACM Press; 1995. 172-179. ISBN: 0-89791-714-6.

WILLETT, PETER. 1988. Recent Trends in Hierarchical Document Clustering: A Critical Review. Information Processing & Management. 1988; 24(5): 577-597. ISSN: 0306-4573.

WITTEN, IAN H.; FRANK, EIBE. 2000. Data Mining: Practical Machine Learning Tools and Techniques with JAVA Implementations. San Francisco, CA: Morgan Kaufmann; 2000. 371p. ISBN: 1-55860-552-5.

WITTEN, IAN H.; MOFFAT, ALISTAIR; BELL, TIMOTHY C. 1994. Managing Gigabytes. New York, NY: Van Nostrand Reinhold; 1994. 429p. ISBN: 0-442-01863-0.

YAGER, R. R.; RYBALOV, A. 1998. On the Fusion of Documents from Multiple Collection Information Retrieval Systems. Journal of the American Society for Information Science. 1998; 49(13): 1177-1184. ISSN: 0002-8231.

YANG, JING-JYE; KORFHAGE, ROBERT R. 1994. Query Modification Using Genetic Algorithms in Vector Space Models. International Journal of Expert Systems. 1994; 7(2): 165-191. ISSN: 0894-9077.

7   Text Mining

WALTER J. TRYBULA
International SEMATECH

INTRODUCTION

The amount of information is exploding. Essayist and scientist Philip Morrison ponders the magnitude of recorded information. The ancient library at Alexandria contained approximately 600,000 scrolls, which Morrison estimates is the equivalent of 50,000 books (or this author's estimate of 50 gigabyes (billion bytes) of information). The Library of Congress contains 20 million books consisting of 20 terabytes (20,000 billion bytes) of information. Sound recordings add another petabyte (million billion bytes) of information. New books and newspapers add another 100 terabytes each year. The century's movies add another petabyte and home movies add 10 petabytes. Television adds 100 petabytes per year and telephony adds several thousand petabytes (or exebytes) of data annually (MORRISON & MORRISON). Many challenges face the information community in being able to effectively manage this accumulation. Many diverse efforts are investigating various aspects of "mining" information. Textual information is expanding beyond the ability of people to manage and understand its content without computer assistance. The impact of information on both governments and industry is large so it is important to focus on obtaining knowledge from disparate sources of information.

This chapter is a review of the state of research in text mining. DIXON defines the process of text mining as finding interesting or useful patterns in a corpus of unstructured textual information, combining many of the techniques of information extraction, information retrieval, natural-language processing, and document summarization. The key use for document mining is to elicit previously unknown knowledge locked away in a volume of text.

Annual Review of Information Science and Technology (*ARIST*), Volume 34, 1999
Martha E. Williams, Editor
Published for the American Society for Information Science (ASIS)
By Information Today, Inc., Medford, NJ

Text mining relies on computers to manipulate documents in electronic textual repositories or textbases. For almost 30 years, computing power has been increasing at approximately 30% per year (Moore's Law). Tasks that were not possible on supercomputers in the early 1980s are now possible on desktop systems, especially the more powerful computers developed in the last two years.

Data storage has become less expensive as computing power has increased, so more information is being stored. Organizations are producing 60% to 100% more data annually (TIOGO). It is predicted that by the year 2000, as much as 75% of investments in information technology will be dedicated to storage. When databases came online, there was an increasing need to mine them for knowledge that is lost in the data. As more information now is in the form of reports and other textual forms, there is an increasing need to mine for knowledge that is lost in the textbase. Text mining can provide a means of developing knowledge links and knowledge sharing among people within organizations. With more powerful computers and a need from government and industry to manage the vast quantity of information, text mining is an area that will have explosive growth in order to address these information challenges.

From another viewpoint, the ability to mine textbases is also becoming more important as more information is created electronically. It has been estimated that over 80% of all written material first occurs in electronic form. In a related statistic, an IBM (1997) article stated that 80% of the world's electronic data is in text form (based on bit count). The ability to evaluate the information in its electronic form can provide an advantage to people who are becoming overwhelmed with information. The popular press has referred to "knowledge storms" to describe the overwhelming amount of information received by the average person. Initial efforts in text mining appear to be promising as methods for uncovering hidden information in textbases. The implications are that the successful implementation of such methods can provide researchers with unsuspected insights into previously published material (SWANSON; TRYBULA, 1997, pp. 203-204).

Scope

This is the second *ARIST* chapter on information mining. The first chapter, by TRYBULA (1997), addressed "Data Mining and Knowledge Discovery." The focus of this chapter is on newer developments in mining information contained in textbases. The primary material for this chapter was published from mid-1997 to early 1999, although some earlier publications that have influenced the development of text mining are included. While there is considerable referencing of data-mining activities, which have continued to escalate, this review concentrates on the state of text mining.

This chapter is organized into six major sections: Introduction, Background, Comparison of Text Mining to Data Mining, Research Areas, Software Products, and Conclusions.

Text mining, document mining, data mining of text, and knowledge discovery in text documents are some of the terms applied to this weakly defined process. The development of text mining has been viewed as an extension of data mining by the research community. This review shows Trybula's 1997 review to be an oversimplification: text mining is significantly more complex than data mining. The intent here is to describe the disparate investigations currently included under the term text mining and provide a cohesive structure for these efforts. A summary of existing research identifies the key organizations responsible for pushing the development of text mining. A section is devoted to text-mining software products. The final section, Conclusions, presents the author's opinion of the research areas that need to be addressed in order to enhance the functionality of text mining.

Terminology

Text mining is a field in its infancy. Terminology is evolving. In order to provide an opportunity for researchers to develop commonality in their descriptions, the text-mining definitions are added to those of data mining and knowledge discovery.

- Database refers to an organized collection of stored data. It normally refers to active data and not to compilations of historical data. The database need not reside in a single location but can reside in numerous, spatially distinct systems. Textbases are repositories of electronic textual information. Textbases are historical compilations of electronic information that previously may not have been organized.
- Data mining (DM) is the basic process employed to analyze patterns in data and extract information. This includes data cleaning (also called cleansing) and validation. The objective is to generate rather than to verify a hypothesis about the selected data. Many applications involve large databases with customer information that can be investigated to glean insights on customer behavior given various marketing incentives. Text mining is the basic process to analyze patterns in text and present information. This process includes cleaning and valida-

tion. Validation is more difficult to develop for text than for data. Text mining requires the ability to perform stemming (isolating roots of words) and, ideally, identifying parts of speech (noun, verb, adverb, etc.).

- Knowledge discovery (KD) is the process of transforming data into previously unknown or unsuspected relationships that can be employed as predictors of future actions. The author proposes the term knowledge discernment for the equivalent process for text mining.

- Knowledge discovery of databases (KDD) is a term that has been employed to encompass both DM and KD. There is no equivalent term for text mining. In order to minimize confusion due to a multiplicity of terms, this review employs the term KDD to describe the entire knowledge acquisition process.

- Undiscovered public knowledge (SWANSON; SWANSON & SMALHEISER) refers to the creation of knowledge by acquiring similar but apparently unrelated information from textbases with different information schemas. The development of novel ideas from text mining and knowledge discernment is precisely the objective of Swanson's work. As is shown later in this chapter, this process is not an automated knowledge process but requires a domain expert to evaluate the results.

BACKGROUND

While the research efforts of text mining are increasing due to the availability of the necessary computing power, the concept of analyzing text with a computer has a long history. In his 1967 book, *Automated Language Processing: The State of the Art*, BORKO (1967a) indicates the idea for the book was suggested in 1964. In the foreword, OETTINGER says Warren Weaver wrote a memorandum in 1950 that urged researchers to find out whether a computer could be employed to translate text from one language to another, a task that would also require an understanding of the structure of language. Borko's book, 17 years later, concentrates on the application of computers to the study of language and the processing of data presented as natural tasks. Three chapters, "Indexing and Classification" (BORKO, 1967b), "Extracting and Abstracting by Computer" (WYLLYS), and "Stylistic Analysis" (SEDELOW & SEDELOW), provide an overview of the state of the art in text analysis in 1967.

When reviewing this material, one must remember that in the late 1960s, computers were massive devices that were available on a very limited basis. Applications (jobs) were billed based on CPU time used, to the hundredth of a second. One hour of processing time in 1970 could exceed the cost of personal computers found on desks throughout businesses in 1999. Processing power was extremely limited compared to 1999. Magnetic memory was also very expensive and physically large because it normally consisted of wound ferrite cores. Programs were run in batch mode, that is, data were submitted together for processing, queued, processed, and results delivered. This sequence of running a program and obtaining results might extend beyond one day, so extensive interactive evaluations were rare. The focus was on devising schemes that would conceptualize the information and present it to the researcher with a minimal amount of computing power.

Today's machines have more computational power and significantly more memory, are interactive, and may be dedicated to a certain task. The emergence of text mining is substantially due to the availability of the computing power that is widespread in the late 1990s, almost 50 years after what is being called text mining was suggested.

In his earlier *ARIST* chapter TRYBULA (1997, p. 223) indicates that there was little published literature on data mining or knowledge discovery in textual databases. One publication by WOLVERTON & HAYES-ROTH was the only article cited. A search of available databases in mid 1998 revealed only 40 applicable citations. A similar search of the World Wide Web resulted in fewer than 1,000 references. However, a culling of duplicate references, student Web pages (mainly pointing to WEBSOM, a Web mapping program), and sites with "mining" in their pathnames resulted in fewer than 100 sites with possible relevant information. A further analysis resulted in fewer than 40 relevant sites. In many cases, the information reflected material presented at conferences and duplicated information from searches of published sources. A search of LEXIS/NEXIS at the end of 1998 resulted in one additional source. With so few direct references, it appears that this can be considered an embryonic field. This is not completely surprising because the computing power to perform the necessary analyses has only recently become available to the mainstream researcher.

Significant research activity is currently published on the Web. Some key sources are indicated in this chapter and in the Bibliography. The author will attempt to maintain a link to the more recent text mining developments by providing a Web page on text mining at http://www.tryb.org/tmkd/default.htm. Company sites are excellent sources of information on the latest developments, as are trade magazines such as *KNOWLEDGE MANAGEMENT* and *KM WORLD*.

There is a Text REtrieval Conference (TREC), which is sponsored by the United States National Institute of Standards and Technology and DARPA. The goal of TREC is to bring research groups together to discuss work on a large test collection using automated thesauri, term weighting, natural-language techniques, relevance feedback, and advanced pattern matching.

COMPARISON OF TEXT MINING TO DATA MINING

In order to understand the development of text mining, it is helpful to consider data mining. The differences are primarily in the information structures being mined and in parts of the mining process itself.

Information Structure

Data mining and knowledge discovery have been proven as a means of uncovering hidden information in alphanumeric databases. These databases are based on fields in relational or flat file structures. There is a correlation between the fields and the information contained in them: the name field contains the person's name, the address fields contain the person's location, another field may contain the person's purchases, etc. Through the process of data mining the data are made consistent in content and character in a given field. The knowledge discovery aspect of this process might be developing a correlation between certain products and a given description of the purchaser that might provide the researcher with insights on buying activities. The connectivity of data is a fundamental property of the database. This fact and the availability of inexpensive computing power have encouraged the widespread application of these tools. There have been many successful implementations of data mining. Computer software programs (tools) automate the process of analyzing data in these databases and delivering information about consumer behavior.

Textbases are collections of free-form connected discourse. Unlike databases, textbases are not fully predictable in content or format. This author separates textbases into two distinct categories. The first is the structured textbase, which contains textual material in consistent locations in documents. Examples are bibliographic records, police reports, product specification sheets, and corporate financial reports. The content may vary, but the structure is relatively consistent, like that of a database, which easily lends itself to mining. The second category is free-form unstructured information. Examples include reports, publications, and the majority of textual documentation.

Both structured and unstructured textbases can be divided into two content categories: fact and fiction. The author does not purport to limit text mining and knowledge discernment to one content category or the other. The desired results from investigating one category may be significantly different from the other. SWANSON's Undiscovered Public Knowledge pursues the obtaining of new insights by examining contextually related but bibliographically distinct fields. This focus assumes that the investigation is examining factual documentation, as evidenced by Swanson's work in the medical field. One can envision a similar examination of works of fiction to find correlations that identify an author or to investigate an author's change in focus over time.

One final aspect of textbases is the actual content that is mined. Historically, the presence of bibliographic metadata has been a tangible asset. Documents published through traditional channels have a series of identifiers that can be employed to locate them, such as a book's ISBN or Library of Congress Control Number, or an article's report number or location in a technical journal. Many Web sites contain documents that have not completed the traditional publication path (often referred to as gray information) and thus may not have permanent identifiers. An example is Web sites at educational institutions. While the author is active at the institution, the site is normally maintained. Shortly after the author leaves, the site first becomes static and then disappears. Today the majority of new material exists in electronic form, and sometimes only in electronic form. Assessing the accuracy and integrity of the textbase is a challenge, but is not part of text-mining tools.

Until tools are readily available, it is difficult to predict the purposes for which they will employed. The focus of this chapter is the state of the research, not predicting applications.

Mining Process

Text mining is very similar to data mining except that the focus is a collection of textual documents (textbase). Employing the terminology presented by the author in "Data Mining and Knowledge Discovery" (TRYBULA, 1997), Figure 1 is a description of the knowledge discernment process. Knowledge discernment develops the evaluation of the results of text mining into some knowledge that might not have been anticipated. The process begins with (1) information acquisition. The text is typically gathered from textbases at various sources. In order to be useful, the text must be found, combined, cleaned, and transformed into an organized document repository (a computer storage textbase that contains both unpublished and published documents). The representation of a single image for the document repository in the figure does not imply that it cannot exist in multiple computers spread across spatially distant locations. Based on a task definition and desired goals, a selection is made of manuscripts from the document repository. These manuscripts are compiled into a preprocessed textbase in a manner similar to building a database repository for data mining. Transforming the resulting manuscripts provides a textbase of usable information for the tools (programs) to evaluate. A key element in the mining process is to determine the characteristics of the textbase. Because the development of the textbase does not require any human classification or categorization of the text, the computer must accomplish the (2) extraction process. Figure 1 shows some elements of the information extraction process that are the focus of research efforts. The purpose of extraction is to provide a means of categorizing the information so that relationships can be identified. The (3) text-mining effort involves clustering in order to provide a manageable size of textbase relationships that can be evaluated during information searches. When the text is analyzed (mined) for relationships, the results are (4) presented in either visualizations or textual summarizations. The person investigating the information must determine whether new knowledge is evident. An alternative outcome is the ability to browse the information and seek new relationships in the text being mined. To date, no methods are available for automatically determining whether new knowledge has been discovered: this requires human intervention.

The differences between data mining and text mining begin with transformation of the data. Data mining can employ algorithms to look for relationships or correlations among data sets to discover novel connections. Text mining can provide similar relationships or correlations of high occurrences of certain text patterns; however, the operator must decide whether there is meaning behind the results and in many cases further explore the results to determine what these correlations actually mean, tasks that require significantly more understanding of the information content.

Text-mining instruments have a variety of means for presenting information. One approach is to provide a visualization of the relationships among various aspects of the text. Some of the concepts in this chapter were reviewed in 1995 by WILLIAMS ET AL. in an *ARIST* chapter, "Visualization." Two years later (1997), WHITE & MCCAIN produced an *ARIST* chapter, "Visualization of Literatures," that examines some of the visualization tools that are now being classified as text-mining instruments. The presentation of the information can be as simple as a series of short summaries of each relevant document or a hierarchical relationship with correlations identified by linkages. Interpretation of the results is still the responsibility of the user. In the case of technical or scientific information, the domain expert has the ability to provide the best insight on the results. It is from the output of text-mining instruments that knowledge discernment occurs.

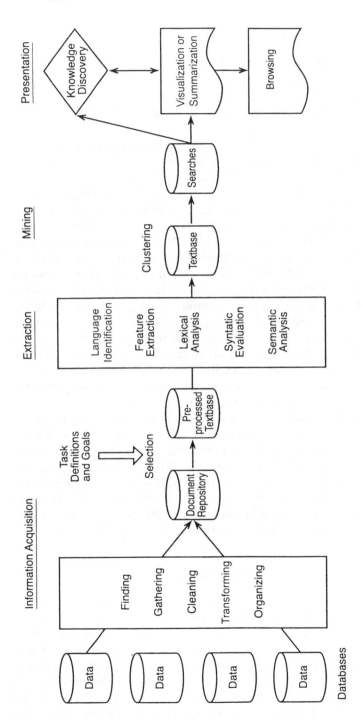

Figure 1. Knowledge discernment process

RESEARCH AREAS

The research efforts are divided into five areas shown in Figure 1: information acquisition, extraction, mining and its subprocess of clustering, and presentation. Extraction and mining can be considered the heart of text mining, while presentation is the key to knowledge discernment.

The best overview description of the text-mining process was published in early 1998 by TKACH. Tkach looks at business applications where e-mail or intranet documents can be mined.

The acquisition of documents and development of a target textbase depend on the type of documents being evaluated. The mining of e-mail provides a good example of a focus on a particular structure. LOTUS DEVELOPMENT CORPORATION has been developing its Lotus Domino Notes program to provide a mechanism for collaboration among workers. The ability to provide a predefined structure for the mining program is a major factor in development of efficient delivery mechanisms. Documents with common formats, such as news feeds, business reports, or product descriptions can be more readily compiled. When the documents include presentation foils, spreadsheets, or detailed technical reports, compilation is more difficult. A problem is determining what documents to include and where to find these documents. With the global nature of communications, it is also important to determine the language of the documents.

A number of higher educational institutions conduct research involving some aspect of text mining. This is not a comprehensive list but represents universities that have published information reviewed in this chapter. These include University of California, Berkeley (USA), Brooklyn Polytechnic (USA), Cornell University (USA), Queens University (Canada), Syracuse University (USA), the University of Freiburg (Germany), the University of Helsinki (Finland), the University of Jena (Germany), and the Vienna University of Technology (Austria).

Information Acquisition

The purpose of information acquisition is to find and bring together textual information that will be later processed and mined for information. The information (or document) acquisition process consists of selecting the correct documents from the entire set available and transforming them into a usable target textbase. The target textbase provides a coherent set of information intended to meet the needs of the desired exploratory investigation. Natural-language technology can be employed to insure that the documents contain the correct characteristics. This may include screening documents to maintain a certain threshold level of terminology, relevance to the user's goals, or new information.

A particular mindset is required for developing a textbase. Historically, one strategy is to group documents according to subject matter. Libraries organize their information this way, using classification systems such as Dewey Decimal. For example, books about European history are placed in one location, and books on computer science in another. If there are, say, 2,000 books on European history, they must be subdivided into finer categories. However, the topic of European history can be subdivided by nation, by economic changes, by political movements, by cultural characteristics, and so on. Although the topics are interrelated, it is necessary to classify books under one subject because books are physical objects that can be in only one place at a time (HEARST, 1997). With electronic textbases, this process is typically not employed in text mining.

Although physical objects can often be assigned one place in a taxonomy (e.g., a truck is a kind of vehicle), textual documents are not so simply classified. Text consists of discussions of multiple abstract ideas and their relationships and of metadata (e.g., source, date, genre, author) (HEARST, 1997). Information extraction must consider the type of information required for the investigation.

Another area for consideration is the electronic format of the text. Some techniques accept only ASCII text (MANAGEMENT INFORMATION TECHNOLOGIES, INCORPORATED). Another technique accepts a variety of formats and converts them to ASCII for mining. A third technique works with SGML-formatted text (AHONEN ET AL., 1997a). SGML provides an advantage in that it systematically indicates text structures, such as headings, that can be employed in mining. The selection of text-handling technique is important not only for mining, but also for presentation of results.

The appropriateness of certain information retrieval techniques for use in textbase compilation and the appropriateness of documents retrieved are not covered in this work. Information retrieval is a separate topic. HARTER & HERT also address approaches to information retrieval in the 1997 volume of *ARIST*. The type of material captured depends on the result desired by the user.

Extraction

The purpose of extraction is to develop a textbase that can be analyzed (mined) for insights into the combined contents of the documents. The process of extracting information from the textbase requires the capability of analyzing the content. This raises several questions.

How does one extract information? What are the guidelines? What type of information? What is the user seeking? What are the important items? These questions, which DIXON calls formalizing the mining problem, are part of the extraction process.

The first step is identification of the language of the documents. Multiple-language documents require the ability to process all the languages involved. For each language separate processing must be performed and the results combined at the conclusion of the processing. The processing of the text starts with the development of tuples that represent content and metadata about the document. Among the analyses performed are feature extraction, which can include names, multiple-word phrases, abbreviations, other specialized vocabulary, and domain-specific knowledge. A lexical analysis provides a syntactic evaluation of the document, which then permits semantic analysis of the terminology. The semantic analysis correlates groups of words appearing in proximity to each other. It eliminates the need to build a lexicon or thesaurus, although it could be structured to provide one if this aids the presentation of information. The semantic analysis also provides the ability to develop a factual integration of document concepts. Having this information about each individual document permits the evaluation of the set of documents in the textbase.

The NATURAL LANGUAGE PROCESSING GROUP (NLPG) of the Artificial Intelligence Laboratory at the Swiss Federal Institute of Technology focuses on knowledge extraction from textual data based on information retrieval techniques using a distributed semantic approach. Semantic proximities are derived from co-frequency matrixes computed on large textual corpora. Different similarity measures are used to characterize the proximity between queries and documents, which are represented as projections in n-dimensional space. Methods for automatic production of syntactic tools are the implementation of probabilistic techniques and models operating on textual corpora to adapt generic algorithms to specific applications, part-of-speech tagging, speech recognition, information retrieval, etc. Applications include user-sensitive structuring of large collections of textual data. Information structuring is essential because it constitutes a necessary basis for efficient visualization of large amounts of textual data. Structuring is a central step toward information clustering and filtering. It is needed to provide efficient access to information and avoid huge amounts of retrieved data. Techniques based on curvilinear analysis are considered for the extraction of the intrinsic topological information from the textbase. Natural-language processing is employed to preprocess the textbase using lemmatization, or identification of syntactic structures. NLPG also uses probabilistic parsing and automatic structuring of textbases. NLPG mentions the GRACE and the ELSE projects. SALTON

& BUCKLEY present natural-language processing in a UNIX program, SMART, where contiguous words are stemmed, sorted in alphabetical order, and joined by an underscore.

TKACH discusses the IBM Intelligent Miner for Text, which contains tools to identify languages, extract key information from text, organize documents by subject, find predominant themes in a collection of documents, and search for relevant documents using flexible queries. The feature extraction component recognizes significant vocabulary items in the text, such as people's names, organization names, places, abbreviations, dates, currency, and multiword items.

AHONEN ET AL. (1998) develops a method that starts with SGML text and preprocesses it, then performs a morphological analysis and selects, filters, and converts it. Perform and episode rule algorithms then convert it again to episode rules. (Episode rules are a modification of association rules and frequent sets applied to sequential data.) The phases of the discovery process are data preprocessing (selection, cleaning, etc.), data transformation and input selection for the discovery phase, discovery of episode and episode rules, presentation of the results, and interpretation and utilization of the results.

SCHNATTINGER & HAHN develop statistical lexical approaches to text analysis that are restricted to simple document referral services to provide references to relevant documents. Text analysis must cope with linguistic knowledge sources (grammars, lexicons) and domain knowledge sources (ontologies). Concept learning is an evidence-based solution that balances clues from the structure of text with conceptual structures in the knowledge base. HAHN & SCHNATTINGER (1997a) develop a method that updates domain knowledge through data mining, interpretation, and cleaning to a terminological reasoning process. HAHN & SCHNATTINGER (1997b) build on Schnattinger & Hahn and generate hypotheses, rank them by plausibility, and select the most credible hypotheses for knowledge extraction.

The COINS (Collaborative Information Acquisition) project develops concept indexes to present information in a personalized manner. The information in a dynamic set of registered documents that have key phrases identified will evolve to text passages and annotations. Nodes are concepts that are paraphrased by sets of synonymous key phrases. The nodes are related through correlations, citations through similarity, or persons by fields of interest. Nodes are cross-referenced with their occurrences and thesauri and ontologies are created to express conceptual knowledge. With automated data mining, COINS is said to be applicable for extracting concepts from documents.

IBM ITALY claims to extract useful information from large electronic textbases. The process requires formatted fields describing the document by terms in descriptor fields. Patents and most technical and research publications satisfy this requirement. The program, which employs relational data analysis by IBM European Centre for Applied Mathematics in Paris, automatically classifies the documents into groups that are as distinct as possible from each other. It provides a visual summary of the analysis, showing different groups in a map with keywords characterizing each group.

Terminology Framework is a generic approach to building thesauri and dictionaries and has developed various tools under the acronym of PaVE (Publication and Visualization Environment). PaVE uses a grammar to parse text files of terminology resources and transform entries into frame-based target models. A graphical interface presents the data and provides a means of manipulating the conceptual net structures (PAVE). Text Analysis Tool with Object Encoding (TATOE) (ALEXA & ROSTEK, 1999) develops pattern concordances that use the XGrammar program from PaVE. The text analysis empirically identifies features that are specific to the text type analyzed. The corpus is automatically tagged with part-of-speech information and then imported into TATOE. The imported text contains structure markers and tags (morphological, content, and discourse markup). TATOE separates the text into a categorization scheme for further analysis. It communicates with external data repositories such as WordNet of the Merged Upper Model linguistic ontology, and exports the text as SGML.

SINGH ET AL. indicate that most data-mining research focuses on generating rules within databases containing structured values. They suggest an approach for generating association rules relating structured values to concepts that includes pointers to a concept hierarchy to help maintain relationships. They also discuss the ABI/Inform information retrieval system, which contains a thesaurus of subject indexing terms. Associated with each concept in this thesaurus is a list of broader, narrower, and related terms. Sets of thesaurus concepts were identified and developed by a domain expert. The thesaurus has three levels of relationships: parent rules, children rules, and sibling (synonym) rules.

AHONEN ET AL. (1997b) state that text may be considered sequential data (a sequence of pairs such as a feature vector or index). It is necessary to preprocess text, select or filter it, and then convert it to provide a morphological analysis. This is followed by needs conversion, postprocessing, pruning, grouping, and ordering. The document has a base form, inflected work form, a stem, a grammatical feature, a question mark or other special character, and an SGML tag. Preprocessing is straightforward. Ahonen et al. have explored grammatical rules that indicate dependency collocations that include predicative relations, rigid noun phrases, and phrasal templates with empty slots, and co-occurring terms.

FELDMAN & DAGAN establish meaningful concepts for text that can be developed as a hierarchical ordering of the concepts and investigate relationships among concepts and among documents. FELDMAN ET AL. present the Document Explorer that can construct a textbase from a document collection. Text mining is achieved through the application of concept graphs. Document Explorer has the ability to work with a wide range of documents.

The DECIDE project, 1994-1996, was directed at designing and evaluating extraction tools for collocations in dictionaries and corpora. Its Lexicon evaluates the function of the word in the language structure and includes the most common forms of collocation and their frequency of occurrence in the corpus.

MCNEMAR discusses a set of tools capable of scanning textbases for references, acronyms, misspellings, and inconsistencies in technical documents. The Acronym Checker defines anything with two or more capital letters as an acronym. The tools examine phrases such as "refer to see" and document serial numbers as references. Word Finder matches a single word or phrase against an input file. Spell Checker checks against a standard list. An HTML converter provides Web document inclusion. There is also a short description of the Automated Requirement Measurement Tool (ARM).

Mining

Mining is the process of analyzing textbases and developing methods for presenting results to the user. Currently the most popular method is clustering, which is discussed in the next section. Other options include employing metadata, developing thesauri, and establishing category labels.

Most documents have some kinds of metadata, such as author(s), date of publication, length, publisher, and genre. BALDONADO & WINOGRAD explore issues associated with table format interfaces for exploiting this kind of information. In searches, metadata are treated as labels and matched against other labels to find documents.

Researchers are investigating automatic thesaurus creation, most often using word co-occurrences. Thesaurus terms are related to category labels. Category labels are used to classify document contents according to general subject areas and other semantic attributes. Categories are created by the set of documents to which they are assigned, and are identified by labels. These labels are used as a kind of metadata, and category labels are matched against other labels in searching.

Category labels or subject codes (such as those in Dewey Decimal numbering) are commonly employed for identification. Some online text collections now have large subject hierarchy codes (also identified as keywords) associated with them. Three to five terms are assigned by authors to their journal articles to indicate the subject matter.

Categories provide a good means of retrieving information. In most systems, including many World Wide Web interfaces, the user must peruse a list of categories to find those of interest. Unfortunately, the user is usually not given an overview of the category space other than a top-level view of the most general labels. Systems that let the user browse category labels present this information as an alphabetical list, with corresponding documents listed under appropriate labels. For text mining, context and structure should play an important role. A critical aspect of a text pattern is the distributions of the terms that comprise it. The frequency of each term, how each term is distributed in the text, and where the terms overlap within the document are especially important in long texts.

Categorization in the context of text mining means automatic assignment of documents to preexisting categories, sometimes called topics or themes. These could be, for example, the folders on a desktop interface, which are usually organized by topics or themes. The categories are chosen to match the intended use of the collection and must be designated beforehand. Any document can be assigned to an organization scheme and linked automatically to its category. Assigning documents to categories helps to organize them. Although automatic categorization cannot replace manual cataloging by a librarian, it does provide a much less expensive alternative. In addition, it can be useful in many other applications. It costs at least $25 to have a librarian manually catalog an item, which is clearly impractical for the millions of documents on the Internet. A negative of automatic categorization is that the text could be assigned to too many schemes.

Clustering

Clustering techniques from data mining have migrated into text mining. In text mining, clustering is used to segment a document collection into subsets, with the members of each subset being similar with respect to certain features. This technique distinguishes text mining from a simple search engine. The ability to retrieve text references is not difficult. The problem is that too large a volume of retrieved documents makes it difficult for users to find information. When searching, the user may move from one document to another looking for dominant themes or similar documents in a collection. Clustering helps this process. Unfortunately, clustering forces a structure onto naturally unstructured documents. The challenge is to find a method that is simple and efficient, yet provides enough structure to reveal interesting information.

Clustering depends on some measure of interdocument similarity. One approach is to represent documents as vectors of equal length, where each component of a vector is associated with one of the unique content words in the document collection. The vector component may indicate the frequency, normalized or not, of a word in the document. Single-linkage hierarchical clustering is a commonly used method. It is, however, too slow for even moderately large document collections. Beginning with individual documents, single-linkage hierarchical clustering iteratively agglomerates the most similar pairs of clusters into a new cluster. The global consideration of all pairwise similarities at each stage of clustering leads to extensive computer run times.

Similarity searching ranks documents according to location proximity. In multidimensional term space, combinations of document terms are matched to combinations of query terms. The closer two documents are to one another in term space, the more topics they are assumed to have in common. This may not be a reasonable assumption for comparing long documents.

Hierarchical clustering develops a tree with related clusters in the same branch of the tree, while the binary relational approach generates a flat cluster structure. The algorithm for a hierarchy starts with a set of singleton clusters, each containing a single document, which appear as leaves at the bottom of the tree. Starting with the leaves, the algorithm identifies the pairs of clusters that are most similar and merges them into a single cluster. This process is iterated until only one cluster, the root, is left. When two clusters are merged, their intracluster similarity is calculated. The singleton clusters have an intracluster similarity of 100% because they contain only one document. The binary tree constructed during the clustering process contains the complete clustering information including all inter- and intracluster similarities. The intercluster similarity between two arbitrary clusters is the intracluster similarity of the first common cluster.

The binary tree can become very deep and contain a lot of clusters with only a few documents. These binary trees are inconvenient to visualize, so a further processing step is applied. Clusters within the same branch that have a comparable intracluster similarity are merged into a single cluster. This reduces the depth of the tree and facilitates browsing or further processing.

To determine document similarity, the vocabulary of the document is analyzed in a linguistic preprocessing step. The identified terms for a document are collected in term vectors. These vectors are compared to each other. The term vector of a cluster is a merge of the term vectors of its subcultures.

A lexical affinity is the correlation of a group of words that appear frequently within short distances of each other throughout the given documents. Examples of lexical affinities are phrases like "online library" or "computer hardware." Lexical affinities are generated dynamically and are specific to each collection.

The notion of similarity between documents and clusters is crucial to obtain high-quality groupings of information. Extracting only single words from documents and using their degree of overlap as a similarity measure is rather imprecise and noisy due to the great amount of lexical ambiguity of single words.

Ideally, a semantic analysis of the documents should be performed to identify the concepts mentioned in the text as a basis for clustering. However, this kind of analysis is very expensive and depends on a lot of domain-specific knowledge that must be constructed manually or obtained from other sources.

The extraction of lexical affinities is superior to an expensive semantic analysis because it is a domain-independent solution. It can derive a set of semantically rich terms without requiring a hand-coded specialized lexicon or a domain-specific thesaurus. For feature extraction in text mining, the following simplified scenario can be assumed: the database is a collection of documents within which the only explicit structure is an unordered set of arbitrarily complex textual data. An important aspect of this scenario is to determine the criteria by which documents are related.

In general, information about common properties of documents can be retrieved from the natural vocabulary of the documents. Often domain terms or names characterize the content of a document. The vocabulary is generated automatically; no predefined vocabulary is necessary.

TURENNE & ROUSSELOT provide an evaluation of four clustering methods used in text mining, based on certain relational characteristics: (1) ascendance, which constructs itself toward a root; (2) hierarchy, which builds closed linked objects into tree-like structures; (3) incremental, which preserves the internal structure; and (4) overlapping, which permits membership in multiple classes. Clustering develops a posteriori definition of information organization, whereas classification requires preexisting classes. The authors describe their program, Classification by Tralogie, as based on the distance between two vectors in the co-occurrence matrix. Their Sampler provides terms with strong statistical links in the corpus. The classification is based on the coefficient of statistical association from the co-occurrences between the two terms. Neurotext is a textual analysis tool that allows indexing, key terms, and content analysis by semantically classed phrases. Alceste is a textual analysis software grouping wherein contexts have similar semantic nature and their corpora are divided into context elements, classified according to syntax.

TKACH discusses clustering documents into groups that correspond to different themes. Hierarchical clustering builds sets of documents. Categorization assigns documents to preexisting topic or theme categories. Multiple types of queries including search engines can be used to interrogate the text. Knowledge management is based on four processes: (1) gathering, or bringing information into the system; (2) organizing by associating items with subjects, giving them context, and making them easier to find; (3) refining, or adding value by discovering relationships, abstracting, synthesizing, and sharing; and (4) disseminating, or getting knowledge to people who can use it.

D'ALESSIO ET AL. describe the assignment of documents to categories in a hierarchically organized taxonomy. This technique employs a training corpus of documents placed in various categories. Vocabulary is extracted and high-frequency words are then categorized. The vocabulary characterizing each subject area is associated with nodes in the hierarchy. The vocabulary is filtered and words are assigned weights with respect to specific categories. The technique is applied in user-sensitive structuring of large collections of textual data. There is a concentration of structuring of textual information according to implicit neighborhood properties (proximities), and a dynamic adaptation of the produced structures according to an implicit model of the user that has been automatically derived from the analysis of interactions with the information system. Information structuring is considered essential because it constitutes a necessary basis for efficient visualization of large amounts of textual data and could lead to the extraction of patterns. Global topological automatic properties are employed for visualization of the textbase as a whole and local properties for portions of the textbase selected after retrieval or during navigation. Syntactical analyses using natural-language processing techniques are also employed to preprocess the textual information base. This work employs a distributional semantic approach, where semantic proximities are derived from co-frequency matrixes computed on large textual corpora.

MERKL (1998) claims that classification is a central issue. He demonstrates an unsupervised neural network for document clustering that employs a hierarchically organized network built from self-organizing maps to represent the contents of a text archive and establish a document taxonomy. SPARKLE produces generic software able to conduct phrasal-level syntactic analysis of naturally occurring free text.

The search begins with a query. The mining retrieval tool must have several capabilities. It must be able to identify single concepts expressed as multiple words or to identify a concept with a category (a person or a phone number). A morphological analysis must be made to recognize synonyms and homonyms. The standard stop words are discarded in any mining. The actual mining query can be formulated for Boolean, free-text, hybrid, phonetic, or fuzzy searching. The results should be presented in a manner that permits access to the specific query-related point in the documents, for example, through use of a visualization map.

Presentation

The development of knowledge from information requires that the user be able to distinguish characteristics of the information being presented and transform that information into knowledge. The challenge is how to perform this task. A search engine that presents 1,000 different links challenges all but the most persistent user. The same problem exists for text-mining tools. A menu of results, even in some ranked order, requires the user to analyze the results and decide which information is useful. There are three different approaches for presenting the information: cross-correlations (full text), summaries (synopses), and visualizations (maps).

Cross-correlations. Full-text retrieval can be expected from a search engine. The user may be presented with the specific reference to a document with the key phrase highlighted. Another approach is to present the full-text document and require the user to search for the occurrence of query terms in the document.

HAHN & SCHNATTINGER (1997b) discuss failure to extract facts based on keywords, which has caused a move toward natural-language processing and machine learning. They describe experiments to develop a knowledge-based approach to the analysis of real-world natural-language texts. AZMY states that data mining is the natural evolution of query and reporting tools. Techniques include queries to extract sample data, classification, graphs and statistics to visualize and explore the data, summaries to group data, fact discovery, and organizers to arrange results. ETZIONI addresses data-mining techniques for HTML documents on the Web.

CHAKRABARTI ET AL. use taxonomy, discriminants, and signatures for navigating in text databases and require a system to search and navigate in taxonomies. Documents must be indexed on topic paths as well as on keywords in the taxonomy. The taxonomy should be employed to present a series of progressively refined views of the collection in response to queries. There should be topical query filtering; otherwise looking for the speed of a jaguar based on the query "jaguar AND speed" will not be effective. Context-sensitive signatures and feature selection are useful when looking for salient distinctions between two or more sets of documents.

Summaries. In existing text-mining efforts, the summary phrase approach permits the user to view a phrase with leading and following sentences or sentence fragments to indicate context. The user may be given the option to click on a highlighted phrase and be directed to the location of the phrase in the document or the user may be directed to the start of the document and be required to search for the occurrence within the document. The latter adds little to current search engine capabilities. Unless the instrument leads to the exact location of the phrase in context, the value of the summary is questionable. (This procedure should not be confused with the algorithmic generation of document summaries.)

Visualizations. Visualization is the presentation of an image that represents the information. This is an area under much development. Some approaches provide contour maps, such as ThemeScape by CARTIA, or provide a surface map without contour lines but with coloration changes, such as WEBSOM. Another approach is the presentation of linked phrases in a hierarchical tree, such as Inxight's Hyperbolic Tree (INXIGHT SOFTWARE INCORPORATED) or SemioMap by SEMIO CORPORATION. The output of these software programs provides the ability to investigate the phrasal relationship in context. The user needs to understand the links in order to follow the relationships indicated in the visualizations.

The development of a map is demonstrated by LAGUS in the Map of WSOM'97 Abstracts. This map contains 58 short abstracts from WSOM'97 that include the titles. In an example of employing the map to analyze information, Lagus observes that not all abstracts fell into their optimal cluster: only two sessions were well clustered, while several sessions did not provide any grouping of information. Lagus supposes that the difference was due to word choices. Many relations among the articles could not be visualized simultaneously, which can be considered a limitation of the tool.

Visualization provides some viewable relationships among phrases or terms that the user must decide how to process. It provides the beginning of the analysis but leaves the final interpretation to the user. At the DECISIONCENTRE, work is being done on visualization of textual relationships. The problem addressed is the definition of similarities of full-text documents based on semantic content for information retrieval. Clustering of texts is based on word categories. WEBSOM (self-organizing maps for Internet exploration) provides an ordered map of information space, where similar documents lie near each other on the map. The location of one document helps in finding related documents. It is possible to label the information space by attributes such as author or content. The process is that a high-level document showing the information space provides descriptions. The general view allows users to explore material instead of or prior to searching full text. Clicking on an area of interest allows the user to zoom in for a closer view. Navigational aids move the user in the information depth directions from the map to the corresponding document lists. The self-organizing process of WEBSOM is discussed by LAGUS. Some manual mapping and the WEBSOM methodology is described by HONKELA ET AL., who show the mapping of postings on the Usenet newsgroup comp.ai.neural-nets.

The presentation of information also has an impact on how the user perceives what is presented. SUGIMOTO ET AL. present the premise that if software can elicit different viewpoints from large information sources, users can reach new understandings that would not have been possible through discussions with other people alone. They propose a system that automatically elicits and visualizes different viewpoints of authors concerning certain topics from a textbase for journal and conference papers. The system consists of an indexed database that allows high-speed full-text searches. The textbase stores 1,300 papers and generates a term-frequency database. The system includes a search request-processing module that performs a full-text search, a browsing module that provides the full paper, and a visualization module that correlates relations among viewpoints of the documents, makes calculations to create visualization space, and displays the results.

HEARST (1997) discusses the impact of the type of material retrieved in Web searches. Popular and well-defined information is not difficult for users to interpret; the challenge is to interpret less-ordinary information. Software that can analyze text and manipulate large hierarchies of data provides different ways of examining text. Hearst's research in information visualization produced several useful techniques for transforming abstract data such as Yahoo's categorized list into displays that can be explored more intuitively. One strategy is to shift the user's mental load from slower thought-intensive processes, such as reading, to faster perceptual processes, such as pattern recognition.

At Xerox Parc (XEROX PALO ALTO RESEARCH CENTER), the Scatter/Gather technique was developed (HEARST, 1998). The user first retrieves the information suggested and has Scatter Gatherer analyze the information and separate it into groups. The user then can scan each cluster to select groups that are relevant and rerun the Scatter Gatherer. The program's TileBars display can aid users in determining which documents to view. This visualizer is an animated three-dimensional tree that permits exploration of the content of the textbase (XRCE).

Not all researchers agree that the only approach is to develop highly visual representations of textbases. An information system's design and functionality change along with changes in the nature of the data, the nature of data association, and the task the user is trying to perform. GUPTA ET AL. examine visual classification of data to help support the system's most important role: to capture the data and its semantic associations so users can perform meaningful tasks with the information. Information delivery is more effective when it can be delivered selectively through an expressive query (p. 40-41). The converse of this is also demonstrated by the fact that search engines are more comprehensive in delivering information but bury the user with meaningless data.

SOFTWARE PRODUCTS

The variety of commercial offerings is increasing rapidly. The descriptions are provided primarily in alphabetical order of the commercial name of the text-mining instrument. These descriptions focus on availability, functionality (retrieval, search, etc.), methodology, textbase format, internal format, and output mechanism.

AUTONOMY is a company that offers a set of knowledge management products that support numerous document formats. The software understands information as it is entered and can categorize it and provide hyperlinks to improve search capabilities. The Agentware software is a neural network that uses a pattern-matching technique to develop signatures of key concepts within text documents.

Cambio is a product of DATA JUNCTION CORPORATION. Cambio provides for the extraction of desired fields in a source file, which is accomplished by the user indicating the desired segments in the text file. Cambio converts files, which range from simple ASCII to complex database and spreadsheet formats, into an internal ASCII script and flattens each file into a table format. The output of this program can input to the Data Junction program for analysis.

CMS TextMap (CMS) is a visual program. The user must select the data sections that are to be analyzed. The program then performs a text parsing and processing function that can be employed to develop business applications, such as billing or shipping address lists.

CONCEPTUAL DIMENSIONS is a company that provides a service for Web-based text searches that includes feasibility analysis of a text search, classification, and routing within a collection. This service has been employed in the pharmaceutical industry.

ConSearch is a product of MANAGEMENT INFORMATION TECHNOLOGIES, INCORPORATED under the functionality of its Readware technology. It handles a large number of input document formats and develops an indexed collection of files. Phrase searching summarizes the usage of a phrase with the ability to view the full context of the phrase.

IBM DB2 Digital Library from IBM CHINA/HONG KONG is directed at multimedia objects and includes collection, organization, management, rights management, and distribution. The product automatically categorizes and indexes objects for later retrieval. The user can search by employing a metadata search or advanced text search to locate objects.

IBM INTELLIGENT MINER FOR TEXT (IBM, 1999), although identified as a single product, is really a series of programs that can be employed to evaluate information in e-mail, insurance claims, news feeds, patent portfolios, customer letters, etc. The system begins with a language identifier so that multiple-language documents can be analyzed. Clustering groups the documents by content and can employ user-specified categories. The output can be directed to specific individuals for further action.

iCrossReader is a proposed product of INSIGHTSOFT-M. The claim for this soon-to-be-released offering is that it develops on-demand results from Internet documents delivered by up to three selected search engines. It is said to develop relationships among information clusters. Its purpose is to compile a document that contains excerpts from the information files that were delivered by the search engines. The program then further develops related queries based on the initial results.

Intext is a program for the analysis of texts in the humanities and social sciences (KLEIN). Standard word-processor input is analyzed and a word list developed that contains single words, word sequences, and permutations. The program can be employed to develop an index or cross-reference list.

Inxight (INXIGHT SOFTWARE INCORPORATED) offers three visualization tools. The Hyperbolic Tree provides the ability to view relationships in an information domain, including contextual relationships along the perimeter. Table Lens is a tool for focusing on a narrow view of spreadsheet data. It provides large-area representations of numerous items by employing tiny lines of varying color and length to indicate feature values. The Cone Tree is a three-dimensional representation of data relationships in a cone shape. Each tool allows the user to focus on selected portions of the data to investigate details. Inxight spun off as a separate company from Xerox Parc (XEROX PALO ALTO RESEARCH CENTER), which originally developed these tools under the concept of Wide Widgets.

KNOWLEDGEX is an information mining company that has been acquired by IBM. All products and research efforts are included in the IBM work.

MITRE CORPORATION is a company that has a project focusing on text mining for intelligence analysis of large data sets. This effort involves work on incomplete information to develop sequences, classifications, associations, or inferences.

Perspecta is a decision-support software program by PERSPECTA directed at building multi-perspective indexes. This effort is directed toward Web-based applications and is intended to gather, organize, analyze, and validate information in order to provide the basis for decision making.

SemioMap is a product of SEMIO CORPORATION and is a graphical tool that undertakes database construction, extraction, navigational maps, and document display. It can select documents in a wide variety of formats, including most of the popular word processors, spreadsheets, and presentation programs. The conceptual map links phrases with a certain level of association to a hierarchical structure for the complete textbase. Multiple "worlds" exist as unrelated associations on a comparable level. The map is linked to a document list. The user can proceed from the list to an entire document or to a representation of phrase usage within the text.

TextAnalyst is a MEGAPUTER INTELLIGENCE, INCORPORATED system for text mining and semantic information searching. It provides for indexing, topic assignment, and abstracting of preselected ASCII text documents.

TextSmart is an offering of SPSS that is a text analyzer. The output is a map that uses color to show frequencies of selected words. The location on the map indicates the relative relationship among terms. Users can employ Boolean operators for searching and can view correlations among words, responses to questions, and categories.

Themescape is a CARTIA product that provides a visualization of textbase information. The visualization is developed through special organization that develops the structural concepts, spatial compression to reduce the structure to two dimensions, and transformation into a topographical map. The map is an active viewing area that shows concentrations of text by topology and provides access to details under the surface by clicking on the desired details.

WEBSOM is a tool that was developed as a self-organizing map for Internet explorations. It presents an ordered map of information space, where similar documents lie near each other on the map (self organizing maps). The SOM is based on an algorithm to visualize multidimensional data sets. Its application to Web-based information provides a demonstration of its potential. It is possible to label documents by author, content, etc. Navigational aids permit moving deeper into the surface when a particular item of interest is found. (With its red and yellow coloration, WEBSOM has been compared to a map of the sun's surface.)

Xcize is a product of BROSIS INNOVATIONS, INCORPORATED. The program can capture text from both Internet sources and text files. Combining various documents provides for the analysis of large amounts of data. By employing keywords or phrases, or locating word clusters graphically, the user is able to access the underlying text.

While not in the category of text mining, two knowledge products, Thinkmap and the Brain, are worth mentioning. Thinkmap is a Java-based application by PLUMB DESIGN, INCORPORATED. The focus of the Thinkmap Web site is to demonstrate the program's capability to represent a dynamic relationship among objects. In this case, Princeton University's WordNet is employed to illustrate the dynamic environment capabilities of the Java code in the COSMOS display environment. WordNet is an online lexical reference system based on current psycholinguistic theories of human lexical memory. English nouns, verbs, and adjectives are organized into synonym sets, where each set represents one underlying lexical concept. Different relations link the synonym sets. Thinkmap provides a browsing interface in which selecting one word of a set changes the perspective, the reference point, and the related words surrounding the one selected. TheBrain (THEBRAIN TECHNOLOGIES CORPORATION) is another relational concept demonstration with output similar to several other text-mining offerings.

CONCLUSIONS

The field of text mining is embryonic and challenging. Many approaches can be employed to develop methods for knowledge discernment in textbases. The problem is that no one general solution applies to all cases.

Researchers are working on specific portions of the problem. This review presents a concept of an overall flow for text mining that represents the first attempt at defining what the process should encompass. Meeting the challenge of retrieving desired information (information acquisition) has been an ongoing effort. Researchers are realizing that construction of the textbase requires some understanding of the content. For complex or long documents, traditional procedures do not necessarily work. Developing the textbase with the proper content (extraction) has been a significant research effort. Mining approaches, specifically clustering, have also been strongly investigated. The various directions of the research efforts provide many opportunities to evaluate the methods with various textbase structures and content. The area that the author considers to be the weakest, and thus worthy of current attention, is presentation. Of the three basic approaches for displaying information (cross-correlations, summaries, and visualizations), no one method delivers information that does not need to be evaluated. Text mining results in a collection of related documents from the textbase, but the assimilation of the information into knowledge requires the user to understand and absorb the information being presented. This last area offers the greatest opportunity for future research.

While the steps involved in text mining are almost identical to those of information retrieval, text mining is directed at presenting information about related topics without attempting to answer a specific question. The reader must decide what is relevant. A major part of the text mining effort is driven by computer scientists, many of whom do not have knowledge of the thirty plus years of information retrieval work. It is important that researchers from the information retrieval community and those of the computer science community communicate their findings.

BIBLIOGRAPHY

AHONEN, HELENA; HEINONEN, OSKARI; KLEMETTINEN, MIKA; VERKAMO, A. INKERI. 1997a. Applying Data Mining Techniques in Text Analysis. Available WWW: http://www.cs.helsinki.fi/u/hahonen/publications.html.

AHONEN, HELENA; HEINONEN, OSKARI; KLEMETTINEN, MIKA; VERKAMO, A. INKERI. 1997b. Mining in the Phrasal Frontier. In: Principles of Data Mining and Knowledge Discovery: 1st European Symposium, PKDD '97; 1997 June 24-27; Trondheim, Norway. Berlin, Germany: Springer-Verlag; 1997. 343-350. ISBN: 3-540-63223-9.

AHONEN, HELENA; HEINONEN, OSKARI; KLEMETTINEN, MIKA; VERKAMO, A. INKERI. 1998. Applying Data Mining Techniques for Descriptive Phrase Extraction in Digital Document Collections. In: IEEE International Forum on Research and Technology Advances in Digital Libraries: ADL '98: Proceedings; 1998 April 22-24; Santa Barbara, CA. Los Alamitos, CA: IEEE Computer Society Press; 1998. 2-11. ISBN: 0-8186-8464-X.

ALBRECHT, RUDOLF; MERKL, DIETER. 1998. Knowledge Discovery in Literature Data Bases. In: Proceedings of the 3rd International Conference on Library and Information Services in Astronomy; 1998 April 21-24; Puerto de la Cruz, Tenerife, Spain. San Francisco, CA: Astronomical Society of the Pacific; 1998. 283-286. ISBN: 1-88673-373-2.

ALEXA, MELINA; ROSTEK, LOTHAR. 1997. Pattern Concordances—TATOE Calls XGrammar. Available WWW: http://www.cs.queensu.ca/achallc97/papers/p028.html.

ALEXA, MELINA; ROSTEK, LOTHAR. 1999. TATOE: Text Analysis Tool with Object Encoding. Available WWW: http://www.darmstadt.gmd.de/~rostek/tatoe.htm.

ALTAVISTA. 1999. AltaVista Web Page Search Engine. Available WWW: http://www.altavista.com.

ARM. 1998. Automated Requirement Measurement Tool. Available WWW: http://satc.gsfc.nasa.gov/tools/arm/index/.html.

AUTONOMY. 1999. The Technology behind Autonomy. Available WWW: http://www.autonomy.com/tech/index.html.

AZMY, ASHRAF. 1998. SuperQuery: Data Mining for Everyone. Available WWW: http://www.azmy.com/wp1.htm.

BALDONADO, MICHELLE; WINOGRAD, TERRY. 1997. Sense Maker: An Information-Exploration Interface Supporting the Contextual Evaluation of a User's Interests. In: CHI '97: Proceedings of the Conference on Human Factors in Computing Systems; 1997 Martch 22-27; Atlanta, GA. New York, NY: ACM Press; 1997. 11-18. ISBN: 0-89791-802-9.

BELKIN, NICHOLAS J.; CROFT, W. BRUCE. 1987. Retrieval Techniques. In: Williams, Martha E., ed. Annual Review of Information Science and Technology: Volume 22. Amsterdam, The Netherlands: Elsevier Science Publishers B.V. for the American Society for Information Science; 1987. 109-145. ISSN: 0066-4200; ISBN: 0-444-70302-0.

BERN, J.; DAMM, C.; MEINEL, CH. 1997. The Electronic Colloquium on Computational Complexity (ECCC): A Digital Library in Use. In: Peters, C.; Thanos, C., eds. 1st European Conference ECDL '97 Proceedings: Research and Advanced Technology for Digital Libraries; 1997 September 1-3; Pisa, Italy. Berlin, Germany: Springer-Verlag; 1997. 405-421. ISBN: 3-540-63554-8.

BORKO, HAROLD, ed. 1967a. Automated Language Processing: The State of the Art. New York, NY: John Wiley & Sons, Inc.; 1967. 386p. OCLC: 306976.

BORKO, HAROLD. 1967b. Indexing and Classification. In: Borko, Harold, ed. Automated Language Processing. New York, NY: John Wiley & Sons, Inc.; 1967. 99-125. OCLC: 306976.

BRACHMAN, RONALD J.; ANAND, TEJ. 1996. The Process of Knowledge Discovery in Databases: A Human-Centered Approach. In: Fayyad, Usama M.; Piatetsky-Shapiro, Gregory; Smyth, Padhraic; Uthurusamy, Ramasamy, eds. Advances in Knowledge Discovery and Data Mining. Menlo Park, CA: AAAI Press/MIT Press; 1996. 59-82. ISBN: 0-262-56097-6.

BROSIS INNOVATIONS, INCORPORATED. 1998. XcizePro Web Home Page. Available WWW: http://www.brosisii.com.

CARTIA. 1999. ThemeScape Web Home Page. Available WWW: http://www.cartia.com.

CHAKRABARTI, SOUMEN; DOM, BYRON; AGRAWAL, RAKESH; RAGHAVAN, PRABHAKAR. 1997. Using Taxonomy, Discriminants, and Signatures for Navigating in Text Databases. In: Proceedings of the 23rd International Conference on Very Large Data Bases; 1997 August 26-29; Athens, Greece. San Francisco, CA: Morgan Kaufmann Publishers; 1997. 446-455. ISBN: 1-55860-470-7.

CHEN, Z. 1994. Let Documents Talk to Each Other: A Computer Model for Connection of Short Documents. Journal of Documentation. 1994 March; 49(1): 44-54. ISSN: 0022-0418.

CLEVERDON, CYRIL W. 1962. Report on the Testing and Analysis of an Investigation into the Comparative Efficiency of Indexing Systems. Cranfield, England: College of Aeronautics; 1962. 311p. OCLC: 41794559.

CMS. 1998. TextMap Web Home Page. Available WWW: http://www.cmshome.com.

COINS. 1999. Collaborative Information Acquisition Web Home Page. Available WWW: http://orgwis.gmd.de/projects/Coins.

CONCEPTUAL DIMENSIONS. 1999. Concept Map Web Home Page. Available WWW: http://www.cdimensions.com.

CRESWELL, JOHN W. 1994. Research Design: Qualitative & Quantitative Approaches. Thousand Oaks, CA: Sage Publications; 1994. 228p. ISBN: 0-8039-5254-6.

D'ALESSIO, STEPHEN; MURRAY, KEITHA; SCHIAFFINO, ROBERT; KERSHENBAUM, AARON. 1998. Category Levels in Hierarchical Text Categorization. Available WWW: http://www.iona.edu/academic/arts_sci/departments/cis/FacultyPublications.htm.

DATA JUNCTION CORPORATION. 1999. Cambio Web Home Page. Available WWW: http://www.datajunction.com/products/cambio.html.

DAVIES, ROY. 1989. The Creation of New Knowledge by Information Retrieval and Classification. Journal of Documentation. 1989 December; 45(4): 273-301. ISSN: 0022-0418.

DAVIES, ROY. 1991. The Chemical Metaphor in Information Retrieval: Reactions between Bibliographic Units of Information. In: Jones, Kevin, P., ed. The Structuring of Information: Informatics 11 Proceedings; 1991 March 20-22; York, England. London, England: Aslib; 1991. 79-91. ISBN: 0-85142-282-9.

DECIDE. 1998. The DECIDE Project: Designing and Evaluating Extraction Tools for Collocations in Dictionaries and Corpora. Available WWW: http://engdepl.philo.ulg.ac.be/decide.

DECISIONCENTRE. 1998. Advanced Enterprise Decision Support on Parallel Servers. Available WWW: http://ruby.doc.ic.ac.uk/.

DIXON, MARK. 1997. An Overview of Document Mining Technology. Available WWW: http://www.software.ibm.com/.

DOYLE, L. B. 1961. Semantic Road Maps for Literature Searchers. Communications of the ACM. 1961; 8: 553-578. ISSN: 0001-0782.

ELDREDGE, JEFFREY. 1998. Text Data Mining: An Overview. Available WWW: http://www.cs.columbia.edu/~radev/cs6998/class/cs6998-09-02.

ETZIONI, OREN. 1996. The World-Wide Web: Quagmire or Gold Mine? Communications of the ACM. 1996 November; 39(11): 65-68. ISSN: 0001-0782.

FAYYAD, USAMA M.; PIATETSKY-SHAPIRO, GREGORY; SMYTH, PADHRAIC. 1996. From Data Mining to Knowledge Discovery: An Overview. In: Fayyad, Usama M.; Piatetsky-Shapiro, Gregory; Smyth, Padhraic; Uthurusamy, Ramasamy, eds. Advances in Knowledge Discovery and Data Mining. Menlo Park, CA: AAAI Press/MIT Press; 1996. 1-36. ISBN: 0-262-56097-6.

FELDMAN, RONEN; DAGAN, IDO. 1995. Knowledge Discovery in Textual Databases. In: Fayyad, U.M.; Uthurusamy, R., eds. KDD-95 Proceedings: 1st International Conference on Knowledge Discovery and Data Mining; 1995 August 20-21; Montreal, Canada. Menlo Park, CA: AAAI; 1995. 112-117. ISBN: 0-929280-82-2.

FELDMAN, RONEN; KLOSGEN, WILLI; DEN-YEHUDA, YANIV; KEDAR, GIL; REZNIKOV, VLADIMIR. 1997. Pattern Based Browsing in Document Collections. In: Principles of Data Mining and Knowledge Discovery; 1st European Symposium, PKDD '97 Proceedings; 1997 June 24-27; Trondheim, Norway. Berlin, Germany: Springer-Verlag; 1997. 112-122. ISBN: 3-540-63223-9.

GOTTHARD, WILLI; MARWICK, ALAN; SEIFFERT, ROLAND. 1997. Mining Text Data. DB2 Magazine Online. 1997 Winter. Available WWW: http://www.db2mag.com/97wiGot.htm.

GUPTA, AMARNATH; SANTINI, SIMONE; JAIN, RAMESH. 1997. In Search of Information in Visual Media. Communications of the ACM. 1997 December; 40(12): 35-42. ISSN: 0001-0782.

HAHN, UDO; SCHNATTINGER, KLEMENS. 1997a. Deep Knowledge Discovery from Natural Language Texts. In: Heckerman, D.; Mannila, H.; Pregibon, D.; Uthurusamy, R., eds. Proceedings of the 3rd International Conference on Knowledge Discovery and Data Mining; 1997 August 14-17; Newport Beach, CA. Menlo Park, CA: AAAI Press; 1997. 175-178. ISBN: 1-57735-027-8.

HAHN, UDO; SCHNATTINGER, KLEMENS. 1997b. Knowledge Mining from Textual Sources. In: CIKM '97: Proceedings of the 6th International Conference on Information and Knowledge Management; 1997 November 10-14; Las Vegas, NV. New York, NY: ACM Press; 1997. 83-90. ISBN: 0-89791-970-X.

HAHN, UDO; SCHNATTINGER, KLEMENS. 1997c. A Qualitative Growth Model for Real-World Text Knowledge Bases. In: RIAO '97: Proceedings of the 5th Conference on Computer Assisted Information Searching on the Internet; 1997 June 25-27; Montreal, Quebec. Available WWW: http://supreme.coling.uni-freiburg.de/publications/textmining.html.

HARTER, STEPHEN P.; HERT, CAROL A. 1997. Evaluation of Information Retrieval Systems: Approaches, Issues, and Methods. In: Williams, Martha E., ed. Annual Review of Information Science and Technology: Volume 32. Medford, NJ: Information Today, Inc. for the American Society for Information Science; 1997. 3-94. ISSN: 0066-4200; ISBN: 1-57387-047-1.

HAVERKAMP, DONNA S.; GAUCH, SUSAN. 1998. Intelligent Information Agents: Review and Challenges for Distributed Information Sources. Journal of the American Society for Information Science. 1998; 49(4): 304-311. ISSN: 0002-8231.

HEARST, MARTI. 1997. Interfaces for Searching the Web. Available WWW: http://www.sciam.com/0397issue/0397hearst.html.

HEARST, MARTI. 1998. About Scatter/Gather. Available WWW: http://www.sims.berkeley.edu/~hearst/sg-overview.html.

HEDBERG, SARA REESE. 1995. The Data Gold Rush. Byte Magazine. 1995 October; 20(10): 83-88. ISSN: 0360-5280.

HEDBERG, SARA REESE. 1996. Searching for the Mother Lode: Tales of the First Data Miners. IEEE Expert. 1996 October; 11(5): 4-7. ISSN: 0885-9000.

HONKELA, TIMO; KASKI, SAMUEL; LAGUS, KRISTA; KOHONEN, TEUVO. 1998. Newsgroup Exploration with WEBSOM Method and Browsing Interface. Available WWW: http://www.cis.hut.fi/~tho/index.html.

IBM. 1997. Speed Reading the Internet. Think 1997; 2: XX. ISSN: 0040-6112.

IBM. 1999. Intelligent Miner for Text Web Home Page. Available WWW: http://www.software.ibm.com/data/iminer/fortext/index.html.

IBM CHINA/HONG KONG. 1999. IBM DB2 Digital Library. Available WWW: http://www-4.ibm.com/software/is/dig-lib.

IBM ITALY. 1998. IBM Technology Watch Home Page. Available WWW: www.synthema.it/tewat/main.htm.

INFORMATION WEEK. 1998. Lotus to Add Data Mining to Notes. Information Week. 1998 June 29; 38. ISSN: 8750-6874.

INSIGHTSOFT-M. 2000. Home Page for iCrossReader. Available WWW: http://www.insight.com.ru/.

INTERCON SYSTEMS. 1999. DataSet Web Home Page. Available WWW: http://ds-dataset.com.

INXIGHT SOFTWARE, INCORPORATED. 1999. Inxight Software Web Home Page. Available WWW: http://www.inxight.com.

KANTOR, PAUL B. 1994. Information Retrieval Techniques. In: Williams, Martha E., ed. Annual Review of Information Science and Technology: Volume 29. Medford, NJ: Learned Information, Inc. for the American Society for Information Science; 1994. 53-90. ISSN: 0066-4200; ISBN: 0-938734-91-1.

KLEIN, HARALD. 2000. Text Analysis Resources. Available WWW: http://www.intext.de/TEXTANAE.HTM.

KM WORLD. 1997(-). Camden, ME: Knowledge Asset Media. ISSN: 1099-8284.

KNOWLEDGE MANAGEMENT. 1998-. New York, NY: Freedom Technology Media Group. Also available WWW: http://www.kmmag.com.

KNOWLEDGEX. 1999. Available WWW: http://www.knowledgex.com/home.htm.

KNOWLES, CHERIE M. 1981. The Bibliographic Presentation of Grey Literature. Brussels, Belgium: Commission of the European Communities; 1981. 43p. OCLC: 10227111.

KRIVDA, CHERYL D. 1995. Data Mining Dynamite. Byte Magazine. 1995 October; 20(10): 97-104. ISSN: 0360-5280.

LAGUS, KRISTA. 1997. Map of WSOM'97 Abstracts—An Alternative Index. Available WWW: http://www.cis.hut.ti/wsom97/abstractmap.

LANCASTER, F. WILFRID; WARNER, AMY J. 1993. Information Retrieval Today. Arlington, VA: Information Resources Press; 1993. 341p. ISBN: 0-87815-064-1.

LE BRET, CHRISTOPHER. 1997. Have You Heard about Data Mining? Science Tribune. 1997 October. Available WWW: http:///www.tribunes.com/tribune/art97/lebe.htm.

LOTUS DEVELOPMENT CORPORATION. 1999. Lotus Web Home Page. Available WWW: http://www.lotus.com.

MACHLUP, FRITZ. 1980. Knowledge: Its Creation, Distribution, and Economic Significance. Vol. 1. Knowledge and Knowledge Production. Princeton, NJ: Princeton University Press; 1980. 272p. ISBN: 0-691-04226-8.

MANAGEMENT INFORMATION TECHNOLOGIES, INCORPORATED. 1999. ConSearch Web Home Page. Available WWW: http://www.readware.com/consearc.htm.

MARTIN, SARAH S. 1978. Managing Reprints and Preprints in an Observatory Library. Paper presented at the Special Libraries Association Annual Meeting; 1978 June; Kansas City, MO. 9p. ERIC: ED 165759.

MATHEUS, CHRISTOPHER J.; PIATETSKY-SHAPIRO, GREGORY; MCNEILL, DWIGHT. 1996. Selecting and Reporting What Is Interesting: The KEFIR Application to Healthcare Data. In: Fayyad, Usama M.; Piatetsky-Shapiro, Gregory; Smyth, Padhraic; Uthurusamy, Ramasamy, eds. Advances in Knowledge Discovery and Data Mining. Menlo Park, CA: AAAI Press/ MIT Press; 1996. 496-516. ISBN: 0-262-56097-6.

MCNEMAR, CHRIS. 1998. Text-Mining the CLCS Web Site. Available WWW: http://research.ivv.nasa.gov/~mcnemar/report.htm.

MEGAPUTER INTELLIGENCE, INCORPORATED. 1999. TextAnalyst and PolyAnalyst Web Home Page. Available WWW: http:// www.megaputer.com/html/products.html.

MERKL, DIETER. 1998. Self-Organizing Maps and Software Reuse. In: Pedrycz, Witold; Peters, James F., eds. Computational Intelligence in Software Engineering. Singapore: World Scientific; 1998. ISBN: 9-8102-3503-8.

MERKL, DIETER. 2000. Text Data Mining. In: Handbook of Natural Language Processing. New York, NY: Marcel Dekker; 2000. ISBN: 0-8427-9000-6.

MERKL, DIETER; RAUBER, ANDREAS. 1998. Cluster Connections: A Visualization Technique to Reveal Cluster Boundaries in Self-Organizing Maps. In: Proceedings of the 9th Italian Workshop on Neural Nets; 1997 May 22-24; Vietri sul Mare, Italy. Berlin, Germany: Springer-Verlag; 1998. 324-329. ISBN: 3-540-76157-8.

MITRE CORPORATION. 1999. Knowledge Discovery from Data and Data Mining. Available WWW: http://www.mitre.org/pubs/showcase/ datamining.

MORRISON, PHILIP; MORRISON, PHYLIS. 1998. Wonders: The Sum of Human Knowledge. Scientific American. 1998 July; 279(1): 115-117. ISSN: 0036-8733.

NATURAL LANGUAGE PROCESSING GROUP. 2000. Research Topics. Available WWW: http://liawww.epfl.ch/Research/research.html.

OETTINGER, ANTHONY G. 1967. Foreword. In: Borko, Harold, ed. Automated Language Processing. New York, NY: John Wiley and Sons, Inc.; 1967. ix. OCLC: 306976.

PAVE. 1999. Publication and Visualization Environment. Available WWW: http://www.darmstadt.gmd.de/publish/pave/pave/pave.html.

PELTON, JOSEPH N. 1997. Cyberlearning vs. The University: An Irresistible Force Meets an Immovable Object. IEEE Engineering Management Review. 1997 Fall; 25(3): 110-113. ISSN: 0360-8581.

PERSPECTA. 1999. Available WWW: http://www.perspecta.com.

PLUMB DESIGN, INCORPORATED. 1998. Thinkmap Web Home Page. Available WWW: http://www.thinkmap.com.

ROUSE, WILLIAM B.; THOMAS, BEVERLY SUTLEY; BOFF, KENNETH R. 1998. Knowledge Maps for Knowledge Mining: Application to R&D Technology Management. IEEE Transactions on Systems, Man, and Cybernetics Part C: Application and Reviews. 1998 April; 28(3): 309-317. ISSN: 1094-6977.

SAATY, THOMAS L. 1990. The Analytic Hierarchy Process: Planning, Priority Setting, Resource Allocation. 2nd ed. Pittsburgh, PA: RWS Publications; 1990. 1 volume. ISBN: 0-962031-72-0.

SALTON, GERARD; BUCKLEY, CHRIS. 1991. Automatic Text Structuring and Retrieval: Experiments in Automatic Encyclopedia Searching. In: SIGIR '91: Proceedings of the Association for Computing Machinery Special Interest Group on Information Retrieval (ACM/SIGIR) 14th Annual International Conference on Research and Development in Information Retrieval; 1991 October 13-16; Chicago, IL. New York, NY: ACM Press; 1991. 21-30. ISBN: 0-89791-448-1.

SCHNATTINGER, KLEMENS; HAHN, UDO. 1998. Intelligent Text Analysis for Dynamically Maintaining and Updating Domain Knowledge Bases. In: IDA '97 Proceedings of the 2nd International Symposium on Intelligent Data Analysis; 1997 August 4-6; London, England. Berlin, Germany: Springer-Verlag; 1997. 409-422. ISBN: 3-540-63346-4.

SCRIVENER, S. A. R.; VERNON, S. 1995. DesignNet: Transnational Design Project Work at a Distance. In: Digital Creativity: Proceedings of the 1st Conference on Computers in Art and Design Education (CADE'95); 1995 April 18-21; Brighton, England. Brighton, England: University of Brighton; 1995. ISBN: 1-87196-672-8.

SEDELOW, SALLY YEATES; SEDELOW, WALTER A., JR. 1967. Stylistic Analysis. In: Borko, Harold, ed. Automated Language Processing. New York, NY: John Wiley and Sons, Inc.; 1967. 181-213. OCLC: 306976.

SEMIO CORPORATION. 1999. SemioMap. Available WWW: http://www.semio.com/products/semiomap.html.

SINGH, LISA; SCHEUERMANN, PETER; CHEN, BIN. Generating Association Rules from Semi-Structured Documents Using an Extended Concept Hierarchy. In: CIKM '97: Proceedings of the 6th International Conference on Information and Knowledge Management; 1997 November 10-14; Las Vegas, NV. New York, NY: ACM Press; 1997. 193-200. ISBN: 0-89791-970-X.

SOTO, PATRICIA. 1998. Text Mining: Beyond Search Technology. DB2 Magazine OnLine. 1998 Fall. Available WWW: http://www.db2mag.com/98fsoto.html.

SPARKLE. 1998. Shallow PARsing and Knowledge Extraction for Language Engineering. Available WWW: http://www.ilc.pi.cnr.it/sparkle.htm.

SPSS. 1999. TextSmart Web Home Page. Available WWW: http://www.spss.com/textsmart/.

SUGIMOTO, MASANORI; HORI, KOICHI; OHSUGA, SETSUO. 1998. A System for Visualizing the Viewpoints of Information and Its Application to Intelligent Activity Support. IEEE Transactions on Systems, Man and Cybernetics Part C Applications and Reviews. 1998 February; 28(1): 124-136. ISSN: 1094-6977.

SWANSON, DON R. 1986. Undiscovered Public Knowledge. Library Quarterly. 1986 April; 56(2): 103-118. ISSN: 0024-2519.

SWANSON, DON R.; SMALHEISER, N.R. 1996. Undiscovered Public Knowledge: A Ten-Year Update. In: Simoudis, E.; Han, J.; Fayyad, U.M., eds. KDD-96: Proceedings of the 2nd International Conference on Knowledge

Discovery and Data Mining; 1996 August 2-4; Portland, OR. Menlo Park, CA: AAAI Press; 1996. 295-298. ISBN: 1-57735-004-9.

TALLMO, KARL-ERIK. 1998. Knowledge-on-Demand. Available WWW: http://art-bin.com/art/akn-on-demande.html.

THEBRAIN TECHNOLOGIES CORPORATION. 2000. TheBrain.com Web Home Page. Available WWW: http://www.thebrain.com.

TIOGO, JON WILLIAM. 1999. Data Deluge Sparks Mass Storage Boom. Washington Technology. 1999 March; 13(23): 30-36. ISSN: 1058-9163.

TKACH, DANIEL. 1998. Text Mining Technology: Turning Information into Knowledge. Available WWW: http//www-4.ibm.com/software/data/iminer/fortext/download/whiteweb.pdf.

TREC. 1998. Text REtrieval Conference. Available WWW: http://trec.nist.gov.

TRYBULA, WALTER J. 1996. Agents in the Net. Unpublished manuscript. 1996 April. 21p. Available from: the author.

TRYBULA, WALTER J. 1997. Data Mining and Knowledge Discovery. In: Williams, Martha E., ed. Annual Review of Information Science and Technology: Volume 32. Medford, NJ: Learned Information, Inc. for the American Society for Information Science; 1997. 197-230. ISSN: 0066-4200; ISBN: 1-573487-047-1.

TURENNE, NICOLAS; ROUSSELOT, FRANÇOIS. 1998. Evaluation of Four Clustering Methods Used in Text Mining. Available WWW: http://www-ensais.u-strasbg.fr/LIIA/publications/1998.htm.

WATTERSON, KAREN. 1995. A Data Miner's Tools. Byte Magazine. 1995 October; 20(10): 91-96. ISSN: 0360-5280.

WEBSOM. 1999. WEBSOM: Self-Organizing Maps for Internet Exploration. Available WWW: http://websom.hut.fi/websom.

WEISS, SHOLOM M.; INDURKHYA, NITIN. 1998. Predictive Data Mining. San Francisco, CA: Morgan Kaufmann Publishers, Inc.; 1998. 228p. ISBN: 1-55860-403-0.

WHITE, HOWARD D.; MCCAIN, KATHERINE W. 1997. Visualization of Literatures. In: Williams, Martha E., ed. Annual Review of Information Science and Technology: Volume 32. Medford, NJ: Learned Information, Inc. for the American Society for Information Science; 1997. 99-168. ISSN: 0066-4200; ISBN: 1-57387-047-1.

WILBUR, W. JOHN. 1998. A Comparison of Group and Individual Performance among Subject Experts and Untrained Workers at the Document Retrieval Task. Journal of the American Society for Information Science. 1998; 49(6): 517-529. ISSN: 0002-8231.

WILLIAMS, JAMES G.; SOCHATS, KENNETH M.; MORSE, EMILE. 1995. Visualization. In: Williams, Martha E., ed. Annual Review of Information Science and Technology: Volume 30. Medford, NJ: Information Today, Inc. for the American Society for Information Science; 1995. 161-207. ISSN: 0066-4200; ISBN: 1-57387-019-6.

WOHL, AMY D. 1998. Intelligent Text Mining Creates Business Intelligence. Available WWW: http://www-3.ibm.com/solutions/businessintelligence/pdf/amipap.pdf.

WOLVERTON, MICHAEL; HAYES-ROTH, BARBARA. 1994. Retrieving Semantically Distant Analogies with Knowledge-Directed Spreading Activation. In: Proceedings of the 12th National Conference on Artificial Intelligence: Volume 1; 1994 July 31-August 4; Seattle, WA. Cambridge, MA: MIT Press; 1994. 56-61. ISBN: 0-262-61102-3.

WORDNET. 1998. WordNet: A Lexical Database for English. Available WWW: http://www.cogsci.princeton.edu/~wn.

WYLLYS, RONALD E. 1967. Extracting and Abstracting by Computer. In: Borko, Harold, ed. Automated Language Processing. New York, NY: John Wiley and Sons, Inc.; 1967. 127-179. OCLC: 306976.

XEROX PALO ALTO RESEARCH CENTER. Available WWW: http://www.parc.xerox.com.

XRCE. 1999. Xerox site for Information Visualizers. Available WWW: http://www.xrce.xerox.com/showroom/techno/iv.htm.

III

Applications

Section III contains one chapter by Donald W. King of the University of Pittsburgh and Carol Tenopir of the University of Tennessee. "Using and Reading Scholarly Literature" is concerned largely with the scholarly, scientific literature. Since the volume of scientific articles doubles every 15 to 17 years and the pressure to keep up is great, scientists face a daunting task of reading at the risk of being inadequately informed for carrying out their research and teaching. On top of that they face: the change of publication from paper to electronic media, preprints and publications stored digitally for electronic access, and conversion of retrospective collections to digital form.

This chapter reviews the events in readership found in the literature, including other reviews of journal use, over the past 40 to 50 years. It deals, for the most part, with demand, use, and readership. Demand is the circulation or number of subscriptions (both personal and library), use is simply picking up an issue or bound volume and perusing it, and reading involves reading at least some of the body of the article. The topics covered by Donald W. King and Carol Tenopir are: journal demand, journal use, use of separate copies of articles, readership of articles, time and cost of reading, usefulness and value of article information, information-seeking patterns, age of articles read, and factors affecting information seeking and reading. The authors support the findings with numeric data found in the literature. For example there are on average 13.4 readings per 123 articles, supporting the estimate that only about 10% to 20% of the articles distributed are actually read. In 1977 King found that there were an estimated 244 million readings of 382,000 scholarly scientific articles for an average of 638 readings per article; in 2000 Tenopir and King found the number of readings per article had increased to 900. Readers of the chapter should, of course, note the various sources for the data and the parameters of each study (time period, age of literature, number of subjects, characteristics of subjects, methodology for gathering data, etc.) in trying to make sense of multiple studies of approximately the same phenomenon.

In concluding their chapter King and Tenopir observe that this historical review indicates that "(1) scientists continue to read a great deal and spend substantial time reading; (2) publications are the principal channel of communication for scientists, and they read scholarly journals far more than any other type of publication; (3) engineers rely more on other channels of communication; and (4) the high levels of usefulness and value of scholarly journals have persisted over the years." Changes have occurred that affect readership patterns and information seeking. Notably, more articles are being identified through computer searches than earlier, yet browsing remains the principal means of identifying new articles; the higher price of subscriptions forces readers to rely more on libraries for articles; and the use of separate copies of articles is increasing. "A variety and combination of distribution means and media are likely to best serve users, distributors, and creators of scholarly journals for a long time to come."

8 Using and Reading Scholarly Literature

DONALD W. KING
University of Pittsburgh

CAROL TENOPIR
University of Tennessee

INTRODUCTION

Scientific scholarly journals have existed for nearly three and a half centuries and have evolved to be the principal formal channel of communication for scientists.[1] Journals are read extensively both by scientists who work in universities and by those who work elsewhere. Reading helps them keep up with the literature of their disciplines and supports lifelong learning, as well as providing an important resource for research, teaching, administration, and other endeavors. There is strong evidence that the information obtained from scholarly articles improves scientists' quality of work and productivity. Scientists whose achievements have been formally recognized tend to read substantially more than others and scientists who are more often consulted for advice by colleagues also tend to read more heavily than others in their organizations. The number of scientific articles doubles approximately every 15 to 17 years, so at the time scientists finish their formal education, they will have been exposed to less than one-sixth of the amount of new knowledge that will be created during their careers. They must keep up or assume the risk of having inadequate knowledge for their research and teaching.

Today scholarly journals are in the midst of profound changes, notably: (1) transformation of published scientific journals to electronic media, (2) digital storage and electronic access to separate copies of preprint and published articles, and (3) retrospective digital conversion

---

[1] We use the term scientists in a generic manner to include all the fields of science as defined by the National Science Foundation, including engineering and social science. Sometimes engineers and social scientists are distinguished from all the other fields of science/scientists.

Annual Review of Information Science and Technology (ARIST), Volume 34, 1999
Martha E. Williams, Editor
Published for the American Society for Information Science (ASIS)
By Information Today, Inc., Medford, NJ

of library collections. Technological innovations are providing an opportunity to improve upon the time-tested values of scholarly journals, as well as facilitating the development of other innovative ways of communicating. Although the advantages of these impending changes are many, there is also the risk of destroying a valuable and time-tested communication system merely for the sake of change. Perhaps the biggest challenge to the scientific community in addressing the future is economic rather than technological. The economic nature of the current journal system is one of its major weaknesses—particularly the general lack of understanding of why journal prices have skyrocketed beyond what might be explained by inflation and increase in journal sizes. The demand for and use of scholarly journal information are important economic aspects of the scholarly journal system.

This chapter reviews the literature dealing with scholarly journal demand, use, and readership over the past 40 to 50 years. An historical perspective is given because so much of the research in these areas dates back to the 1960s and 1970s and a great deal can be learned from this past research. Furthermore, current evidence suggests that the use, usefulness, and value of scholarly journals have remained intact over this time period, which reinforces the notion that any tampering with the journal system must be undertaken cautiously. Finally, there are aspects of readership patterns over the years that should be considered carefully in development of electronic journals and digital full-text article databases.

CHAPTER SCOPE

Two previous *Annual Review of Information Science and Technology* (*ARIST*) chapters are particularly relevant to our discussion. PEEK & POMERANTZ provided an overview of the literature relating to electronic journals, although they did not focus on issues surrounding readership. Earlier BISHOP & STAR provided detail on the sociological and behavioral aspects of journal and digital library use. In contrast, this chapter emphasizes the quantitative aspects of scholarly readership. This is done to show trends, to provide a benchmark from which to assess future changes, and to examine use-related factors that innovators should consider in creating change.

This chapter deals largely with demand, use, and readership of scholarly literature, with an emphasis on scholarly journals and information found in articles. By demand we mean the circulation or number of subscriptions to scientific scholarly journals. Use and readership of journals and articles are terms that are sometimes used synonymously. For example, some library studies count picking up and scanning an issue or bound volume as being a use, although some confuse this with reading an article. In this chapter, we define reading as going beyond the table of contents, title, and abstract to the body of an article. Journal use is defined as an incident of use made of a journal issue, bound copy, or separate copy of an article by a scientist (or other user). A use of a journal or separate copy of an article could be the same as a reading but this is unlikely. There may be many more readings than uses, since using an issue or volume may result in reading several articles. On the other hand, it could involve no reading.

The chapter is organized into the following topics:

- *Journal demand.* We present evidence of trends and factors that affect demand with particular emphasis on price-demand relationships. We also review several methods used to estimate demand and price-demand relationships.
- *Journal use.* There are basically three types of journal use studies. One type establishes the sources of information used to solve problems, make decisions, and so on, where one source is journals (or "the literature"). These studies tend to estimate the number or proportion of instances for which journals are used and compare such use with other sources. The second type of study involves use of journals in libraries, as defined above, to see if amount of use is sufficient to warrant purchase of the journals or, instead, to rely on interlibrary loan or document delivery. The third type of study is of the use of electronic journals and digital databases in which hits and/or number of downloads are counted.
- *Use of separate copies of articles.* There is a long history of a largely subterranean use of separate copies of articles obtained through interlibrary loan, document delivery, and distribution of preprints, reprints, and photocopies made by colleagues. Emergence of digital databases of full-text articles has made the use of separate copies an important topic, although definition of use from these digital databases is still a question. That is, should a search hit be counted as a use or should a use only be counted when an article is downloaded?
- *Readership of articles.* There are two aspects to readership of articles. The first is the extent to which individual articles, and therefore journals, are read. The second is the extent to which individual scientists read scholarly articles.
- *Time and cost of reading.* Time spent reading scholarly articles is a useful cross-check on estimates of amount of

reading, but more importantly, scientists' time is such a critical resource that consideration of any alternative to current practices must take into account the effect on the time required to identify, locate, obtain, and read articles. Finally, the time and dollar cost scientists are willing to pay for article information is an indicator of its value to them.

- *Usefulness and value of article information.* Many studies over the years have examined the usefulness and value of journal information in terms of the purposes for which information is obtained, the importance of the information to these purposes, and the consequences of reading on scientists' creativity, performance, achievement, productivity, decision-making, and so on.
- *Information-seeking patterns.* Some studies have addressed how scientists identify and locate articles, such as through browsing, citations in other literature, automated searching, and recommendations by colleagues. Other studies establish the sources of articles, including personal subscriptions, library copies, and various forms and sources of separate copies of articles. Some of these studies provide important insights as to how much time is required by scientists and by others on scientists' behalf to identify and obtain articles.
- *Age of articles read.* The age of articles read is treated as a separate topic because of the enormous expenditures for retrospectively digitizing texts of articles. One must ask whether older articles are read and, if so, whether their usefulness and value justify such expenditures.
- *Factors affecting information seeking and reading.* There appear to be many factors that affect scientists' choices from among information-seeking alternatives and, ultimately, whether journals are read. Perhaps the most important factor involves attributes of the information found in articles, such as quality, conciseness, and readability. Other factors include attributes of journal distribution means and media, the ease of use or time required to use, and awareness of journals and the services used to identify, locate, and provide access to them.

Throughout the chapter, examples of quantitative results are given to demonstrate trends in use, usefulness, and value of the literature—particularly regarding scholarly journals.

A CONTEXT FOR JOURNAL USE

GARVEY & GRIFFITH (1972) and others provide sound and useful evidence of the extent to which information about a research project is communicated through many written and oral channels, such as personal correspondence, internal and external technical reports, conference presentations and published proceedings, journal articles, and books, to name a few. Nearly all these channels are used by individual scientists, but they are used to a varying degree depending on the scientists' field of interest, type of research or other work being performed, stage of the research, role played in an organization, resources available to obtain information, and so on.

Scientists have several alternative distribution means from which to choose in obtaining journal articles. For example, they can subscribe, use library-provided articles, or obtain separate copies of articles from a number of sources. They also have several media from which to obtain articles, such as traditional print on paper, microform, and electronic on CD-ROM or online. The fact that so many communication channels (as well as distribution means and media within channels) have evolved and survived suggests that each has carved a niche where features and ease of use are needed by certain groups of scientists or by scientists at different times. This does not mean that each channel, distribution means, and medium is perfect, nor does it imply that substantial improvement cannot be achieved. It does suggest, however, that future communication will not readily evolve into a single channel, distribution means, or medium.

OTHER LITERATURE REVIEWS OF JOURNAL USE

As mentioned earlier, two *ARIST* chapters are particularly germane to this chapter. PEEK & POMERANTZ in 1998 discuss briefly user and social implications in their chapter, "Electronic Scholarly Journal Publishing." BISHOP & STAR in 1996 review literature covering the "Social Informatics of Digital Library Use and Infrastructure." This in-depth discourse covers a wide range of sociological and behavioral aspects of searching and using databases of full-text articles. Earlier chapters by CRANE (1971), CRAWFORD (1978), DERVIN & NILAN, HEWINS, and METOYER-DURAN review the topic of information needs and uses from a sociological and behavioral perspective, but with little discussion of the use and needs of primary literature or scholarly journals. Chapters in the first five *ARIST* volumes by ALLEN (1969), HERNER & HERNER, LIPETZ, MENZEL (1966), and PAISLEY (1968) all provide substantial information and data concerning journal use and methods involved in studying its use. Other chapters, notably KUNEY, LANDAU, LANCASTER & GILLESPIE, COOPER, LIN &

GARVEY (1972), MARTYN, HILLS (1983), LERNER ET AL., MAILLOUX, and KOENIG, provide some insights concerning scholarly journal use.

Apart from the *ARIST* volumes, several books serve as literature reviews or have a useful range of information needs and uses chapters prepared by knowledgeable researchers. Examples include *Key Papers in Information Science* (GRIFFITH); *Encyclopedia of Library and Information Science* (KENT); *Communication Among Scientists and Engineers* (NELSON & POLLOCK); *Scientific Communications and Informatics* (MIKHAILOV ET AL.); *Technology Transfer: A Communication Perspective* (F. WILLIAMS & GIBSON); *The Future of the Printed Word* (HILLS, 1980); and *Managing Professionals in Innovative Organizations* (KATZ).

PINELLI provides a useful review of the literature dealing specifically with information-seeking processes of engineers. Part of Pinelli's review deals with the nature of science and technology, differences between engineers and scientists, and factors that affect use of information and information sources. He also reviews the research literature and comments on a research agenda for scientific and technical information with a focus on users. KING ET AL. (1994) provide a literature review and an extensive annotated bibliography of engineers' information seeking and use behavior from the late 1960s to 1994. POLAND reviews the literature concerning communication among scientists and engineers, while ALONI discusses literature dealing primarily with informal and formal communication among engineers in research and development (R&D) organizations. The extensive ALONI analytical review is useful to those interested in information-seeking processes, gatekeepers, boundary spanning, and related issues. B.M. GUPTA does a good job of showing comparative data from studies performed prior to 1981, particularly regarding types of information, sources (e.g., internal or external), and factors related to sources used. In 1974, KING & PALMOUR provide an early review of user behavior and WOOD covers user studies from 1966 to 1970. Prior to 1965, reviews concerning journal use by scientists were prepared by AUERBACH CORPORATION, DAVIS & BAILEY, MENZEL (1962), and PAISLEY (1965).

DEMAND, USE, AND READERSHIP OF
SCHOLARLY JOURNALS
Scholarly Journal Demand

Journal demand is characterized by the number of personal and library subscriptions. Unfortunately, there is little data on the circulation of scientific scholarly journals and some of what is available is questionable. MACHLUP & LEESO (1980) and FRY & WHITE both provide circulation data from surveys of publishers in the 1970s. The annual *ULRICH'S INTERNATIONAL PERIODICALS DIRECTORY* provides circulation data by journal title, but not for every title and, since the reported circulation figures sometimes remain the same across years for the same titles, the data that are reported are questionable. TENOPIR & KING (1997) report 1975 and 1995 circulation data for journals published in nine fields of science and for four types of publishers (commercial, society, educational, and other). These data are derived from a combination of *Ulrich's* data, reported circulation in the journals, and data provided by a few large publishers. These data show that 4,175 scientific scholarly journals published in the United States in 1975 had an average of 6,100 subscribers and the estimated 6,771 journals published in 1995 had an average of 5,800 subscribers, but the median number of subscribers dropped from 2,900 to 1,900. This suggests that the rich are getting richer and the poor are getting poorer in terms of journal circulation.

Another aspect of circulation is taken from the perspective of subscribers: individual (personal) and institutional (library). There is little statistical evidence over the years about the extent to which either type subscribes to journals. TENOPIR & KING (2000) show that the average number of personal subscriptions for scientific scholarly journals appears to have decreased from about 5.8 to 2.7 subscriptions per scientist per year over the period 1975 to 1995.[2] However, in 1948, BERNAL (cited by MEADOWS, 1974) reports that pure scientists subscribed to 3 journals, but read from about 9 journals in any given week. Engineers, on the other hand, subscribed to an average of 1.3 journals and read from about 4 journals. In 1963, MARTIN & ACKOFF say that chemists owned one-third of the journals they read and physicists about one-half.

The ASSOCIATION OF RESEARCH LIBRARIES provides some evidence of subscription trends over the years, but does not break the number down by type of journal (i.e., scholarly or trade; scientific or other). While the total number of library subscriptions increased over the twenty-year period, the increase does not reflect increases in number of journals, libraries, and scientists. Several authors (D.J. BROWN; A.M. CUMMINGS ET AL.; M.M. CUMMINGS; HAWKINS; HENDERSON) point out that library budgets have not increased at the rate of R&D expenditures nor number of scientists, contributing to dampened library demand for scholarly journals and other materials.

Many factors affect circulation of scholarly journals. One is the size of the audience served by the journal. Journals over the past decade tend

---

[2]For 2.64 million U.S. scientists in 1975, the total number of personal subscriptions was 15.3 million. In 1995 the number was 15.5 million subscriptions received by 5.74 million scientists. However, had the number of subscriptions remained at 5.8 per scientist, the total would have been 33.3 million or 17.8 million more or 2,600 per journal on average.

either to become larger in size in an apparent attempt to attract a larger readership or to become very specialized, serving a potentially smaller audience. This partially explains the decrease in median circulation mentioned above (i.e., 2,900 in 1975 to 1,900 in 1995). Three studies in the 1970s examined factors that affect readers' decision to subscribe to journals (CHARLES RIVER ASSOCIATES; INSTITUTE OF PHYSICS; MCDONALD). All of these studies—two in the United States and one worldwide—involved surveys of physicists. The Institute of Physics and McDonald both found that versions of attributes of information content, refereeing, and reputation of authors were the most important reasons to subscribe to a journal, while price, at that time, was rated relatively low. Charles River Associates developed a stochastic model to determine factors that explain the probability that readers will subscribe to journals. These factors, in order of contribution to the probability, are: (1) availability of the journal in a library frequently used by them, (2) convenience of location of their library, (3) the subscription price, (4) proportion of articles read, (5) whether a journal is an association journal, and (6) amount of discretionary or "out-of-pocket" expenditures available for information services.

In the late 1970s prices began to increase dramatically for a number of reasons (ECONOMIC CONSULTING SERVICES INCORPORATED; OKERSON; TENOPIR & KING, 2000). Many studies demonstrate that there is little doubt that price increases influence demand. There are four types of price-demand studies. One type displays the price and demand (circulation) of a sample of journals. For example, NOLL & STEINMUELLER provide plots of 1,400 journals that demonstrate the wide (shotgun-like) variation among journals, although generally inversely related. The second type of study involves variations of multiple regression modeling and analyses. Examples, from among hundreds of such studies (mostly in the economics literature), include BERG who shows that personal subscriptions to scientific journals are much more sensitive to price than library subscriptions. Others look for variables that are related to price. For example, PETERSEN found that increases in size, number of issues, and special graphics increase price whereas advertising helps reduce price. When cost factors are held constant, journals from commercial publishers, non-U.S. publishers, and physical sciences tend to have higher prices. Studies by CHRESSANTHIS & CHRESSANTHIS (1994a; 1994b) and STOLLER ET AL. examined similar variables. The latter conclude that a few commercial publishers (primarily from Western Europe) tend to contribute to the current high prices, but the Chressanthis & Chressanthis studies conclude that the profit-making status of publishers is less important than other factors. MCCABE (1998; 2000) provides convincing evidence that increased size of publishers (largely through merger) is related to increased prices of scholarly journals.

Another approach to examining price-demand relationships is to observe price and circulation changes of individual journals over time (taking inflation rates into account). This approach was taken by KING & RODERER (1981) for 19 physics journals. Like BERG, they found that personal subscriptions are much more sensitive to price than library subscriptions. They also examined the economic interdependencies among personal subscriptions (and factors related to them), library subscriptions, interlibrary borrowing, distribution of preprints and reprints, and page charges (see also TENOPIR & KING, 2000).

A final way of explaining price and demand sensitivities is to determine how readers and librarians choose between purchasing journals and using alternative sources of the articles (TENOPIR & KING, 2000). From a cost standpoint, it is generally less expensive for a reader to use a library for infrequently read journals and subscribe to frequently read ones. One can establish break-even points in amount of reading for journals priced at various values and at different distances to a library, thus taking into account the factors reported by CHARLES RIVER ASSOCIATES. Similarly, libraries generally should subscribe to frequently read journals and rely on interlibrary loan or document delivery for infrequently read ones, depending on the journal price (and processing costs) and the total cost for obtaining separate copies of articles (including fees). The break-even point for a $100 journal would typically be about 13 readings and for a $1,000 journal about 120 readings.

The price-demand sensitivity can be established through the distribution of reading levels of library-provided journals (CHEN; KENT ET AL.; KINGMA) and knowing the costs of processing journals (GRIFFITHS & KING, 1993; KINGMA) and the costs of borrowing (GETZ; GRIFFITHS & KING, 1993; JACKSON; KINGMA). TENOPIR & KING (2000) developed a model for simulating price increases. This model shows that increases from $250 to $500 would result in a journal with 2,500 library subscriptions losing about 400 subscriptions (i.e., to 2,100 subscriptions). Yet, with the same price increase, a journal with 2,500 personal subscriptions would decrease by 1,950 subscriptions (i.e., to 550 subscribers). This evidence helps explain why personal subscriptions dropped so dramatically when prices accelerated in the late 1970s, but the number of library subscriptions was less affected.

There is little evidence in the literature concerning circulation of electronic journals, although KIERNAN (1999b) reports that many electronic journals have disappointingly low circulation. WALKER describes trends for the circulation of a small electronic journal, *Florida*

Entomologist, which was provided free on the Web in 1994. Over the first four years circulation declined 3%, but then gained 5% the next year. ROUS reveals that the electronic ACM initiative (Digital Library) actually gained 30,000 paying subscribers in little over a year, although with a decline in print subscriptions. He emphasizes that the Digital Library serves users who need to search and retrieve additional articles from journals they cannot afford, much like the long tradition of interlibrary loan and document delivery. The Digital Library is not necessarily a substitute for traditional print subscriptions. TENOPIR & KING (2000) provide quantitative reasons that such a system should work.

Several recent studies asked respondents (usually academicians) about subscribing to electronic journals. For example, in 1994 BERGE & COLLINS asked *IPCT Journal* users how many electronic journals they subscribed to or received in addition to *IPCT Journal.* Of the 390 respondents, 14.6% said none, 35.5% said one or two, 34.4% said three to five, 15.1% said over five. Including *IPCT Journal,* the average would be about four journals per respondent (keeping in mind that this sampled universe is all electronic journal users). In 1995 BUDD & CONNAWAY surveyed faculty of eight universities and received 651 responses (48% response rate). When asked whether they subscribed to electronic journals (excluding listservs, bulletin boards, Usenet), 13.7% of respondents said yes, and of those who didn't, 23.4% said they occasionally read electronic journals. Presumably, the proportion of subscribers has increased since that time because the number of electronic journals has increased.

Scholarly Journal Use

The section above provides some evidence of trends in scholarly journal demand (circulation) and factors that affect price-demand relationships in both the personal and library market. This section deals with the use of scholarly journals in comparison with other communication channels. It also provides evidence of the total amount of use of articles and journals and the number of articles read by scientists and others.

Many studies over the years have established the extent to which various channels are used to obtain needed information. These channels are sometimes generically characterized as formal (e.g., publications) and informal (e.g., conversations), oral versus written, internal to a parent organization (i.e., technical reports, discussions with colleagues), and external (i.e., journals, attendance at meetings). Sometimes scholarly journals are not specified, but are included in a broader class of "the literature." Use of channels is often established by determining what information sources were used for various critical incidents such as successful events, generation of ideas, creation or innovation, or problems solved (R.C. GUPTA). It is clear that various channels are used for different purposes by scientists in different disciplines. In particular, scientists tend to use different channels than do engineers (or technologists, as they are called by several authors).

Studies of journal use have been conducted since the 1950s (Table 1). Journals remain an extremely important source of information for scientists. Research results consistently show that scientists rely more on journals than on other sources. RAITT and others also report that written sources are more important than oral sources for scientists (FLOWERS; MICK ET AL.; RITCHIE & HINDLE; SUTTON). A recent (1998) SUPERJOURNAL Project found that scientists not only frequently read journal articles (29% daily, 57% weekly), but they also consider journals to be important to their work (i.e., 84% strongly agreed that "journals are important to my work" and another 14% agreed with the statement). B.M. GUPTA provides an excellent review of this topic.

Some of the results above apply to scientific literature in general and not just scholarly journals. However, over the years studies have shown that journal reading accounts for most reading by scientists. For example, in 1956 SHAW (cited by MEADOWS, 1974) found that 70% of all reading was from journals. In 1968, GERSTBERGER & ALLEN compared the use of several types of literature: books, professional journals, technical and trade journals, and other publicly accessible written material. They observed that engineers used professional journals most frequently and found them to have the highest technical quality, however, they were found to be third in accessibility and ease of use. WEIL (1977) reports that journals were read most and provided the most benefits. A later study by WEIL (1980) showed the same kind of results. For the years 1984 to 1998, scientists in several surveys reported amount of reading of different materials; scholarly journals were always read far more frequently than others documents (TENOPIR & KING, 2000).

On the other hand, engineers (and technologists) said journals were a much less important source of information than interpersonal communication and even technical reports. However, these conclusions depend some on the type of organization of engineers. For example, a 1989 survey of aerospace engineers (PINELLI ET AL., 1991a) found that engineers in academia used journal articles much more than conference papers, in-house technical reports, and government technical reports (i.e., 26.6 times in a six-month period, 18.0 times, 9.2 times, and 10.0 times respectively). The use reflected the engineers' ratings of importance ranging from 4.35 (on a scale of 1 to 5) for journal articles to 3.02 for in-house technical reports. Use of journal articles in a six-month period by engineers in government was 15.4 times and by engineers in industry was 10.0 times. RAITT's 1984 survey revealed that oral sources

Table 1. Journal Uses and Usage

Year	Type of Scientist	Focus of Study	Author
1959	Medical	To keep abreast of developments	HERNER
1965	Psychologists	Channel used for activity that exerts greater (and 2nd greatest) demand for scientific information	AMERICAN PSYCHOLOGICAL ASSOCIATION (1966) (#14)
1965	Chemists and Metallurgists	Importance in calling attention to current developments	WUEST
1966	Scientists	Idea generation, problem definition	ALLEN (1966b)
1967	Physicists	Proportion who use	KEENAN & SLATER
1967	High-Energy Physicists	Proportion who use	LIBBEY & ZALTMAN
1967	Scientists	Critical incident where proved to be useful in work	ROSENBLOOM & WOLEK
1967	R&D	Idea-generating functions	BAKER ET AL.
1969	R&D	Idea-generating functions	UTTERBACK
1972	Engineers	Types of use	BEARDSLEY
1973	Research Lab	Types of use	WHITLEY & FROST
1974	Basic	Importance of furnishing needed scientific information	GARVEY ET AL.
1975	Hard Science	Source of most useful ideas	GLUECK & JAUCH
1975	R&D	Resolution of technical problems	JOHNSTON & GIBBONS
1976	R&D	Production innovations	ETTLIE
1976	Scientists (Australia)	Proportion who use	SUTTON
1989	Geoscientists	Ranked importance of journals	BICHTELER & WARD
1991	R&D	Frequency of use, importance	HOLLAND ET AL.
1991	Chemists, geneticists, computer scientists	Important source of information	ALMQUIST
1996	Scientists	Use in last six months	VON SEGGERN & JOURDAIN

of information were more used by engineers and that others reported the same results (GERSTL & HUTTON; LADENDORF; MARQUIS & ALLEN; SHUCHMAN). Nearly all studies support the finding of ALLEN & COHEN that "the average engineer makes little or no use of the scientific and professional engineering literature" (p. 12). Instead engineers rely heavily on internal technical reports and personal contacts, although ALLEN (1964) found an inverse relationship between performance and use of outside persons (e.g., consultants). Similar conclusions were made by SHILLING & BERNARD in 1964; AUERBACH CORPORATION in 1965; ROSENBLOOM & WOLEK in 1967; GERSTBERGER & ALLEN in 1968; ALLEN ET AL. in 1968; BEARDSLEY in 1972; GERSTENFELD & BERGER in 1977-79; KRIKELAS in 1983; and PINELLI ET AL. in 1989.

Several studies over the years report the number of journals used by scientists. For example, in 1948 BERNAL (cited by MEADOWS, 1974) reports that the average number of journals consulted per week was 5 to 15 according to the group surveyed (9 for scientists and 5 for engineers). MENZEL ET AL. in 1960 found that 60% of reading by chemists was from 3 main journals and 25% of reading by zoologists was from 3 journals. MARTIN in 1962 (cited by MEADOWS, 1974) indicates that 10 journals accounted for half the reading done by chemists and physicists. ALLEN & COHEN in 1969 indicate that "stars" in one organization read an average of 8.2 journals in one setting and 4.4 journals in another setting. Others, in both settings, read 3.6 journals on average. FROST & WHITLEY in 1971 found similar results; that is, "stars" read 6 scientific journals regularly and others 3.1 (median). In 1970 WOLEK observed the ranges in number of publications that are read regularly by researchers and engineers. These average 6 publications for researchers and 4.3 for engineers. TAYLOR in 1975 found that the number of periodicals read regularly was 18 for technical discipline choices, 29 for testing technical idea choices, and 14 by technical discipline "stars." A 1990 survey of 156 researchers in 6 companies found they had reviewed journals, but they shared an average of 8.3 papers and journals with colleagues (MONDSCHEIN). In response to the question: "On average, how often do you use electronic journals?", scientists in 1999 answered 8 daily, 30 weekly, 9 monthly, 13 occasionally, and 10 never (PULLINGER, 1999). Surveys of scientists in 1977 observed that scientists read at least one article from 13 journals; in a series of surveys in the 1990s that number increased to 18 journals (TENOPIR & KING, 2000). It appears that scientists are reading a wider range of journals now than in the past.

Many studies observe use of journals in libraries. Usually the use is observed by asking library users to not reshelve issues or bound copies of journals and then counting the number that need to be shelved. Three studies in particular provide observations of the distribution of use across journals (CHEN; KENT ET AL.; KINGMA). This is a useful set of measures because it can help determine the journal titles that might be purchased instead of relying on obtaining separate copies of articles in the future. Some studies have made the important distinction between use of unbound issues and bound volumes of journals. This distinction is important because electronic journal subscriptions, online access to current digital databases, and access to retrospective digital databases may vary by these two categories, which reflect age of use. TSAY in 1998 counted the number of bound and unbound journals requiring shelving in a veterans' hospital library and found an average of 50 uses per journal. GOODMAN also makes this distinction and shows the relationship among use of bound volumes, unbound issues, and citation counts for several highly used journals. One remarkable observation is that unbound issues are "used" far less than bound volumes. This is contrary to what age of reading observations show and is not what Goodman expected. He gives some reasons for this unexpected result and also discusses the implications of his library observations and electronic publishing. About 150,000 uses were observed for 59 days by BLECIC in 1999. Thus, for 5,370 titles the average would be about 120 uses per title (assuming 260 days of library opening). TENOPIR & KING (2000) report about 137 readings per title from more than 50 special libraries observed from 1993 to 1998.

Several recent studies observed the use of electronic journals. In 1997 GRAJEK found that about one-half of faculty and staff at the Yale University Medical Center used their computers to access electronic journals. In 1999, MACLENNAN tracked electronic journal usage at the University of Vermont, including hits from Project Muse, SIAM Journals Online, Springer-Verlag Online Journals, and HighWire Press. LENARES found that 48% of faculty from a sample of Association of Research Libraries (ARL) institutions used electronic journals in 1998, but 61% said they did so in 1999, with the largest increase in physical sciences (from 60% to 90%). C.M. BROWN in 1998 established the proportion of chemists and biochemists, mathematicians, and physicists and astronomers at the University of Oklahoma who had personal subscriptions to electronic versions of journals or used library electronic versions, free electronic versions, and electronic (or paper) document delivery. In the Netherlands a nationwide survey of university faculty, researchers, and students established that more than half used electronic journals and that those who used the Internet for this purpose regularly consulted an average of 1.2 journals (VOORBIJ). However, business school faculty were found to use electronic journals less (SPEIER ET AL.).

ODLYZKO discusses the distinction between counting hits and number of downloads as measures of use. He also gives some extremely useful data on use of electronic journals. For example, *The Electronic Journal of Combinatorics* had published 200 articles by early 1999, and had 30,000 full article downloads from its main site each year (i.e., 150 downloads per article, or perhaps, about 300 including mirror sites). *First Monday* (a journal of the Internet) reported between 110,000 and 120,000 full paper downloads per month (an increase of 100% in a year). These accesses came from over 20,000 hosts each month, even though there are only 3,600 subscribers.

Use of Separate Copies of Articles

One of the most discussed phenomena in the current literature deals with the large number of published articles (and preprints) that are being accessed online. The number of separate article copies distributed in the U.S. and elsewhere has always been extensive, but largely undetected and unmeasured. For example, it was estimated that in 1977 about 43 million copies of articles were distributed to scientists, including 5 million preprints, 7 million reprints, and 31 million photocopies of articles sent through interlibrary loan (4 million) and by authors (20 million) and colleagues (7 million) (KING ET AL., 1981). In addition, 32.5 million photocopies were made by scientists themselves (25 million) or by library staff (7.5 million). Currently, the separate copy amount is thought to be well over 100 million—mostly interlibrary loan/document delivery and copies from colleagues and, to a lesser degree, paper versions of preprints and reprints (TENOPIR & KING, 2000).

A survey of interlibrary loan requests in academic libraries in 1971 estimated that there were about 630,000 loan requests involving scientific periodicals—recognizing that some requests involve more than one article (PALMOUR ET AL.). Surveys of libraries done for the U.S. Copyright Office showed that there were about 4 million interlibrary loan/document delivery copies of scientific articles in 1977 (KING ET AL., 1977) and 7.5 million in 1982 (MCDONALD & BUSH). Currently, based on surveys of scientists in organizations, it appears that the number exceeds 40 million copies for scholarly scientific articles, while surveys over the years show steady increases in the number of interlibrary loans/document deliveries per scientist (TENOPIR & KING, 2000). Such results reflect relative decreases in demand of journals due to price increases. KASER provides an excellent summary of reported numbers of interlibrary loans and trends; for example, British Library interlibrary loan increased from 229,000 in 1962 to 3.6 million in 1993 (CARRIGAN) and ARL libraries increased from 2.8 million in 1983-84 to 4.3 million in 1992-93. Current amounts of photocopying done by scientists or by others on their behalf (e.g., libraries) are discussed by TENOPIR & KING (2000).

There is less detailed information on distribution of preprints and reprints in the literature, especially recently. In 1963 the GARVEY & GRIFFITH studies showed that about one-third of university authors distributed preprints (median of 9 preprints sent per author) and half of non-university authors generally did so (median of 8 copies). About 60% of the preprints distributed resulted in some feedback to the authors (LIN ET AL.). In 1966, HAGSTROM reports a high proportion of authors who distributed preprints and the average number of preprints they sent: 46% of mathematics authors sent an average of 13.8 copies; 73% theoretical physics, 38 copies; 66% experimental physics, 19.8 copies; 48% chemistry, 5.6 copies; 29% experimental biology, 5.7 copies; and 25% other biology, 8 copies. Theoretical physics has by far the largest distribution of preprints, which continues today with the Los Alamos National Laboratory (LANL) digital preprint and archives system (GINSPARG, 1994, 1996). In 1977 physical scientists distributed about 110 preprints per article (KING & RODERER, 1982). In 1967 LIBBEY & ZALTMAN identified the world population of theoretical high-energy physicists and surveyed a sample of them concerning information exchange patterns. They found that, on average, these physicists received 7 manuscripts in a two-week period (or, perhaps, about 180 per year per physicist).

At least two formal preprint exchange groups formed in the 1960s. In biomedicine the Information Exchange Group began in 1961, sponsored by the National Institutes of Health (ALBRITTON). Before it was terminated in 1966, the service received new papers at a rate of 36 per week and distributed approximately 6 preprints each to each of more than 3,600 recipients at a rate of about 24,000 total copies per week (BEVER). This amount extrapolates to about 1.2 million distributed copies per year. In 1965 a Physics Information Exchange was suggested by MORAVCSIK and the U.S. Atomic Energy Commission agreed to sponsor preprint exchange for high-energy physics theorists. However, after a "counter-revolution" was led by PASTERNACK, who suggested that such a system would damage primary journals, the idea was scrapped.

In a sense history is repeating itself. The proposal for a high-energy physics preprint exchange has been realized in the highly publicized LANL preprint and archives system, arXive (GINSPARG, 1994, 1996). This system is said to have a large number of submissions (100,000 in 1999) and an average number of hits of about 140 downloads per year per article plus, perhaps, 20 to 30 times a year in subsequent years (ODLYZKO). The National Institutes of Health has also contemplated a preprint system much like that of LANL and not too different from the concept of the early 1960s Information Exchange Group (KIERNAN, 1999a; TURNER). Other systems such as the ACM Digital Library, the

Netlib system, American Mathematical Society, American Chemical Society, several aggregators, and some large publishers are also showing success.

Reprints are also frequently distributed. MEADOWS (1998) reports that 60% of a sample of biologists sent out more than 100 copies of article reprints. HAGSTROM showed nearly twice as many reprints as preprints distributed: 79% of mathematics authors sent an average of 26.6 copies; 93% theoretical physics, 50.9 copies; 94% experimental physics, 34 copies; 92% chemistry, 48.7 copies; 98% experimental biology, 111.8 copies; and 97% other biology, 104.3 copies. LIBBEY & ZALTMAN found that physicists, on average, received 5 reprints over a two-week period. Altogether, about 17% of the readings in 1977 were from preprints, reprints, and photocopies provided to scientists (KING ET AL., 1981) and in the period from 1993 to 1998 the proportion of the readings was about 18% (TENOPIR & KING, 2000), thus suggesting a consistency in this distribution channel over the years.

Scholarly Journal Reading

One problem with measuring use of scholarly journals is that one does not know the extent to which a journal issue or annual subscription that is used is actually read. Measures of actual reading, depth of reading, and consequences of reading reveal a great deal more about the usefulness and value of scholarly articles and journals. Two survey methods have been used in the past to observe amount of reading. The first method involves providing survey respondents with a list of article titles and asking them which articles they had read. One type of list is the table of contents from journals (GARVEY & GRIFFITH, 1963; KING ET AL., 1978; MACHLUP & LEESON, 1978). This method provides a useful indicator of the extent to which individual articles and, thus journals, are read. However, the measure of reading observed in this way underestimates total reading of an article because (1) an article may be read multiple times for various purposes by a scientist; (2) there may be subsequent first readings of articles following the time of observation (usually about two months following publication), although this source of bias can be addressed through knowledge of age of reading distribution; (3) a substantial amount of reading of articles comes from sources other than original published issues (e.g., preprints, reprints, interlibrary loan, document delivery, and distributed photocopies); and (4) the article information content is passed on by informal/interpersonal means.

A second method involves combining two estimates: total amount of reading observed from surveys of scientists (i.e., average readings per scientist times total number of scientists) divided by total number of articles published as observed from a sample of scholarly journals. While there may be sampling bias involving this estimate,[3] it does take into account reading that would not appear in the GARVEY & GRIFFITH (1963) survey method mentioned above.

An important issue involves the definition of reading. GARVEY & GRIFFITH (1971) refer to a reading as an article being partially or entirely read. MACHLUP & LEESON (1978) conducted a survey of reading by economists (as part of a larger National Science Foundation study), where they defined reading as "going beyond the table of contents, title and the abstract to the body of the article." They established the depth of reading by asking if the article was read: (1) with great care, (2) with attention to the main points, or (3) just to get the idea. This wording was adopted in a later 1977 NSF-sponsored survey (KING ET AL., 1981) in order to provide comparable data, and it was used in more than 13,500 survey responses from scientists from 1977 to 1998 (TENOPIR & KING, 2000). MEADOWS (1998) cites the definition above, but suggests that perhaps a third of the readings might involve half or more of an article and this amount can be reasonably used as a definition of a reading. An indicator of amount of reading is the time spent reading a scholarly article or the total time spent over a period of time, say, the last month reading articles (see below). There appear to be more surveys that ask about time spent reading than about the number of articles read, but the two estimates serve as a good cross-check against one another.

Amount of Reading of Articles and Journals

There is substantial misconception or misunderstanding concerning the extent to which articles and journals are read, based primarily on three sources of information. The first source of misleading information is that some have assumed that the number of citations to an article represents the extent to which an article is read. That number is in the range of 10 to 20 readings per article, for citation purposes, but growing over time. This amount is fallacious for two reasons: (1) only a small proportion of readings are done for the purpose of writing articles and (2) most readings of articles are done by non-authors (TENOPIR & KING, 2000). Furthermore, it has been found that cited articles are different from typical article readings in that they have different identification patterns, are obtained from different sources, and are, on average, much older (HALLMARK; KING ET AL., 1976).

---

[3]While one can sample scientists from lists of known scientists, there is no known universe of scientists from which to sample and one must take care to weight properly for overlapping strata (GRIFFITHS & KING, 1991). National estimates of the number of scientists are made by the U.S. Census Bureau, but even here there are definitional issues.

The second source of misunderstanding comes from interpretation of the Garvey & Griffith surveys, in which they asked scientists to report the number of articles they read from a list provided to them. For example, from one survey it was found that:

> During the two months after publication, the audience for most articles is very small. About half of the research reports in core psychology journals are likely to be read (partially or entirely) by 1% or less of a random sample of psychologists. No research report is likely to be read during this period by more than 7% of a random sample of psychologists (GARVEY & GRIFFITH, 1971, p. 358).

They go so far as to suggest that the publication of journals is unnecessary because of the efficiency of alternative informal channels of communication. This, and other of their sample results, have been widely reported in the literature and treated as though the results for the sample apply to the entire population from which the sample was drawn (e.g., LANCASTER; MERTON; G.R. WILLIAMS). G.R. WILLIAMS (cited by SCHAUDER) reports that "the average article in the American Psychological Association's journals was read by only 17 people. A similar study of chemical journals showed an average readership of only ten persons" (p. 84). GROGAN also presents the results in this way. This reporting of 17 persons reading an article on average ignores or overlooks the fact that GARVEY & GRIFFITH in 1971 report a median of 200 readings (i.e., half of the articles were read fewer than 200 times and half read more than 200) and in 1963 report that these journal articles were read an average of 520 times by psychologists.[4] KING ET AL. (1981) report the average number of readings per psychology article, which was estimated by the second method mentioned above to be 858 readings per article, with readings from other sources together accounting for about 30% to 35% of all readings. Thus, the averages using the two methods appear to validate one another.

MACHLUP & LEESON (1978) performed a similar survey with economists who were provided lists of articles from eight recently published economics journals. Their sample responses yielded an average of 24 readings per article, but when projected to the population from which the sample was drawn, the average was 1,240 readings per article.

---

[4]The median of 200 and mean of 520 illustrates that the distribution of article reading is highly skewed; that is, some articles are frequently read while many others are infrequently read. Many library studies have highlighted the phenomenon for use of library journals (e.g., CHEN; KENT ET AL.; KINGMA). Journal readership reflects the highly skewed distribution of circulation of journals, that is, 25% below 900 subscribers, 50% below 1,900, and 25% above 5,700.

In 1978 the Garvey & Griffith method was replicated by KING ET AL. (1978) for an evaluation of the *Journal of the National Cancer Institute* in which a table of contents of 37 articles was provided to a sample of cancer researchers (521 respondents, 63% response rate). Respondents were asked to "circle the page numbers of all the items which you read in this issue of *JNCI*." The average number of readings per article by the 521 respondents was 52 (46 median), all articles were read at least 11 times, and one was read by 151 of the 521 respondents. Projected over the entire population sampled and over time, the average readings per article was estimated to be 1,800 or 756,000 for the entire journal (12 issues). Other evidence in the survey suggested that other leading journals reporting results of cancer research were read extensively as well.

The journal research community is concerned because it appears that a low proportion of articles received through personal (and library) subscriptions are read (see AMERICAN PSYCHOLOGICAL ASSOCIATION studies mentioned above). For example, ELSDON-DEW (cited by ASTLE; LAMBERT; LANCASTER) reports a 1955 study that found that "a single article in a specialized periodical is of interest to only 10% of the workers in the subject area covered by the journal" (p. 51). A 1970s readership study by Kuney & Weisberger of the *Journal of Organic Chemistry* showed that the average subscriber glanced at or began to read about 17% of the papers in a typical issue, and read half or more of only 4% of the articles[5] in the issue (MOORE, cited by LANCASTER and SCHAUDER). LONGUET-HIGGINS states that 90% of all scientific papers are unread by anyone but their authors. Wass (cited by LANCASTER) developed a simple Makulatorfactor formula, which shows that about 85% of the articles distributed in 1960 were not read.[6] BARUCH & BHAGAT claim that journal subscribers on average read fewer than 1% of the articles they receive, while WILSON ET AL. (cited by SCHAUDER) indicate that only 6% of articles in libraries were consulted twice or more during an academic year.

Dividing estimated total number of readings by total number of articles distributed, the proportion of articles read was 12% in 1977 (KING ET AL., 1981) and 11% in 1995 for personal subscriptions; that is, there are 13.4 average readings from an average of 123 articles per journal (TENOPIR & KING, 1997). Thus, evidence over the years suggests that only about 10% to 20% of articles distributed are actually read, yet the same is likely to be true of most printed materials such as newspapers and magazines, which are not thoroughly read. Even print-

---

[5]Note that GANNETT cites the 4% as being 10%.
[6]LANCASTER and many others have summarized or discussed the various mathematical models, which show the distribution of article coverage, which partially explains the phenomenon reported.

outs from automated searches involve a fairly low proportion of items that are actually read. For example, WANG & WHITE report that automated search outputs had 154 articles retrieved, but only 46 of them are selected, 27 actually read (i.e., 17.5%), and just 1 used as a citation. GRIFFITHS & KING (1993) observed 613 automated searches done by special librarians and found that the searches identified an average of 19.2 articles, of which 8.3 were obtained and 6.7 read (or intended to be read). However, while journals appear to be an inefficient means of communication, it appears to be reasonably efficient when compared with other means of grouping or bundling articles. Also, other print media, such as newspapers and magazines, are not normally thoroughly read. This evidence of low proportions of reading does not mean that scholarly journals are not useful and valuable.

GARVEY & GRIFFITH (1971) recognize that actual reading does not reflect fully the use of information found in articles. In their study of psychologists they conclude that the journal article is "no longer the medium for disseminating *current* scientific findings to researchers active on the research front" (p. 359). However, "this is only a minor portion of the use to which journal articles are ultimately put" (p. 359). That is, the information is also used at a later time following publication and, perhaps more importantly, it is used in subsequent publications and other channels. Also, information read by one scientist is often passed on by him/her to colleagues. The early GARVEY & GRIFFITH (1963) study showed that, for 13% of readings, some information is passed on. BERGE & COLLINS indicate that 53% of their respondents said that they passed on articles to colleagues. ALLEN & COHEN found that a few gatekeepers in some R&D laboratories read journals (and other external materials) far more than others, but keep the others informed about what the literature is saying. TENOPIR & KING (2000) report that about 11% of reading comes from sources such as colleagues.

In 1977 there were estimated to be 382,300 articles published in U.S. scientific scholarly journals and 244 million readings by U.S. scientists, thus yielding an estimated 638 average readings per article (KING ET AL., 1981). (Readings were adjusted to reflect estimated future readings of current articles.) The current estimate using updated measures is about 900 readings per article (TENOPIR & KING, 2000). Since the average number of articles published per journal is 123, the total readings are about 110,000 per journal.

There are also some estimates of the average number of readings per journal subscription received by a scientist. The Garvey & Griffith (1963) survey showed that only 30% of respondents had read any of the listed articles, but those 30% had read more than 6 articles. Depending on the number of issues in a journal, the total for a year would be in the

10 to 20 readings range. A 1977 survey found an average of about 12 readings per personal subscription (KING ET AL., 1981) and surveys in the 1990s found an average of 13.4 readings (TENOPIR & KING, 2000).

Scientists' Amount of Reading

Above we provide a review of estimates of the use and readership of scholarly journals and articles. In this section we review studies that provide estimates of the extent to which individual scientists read scholarly journals. These studies invariably involve surveys of scientists, although the way in which the questions of readership and time are asked varies somewhat. Surprisingly few of the many surveys of scientists' information-seeking behavior ask about the number of articles read. The Garvey & Griffith survey method that uses lists of articles does not provide accurate estimates of total readership per scientist because it is limited to the journals involved. In 1948 BERNAL (cited by MEADOWS, 1974) estimated that medical researchers read an average of 7.4 papers per week (perhaps 340 to 380 per year) and engineers read 1.5 papers per week (about 70 to 80 per year). A 1977 national survey showed that scientists averaged 105 article readings per scientist (KING ET AL., 1981), while a follow-up survey in 1984 showed about 115 readings, and several surveys in organizations from 1993 to 1998 yielded combined estimates of about 120 readings per scientist (TENOPIR & KING, 2000). Engineers are found to read less than other scientists. For example, PINELLI ET AL. (1989) estimated that engineers read an average of 6.7 articles per month (or about 80 readings per year) and the engineers in the surveys above also averaged 80 readings per year (both of these results are about the same as the 1948 Bernal observations). Thus, evidence suggests that scientists' amount of reading has not changed much over the years.

Several studies have shown that academicians read more than non-university scientists. In 1969 MEADOWS & O'CONNOR revealed that university scientists use journals more than those in government establishments. KING ET AL. (1981) estimated that university scientists read scholarly journals an average of 150 times per year versus 90 times by other scientists. In the period 1993 to 1998 several surveys produced averages of 188 and 106 readings of scholarly journals per university and non-university scientist respectively (TENOPIR & KING, 2000). However, since there are many more scientists working outside of universities, they account for about 70% of all readings. The Association for Computing Machinery (ACM) provides some confirmation of these results (DENNING & ROUS). They say that most ACM "journals are written by experts for other experts, but these experts constitute less than 20% of the readership" (p. 99). Note that most scientific scholarly articles are written by university scientists. The other 80% of readers of ACM journals are said to be experts from other disciplines or practitioners.

COMMUNICATION TIME OF SCIENTISTS

Proportion of Time Spent Communicating

Studies reviewed above show that journals are but one of many channels of communication used by scientists, although journals are preferred over other channels, depending on several factors including scientific discipline and ease of access. (More is said about such factors later in this chapter.) One indicator of the value of information and its communication is the amount of time scientists are willing to spend in this activity. Several studies have examined how much time scientists spend communicating. These studies used a variety of methods ranging from having scientists carry random alarm devices (to determine the proportion of time spent in various activities) to simply asking scientists to indicate the proportion of time they spent in various activities. ORR provides some discussion of methods used to estimate time spent in various activities.

A summary of observations of the proportions of time spent communicating is given in Table 2. PINELLI ET AL. (1991b) report differences in time spent communicating by aerospace scientists and engineers around the world: U.S. 50%, Western Europe 40%, Japan 37.5%, and Israel 37.5%. Twenty years earlier BAYER & JAHODA found that 60%

Table 2. Time Spent Communicating

Year	Type of Scientist	Proportion of Time (%)	Author
1958	Chemists	44%	HALBERT & ACKOFF
1960	University chemists	25%	MENZEL ET AL.
	Industry chemists	33%	MENZEL ET AL.
	Physical scientists	42%	CASE INSTITUTE OF TECHNOLOGY
1964	Chemists	61%	HINRICHS
1975	Scientists	67%	TUROFF & SCHER
	Scientists	55%	DAVIS
1979	R&D	40%	MICK ET AL.
1988	R&D	48%	ALLEN
1991	Engineers	50%	PINELLI ET AL., 1991b
1994-1998	R&D	58%	TENOPIR & KING, 2000

of academic chemists spent four or more hours per week in discussion with colleagues and nearly half of industry chemists spent more than that amount. RAITT observed that 50% of aerospace engineers spent less than one-third of their time communicating and 8% spent more than two-thirds of their time communicating.

From these observations it is difficult to detect any trends in amount of time spent communicating, although it is clear that these activities occupy a substantial proportion of scientists' time. TENOPIR & KING (2000) report that there is some evidence that the total amount of time spent on work-related activities increased about 150 hours over a 15-year period, most of this time attributable to additional time spent communicating. One set of studies asked aerospace engineers and scientists whether there were changes in the past five years in amount of time spent communicating technical problems (PINELLI ET AL., 1991b). In the United States, 42% said time increased, 45% said it stayed the same, and 13% said it decreased. In Japan, results were about the same, but in Western Europe 60% said the time increased. Several of the studies specify proportions of time spent reading; these results are discussed below.

Time Spent Reading Journal Articles

Several studies have investigated the hours or proportion of time spent reading the literature. For example, HALBERT & ACKOFF estimated that in 1958 physical scientists spent about 37 hours per month reading. In the 1960s, the CASE INSTITUTE OF TECHNOLOGY Operations Research Group reports 24 hours per month. HALL ET AL. report 45 hours, ALLEN (1966a) reports 8.6 to 13.8 hours, and GARVEY & GRIFFITH (1963) report 27.7 hours for psychologists and 15.6 to 20.8 hours for other fields of science. RAITT in 1984 reports time in increments, which roughly convert to 15 hours per month for background reading by aerospace engineers, and HOLLAND & POWELL indicate that University of Michigan engineering graduates spend about 22.9 hours per month reading. Results, while varied, do indicate an appreciable amount of time spent reading. HINRICHS in 1964 reports 10% of time, MICK ET AL. in 1979 report 9.8%, ALLEN (1966a) reports 7.9% for engineers and in 1988 18.2% for scientists, and TENOPIR & KING in 2000 report 20.6% for scientists (including about 5% involving electronic messages). Again, scientists' time is a scarce resource that is carefully utilized. A decision to spend an appreciable amount of time reading suggests that they place considerable value on the information received.

While not all reading involves scholarly journals, studies suggest that amount of time spent reading journals is substantial, as shown in

Table 3 by field of science (TENOPIR & KING, 2000). LUFKIN & MILLER estimated that scientists and engineers in two companies in 1966 averaged about 10 minutes a day reading (or about 3.6 hours per month), although 40% of them spent 1 to 5 hours per week.

As mentioned earlier, estimates of time spent reading journal articles is a good cross-check on the estimate of amount of reading. Among the observations in Table 3, the median estimate of hours spent per month reading journals is 9, or about 108 hours per year. In 1956 SHAW (cited by MEADOWS, 1974) estimated that the average time spent for each reading was 20 minutes. In 1977 the estimate was 45 minutes per reading (KING ET AL., 1981) and in the period 1993 to 1998 the estimate was 52 minutes per reading (TENOPIR & KING, 2000). Thus, one would expect there to be anywhere from 10 readings per month (120 per year) at 52 minutes per reading to 27 readings per month (324 per year) at 20 minutes per reading, which are in the ranges reported earlier.

Table 3. Time Spent Reading Journals

Field	Hours/Month	Year	Author(s)
Physical sciences	25.1	1958	HALBERT & ACKOFF
	11.7	1960	CASE INSTITUTE OF TECHNOLOGY
	4.8-11.7	1977	WEIL
	9.0	1977	KING ET AL., 1981
	24.0	1999	BROWN, C.M.
Mathematics	19.1	1977	KING ET AL., 1981
Computer sciences	3.4	1977	KING ET AL., 1981
Environmental sciences	4.2	1977	KING ET AL., 1981
Engineering	2.2-3.5	1966	ALLEN, 1966a
	19.1	1972	HALL ET AL.
	5.0	1977	KING ET AL., 1981
	4.0	1989	PINELLI ET AL., 1989
Life sciences	8.1	1977	KING ET AL., 1981
Cancer research	24.1	1978	KING ET AL., 1978
Psychology	13.9	1963	GARVEY & GRIFFITH, 1963
	4.8	1977	KING ET AL., 1981
Social Sciences	11.3	1977	KING ET AL., 1981
All fields	11.7	1963	GARVEY & GRIFFITH, 1963
	6.8	1977	KING ET AL., 1981
	9.2	1994-98	TENOPIR & KING, 2000

USEFULNESS AND VALUE OF SCHOLARLY JOURNALS

Purposes of Reading

The purposes for which scholarly journals are used have been described in a variety of ways over the years. For example, ALLEN (1966b) determined the proportion of times information sources were used for various purposes on research projects. The proportion of times the literature is used for various purposes is as follows: expand alternatives (60%), generate alternative approaches (58%), generate critical dimensions (54%), set limits of acceptability (50%), test alternatives against dimensions (27%), and reject alternative approaches (13%). Literature is the most frequently used source for all purposes except the last two. In 1967 ROSENBLOOM & WOLEK found that in central laboratories, professional documents are used for research (48%), design and development (33%), and analysis and testing (48%), and that they are the most frequently used channel for all three purposes. GARVEY ET AL. in 1974 revealed that journal articles are used to: (1) form a basis for instruction of new scientists, (2) acquaint themselves with the accumulated knowledge that exists when embarking on new research or inquiry, (3) facilitate day-to-day scientific work, and (4) advance the research front.

Others also provide data on use of journal literature. MACHLUP & LEESON (1978) found in their survey of economists that general interest is the most prominent purpose (46%), followed by research (33%), teaching (15%) and coursework and other purposes (6%). More recently SABINE & SABINE established that journals in 50 libraries were used for current research (38%), help on the job (25%), writing a paper or speech (13%), general information (10%), and teaching (5%). BERGE & COLLINS observed that electronic journals were used because of interest in a topic (68%), to help in work (25%), or for researching a topic (14%). In 1998 SHOHAM showed that purposes vary by type of scientist (Table 4).

Table 4. Purpose of Journal Use

Purpose of Use	Engineers	Scientists	Social Scientists
Research	78.6%	94.9%	90.1%
Instruction	21.4%	41.8%	72.7%
General Updating	71.4%	75.9%	79.1%
Obtain Research Funds	14%	10.1%	14.5%

Source: SHOHAM

TENOPIR & KING (2000) make a distinction between university and non-university scientists' purposes for using scholarly journal articles. In 1993 over 50% of readings by University of Tennessee scientists were for current awareness or professional development. Other readings were used to support research (75%), teaching (41%), to prepare formal publications and formal talks or presentations (32%), and administration (13%). C. M. BROWN also found that scientists at the University of Oklahoma relied on journals more for research than for teaching. On the other hand, GRIFFITHS & KING (1993) found that scientists in 32 non-university settings (e.g., AT&T Bell Laboratories, National Institutes of Health, Oak Ridge National Laboratory) used journals differently: for current awareness or professional development (30%), background information research (26%), conducting primary research (17%), conducting other R&D activities (11%), and management or other (3%). Their readings for communications-related activities were: consulting or giving advice (4%), writing (7%), and making presentations (3%).

Importance of Reading

Information in journal articles is found to be important for a number of reasons. SCOTT reports that literature serves as the primary source of creative stimulation. CHAKRABARTI & RUBENSTEIN found that the quality of the information as perceived by the recipient is a major factor in the adaptation of innovation. ETTLIE also found that the literature was the single most important source of information in achieving product innovations. Another aspect of the usefulness of scholarly journals is their importance to scientists. MACHLUP & LEESON (1978) report that economists found 32% of their readings to be useful or interesting, 56% moderately useful, and 12% not useful. TENOPIR & KING (2000) indicate the importance of journal article readings to the purposes mentioned above. University scientists rated importance from not at all important (1) to somewhat important (4) to absolutely essential (7). For readings done for teaching, the scientists rated the importance of the information to achieving teaching objectives as 4.83 on average, while importance to research was given an average rating of 5.02. Over a period of a year, the scientists indicated that, of a total of 188 readings, an average of 13 readings per scientist were absolutely essential to their teaching and 23 were absolutely essential to research. Non-university scientists were asked to rate the importance of several resources (e.g., computing equipment/workstations, instrumentation, documents, advice from others, etc.) used to perform various activities. The ratings were from 1 (not at all important) to 5 (absolutely essential). The average ratings of journals for activities performed are as follows: professional development (4.05, highest), primary research (4.03, second highest), other R&D activities (3.87, highest), writing (3.76, highest), consulting/advising (3.60, second highest), and presentations (3.31, third highest).

Value of Scholarly Journals

Value of information provided by journal articles can be measured in many ways. However, in 1974 MARTYN (in quoting KING & PALMOUR) makes the point that: "The ultimate value of any information communication system should be thought of in terms of the uses that are made of the information and the subsequent impact of the information on users' scientific and technical activities . . . Although this is the critical function of user behavior, it is rarely measured, let alone even considered in many user studies" (p. 17). This holds true today.

MACHLUP points out that there are two types of value of the information provided by scholarly journals: purchase value and use value. The purchase value is what scientists are willing to pay for the information in terms of money exchanged and the time expended in obtaining and reading the information, whereas use value is the consequence of using the information. The average purchase value expended per scientist on journals is at least $6,000 per year and the use value exceeds $25,000 per year per scientist (TENOPIR & KING, 2000). The price paid in scientists' time tends to be five to ten times the price paid in purchasing journals and separate copies of articles.

There are many ways in which the consequences of reading can be expressed. For example, TENOPIR & KING (2000) showed that nearly all readings by university scientists (95%) resulted in some favorable outcomes. Readings improved quality of teaching, research, or other activities for which the reading was done (66% of readings); and helped them to perform the activity better (33%), faster (14%), or at a lower cost in time or money (19%). With non-university scientists, consequences were established for the principal activity for which the reading is done (GRIFFITHS & KING, 1993). For example, 67% of the readings resulted in higher quality, 32% in faster performance, 42% helped reinforce hypotheses or increased confidence in one's work, 26% resulted in initiating ideas or broadened options concerning work.

There has been ample evidence over the years that amount of reading and productivity of scientists are positively correlated. In 1958 MAIZELL established an association between the numbers of journals the scientists read and productivity measured in terms of publications. ORR cites several studies in the 1960s that suggest similar relationships. The Operations Research Group of the CASE INSTITUTE OF TECHNOLOGY concludes that physicists and chemists who publish read more than non-publishers. SHILLING & BERNARD and BERNARD ET

AL. established a strong positive correlation between various measures of the productivity of biological R&D labs and indices of communication. ALLEN & ANDRIEN compared differences among engineering teams with regard to (1) the proportion of time spent with various types of input channels (and also the phasing of the use of these channels) and (2) the quality of their output or performance and of publications. PARKER ET AL. found that the strongest single predictor of production was the number of informal contacts with other scientists. MEADOWS (1974) cites MENZEL ET AL. as providing evidence that chemists who were rated as highly creative typically consulted twice as much literature as those having low creativity. Later WEIL (1980) states that journals, when compared to other published materials and computerized information, provided by far the greatest benefits to current work. GRIFFITHS & KING (1993) established in each of six organizations that amount of reading is positively correlated with five indicators of productivity (i.e., outputs measured in five ways).

Another indicator of the use value of scholarly journals is that scientists whose work has been formally recognized tend to read more than others. For example, LUFKIN & MILLER in the 1960s report from surveys in two companies that "People who have been singled out for excellence, whether by promotion, or by publication, or by special recognition for creativity, all read a great deal more than the average" (p. 180). Surveys by GRIFFITHS & KING (1993) in the 1980s and 1990s invariably showed that winners of achievement, technical, and patent awards read 53% more articles than non-awardees. Similar results were observed for those chosen to serve on high-level projects or problem-solving teams. In one company, 25 persons who were considered particularly high achievers read 59% more articles than their colleagues. TENOPIR & KING (2000) report University of Tennessee scientists who received achievement awards or special honors read more; that is, those recognized for their teaching read 26% more articles and those recognized for research read 33% more articles.

INFORMATION-SEEKING PATTERNS

Identification and Location of Articles Read

Articles that are read are identified and located in several ways as shown from surveys over the years (Table 5). Browsing is the principal means of identifying articles that are read, mostly for current articles (i.e., 81% of articles found this way are a year or less old). In 1986 WILSON ET AL. also report that 53% of articles are found by browsing. Browsing is done in different ways. For example, GUSHEE concludes that scientists select the articles they read by scanning the contents,

Table 5. Ways Journal Articles Are Identified

Means of Identifying	King et al. (1981) 1977	Tenopir & King (2000) 1993-1998	L.A. Williams 1993
Browsing	52.3%	62.4%	56%
Other persons	18.0%	11.4%	8%
Cited in article	9.9%	6.6%	—
Cited in printed index	—	—	9%
Automated search	0.3%	12.1%	11%
Other means	19.5%	7.5%	16%

engineers by scanning the text pages, and organic chemists by examining structures and diagrams. Browsing takes some of scientists' valuable time. MARTIN & ACKOFF found that one-half of the reading time of chemists and two-thirds of the time of physicists is spent browsing.

Sources of Articles Read

There are several distribution means or sources for articles that are read. In addition to the personal or library subscriptions to journals mentioned earlier, well over 100 million separate copies of articles are distributed through interlibrary loan, document delivery, preprints, reprints, and photocopies or electronic copies provided by authors and colleagues. KING ET AL. (1981) estimated that in 1977, 68% of readings came from a reader's own subscription copy, while 15% were from library copies. The remaining 17% of readings came from separate copies of articles characterized (1) by the source (author 12%, coworker 4%, and other 1%) or (2) by the form of the separate copy (preprint 3%, reprint 2%, and photocopy 12%). In recent years the proportion of readings from personal subscriptions dropped to about 27%, which reflects the fact that the number of personal subscriptions decreased from 5.8 to 2.7 per scientist over the same time period (TENOPIR & KING, 2000). Scientists replaced their cancelled personal subscriptions with library copies as a source: 14% of readings in 1977 came from library copies compared to 55% in the 1993-to-1998 period. The proportion of readings from separate copies of articles remained at about 18%, with about 33% of these from interlibrary loan and document delivery. Surveys of scientists from non-universities in the late 1990s showed that 9.8% of the readings were obtained online; however, it is not known if these were from subscriptions or document delivery services. Sources of articles vary by age of articles when read. For example, 88% of readings from personal subscriptions were of articles one year old or less. Of articles over one year old, 71% were read from library copies, 9% from personal subscriptions, and 20% from separate copies of articles.

Age of Articles Read

Several studies over the years have established the age of articles when they are read. Some provide a distribution of age of articles (Table 6). Thus, it seems clear that age of articles read has not changed much over the years. Other studies showed somewhat similar results. For example, in 1956 SHAW (cited by MEADOWS, 1974) indicated that 80% of materials read appeared within 12 months and that half of them were just published. WERLER in 1975 says that 85% of articles read from libraries were published five years ago or less. PALMOUR ET AL. found that library use was from articles less than 25 years old and GERSTENFELD & BERGER showed that 56% of the information used from written materials was used at a time later than its receipt.

Newer articles are more likely to be read for casual interest and older articles to apply to one's work. This conclusion is supported by results showing that older articles were rated more important than new articles and more time was spent reading them (TENOPIR & KING, 2000). Interestingly, newer articles were more likely to be read for teaching purposes and older ones for research.

ODLYZKO makes a strong argument that use of electronic journal articles has a substantially different pattern over time than observed

Table 6. Age of Journal Articles Read

Age[1]	Case Institute of Technology 1960	Tenopir & King (2000) 1993-1998
1	61.5%	64.4%
2	13.3%	14.3%
3	2.6%	3.1%
4-5	8.4%	6.0%
6-10	10.2%	4.8%
11-15	1.7%	2.3%
>15	2.3%	5.0%

[1]Years since publication

with print journals. Electronic use continues for a much longer period of time, which is true for formal electronic subscription sites as well as articles appearing on personal Web pages.[7]

FACTORS AFFECTING SEEKING AND READING PATTERNS

ORR points out that when information is needed one can get it by: (1) experimentation, observations, and so on; (2) from contemporaries' brains; and/or (3) from the pool of recorded knowledge (i.e., the past effort of others). The choice among these three options depends on one's assessment of the likelihood of success within an acceptable time period and on perception of relative accessibility, cost (i.e., time and expenditure), and effort necessary to obtain the information. Variations of this theme are to weigh the amount of information versus cost (GRIFFITHS & KING, 1993; TENOPIR & KING, 2000) and to consider what is "good enough" or "not good enough" versus some variables that contribute to this assessment (ORR). On the other hand, ALLEN & GERSTBERGER found that engineers appear to act in a manner so as not to maximize gain (i.e., benefits), but rather to minimize loss (i.e., cost). Yet, MEADOWS (1998) summarizes the many surveys as follows: "One of the firmest conclusions of information usage surveys seems to be, indeed, that the intrinsic value of an information channel has little, or no, bearing on the frequency with which it is used. The ultimate factor is always its accessibility" (p. 124).

Personal and Situational Factors

ORR sets forth two types of variables or factors that are related to choices of communication channels, which probably also apply to scholarly journal distribution means and media. These two types of factors are given below with expansion and with some examples of studies over the years that support them.

Personal factors.

    (1)   education, training and past work, including discipline/ profession, level of training, nature of work, experience with channels: CRANE (1969) (stage of growth of disciplines, "soft" versus "hard" disciplines); ROSENBLOOM & WOLEK (discipline, degree, and experience); GARVEY

---

[7]For example, we asked Odlyzko about continued use of his five-year-old article "Tragic Loss or Good Riddance? The Impending Demise of Traditional Scholarly Journals." (*International Journal of Human-Computer Studies* 42 (1995): 71-122). For the first six months of 2000 he continued to receive an average of 175 full article downloads per month from an average of 111 unique hosts.

& GRIFFITH (1963) (education level, area of specialization); HAZELL & POTTER (education)

(2) status and stage of career: ROSENBLOOM & WOLEK (job rank, seniority); GERSTBERGER (time in a firm)

(3) demographics: MEADOWS & BUCKLE and MEADOWS (1998) (age, sex, etc.); BERNARD ET AL. (age)

(4) inherent capabilities: ROTHWELL (ability to understand messages); CARTER ET AL. and CHAKRABARTI ET AL. (skills needed to use sources); DOSA ET AL. and BORGMAN (cognitive styles); ANTHONY ET AL. (psychological traits)

(5) personality/work style: HOBAN and LOHMANN (character, maturity); ANTHONY ET AL. (predisposition to problem-solving approaches); BORGMAN (motivation)

Situational factors.

(1) nature of need, including functions served; kind of information (i.e., theories, methods, data/results); information attributes (i.e., precision, quality, specificity, complexity, urgency): GRIFFITHS & KING (1993) (information attributes); PINELLI (information content and attributes)

(2) current project, including nature of work, stage of the project: ALLEN & ANDRIEN; ACKOFF; and DUBINSKAYA (nature of work); ALLEN (1966b) and AMERICAN PSYCHOLOGICAL ASSOCIATION (1966) Report 11 (phase of research); BAKER ET AL. and UTTERBACK (problem definition versus idea generation)

(3) work setting, including structure, reward/control system, size of organization, information infrastructure, prestige of setting: HAGSTROM; ROTHWELL & TOWNSEND; GRANT; and LISTON ET AL. (size of firm); MARQUIS & STRAIGHT and ALLEN (1969) (physical location); ALLEN (1966b) and SMITH (rating of project teams)

(4) sponsor/funder characteristics: ALLEN (1965) and LIPETZ (different values than other participants); MILLER (spatial orientation)

(5) peer communities: CRAWFORD (1971) (communication ties); PRICE (invisible colleges); AMERICAN PSYCHO-LOGICAL ASSOCIATION (1965) and GARVEY & GRIFFITH (1963; 1971) (professional membership); ALLEN & COHEN (friendships)

(6) channel capabilities and attributes: PAISLEY (1965, 1968)
(10 communication systems and subsystems ranging
from the scientist within own head, scientist within a
work team, to scientist within his culture);
GERSTBERGER & ALLEN; ALLEN (1988); MEADOWS
(1998); RATH & WERNER; and ROSENBERG (accessibility, ease of use); LINE (availability); JOHNS HOPKINS
UNIVERSITY SOGIP STUDY GROUP (information content, relevance, writing); LIN & GARVEY (1972) and
LIN & NELSON (prestige of authors); HUTH (barriers
to the use of the literature); KATZEN (factors that govern the effect of research articles on their readers);
REYNOLDS (legibility); BUXTON & MEADOWS (formatting of titles, abstracts, text)

Factors Related to Electronic Journals

Several recent studies examined factors involving use of electronic
journals. The principal issues concern quality of electronic journals and
reading them on the screen. SPEIER ET AL. asked respondents to rate
the quality of peer-reviewed electronic journals versus paper, from
those of substantially lesser quality (1) to those of substantially greater
quality (7). About 61% rated electronic journal quality in the three
lowest ratings, 28% in the middle, and only 3% in the highest three
ratings (average rating of 2.9 excluding nonresponses). When the top-
quality electronic journal was compared with paper-based journals, the
ratings increased to an average of 3.79. BUDD & CONNAWAY also
asked about the quality of electronic and print journals. Of the survey
respondents, 1.9% said electronic journals were equal to the best print
journals; 6.5% said they were equal to acceptable print journals; 4.2%
said they were equal to lesser print journals; and 10.2% said they were
inferior to most print journals. However, most (77.1%) said they could
not judge. Some (12.4%) felt that electronic journals were improving,
but 85% said they could not judge. BERGE & COLLINS found that 84%
of survey respondents felt that quality of electronic journals was the
same or better than print journals and 14% said they cited electronic
journal articles.

BUTLER took another approach by asking contributors to electronic
journals (mostly affiliated with academic institutions) about their perceptions of the advantages and disadvantages of publications in electronic journals. The top five advantages reported were speed of publication (71% of respondents), reach the best audience (55%), enhance
scholarly dialogue (48%), low cost to readers (35%), and remote geographic access (33%). The five top disadvantages reflect variations of

some of those disadvantages observed by others including: perceived as not "real" publications (63%), less prestigious (54%), inadequate graphics (38%), inadequate indexing (38%), and archival instability (35%). Butler also asked about feedback to authors. Although amount of feedback seemed about the same compared with print (34% more, 28% same, 38% less), the substance of feedback appeared to compare favorably with print (37% more, 49% same, 14% less). Furthermore, speed of feedback was considered faster than print (84% faster, 14% same, 2% slower). Most of the feedback was through email/listserv (55%), although traditional channels were used as well (e.g., 17% face-to-face, 10% telephone, 8% mail, 6% publication, and 4% other channels). In evaluating one's career performance, the electronic journal contributors generally perceived electronic publication to be less important than print.

The SUPERJOURNAL Project took a similar approach, but found other kinds of advantages: the top five reasons being easy access (30% of respondents); convenience, desktop access (29%); searchable (25%); quick or direct access (19%); and good printouts, better than photocopy (15%). Disadvantages included slow access, downloading (42%); journal coverage, breadth or depth (27%); don't like to read on screen (27%); presentation, graphics (12%); and access problems, passwords (8%).

STEWART interviewed 39 chemists who used Chemistry Online Retrieval Experiment (CORE) and found that the most important capability was creation of a print copy (80.0% very important, 14.3% important). Other features of importance were browsing graphics to determine the value of an article (72.7% very important, 15.2% important); and browsing that could support ongoing education and generate new ideas (65.8% very important, 21.1% important). She found that users would browse a page or two and then print. Of 154 viewing occasions, 75% looked at one page and then printed. Printing capabilities are evidently essential. Even in 1983, PULLINGER found in evaluation of Birmingham Loughborough Electronic Network Development (BLEND) that 65% of browsing and 85% of reading of entire papers took place outside office hours. Reading on a screen presents some problems to users. RICHARDSON found that none of his survey respondents appeared to have read articles on the screen. SCHAUDER indicated that 75% of respondents preferred to read printouts. SIMPSON observed similar results. In the ADONIS Project, RICHARDSON found that portability was important.

KLING & MCKIM provide an analysis of 16 journal media and distribution means in terms of communication attributes: publicity, access, and trust. STEWART found that dates of coverage were important in electronic databases, but exact page images were not required. She also found that many chemists she interviewed felt that electronic journals could be used for all scholarly journal reading: of 39 chemists, 16 said they could be, 5 said maybe, and 5 said no. The rest were uncertain or not clear.

TENOPIR & KING (2000) examined the alternative costs of electronic versus print personal subscriptions, electronic versus print library subscriptions, electronic personal subscriptions versus electronic document delivery, and electronic library subscriptions versus electronic document delivery. These analyses demonstrate that the amount of readership of a journal is an important criterion, as is users' time (i.e., cost must be seriously considered). They also suggest that print and electronic journals may coexist and complement one another over the short term.

Awareness of electronic journals may still be an issue. SPEIER ET AL. asked respondents in ARL institutions to rate their awareness, with the following rating results: 1 (not aware), 7%; 2, 18%; 3 (somewhat aware), 35%; 4, 11%; 5 (fairly aware), 17%; 6, 5%; 7 (aware), 7%. These results are partially reflected in use of electronic journals by these respondents: 1 (never), 35%; 2, 21%; 3 (rarely), 21%; 4, 7%; 5 (sometimes), 11%; 6, 4%; 7 (frequently), 1%. In the same year LENARES reports that 54% of academics in her survey "did not know of respected e-journals in my field," down from 61% in the previous year.

MERCER proposes using automatically captured usage reports to measure patterns of use of electronic journals through a digital library. Analysis of information captured by both HighWire Press and Ovid Technologies can provide a detailed picture of use that has not before been available to libraries. Not only are number of hits or downloads recorded for each journal title, but also more detailed information on such things as users' format preferences (HTML or PDF), what sections of a journal are read most frequently, and what searches or paths were taken by users to access an article. The ARL (at the Spring 2000 Coalition for Networked Information conference in Washington, D.C.) reported a project to examine measures of the use and impact of electronic services.

CONCLUSIONS

An historical review of the literature on the use and readership of the scholarly literature clearly shows that (1) scientists continue to read a great deal and spend substantial time reading; (2) publications are the principal channel of communication for scientists, and they read scholarly journals far more than any other type of publication; (3) engineers rely more on other channels of communication; and (4) the high levels of usefulness and value of scholarly journals have persisted over the years. However, information-seeking and readership patterns have changed in several ways. While browsing remains the principal means of identifying recently published articles that are read, substantially more articles are now being identified through automated searches. Also, high prices of subscriptions have forced scientists to cancel subscriptions and rely much more on library-provided articles, while libraries have cancelled subscriptions to rely more on separate copies of articles. Scientists now read from more journals, probably due to increased use of automated searches and library services and, while use of separate copies of articles has always been high, it appears to be increasing on a per-scientist basis.

There are many information channels and within the scholarly journal channel, several distribution means and media. All of these ways of communicating information have survived because they fill their own niches to satisfy the range of user needs and requirements. It appears that electronic scholarly journals will play an increasingly important role in the future. However, all those involved in the journal system (authors, readers, publishers, libraries, and other intermediaries) must take into account factors that are likely to have a significant bearing on the success of the electronic journal system. These include pricing factors, such as pricing of journal subscriptions and access to separate copies of articles, and other factors, such as availability of older articles and high-quality means of identifying, locating, and retrieving needed articles. Any future changes will be influenced by their effect on readers' time and ease of use.

Finally, for the continued success of the scientific journal system in a time of change, all participants in the system must recognize factors that affect selection of various channels, distribution means, and media. A variety and combination of distribution means and media are likely to best serve users, distributors, and creators of scholarly journals for a long time to come.

BIBLIOGRAPHY

ACKOFF, RUSSELL. 1967. Choice, Communication, and Conflict. Philadelphia, PA: Management Science Center, University of Pennsylvania; 1967. 433p. NTIS: PB-178335.

ALBRITTON, EVERETT C. 1965. The Information Exchange Groups—An Experiment in Communication. Paper presented at the Institute on Advances in Biomedical Communication; 1965 March 9; Washington, DC.

ALLEN, THOMAS J. 1964. The Utilization of Information Sources during R&D Proposal Preparation. Cambridge, MA: Sloan School of Management, Massachusetts Institute of Technology; 1964. 31p. (Working paper 97-64). OCLC: 14366743.

ALLEN, THOMAS J. 1965. Sources of Ideas and Their Effectiveness in Parallel R&D Projects. Cambridge, MA: Sloan School of Management, Massachusetts Institute of Technology; 1965. 23p. (Working paper 130-65). OCLC: 14367409.

ALLEN, THOMAS J. 1966a. Managing the Flow of Scientific and Technical Information. Cambridge, MA: Massachusetts Institute of Technology; 1966. 224p. (Ph.D. dissertation). NTIS: PB-174440.

ALLEN, THOMAS J. 1966b. Studies of the Problem Solving Process in Engineering Design. IEEE Transactions on Engineering Management. 1966; 13(2): 73-83. ISSN: 0018-9391.

ALLEN, THOMAS J. 1969. Information Needs and Uses. In: Cuadra, Carlos A., ed. Annual Review of Information Science and Technology: Volume 4. Chicago, IL: Encyclopaedia Brittannica for the American Society for Information Science; 1969. 3-29. ISBN: 0-85229-147-7.

ALLEN, THOMAS J. 1988. Distinguishing Engineers from Scientists. In: Katz, Ralph, ed. Managing Professionals in Innovative Organizations: A Collection of Readings. Cambridge, MA: Ballinger Publishing Co.; 1988. 3-18. ISBN: 0-88730-351-X.

ALLEN, THOMAS J.; ANDRIEN, MAURICE P., JR. 1965. Time Allocation among Three Technical Information Channels by R&D Engineers. Cambridge, MA: Sloan School of Management, Massachusetts Institute of Technology; 1965. 20p. (Working paper 131-65). OCLC: 14367459.

ALLEN, THOMAS J.; COHEN, STEPHEN I. 1969. Information Flow in Research and Development Laboratories. Administrative Science Quarterly. 1969 March; 4: 12-19. ISSN: 0001-8392.

ALLEN, THOMAS J.; GERSTBERGER, PETER G. 1967. Criteria for Selection of an Information Source. Cambridge, MA: Sloan School of Management, Massachusetts Institute of Technology; 1967. 24p. (Working paper 284-67). OCLC: 14369805.

ALLEN, THOMAS J.; GERSTENFELD, ARTHUR; GERSTBERGER, PETER G. 1968. The Problem of Internal Consulting in R&D Organizations. Cambridge, MA: Sloan School of Management, Massachusetts Institute of Technology; 1968. 44p. (Working paper 319-68). OCLC: 14369156.

ALMQUIST, E. 1991. An Examination of Work-Related Information Acquisitions and Usage among Scientific, Technical and Medical Fields. In: The Faxon Institute 1991 Annual Conference: Creating Pathways to Electronic Information: Electronic Conferencing System; 1991 April 28-30; Reston, VA. Westwood, MA: Faxon Institute for Advanced Studies in Scholarly and Scientific Communication; 1991. 1 volume. OCLC: 23853493.

ALONI, MICHAEL A. 1985. Patterns of Information Transfer among Engineers and Applied Scientists in Complex Organizations. Scientometrics. 1985; 8(5-6): 279-300. ISSN: 0138-9130.

AMERICAN PSYCHOLOGICAL ASSOCIATION. 1965. Reports of the American Psychological Association's Project on Scientific Information Exchange in Psychology: Volume 1, Overview Reports, no. 1-9. Washington, DC: American Psychological Association; 1965. NTIS: PB 164496.

AMERICAN PSYCHOLOGICAL ASSOCIATION. 1966. Reports of the American Psychological Association's Project on Scientific Information Exchange in Psychology: Volume 2, Report no. 10-15. Washington, DC: American Psychological Association; 1966. NTIS: PB 169005.

AMERICAN PSYCHOLOGICAL ASSOCIATION. 1968. Reports of the American Psychological Association's Project on Scientific Information Exchange in Psychology: Volume 3, Report no. 16-19. Washington, DC: American Psychological Association; 1968. NTIS: PB 182962.

ANTHONY, L. J.; EAST, H.; SLATER, M. J. 1969. The Growth of Literature in Physics. Reports of Progress in Physics. 1969; 32: 709-767. ISSN: 0034-4885.

ASSOCIATION OF RESEARCH LIBRARIES. 1989. Report of the ARL Serials Project. Washington, DC: Association of Research Libraries; 1989. 1 volume. OCLC: 19882948.

ASTLE, D. L. 1989. The Scholarly Journal: Whence or Whither? Journal of Academic Librarianship. 1989 July; 15(3): 151-156. ISSN: 0099-1333.

AUERBACH CORPORATION. 1965. DOD User Needs Study, Phase I, Final Technical Report. Philadelphia, PA: Auerbach Corporation; 1965. 2 volumes. NTIS: AD615501; AD615502.

BAKER, NORMAN R.; SIEGMANN, JACK; RUBENSTEIN, ALBERT H. 1967. The Effects of Perceived Needs and Means on the Generation of Ideas for Industrial Research and Development Projects. IEEE Transactions on Engineering Management. 1967; 14: 156-163. ISSN: 0018-9391.

BARUCH, JORDAN J.; BHAGAT, NAZIRA. 1975. The IEEE Annals: An Experiment in Selective Dissemination. IEEE Transactions on Professional Communication. 1975 September; PC-18(3): 296-300. ISSN: 0361-1434.

BAYER, ALAN E.; JAHODA, GERALD. 1979. Background Characteristics of Industrial and Academic Users and Nonusers of Online Bibliographic Search Services. Online Review. 1979 March; 3(1): 95-105. ISSN: 0309-314X.

BEARDSLEY, CHARLES W. 1972. Keeping on Top of Your Field. IEEE Spectrum. 1972 December; 9(12): 68-71. ISSN: 0018-9235.

BERG, SANFORD V. 1972. An Economic Analysis of the Demand for Scientific Journals. Journal of the American Society for Information Science. 1972 January/February; 23(1): 23-29. ISSN: 0002-8231.

BERGE, Z. L.; COLLINS, M. P. 1996. IPCT Journal Readership Survey. Journal of the American Society for Information Science. 1996 September; 47(9): 701-710. ISSN: 0002-8231.

BERNAL, J. D. 1948. Report on the Royal Society Scientific Information Conference. London, England: Royal Society; 1948.

BERNARD, JESSIE; SHILLING, CHARLES W.; TYSON, JOE W. 1963. Informal Communication among Bioscientists. Washington, DC: George Washington University; 1963. 1 volume. OCLC: 9562671.

BEVER, ARLEY T. 1969. The Duality of Quick and Archival Communication. Journal of Chemical Documentation. 1969 February; 9(3): 3-6. ISSN: 0021-9576.

BICHTELER, JULIE; WARD, DEDERICK. 1989. Information-Seeking Behavior of Geoscientists. Special Libraries. 1989 Summer; 80(3): 169-178. ISSN: 0038-6723.

BISHOP, ANN PETERSON; STAR, SUSAN LEIGH. 1996. Social Informatics of Digital Library Use and Infrastructure. In: Williams, Martha E., ed. Annual Review of Information Science and Technology: Volume 31. Medford,

NJ: Information Today, Inc. for the American Society for Information Science; 1996. 301-401. ISSN: 0066-4200; ISBN: 1-57387-033-1.

BLECIC, DEBORAH D. 1999. Measurements of Journal Use: An Analysis of the Correlations between Three Methods. Bulletin of the Medical Library Association. 1999 January; 87(1): 20-25. ISSN: 0025-7338.

BORGMAN, CHRISTINE L. 1989. All Users of Information Retrieval Systems Are Not Created Equal: An Exploration into Individual Differences. Information Processing & Management. 1989; 25(3): 237-251. ISSN: 0306-4573.

BROWN, CECELIA M. 1999. Information Seeking Behavior of Scientists in the Electronic Information Age: Astronomers, Chemists, Mathematicians, and Physicists. Journal of the American Society for Information Science. 1999 August; 50(10): 929-943. ISSN: 0002-8231.

BROWN, DAVID J., comp. 1996. Electronic Publishing and Libraries: Planning for the Impact and Growth to 2003. London, England: Bowker-Saur; 1996. 200p. ISBN: 1-85739-166-7.

BUDD, JOHN M.; CONNAWAY, LYNN SILIPIGNI. 1997. University Faculty and Networked Information: Results of a Survey. Journal of the American Society for Information Science. 1997 September; 48(9): 843-852. ISSN: 0002-8231.

BUTLER, H. JULENE. 1995. Where Does Scholarly Electronic Publishing Get You? Journal of Scholarly Publishing. 1995 July; 26(4): 174-186. ISSN: 1198-9742.

BUXTON, A. B.; MEADOWS, ARTHUR JACK. 1978. Categorization of the Information in Experimental Papers and Their Author Abstracts. Journal of Research Communication Studies. 1978 August; 1(2): 161-182. ISSN: 0378-5939.

CARRIGAN, DENNIS. 1993. From Interlibrary Lending to Document Delivery: The British Library Document Supply Centre. Journal of Academic Librarianship. 1993 September; 19(4): 220-224. ISSN: 0099-1333.

CARTER, LAUNOR; CONTLEY, GORDON; ROWELL, JOHN T.; SHULTZ, LOUISE; SEIDEN, HERBERT R.; WALLACE, EVERETT; WATSON, RICHARD; WYLLYS, RONALD E. 1967. National Document-Handling Systems for Science and Technology. New York, NY: Wiley; 1967. 349p. OCLC: 575441.

CASE INSTITUTE OF TECHNOLOGY. 1960. An Operations Research Study of the Dissemination and Use of Recorded Scientific Information. Cleveland, OH: Operations Research Group, Case Institute of Technology; 1960. 63p. OCLC: 4398360.

CHAKRABARTI, ALOK K.; FEINEMAN, STEPHEN; FUENTEVILLA, WILLIAM. 1983. Characteristics of Sources, Channels, and Contents for Scientific and Technical Information Systems in Industrial R&D. IEEE Transactions on Engineering Management. 1983 May; EM-30(2): 83-88. ISSN: 0018-9391.

CHAKRABARTI, ALOK K.; RUBENSTEIN, ALBERT H. 1976. Interorganization Transfer of Technology: A Study of Adoption of NASA Innovations. IEEE Transactions on Engineering Management. 1976 February; EM-23(1): 20-34. ISSN: 0018-9391.

CHARLES RIVER ASSOCIATES. 1979. Development of a Model of the Demand for Scientific and Technical Information Services. Boston, MA: Charles River Associates; 1979. 112p. NTIS: PB-297826.

CHEN, CHING-CHIH. 1972. The Use Patterns of Physics Journals in a Large Academic Library. Journal of the American Society for Information Science. 1972 July/August; 23(4): 254-270. ISSN: 0002-8231.

CHRESSANTHIS, GEORGE A.; CHRESSANTHIS, JUNE D. 1994a. The Determinants of Library Subscription Prices of the Top-Ranked Economics Journals: An Econometric Analysis. The Journal of Economic Education. 1994 Fall; 25(4): 367-382. ISSN: 0022-0485.

CHRESSANTHIS, GEORGE A.; CHRESSANTHIS, JUNE D. 1994b. A General Econometric Model of the Determinants of Library Subscription Prices of Scholarly Journals: The Role of Exchange Rate Risk and Other Factors. Library Quarterly. 1994 July; 64(3): 270-293. ISSN: 0024-2519.

COOPER, MICHAEL D. 1973. The Economics of Information. In: Cuadra, Carlos A., ed. Annual Review of Information Science and Technology: Volume 8. Washington, DC: American Society for Information Science; 1973. 5-40. ISBN: 0-87715-208-X.

CRANE, DIANA. 1969. Social Structure in a Group of Scientists: A Test of the "Invisible College" Hypothesis. American Sociological Review. 1969; 34(3): 335-352. ISSN: 0003-1224.

CRANE, DIANA. 1971. Information Needs and Uses. In: Cuadra, Carlos A., ed. Annual Review of Information Science and Technology: Volume 6. Chicago, IL: Encyclopaedia Britannica for the American Society for Information Science; 1971. 3-39. ISBN: 0-85229-166-3.

CRAWFORD, SUSAN. 1971. Informal Communication among Scientists in Sleep Research. Journal of the American Society for Information Science. 1971; 22(5): 301-310. ISSN: 0002-8231.

CRAWFORD, SUSAN. 1978. Information Needs and Uses. In: Williams, Martha E., ed. Annual Review of Information Science and Technology: Volume 13. White Plains, NY: Knowledge Industry Publications, Inc. for the American Society for Information Science; 1978. 61-81. ISSN: 0066-4200; ISBN: 0-914236-21-0.

CUMMINGS, ANTHONY M.; WITTE, MARCIA L.; BOWEN, WILLIAM G.; LAZARUS, LAURA O.; EKMAN, RICHARD H. 1992. University Libraries and Scholarly Communication: A Study Prepared for the Andrew W. Mellon Foundation. Washington, DC: Association of Research Libraries; 1992 November. 205p. ISBN: 0-918006-22-8.

CUMMINGS, MARTIN M. 1986. The Economics of Research Libraries. Washington, DC: Council on Library Resources; 1986. 216p. LC: 86-2321.

DAVIS, RICHARD A.; BAILEY, CATHERINE A. 1964. Bibliography of Use Studies. Philadelphia, PA: Graduate School of Library Science, Drexel Institute of Technology; 1964. 98p. OCLC: 9703337.

DAVIS, RICHARD M. 1975. Technical Writing: Its Importance in the Engineering Profession and Its Place in Engineering Curricula: A Survey of the Experience and Opinions of Prominent Engineers. Wright-Patterson Air Force Base, OH: Air Force Institute of Technology; 1975. 86p. NTIS: ADA015906.

DENNING, PETER J.; ROUS, BERNARD. 1995. The ACM Electronic Publishing Plan. Communications of the ACM. 1995 April; 38(4): 97-103. ISSN: 0001-0782.

DERVIN, BRENDA; NILAN, MICHAEL. 1986. Information Needs and Uses. In: Williams, Martha E., ed. Annual Review of Information Science and Technology: Volume 21. White Plains, NY: Knowledge Industry Publications, Inc. for the American Society for Information Science; 1986. 3-33. ISSN: 0066-4200; ISBN: 0-86729-209-1.

DOSA, MARTA; FARID, MONA; VASARHELYI, PAL. 1989. From Informal Gatekeeper to Information Counselor: Emergence of a New Professional Role. The Hague, The Netherlands: FID; 1989. 54p. (FID Publication no. 677). ISBN: 92-660-0677-7.

DUBINSKAYA, S. A. 1967. Investigation of Information Service Needs of Chemical Specialists. Nauchno-Tekhnicheskaya Informatsiya. 1967; 2(4): 3-6. ISSN: 0548-0027.

ECONOMIC CONSULTING SERVICES INCORPORATED. 1989. A Study of Trends in Average Prices and Costs of Certain Serials over Time. In: Report of the ARL Serials Prices Project. Washington, DC: Association of Research Libraries; 1989. Section II: 1-43. OCLC: 19882948.

ELSDON-DEW, R. 1955. The Library from the Point of View of the Research Worker. South African Libraries. 1955; 23: 51-54. ISSN: 0038-240X.

ETTLIE, JOHN E. 1976. The Timing and Sources of Information for the Adoption and Implementation of Production Innovations. IEEE Transactions on Engineering Management. 1976 February; 23(1): 62-68. ISSN: 0018-9391.

FLOWERS, B. H. 1965. Survey of Information Needs of Physicists and Chemists. Journal of Documentation. 1965 June; 21(2): 83-112. ISSN: 0022-0418.

FROST, PENELOPE A.; WHITLEY, RICHARD. 1971. Communication Patterns in a Research Laboratory. R&D Management. 1971; 1: 71-79. ISSN: 0033-6807.

FRY, BERNARD M.; WHITE, HERBERT S. 1976. Publishers and Libraries: A Study of Scholarly and Research Journals. Lexington, MA: Lexington Books; 1976. 166p. ISBN: 0-669-00886-9.

GANNETT, ELWOOD K. 1973. Primary Publication Systems and Services. In: Cuadra, Carlos A., ed. Annual Review of Information Science and Technology: Volume 8. Washington, DC: American Society for Information Science; 1973. 243-275. ISBN: 0-87715-208-X; LC: 66-25096.

GARVEY, WILLIAM D.; GRIFFITH, BELVER C. 1963. The American Psychological Association's Project on Scientific Information Exchange in Psychology. Washington, DC: American Psychological Association; 1963. (Report No. 9).

GARVEY, WILLIAM D.; GRIFFITH, BELVER C. 1971. Scientific Communication: Its Role in the Conduct of Research and Creation of Knowledge. American Psychologist. 1971; 26(4): 349-362. ISSN: 0003-066X.

GARVEY, WILLIAM D.; GRIFFITH, BELVER C. 1972. Communication and Information Processing within Scientific Disciplines: Empirical Findings for Psychology. Information Storage and Retrieval. 1972; 8: 123-136. ISSN: 0020-0271.

GARVEY, WILLIAM D.; TOMITA, KAZUO; WOOLF, PATRICIA. 1974. The Dynamic Scientific-Information User. Information Storage and Retrieval. 1974; 10: 115-131. ISSN: 0020-0271.

GERSTBERGER, PETER G. 1971. The Preservation and Transfer of Technology in Research and Development Organizations. Cambridge, MA: Sloan School of Management, Massachusetts Institute of Technology; 1971. 271p. (Ph.D. dissertation). OCLC: 23813070.

GERSTBERGER, PETER G.; ALLEN, THOMAS J. 1968. Criteria Used by Research and Development Engineers in the Selection of an Information Source. Journal of Applied Psychology. 1968 August; 52(4): 272-279. ISSN: 0021-9010.

GERSTENFELD, ARTHUR; BERGER, PAUL. 1980. An Analysis of Utilization Differences for Scientific and Technical Information. Management Science. 1980 February; 26(2): 165-179. ISSN: 0025-1909.

GERSTL, JOEL EMERY; HUTTON, STANLEY PEERMAN. 1966. Engineers: The Anatomy of a Profession. London, England: Tavistock Publications; 1966. 229p. OCLC: 954134.

GETZ, M. 1991. Document Delivery. Bottom Line. 1991; 5(4): 40-44. ISSN: 0888-045X.

GINSPARG, PAUL. 1994. First Steps towards Electronic Research Communication. Computers in Physics. 1994 July/August; 8(4): 390-396. ISSN: 0894-1866.

GINSPARG, PAUL. 1996. Winners and Losers in the Global Research Village. Available WWW: http://xxx.lanl.gov/blurb/pg96unesco.html.

GLUECK, WILLIAM F.; JAUCH, LAWRENCE R. 1975. Sources of Research Ideas among Productive Scholars. Journal of Higher Education. 1975 January/February; 46(1): 103-114. ISSN: 0022-1546.

GOODMAN, DAVID. 2000. What Journals, If Any, Should STILL Be Printed? In: Williams, Martha E., ed. Proceedings of the 21st Annual National Online Meeting; 2000 May 16-18; New York, NY. Medford, NJ: Information Today, Inc.; 2000. 129-136. ISBN: 1-57387-102-8.

GRAJEK, SUSAN. 1998. Annual School of Medicine, Questionnaire of Library and Computer Use. Available WWW: http://its.med.yale.edu/about_itsmed/research/index.html.

GRANT, JOAN. 1964. Information for Industry—A Study in Communications. Pretoria, Republic of South Africa: Council for Scientific and Industrial Research; 1964.

GRIFFITH, BELVER C., ed. 1980. Key Papers in Information Science. White Plains, NY: Knowledge Industry Publications, Inc.; 1980. 439p. ISBN: 0-914236-50-4.

GRIFFITHS, JOSÉ-MARIE; KING, DONALD W. 1991. A Manual on the Evaluation of Information Centers and Services. New York, NY: American Institute of Aeronautics and Astronautics; 1991. 118p. ISBN: 9-28350-614-6; NTIS: AD-A237321.

GRIFFITHS, JOSÉ-MARIE; KING, DONALD W. 1993. Special Libraries: Increasing the Information Edge. Washington, DC: Special Libraries Association; 1993. 194p. ISBN: 0-87111-414-3.

GROGAN, D. J. 1982. Science and Technology: An Introduction to the Literature. 4th ed. London, England: Bingley; 1982. 400p. ISBN: 0-85157-315-0.

GUPTA, B. M. 1981. Information, Communication and Technology Transfer: A Review of Literature. Annals of Library Science and Documentation. 1981; 28(1-4): 1-13. ISSN: 0003-4835.

GUPTA, R. C. 1988. Skill Development to Assess Information Needs and Seeking Behavior. Lucknow Librarian. 1988; 20(2): 52-58. ISSN: 0024-7219.

GUSHEE, DAVID E. 1968. Reading Behavior of Chemists. Journal of Chemical Documentation. 1968 November; 8(4): 191-194. ISSN: 0021-9576.

HAGSTROM, WARREN O. 1970. Factors Related to the Use of Different Modes of Publishing Research in Four Scientific Fields. In: Nelson, Carnot E.; Pollock, Donald K., eds. Communication among Scientists and Engineers. Lexington, MA: Heath Lexington Books; 1970. 85-124. LC: 71-129156; OCLC: 97550.

HALBERT, MICHAEL H.; ACKOFF, RUSSELL L. 1959. An Operations Research Study of the Dissemination of Scientific Information. In: Proceedings of the International Conference on Scientific Information: Volume 1; 1958 November 16-21; Washington, DC. Washington, DC: National Academy of Sciences, National Research Council; 1959. 87-120. OCLC: 1240710.

HALL, ANGELA M.; CLAGUE, P.; AITCHISON, T. M. 1972. The Effect of the Use of an SDI Service on the Information-Gathering Habits of Scientists and Technologists. London, England: The Institution of Electrical Engineers; 1972. 175p. ISBN: 0-85296-412-9.

HALLMARK, JULIE. 1994. Scientists' Access and Retrieval of References Cited in Their Recent Journal Articles. College & Research Libraries. 1994 May; 55(3): 199-209. ISSN: 0010-0870.

HAWKINS, BRIAN L. 1998. The Unsustainability of the Traditional Library and the Threat to Higher Education. In: Hawkins, Brian L.; Battin, Patricia, eds. The Mirage of Continuity: Reconfiguring Academic Resources for the 21st Century. Washington, DC: Council on Library and Information Resources and the Association of American Universities; 1998. 129-153. ISBN: 1-85739-166-7.

HAZELL, J. C.; POTTER, J. N. 1968. Information Practices of Agricultural Scientists. Australian Library Journal. 1968 June; 17(5): 147-159. ISSN: 0004-9670.

HENDERSON, ALBERT. 1999. Information Science and Information Policy: The Use of Constant Dollars and Other Indicators to Manage Research Investments. Journal of the American Society for Information Science. 1999 April; 50(4): 366-379. (Previously published by the National Science Board in 1996). ISSN: 0002-8231.

HERNER, SAUL. 1959. The Information-Gathering Habits of American Medical Scientists. In: Proceedings of the International Conference on Scientific Information: Volume 1; 1958 November 16-21; Washington, DC. Washington, DC: National Academy of Sciences, National Research Council; 1959. 277-285. OCLC: 1240710.

HERNER, SAUL; HERNER, MARY. 1967. Information Needs and Uses in Science and Technology. In: Cuadra, Carlos A., ed. Annual Review of

Information Science and Technology: Volume 2. New York, NY: John Wiley & Sons, InterScience Publishers for the American Documentation Institute; 1967. 1-34. LC: 66-25096.

HEWINS, ELIZABETH T. 1990. Information Needs and Use Studies. In: Williams, Martha E., ed. Annual Review of Information Science and Technology: Volume 25. Amsterdam, The Netherlands: Elsevier Science Publishers for the American Society for Information Science; 1990. 145-172. ISSN: 0066-4200; ISBN: 0-444-88531-5.

HILLS, PHILIP J., ed. 1980. The Future of the Printed Word: The Impact and the Implications of the New Communications Technology. Westport, CT: Greenwood Press; 1980. 172p. ISBN: 0-313-22693-8.

HILLS, PHILIP J. 1983. The Scholarly Communication Process. In: Williams, Martha E., ed. Annual Review of Information Science and Technology: Volume 18. White Plains, NY: Knowledge Industry Publications, Inc. for the American Society for Information Science; 1983. 99-125. ISSN: 0066-4200; ISBN: 0-86729-050-1.

HINRICHS, J. R. 1964. Communications Activity of Industrial Personnel. Personnel Psychology. 1964; 17: 193-204. ISSN: 0031-5826.

HOBAN, CHARLES F. 1967. Survey of Professional Journals in Field of Public Communication, Including New Media in Education. Philadelphia, PA: University of Pennsylvania; 1967. 49p. OCLC: 133817.

HOLLAND, MAURITA PETERSON; PINELLI, THOMAS E.; BARCLAY, REBECCA O.; KENNEDY, JOHN M. 1991. Engineers as Information Processors: A Survey of U.S. Aerospace Engineering Faculty and Students. European Journal of Engineering Education. 1991; 16(4): 317-336. ISSN: 0304-3797.

HOLLAND, MAURITA PETERSON; POWELL, CHRISTINA KELLEHER. 1995. A Longitudinal Survey of the Information Seeking and Use Habits of Some Engineers. College & Research Libraries. 1995 January; 56: 7-15. ISSN: 0010-0870.

HUTH, EDWARD J. 1989. The Underused Medical Literature. Annals of Internal Medicine. 1989 January 15; 110(2): 99-100. ISSN: 0003-4819.

INSTITUTE OF PHYSICS. 1976. Author/Subscribers Survey: Summary of Results. Bristol, England: The Institute of Physics; 1976.

JACKSON, MARY E. 1997. Measuring the Performance of Interlibrary Loan and Document Delivery Services. ARL: A Bimonthly Newsletter of Research Library Issues and Actions. 1997; 195: 1-3. ISSN: 1050-6098.

JOHNS HOPKINS UNIVERSITY SOGIP STUDY GROUP. 1971. Some Preliminary Results from a Survey of Graduate Students in Psychology. Washington, DC: American Psychological Association; 1971. 93p. OCLC: 41682187.

JOHNSTON, RON; GIBBONS, MICHAEL. 1975. Characteristics of Information Usage in Technological Innovation. IEEE Transactions on Engineering Management. 1975 February; EM-22(1): 27-34. ISSN: 0018-9391.

KASER, DICK, ed. 1995. Document Delivery in an Electronic Age: A Collection of Views and Viewpoints. Philadelphia, PA: National Federation of Abstracting and Information Services; 1995. 124p. ISBN: 0-942308-46-8.

KATZ, RALPH, ed. 1988. Managing Professionals in Innovative Organizations. Cambridge, MA: Ballinger Publishing Co.; 1988. 593p. ISBN: 0-88730-351-X.

KATZEN, MAY. 1977. The Visual Impact of Scholarly Journal Articles: Report of a Feasibility Study to Isolate the Factors Which May Govern the Impact of Research Articles on Readers and to Outline a Methodology for Their Determination. Leicester, England: University of Leicester Primary Communications Research Centre; 1977. 99p. ISBN: 0-906083-02-8.

KEENAN, STELLA; SLATER, MARGARET. 1967. Results of a Questionnaire on Current Awareness Methods Used by Physicists. London, England: Institution of Electrical Engineers; New York, NY: American Institute of Physics; 1967. 36p. OCLC: 226988.

KENT, ALLEN, ed. 1968-. Encyclopedia of Library and Information Science. 1968-. New York, NY: Marcel Dekker, Inc.; 1968-.

KENT, ALLEN; MONTGOMERY, K. LEON; COHEN, J.; WILLIAMS, JAMES G.; BULICK, S.; FLYNN, R.; SABAR, W. N.; KERN, J. R. 1978. A Cost-Benefit Model of Some Critical Library Operations in Terms of Use of Materials. Pittsburgh, PA: University of Pittsburgh; 1978. 243p. NTIS: PB-282059.

KIERNAN, VINCENT. 1999a. NIH Proceeds with On-Line Archive for Papers in the Life Sciences. Chronicle of Higher Education. Available WWW: http://chronicle.com/infotech.

KIERNAN, VINCENT. 1999b. Why Do Some Electronic-Only Journals Struggle, While Others Flourish? Chronicle of Higher Education. 1999 May 21; 45(37): A25-A27. ISSN: 0009-5982.

KING, DONALD W.; CASTO, JANE; JONES, HEATHER. 1994. Communication by Engineers: A Literature Review of Engineers' Information Needs, Seeking Processes and Use. Washington, DC: Council on Library Resources; 1994. 198p. LC: 94-39693.

KING, DONALD W.; DOWD-REISIN, PATRICIA M.; LADD, R. BOYD; MCDONALD, DENNIS D.; PALMOUR, VERNON E.; RODERER, NANCY K. 1977. Library Photocopying in the United States. Washington, DC: U.S. Government Printing Office; 1977. 251p. LC: 77-91033; OCLC: 3413722.

KING, DONALD W.; MCDONALD, DENNIS D.; OLSEN, CANDACE H. 1978. A Survey of Readers, Subscribers, and Authors of the Journal of the National Cancer Institute. Washington, DC: National Cancer Institute; 1978. Available from: dwking@umich.edu.

KING, DONALD W.; MCDONALD, DENNIS D.; RODERER, NANCY K. 1981. Scientific Journals in the United States: Their Production, Use, and Economics. Stroudsburg, PA: Hutchinson Ross Publishing Co.; 1981. 319p. ISBN: 0-87933-380-4.

KING, DONALD W.; MCDONALD, DENNIS D.; RODERER, NANCY K.; WOOD, BARBARA L. 1976. Statistical Indicators of Scientific and Technical Communication. Volume II: A Research Report. Rockville, MD: King Research; 1976. NTIS: PB-254060.

KING, DONALD W.; PALMOUR, VERNON E. 1974. User Behavior. In: Fenichel, Carol, ed. Changing Patterns in Information Retrieval. Philadelphia, PA: American Society for Information Science; 1974. 7-33. ISBN: 0-87715-106-7.

KING, DONALD W.; RODERER, NANCY K. 1981. The AIP Journal System: Relationship of Price, Page Charges, Demand, Cost, and Income. In: AIP

Function Planning, Appendix B. New York, NY: American Institute of Physics; 1981. Available from: dwking@umich. edu.

KING, DONALD W.; RODERER, NANCY K. 1982. Communication in Physics: The Use of Journals. Physics Today. 1982 October; 35(10): 43-45. ISSN: 0031-9228.

KINGMA, BRUCE R. 1996. Economics of Access Versus Ownership: The Costs and Benefits of Access to Scholarly Articles Via Interlibrary Loan and Journal Subscriptions. New York, NY: Haworth Press; 1996. 79p. ISBN: 1-56024-809-2.

KLING, ROB; MCKIM, GEOFFREY. 1999. Scholarly Communication and the Continuum of Electronic Publishing. Journal of the American Society for Information Science. 1999 August; 50(10): 890-906. ISSN: 0002-8231.

KOENIG, MICHAEL E. D. 1990. Information Services and Downstream Productivity. In: Williams, Martha E., ed. Annual Review of Information Science and Technology: Volume 25. Amsterdam, The Netherlands: Elsevier Science Publishers for the American Society for Information Science; 1990. 55-86. ISSN: 0066-4200; ISBN: 0-444-88531-5.

KRIKELAS, JAMES. 1983. Information-Seeking Behavior: Patterns and Concepts. Drexel Library Quarterly. 1983 Spring; 19(2): 5-20. ISSN: 0012-6160.

KUNEY, JOSEPH H. 1968. Publication and Distribution of Information. In: Cuadra, Carlos A., ed. Annual Review of Information Science and Technology: Volume 3. Chicago, IL: Encyclopaedia Britannica for the American Society for Information Science; 1968. 31-59. LC: 66-25096.

LADENDORF, JANICE M. 1970. Information Flow in Science, Technology and Commerce: A Review of the Concepts of the Sixties. Special Libraries. 1970 May-June; 61(5): 215-222. ISSN: 0038-6723.

LAMBERT, JILL. 1985. Scientific and Technical Journals. London, England: Clive Bingley; 1985. 191p. ISBN: 0-85157-375-4.

LANCASTER, F. W. 1978. Toward Paperless Information Systems. New York, NY: Academic Press; 1978. 179p. ISBN: 0-12-436050-5.

LANCASTER, F. W.; GILLESPIE, CONSTANTINE J. 1970. Design and Evaluation of Information Systems. In: Cuadra, Carlos A., ed. Annual Review of Information Science and Technology: Volume 5. Chicago, IL: Encyclopaedia Britannica for the American Society for Information Science; 1970. 33-70. ISBN: 0-85229-156-6.

LANDAU, HERBERT B. 1969. Document Dissemination. In: Cuadra, Carlos A., ed. Annual Review of Information Science and Technology: Volume 4. Chicago, IL: Encyclopaedia Britannica for the American Society for Information Science; 1969. 229-270. ISBN: 0-85229-147-7; LC: 66-25096.

LENARES, DEBORAH. 1999. Faculty Use of Electronic Journals at Research Institutions. In: Thompson, Hugh A., ed. Racing Toward Tomorrow: Proceedings of the 9th National Conference of the Association of College and Research Libraries; 1999 April 8-11; Detroit, MI. Chicago, IL: Association of College and Research Libraries; 1999. 329-334. ISBN: 0-83898-015-5.

LERNER, RITA; METAXAS, TED; SCOTT, JOHN T.; ADAMS, PETER D.; JUDD, PEGGY. 1983. Primary Publication Systems and Scientific Text Processing. In: Williams, Martha E., ed. Annual Review of Information Science and Technology: Volume 18. White Plains, NY: Knowledge Industry

Publications, Inc. for the American Society for Information Science; 1983. 127-149. ISSN: 0066-4200; ISBN: 0-86729-050-1.

LIBBEY, MILES A.; ZALTMAN, GERALD. 1967. The Role and Distribution of Written Informal Communication in Theoretical High Energy Physics. New York, NY: American Institute of Physics; 1967. 1 volume. OCLC: 1859932.

LIN, NAN; GARVEY, WILLIAM D. 1971. The Formal Communication Structure in Science. In: American Sociological Association Annual Meeting; 1971 August/September; Denver, CO. Washington, DC: American Sociological Association; 1971. 45p.

LIN, NAN; GARVEY, WILLIAM D. 1972. Information Needs and Uses. In: Cuadra, Carlos A.; Luke, Ann W., eds. Annual Review of Information Science and Technology: Volume 7. Washington, DC: American Society for Information Science; 1972. 5-37. ISBN: 0-87715-206-3.

LIN, NAN; GARVEY, WILLIAM D.; NELSON, CARNOT E. 1970. A Study of the Communication Structure of Science. In: Nelson, Carnot E.; Pollock, Donald K., eds. Communication among Scientists and Engineers. Lexington, MA: Heath Lexington Books; 1970. 23-60. LC: 71-129156; OCLC: 97550.

LIN, NAN; NELSON, CARNOT E. 1969. Bibliographic Reference Patterns in Core Sociological Journals, 1965-1966. The American Sociologist. 1969 February; 4(1): 47-50. ISSN: 0003-1232.

LINE, MAURICE B. 1971. The Information Uses and Needs of Social Scientists: An Overview of INFROSS. Aslib Proceedings. 1971 August; 23(8): 412-434. ISSN: 0001-253X.

LIPETZ, BEN-AMI. 1970. Information Needs and Uses. In: Cuadra, Carlos A., ed. Annual Review of Information Science and Technology: Volume 5. Chicago, IL: Encyclopaedia Britannica for the American Society for Information Science; 1970. 3-32. ISSN: 0066-4200; ISBN: 0-85229-156-6.

LISTON, D. M.; KING, DONALD W.; KUTNER, GAIL L.; HAVELOCK, RONALD G. 1985. Analysis of Technology Assistance Available to Small High Technology Firms. Prepared for the Small Business Administration. 1985. Available from: dwking@umich.edu.

LOHMANN, VICTOR L. 1969. How to Identify the Special Reading Needs of Library Users. AHIL Quarterly. 1969; 9(2): 40-46. ISSN: 0001-1428.

LONGUET-HIGGINS, H. C. 1970. The Language of Science. Times Literary Supplement (UK). 1970 May 7; 3558: 505-506. ISSN: 0040-7895.

LUFKIN, JAMES M.; MILLER, E. H. 1966. The Reading Habits of Engineers: A Preliminary Study. IEEE Transactions on Education. 1966 December; E-9(4): 179-182. ISSN: 0018-9359.

MACHLUP, FRITZ. 1979. Uses, Value, and Benefits of Knowledge. Knowledge: Creation, Diffusion, and Utilization. 1979; 1(1): 62-81. ISSN: 0164-0259.

MACHLUP, FRITZ; LEESON, KENNETH W. 1978. Information through the Printed Word: The Dissemination of Scholarly, Scientific, and Intellectual Knowledge: Volume 2: Journals. New York, NY: Praeger; 1978. 338p. OCLC: 38011139.

MACHLUP, FRITZ; LEESON, KENNETH W. 1980. Information through the Printed Word: The Dissemination of Scholarly, Scientific, and Intellectual Knowledge: Volume 4: Books, Journals, and Bibliographic Services. New York, NY: Praeger; 1980. 313p. OCLC: 27776155.

MACLENNAN, BIRDIE. 1999. From Print to Cyberspace: Presentation and Access Issues for Electronic Journals in a Medium-Sized Academic Institution. Journal of Electronic Publishing. 1999 September; 5(1). Available WWW: http://www.press.umich.edu/jep/05-01/maclennan.html.

MAILLOUX, ELIZABETH N. 1989. Engineering Information Systems. In: Williams, Martha E., ed. Annual Review of Information Science and Technology: Volume 24. Amsterdam, The Netherlands: Elsevier Science Publishers for the American Society for Information Science; 1989. 239-266. ISSN: 0066-4200; ISBN: 0-444-87418-6.

MAIZELL, R. E. 1958. The Most Creative Chemists Read More. Industrial and Engineering Chemistry. 1958 October; 50: 64a-65a. ISSN: 0019-7866.

MARQUIS, DONALD G.; ALLEN, THOMAS J. 1966. Communications Patterns in Applied Technology. American Psychologist. 1966 November; 21(11): 1052-1060. ISSN: 0003-066X.

MARQUIS, DONALD G.; STRAIGHT, D. M. 1966. Organizational Factors in Project Performance. In: Yovits, M. C., ed. Proceedings of the Conference on Research Program Effectiveness; 1965; Washington, DC. New York, NY: Gordon & Breach; 1966. 441-458. OCLC: 350141.

MARTIN, MILES W. 1962. The Use of Random Alarm Devices in Studying Scientists' Reading Behavior. IEEE Transactions on Engineering Management. 1962; 9: 66-71. ISSN: 0018-9391.

MARTIN, MILES W.; ACKOFF, RUSSELL L. 1963. The Dissemination and Use of Recorded Scientific Information. Management Science. 1963; 9: 322-336. ISSN: 0025-1909.

MARTYN, JOHN. 1974. Information Needs and Uses. In: Cuadra, Carlos A., ed. Annual Review of Information Science and Technology: Volume 9. Washington, DC: American Society for Information Science; 1974. 3-23. ISBN: 0-87715-209-8.

MCCABE, MARK J. 1998. The Impact of Publisher Mergers on Journal Prices: A Preliminary Report. Washington, DC: Association of Research Libraries; 1998 October. Available WWW: http://www.arl.org/newsltr/200/mccabe.html.

MCCABE, MARK J. 2000. Academic Journal Pricing and Market Power: A Portfolio Approach. In: Conference on the Economics and Usage of Digital Library Collections; 2000 March 23-24; Ann Arbor, MI. Available WWW: http://www.si.umich.edu/PEAK-2000/program.htm.

MCDONALD, DENNIS D. 1979. Interactions between Scientists and the Journal Publishing Process. College Park, MD: University of Maryland; 1979. 260p. (Ph.D. dissertation). Available from: UMI, Ann Arbor, MI. (UMI order no. AAD79-25747).

MCDONALD, DENNIS D.; BUSH, COLLEEN G. 1982. Libraries, Publishers and Photocopying: Final Report of Surveys Conducted for the U.S. Copyright Office. Washington, DC: U.S. Copyright Office; 1982. 1 volume. ERIC: ED 226-732.

MEADOWS, ARTHUR JACK. 1974. Communication in Science. London, England: Butterworths; 1974. 248p. ISBN: 0-408-70572-8.

MEADOWS, ARTHUR JACK. 1998. Communicating Research. San Diego, CA: Academic Press; 1998. 266p. ISBN: 0-12-487415-0.

MEADOWS, ARTHUR JACK; BUCKLE, P. 1993. Changing Communication Activities in the British Scientific Community. Journal of Documentation. 1993 September; 48(3): 276-290. ISSN: 0022-0418.

MEADOWS, ARTHUR JACK; O'CONNOR, JEAN G. 1969. An Investigation of Information Sources and Information Retrieval in Astronomy and Space Science. Leicester, England: Astronomy Department, Leicester University; 1969. 1 volume. OCLC: 15273863.

MENZEL, HERBERT. 1962. Planned and Unplanned Scientific Communication. In: Barber, Bernard; Hirsch, Walter, eds. Sociology of Science. New York, NY: Macmillan Free Press; 1962. 417-441. OCLC: 253942.

MENZEL, HERBERT. 1966. Information Needs and Uses in Science and Technology. In: Cuadra, Carlos A., ed. Annual Review of Information Science and Technology: Volume 1. New York, NY: InterScience Publishers for the American Documentation Institute; 1966. 41-69. LC: 66-25096.

MENZEL, HERBERT; LIEBERMAN, LOUIS; DULCHIN, JOAN. 1960. Review of Studies in the Flow of Information among Scientists. New York, NY: Bureau of Applied Social Research, Columbia University; 1960. 2 volumes. OCLC: 21986258.

MERCER, LINDA S. 2000. Measuring the Use and Value of Electronic Journals and Books. Issues in Science and Technology Librarianship. 2000 Winter; 25. ISSN: 1092-1206. Available WWW: http://www.library.ucsb.edu/istl/00-winter/article1.html.

MERTON, ROBERT K. 1968. Social Theory and Social Structure. 3rd edition. New York, NY: Free Press; 1968. 702p. OCLC: 25520736.

METOYER-DURAN, CHERYL. 1993. Information Gatekeepers. In: Williams, Martha E., ed. Annual Review of Information Science and Technology: Volume 28. Medford, NJ: Learned Information, Inc. for the American Society for Information Science; 1993. 111-150. ISSN: 0066-4200; ISBN: 0-938734-75-X.

MICK, COLIN K.; LINDSEY, GEORG N.; CALLAHAN, DANIEL; SPIELBERG, FREDERICK. 1979. Towards Usable User Studies: Assessing the Information Behavior of Scientists and Engineers. Stanford, CA: Applied Communication Research; 1979 December. 230p. NTIS: PB80-177165.

MIKHAILOV, A. I.; CHERNYI, ARKADII IVANOVICH; GILIAREVSKII, R. S. 1984. Scientific Communications and Informatics. Arlington, VA: Informations Resources Press; 1984. 402p. (Translated from Russian). ISBN: 0-87875-046-3.

MILLER, GEORGE A. 1968. Psychology and Information. American Documentation. 1968 July; 19(3): 286-289. ISSN: 0096-946X.

MONDSCHEIN, LAWRENCE G. 1990. Selective Dissemination of Information (SDI) Use and Productivity in the Corporate Research Environment. Special Libraries. 1990 Fall; 81(4): 265-279. ISSN: 0038-6723.

MOORE, J. A. 1972. An Inquiry on New Forms of Primary Publications. Journal of Chemical Documentation. 1972 May; 12(2): 75-78. ISSN: 0021-9576.

MORAVCSIK, MICHAEL J. 1965. Private and Public Communication in Physics. Physics Today. 1965 May; 18: 23-26. ISSN: 0031-9228.

NELSON, CARNOT E.; POLLOCK, DONALD K. 1970. Communication among Scientists and Engineers. Lexington, MA: Heath Lexington Books; 1970. 346p. OCLC: 97550.

NOLL, ROGER; STEINMUELLER, W. EDWARD. 1992. An Economic Analysis of Scientific Journal Prices: Preliminary Results. Serials Review. 1992; 18(1-2): 32-37. ISSN: 0098-7913.

ODLYZKO, ANDREW M. 2000. The Rapid Evolution of Scholarly Communication. In: Conference on the Economics and Usage of Digital Library Collections; 2000 March 23-24; Ann Arbor, MI. Available WWW: http://www.si.umich.edu/PEAK-2000/program.htm.

OKERSON, ANN. 1989. Of Making Many Books There Is No End: Report on Serial Prices. In: Report of the ARL Serials Prices Project. Washington, DC: Association of Research Libraries; 1989. Section III: 1-46. OCLC: 19882948.

ORR, RICHARD H. 1970. The Scientist as Information Processor: A Conceptual Model Illustrated with Data on Variables Related to Library Utilization. In: Nelson, Carnot E.; Pollock, Donald K., eds. Communication among Scientists and Engineers. Lexington, MA: Heath Lexington Books; 1970. 143-189. LC: 71-129156; OCLC: 97550.

PAISLEY, WILLIAM J. 1965. The Flow of (Behavioral) Science Information: A Review of the Research Literature. Stanford, CA: Stanford University, Institute for Communication Research; 1965. 1 volume. OCLC: 10097915.

PAISLEY, WILLIAM J. 1968. Information Needs and Uses. In: Cuadra, Carlos A., ed. Annual Review of Information Science and Technology: Volume 3. Chicago, IL: Encyclopaedia Britannica for the American Society for Information Science; 1968. 1-30. ISSN: 0066-4200; ISBN: 0-87815-035-8.

PALMOUR, VERNON E.; BELLASSAI, MARCIA C.; GRAY, LUCY M. 1974. Access to Periodical Resources: A National Plan. Washington, DC: Association of Research Libraries; 1974. 171, 48p. OCLC: 9755258.

PARKER, EDWIN B.; LINGWOOD, DAVID A.; PAISLEY, WILLIAM J. 1968. Communication and Research Productivity in an Interdisciplinary Behavioral Science Research Area. Stanford, CA: Stanford University, Institute for Communication Research; 1968. iii, 85p. OCLC: 852721.

PASTERNACK, SIMON. 1966. Criticism of the Proposed Physics Information Exchange. Physics Today. 1966 June; 19: 63-69. ISSN: 0031-9228.

PEEK, ROBIN P.; POMERANTZ, JEFFREY P. 1998. Electronic Scholarly Journal Publishing. In: Williams, Martha E., ed. Annual Review of Information Science and Technology: Volume 33. Medford, NJ: Information Today, Inc. for the American Society for Information Science; 1998. 321-356. ISSN: 0066-4200; ISBN: 1-57387-065-X.

PETERSEN, H. CRAIG. 1989. Variations in Journal Prices: A Statistical Analysis. Serials Librarian. 1989; 17(1-2): 1-9. ISSN: 0361-526X.

PINELLI, THOMAS E. 1990. The Relationship between the Use of U.S. Government Technical Reports by U.S. Aerospace Engineers and Scientists and Selected Institutional and Sociometric Variables. Bloomington, IN: Indiana University; 1990. 354p. (Ph.D. dissertation). Available from: UMI, Ann Arbor, MI. (UMI order no. AAD 91-19754).

PINELLI, THOMAS E.; BARCLAY, REBECCA O.; HOLLAND, MAURITA PETERSON; KEENE, MICHAEL L.; KENNEDY, JOHN M. 1991a. Technological Innovation and Technical Communications: Their Place in Aerospace Engineering Curricula. A Survey of European, Japanese and U.S. Aerospace Engineers and Scientists. European Journal of Engineering Education. 1991; 16(4): 337-351. ISSN: 0304-3797.

PINELLI, THOMAS E.; BARCLAY, REBECCA O.; KENNEDY, JOHN M.; GLASSMAN, NANCI A.; DEMERATH, LOREN. 1991b. The Relationship between Seven Variables and the Use of U.S. Government Technical Reports by U.S. Aerospace Engineers and Scientists. Hampton, VA: NASA Langley Research Center; 1991. 10p. (NASA/DOD Aerospace Knowledge Diffusion Research Project, Report No. 17). NTIS: N92-28115.

PINELLI, THOMAS E.; GLASSMAN, MYRON; OLIU, WALTER E.; BARCLAY, REBECCA O. 1989. Technical Communications in Aeronautics: Results of Phase 1 Pilot Study. Report 1, parts 1 and 2. Washington, DC: National Aeronautics and Space Administration; 1989 February. Part 1, 106 p. NTIS: 89N26772; Part 2, 83p. NTIS: 89N26773.

POLAND, JEAN. 1991. Informal Communication among Scientists and Engineers: A Review of the Literature. Science & Technology Libraries. 1991; 11(3): 61-73. ISSN: 0194-262X.

PRICE, DEREK J. DE SOLLA. 1963. Little Science, Big Science. New York, NY: Columbia University Press; 1963. 119p. OCLC: 522357.

PULLINGER, DAVID J. 1983. Attitudes towards Traditional Journal Procedures. Electronic Publishing Review. 1983; 3: 213-222. ISSN: 0260-6658.

PULLINGER, DAVID J. 1999. Academics and the New Information Environment: The Impact of Local Factors on Use of Electronic Journals. Journal of Information Science. 1999; 25(2): 164-172. ISSN: 0165-5515.

RAITT, DAVID IAIN. 1984. The Communication and Information-Seeking and Use Habits of Scientists and Engineers in International Organizations Based in European National Aerospace Research Establishments. Loughborough, England: Loughborough University of Technology; 1984. (Ph.D. dissertation). Available from: British Library Document Supply Centre D52651/84.

RATH, GUSTAVE J.; WERNER, DAVID J. 1967. Infosearch: Studying the Remote Use of Libraries by Medical Researchers. In: Proceedings of the American Documentation Institute (ADI) 30th Annual Meeting: Volume 4; 1967 October 22-27; New York, NY. Washington, DC: Thompson Book Co. for ADI; 1967. 58-62. OCLC: 8415964.

REYNOLDS, LINDA. 1979. Legibility Studies: Their Relevance to Present Day Documentation Methods. Journal of Documentation. 1979 December; 35(4): 307-340. ISSN: 0022-0418.

RICHARDSON, ROBERT J. 1981. End-User Online Searching in a High-Technology Engineering Environment. Online. 1981 October; 5(4): 44-57. ISSN: 0146-5422.

RITCHIE, E.; HINDLE, A. 1976. Communication Networks in R&D: A Contribution to Methodology and Some Results in a Particular Laboratory. Lancaster, England: Department of Operational Research, University of Lancaster; 1976. 65p. (BLRD Report 5291). OCLC: 4926960.

ROSENBERG, VICTOR. 1967. Factors Affecting the Preferences of Industrial Personnel for Information Gathering Methods. Information Storage and Retrieval. 1967 July; 3(3): 119-127. ISSN: 0020-0271.

ROSENBLOOM, RICHARD S.; WOLEK, FRANCIS W. 1967. Technology, Information & Organization: Information Transfer in Industrial R&D. Boston, MA: Graduate School of Business Administration, Harvard University; 1967. 255p. OCLC: 3535083.

ROTHWELL, ROY. 1975. Patterns of Information Flow during the Innovation Process. Aslib Proceedings. 1975; 27(5): 217-226. ISSN: 0001-253X.

ROTHWELL, ROY; TOWNSEND, J. 1973. The Communication Problems of Small Firms. R&D Management. 1973; 3(3): 151-153. ISSN: 0033-6807.

ROUS, BERNARD. 1999. ACM: A Case Study. Journal of Electronic Publishing. 1999; 4(4). ISSN: 1080-2711. Available WWW: http://www.press.umich.edu/jep/04-04/rous.html.

SABINE, GORDON A.; SABINE, PATRICIA L. 1986. How People Use Books and Journals. Library Quarterly. 1986 October; 56(4): 399-408. ISSN: 0024-2519.

SCHAUDER, DON. 1994. Electronic Publishing of Professional Articles: Attitudes of Academics and Implications for the Scholarly Communication Industry. Journal of the American Society for Information Science. 1994 March; 45(2): 73-100. ISSN: 0002-8231.

SCOTT, CHRISTOPHER. 1959. The Use of the Technical Literature by Industrial Technologists. In: Proceedings of the International Conference on Scientific Information; 1958 November 16-21; Washington, DC. Washington, DC: National Academy of Sciences, National Research Council; 1959. 245-266. OCLC: 1240710.

SHAW, R. R. 1956. Pilot Study on the Use of Scientific Literature by Scientists. New Brunswick, NJ: Rutgers University; 1956. 139p. OCLC: 8426449.

SHILLING, CHARLES W.; BERNARD, JESSIE. 1964. Informal Communication among Bioscientists. Washington, DC: Biological Sciences Communication Project, George Washington University; 1964. 1 volume. OCLC: 6210176.

SHOHAM, SNUNITH. 1998. Scholarly Communication: A Study of Israeli Academic Research. Journal of Librarianship and Information Science. 1998 June; 30(2): 118-121. ISSN: 0961-0006.

SHUCHMAN, HEDVAH L. 1981. Information Transfer in Engineering. Glastonbury, CT: The Futures Group; 1981. 265, [78]p. ISBN: 0-960519-60-2.

SIMPSON, ANNETTE. 1988. Academic Journal Usage. British Journal of Academic Librarianship. 1988 Spring; 3: 25-36. ISSN: 0269-0497.

SMITH, CLAGETT G. 1966. Organizational Factors in Scientific Performance in an Industrial Research Laboratory. Madison, WI: Center for Advanced Study in Organization Science, University of Wisconsin; 1966. 172p. OCLC: 7872642.

SPEIER, CHERI; PALMER, JONATHAN; WREN, DANIEL; HAHN, SUSAN. 1999. Faculty Perceptions of Electronic Journals as Scholarly Communication: A Question of Prestige and Legitimacy. Journal of the American Society for Information Science. 1999 May 1; 50(6): 537-543. ISSN: 0002-8231.

STEWART, LINDA. 1996. User Acceptance of Electronic Journals: Interviews with Chemists at Cornell University. College & Research Libraries. 1996 July; 57(4): 339-349. ISSN: 0010-0870.

STOLLER, MICHAEL A.; CHRISTOPHERSON, ROBERT; MIRANDA, MICHAEL A. 1996. The Economics of Professional Journal Pricing. College & Research Libraries. 1996 January; 57(1): 9-21. ISSN: 0010-0870.

SUPERJOURNAL. 1999. SuperJournal Baseline Studies Report. Available WWW: http://www.superjournal.ac.uk/sj/baserept.htm.

SUTTON, J. R. 1976. Information Requirements of Engineering Designers. In: The Problem of Optimization of User Benefit in Scientific and Technical Information Transfer; 1975 October 8-9; Copenhagen, Denmark. Neuilly sur Seine, France: AGARD; 1976. 12.1-12.8. (AGARD Conference Proceedings no. 179). NTIS: AD-A024494.

TAYLOR, ROBERT L. 1975. The Technological Gatekeeper. R&D Management. 1975 June; 5(3): 239-242. ISSN: 0033-6807.

TENOPIR, CAROL; KING, DONALD W. 1997. Trends in Scientific Scholarly Journal Publishing in the United States. Journal of Scholarly Publishing. 1997 April; 28(3): 135-170. ISSN: 1198-9742.

TENOPIR, CAROL; KING, DONALD W. 2000. Towards Electronic Journals: Realities for Scientists, Librarians, and Publishers. Washington, DC: Special Libraries Association; 2000. 488p. ISBN: 0-87111-507-7.

TSAY, MING-YUEH. 1998. The Relationship between Journal Use in a Medical Library and Citation Use. Bulletin of the Medical Library Association. 1998 January; 86(1): 31-39. ISSN: 0025-7338.

TURNER, JUDITH AXLER. 2000. PubMed Central: A Good Idea. Journal of Electronic Publishing. 2000; 5(3). ISSN: 1080-2711. Available WWW: http://www.press.umich.edu/jep/05-03/turner0503.html.

TUROFF, MURRAY; SCHER, JULIAN. 1975. Computerized Conferencing and Its Impact on Engineering Management. In: Effective Management of Engineering Resources: Joint Engineering Management Conference; 1975 October 9-10; Washington, DC. New York, NY: American Society of Mechanical Engineers; 1975. 59-70. OCLC: 1920185.

ULRICH'S INTERNATIONAL PERIODICALS DIRECTORY. 2000. New York, NY: Bowker; 2000. 5 volumes. ISSN: 0000-0175.

UTTERBACK, JAMES M. 1969. The Process of Technical Innovation in Instrument Firms. Cambridge, MA: Sloan School of Management, Massachusetts Institute of Technology; 1969. 134p. OCLC: 23884946.

VON SEGGERN, MARILYN; JOURDAIN, JANET M. 1996. Technical Communications in Engineering and Science: The Practices within a Government Defense Laboratory. Special Libraries. 1996 Spring; 87(2): 98-119. ISSN: 0038-6723.

VOORBIJ, HENK J. 1999. Searching Scientific Information on the Internet: A Dutch Academic User Survey. Journal of the American Society for Information Science. 1999; 50(7): 598-615. ISSN: 0002-8231.

WALKER, THOMAS J. 1998. Free Internet Access to Traditional Journals. American Scientist. 1998; 86(5): 463-471. ISSN: 0003-0996. Also available WWW: http://www.amsci.org/amsci/articles/98articles/walker.html.

WANG, PEILING; WHITE, MARILYN D. 1999. A Cognitive Model of Document Use during a Research Project. Study II. Decisions at the Reading and Citing Stages. Journal of the American Society for Information Science. 1999; 50(2): 98-114. ISSN: 0002-8231.

WEIL, BEN. 1977. Benefits from Researcher Use of the Published Literature at the Exxon Research Center. Paper presented at National Information Conference and Exposition; 1977; Washington, DC.

WEIL, BEN H. 1980. Benefits from Researcher Use of the Published Literature at the Exxon Research Center. In: Jackson, Eugene B., ed. Special Librarianship: A New Reader. Metuchen, NJ: Scarecrow Press; 1980. 586-594. ISBN: 0-8108-1295-9.

WERLER, RUTH W. 1975. Hospital Journal Title Use Study. Special Libraries. 1975 November; 66(11): 532-537. ISSN: 0038-6723.

WHITLEY, RICHARD; FROST, PENELOPE A. 1973. Task Type and Information Transfer in a Goverment Research Laboratory. Human Relations. 1973 August; 25(4): 537-550. ISSN: 0018-7267.

WILLIAMS, FREDERICK; GIBSON, DAVID V., eds. 1990. Technology Transfer: A Communication Perspective. Newbury Park, CA: Sage Publications; 1990. 302p. ISBN: 0-8039-3740-7.

WILLIAMS, G. R. 1975. Library Subscription Decisions. IEEE Transactions on Professional Communication. 1975 September; 18(3): 207-209. ISSN: 0361-1434.

WILLIAMS, L. A. 1993. How Chemists Use the Literature. Learned Publishing. 1993; 6(2): 7-14. ISSN: 0953-1513.

WILSON, J. M.; MACDOUGAL, A. F.; WOODWARD, H. M. 1986. Economic Consequences of Libraries Acquiring Electronic Journal Articles. British Journal of Academic Librarianship. 1986 Winter; 1(3): 228-235. ISSN: 0269-0497.

WOLEK, FRANCIS W. 1970. The Complexity of Messages in Science and Engineering: An Influence on Patterns of Communication. In: Nelson, Carnot E.; Pollock, Donald K., eds. Communication among Scientists and Engineers. Lexington, MA: Health Lexington Books; 1970. 233-265. OCLC: 97550.

WOOD, D. N. 1971. User Studies: Review 1966-1970. Aslib Proceedings. 1971; 21: 233-265. ISSN: 0001-253X.

WUEST, FRANCIS JOSEPH. 1965. Studies in the Methodology of Measuring Information Requirements and Use Patterns: Report No. 1. Bethlehem, PA: Center for the Information Sciences, Lehigh University; 1965. 143p. OCLC: 5970170.

Introduction to the Index

Index entries have been made for names of individuals, corporate bodies, subjects, geographic locations, and author names included in the text pages and for author and conference names from the bibliography pages. The page numbers referring to the bibliography pages are set in italics, and are listed after the page numbers relating to the text pages. This format allows one to distinguish references to bibliographic materials from references to text.

Acronyms are listed either under the acronym or under the fully spelled-out form, depending on which form is more commonly used and known. In either case a cross reference from the alternative form is provided. Postings associated with PRECIS, for example, would be listed under PRECIS as readers are generally less familiar with the full name "Preserved Context Index System." In a few cases, such as names of programs, systems, and programming languages, there is no spelled-out form either because there is none or because the meaning has been changed or is no longer used.

The Index is arranged on a word-by-word basis. The sort sequence places special characters first, followed by alpha characters, then numbers. Thus, O'Neill would precede Oakman and 3M Company would file after the Zs. Government organizations are generally listed under country name, with *see* references provided from names of departments, agencies, and other subdivisions. While index entries do correspond precisely in spelling and format, they do not follow the typographical conventions used in the text. Author names, which are all upper case in the text, and both programming languages and software packages (such as expert system shells), which are in small caps in the text, are in upper and lower case or normal upper case in the Index.

Subject indexing is by concepts rather than by words. When authors have used different words or different forms of the same word to express the same or overlapping concepts, the terminology has been standardized. An effort has been made to use the form of index entries for concepts that appear in previous *ARIST* Indexes and in the 1994 *ASIS Thesaurus of Information Science and Librarianship.** See also* references are used for overlapping or related (but not synonymous) concepts; *see* references are used to send the reader to the accepted form of a term used in the Index.

---

* Milstead, Jessica L., ed. 1994. *ASIS Thesaurus of Information Science and Librarianship.* Medford, NJ: Learned Information, Inc., for the American Society for Information Science; 1994. 139p. ISBN: 0-938734-80-6.

The Index was prepared by Debora Shaw, using the MACREX Plus Indexing Program, version 5.10 developed by Hilary and Drusilla Calvert and distributed in the United States by Bayside Indexing. The overall direction and coordination of the Index were provided by Martha E. Williams. Comments and suggestions should be addressed to the Editor.

Index*

---

* Italicized page numbers refer to Bibliography pages.

Introduction to the Cumulative Keyword and Author Index of *ARIST* Titles: Volumes 1-34

The following section is a Cumulative Keyword and Author Index (both single word and multiword terms have been used) to *ARIST* chapters for Volumes 1 through 34. Terms are largely based on the titles of *ARIST* chapters, with editing for consistency. It has been produced to assist users in locating specific topics and author names (in bold when at the entry position) for all *ARIST* volumes to date. The index terms are sorted alphabetically. Multiple forms (e.g., adjective, verb, and noun forms) of the same word have been combined, and *see* and *see also* references are provided. The sort word is followed by the author(s) name(s) and the *ARIST* citation. This Cumulative Keyword and Author Index was totally reworked in Volume 30 and the new indexing procedures have been employed in succeeding volumes.

Cumulative Keyword and Author Index of *ARIST* Titles: Volumes 1-34

Abstracting and Indexing Services *see* Secondary Information Systems and
Services
Acquisition and Use of Information
Choo, Chun Wei and Ethel Auster. Environmental Scanning: Acquisi-
tion and Use of Information by Managers. **28**, p279
Adams, Peter D. Lerner, Rita G., Ted Metaxas, John T. Scott, Peter D. Adams
and Peggy Judd. Primary Publication Systems and Scientific Text
Processing. **18**, p127
Adams, Scott and Judith A. Werdel. Cooperation in Information Activities
through International Organizations. **10**, p303
ADI (American Documentation Institute)
Cuadra, Carlos A. Introduction to the ADI Annual Review. **1**, p1
Adkinson, Burton W. Berninger, Douglas E. and Burton W. Adkinson.
Interaction between the Public and Private Sectors in National Informa-
tion Programs. **13**, p3
Agriculture
Frank, Robyn C. Agricultural Information Systems and Services. **22**,
p293
Aines, Andrew A. and Melvin S. Day. National Planning of Information
Services. **10**, p3
Allen, Bryce L. Cognitive Research in Information Science: Implications for
Design. **26**, p3; Kinnucan, Mark T., Michael J. Nelson and Bryce L.
Allen. Statistical Methods in Information Science Research. **22**, p147
Allen, Thomas J. Information Needs and Uses. **4**, p3
Alper, Bruce H. Library Automation. **10**, p199
Alsberg, Peter A. Bunch, Steve R. and Peter A. Alsberg. Computer Commu-
nication Networks. **12**, p183
American Institute of Physics Staff. Techniques for Publication and Distri-
bution of Information. **2**, p339
Amsler, Robert A. Machine-Readable Dictionaries. **19**, p161
Analysis Methods
Sugar, William. User-Centered Perspective of Information Retrieval
Research and Analysis Methods. **30**, p77
Annual Review
Cuadra, Carlos A. Introduction to the ADI Annual Review. **1**, p1
Annual Review Staff. New Hardware Developments. **1**, p191
Applications *see also* Information Services; Information Systems and Services;
Information Technology
Baruch, Jordan J. Information System Applications. **1**, p255;
Beard, Joseph J. Information Systems Application in Law. **6**, p369;

About the Editor. . .

Professor Martha E. Williams assumed the Editorship of the *ANNUAL REVIEW OF INFORMATION SCIENCE AND TECHNOLOGY* with Volume 11 and has produced a series of books that provide unparalleled insights into, and overviews of, the multifaceted discipline of information science. Professor Williams held the positions of Director of the Information Retrieval Research Laboratory and Professor of Information Science in the Coordinated Science Laboratory (CSL) from 1972-2000. She was also Professor of Information Science in the Graduate School of Library and Information Science and affiliate of the Computer Science Department at the University of Illinois, Urbana-Champaign, Illinois. As a chemist and information scientist Professor Williams has brought to *ARIST* a breadth of knowledge and experience in information science and technology.

She has served as a Director and Chairman of the Board of Engineering Information, Inc.; she was founding editor of *Computer-Readable Databases: A Directory and Data Sourcebook*; was editor of *Online & CDROM Review* (now *Online Information Review*); and was Program Chairman for the National Online Meetings, 1980-2001. She was appointed by the Secretary of Health, Education and Welfare, Joseph Califano, to be a member of the Board of Regents of the National Library of Medicine (NLM) in 1978 and has served as Chairman of the NLM Board. She has been a member of the Numerical Data Advisory Board of the National Research Council (NRC), National Academy of Sciences (NAS). She was a member of the Science Information Activities task force of the National Science Foundation (NSF), was chairman of the Large Database subcommittee of the NAS/NRC Committee on Chemical Information, and was chairman of the Gordon Research Conference on Scientific Information Problems in Research in 1980.

Professor Williams is a Fellow of the American Association for the Advancement of Science, Honorary Fellow of the Institute of Information Scientists in England, Honorary Fellow of the National Federation of Abstracting and Information Services (NFAIS), recipient of the 1984 Award of Merit of the American Society for Information Science (ASIS), and recipient of the 1995 Watson Davis Award of ASIS. She is a member of, has held offices in, and/or is actively involved in various committees of the American Association for the Advancement of Science (AAAS), the American Chemical Society (ACS), the Association for Computing Machinery (ACM), and served as president of the American Society for Information Science (ASIS). She has published numerous books and papers, has maintained worldwide statistics on databases for over 25 years, and serves on the editorial boards of several journals. She is the founder and President of Information Market Indicators, Inc., and consults for many governmental and commercial organizations.

More ASIST titles from Information Today, Inc.

ARIST 35
Annual Review of Information Science and Technology
Edited by Martha E. Williams

Contents of Volume 35 include:
- *The Concept of Situation in Information Science*, by Colleen Cool
- *Conceptual Frameworks in Information Behavior*, by Karen E. Pettigrew, Raya Fidel, and Harry Bruce
- *Distributed Information Management*, by William M. Pottenger, Miranda R. Callahan, and Michael A. Padgett
- *Digital Privacy: Toward a New Politics and Discursive Practice*, by Philip Doty
- *Subject Access Points in Electronic Retrieval*, by Birger Hjorland and Lykke Kyllesbech Nielsen
- *Methods of Generating and Evaluating Hypertext*, by James Blustein and Mark S. Staveley
- *Digital Preservation*, by Elizabeth Yakel
- *Knowledge Management*, by Noreen Mac Morrow
- *Library and Information Science Education in the Nineties*, by Elisabeth Logan and Ingrid Hseieh-Yee

2001/hardbound/ISBN 1-57387-115-X
$79.95 ASIST Members   **$99.95 Non-Members**

The Web of Knowledge
A Festschrift in Honor of Eugene Garfield
Edited by Blaise Cronin and Helen Barsky Atkins

Dr. Eugene Garfield, the founder of the Institute for Scientific Information (ISI), has devoted his life to the creation and development of the multidisciplinary Science Citation Index. The index, a unique resource for scientists, scholars, and researchers in virtually every field of intellectual endeavor, has been the foundation for a multidisciplinary research community. This ASIS monograph is the first to comprehensively address the history, theory, and practical applications of the Science Citation Index and to examine its impact on scholarly and scientific research 40 years after its inception. In bringing together the anaylses, insights, and reflections of more than 35 leading lights, editors Cronin and Atkins have produced both a comprehensive survey of citation indexing and analysis and a beautifully realized tribute to Eugene Garfield and his vision.

2000/544 pp/hardbound/ISBN 1-57387-099-4
$39.60 ASIST Members   **$49.50 Non-Members**

Evaluating Networked Information Services
Techniques, Policy, And Issues
By Charles R. McClure and John Carlo Bertot

As information services and resources are made available in the global networked environment, there is a critical need to evaluate their usefulness, impact, cost, and effectiveness. This new book brings together an introduction and overview of evaluation techniques and methods, information policy issues and initiatives, and other critical issues related to the evaluation of networked information services.

2001/300 pp/hardbound/ISBN 1-57387-118-4
$35.60 ASIST Members   **$44.50 Non-Members**

Advances in Classification Research, Volume 10
Edited by Hanne Albrechtsen and Jens-Erik Mai

Advances in Classification Research, Volume 10 is a compilation of papers prepared for the 10th ASIS SIG/CR Workshop of Classification Research. Contents include:
- *Wittgenstein and Indexing Theory*
- *Implicit Orders: Documentary Genres and Organizational Practice*
- *A Universal Classification System Going Through Changes*
- *Non Traditional Indexing Structures for the Management of Electronic Resources*
- *Combining Machine Learning and Hierarchical Indexing Structures*
- *Local Practice and the Growth of Knowledge: Decisions in Subject Access to Digitized Images*

2001/150 pp/softbound/ISBN 1-57387-105-2
$31.60 ASIST Members $39.50 Non-Members

Intelligent Technologies in Library and Information Service Applications
By F. W. Lancaster and Amy Warner

Librarians and library school faculty have been experimenting with artificial intelligence (AI) and expert systems for 30 years, but there has been no comprehensive survey of the results available until now. Here, authors Lancaster and Warner report on the applications of AI technologies in library and information services, assessing their effectiveness, reviewing the relevant literature, and offering a clear-eyed forecast of future use and impact.

2001/214 pp/hardbound/ISBN 1-57387-103-6
$31.60 ASIST Members $39.50 Non-Members

Statistical Methods for the Information Professional
By Liwen Vaughan

In this unique and useful book, Liwen Vaughan clearly explains the statistical methods used in information science research, focusing on basic logic rather than mathematical intimacies. Her emphasis is on the meaning of statistics, when and how to apply them, and how to interpret the results of statistical analysis. Through the use of real-world examples, she shows how statistics can be used to improve services, make better decisions, and conduct more effective research. Includes more than 80 helpful figures and tables, 7 appendices, bibliography, and index.

2001/240 pp/hardbound/ISBN 1-57387-110-9
$31.60 ASIST Members $39.50 Non-Members

Editorial Peer Review: Its Strengths and Weaknesses
By Ann C. Weller

This book is the first to provide an in-depth analysis of the peer review process in scholarly publishing. Author Weller offers a systematic review of published studies of editorial peer review in the following broad categories: general studies of rejection rates, studies of editors, studies of authors, and studies of reviewers. The book concludes with an examination of new models of editorial peer review intended to enhance the scientific communication process as it moves from a print to an electronic environment.

2001/360 pp/hardbound/ISBN 1-57387-100-1
$35.60 ASIST Members $44.50 Non-Members

To order directly from the publisher, include $3.95 postage and handling for the first book ordered and $3.25 for each additional book. Catalogs also available upon request.

Information Today, Inc.
143 Old Marlton Pike • Medford, NJ 08055 • (609) 654-6266
www.infotoday.com